**新视角英语文学与文化系列教材**
丛书主编 刘 岩
Readings in Intercultural Studies

# 跨文化研究读本

余卫华 主编

顾　问　何其莘　陈建平
编委会　（按姓氏笔画排序）
　　　　马建军　王　虹　卢红梅　平　洪
　　　　仲伟合　余卫华　李　明　沈三山
　　　　郑　超　金李俪　黄家修　傅文燕
　　　　彭保良　管建明

武汉大学出版社

图书在版编目(CIP)数据

跨文化研究读本/余卫华主编. —武汉:武汉大学出版社,2006.2
新视角英语文学与文化系列教材/刘岩主编
ISBN 7-307-04872-8

Ⅰ.跨… Ⅱ.余… Ⅲ.文化交流—教材 Ⅳ.G115

中国版本图书馆 CIP 数据核字(2005)第 155891 号

责任编辑:谢群英　　责任校对:程小宜　　版式设计:支　笛

出版发行:武汉大学出版社　(430072　武昌　珞珈山)
（电子邮件:wdp4@whu.edu.cn 网址:www.wdp.com.cn）
印刷:武汉凯威印务有限公司
开本:880×1230　1/32　印张:25.75　字数:713 千字
版次:2006 年 2 月第 1 版　2006 年 12 月第 2 次印刷
ISBN 7-307-04872-8/G·768　　定价:36.00 元

版权所有,不得翻印;凡购买我社的图书,如有缺页、倒页、脱页等质量问题,请与当地图书销售部门联系调换。

# Contents

总序 ········· 1
前言 ········· 1
作者简介 ········· 1
**Introduction** ········· 1
    Concepts and Terms (Michael Byram) ········· 1

**Globalisation, Internationalisation and Post-modernism** ··· 45
    Globalisation and Internationalism: Democratic Prospects for
        World Education (Phillip W. Jones) ········· 45
    Globalisation and Education in the Post-colonial World:
        Towards a Conceptual Framework (Leon Tikly) ········· 74
    Internationalisation and Globalisation: Rethinking a Curriculum
        of Communication (Gunther Kress) ········· 124
    Post-modernity, Cultural Pluralism and the Nation-state:
        Problems of Language Rights, Human Rights, Identity and
        Power (Naz Rassool) ········· 153

**Language, Society and Identity** ········· 180
    Language Society and Identity
        (J. Edwards) ········· 180
    Educational Language Planning and Linguistic Identity

（Peter Sutton） ............ 221
　　Socialisation and Classification：Understanding
　　　　Japanese Society（J. Hendry） ............ 244
　　National and Other Identities（A. D. Smith） ............ 265
　　Ethnic Groups and Boundaries.（Fredrik Barth） ............ 291
　　The Stranger（G. Simmel） ............ 335

## Stereotype and Prejudice ............ 346
　　The Nature of Prejudice（G. W. Allport） ............ 346
　　Prejudice and Intergroup Conflict（James Vivian and Rupert
　　　　Brown） ............ 402

## Intercultural Communication and Intercultural Education ............ 439
　　Cross-cultural Adaptation：Axioms（Y. Y. Kim） ............ 439
　　Toleration and Recognition（Susan Mendus） ............ 467
　　Describing Intercultural Communication and the
　　　　Intercultural Speaker（Michael Byram） ............ 486
　　Culture Shock：Psychological Reactions to Unfamiliar
　　　　Environments（A. Furnham & S. Bochner） ............ 499
　　A Survey of Intercultural Communication Courses
　　　　（A. E. Fantini & E. M. Smith） ............ 537
　　Preparing Teachers for an Intercultural Context
　　　　（Kenneth Cushner） ............ 580
　　Intercultural Education at the University Level：
　　　　Teacher-Student Interaction（Neal R. Goodman） ............ 613
　　Human Rights and Intercultural Education
　　　　（Micheline Rey） ............ 645

# Intercultural Understanding and Intercultural Competence ····· 675

    Becoming an Intercultural Mediator: A Longitudinal Study
        of Residence Abroad (Geof Alfred & Michael Byram) ··· 675
    Searching for the Intercultural Person (Phyllis Ryan) ········· 687
    Defining and Describing Intercultural Communicative
        Competence (Michael Byram) ····························· 719
    For a Flexible Model of Intercultural Understanding
        (Lothar Bredella) ·········································· 759
    Tandem Learning as an Intercultural Activity
        (Jane Woodin) ············································· 790

# 总　序

我们所处的时代是一个多元共生的时代。国际政治的多极化走向、经济的全球化趋势、社会的信息化局面以及文化的多元化态势正以毋庸置疑的速度改变着我们的生活。科学技术的高速发展以及新兴学科的不断涌现加剧了世界各国文化的交流、碰撞和合作。如何培养适应新时代发展和需要的人才，这是我们这一代教育工作者面临的新的课题和挑战。

高等学校外语专业教学指导委员会英语组于 2000 年 3 月修订的《高等学校英语专业英语教学大纲》明确规定了高等学校英语专业的培养目标："高等学校英语专业培养具有扎实的英语语言基础和广博的文化知识并能熟练地运用英语在外事、教育、经贸、文化、科技、军事等部门从事翻译、教学、管理、研究等工作的复合型英语人才。"这样的描述为我们编写英语专业教材和组织英语专业教学提供了重要依据。我校在长期的外语教学和研究实践中践行"明德尚行，学贯中西"的校训，着力推进外语与专业的融合，致力于培养一专多能、"双高"（思想素质高、专业水平高）、"两强"（外语实践能力强、信息技术运用能力强）、具有国际视野和创新意识的国际通用型人才。这要求全面提高学生的综合素质，包括拓宽人文学科知识，加强人文素质，培养创新精神，提高独立分析问题和解决问题的能力。

正是在这样的环境和背景下，我院精心策划并组织骨干教师编写了这套《新视角英语文学与文化系列教材》。这套教材可以用于英语专业高年级文学、文化、翻译等专业课和选修课的教学，也可以为其他专业的学生提供必要的相关专业知识。我们期待这套教材能够以培养学生人文素质为根本原则，以加强学生人文修养、增强学生创新能力为目标，帮助学生批判地吸收世界文化精髓并弘扬中国优秀文化传统。

这套教材的策划和出版得到武汉大学出版社的积极推动和热情支持，没有他们的努力就不会有这套教材的问世。我院教师把多年教学经验积淀成书，每一本教材都凝结着他们的智慧和心血。还有我院一批渴求知识的学生，是他们的勤学好问让我们看到了工作的价值，也正是在教学相长的过程中我们的教材得到了不断的完善。在这套教材即将面世之际，让我们对所有参与教材编写和出版的人士表示衷心的感谢和敬意！也请同行专家对教材的缺憾不吝赐教。

广东外语外贸大学英语语言文化学院　刘岩博士<br>2005 年 12 月于白云山校区

# 前　言

现有高等学校英语院系开设的"跨文化交际"课程的教材，"概论"型的居多，论述"语言与文化"的居多，而从培养学生综合型"跨文化能力"（Intercultural competence）的视角着眼的教材不多，这方面的原著读本更为少见。鉴于此，我们决定尝试编选这样一部读本。同时，我们深信：让读者和学生直接精读原著、体会原著的精神，才是最有效的学习跨文化理论的捷径，这也是我们编选本书的初衷。但是跨文化研究的书籍和文章不说是浩如烟海，其中值得一读的也确实不少。编选一部这样的读本，自然只能是见仁见智，难以求全。正是有这个冠冕堂皇的借口，编者才敢抛开"献丑不如藏拙"的古训，作一尝试。

全书包含以下六大部分内容：第一部分内容为文化研究、跨文化意识、跨文化交际、跨文化能力等术语的基本定义和基本概念。第二部分内容为国际化和全球化的性质、特点、含义及其异同。第三部分内容为语言、社会与文化身份之间的关系。第四部分内容为思维定势与偏见。第五部分内容为跨文化交际的研究范围以及跨文化交际与教育的关系。第六部分内容为跨文化能力及其培养，如何成功地实现不同文化之间的相互交际与理解以及跨文化交际与理解的各种前提条件等。

编者根据上述六大范畴，总共选取了 26 篇相关文献。这些文献的出版时间和跨度主要集中在上世纪末和本世纪初。选材范围既包括了主流期刊杂志上的文章，也包含了跨文化研究方面的主流著作。所选文献绝大部分出自英美学者之手。编者在每篇文献的后面列出了该篇文献的出处。对本书所选的 27 篇文献的原作者及其相关出版社和杂志社我们表示衷心的感谢！

本书出版前曾在广东外语外贸大学英语语言文化学院英语专业（新闻传播方向）四年级和语言学及应用语言学硕士研究生的"跨文化交际"课程中试用过二年。此次出版时编者对相关文献作了一定调整。同时为方便读者和学生进一步理解相关文献，我们在每篇文献的后面写了一个简单的导读并给出了几道思考题。编者的两位硕士生李毓娟和王艳萍同学参加了部分导读的初稿的编写工作。

限于编者水平，本书的编选内容肯定会有不妥、疏漏甚至错误之处，我们恳请读者、专家和学者不吝赐教，待有机会再版时予以修正。

编　者

2006 年 3 月

# 作者简介

**余卫华**：博士、教授，出生于20世纪60年代的湖北省大冶市。现任教于广东省广东外语外贸大学英语语言文化学院。1979～1993年在武汉大学学习、任教并获英语文学硕士学位。1998～2001年师从语言教育与跨文化研究方面的国际著名学者Michael Byram教授，在英国杜伦大学（University of Durham）教育学院攻读语言教育专业，获教育学博士学位。现从事的研究方向和兴趣为：跨文化研究与双语教育、比较教育学等。近年来，多次在国内外出版社和学术刊物发表学术著作和论文。

# Introduction

## Concepts and Terms

Michael Byram

### Cultural Studies

Cultural Studies is an umbrella term for multi-or interdisciplinary analyses of cultural phenomena (products, processes, problematics) which was first used and developed in Britain and has spread to many parts of the world over the last thirty years.

### Origins and Development

The term was first used to characterise the works of Richard Hoggart and Raymond Williams, who continued the British tradition of cultural criticism (Matthew Arnold, T. S. Eliot, I. A. Richards, E. R. Leavis) and expanded as well as transformed it by democratising its concept of culture. The focus was no longer on a selective and elitist ('high') culture, but on the multiplicity of cultures within British society. This change of perspective was owed to a number of social, political and cultural transformations in post-war Britain. These included the expansion of the welfare state, the embourgeoisement of the working classes, the

Labour Party in office, the decline of the British Empire, the increasing equality in educational opportunities, the coming into existence of a multicultural British society.

The rise, development and institutionalisation of British Cultural Studies was initiated by a number of foundational texts (such as Hoggart, 1957, Williams, 1958, 1961, and Thompson 1963) which tried to make sense of (some of) these transformations. It was implemented by the Centre for Contemporary Cultural Studies (CCCS) at the University of Birmingham, founded by Richard Hoggart in 1964 to carry out theoretical and empirical analyses of related problematics. Under Hoggart's directorship (1964-1968) the CCCS concentrated on problems of literary and cultural sociology; under Stuart Hall's directorship (1968-1979) questions related to the media, popular cultures, youth and working-class cultures, feminism, racism, as well as theory and ideology were added to the agenda. These studies subscribed to more than one particular theoretical approach: French Structuralism (SAUSSURE, Levi-Strauss, Barthes), Marxism (Lukics, Althusser, Gramsci), the Frankfurt School and the specific British brand of Cultural Materialism (derived from Williams's work—see Williams, 1977:5) were particularly influential. Until 1979, the CCCS was associated with the university's English Department. When Hall left to join the Open University, the Centre became an 'independent research and postgraduate unit in the Faculty of Arts' under Richard Johnson's directorship. In 1988 the Centre and the Department of Sociology were combined into a 'Department of Cultural Studies ... within the Faculty of Commerce and Social Science' (CCCS, Nineteenth Report 1987-1988).

Although other groups and institutions with similar interests came into existence in the 1960s and have produced a substantial output (e.g., the

Centre for Television Research, Leeds, the Centre for Mass Communication Research, Leicester, the Glasgow Media Group), it is legitimate to equate the development of Cultural Studies in Britain with that of the CCCS until the late 1970s. Around 1980 the 'moment of autonomy' (Hall) came. Despite massive cuts in the tertiary sector, student demands led to the creation of a great diversity of Cultural Studies programmes and courses, first in the polytechnics and then in the universities. From 1982 to 1987 the Open University offered a course on 'Popular Culture' (U203) which was produced by a number of academics who, together with the graduates of the CCCS, were to decisively influence the further development of Cultural Studies in Britain (see Bassnett, 1997) and elsewhere.

Parallel to these developments, British Cultural Studies was received, assimilated to particular indigenous traditions and re-worked according to the specific NEEDS of its users in the United States (see Nelson and Grossberg, 1988; Grossberg, Nelson and Treichler, 1992), Australia (see Turner, 1991, 1992), Taiwan (see Chen, 1992), Italy (see Baransky and Lumley, 1990), Germany (see Kramer, 1983, 1997) and other countries in Europe (see Journal or the Study of British Cultures, 1999) and the world (see British Studies : Volume 1992 ; International Journal of Cultural Studies, 1998-). Almost at the same time, Cultural Studies was introduced (in some cases also re-introduced) into the teaching of foreign languages (see Buttjes, 1981; Byram, 1989, 1994; Kramer, 1990) and other subjects (see Aronowitz and Giroux, 1991).

## Definitions and Contemporary Issues

But what exactly is Cultural Studies? The modern concept of culture (on which Cultural Studies is based) is composed of five different elements which have come into existence one after the other but which still inform our present understanding of the term. First, culture was used in the context of cultivating the land, crops and animals; later, this meaning was extended to the cultivation of the mind. Then, the meanings, values and ways of life of particular, highly regarded groups were seen as setting the cultural standard for society as a whole. Under the influence of J. G. Herder in the late eighteenth century, a process of relativisation set in which made it possible to speak of cultures (in the plural) as different ways of life within a particular society and between different societies. This idea led to the formation of the anthropological concept of culture. And finally, out of particular interest in the symbolic dimension, i. e. the signs and meanings a particular group shares, the semiotic concept of culture was developed.

This concept itself has undergone significant transformations. While structuralist approaches relied on the relative stability of meaning, post-structuralist approaches have confronted the fundamental instability of the relationship between signifier and signified. More recently, an interest in the production of knowledge and its relationship to social power structures has superseded the interest in meaning. Parallel to these developments a partial convergence of the anthropological and semiotic concepts of cultures has resulted in the fact that signifying processes, by and through which a particular social group represents, experiences and communicates itself, are no longer regarded as derived (as in traditional base-superstructure models) or as reflexive (as in traditional theories of ideology), but as constitutive elements of the socio-cultural system.

The central question of Cultural Studies — 'How, where, when and to what effect are the shared meanings of particular groups produced, circulated and consumed?' can be demonstrated by a 'circuit of culture' and its five dimensions: representation, production, consumption, identity, regulation.

1. **Representation**: Meanings can only be produced because human beings possess two interdependent systems of representation. The first enables us to make connections between the 'things' of the world and our mental concepts; the second enables us to connect our mental concepts with particular signs or sign sequences. "The relation between 'things', concepts and signs lies at the heart of the production of meaning in language. The process which links these three elements together is what we call 'representation'" (Hall, 1997:19).
2. **Production—Consumption**: Meanings are produced (and circulated) by individuals, collectives and social institutions; but they are also created in processes of consumption: people listen to a particular kind of music, read certain texts, watch specific films, wear certain clothes, attend particular events—and by doing so, they attach certain meanings to these cultural products which are constitutive of their identities.
3. **Identity—Regulation**: In and through producing shared meanings the members of a group create a sense of identity. These meanings can (and do) serve as a means of regulation: as they 'work' by including or excluding others, they regulate the identity of the group.

There is no consensus in Cultural Studies about the theories and methods to be applied in the concrete analyses of these questions; in the best studies a productive kind of eclecticism prevails, combining phenomenology, structuralism, post-structuralism, deconstruction, psychoanalysis, gender feminism, queer theory, Marxism, new historicism, cultural materialism and post-colonial theory.

Although it is by no means clear why Cultural Studies in its diversity has experienced such an upturn and expansion, one may safely point to the truism that the need to debate culture arises when its meaning is no longer self-evident. In this sense the following reasons for the rise of Cultural Studies can be given without claiming to be exhaustive:

1. A growing interest in the social and political implications of the humanities made itself felt when the immediate after-effects of World War Two had worn off and the social and psychological resources had been filled again. This made it possible to reflect on, discuss and possibly transform those norms and values which had not been able to prevent Fascism and the war. In Europe (and other Western countries) these processes surfaced in the 'crisis of the humanities' (of the 1950s) and again in the student unrest and its related political and cultural transformations (of the 1960s). While the first problematic affected mainly the academic discourses, the second changed the political and cultural outlook of a whole generation.

2. The growing number of migrant workers that began to enter first Britain and then other European countries in the 1950s and 1960s at least implicitly influenced the debates around culture and politics, although they were hardly perceived and acknowledged as political or cultural factors in those days. This was to change decisively, when the second and third generations entered the schools and, even more importantly, the process of European integration intensified.

3. Similarly, the success of cultural studies in the United States coincided with the historical loss of the ability of that country to control the global economy and the increasing recognition that it can no longer dictate the terms of the 'new world order', which, to a certain extent, has sustained the cohesion of American national identity (Stratton and Ang, 1996:376-377).

4. In a more global perspective it seems evident that a number of irreversible and transformative processes in the economy (globalisation, migration), politics (international integration, devolution, 'new'

nationalisms) and culture (trans-national communication, 'clash of cultures') have rendered culture a matter of necessarily constant debate. (Jurgen Kramer, in Byram: 2000:162-165)

## References

Aronowitz, S. and Giroux, H. A. (1991) *Postmodern Education: Politics, Culture, and Social Criticism*, Minneapolis and Oxford: University of Minnesota Press.

Baransky, Z. and Lumley, B. (eds.) (1990) *Culture and Conflict in Post-war Italy: Essays in Popular and Mass Culture*, London: Macmillan.

Bassnett, S. (ed.) (1997) *Studying British Cultures*, London and New York: Routledge. *British Studies Now* (1992-).

Buttjes, D. (ed.) (1981) *Landeskundliches Lernen ira Englischunterricht (Cultural Learning in EFL)*, Paderborn.

Byram, M. (1989) *Cultural Studies in Foreign Language Education*, Clevedon and Philadelphia: Multilingual Matters.

Byram, M. (ed.) (1994) *Culture and Language Learning in Higher Education*, Clevedon and Philadelphia: Multilingual Matters.

Chen, K. H. (1992) *Media/Cultural Criticism: A Popular-democratic Line of Flight*, Taipei.

Grossberg, L., Nelson, C. and Treichler, P. (eds.) (1992) *Cultural Studies*, New York and London: Routledge.

Hall, S. (1997) *The Work of Representation*, in S. Hall (ed.) *Representation: Cultural Representations and Signifying Practices*, London, Thousand Oaks and New Delhi: Sage.

Hall, S., Hobson, D., Lowe, A. and Willis, P. (eds.) (1980) *Culture, Media, Language*, London: Hutchinson.

Hoggart, R. (1957) *The Uses of Literacy*, London: Chatto and Windus. *International Journal of Cultural Studies* (1998-).

*Journal for the Study of British Cultures* 1 / 1999: Special Issue on "British Studies: European Perspectives".

Kramer, J. (1983) *English Cultural and Social Studies*, Stuttgart: Metzler.

Kramer, J. (1990) *Cultural and Intercultural Studies*, Frankfurt: Peter Lang.

Kramer, J. (1997) *British Cultural Studies*, Munich: W. Fink.

Nelson, C. and Grossberg, L. (eds.) (1988) *Marxism and the Interpretation of Culture*, Basingstoke and London: Macmillan.

Stratton, J. and Ang, I. (1996) *On the Impossibility of a Global Cultural Studies: "British" Cultural Studies in an "International" Frame*, in D. Morley and K. H. Chen (eds.), *Stuart Hall: Critical Dialogues in Cultural Studies*, London and New York: Routledge.

Thompson, E. P. (1963) *The Making of the English Working Class*, London: Victor Gollancz.

Turner, G. (1991) "*Return to Oz: Populism, the Academy, and the Future of Australian Studies*", *Meanjin* 50 (Autumn).

Turner, G. (1992) "*It Works for Me*": *British Cultural Studies, Australian Cultural Studies, Australian Film*, in L. Grossgerg, C. Nelson and P. Treichler (eds.), *Cultural Studies*, New York and London: Routledge

Williams, R. (1958) *Culture and Society* 1780-1950, London: Chatto and Windus.

Williams, R. (1961) *The Long Revolution*, London: Chatto and Windus.

Williams, R. (1976) *Keywords: A Vocabulary of Culture and Society*, Glasgow: Fontana/Croom Helm.

Williams, R. (1977) *Marxism and Literature*, Oxford: Oxford University Press.

Williams, R. (1981) *Culture*, Glasgow: Fontana.

**Further reading**

Branlinger, P. (1990) *Crusoe's Footprints: Cultural Studies in Britain and America*, New York and London: Routledge.

During, S. (ed.) (1993) *The Cultural Studies Reader*, London and New York: Routledge.

Hall, S. (1997) "*The Centrality of Culture: Notes on the Cultural Revolutions of Out Time*", in K. Thompson (ed.) *Media and Cultural Regulation*, London, Thousand Oakes and New Delhi: Sage.

Turner, G. (1990) *British Cultural Studies: An Introduction*, London and New York: Routledge.

## Cultural Awareness

Cultural awareness (CA) is a concept which became popular within education in most Anglophone parts of the world in the 1980s and 1990s, and it has near-synonyms in many languages. It is used especially in connection with languages, but, seen in a wider perspective, it is evident that the concept was born of the 'cultural turn' in the human and social sciences, and in the general social debate of the 1980s. Thus CA is closely linked with the development of post-modern society with its interest in cultural difference and the relationship to 'the Other', no matter whether the latter is different from a national, ethnic, social, regional or institutional point of view. An important dimension of CA is the concept of reflexivity, i. e. the idea that insight into or experience of the practices or systems of meaning of other cultures is of significance for the individual's cultural understanding of self and their own identity.

In education the concept is widely used in connection with a number of subjects, for example geography and social studies, which have both seen a prioritisation of the cultural dimension. In the subject history, it is also possible to see a parallel to CA in the concept of historical awareness, i. e. the consciousness of the differences in historical periods and of one's own historical identity. The concept is also sometimes used in connection with MOTHER TONGUE teaching, but it is in foreign and second language teaching that it is used most.

The fact that CA has acquired a relatively major significance in language teaching is related to its being linked with a wish for a broad and more explicit focus on ordinary language teaching's cultural content at all levels, including BEGINNER level. This does not mean that it was without importance in teaching before the 1980s, since language teaching has included work with literature and realia since the 1800s in varying degrees (see Buttjes, 1991), and thereby given a certain limited impression of the cultural and social context in target countries. Moreover, in connection with COMMUNICATIVE LANGUAGE TEACHING, there has always been an assumption that there has to be a content to communicate about.

However, it was not until the 1970s and especially in the 1980s that attempts were made to make explicit that part of cultural content which goes beyond literature (e. g. Byram, 1989; Zarate, 1986), and only in the 1990s has the question of ASSESSMENT of this dimension of learning come onto the agenda, and this in turn requires a much higher degree of explicitness. In this pedagogical development, CA is a key concept which emphasises both cultural insight and ATTITUDE and identity development.

Among the many other terms in this same semantic field, some of which emphasise the subject content, others the processes, others the outcomes, there are the following: CULTURAL STUDIES (English), CIVILISATION (French), kulturelle Bildung, LANDESKUNDE (German), stranovedenie (Russian), kulturforstaelse (Danish), and 'realia'.

The understanding of what more precisely is contained in the concept of CA depends on which interpretation of culture it represents. There has not been a comprehensive theoretical discussion of the concept of culture itself in this field, but there are a number of themes which characterise the discussion. These themes are essentially developed from various conceptions of the aims of developing CA, and thereby reflect various priorities in the definition of culture:

  \* **the reflexive role**: How much emphasis should be given to understanding the culture and society of the target country, in relation to understanding one's own country? What role should be given to cultural comparison?
  \* **the cognitive and the affective**: How much emphasis should be given to the cognitive dimension (knowledge, insight, understanding) in relation to the affective (attitudes, representations, feelings)?
  \* **the content of the cognitive dimension**: Which cultural and social issues is it important to know about? What weight should be given to knowledge of facts in comparison to understanding of relationships?
  \* **the relationship to the historical dimension and the historical awareness** mentioned earlier: What emphasis should be given to historical as opposed to contemporary issues?
  \* **the relationship to literature**: Does CA also include the LITERARY content of a course?
  \* **national versus other communities**: Is CA concerned primarily with cultural content and cultural identity at the national/ethnic level, or does it also include multicultural communities and transcultural relationships and processes?
  \* **the relationship to the linguistic dimension and LANGUAGE**

**AWARENESS**: In what sense is language awareness a part of cultural awareness, and in what sense not?

* **the distance from target countries in foreign language teaching**: Is it possible to develop CA at a distance? Some people differentiate between CA, which can primarily be developed in the school or the classroom, and cultural experience which is primarily developed during a stay in the target country (Byram, 1989; several articles in Byram and Fleming, 1998).

Furthermore, the concept CA is on a par with language awareness, which is also used in language teaching. Byram has developed a model for language and culture teaching which includes language learning, language awareness, cultural awareness and cultural experience (Byram, 1989).

In general the pedagogical discussion about culture is much influenced by the American anthropologist Geertz's semiotic interpretative perspective on culture (Geertz, 1973). There are also examples of views inspired by DISCOURSE ANALYSIS, hermeneutics and post-modern thinking (Kramsch, 1993), or views inspired by theories of globalisation and the dissemination of culture, which are concerned with the cultural political significance of language teaching (Risager, 1998; Byram and Risager, 1999). Apart from the latter, there are very few approaches to what can be called critical cultural awareness (by analogy with critical language awareness, cf. Fairclough, 1992), i.e. a consciousness of the social and political dimensions of the cultural landscape, and of power and hegemonic relationships between various cultural practices and universes of significance.

As indicated earlier, one important aspect of CA is reflexivity. The development of CA is a development from ethnocentrism to relativity, including among other things an engagement with national STEREOTYPES (e. g. Zarate, 1986), or a development of the realisation that the world can be seen from many different perspectives, e. g. national perspectives (Byram, 1989). In this way two different disciplinary traditions are connected in the interpretation of CA: on the one hand the anthropological discussion of cultural representations and cultural relativism; on the other hand the social psychological discussion of prejudice, stereotypes and social cognition as a whole (see Tomalin and Stempelski, 1993, a practical handbook inspired by a mainly social psychological approach to cross-cultural interaction and communication).

CA is a concept which describes one of the aims of foreign and second language teaching. It thereby stands in a certain competitive relationship to another concept, INTERCULTURAL COMPETENCE. The latter refers to and supplements the concept of communicative competence, and therefore includes a SKILLS dimension. It is also a concept which is theoretically more developed and one which has been preferred in connection with the development of assessment criteria, including at the European level. In comparison to intercultural competence, CA is a more general, non-technical term liable to many different interpretations, which have to exist given the manifold nature of the contexts and interests connected with the content dimension of language teaching. (Karen Risager in Byram 2000:159-162)

**References**

Buttjes, D. (1991) *Culture in German Foreign Language Teaching: Making Use of an Ambiguous Past*, in M. Byram and D. Buttjes (eds.), *Mediating Languages and Cultures*, Clevedon: Multilingual Matters.

Byram, M. (1989) *Cultural Studies in Foreign Language Education*, Clevedon: Multilingual Matters.

Byram, M. and Fleming, M. (1998) *Language Learning in Intercultural Perspective*, Cambridge: Cambridge University Press.

Byram, M. and Risager, K. (1999) *Language Teachers, Politics and Cultures*, Clevedon: Multilingual Matters.

Fairclough, N. (ed.) (1992) *Critical Language Awareness*, London: Longman.

Geertz, C. (1973) *Thick Description: Toward an Interpretive Theory of Culture*, in C. Geertz, *The Interpretation of Cultures. Selected Essays by Clifford Geertz*, New York: Basic Books.

Kramsch, C. (1993) *Context and Culture in Language Teaching*, Oxford: Oxford University Press.

Risager, K. (1998) *Language Teaching and the Process of European Integration*, in M. Byram and M. Fleming (eds), *Language teaching in Intercultural Perspective*, Cambridge: Cambridge University Press.

Tomalin, B. and Stempelski, S. (1993) *Cultural Awareness*, Oxford: Oxford University Press.

Zarate, G. (1986) *Enseigner une Culture Etrangere*, Paris: Hachette.

**Further reading**

Byram, M. (1989) *Cultural Studies in Foreign Language Education*, Clevedon: Multilingual Matters.

Kramsch, C. (1993) *Context and Culture in Language Teaching*, Oxford: Oxford University Press.

## Acculturation

Acculturation is the process an individual needs to go through in order to become adapted to a different culture. For this to take place there will need to be changes in both social and psychological behaviour. Where the target culture involves a different language, a key part of the acculturation process will involve language learning. Research has concentrated on the acculturation of immigrant workers to their host country. The fact that many of the learners in this category fail to master the target language is associated with their isolation and lack of social contact with the host population. This lack of progress and the FOSSILISATION of their language SKILLS has been linked to pidginisation (Schumann, 1976). Acculturation is not generally associated with foreign language learning because this can take place without any direct contact with the target country. Where pupils do have contact with the target language and culture, for example through a pupil exchange, some of the features of acculturation could be seen to have relevance for foreign language learning.

Acculturation requires the learner to adjust their social and psychological behaviour in order to become more closely integrated with the target culture. This distance which separates the learner from the target culture is a measure by which acculturation can be assessed. Byram (1989) talks about the outsider beginning to become an insider, and how critical the move is '... from noticing the boundary markers to appreciating the whole complexity of the way of life'. The initial contact in this process of adaptation may be associated with CULTURE SHOCK as the learner discovers that they need to accept differences in behaviour from those with which they are familiar from their own culture. The learner's MOTIVATION to become more closely integrated with the target culture will be associated with their individual NEEDS.

Acculturation theory originated with the ethnographic work of Linton (1960), who studied the changes Native Americans needed to make in order to become more integrated into mainstream American society. He identified the notion of the distance separating the two cultural groups and the social and psychological changes which would be necessary for closer integration to take place. Social distance would be associated with the actual contact which was available between the two cultures, while psychological distance represented the extent to which the learner wanted to become more closely adapted to the dominant culture. Where differences in language existed between the two cultures, language learning was clearly an important part of the acculturation process.

For Schumann (1978), acculturation theory provided an explanation for individual differences in second language learning and represented the causal variable in the second language ACQUISITION process. In his model of the factors determining social and psychological distance, Schumann established the positive and negative elements of acculturation. So, for example, the ATTITUDE of the learner to the target social group could be a positive or negative factor while, psychologically, MOTIVATION would be seen as a key factor. For him, the first stages of language acquisition are 'characterised by the same processes that are responsible for the formation of PIDGIN languages. When there are hindrances to acculturation—when social or psychological distance is great—the learner will not progress beyond the early stages and the language will stay pidginized' (McLaughlin, 1987). The learner's language will therefore fossilise due to the lack of contact with the target language group. Further research (Andersen, 1981), has described in more detail these characteristics, identifying a number of different stages in the process of pidginization and creolisation (development of a more complex form of pidgin). So, nativisation 'involves assimilation as the learner makes the input conform to an internalized view of what constitutes the second language system', while denativisation represents the next stage when the learner adjusts this early language to external input.

The first stage of second language learning involves, therefore, simplification and regression, while later learning is concerned with replacement and restructuring. McLaughlin (1987) describes nativisation as "perhaps the most interesting aspect of Acculturation/Pidginization theory as it relates to the mechanisms of learning".

The theory of acculturation as developed by Schumann is proposed to explain the factors affecting ADULT second language ACQUISITION taking place without formal instruction, in naturalistic situations. As the theory stands, then, it would appear to have little to offer instructed second or foreign language learning (McLaughlin, 1987; Ellis, 1994). However, McLaughlin has pointed to the probable relevance of the notion of psychological distance for foreign language learning in the classroom. Attitude to the target culture and pupil motivation are likely to be key factors in classroom foreign language learning. Moreover, where pupils have the possibility of direct contact with the target country through a period of exchange or work experience abroad, they are in a situation where they will need to adapt to new and different cultural situations. The extent to which they are able to become integrated with the family with whom they are staying approximates, even for a limited period, the kind of changes emphasised by the acculturation theory. The theory provides, therefore, a useful means of assessing the adaptation of exchange pupils to their new environment which could be measured through the use of questionnaires.

Acculturation theory clearly matches, in a number of important areas, the fossilisation theory of Selinker (1972), which pre-dates it. Both theories seek to explain incomplete language learning and the fact that most learners do not achieve mastery of the target language. In their descriptions of simplified and reduced forms of speech not matching target language norms, they are describing similar phenomena. However, whereas fossilisation theory is based on a linguistic analysis of second language development as identified through examples of usage, acculturation begins with the notion of a single external factor-relationship to the target culture—which leads to these recognized limitations in learner INTERLANGUAGE. Acculturation, centred on the degree to which learners are in contact with the target culture, is largely, in contrast with the fossilisation theory, concerned with naturalistic and not instructed language learning. While they differ in the learning environment they describe, both theories have concentrated on the permanence of the language features identified. This is a point which McLaughlin takes up in his EVALUATION of the acculturation theory: '... relatively little attention has been given to the possibility of changes in individual motivation and attitude as they relate to second language acquisition' (McLaughlin, 1987). Changes in fossilization theory have begun to address this problem and Selinker (Selinker and Lakshmanan, 1993), recognising the difficulties of identifying a point when language development stops, no longer sees the process as necessarily permanent and identifies the concept of 'plateaus in L2 learning rather than cessation of learning'.

The acculturation/pidginization theory provides a powerful means for assessing a learner's involvement with the target culture. By extending the scope of the theory to include instructed language learning, it would certainly have, as McLaughlin (1987) suggests, '... something to say to teaching practitioners' (John Daniels in Byram 2000:1-3)

## References
Andersen, R. (1981) *Two Perspectives on Pidginization as Second Language Acquisition*, in R. Andersen (ed.), *New Dimensions in Second Language Acquisition Research*, Rowley, MA: Newbury

House.

Byram, M. (1989) *Cultural Studies in Foreign Language Education*, Clevedon: Multilingual Matters.

Ellis, R. (1994) *The Study of Second Language Acquisition*, Oxford: Oxford University Press.

Klein, W. (1986) *Second Language Acquisition*, Cambridge: Cambridge University Press.

Linton, W. (1960) *Acculturation in Seven American Indian Tribes*, Gloucester: Smith.

McLaughlin, B. (1987) *Theories of Second Language Learning*, London: Edward Arnold. Schumann, J. (1976) "Second Language Acquisition: The Pidginization Hypothesis", *Language Learning* 26: pp. 391-408.

Schumann, J. (1978) *The Pidginization Process: A Model of Second Language Acquisition*, Rowley, MA: Newbury House.

Selinker, L. (1972) "Interlanguage", *International Review of Applied Linguistics*, X: pp. 209-230.

Selinker, L. and Lakshmanan, U. (1993) "Language Transfer and Fossilization: The Multiple Effects Principle", in S. Gass and L. Selinker (eds.), *Language Transfer in Language Learning*, Philadelphia: Benjamin.

**Further reading**

Aitchison, J. (1996) *The Seeds of Speech, Language Origin and Evolution*, Cambridge: Cambridge University Press.

# Intercultural Communication

The interest in intercultural communication (IC) is an outcome of the ongoing globalization of academic studies, professional training and cooperation. Intercultural contacts become less intermittent and time bound, demanding more and more specific communication strategies for mastering the processes of mutual adaptation, integration and mediation.

The term IC in its narrow sense was introduced into the foreign language and communication training literature in the 1970s (Samovar and Porter 1972). IC denotes a peculiar communication situation: the varied language and discourse strategies people from different cultural backgrounds use in direct, face-to-face situations. As this term became more popular, it was also used to refer to studies in translation, in contrastive linguistics (pragmatics), in reading foreign literature or in comparative analysis of cultural meanings. In this broad sense, the term IC faced some criticism since similar studies had been carried out before using the same methodological tools so that this labelling did not reveal important new issues to the respective fields. While this is certainly correct, research and its applications in the narrow sense of the term developed into a specific field of interest, namely the discourse analysis of communicative events, where people from different cultural backgrounds engage in face-to-face communication.

The current focus of IC is on how people handle differences in linguistic behaviour and the various effects. The analyses result in descriptions of culturally specific ways of expressing and interpreting the situated linguistic action of the co-participants. Discourse analysis of this process of negotiation of meaning under multicultural conditions was supported by the development of low cost and mobile video technologies allowing researchers to record authentic IC and to work out micro-analyses of the specific rules of interaction under the conditions of multicultural influences. This research on discourse in intercultural situations has become increasingly important to the field of FL teaching, since the analyses have provided the linguistic grounds of the competencies FL learners need when they want to apply their acquired classroom knowledge in real intercultural communication situations.

This concept of 'intercultural situations' (IS) is tightly connected to intercultural communication because it indicates the framing activities co-participants apply in order to build up a 'common' base of understanding. IS arise under the following conditions: speakers 1-n from different cultures $C_2$-$C_n$. They communicate various 'things', i.e. while conversing they refer to <u>abstract concepts</u> (freedom, warm-heartedness, enjoyment, etc.), <u>concrete objects</u> (child, dog, apartment, etc.), <u>institutions</u> (school, café, etc.), or <u>perceptions</u> (pretty, unfriendly, extraordinary, etc.). According to their intentions they realize utterances, carrying out <u>speech acts</u> (promising, confirming, evaluating, presuming, etc.) in order to gain purposes like convincing, criticizing, etc. Normally, the presence alone of an interlocutor from a foreign culture (as a co-participant, not a bystander) determines sufficiently a situation as being intercultural. In an IS, co-participants need to apply metacognitive thinking and master specific, non-face threatening actions to index or to monitor the mutual culture-specific production and reception of linguistic actions and knowledge bases.

However, intercultural situations are not simply the merging of different cultures. The IS are constituted by the co-participants themselves by using various components of the given situation for setting third-cultural grounds and creating a 'situated talk'. For example, in a given situation, a group of people from Great Britain, France, Sweden and Germany meet in Frankfurt in order to discuss business arrangements. In this IS various cultural systems are involved that determine the situation consciously or unconsciously as being intercultural. In the given IS the following cultures can be used as common frames of interaction: (a) Culture $C_1$: Country of origin/cultural background of speaker $C_1$ (Great Britain); (b) Culture $C_2$: Country of origin/cultural background of speaker $C_2$ (France); (c) Culture $C_{n-1}$: Country of origin/cultural background of speaker $C_{n-1}$ (Sweden); (d) Culture $C_n$: Country of origin/cultural background of speakers $C_n$ (Germany); (e) Culture $C_S$: Cultural domain in which the speakers $C_1$-$C_n$ are currently interacting, i.e. the cultural domain of the current communication situation $C_S$ (Germany); (f) Culture CM: Cultural domain of the foreign language being used as a medium of communication CM, e.g. English, the form of expression of the cultural domains of Great Britain, the USA, etc. or (g) Culture $C_n$: Domain of an often neutrally perceived culture of the Anglo-American business world (CN).

The task of the participants in such an intercultural situation would be to negotiate, by means of implicit or explicit cues, a situationally adequate system of (inter-) cultural standards and linguistic rules of interaction. In practice, the grounds of this situation can be established within the following frames: (a) the above-mentioned cultural domain $C_S$, that is, the current communication situation ('We are having our meeting in Germany, and I propose we go the German way, establishing time limits for our discussion points and ...'); (b) using the cultural domain $C_2$ of one of the participants ('As a Frenchman I feel bad about this procedure and I propose to handle this problem as we always do in France, that is, to ...'); (c) the domain $C_n$ of the 'Anglo-American business world', often considered to be culturally neutral as an artificial cultural background when English is used as a lingua franca; (d) a new cultural framework IC, created ad hoc by the participants and including profitable aspects of several cultural domains for the benefit of the group, the situation and the communicative goals.

This last example shows a vision of intercultural understanding: the participants in IC situations are aware of the culture-bound character of meanings and try constructively, in the sense of the original meaning of (lat.) <u>communicare</u>, to create for themselves a comprehension base for jointly defined frames, meanings, linguistic action and procedures. According to Koole and ten Thije (1994) this common knowledge and action practice can be called discoursive interculture.

Sarangi (1994) and Clyne (1994) divide the attempts of analysing IC into three basic approaches: the 'cultural anthropological perspective' (where persons 'represent' different cultures and, therefore, cause various communication problems out of their different cultural background e. g. Asante and Gudykunst 1989; Brislin 1981; Prosser 1978), the 'cross-cultural pragmatic perspective' (looking for different realizations of predefined patterns of linguistic action; e. g. Blum-Kulka et al. 1989; Kasper / Blum-Kulka 1993), and the 'interactional sociolinguistic perspective' (providing data of IS that create culturally shaped communicative styles which might cause interethnic misunderstanding; e. g. Gumperz 1982; Scollon and Scollon 1994). Some critical discourse analysts (Sarangi 1994; Blommaert and Verschuren 1991) question the tendency of all three schools to claim for the manifestations of miscommunication a culture oriented reason. As can be seen in the data and in follow-up interviews, most co-participants attribute them in this way and react correspondingly. Thus, in IC, the emerging situated discourse and its third-culture effects are not only determined by the composition of cultural backgrounds and linguistic behaviour of the co-participants, but to a great extent by their (mis)interpretation and their attributions of linguistic action.

Any valuable research on IC, therefore, has to focus on how the participants perceive the linguistic manifestations of others, how they create 'new' meanings, adapted to be valid for the particular situation they are constituting. This means that persons do not rely entirely on their cultural norms but take into account other values and adapt eventually to what they assume as the foreign cultural norms and actions that others orient their talk to. Any attempt, for example in the FL classroom, to improve IC not only depends on the amount of FL teaching input but on the intercultural competencies of the co-participants. (Bernd Müller-Jacquier in Byram 2000:295-297)

**References**

Asante, M. K. and Gudykunst, W. B. (eds.) (1989) *Handbook of International and Intercultural Communication*, Newbury Park: Sage.

Blommaert, J. and Verschueren, J. (eds.) (1991) The *Pragmatics of Intercultural and International Communication*, Amsterdam/Philadelphia: John Benjamins.

Blum-Kulka, S. et al. (eds.) (1989) *Cross-Cultural Pragmatics: Requests and Apologies*, Norwood, NJ: Ablex.

Brislin, R. W. (1981) *Cross-Cultural encounters*, New York: Pergamon Press.

Clyne, M. (1994) *Intercultural Communication in the Workplace: Cultural Values in Discourse*, Cambridge: CUP.

Gumperz, J. (1982) *Discourse Strategies*, Cambridge: CUP.

Kasper, G. and Blum-Kulka, S. (eds.) (1993) *Interlanguage Pragmatics*, New York / Oxford: OUP.

Koole, T. and Ten Thije, J. D. (1994) *The Construction of Intercultural Discourse. Team Meeting of Education Advisers*, Amsterdam / Atlanta: RODOPI.

Prosser, M. H. (1978) *The Cultural Dialogue: An Introduction to In-*

tercultural Communication, Washington: SIETAR.

Samovar, L. A. and Porter, R. E. (1972) (eds.) Intercultural Communication: A Reader, Wadsworth: Belmont Ca.

Sarangi, S. (1994) Intercultural or Not? Beyond Celebration of Cultural Differences in Miscommunication Analysis, Pragmatics 3, 409-427.

Scollon, R. and Scollon Wong, S. (1995) Intercultural Communication. A Discourse Approach, Oxford: Blackwell.

## Intercultural Competence

Intercultural Competence (IC) is the ability to interact effectively with people from cultures that we recognise as different from our own. Cultures simultaneously share and differ in certain aspects, e. g. beliefs, habits and values. The so-called culture-general aspects are those they share while the aspects in which they differ are usually reckoned as culture-specific (Brislin and Yoshida, 1994: 37-55). The fewer culture-general aspects shared and the more culture-specifics identified, the more we perceive a culture as different.

Interacting effectively across cultures means accomplishing a negotiation between people based on both culture-specific and culture-general features that is on the whole respectful of and favourable to each. Smith, Paige and Steglitz provide a definition of 'effectiveness' and 'appropriateness' with respect to communication: 'Communication is *appropriate* when it meets contextual and relational standards (you did it right given the context); *effective* when it achieves desired ends or goals or provides satisfaction of both communicators' needs and concerns.' (1998:71-72).

Therefore, IC may have different meanings according to the type of relationship established between Self and Other. Either Self is expected to adjust to Other, or Self is expected to accomplish strategic goals on their or someone else's behalf with regard to Other, or Self and Other are expected to negotiate a cultural platform that is satisfactory for all parties involved (the preferable alternative). According to Byram, IC is more complex than Communicative Competence precisely because it focuses on 'establishing and maintaining relationships' instead of merely communicating messages or exchanging information (Byram, 1997b: 3). Therefore, 'adequacy and flexibility' are, according to Meyer, abilities that should be developed among foreign language/culture learners because they help them to be aware of differences and able to deal with them (Meyer, 1990: 137).

The difficulty in achieving a successful intercultural interaction does not necessarily correspond to the gap between cultural backgrounds. There are several factors involved, not all of them cultural, e.g. personality. The linguistic element is also most important for developing and achieving IC. An intercultural interaction is generally accomplished in one language that may be either native or foreign to all speakers or simultaneously native for some and foreign for others. Therefore, Byram distinguishes between 'Intercultural Competence' as the 'ability to interact in their own language with people from another country and culture' and 'Intercultural Communicative Competence' which means performance in a foreign language (1997b: 70).

### The 'intercultural speaker'

Thus, the foreign language/culture learner is viewed by Byram and Zarate as an 'intercultural speaker', defined as someone who 'crosses frontiers, and who is to some extent a specialist in the transit of cultural property and symbolic values' (1997:11). The notion of an 'intercultural speaker' responds to contemporary theories of cultural identity as socially constructed, always in the process 'of "becoming" as well as of "being"' (Hall, 1990: 225).

The 'intercultural speaker' mediates between two, or more, cultural identifications. These include the crisis-crossing of identities and 'the "positions" to which they are summoned; as well as how they fashion, stylize, produce and "perform" these positions' (Hall, 1996:13-14). Therefore, the 'intercultural speaker' has to negotiate between their own cultural, social and political identifications and representations with those of the other, that is, they must be critical. The *critical* 'intercultural speaker' takes critical advantage of the world opened wide to them by appreciating the different narratives available, by reflecting upon how they articulate, how they are positioned and how their positions affect their perspectives.

An intercultural encounter encompasses an interaction between the multiple identities of social actors, their perceptions of each other's identities (Byram 1997a: 56) and the fact that some are more dominant in particular circumstances (Byram and Fleming, 1998:7). However, eventually the interaction is more than the sum of its parts because the intercultural encounter stretches the cultural identities involved and the exchange takes place 'in-between' them or at their extremities. This 'open-country' where the extensions of our selves meet is identified by Bhabha as the 'Third Space' and described as 'unrepresentable in itself', a place where 'the meaning and symbols of culture have no primordial unity or fixity' and where 'the same signs can be appropriated, translated, rehistoricized and read anew' (1994:37-38).

## Learning intercultural competence
The idea of the 'intercultural speaker' confirms the description of learn-

ers as 'border crossers' (Giroux, 1992), who make full use of the opportunities for establishing various, formal or informal, cross-cultural contacts that enable them to gather a variety of experiences. However, the 'intercultural speaker' is not a cosmopolitan being who floats over cultures, but someone committed to turning intercultural encounters into intercultural relationships. Therefore, the process of becoming interculturally competent is more complex than just realising that there is a 'They' and a 'We'. It entails awareness of the ever-evolving and struggling web of intra-and intercultural meanings. Accordingly, Byram and Zarate (1997) identify several factors/ '*savoirs*' —*savoirs*, *savoir être*, *savoir comprendre*, *savoir faire/apprendre*—for developing intercultural competence within foreign language/culture education. Furthermore, Byram distinguishes '*savoirs' engager*' /critical cultural awareness as the centre of his model, which he describes as 'a rational and explicit standpoint from which to evaluate' (Byram, 1997b: 54). This is a world where identifications and representations are in constant contact and change and foreign language/culture has an important role to play in helping young citizens to consciously differentiate and mediate between competing identity loyalties.

## Teaching intercultural competence

The main target for the foreign language/culture learner/teacher is no longer to imitate a circumscribed and standardized model of a native speaker (Kramsch, 1993; Byram, 1997b; Byram and Zarate, 1997). Therefore, teachers need to discard their role as ambassadors of a foreign culture and the concept of a static, self-contained, and strange culture. Instead, they must acknowledge the interactive nature and the social, political, and ethical implications of learning/teaching about culture. Such an understanding of foreign language/culture education has profound consequences for teacher development due to its effect on teachers' 'professional identity' (Byram and Risager, 1999:79). Interdisciplinary research and intercultural training are becoming more visible in teacher development programmes. University-based and experiential learning are important and complement each other since they prompt alternative cognitive, affective and behavioural outcomes. Therefore, integration of theory and practice-*praxis*-performed in an interpretive, reflexive, exploratory, and pragmatic way in teacher education is fundamental in order to induce teachers to promote it in their classes. Consistent preparation and follow-up to experiential learning have been achieved through the combination of 'home ethnography' and field work abroad (Roberts, 1993). Teachers are not acculturated into the target culture, but instead develop a critical spirit towards foreign culture teaching/learning, target and native cultures, intercultural interaction and exchange itself. (Manuela Guilherme in Byram 2000:297-300)

## References
Bhabha, H. (1994) *The Location of Culture*, London: Routledge.
Brislin, R. and Yoshida, T. (1994) *Intercultural Communication Training: An Introduction*, Thousand Oaks: Sage.
Byram, M. (1997a) *Cultural Studies and Foreign Language Teaching*, in S. Bassnett (ed.) *Studying British Cultures: An Introduction*, London: Routledge.
Byram, M. (1997b) *Teaching and Assessing Intercultural Communicative Competence*, Clevendon: Multilingual Matters.
Byram, M. and G. Zarate (eds.) (1997) *The Sociocultural and Intercultural Dimension of Language Learning and Teaching*, Strasbourg: Council of Europe.
Byram, M. and Fleming, M. (eds.) (1998) *Language Learning in Intercultural Perspective*. Cambridge: Cambridge University Press.
Byram, M and Risager, K. (1999) *Language Teachers, Politics and*

*Cultures*, Clevedon: Multilingual Matters.

Meyer, M. (1990) *Developing Transcultural Competence: Case Studies of Advanced Foreign Language Learners*, in D. Buttjes and M. Byram (eds.) *Mediating Languages and Cultures: Towards an Intercultural Theory of Foreign Language Education*, Clevedon: Multilingual Matters.

Giroux, H. A. (1992) *Border Crossings—Cultural Workers and the Politics of Education*, New York: Routledge.

Hall, S. (1990) *Cultural Identity and Diaspora*, in J. Rutherford (Ed.) *Identity: Community, Culture, Difference.* London: Lawrence & Wishart.

Hall, S. (1996) *Introduction: Who Needs 'Identity'*? in S. Hall and P. du Gay (eds.) *Questions of Cultural Identity*, London: Sage.

Kramsch, C. (1993) *Context and Culture in Language Teaching*, Oxford: Oxford University Press.

Roberts, C. (1993) *Cultural Studies and Student Exchange: Living the Ethnographic Life, Language, Culture and Curriculum* 6, 1: pp. 11-17.

Smith, S. L., Paige, R. M., and Steglitz, I. (1998) *Theoretical Foundations of Intercultural Training and Applications to the Teaching of Culture*, in D. L. Lange, C. A. Klee, R. M. Paige, and Y. A. Yershova (eds.) *Culture as the Core: Interdisciplinary Perspectives on Culture Teaching and Learning in the Language Curriculum*, Center for Advanced Research on Language Acquisition, Working Paper Series: University of Minnesota.

**Further reading:**

Bhabha, H. (1994) *The Location of Culture*, London: Routledge.

Brislin, R. and Yoshida, T. (1994) *Intercultural Communication Training: An Introduction*, Thousand Oaks: Sage.

Byram, M. (1997) *Teaching and Assessing Intercultural Communicative Competence*, Clevendon: Multilingual Matters.

Byram, M. and G. Zarate (eds.) (1997) *The Sociocultural and Intercultural Dimension of Language Learning and Teaching*, Strasbourg: Council of Europe.

Hall, S and du Gay, P. (eds.) (1996) *Questions of Cultural Identity*, London: Sage.

[From: Byram, M. (2000) *Routledge Encyclopedia of Language Teaching and Learning*, London: Routledge]

## 导读：概念与术语

本章主要介绍跨文化交际所涉及的几个重要概念和术语，包括文化研究、文化意识、文化适应、跨文化交际、跨文化能力等。这些概念对于跨文化交际这门学科的理解具有重要意义。本章的几个概念和术语均选自 Byram 的《语言教学百科全书》（*Routledge Encyclopedia of Language Teaching and Learning*, London: Routledge, 2000）。

### 1. 文化研究

文化研究是关于文化现象的多学科或跨学科分析的涵盖性术语。它最早始于英国，尔后在近 30 年发展到世界各地。

**文化研究的起源和发展**：该术语第一次出现在 Richard Hoggart 和 Raymond Williams 的作品中，两位作者传承了文化批评的英国传统，并通过文化概念的贫民化使其发扬光大。从此文化研究不再只是集中研究那些精英文化和高层文化，而是社会内部所有纷繁复杂的种种文化。这种观察视角的转换归因于战后英国社会在社会政治和文化方面的变化。这些变化包括社会福利的扩大、工薪阶层向中产阶层转化、劳动党执政、大英帝国的衰落、教育机会的增加以及英国多元文化社会的到来。

英国文化研究的发展和规范发端于一些研究社会变化的基本文本。1964年Richard在伯明翰大学建立了"当代文化研究中心",主要对相关文化问题进行了理论和实证研究。在Hoggart领导期间该中心主要研究文化社会学问题。到了Stuart Hall负责时期则把传媒、大众文化、青年和工薪阶层文化、女权主义、种族主义以及理论和意识形态等也纳入到研究日程。这些研究不局限于一种理论:法国的结构主义、马克思主义、Frankfurt学派和文化实物主义等在研究中都产生过深远的影响。1979年该中心与其所在大学的社会学系合并,而Hall本人也离开了该中心去伦敦的公开大学单独开设"大众文化"课程。尽管有不少其他与文化研究相关的机构和团体的存在,但是直到20世纪70年代后期,人们提起英国的文化研究的发展就不可能忽视该中心的存在。该中心在英国文化研究的发展史上最具代表性和影响力。

全球各国的文化研究也在与英国的文化研究同步发展。美国、澳大利亚、中国的台湾地区、意大利、德国、欧洲,甚至是世界各国在此期间都在根据各自的需求开展文化研究。在文化研究向纵深发展的同时,它也被引入外语教学与其他学科之中。

**文化的界定和研究主题**:对文化的定义可谓千姿百态,已逾400多种,其博大精深可见一斑。文化通常有广义和狭义之分。广义的文化几乎囊括了人类的整个社会生活,可用黑格尔的名言"文化是人类创造的第二自然"来说明;狭义的文化指意识形态,以及与之相适应的制度和组织结构。当今文化概念主要包括五个方面的内容:最初文化是指耕作和畜牧;后来意义扩大到精神文明方面;接着是指特定的上层社会群体的意义、价值观和生活方式被看做是为整个社会创建了文化标准;18世纪末,在Herder的影响下,文化的相对性的观点的出现使文化被看做是特定社会内部和不同社会之间的不同的生活方式。这些观念导致了文化人类学观念的形成;最后,由于对符号学的兴趣,文化的符号概念得以形成和发展。

文化概念本身也在经历着深刻的变化。当结构主义的研究依赖词义的稳定性时,后结构主义已经面临所指和能指之间的不稳定关系。再后来人们的关注点转移到了知识的生产以及它和社会权利结构之间的关系。与此同时,人类学和符号学观点也成了社会文化系统的主要组成部分。

文化研究的核心问题:特定群体的共有意义是何时,何地,怎样,有何效果地产生、传播和接受的?该问题也可以用文化轮回的五个方面表示:表征,产生,接收,身份认同和规范。

表征:意义的产生是因为人类有两种相依的表达系统。第一个系统使我们的思想概念与世界中的事物联系起来,而第二个系统把我们的概念和特定的符号或符号串联系起来。事物、概念和符号的关系存在于语言意义产生的中心位置。把这三个成分联系起来的过程就是我们所谓的表征(Hall, 1997)。

产生和接收:意义被个体、集体或社会组织产生出来时同时也处在被接收的过程当中:欣赏音乐,阅读文本,观看电影,穿着打扮以及参与各项社会事件等,人们在做诸如此类事情的同时为构成他们所认同的文化产物赋予某种意义。

身份认同和规范:文化群体中的成员在产生共有意义的同时已通过这种生产创立了身份认同感,而这些全都成为某种规范方式:他们通过纳入或排除异己,来规范群体的同一身份。

在文化研究中对这些问题的具体分析没有一致的理论和方法。研究中一般折中主义较为盛行,它综合了诸多理论:如现象学、结构主义、后结构主义、解构主义、心理分析、性别研究、女权主义、酷儿理论、马克思主义、新历史主义、文化唯物主义和后殖民主义等。

尽管文化研究在其多样性方面经历着上升和扩展,但我们能有把握地说,当那些所谓的自明之理的意义不再是不言而喻时,对文化的讨论便会自然而然产生。正是从这个意义上来说,以下所提出的文化研究兴起的原因是可以让人窥见一斑:①当第二次世界大战的后遗症逐渐消失,当社会和心理资源再一次得以充实时,人们越来越对人性的社会和政治意义感兴趣。这就使得人们可能再一次去反思、探讨和彻底改变那些曾经无法与法西斯和战争抗衡的社会准则和价值观。在欧洲，这些过程逐渐在"人性的危机"中显现出来，也再一次表现在20世纪50年代学生动乱及相关的政治、文化转型之中。它们分别对学术观点以及整个一代人的政治、文化观产生了影响。②20世纪50年代到60年代移民到英国和其他欧洲国家的工人数量逐渐增加。在当时的社会这些移民并未被认为是影响政治文化的因素，但是他们至少微妙地影响了关于文化和政治的讨论。当这些移民的第二代和第三代进入学校时，他们对欧洲政治文化的统一就产生了决定性影响。③很巧合的是，美国在文化研究成功发展的同时，丧失了控制全球经济的能力。人们也意识到美国再也不可能为了确立自己的大国地位建立"世界新秩序"了。从全球视角来看，经济、政治、文化发展的不可逆转的变化过程给文化带来了一场必然的持久的论战。

**Questions for reflection：**
1. What is culture?
2. What is the central question of cultural studies?
3. Why can't we claim that cultural studies are exhaustive?

## 2. 文化意识

虽然在20世纪80年代至90年代，文化意识盛行于世界上大多数以英语为本土语的教育领域而且在许多语言中它还以不同的近义词出现，但这一概念还是与语言联系最为密切的。从更广的视角来看，文化意识这一概念产生于人文和社会科学以及20世纪80年代社会讨论的"文化大转型"之中。文化意识和对文化差异以及不同文化感兴趣的后现代社会的发展紧密相关。尽管和不同文化的关系会因民族、种族、社会，地域或制度上的不同观点而不同，文化意识的一个很重要的方面就是概念的内省性或反思性，也就是说，洞察和感受它国文化的运作方式或文化系统对于个人从文化上认识自我和自我身份具有重要意义。

教育中的文化意识这个概念被广泛应用于许多相关学科之中，比如说，地理学和社会学研究就会优先从文化角度来看待文化方面的问题。学科史也能够看出文化意识和历史并存，比如对不同历史时期的区别认识和自我历史身份的认识。文化意识虽然常用于母语教学中，但在二语和外语教学中更为突出。

文化意识在外语教学上具有相对的重要性是因为各个层次的语言教学越来越广泛、直接、具体地集中于文化内容上而且与文化内容的关系越来越密切。这并不意味着20世纪80年代以前文化意识就不重要，因为从19世纪开始语言教学的内容就不同程度地包括了文化著作和各种直观教具，语言教学早就烙上了国家文化和社会的印记。此外，交际语言教学首先假定要有交流内容。在教学法的发展史上，文化意识是一个既强调发展文化洞察、文化态度又强调发展文化身份的一个关键概念。

从比较准确的角度来看待文化意识的内容主要基于对文化的理解。目前对文化意识的内容未形成综合的理论性的讨论，但是确实已经存在一些经过讨论后构成文化特征的主题。它们分别从培养文化意识的不同的目的观念入手，因而反映了在文化界定上对不同方面的优先考虑：

反思作用：在涉及了解本国文化时我们该多大程度地强调对目的国的文化和社会的理解？

认知和情感作用：在考虑情感作用时，我们该多大程度强调文化意识的认知功能？

认知方面的内容：哪些社会文化问题是我们所必须了解的，应该给予它们多重分量？

与历史和历史意识的关系：与当代事件比较而言，我们应多大程度地强调历史事件？

与文学的关系：文化意识是否也包括文学的内容？

民族和其他社团：在民族层面上，文化意识是主要关注文化内容和文化地位还是也应该包括多元文化社会以及跨文化关系和过程？

与语言及语言意识的关系：从什么意义上来说语言意识是或不是文化意识的一部分？

外语教学上与目的国的距离：远距离培养文化意识是否可能？有些人把学校和课堂培养起来的文化意识和在目的文化国居住的文化经历所建立的文化意识区分开来。

此外，语言教学上的文化意识和语言意识处在同等位置。Byram 建立了一种语言与文化教学的模式，它包括语言学习、语言意识、文化意识和文化经历。一般说来，对文化和教学论的讨论主要受美国人类学家 Geertz 的影响。他从符号学角度对文化进行解释。也有一些观点源于话语分析，圣经阐释学和后现代思维（Kramsch, 1993），或者是那些语言教学的文化政治意义的全球化理论和文化传播理论（Risager, 1998; Byram and Risager, 1999）。除此之外还有少数被称为批评性质的文化意识的方法。如前所述，文化意识的一个重要方面是其反思性。文化意识的发展就是从民族中心主义向相对性的观点发展，包括从民族的文化定势向从多角度看世界的方面发展（Byram, 1989）。因此，文化意识的解释把两个不同的传统学科联系起来：一方面是人类学有关文化的代表性和文化的相对性的讨论，另一方面是社会心理学关于偏见、文化定势和整体社会认知的讨论。

文化意识描述了外语和二语教育的目的，因此文化意识这一概念与另一概念——跨文化能力的概念存在某种竞争关系。它的理论发展得更成熟、更多地被用在评价标准上。与跨文化能力相比，文化意识是一个更为普遍、不太学术化的概念。它往往有许多不同的解释，常常有存在于多样化的语境和对语言教学的内容感兴趣的方面。

**Questions for reflection:**

1. What is the importance of cultural awareness?
2. Illustrate the relation between cultural awareness and linguistic awareness?

3. Why can we say that cultural awareness is based on culture understanding?

## 3. 文化调适

文化调适是指个人在适应不同文化时所必须经历的一个过程。要适应不同的文化就势必需要改变社会行为和心理行为。语言是文化的载体，当目的文化是一门不同于母语的文化时，语言学习就成了文化调适的重要一环，语言无法沟通交际就无法进行，个体就会孤立于文化圈之外。Schumann（1976）把语言学习过程的缺失及语言技能的僵化和洋泾浜化联系起来。当然文化调适不仅仅通过语言学习就可以完成，它还需要学习者适当调整社会行为和心理行为，以便与目的文化达成统一。从原有的文化递进到适应新的文化即从文化圈外人变成圈内人，其中的距离是显而易见的。当所熟悉的文化从眼前消失去接触另一种新文化时，人们常常会不同程度地产生一种心理反应即文化休克或文化震荡。文化人类学家 Kalvero Oberg（1960）把文化休克定义为"由于失去了自己熟悉的社会交往信号或符号，因对于对方的社会符号不熟悉而在心理上产生的深度焦虑症"。面对文化休克不同学习者会根据自己的不同需要产生不同的文化调适动机。

文化调适理论源自 Linton（1960）在研究美国本地人适应主流文化的人种学著作中。他指出两个文化之间存在距离，要达到较一致就必须发生社会和心理变化，社会距离可以通过实际接触变近，而心理距离则代表着学习者与主流文化接近的愿望的强烈程度。

Schumann（1978）的文化调适理论为二语习得的个体差异提供了解释，也说明了二语习得的原因变量。在决定社会和心理距离模式中，Schumann 创立了文化调适的积极因素和消极因素这一对立体。比如说学习者对目的社会群体所持的态度既可以是积极的因素也可以是消极的因素。而动机则是至关重要的一个因素。学习第二语言的过程都会经历洋泾浜语这一阶段。如果文化调适过程出现阻碍，语言学习也会受到阻碍，导致语言学习停滞在洋泾浜语的状态。非本土化会使语言学习的早期阶段简化和倒退，学习后期则出现替代和重构。所以 McLaughlin（1987）认为本土化可能是与学习机制相关的文化调适理论中最为有趣的一个方面。

Schumann 的文化调适理论还可以用于解释在自然环境里和不接受正规教育的情况下影响成人二语习得的因素。而 McLaughlin 指出了在二语或外语学习课堂里心理距离与语言学习的相关性。学习者对目的文化的态度和动机可能是课堂二语或外语学习的主要因素。

在一些重要领域里文化调适理论显然与僵化理论一致，因而这两种理论都试图解释语言学习的不完全及大多数学习者不能很好掌握目的语的原因。他们同样都描述了语言的简化或压缩形式与目的语标准不一致的现象。然而僵化理论是基于通过语言运用实例对二语发展进行的语言分析。文化调适始于一个外在因素——与目的文化的关系。这一关系导致了学习者的中介语言的局限性。而文化调适理论则以学习者与目的文化接触程度为中心，主要探讨了自然的非正规教育条件下的语言学习。尽管两种理论描述的语言学习环境有差异但是两者都集中描述已知的语言特性的恒定性。文化调适理论为跨文化语言学习者的评估提供了一套强有力的方法。随着理论视野的扩大，正规教育条件下的语言学习也被纳入研究范围之列。语言僵化理论的最新发展也开始探讨类似于文化调适方面的问题，譬如：Selinker（Selinker & Lakshmanan, 1993）认为语言学习确实存在一个艰难的停留阶段，但是这个阶段不会是永久的，它是二语学习中的"学习高原反应"，而非语言学习中的停滞。

**Questions for reflection：**
1. What is acculturation and culture shock?
2. Discuss the relation between acculturation and second or foreign language learning?
3. Discuss the similarities and differences between fossilization theory and acculturation theory.

## 4. 跨文化交际

跨文化交际指具有不同文化背景的人士之间的交际。随着通信交通工具的迅速发展和全球化趋势的增强，跨文化交往变得更为直接而且不受时间约束。同时为了达到相互适应，融合和调和跨文化交往需要更多的特定的交流策略，跨文化交际学已经成为一门非常重要的学科。

狭义上的跨文化交际在20世纪70年代初被引入有关外语和交际培训的文献中。跨文化交际意味着一种特定的交际情境：在进行直接的面对面的交流的情景中来自不同文化背景的人用不同语言和话语策略进行交流。随着该术语的普遍使用，它也被用于翻译研究、对比语言学（语用学）、外国文学阅读以及文化意义的比较分析中。广义上的跨文化交际经受过一些批评，因为在未应用新的方法论的前提下开展了一些相似研究，结果使得这一术语没有揭示其相关领域的一些重要问题。而狭义的跨文化交际研究和应用已经拓展为对相对特定的兴趣领域，也即对来自不同文化背景的人士的面对面的交流所开展的话语分析。

目前跨文化交际的研究集中在人们如何处理语言行为的差异及其不同的效果上，以特定的文化方法描述并探讨交际参与者在特定情境下的语言行为。在多元文化相互影响的条件下对意义的交流过程所开展的话语分析得益于低成本移动摄像技术的发展。研究者可以通过录下真正的跨文化交际过程，对多种文化相互影响的情景下的特定交流开展微观分析。跨文化中的话语研究对外语教学领域变得日益重要，因为当外语学习者想把课堂知识应用到真实的跨文化交际情境中时，这些分析给他们提供了所需要能力的语言基础。

跨文化情境这一概念与跨文化交际是密不可分的，因为交际的参与者为建立共识基础而必须开展一些框架性的交际活动。交际情境（IS）产生于如下条件：来自不同的文化（$C_1$-$C_n$）讲不同语言的人（1-n），他们交流不同的内容，可以谈论抽象的概念或具体的实物，也可以是社会机制或体制或人的感知。根据不同目的，交谈者进行交流，执行言语行为以便达到说服或批评等目的。一般说来只要出现来自不同文化的交流者就决定了交际情境的文化多样性。在交际情境中，合作者需要利用元认知思维和掌握特定的坦诚的行为来协商和控制相互之间特定文化的表述以及对语言行为和知识基础的接受。当然跨文化情境并不是不同文化的简单的混合，它是由参与合作者本人通过利用不同的场景的不同成分设立第三种文化基础并创造情景对话的情况下构建而成。

譬如说在某个特定情景下一群来自英、法、瑞典和德国的人士为了讨论一些商务活动，安排在 Frankfurt 相聚。在这个跨文化交际中，聚会所涉及的不同文化系统有意无意地决定了这一情景的跨文化性。在已知的跨文化情境中，以下不同的文化可被视为相互交流的共同框架：文化 1（$C_1$）：第一位说话者的背景文化（英国）；文化 2（$C_2$）：第二位说话者的背景文化（法国）；文化 n-1（$C_{n-1}$）：第 n-1 位说话者的背景文化（瑞典）；文化 n（$C_n$）：第 n 位说话者的背景文化（德国）；文化 s——特定文化领域（$C_S$）：来自不同文化讲不同语言地的人士（$C_1$-$C_n$）当前相互交流时所处在的特定文化领域（此例中为德国）；文化 m——交流工具（CM）：作为共同的交流工具的外语文化领域，比如说英国；文化 n（$C_n$）——中性文化：跨文化交流时所使用的英美商界共同使用的中性文化。

跨文化交际参与者的任务是基于相互交流的跨文化标准和语言规则，利用微妙的或明确的暗示在跨文化情境中进行磋商。实际上跨文化情境的基础可建立在如下框架之中：(1) 上面所提到的特定文化领域（$C_S$），也就是当前的交际情境（既然本次商务活动在德国，提议以德国文化模式作为当前交际情景文化）；(2) 用某位参与者的文化领域（$C_2$）（譬如法语）；(3) 把英语作为一门共同语，使用英美商界文化领域常被视为中立性的人为的文化背景（$C_n$）；(4) 新的文化框架 IC，即由参与者特别创立并包括那些对该群体、情境和交际目的等多个文化领域均有利的方面。

上述范例也显示了跨文化交流相互理解的某种趋势：跨文化情境中的参与者意识到不同文化所表述的意义的文化局限，并试图在原文化交流的意义基础上为共同定义的框架、意义、语言行为和语言过程建设性地创立一个理解基础。根据 Koole & Ten Thije (1994) 的观点,这种共同知识和行为的实施被称为话语跨文化。

跨文化的参与者在跨文化情境中的任务就是利用明确的或含糊的暗示,以及充分的文化标准系统和语言交流规则来进行协商。Sarangi (1994) 和 Clyne (1994) 把对跨文化交流的分析尝试性地分为三种基本方法:文化人类学视角(不同人士代表不同文化。正因为来自不同文化背景,所以不同文化之间的交际会产生各种不同的交际问题);跨文化语用学视角(寻求对语言行为的预设模式的不同再现);互动型的社会语言学视角。这三个学派都宣称跨文化交际中的误解是文化定位的原因。一些话语分析专家对这一宣称提出了质疑和批评。其实正如一些访谈和数据资料所示,大多数跨文化交际中的合作参与者都是按此行事并做出相应反应的。因此在跨文化交际中,具体情景中的话语和它的第三方文化效应并不只是由合作参与者的文化背景和语言行为共同决定,而是在很大程度上由他们的理解(或误解)和语言行为的归因决定的。任何有价值的跨文化交际研究都应该集中在参与者如何感知其他文化的语言表现,如何创造"新"意义,有效地适应交际时所构建的新的情景。因此跨文化交际有价值的研究大多集中在以下两个方面:参与者如何理解他人一方的语言现象;如何为了适应所创造的特定情景而创造新的意义。这意味着人们不只依靠他人的文化标准还要考虑他人的价值观,最终适应说话对方的外国文化标准和行为。任何努力和尝试(比如研究在外语课堂里如何改善跨文化交际)不只是依靠教学输入的量而要依靠合作参与者的跨文化能力。

## Questions for reflection:

1. Is intercultural situation simply the merging of different cultures? Why?
2. What is the task of the participants in the intercultural communication?

3. What should intercultural communication research focus on?

## 5. 跨文化能力

跨文化能力指与来自不同文化背景的人士进行有效的相互交流的能力。文化之间总是在一些方面共通而另一些方面相异，比如人的信仰、习惯和价值观。所谓文化的普遍性或共同性方面是指那些共有的又具有各自文化特性的方面。文化的共通性越少而特定性越多，文化就越被视为相异。

有效的跨文化交流指那些既有文化共同性又有文化相异性的人士在彼此互尊互利的基础上进行的成功磋商。Smith, Paige 和 Steglitz 给交流的"有效性"和"恰当性"作了如下界定：恰当性指交流符合语境和关系标准。有效性指交流达到预期的结果和目的或满足交流双方的需要或关注。因此根据自我与他人的关系的不同类型，跨文化能力具有不同的含义。

根据 Byram 的观点，跨文化能力比交际能力更为复杂，准确地说是因为它主要集中在"建立和保持关系"，而不只是交流或交换信息（Byram，1997）。因此在 Meyer 看来，"充分和灵活"是指外语或外国文化学习者应该培养的能力，因为这些能力能帮助学习者意识到文化差异并能够解决差异所引起的矛盾。

达到成功的跨文化交流的困难不一定在于文化背景的隔阂，还存在一些非文化的因素，比如说人格。语言因素也是发展和获得跨文化能力的一个重要方面。跨文化交流可以指进行交流的语言是所有交流者的母语或外语的情况，也可以指该语言是部分人的母语而是另外一些人的外语的情况。因此 Byram 把"跨文化能力"界定为"用母语与来自不同国家和文化的人进行交流的能力"，而把"跨文化交流能力"界定为用外语与来自不同国家和文化的人士进行交流的能力。他把两个概念区分开来。

**跨文化代言者：**

Byram 和 Zarate 把外语学习者或外国文化的学习者看成跨文化代言者，即指那些跨越国界和文化的界限，在某种程度上传播文化特征和象征性的价值观的专业人士（1997）。跨文化代言者斡旋于两种或多种文化身份之间，在自我和他人的文化之间、社会和政治之间进行协调。也就是说跨文化代言者必须具有批判性。批判性质的跨文化代言者通过领会不同的话语、通过对他人的说话方式如何定位以及定位如何影响他们的视角等的思考来批判地利用这个开放的世界。

**跨文化能力的学习：**

跨文化代言者作为文化界限的跨越者，充分利用了建立不同的、正式的或非正式的跨文化交流机会来感受各种不同的经历。然而跨文化代言者并非游移于各种文化之上的世界居民。有些跨文化代言者也在致力于把各种跨文化交流的经历转换为各种跨文化关系。因此跨文化能力的获得是一个复杂的过程。它不仅仅是意识到"他人"和"自我"的区别，还包括逐渐养成的、在内文化与跨文化的意义之间挣扎的一张网。Byram 和 Zarate 指出了影响外国语言文化教育中培养跨文化能力的诸因素。Byram 把批判性的文化意识（评价文化的理性的明确的观点）作为跨文化能力模式的重点。

**跨文化能力的教育：**

传授外国语言文化的教师或学习外国语言文化的学生的主要目的不再只是模仿那些以外语为母语的人的标准说话模式（Byram and Zarate, 1997）。教师应该放弃自己作为目的语文化使者的身份，摒弃外国文化是静态、独立、奇特的文化的观念，应该了解文化之间相互影响的本质及其社会、政治、道德上的各种含义。对外国语言文化教育的这种认识由于会对教师职业身份的认同产生影响从而会对教师自身的发展产生深刻的影响（Byram and Risager, 1999）。在教师发展项目中，跨学科研究和跨文化训练已日益显著地呈现出来。以大学课堂教育为基础的跨文化能力教育和直接的跨文化的经验性的学习非常重要而且是互补的，因为二者都会产生一些认知的、情感的和行为上的结果。为了激励教师在课堂上进一步培养学生的跨文化能力，在教师培训中采取深度理解、反思、探索式研究，实证式应用等方式把跨文化的理论和实践结合起来显得非常重要。理论联系实际可以通过结合国内的人类文化学的学习和去国外进行跨文化实践而实现。教师绝不是要被目的文化同化掉，而是要在对待外国文化教学、本土文化和目的文化及跨文化交流时培养一种批判精神。

**Questions for reflection:**

1. Compare the two concepts of "intercultural competence" and "communicative competence".
2. How do you learn intercultural competence?
3. Why should intercultural speaker be critical?
4. What is the main target of teaching intercultural competence?

# Globalisation, Internationalisation and Post-modernism

## Globalisation and Internationalism: Democratic Prospects for World Education

Phillip W. Jones

*ABSTRACT: The logic of globalisation contrasts markedly with that of internationalism. The latter, with its intrinsically democratic foundation, looks to a world ordered by structures supportive of that functionalism which is embedded in accountability. Globalisation, by contrast, implies few logical imperatives in favour of accountability, but rather looks to the pursuit of interest on the global level through the operation of unfettered capitalism. Implications for the sustaining of multilateral post-war arrangements are explored and analysed particularly in terms of war, its causes and its prevention. The notion of peace as human rights in action leads to the consideration of multilateral agenda in education, and the stances in a globalising world of the key multilaterals in education—UNICEF, UNESCO and the World Bank—with conclusions put forward concerning their relative grounding in the logic of internationalism or, alternatively, in the logic of globalisation.*

## Introduction

My intention is to explore the tension between globalisation and internationalism. Each relates to education in quite different ways, particularly with respect to the expectations implied in each about the social functions of education. In essence, globalisation is seen as economic integration, achieved in particular through the establishment of a global marketplace marked by free trade and a minimum of regulation. In contrast, internationalism refers to the promotion of global peace and well-being through the development and application of international structures, primarily but not solely of an intergovernmental kind. Despite important conceptual difficulties in formulating the case for internationalism and despite the world's patchy record in putting its principles into effect, the essentially pro-democratic logic of internationalism stands in sharp contrast to the logic of globalisation. To the extent that choice is feasible, the argument here supports the accountability implied by internationalism. Implications are acknowledged not only at the level of international cooperation in education, but also and perhaps more importantly in terms of the out-workings at local levels of the international dynamics of education.

## The Concept of Globalisation

I am using here a model of globalisation which starts with its most obvious and fundamental feature—the organisation and integration of economic activity at levels which transcend national borders and jurisdictions. I use the word jurisdictions advisedly, given the sheer force of much of the globalisation process as it transcends the taxation and regulatory discipline which is conventionally the concern and responsibility of national governments. This is the sense taken up by such analysts as Hirst & Thompson (1996) who saw in globalisation the attainment of century-old ideals of the free-trade liberals and who looked to 'a demilitarized world in which business activity is primary and political power has no other tasks than the protection of the world free trading system' (p. 176). In highlighting the essentially ungovernable quality of any emerging globalised economy, I do not join those who see in globalization the collapse of the state or the erosion of governmental participation in economic life. On the contrary, the logic of globalisation implies the active involvement of state mechanisms in order to ensure the unfettered operation of markets, both capital and labour. Reconstituted states, in fact, begin to behave like economic entrepreneurs in a free market. One of the ironies of globalisation is its reliance on the state to make possible the free operation of markets implying, as Hirst & Thompson (1996) put it, that global markets are 'by no means beyond regulation and control' (p. 3).

The use of the term globalisation in this focused sense began, of course, within the business world itself and referred to globalisation as a means of conducting business more efficiently, more profitably and more discreetly. It will cause no surprise to claim that an integral part of this aim was the intention to open up the world's markets and minimise the supervisory role of public authorities within them. Much of the globalisation process came to be dependent on the adoption of reduced roles for government, not only as a regulator but also as a provider of public services funded in large measure through taxation. With many nations revealing interesting differences in how economic rationalist agendas were promoted and applied within them, at a global level the promotion of a 'New World Order' took on a distinct form and character of its own. While arguments might rightly persist about the current and likely extent or intensity of globalisation, clarity is needed when considering the logic of globalisation and any claims made about its effects. A new division of labour between nations is only one aspect of this, whereby the economic outlook for various groups of nations varies enormously.

At its heart, the story of globalisation is as much the story of changes within individual nations as changes in economic relations between and among them. This is an emphasis taken up by many commentators who, like Robertson (1991) see a tying up of the universal and the particular as part of a 'globewide cultural nexus [bound up by a] universality of experience' (p. 76). Here we see how necessary it becomes to move beyond a straight forward reductionist view of economic integration in any analysis of globalisation. Hall (1991 a, b), for example, insisted upon an emphasis on how the global articulates with the local and upon a view of globalisation that recognises the inevitability of persistent multiplicity and diversity among cultures rather than the inevitability of bland homogenisation. Adopting a bottom-up view of globalisation is necessary, claimed Hall (1991a), if we are to avoid the simplicity of a reductionist view of globalisation as 'monolithic, non-contradictory, uncontested' (p. 32). At the same time, Hall (1991b) and I seem aligned on how the global affects the local:

> I think of the global as something having more to do with the hegemonic sweep at which a certain configuration of local particularities try to dominate the whole scene, to mobilize the technology and to incorporate, in subaltern positions, a variety of more localized identities to construct the next historical project. (p. 67)

What made globalisation agendas feasible were, of course, the communications and information revolutions, combined with an increased mobility of persons, services and goods. They can usefully be seen as the tools of economic integration, as prominent means whereby the creation of a new world economic order is facilitated. Much discussion of globalization and its effects cannot get far without reference to them and it becomes problematic if we insist too much that they be recognised as conceptually distinct from globalisation itself. Their own logic does not imply globalisation, yet globalisation as we are experiencing it would not be possible without them. Such issues come to the heart of the ultimate incompatibility of world systems' understandings of globalisation as championed by Wallerstein (1991a) and his followers with what Robertson (1992) claimed to be 'more wideranging, open and fluid' (p. 15) concepts of global unification, demanding not an economic focus but a 'cultural focus':

> We have come increasingly to recognize that while economic matters are of tremendous importance in relations between societies and in various forms of transnational relations, those matters are increasingly subject to cultural contingencies and cultural coding. Even more relevant in the present context, it is becoming more and more apparent that no matter how much the issue of 'naked' national self-interest may enter into the interactions of nations there are still crucial issues of a basically cultural nature which structure and shape most relations, from the hostile to the friendly, between nationally organized societies. (Robertson, 1992, p. 4; see also Robertson, 1990)

If classical Marxism has inspired those who, like Wallerstein (1991a, b), insist on the primacy of the economic as the determinant of the political and the cultural, the legacy of Parsons (1996, 1997) in the work of Robertson (1990, 1991, 1992) and others cannot be overlooked either, with its insistence on culture as the engine of the economic and the political. Waters (1995, p. 3) perhaps made some progress: while he characterised globalisation as a weakening of the constraints of space and time on economic, political and cultural arrangements, he suggested that the dominances of the relationships between the three 'systems' are themselves determined by space and time. Waters (1995), like Hall (1991a, b), in looking to the transcending of national boundaries, accepted the likelihood of a single world society and culture, territoriality being an increasingly weak organising principle. However, at the same time, Waters (1995) insisted on how 'extremely abstract' this universality was likely to be, being erected on a fundamental 'tolerance for diversity and individual choice'. He saw a globalised world as unlikely to be 'harmoniously integrated although it might conceivably be. Rather it will probably tend towards high levels of differentiation, multicentricity and chaos' (Waters, 1995, p. 3). Little (1996, p. 428) succinctly organised various aspects of Waters' (1995, pp. 96, 127 and 157) ideal typical patterns of globalisation along the following lines.

*Economic Globalisation*
(1) Freedom of exchange between localities with indeterminate flows of services and symbolic commodities.
(2) The balance of production activity in a locality determined by its physical and geographical advantages.
(3) Minimal direct foreign investment.
(4) Flexible responsiveness of organisations to global markets.
(5) Decentralised, instantaneous and 'stateless' financial markets.
(6) Free movement of labour.

*Political Globalisation*
(1) An absence of state sovereignty and multiple centres of power at global, local and intermediate levels.
(2) Local issues discussed and situated in relation to a global community.
(3) Powerful international organisations predominant over national organisations.
(4) Fluid and multicentric international relations.
(5) A weakening of value attached to the nation-state and a strengthening of common and global political values.

*Cultural Globalisation*
(1) A deterritorialised religious mosaic.
(2) A deterritorialised cosmopolitanism and diversity.
(3) Widespread consumption of simulations and representations.
(4) Global distribution of images and information.
(5) Universal tourism and the 'end of tourism'.

Although it is easy to overstate the speed and intensity of economic globalisation, it is important to appreciate its impact to date. The various agendas of globalisation by nature are mutually reinforcing and increasingly leave participants who refuse to 'play ball' isolated and, yet, at a comparative disadvantage. Second and in the same way can be seen the multiplier effect of globalisation on the processes which promote it—communications, information technology (IT), and mobility. Each intensifies as it is called into play and each becomes a more dominant aspect of our lives and of the world scene. The enormous implications for culture have, rightly, been the object of much consideration [if somewhat restricted in the Waters' (1995) typology just considered].

The political character and consequences of globalisation are also the object of a great deal of discussion. Conventions of the nation-state, of governance, of accountability and of the public versus private domain become unsettled. Governments are called upon to and indeed do revise their role and reduce the scope of their work. Notions of the public good shift in order to accommodate reduced expectations about accountability, regulation and taxation, which in turn lead to not only reduced but transformed expectations about what public services and infrastructure consist of. Social relations are scrambled, frequently in ways which promote reckless individualism. Identity, diversity, responsibility, and accountability—each fails to escape the impact of fundamental assaults on democratic institutions and on the careful balances of self-determination at the individual, communal and national levels [a useful discussion is Strange (1997)].

What I particularly wish to take up here are the effects of globalisation on international order. I have already referred to the establishment and reinforcement of divisions of labour which impose structural divisions between winners, losers and those somewhere in between, contrary to the 'win-win' rhetoric so prevalent in globalisation discourse (for an extended analysis see Burbach et al. (1996)). Such structural inequalities can only have profound implications for the world's prospects for peace, the acceptance of human rights, environmental integrity and the self-determination of peoples. The yawning chasm between individualistic capitalism and democracy gives rise to concern about the application of democratic principles and practices at the international level as well as the local. Further, the effects of globalisation upon those fragile commitments to international peace and well-being effected through international organisations, the promotion of international standards and norms, and the promotion of international law need to be considered (for an overview see Cox, 1994, 1997). Globalisation has collided with them front on and it is a far from trivial matter to gauge the damage done to the world's prospects.

## Internationalism and Global Order

The vast literature on internationalism is bound together by its focus on international order, with its traditions revealing varying degrees of both idealism and practicability. Bull's (1977, pp. 3-22) famous characterisation of international order cannot be ignored—as activity (and commitment to activity) designed to promote the specified goals of the 'society of states', goals which he ranked in descending order of priority: first, preserving commitment to the society of states itself; second, preserving the sovereignty and independence of individual states; and third, promoting peace (see also Goldmann, 1994, p. 210). Permeating this focus on international order are what might be called common-sense notions of international community, international cooperation, international community of interests and international dimensions of the common good, of the kind which frequently find their way into dictionary definitions of internationalism.

Given the idealism surrounding much of the internationalist stance, it is important to appreciate the degree to which its focus on order enables consideration to proceed of means as well as ends. Whether emphasis is placed on the creation and application of international law or on communications and exchanges at the international level or the conduct of business through international organisational frameworks, internationalism looks to ordered, structural means of giving practical expression to outward-looking, universalist stances. They stand in stark contrast to both vague Utopianism and inward-looking isolationism.

If deterrence lies at the heart of conventional interpretations of the internationalist ideal and their applications in international order, the problem of the causes of war remains as a separate and crucial issue. If the early advocates of international organisation promoted agendas based on disincentives to embark on war, they overlooked much of the classical liberal explanation of war and its causes that was developing at the same time. The promotion of peace by the promotion of free trade comes to the heart of matters when the tensions between globalisation and internationalism are considered. Goldmann (1994) summed it up well, drawing on the work of Silberner (1946, pp. 280-283):

> The key to the classical liberal analysis of war was the conviction that war was due to a false conception of the national interest. Free trade was immensely preferable to war, it was argued, contributing not only to the material prosperity of nations but also to the intellectual and moral progress of mankind [sic]. It would strengthen the peaceful ties that unite nations and the pacific spirit among men [sic]. Freedom of commerce would thus substantially reduce the risk of war or even eliminate it altogether. (p. 10)

Goldmann (1994) went on to sum up some key ideas in classical liberal-economic pacifism. 'Uninhibited international commerce, to the minds of many liberals', (Goldmann, 1994, p. 12) was associated with the following.

(1) The growing realisation that, in each nation, free trade was to the advantage of everybody but a small minority.

(2) The growing realisation that nations had a common interest in peaceful relations with one another and in each other's welfare.

(3) The growth of those forces or classes in society with particular interest in peaceful international discourse and the decline of elements less interested in the maintenance of peace (the state apparatus, particularly the military).

Over a century later, such a summary seems fresh and relevant to current debates. At the heart of such thinking was the severing of the link between economic development and military opportunism. Balances of power, at the end of the day, would shift in favour of those with vested interests in peace. I have argued elsewhere how such expressions came to be interpreted in light of the League of Nations experience, the breakdown of economic order associated with the depression of the late 1920s and 1930s and World War II itself (Jones, 1993). The major conceptual development, in terms of the mid-century ordering of the international world, was the emphasis placed on functionalism, seen profoundly in the design of the United Nations system. Not only did functionalism provide the emerging system with a practical emphasis, it also bedded down the principle of the transfer (or, at the very least, the replication) of state functions to international organisations, in the name of the great quantity of business that governments needed to transact between themselves at more than the bilateral level. The great pillars of peace, progress and human rights emerged as the cornerstones of what international organisation was there to promote and, despite disappointments about degrees of success, it is fair to say that such impulses remain at the heart of popular folklore about the purposes and functions of the international system.

## Democracy, Order and Prospects for Peace and Well-being

An essential element in much thinking on the logic of internationalism is its affinity with democracy, to the extent that internationalism is, for many, best understood as a product of democratic institutions at work. As soon as internationalism finds expression in ordered, structural ways, the democratic requirement is readily accommodated, it being evident that just as domestic political institutions might be shaped along democratic lines, so too can those which make and give effect to decisions at the international level. Goldmann (1994) took up the point:

> Just as opinions are freely formed and expressed within democracies, and just as democratic leaders are expected to be influenced by them, opinions can be formed at the international level and ought to influence international politics—an assumption to this effect is implicit in internationalist reasoning.... And just as democracy presumes pluralistic diversity within a consensual framework, cooperative links ought to multiply across national borders so as to promote both transnational diversity and consensus on fundamentals. (p. 53)

This stance leaves considerable room for internationalists to disclaim any interest in establishing a world state, democratic or otherwise. It is a peaceful and cooperative interstate system which defines international order, despite the inevitable tensions between respecting sovereign independence while applying democratic principles at the international level (Goldmann, 1994, p. 54). Invoking both Immanuel Kant and Woodrow Wilson, Goldmann (1994) acknowledged the ways in which internationalist agendas go hand in hand with democratic change at the domestic level: ' [It is part of] the tradition of internationalist thinking to consider law, organization, exchange, and communication to be more likely to lead to peace and security if states are democratic than if they are authoritarian' (p. 54).

This comes to the heart of the matter if the negative impact of globalisation on domestic democratic institutions is extended to the international arena. It is of fundamental interest to consider the extent to which international peace, security and well-being depend upon the maintenance of democratic institutions and practices at the domestic level. The question also brings us to consider the possibility and extent to which the international framework as currently and recently effected (since 1945) is an expression of hegemony exercised on behalf of Western capitalism. If so, it is also worth considering whether globalisation, by weakening international frameworks, is in fact pushing them into less powerful and thereby less hegemonic positions. The post-hegemonic character of emerging international frameworks becomes a key element in any consideration. The way forward may well be to consider which elements of present-day international structures are best seen as aligned with the democratic impulses of the internationalist ideal and which others can only be seen as the vanguards of globalisation. The likelihood is strong that a highly differentiated system of intergovernmental structures is emerging, some elements lying beyond the accountability demanded by the logic of internationalism.

My concern with the preservation of democracy brings me back to the interplay between the global and the local. My starting point here is to dissuade any reader of the notion that the international economic interdependence deriving from globalisation has anything to do with the logic of internationalism, that is the free association of sovereign states. On the contrary, globalisation brings with it an economic dynamic that is associated with a profound shift in how we regard sovereignty and the very idea of statehood. They are eroding, and quickly. It is an extremely complex moment in history, to see the erosion of national economies, of national identities and cultures and of nationhood. Hall (1991a) thoughtfully invited us to compare the rise of nationhood, with its aggressive and frequently racist stances, with responses to its decline, which indeed might be similarly aggressive and xenophobic:

> One of the things which happens when the nation-state begins to weaken, becoming less convincing and less powerful, is that the response seems to go in two ways simultaneously. It goes above the nation-state and it goes below it. It goes global and local in the same moment. (pp. 26-27)

Going global implies, perforce, the emergence of new patterns of economic organization—new structures, new systems, new modalities. The primary criterion which seems to be applied to them is that of freedom from state supervision and regulation, both domestically through (national) governments and internationally through intergovernmental mechanisms. However, such patterns produce—require—their own forms of cultural expression. We see emerging a global culture which, as a form of mass culture, is intimately bound up with the economics and politics of globalisation. To call it a homogenised culture, however, may be grossly misleading. While such populist writers in organisation 'theory' as Schwartz (1996, pp. 118-134) propelled us into coming to terms with the mass culture of the 'new global teenager' we might be better advised to ponder the tolerance of cultural globalisation for diversity. That is to say, while capital and power remain uncompromisingly centred, that concentration requires no mandatory expression in narrow cultural terms. Hall (1991a) also took up the point, referring to the dynamics of global mass culture and whether it is usefully seen as 'homogenisation':

> It does not attempt to obliterate.... It has to hold the whole framework of globalization in place and simultaneously police that system; it stage-manages independence within it, so to speak. You have to think about the relationship between the United States and Latin America to discover what I am talking about, how those forms which are different, which have their own specificity, can nevertheless be repenetrated, absorbed, reshaped, negotiated, without absolutely destroying what is specific and particular to them. (pp. 28-29)

The logic of globalisation tolerates, indeed requires, the promotion of cultural (and possibly political) difference and diversity. Globalisation will build on diversity and needs to work through patterns that seem paradoxical—both global and decentred—forms of social organisation which convey powerful symbolic images of choice, freedom and diversity.

Globalisation might build a unitary world, but one which celebrates difference while at the same time neutralising it—reducing difference and diversity ultimately to matters of lifestyle, consumption, and seeking pleasure, rather than the essential requirements of democracy? Will globalisation's embracing of difference and diversity foster a cruel misunderstanding of freedom?

At this point I wish to return to the question of war and take up once again the question of which patterns of world order might be more likely to prevent outbreaks of war. In fact, I would prefer to push the matter more vigorously and ask more positively about the world's prospects for peace, attracted as I am to that notion of peace as 'human rights in action'. The classical liberal agenda for peace, to make the point again, looks to economic incentives, whereby a free, global market-place makes warfare superfluous. It is here that a fascinating juxtaposition between globalisation and internationalism can be contemplated. Let me use Goldmann (1994) to set the scene:

> The fact that democratic states do not fight each other has been characterized as 'one of the strongest nontrivial or nontautological generalizations that can be made about international relations' [Russett, 1990, p. 123]. The absence of war between democratic states, in the words of another scholar, 'comes as close to anything we have to an empirical law in international relations' [Levy, 1989, p. 270].... The association between democracy and absence of war cannot be accounted for in terms of other variables like wealth, economic growth, and common alliances.... insofar as can be ascertained, the absence of war between democracies is in fact related to the democratic form of government. (p. 158)

A range of explanations is evident, naturally enough, it being remembered that the point being made is that democracies appear unlikely to wage war upon each other (we need little reminding of their capacity to embark on hostilities with others). Nineteenth-century pacifism emphasised the popular will, the disinclination of citizens to agree that war was in their interest, whereas more contemporary explanations might look more to institutional checks and balances in democratic states, that division of powers that includes the need for public debate, making it 'difficult for democratic leaders to move their countries into war' (Ember et al., 1992, p. 576). The democratic impulse, it can be assumed, revolves around norms of tolerance and mutual respect. Democratic institutions, at the same time, can be relied upon to be more cautious or at least to be less inclined to impulsive or hasty actions. If such are 'rules of thumb' within democratic societies, can such norms be expected to prevail between democratic peoples?

Such reasoning, when pushed, can take us into very dangerous territory, with its implied dismissal of international peace building in favour of appeals to democracy pure and simple, that is, that international peace is a matter of domestic politics after all. Where the argument is misleading, in my view, is that it fails to distinguish precisely enough between the operation of democratic principles at the international and with the openness of international relationships. Openness (of markets, of communications, etc.) is not to be understood as democracy and the blurring of the two has led directly to a recycling of the neoliberal evocation of the operation of untrammelled free markets as the world's best hope for peace and security.

Goldmann's (1994) reminder that 'it is not necessary that all or even most states are democratic in order for internationalism to work' (p. 160) is useful in this context. Yet it is a giant leap to proceed from the premise that universal democracy is not a necessary precondition for internationalism to work to any claim that widespread economic integration might suffice. Rightly, Goldmann (1994) called for further research on how domestic and international relations interact in order to produce certain policy outcomes:

The old issue of cooperation and war is linked to one that is more up-to-date: the internationalization of domestic politics and the domestic-politicization of international politics. The more politics become what Putnam calls a two-level game [Putnam, 1988], and the more intertwined international and domestic politics become in other ways, the greater the likelihood that peace and security will be affected by international cooperation. By the same token, the more we learn about the links between politics at the international and national levels in different types of political systems, the greater our ability to specify the conditions under which cooperation will play a part in inhibiting war. (p. 161)

## Multilateral Agenda in Education

Education has not remained innocent of the differentiation now so evident within the present-day multilateral system. I have outlined elsewhere the essence of the multilateral argument as it affects education, as well as outlining the prominent organisational arrangements (Jones, 1993). Part of the picture is the stark contrast between the declared educational policies of several agencies, whose differences stem not so much from their constitutional mandates as their funding bases. In fact, a compelling case can be made that each agency's policy is a direct product of how its funds are secured, an understanding of which can also provide insight into an agency's stance in relation to the globalization/internationalism divide.

The United Nations Children's Fund (UNICEF), for example, relies massively upon voluntary contributions (whether from governments, non-government organisations (NGOs) or private bodies and individuals). Accordingly, its analyses of need tend to be dramatic, its projections tend to be alarmist and its solutions tend to be populist. Its annual survey *The State of the World's Children* can be relied upon to provide a strong example (for example United Nations Children's Fund, 1997). Importantly, UNICEF rhetoric about prospects for the well-being of children and their carers is notable for the way in which the agency's sources of funds mirrors the agency's view about the provision of social services.

The United Nations Educational, Scientific and Cultural Organisation (UNESCO), in contrast, relies on compulsory levies imposed by formula upon governments, the wealthiest of which invariably combine to render UNESCO as lowcost an organisation as possible. Accordingly, the cash-strapped UNESCO can afford expansive rhetoric it need not match with funded operations. Further, UNESCO's insistence that its policies and programmes be constructed on the basis of universality and consensus renders inevitable the much-vaunted generality of UNESCO stances. A good example is the report on education for the twenty-first century prepared by Jacques Delors and the commission he chaired, a report which projected a concern for democracy, social inclusion and human-centred development in a way which reflects UNESCO's 'niche' in the international system (United Nations Educational, Scientific and Cultural Organisation, 1996).

In contrast again, the World Bank, which raises its loanable capital commercially and administers itself through its trading profits, can remain aloof from the need to ask any government, NGO or private entity for funds [although its soft credit arm, the International Development Association (IDA), is so dependent]. The World Bank is a free agent as far as intergovernmental structures are concerned, its obligations resting with the international markets which provide its loanable capital.

Today, the matter might well involve the extent to which this or that agency is better seen as an expression of conventional internationalism or has shifted ground in terms of its place in a globalised world. To risk bluntness, the World Bank provides a clear-cut example of how the logic of internationalism can be disposed of, in favour of the logic of globalisation. Not that this has recently occurred, the essentially banking nature of the World Bank determining its fundamental character at its conception at Bretton Woods.

Despite the often neglected fact that it is both an intergovernmental organisation and a specialised agency of the United Nations, the World Bank functions with a stark degree of independence. At the same time, it provides a fascinating window onto the world of international finance, a world which lacks a shopfront but which nevertheless operates in terms of ideology with strong social content. I have argued at length, in fact, that we cannot understand World Bank education policy independently of its position as a bank (Jones, 1992). What has recently emerged, however, is a willingness to bring its ideology of globalisation to centre stage in its statements of education policy. This stands in stark contrast to the three earlier decades of educational involvement, when World Bank rhetoric about its education portfolio failed to acknowledge its fundamental debt to its economic and fiscal basis (see also Jones, 1997).

This basis establishes, in the view of the World Bank, a set of preconditions for successful educational policy and practice and which override any views about educational processes the bank might wish to promote. These preconditions, of course, are precisely the agenda of globalisation, championed by a bank which seeks to consolidate its own role at the heart of an integrated world economy. Its chance came in large measure with the end of the Cold War, at which time the bank rapidly switched to the 'transition economies' of Eastern Europe as its priority region, displacing sub-Saharan Africa with its chronic debt and persistently negative growth rates (although its enthusiasm for 'structural adjustment' along the logical lines of globalisation was universally applied to its member countries from the early 1980s). Yet it was only in 1995 that World Bank education policy, as officially codified, embraced the globalisation agenda in its *Policies and Strategies for Education: A World Bank Review*, the first formal statement of bank education policy since 1980 (World Bank, 1995; for extended commentary see Bennell, 1996; Burnett, 1996; Burnett & Patrinos, 1996; Lauglo, 1996; Samoff, 1996; Jones, 1997).

The World Bank's preconditions for education can only be understood as an ideological stance in promoting an integrated world economic system along market lines. It attempts to find intellectual grounding in human capital theory, an attempt I have discussed earlier (Jones, 1992, pp. 233-238) and champions public austerity and a reduced role for government in the provision of education. In painting a picture of the preconditions for successful educational development, the World Bank is in effect depicting its view of the ideal economy.

It is an economy which at best can only tolerate public education. The role of government is that of protector of the poor and the disadvantaged, provider of market information about educational provision, as 'compensator' for market failures in education and setter and monitor of standards in education. It is an economy in which the management of education 'by central or state governments which allows little room for the flexibility that leads to effective learning' (World Bank, 1995, pp. 3-6). It is an economy in which 'educational priorities should be set with reference to outcomes, using economic analysis, standard setting, and measurement of achievement through learning assessments' (World Bank, 1995, p. 8). What is euphemistically termed 'household involvement' in education, understood in terms of maximising household choice in education, is placed at a premium in such an economy. The 'risks' involved are easily identified and it is, accordingly, an economy in which fundamental difficulties and obstacles to equity can be easily managed. It is an economy which can afford to pass to communities and households some of the costs of education. 'Even very poor communities are often willing to contribute toward the cost of education, especially at the primary level' (World Bank, 1995, p. 105). It is an economy which has shed the disagreeable effects of centralised control over education. Centralised control only fosters centralised teachers' unions, for example, which 'can disrupt education and sometimes lead to political paralysis' (World Bank, 1995, p. 137). It is an economy in which decentralisation fosters reform, in which parental and community control, 'when accompanied by measures to ensure equity in the provision of resources, can offset much of the power of vested interests, such as teachers' unions and the elite' (World Bank, 1995, p. 140). At least in urban areas, decentralization 'can be enhanced by the use of market mechanisms that increase accountability and choice' (World Bank, 1995, p. 140).

For the first time there is unambiguous consonance between the World Bank's economic, political and ideological goals and those of its education sector. Explicitly, the market is looked to for provision of accountability. Choice transcends democracy. Freedom is trivialised.

What I have not attempted here is a comprehensive survey of multilateral frameworks in order to assess the differential alignments within them in terms of the globalization-internationalism divide. However, it is no trivial matter to ponder their democratic bases and to consider which elements might or might not contribute to a post-hegemonic future. Also remaining for consideration is the emergence of a large array of international nongovernmental organisations (INGOs) many of which, although by definition outside formal intergovernmental structures, are nevertheless beginning to exercise considerable economic, political and cultural influence. With rapidly shifting balances of power, important issues arise about the world's prospects for peace, security and well-being. Should the domestic operation of the market-place be deemed a threat to the application of democratic principles to the decisions that concern people and the lives they lead, then the global market-place should come under the same scrutiny insofar as the people of the world look to some form of international order to enhance the prospects for putting human rights into action.

Those interested in promoting or studying education in international perspective will find a more complex world order than ever before, with the logic of internationalism under threat from an increasingly differentiated and anarchic framework for the conduct of international relations (for discussions see Albrow & King, 1990; Brown & Lauder, 1996; Pannu, 1996; Stewart, 1996). Of particular importance is the need to think afresh about the nature and importance of democracy, democratic institutions and accountability as a basis for democracy. Should our past reliance—at the international level— have been placed in intergovernmental structures and mechanisms in order to safeguard and promote democracy, it will be important to assess the democratic prospects of a globalising world and to think afresh about education and its interactions with nationalism, statism, governmentalism and internationalism.

# References

Albrow, M. & King, E. (eds.) (1990) *Globalization, Knowledge and Society* (London, Sage).

Bennell, P. (1996) *Using and Abusing Rates of Return: A Critique of the World Bank's Education Sector Review*, International Journal of

*Educational Development*, 16, pp. 235-248.

Brown, P. & Lauder, H. (1996) *Education, Globalization and Economic Development*, Journal of Educational Policy, 11, pp. 1-26.

Bull, H. (1977) *The Anarchical Society: A Study of Order in World Politics* (London, Macmillan).

Burach, R., Nunez, O. & Kagarlitsky, B. (1996) *Globalisation and Its Discontents: the Rise of Postmodern Socialism* (London, Pluto Press).

Burnett, N. (1996) *Priorities and Strategies for Education, A World Bank Review: the Process and the Key Messages*, International Journal of Educational Development, 16, pp. 215-220.

Burnett, N. & Patrinos, H. A. (1996) *Response to Critiques of Priorities and Strategies for Education: A World Bank Review*, International Journal of Educational Development, 16, pp. 273-276.

Cox, R. W. (1994) *The Crisis in World Order and the Challenge to International Organization*, Cooperation 29, pp. 99-113.

Cox, R. W. (ed.) (1997) *The New Realism: Perspectives on Multilateralism and World Order* (London, Macmillan for the United Nations University Press).

Ember, C. R., Ember, M. & Russett, B. M. (1992) *Peace between Participatory Polities: A Cross-cultural Test of the Democracies Rarely Fight Each Other's Hypothesis*, World Politics, 44, pp. 573-599.

Goldmann, K. (1994) *The Logic of Internationalism: Coercion and Accommodation* (London and New York, Routledge).

Hall, S. (1991a) *The Local and the Global: Globalization and Ethnicity*, in: A. D. King (ed.) *Culture, Globalization and the World System: Contemporary Conditions for the Representation of Identity*, pp. 19-39 (Binghamton, NY, Department of Art and Art History, Suny).

Hall, S. (1991b) *Old and New Identities, Old and New Ethnicities*, in:

A. D. King (ed.), *Culture, Globalization and the World System: Contemporary Conditions for the Representation of Identity*, pp. 41-68 (Binghamton, NY, Department of Art and Art History, Suny).

Hirst, P. & Thompson, G. (1996) *Globalization in Question* (Cambridge, Polity Press).

Jones, P. W. (1992) *World Bank Financing of Education: Lending, Learning and Development* (London and New York, Routledge).

Jones, P. W. (1993) United Nations Agencies, in: *Encyclopedia of Educational Research*, 6th edn, pp. 1450-1459 (New York, Macmillan).

Jones, P. W. (1997) On World Bank Education Financing, *Comparative Education*, 33, pp. 117-129.

Lauglo, J. (1996) Banking on Education and the Uses of Research: A Critique of World Bank Priorities and Strategies for Education, *International Journal of Educational Development*, 16, pp. 221-233.

Levy, J. S. (1989) The Causes of War: A Review of Theories and Evidence, in: P. E. Tetlock, J. L. Husbaaands, R. Jervis, P. C. Stern & C. Tilly (eds.), *Behavior, Society, and Nuclear War*, Vol. 1 pp. 209-333 (New York, Oxford University Press).

Little, A. W. (1996) Globalisation and Educational Research: Whose Context Counts? *International Journal of Educational Development*, 16, pp. 427-438.

Pannu, R. S. (1996) Neoliberal Project of Globalization: Prospects for Democratization of Education, *Alberta Journal of Educational Research*, 42, pp. 87-101.

Parsons, T. (1966) *Societies* (Englewood Cliffs, Prentice-Hall).

Parsons, T. (1977) *The Evolution of Societies* (Englewood Cliffs, Prentice-Hall).

Putnam, R. D. (1988) Diplomacy and Domestic Politics: *the Logic of Two-level Games, International Organization*, 42, pp. 427-460.

Robertson, R. (1990) *Mapping the Global Condition: Globalization As the Central Concept*, Theory, Culture & Society, 7 (2-3), pp. 15-30.

Rorbertson, R. (1991) *Social Theory, Cultural Relativity and the Problem of Globality*, in: A. D. King (ed.), *Culture, Globalization and the World System: Contemporary Conditions for the Representation of Identity*, pp. 69-90 (Binghamton, NY, Department of Art and Art History, Suny).

Robertson, R. (1992) *Globalization: Social Theory and Global Culture* (London, Sage).

Russett, B. M. (1990) *Controlling the Sword: the Democratic Governance of National Security* (Cambridge, MA, Harvard University Press).

Samoff, J. (1996) *Which Priorities and Strategies for Education? International Journal of Educational Development*, 16, pp. 249-271.

Schwartz, P. (1996) *The Art of the Long View: Planning for the Future in an Uncertain World* (New York, Doubleday).

Silberner, E. (1946) *The Problem of War in Nineteenth Century Economic Thought* (Princeton, NJ, Princeton University Press).

Stewart, F. (1996) *Globalisation and Education*, International Journal of Educational Development, 16, pp. 327-333.

Strange, S. (1997) *Territory, State, Authority and Economy: A New Realist Ontology of Global Political Economy*, in R. W. Cox (ed.), *The New Realism: Perspectives on Multilateralism and World Order*, pp. 3-19 (London, Macmillan for the United Nations University Press).

Uuited Nations Children's Fund (1997) *The State of the World's Children* (New York, United Nation's Children's Fund).

United Nations Educational, Scientific and Cultural Organisation (1996) *Learning : The Treasure within. Report of the International Commis-*

sion on Education for the Twenty-first Century Chaired by Jacques Delors (Paris, United Nations Educational, Scientific and Cultural Organisation).

Wallerstein, I. (1991a) Culture as the Ideological Battleground of the Modern World-system, in M. Featherstone (ed.), *Global Culture: Nationalism, Globalization and Modernity*, pp. 31-56, (London, Newbury Park).

Wallerstein, I. (1991b) *The National and the Universal: Can There Be Such a Thing As World Culture*? in A. D. King (ed.), *Culture, Globalization and the World System: Contemporary Conditions for the Representation of Identity*, pp. 91-105, (Binghamton, NY, Department of Art and Art History, Suny).

Waters, M. (1995) *Globalisation* (London and New York, Routledge).

World Bank (1995) *Policies and Strategies for Education: A World Bank Review* (Washington, DC, World Bank).

[From: *Comparative Education*, *Volume* 34, *No.* 2, 1998, *pp.* 143-155]

## 导读：全球化与国际化：世界教育的民主化前景

### 1. 引言

本文介绍了全球化（globalization）和国际化（internationalism）这两个概念的区别，以及它们与教育之间的关系。首先，作者从概念含义的角度谈到两者在对待责任（accountability）和态度上的区别。作者认为，相比于倡导在全球范围内追逐利益而忽视责任的全球化而言，国际化更加注重通过建立一种国际秩序来行使其责任，倡导世界和平。在谈到国际化与全球教育民主化问题的时候，作者通过引述世界儿童基金组织（UNICEF）、联合国教科文组织（UNESCO）、世界银行（the World Bank）等机构和组织所发表的不同的教育观来讨论全球化或者国际化的不同立场对其所起的作用。

## 2. 全球化

全球化最明显和根本的特征是经济活动的组织和一体的程度超越了国别和国家管辖权,这也就意味着过去属于政府职能范围的税收和管理规定已经开始为经济铺路。政府的职责在于充当协调人的角色并通过征税提供各种服务。尽管如此,作者并不认为在全球化过程中,政府在经济活动中无所作为,相反,政府与国家参与经济的活动不仅不会削弱而是会变得更加积极主动来保证市场资本和人力的顺利运作。Little(1996)把全球化分为经济、政治、文化的全球化。经济全球化是全球化进程的核心和基础;政治全球化主要是经济全球化在政治层面的反映;而文化全球化是技术全球化的副产品。

全球化所带来的不仅是各国国内的变化,同时也是国与国之间经济关系的变化。全球化并不等同于一体化,也不是一元化、霸权化,而是承认多元化和多样性。全球化进程得以实现主要得益于信息革命的发展和人员、服务和商品的自由流动。全球化带来了政府职能的转变,而政府的职能逐步转向为经济服务,正因为如此,人们对什么是公众服务和基础设施产生了不同的理解。政府职能的缩小一定程度上影响了社会关系,尤其是容易引发不考虑后果的个人主义,因而严重影响了民主制度和在个人、集体和国家层面的自制的平衡状态。

全球化给国际秩序也带来了影响。尤其是在社会分工问题上,全球化进程并没有带来像它所鼓吹的那种"双赢"的状态,而是加剧了社会强势群体和弱势群体之间的分化。这种结构上的不平等为世界和平和稳定带来了一定威胁,也加剧了个人主义与民主之间的矛盾,使得民主原则在地方和世界范围内的实行遇到了阻力。

## 3. 国际化和世界秩序

国际化强调各国之间的关系和贸易,并不强调超越国界的发展。与全球化不同的是,国际化并非打破其国家界域,是纯属国家与国家之间的关系与贸易。国家的疆域与界限仍存在,讲求多国性质或特色的现象,并希望达成以国家为单位的合作与贸易。

关于国际化的文献多集中于世界秩序的建立。Bull（1977）谈到了世界秩序的重要特征,他认为世界秩序的建立是一种旨在建立"国家社会"的活动。Goldmann（1994）认为国际化有三个不同层次的目标：第一是维护自己国家内部和地区的社会职责；其次是维护各国的主权独立和完整；然后是推动世界和平与发展。在谈到国际化的这些目标的时候,很多人会把国际化认为是太过理想主义。作者在谈到这一问题时也谈到要把这些目标努力转化成最终的结果。

## 4. 国际化与全球教育

一些学者认为全球教育使全世界的人能够学习与参与到全球社群、系统中。人们之间互为依赖,以达成互相理解。全球系统包括生态、社会、经济与科技。全球教育是关系到人类种族的生存、个人前途以及人类生活品质发展的教育。全球教育成为一种促进国际理解与合作的势力。全球教育是一种对学术卓越的认同,而且也是一种社会责任。

国际化主要是通过人性化教育来实现国与国之间相互依存的关系。其主要特点是：关心、了解世界各国及其种族和人民的历史和文化并采取积极的态度和行为。国际化旨在通过国际合作与努力使最贫穷国家的人民也能有机会接受最基本的国际化教育。国际化所倡导的教育的功能和作用就在于强调人的"自我发展",把教育和学校看成是实现"自我发展"的工具和手段。

## 5. 国际组织的多元化教育观

文章介绍了世界儿童基金组织（UNICEF）、联合国教科文组织（UNESCO）、世界银行（the World Bank）三种不同国际组织在教育观上不同的立场。作者认为以上国际组织教育观的不同主要是源于赞助方的不同，从中我们可以进一步了解全球化与国际化的区别。

由于资金主要来源于志愿捐助，世界儿童基金组织（UNICEF）的教育资助项目倾向于走平民路线。联合国教科文组织（UNESCO）的资金来源主要是各国政府，因此政策倾向于普遍性和共识。而世界银行（the World Bank）由于通过借贷和贸易盈利，因此可以从一定程度上脱离政府，其教育资助也主要是受市场化驱使，以盈利为目的。如今，世界银行把其全球化意识带入其教育政策中，目的是为了巩固在世界经济一体化中的地位。这种做法为我们提供了一个国际化思维为全球化所用的极好范例。

## 6. 结束语

全球化问题是世界各国的教育决策者、专家学者辩论的焦点。在经济全球化的社会里，人被看做是资本和资源。而在国际化的社会里，人的生存是人类存在的本质。教育是为了个人的自我发展和完善。学校教育是工具和手段，是为了创造一个自由与民主的社会。

应该说，教育，尤其是高等教育，作为一个更加全球化社会的作用因素和反应因素，面临着更大的机遇和挑战。全球化社会中的高等教育应该保证平等接受教育、尊重文化多样性和国家主权。保证高等教育质量、促进平等接受高等教育和赋予学习者做出决策的能力是高等教育在日趋全球化环境中面临的主要挑战。因此，我国应将高等教育置于全球化社会中可持续发展的核心地位，鼓励跨国办学，包括提供信息和传播技术辅助的高等教育，加强国家的高等教育能力。

**Questions for reflection:**
1. According to the author, what's the difference between globalization and internationalism?
2. What's the relationship between internationalism and global order?
3. What impact has globalization brought on the democracy and global order?
4. What caused the different educational policies of UNICEF, UNESCO and the World Bank?
5. Why does the author think that democracy is important?

# Globalisation and Education in the Post-colonial World: Towards a Conceptual Framework

Leon Tikly

ABSTRACT: *The article examines the relevance of existing accounts of globalisation and education for low income, postcolonial countries, with special reference to the education systems of sub-Saharan Africa. Using recent developments in globalisation theory, existing accounts are analysed in relation to their view of the origins, nature and future trajectory of globalisation and the implications for education. It is argued that most of the recent literature deals with Western industrialised countries and the newly industrialised countries of the Pacific Rim and therefore has limited relevance for low income countries. The literature that is concerned with low income countries often lacks a firm theoretical basis and has been limited to a discussion of the impact of economic globalisation on education. Drawing on recent work on the political economy of development and the state in Africa, the article sets out a conceptual framework for understand-*

*ing various aspects of the education and globalisation relationship in low income, postcolonial countries including economic, political and cultural aspects.*

##  Introduction

This article develops a conceptual framework for understanding the relationship between globalisation and education in low income, postcolonial countries. There has been much written in this journal and in the broader educational literature in recent years about globalisation and education. In his recent editorial for *Comparative Education*, for example, Ball (1998) made use of globalisation theory to analyse contemporary, international education policy whilst in the same issue Jones (1998) used it to discuss the democratic prospects for world education. Within the broader educational literature globalisation theory has been used to explain a range of diverse and complex phenomena and has assumed a central position within the comparative and international education canon.

Yet how useful are existing accounts of globalisation and education as a tool for comparative thinking and research in postcolonial contexts? After all, much of the more recent, groundbreaking educational literature on education and globalisation focuses on Western industrialised countries and their 'significant others', i. e. the newly industrialized countries of the Pacific Rim. This raises questions about the relevance of this work for understanding globalisation and education policy in countries on the periphery of the global economy and politics. Further, where the effects of globalisation on education in these countries are considered, limited attention is given to the underlying view of the globalization process or to the highly contested nature of the term. The need to broaden our understanding of the implications of globalisation theory for education is underlined by the crises affecting more traditional ways of theorising education and 'development', including modernisation, human capital and dependency theories. In this respect, globalisation theory should be located within a broader attempt to reconceptualise the field of comparative and international education (Crossley, 1999).

It has been a shortcoming of much of the existing literature on globalisation and education that the specific *contexts* to which the theory is assumed to be applicable have not been specified. It is problematic to assume that there is one superior vantage point from which global forces can best be understood. Although the present article will contribute towards an analysis of the relevance of globalisation theory for understanding education policy in low income, postcolonial countries, it will take as its focus the education systems of sub-Saharan Africa. This is to acknowledge on the one hand a general level of commonality between all postcolonial, low income countries in terms of their experiences of globalisation. It is also to recognise, however, differences in the specific responses to globalisation in different regions of the postcolonial world. Here Hoogvelt's (1997) description of distinct 'postcolonial formations' is relevant. Hoogvelt describes four such formations, including sub-Saharan Africa, Militant Islam, East Asia and Latin America. The response to globalization in each is a product of economic, political and cultural factors and studying the impact of globalisation on each region draws attention to different aspects of the postcolonial condition. In sub-Saharan Africa, given the catastrophic impact of structural adjustment programmes and the growing chasm between the 'haves' and 'have nots', the focus is on the *management of exclusion*, a point that will be developed below.

The mode of critique adopted in this article will be a 'postcolonial' one (Tikly, 1999). Central to this mode is a concern to 're-narrativise'

(Hall, 1996) the globalisation story in a way that places historically marginalised parts of the world at the centre, rather than at the periphery of the education and globalisation debate. Such a critique is also centrally concerned with the continuing impact on education systems of European colonialism, and with issues of race, culture, language, as well as other forms of social stratification including class and gender in postcolonial contexts. A postcolonial critique draws attention to the transnational aspects of globalisation and of social inequalities and seeks to highlight forms of resistance to Western global hegemony as they have manifested themselves in education.

## The Relevance of Existing Accounts of Globalisation and Education

A problem with many accounts of globalisation and education is that they lack a precise definition of the term 'globalisation'. The lack of precise definition is unfortunate given the slippery nature of the term and makes it difficult to assess the usefulness of the concept. An attempt at defining globalisation will be given below. Related to the problem of definition has been the tendency in the educational literature to keep the underlying view of the *nature*, *extent* and *future trajectory* of globalisation implicit rather than explicit. This is despite the existence of a plurality of views within the social sciences and of the varying implications of different views for education. Held et al. (1999) distinguish between three broad approaches within the social sciences. Although the approaches are not themselves homogenous and subsume a plurality of viewpoints and ideologies, they do serve as a useful analytical tool and are reflected (albeit implicitly) in the educational literature. In the paragraphs that follow, an attempt is made to assess the relevance of each approach for understanding globalisation in low income, postcolonial countries.

*The Hyperglobalist Approach*

The 'hyperglobalist' approach is premised on the idea that we are entering a truly 'global age' involving the triumph of global capitalism and the advent of distinctively new forms of global culture, governance and of civil society. In this view we are witnessing the demise of the nation state (see, for example, Ohmae, 1995; Strange, 1996). This approach is exemplified within the educational literature by writers such as Donald (1992), Usher & Edwards (1994) and, in this journal, by Kress (1996). These authors have argued that global postmodernity has undermined the modernist goals of national education and of creating a national culture. Also within this group is Edwards' (1994) work on new technologies and globalisation in which he argues that the information superhighway and the way that it interacts with global markets will lead to the demise of schooling in its traditional forms.

As Green (1997) has pointed out, however, such claims are overstated and national governments still hold primary responsibility for providing education. He also points out that information technologies are relatively underdeveloped in relation to schooling and that (even in the affluent North) schools are unlikely to be replaced by virtual networks. A hyperglobalist approach to education in the context of low income, postcolonial countries such as those of sub-Saharan Africa is even more implausible. To begin with, the advent of globalisation in the post Second World War period has coincided in many parts of the postcolonial world with the processes of democratic transformation and national liberation from colonialism. In this context, postcolonial governments have often used education as a principal means to forge national unity and a common citizenship and have in fact strengthened rather than loosened their grip on education systems. Furthermore, in most low income countries of the world, access to computers and the information superhighway is limited to a postcolonial elite who, through access to prestigious schools and international educational experiences, are 'keyed into' the information revolution whilst the majority of learners are not (Kenway, 1996).

*The Sceptical Approach*

Green's work itself can be most easily located within what Held et al. (1999) describe as a 'sceptical' approach to globalisation. Advocates of this approach argue that trading blocs are in fact weaker now than in earlier periods of history (such as during the height of European imperialism), although there has been a growing trend towards 'regionalisation' in trade and politics. In this formulation the logic of global capitalism has led to greater polarization between the 'developed' and 'developing' countries. It has also led, paradoxically, to a greater significance for the nation state in managing the deepening crisis tendencies of capitalism (see, for example, Hirst & Thompson, 1996; Boyer & Drache, 1996). This view is reflected in Green's work by the assertion that there has not been any meaningful globalisation of education. Green bases his claim on the view that although national education systems have become more 'porous', and 'have become more like each other in certain important ways', there is 'little evidence that national education systems are disappearing or that national states have ceased to control them'. Rather, he suggests there has been a more modest process of 'partial internationalisation' of education involving increased student and staff mobility, widespread policy borrowing and 'attempts to enhance the international dimension of curricula at secondary and higher levels' (Green, 1997, p. 171).

The sceptical approach, particularly with its references to the increasing polarization between high and low income countries, would seem to have a lot to commend it for an analysis of the education systems of sub-Saharan Africa. Structural adjustment and austerity, along with rising populations, have led to a decline in enrolment rates and in the quality of education in much of the sub-continent. More than 40 million children are estimated to be out of school (a figure only paralleled in South Asia) and the region has the lowest primary enrolment rates in the world, estimated at 60% in 1999 (World Bank, 1999).

There are, however, other aspects of the sceptical approach and Green's work in particular that are less helpful when applied to sub-Saharan Africa. The chief problem arises from the fact that despite the title of his book, Green's analysis is not 'global' at all, but rather focuses on the Western industrialised countries and those of the Pacific Rim. Scant mention is made of the situation in low income countries except to the extent that they provide an aberration to the 'normal' pattern of educational development. For example, Green's emphasis on the role of the state in managing crisis simply does not fit with recent reality in the sub-continent. As will be discussed below, a feature of structural adjustment programmes has been to undermine the role of the state in managing crisis. Rather, it has been multilateral agencies and NGOs that have often taken a lead. This amounts to more than just a 'partial internationalisation' of education as Green would suggest. Rather, structural adjustment policies are global in origin and affect many more people than the examples of limited policy transfer that Green describes. Finally, although Green does acknowledge increasing polarization between rich and poor *within* the more affluent countries, he does not extrapolate the implications of this uneven intra-national development for education, a point that will be developed below.

*The Transformationalist Approach*

These criticisms of Green's work lead to a consideration of the third broad approach within the social science literature and its offshoots in education studies, namely, the 'transformationalist' approach. Like the hyperglobalists, this approach suggests that we are indeed experiencing unprecedented levels of global interconnectedness (Giddens, 1990; Castells, 1996). Unlike the hyperglobalists, however, transformationalists question whether we are entering a totally new 'global age' of economic, political and cultural integration. Rather, they see globalisation as an historically contingent process replete with contradictions. Thus, although globalisation *is* resulting in greater integration in some areas of the economy, politics and culture, it is also resulting in greater fragmentation and stratification in which 'some states, societies and communities are becoming increasingly enmeshed in the global order while others are becoming increasingly marginalised' (Held et al., 1999, p. 8).

In contrast to the sceptics, transformationalists argue that these contradictory processes are linked to a transformation in the global division of labour such that the core-periphery relationship is not just about relationships between nation states but involves new social relationships that cut across national boundaries. According to Hoogvelt (1997), for example, the 'core' of the world economy now includes not just the wealthy nations (including the newly industrialised nations) but elites in the poorer nations as well. Conversely, the periphery now increasingly includes the poor and the socially excluded in the more affluent nations. Similarly, transformationalists take the view that although nation states have retained much power over what happens within their territories, their power is being transformed in relation to new institutions of international governance and international law.

Finally, writers such as Hall (1992, 1996) and Hoogvelt (1997), writing within a transformationalist framework, have commented on how processes of migration, diaspora formation and cultural hybridisation have transformed individual and group identities and created 'new ethnicities'. Rather than being fixed and essentialised, these new forms of cultural identity are contingent and fluid.

Within the education literature the transformationalist perspective is reflected in the work of Stephen Ball (1998), Philip Jones (1998), Brown & Lauder (1997), Dale (1999), Marginson (1999), Blackmore (1999), Henry et al. (1999) and others. Although these authors deal with quite different aspects of globalisation and education, they share a common view of the contingency of the effects of globalisation on education. The thesis is summed up by Marginson:

> Globalization is irreversibly changing the politics of the nation-state and its regional sectors, domestic classes and nationally-defined interest groups. It is creating new potentials and limits in the politics of education. Its effects on the politics of education are complex ... Increasingly shaped as it is by globalization—both directly and via the effects of globalization in national government—education at the same time has become a primary medium of globalization, and an incubator of its agents. As well as inhibiting or transforming older kinds of education, globalization creates new kinds. (1999, p. 19)

What distinguishes this view is the idea that globalisation works both on and through education policy, i.e. that not only is education affected by globalisation but it has also become a principle mechanism by which global forces affect the daily lives of national populations.

There are many advantages of a transformationalist approach from the point of view of a postcolonial reconceptualisation of globalisation theory and these will be discussed and developed through the remainder of the article. They revolve chiefly around the extent to which the approach allows for a complex and contingent view of the relationship between education and different aspects of globalisation; the role of the state and of civil society in mediating the influence of global forces; and an exploration of issues relating to culture, language and identity.

Further, those who have adopted a transformationalist perspective within education do try to relate the emerging global division of labour and increased social stratification within and between countries to developments in education policy. Thus Ball (1998) presents the emergence of 'star' and 'sink' schools within the new educational quasi-markets in Western industrialised countries as examples of how growing social stratification is mirrored in educational terms. Similarly, Blackmore (1999) argues that the state's reduced role in relation to education provision places a heavy burden on women, regardless of geographical location, who are left to 'take up the slack'.

It is argued, however, that the transformationalist perspective has not gone nearly far enough in extrapolating the educational implications of increasing stratifications along the lines of race, culture, class and gender and that this analysis will need to be deepened in relation to the postcolonial and highly stratified countries of sub-Saharan Africa. Secondly, it is argued that exponents of the transformationalist perspective fail to acknowledge the continuing impact and relevance of *prior forms* of globalisation, especially those associated with European colonialism.

## Towards a Reconceptualisation

In this section a new framework for understanding the effects of globalisation on education policy in postcolonial contexts will be set out. The analysis draws on the strengths of previous models whilst trying to address some of the weaknesses. First, a definition and account of globalisation is suggested. This will be followed by an attempt to elaborate those areas that a comprehensive account of globalisation and education needs to address.

*Globalisation*

The definition of globalisation offered here is taken from recent work by Held et al. (1999). The authors define globalisation as:

> A process (or set of processes) which embodies a transformation in the spatial organization of social relations and transactions—assessed in terms of their extensity, intensity, velocity and impact—generating transcontinental or interregional flows and networks of activity, interaction, and the exercise of power. (p. 16)

The authors explain that by 'flows' they refer to 'the movements of physical artefacts, people, symbols, tokens and information across space and time', whilst 'networks' is used to refer to 'regularized or patterned interactions between independent agents, modes of activity, or sites of power' (p. 16).

In important respects, the authors definition and understanding of globalisation develops the insights of the transformationalist perspective. It is based on an understanding of globalisation as a set of *processes* rather than a single 'condition', involving interactions and networks within the political, military, economic and cultural domains as well as those of labour and migratory movements and of the environment. These processes are fractured and uneven rather than linear and involve a complex 'deterritorialisation' and 'reterritorialisation' of political and economic relations. In this view power is a fundamental attribute of globalisation, and 'patterns of global stratification mediate access to sites of power, while the consequences of globalisation are unevenly experienced. Political and economic elites in the world's major metropolitan areas are much more tightly integrated into, and have much greater control over, global networks than do the subsistence farmers of Burundi' (Held et al., 1999, p. 28).

Held et al. 's (1999) analysis seeks to go beyond a transformationalist perspective, however, in their attempt to provide an historical periodisation of *different forms* of globalisation, in the pre-modern, early modern, modern and contemporary periods. They argue that international and global interconnectedness is by no means a novel phenomenon and seek to advance understanding by providing a framework for assessing the qualitative and quantitative differences between the forms taken by globalisation in different eras. Of particular relevance here is their analysis of the global flows and networks associated with *modern* globalisation (1859-1945). Here the focus is on the enormous expansion of global, political and military relations associated with Western global empires and the soaring of global trade and investment during this period. It will be argued below that an important global network established during this period was that of education.

*Contemporary* globalisation is, according to the authors, historically unprecedented in terms of its extensity, intensity, velocity and impact. Held et al. (1999) distinguish the current (post -1945) phase as one in which

> empires, once the principal form of political rule and world political organization, had given way to a worldwide system of nation-states, overlaid by multila-

teal, regional and global systems of regulation and governance. Moreover, whereas previous epochs were dominated by the collective or divided hegemony of western powers, the contemporary era can claim to have only a single potential hegemonic power: the United States ... [whose] ... enormous structural power has remained deeply inscribed in the nature and functioning of the present world order. (p.425)

American hegemony has been accompanied by ever tightening systems of economic regulation (first through the Bretton Woods system and more recently through the World Trade Organisation) alongside a more liberal world economic order. Contemporary globalization has also involved a massive increase in migrations of populations, the increasing significance and impact of environmental issues and concerns and developments in mass media and technologies. Contemporary globalisation involves reflexivity on the part of a growing worldwide elite as well as popular consciousness of global interconnectedness. It is also contested as states, citizens and social movements resist or manage its impacts.

Whilst such an account provides a suitably complex account of contemporary globalisation, the authors acknowledge that their own empirical evidence is based largely on a study of Western industrialised nations. As such it paints a picture of globalisation as experienced 'inside' the dominant economic, political and cultural flows and networks that they describe. Less account is taken in the analysis of those countries and populations 'outside' these flows and networks, and at the sharp end of an increasingly polarised world order. Here recent work on global political economy has been found more useful and will be discussed in later sections.

*The Significance of Previous Forms of Globalisation for Education*

It will be argued in this section that it is important to take account of previous forms of globalisation if the relationship between education and contemporary globalisation in the postcolonial context is to be understood. Held et al. 's (1999) analysis provides a rich framework from which to begin such an endeavour, although anything resembling a full account of these processes is beyond the scope of the present article. Interesting examples of how global flows and networks from pre-modern and early modern times left their mark on the education systems of sub-Saharan Africa abound. The spread of global religions, especially Islam and Christianity, brought with them their own educational forms and systems of schools and universities. These interacted with and often disrupted and displaced indigenous forms of education, ceremonies, skills and crafts training. Educational globalization really developed and intensified, however, during the early modern and modern periods with the advent of European colonialism. The significance of colonial education from the point of view of this paper is threefold.

First, it provided a key mechanism and template for the spread of contemporary forms of education. The form that colonial education systems took in sub-Saharan Africa depended on the form of colonialism adopted, e. g. 'classical' or 'internal' colonialism (Altbach & Kelly, 1978) and on the nature of the educational programme of the colonising power which differed in some important respects (White, 1996). Nonetheless, colonial education spread a common structure of schooling throughout the region. It also spread a form of curriculum based on an *episteme* (ground base of knowledge) with its roots in the Graeco-Roman tradition. Colonial education either superseded or worked alongside earlier forms and has provided the basis on which postcolonial reform efforts have had to build. In this respect, colonial forms of schooling and the pedagogies and forms of knowledge that they engendered have proved remarkably resistant to change.

Second, in a reversal of previous eras, colonial education was itself a key site for the spread of global flows and networks in the economic, cultural and political spheres both in the modern and contemporary periods. In the modern period education was a key mechanism for the imposition and diffusion of global religions throughout sub-Saharan Africa, especially Christianity. It also directly contributed to the development of global trade and commerce in the colonial era (albeit with varying degrees of success) by providing indigenous labourers with the basic skills and dispositions required by the colonial economic and administrative systems. However, because colonial education only typically offered a very limited basic education and was never universally provided a limited human resource base on which postcolonial governments could draw on in their endeavours to become globally competitive. In this way colonial education contributed to the marginalisation of African economies in the contemporary period (see below). Colonial education was also highly selective and elitist in the opportunities it offered for secondary and higher education and was, therefore, deeply implicated in the formation of indigenous elites who in turn have become part of the emerging global elite. Further, colonial education was instrumental in the globalisation of English and other European languages. This has directly facilitated the commodification of, and the creation of markets for, Anglo-American cultural forms in the contemporary period (Philipson, 1998).

Third, colonial education has provided an important seedbed for local *resistance* to contemporary global forces. Many leading intellectuals and revolutionaries during the heyday of national liberation struggles on the sub-continent were products of colonial education. Some Western intellectual traditions such as Marxism have also inspired and influenced African revolutionary thinking. Mazrui (1978) has described also how the 'mystique' of the Graeco-Roman tradition provided not only a key point of reference for European identity and 'colonial arrogance' but also, ironically, became an inspiration for its antithesis in the negritude movement (itself based on the 'mystique' of ancient Africa). Thabo Mbeki's recent calls for an 'African renaissance' as an alternative to Western global hegemony build on and develop these and other intellectual currents.

*Understanding the Relative Importance for Education of Different Global Forces*
Most authors agree that globalisation is multidimensional, involving a range of global flows and networks. Yet much of the first wave of literature on education and globalisation in low income, postcolonial countries tended to highlight the implications for education and training of *economic* globalisation and in particular the impact of structural adjustment policies. This was evident, for example, in many of the contributions to special editions of the *International Journal of Educational Development* (1996) and of *Prospects* (1997) which were devoted to the theme of globalisation and education in 'developing countries'. On the one hand, such an emphasis is understandable given the devastation wreaked by structural adjustment policies on education and training systems of the South during the 1980s and 1990s.

On the other hand, an economic focus is also indicative of a certain reductionism in the literature and the often implicit view that 'globalization has been promoted primarily by economic agents' (Carton & Tawil, 1997, p. 21). Such an approach limits understanding of the impact of political, cultural and other aspects of globalisation on education systems. Little indication is given in this body of work, for example, of the role of the state in low income countries in mediating and/or contesting structural adjustment policies or of the significance of cultural issues such as language policy in global perspective. This reductionism also does not allow for an analysis of the impact of epidemiological aspects of globalisation such as the HIV/AIDS pandemic that is sweeping across sub-Saharan Africa. Nor does it allow for an analysis of the impact of the global arms trade. This trade impacts on education systems because children have been dragged into conflicts facilitated by arms dealing. Indeed, it is often at the point where all of these global forces intersect that the true magnitude and tragedy of the crisis in African education can be comprehended. Unfortunately, space does not permit a consideration of the impact of all of these factors and in the remainder of the article attention will be given to economic, political and cultural aspects of the globalisation/ education relationship.

How can the relationship and relative impact of different aspects of globalisation on education be understood in a way that avoids a crude economism? In answering this question, Bayart's (1993) work on the postcolonial state in Africa has been found useful. Drawing on Gramsci, Bayart introduces the idea of the 'postcolonial historical bloc'. This is used to describe a unity of economic, political and cultural relationships which together constitute the basis for the maintenance of social order in postcolonial sub-Saharan Africa. What is important for our purposes is the idea underlying the concept that economic, political and cultural factors articulate together in maintaining the status quo. Although economic imperatives may 'determine' what transpires culturally and politically, economic policies and strategies can also be influenced by cultural and political factors. The question of determination becomes a matter for empirical investigation at any stage in the development of an historical bloc and cannot be taken as a pre-given. In this sense the idea of the postcolonial historical bloc is similar to Hoogvelt's (1997) concept of 'postcolonial formations' discussed earlier. An important implication of the use of Gramsci's ideas is that history becomes 'open ended' rather than predetermined. This is particularly pertinent to sub-Saharan Africa where change is multicausal and inherently unpredictable.

*Economic Globalisation and Education*
To understand the significance of economic globalisation for education in the postcolonial context, it is necessary to have an idea of the position of postcolonial economies in relation to global economic flows and networks. Recent literature written within a political economy perspective has been useful in this regard. In her discussion of the position of Africa, Hoogvelt (1997) takes as her starting point three distinctive features of economic globalization in the contemporary period. First, she describes the advent of a *new market discipline* which, within an increasingly shared phenomenal world, creates an 'awareness of global competition which constrains individuals and groups, and even national governments, to conform to international standards of price and quality' (p. 124). Second, she describes *flexible accumulation through global webs* by which she refers to the 'way in which the fusion of computer technology with telecommunications makes it possible for firms to relocate an everwidening range of operations and functions to wherever cost-competitive labour, assets and infrastructure are availale' (p. 126). Finally, Hoogvelt describes *financial global deepening* which has involved a 'tremendous increase in the mobility of capital. This mobility refers not only to the speed and freedom with which money can move across frontiers at the press of a computer button, it also, more significantly, refers to the way it is being disconnected from social relationships in which money and wealth were previously embedded' (p. 129). Crucially, for the analysis presented here, financial deepening has involved the concentration and increased flow of capital within a geographically confined

area including the Western and newly industrialised countries. Large sections of the globe, including Africa, are increasingly on the periphery of these processes.

These aspects of globalisation shape the emerging global division of labour and redefine the 'core-periphery' relationship. The global division of labour, developed under colonialism, was based on the production of primary commodities in the South and their conversion to manufactured products in the North. Now, however, much of the labour intensive manufacturing is being relocated to wherever in the world production costs are lowest. Further, the development of new materials has undermined the market for primary commodities traditionally produced in the South. Consequently, the high levels of economic growth associated with financial deepening and the increased trade in new commodities and financial services have principally benefited Western and newly industrialised nations who are integrated into these new global networks. For authors such as Castells (1993) and Amin (1997), the upshot of the new technologies has been to create pockets of the 'Fourth World' in the former First, Second and Third Worlds. Much of sub-Saharan Africa is included in this emerging 'Fourth World' with the consequence that a significant part of the region's population has shifted 'from a structural position of exploitation to a structural position of irrelevance' within the new world economy (Castells, 1993, p. 37). Importantly, however, many postcolonial elites in sub-Saharan Africa 'bought into' this emerging global economy. This was often achieved by using money fraudulently diverted from overseas loans and from government funds (Hoogvelt, 1997).

How have these key elements of economic globalisation affected Africa specifically? The principal response, advocated by the World Bank and

International Monetary Fund (IMF) since the 1980s, has been to impose structural adjustment policies on many countries of sub-Saharan Africa (although in some instances such as South Africa, many aspects of structural adjustment have also been self-imposed (Marais, 1997). The main ingredients of these policies are well-known and documented and have included cuts in government expenditure, trade liberalisation policies, currency devaluation, reduction of price controls, a shift to export oriented policies, revised fiscal policies to increase government revenue, user charges for public services like education and increased privatisation (see Samoff, 1994, for full account). Structural adjustment policies relate to the new market principle because they intended to make countries more competitive through lowering production costs (through cuts in social welfare and reduced unit costs) and through making Africa more attractive to foreign investors (by means of trade liberalisation, reduced tax and other macro-economic reforms) (Ndoye, 1997).

For authors such as Hoogvelt (1997) and Chossudovsky (1997), however, the impact of structural adjustment has been economic catastrophe, the slowing down and even reversal of human development—in short what Chossudovsky has described as 'the globalisation of poverty 1997, p. 34). In Hoogvelt's analysis, structural adjustment policies served a dual function, namely, to enable the periphery of the world capitalist system to be 'managed' in the interest of the core countries, and to attract an economic surplus from it more effectively. She argues that:

> Even if structural adjustment programmes have achieved little or nothing from the point of view of national territorial development and the improvement of standards of living of the masses in African countries, the programmes have been of resounding success when measured in terms of the acceleration of the process of globalisation. Structural adjustment has helped to tie the physical e-

conomic resources of the African region more tightly into servicing the global system, while at the same time oiling the financial machinery by which wealth can be transported out of Africa and into the global system (p. 171)

How do existing accounts of education in low income, postcolonial countries fit in with the above picture? Broadly speaking, the relevant educational literature has focused on two aspects, namely, the implications of economic globalisation for education provision and the relationship between education, skills formation and global labour markets. The former literature has provided a critique of the negative impact of structural adjustment policies on enrolment rates and on the quality of educational provision (see Samoff, 1994; Colclough & Manor, 1991; Tilak, 1997, for example). The latter has tended to underline the contradiction between the negative effects of structural adjustment on education provision on the one hand, and the need for countries to invest in human resource development in order to become 'globally competitive' on the other. Here the emphasis has been on the need for basic literacy, the formation of 'appropriate' skills for new global production processes and the development and enhancement of technological capabilities in countries of the South (see Riddell, 1996; Stewart, 1996, for example).

Although the literature provides a useful critique of the effects of structural adjustment on education it does not sufficiently problematise the position of low income, postcolonial countries within the emerging global economy. Much of the literature either explicitly or implicitly works within a human capital framework that assumes that investment in human resources can facilitate a smooth, 'linear' model of economic growth. In this respect it shares similar premises to the policy discourses of governments and of multilateral organizations such as the World Bank (although it is often highly critical of these discourses). These discourses do not allow for a consideration of economic crisis and the highly differentiated and inequitable impact of economic globalisation on the education of the poor and of elites. Nor do they allow for a consideration of education's role in legitimising the emerging global division of labour and the 'new world order'.

Ilon's (1994) work provides one alternative starting point for such an analysis. Here Ilon paints a future scenario involving a growing gulf in educational opportunities between emerging global elites and the rest of the population. According to Ilon, 'a national system of schooling is likely to give way to local systems for the poor and global systems for the rich' (p. 99). Within this highly differentiated environment, a top tier will benefit from a private education that will make them globally competitive; a middle tier will receive a 'good' but not 'world class' education, whilst the majority, third tier, will have a local, state education that will make them 'marginally competitive for low-skill jobs' (p. 102).

Ilon's ideas are interesting because they seem to correspond to the reality of education in many countries of sub-Saharan Africa (although they need to be supported by more empirical research). There is also a need to avoid crude functionalism and the idea of a clear-cut 'correspondence' between education and the emerging global division of labour. Following Fritzell (1987) and Ball (1990), it is possible to conceive of different sectors within education having more or less *positive* or *negative* correspondences with the global economy at different times. This is to suggest that at times education may be highly 'functional' for global capitalist accumulation as well as for the legitimisation of the capitalist system and at other times not. Education can also have a *critical* correspondence with the global economy because of its role in providing a focus and forum for the development of resistance to the status quo (Tikly, 1994).

It has been suggested above, for example, that colonial education was at times 'functional' for the national and global division of labour under colonialism through its ability to provide the skills required by different sectors and areas of the colonial economy. It also provided some legitimacy for the colonial order through opportunities for limited social mobility. As Dore (1997) and others have argued, however, colonial education and the 'diploma disease' were in other respects highly dysfunctional for national development and, in the heat of the anti-colonial struggles for independence, actually developed a critical correspondence with the colonial project.

The nature of the correspondence between education and contemporary economic globalisation remains contradictory. For a tiny minority, access to prestigious private education has provided the forms of socialisation and high skills development required for integration and participation in the global economy. The inclusion of individuals from the South within the board rooms and debating chambers of transnational corporations and global political institutions also helps to legitimise the global capitalist system. This 'positive correspondence' can, however, turn critical. This is to assert that although there exists at one level a commonality of interests, the economic and political interests of the global elite are not always of a piece. In order to secure their own position within the emerging historical bloc, postcolonial elites from sub-Saharan Africa may also use their participation in global forums to form a bulwark against Western economic and political hegemony, e. g. in demands to end Third World debt.

Lower down the system, in relation to Ilon's second tier, the picture is more patchy. Although many transnational corporations currently provide their own education and training for their national operatives, there remains a negative correspondence between the high skill requirements of business and the public sector at the national level and skills that the indigenous education system is able to produce. This mismatch is exacerbated by the crippling 'brain drain' that affects most high skill occupations in sub-Saharan Africa.

It is in relation to Ilon's third tier, however, that the problem of correspondence becomes most serious. Here at least 50% of the population in low income countries (such as those of sub-Saharan Africa) can expect to be permanently excluded from employment with another 20% in low income, insecure employment (Hoogvelt, 1997). These figures are unlikely to change so long as the West's relationship with Africa remains premised on the extraction of surplus through the system of debt peonage and the fate of African economies remains subject to pressures and decisions made elsewhere in the globe. It is at this point that the analysis breaks most sharply with the assumptions of human capital theory for sustained economic growth is basically unachievable in this context, *regardless of the skills base of the economy*. In terms of the outputs of education then, the pathetic educational opportunities offered to most children on the sub-continent can actually be perceived to have a positive correspondence with the global division of labour.

This may not be the case, however, in relation to education's role in legitimising the global division of labour. Here a more negative correspondence is developing and there is evidence that the traditional legitimatory role of education may be coming under threat. The slow down in enrolment and the increase in dropout rates in primary and secondary schooling on the sub-continent reflects in part a growing view on the part of communities that there is a declining economic benefit, or rate of return from schooling, particularly for girls. The growing number of street children in the urban areas, child soldiers and levels of juvenile crime also attest to some extent at least to a despondency with schooling as a way out of poverty.

Despite what has been argued above, it remains the case that many parents and children continue to hold out hope of a better future through education. It is also not being suggested that education cannot play a role in reducing poverty and promoting sustained growth in a global economy (although more research is required about the kinds of skills and attributes actually required for this). What is being argued is that education can only begin to play such a role if there is a fundamental change in the nature of the West's economic relationship with Africa and to the global (and national) division of labour. In the next section, it is argued that meaningful change through education is also contingent on political factors and in particular a reconceptualisation of the role of the state.

*Globalisation and the Politics of Education*
Central to a transformationalist perspective is the view that the role of the state has been redefined in relation to education provision as a result of the political effects of globalisation. This new role has been described as involving a 'new orthodoxy' aimed at making nations more competitive within the global economy (Carter & O'Neil, 1995; Ball, 1998). Accounts within this perspective typically see education policy as the outcome of contestation between competing interest groups within the state over accumulation strategies (aimed at proposing solutions to economic crisis) and hegemonic projects (primarily concerned with the construction and maintenance of the social basis of support for a particular form

of state). Different groupings propose different 'solutions' to crises with implications for education policy (see Brown & Lauder, 1997, for example).

The transformationalist view of the state in relation to education policy has some positive implications for a consideration of low income countries, because it allows for the possibility that the educational responses of different states to global forces will vary. In other words the form that particular hegemonic projects will take within the state will depend on the outcome of political struggles at the national level and of the particular construction of the national identity and the nature of policies aimed at managing cultural diversity. The analysis also allows for the possibility that the adverse effects of globalisation can be resisted and even modified at the national level. This latter point is important if the responses of countries such as South Africa or Eritrea that have been able to modify and/or resist structural adjustment policies are to be appreciated.

There are also important limitations to the transformationalist view of the state (as it has developed so far) for our purposes. Chief amongst these is the use of regulation theory and the implications that have been drawn from this for education policy. Based on empirical research in Western industrialised countries, regulation theory has attempted to draw out the implications for the role of the state of the shift from old style 'Fordist' mass production techniques to 'post-Fordist' production methods based on new technologies. The 'new orthodoxy' in education rests on the idea that there has been a shift from a Keynesian/welfarist model of the state to a neo-liberal one. Unlike many of their followers in education, however, exponents of the regulation approach have pointed to the limited geographical applicability of their work. In this respect, many countries in Africa generally mix more traditional, pre-Fordist and Fordist production methods and (as we have seen above) have a limited involvement with post-Fordist methods. Furthermore, except to a very limited degree, there has not been anything approaching a welfare state like that in Western industrialized countries.

Many exponents of the transformationalist thesis in education also assume a common experience in their analyses regarding the history of the role of the state in relation to education policy. Marginson (1999), for example, assumes that education systems emerged as an aspect of state formation. This view is also shared by sceptics such as Green (1997, 1999) and has its origins in older work such as that of Archer (1984). In this view, education systems developed as an aspect of emerging national identity and citizenship rights. In the case of much of the formerly colonised world, however, mass schooling emerged as an aspect of colonial domination although this took a different form depending on the type of colonialism involved (Altbach & Kelly, 1978). In general, however, the dynamics of the emergence and spread of mass systems in colonised countries were entirely different from those in Western countries as were the motives of its perpetrators. In Cowen's (1996) terms, colonial education systems were a 'distortion' of modern forms that developed in Europe and only truly became national once liberation from colonialism had been achieved.

Thus it is important to separate the general from the specific when considering the relevance of the transformationalist approach to the state. At the general level, to see education policy as the outcome of contestation between competing hegemonic projects and accumulation strategies within the state is useful. Indeed, I have used such an approach in my own earlier work on education policy in South Africa (Tikly, 1997). It is also possible to begin to identify a 'new orthodoxy' regarding education as it has emerged on the sub-continent although this differs markedly from that described by Ball (1998) and others. At the specific level, however, it is important to relate the use of such concepts to the history of the state in Africa and to the present political milieu. This involves considering the form of the state and its relationship to civil society, along with the specific nature of hegemonic projects and accumulation strategies. In Bayart's (1993) terms it involves seeing the changing role of the state as an aspect of the emergence in sub-Saharan Africa of a postcolonial historical bloc.

How can the state in Africa be described and what implications does this have for its relationship to globalisation on the one hand and education policy on the other? A useful starting point is Bayart's insistence on the 'historicity' of the African State. Rather than see the modern African State (as exponents of dependency theory do) as simply an invention and tool of colonialism and neo-colonialism, Bayart prefers to see the African State as the outcome of political struggles and developments dating from pre-colonial times. This helps to explain the diversity of forms of the state in Africa but also the continued existence of systems of lineage and other pre-colonial political forms, which influence it and give it shape. In this conception of the state, assertive postcolonial groups have mobilised different constructions of ethnicity and of Africa's past in the pursuance of hegemony. The specific nature of past cultural and political forms has also given rise to unique kinds of social stratification and the emergence of special categories of subordinated subjects such as 'youth' and 'women'.

Bayart (1993) identifies two conflicting 'ideal type' hegemonic projects that have unfolded during the last century and have shaped the pre-and postcolonial state, namely, 'conservative modernisation' and 'social revolution'. Each of these projects can be seen to have articulated with both 'capitalist' and 'socialist' growth paths and with single and multi-party systems. The former has emerged where already established elites have maintained their power (such as in Senegal, Cameroon, Botswana and Burundi) and the latter has involved the rise of at least a section of the subordinate groups (e. g. Angola, Mozambique, Kenya and Tanzania). Both projects have had at their centre concepts of 'development' and of 'nation building' although they have differed in their specific character (see also Mkandawire, 1996). Where hegemony has been maintained in both cases it has involved the 'reciprocal assimilation of elites', i. e. a process of ameliorating emerging or existing elites through granting limited access to status and wealth.

As in other parts of the world, the state has proved a key mechanism for accumulation and the emergence of national and global elites as well as for the maintenance of the status quo. Access to state power gives access to material and cultural resources which can be mobilised to alter the domestic power relationship. A job in the public service also carries a salary, which even if modest and paid irregularly is no trivial thing, and can be used to invest in other economic activities. Holders of positions of power can also use their position to demand goods, cash and labour without recourse to violence and can supplement their salaries with bribes (practices that have their origins in colonial times).

Education plays a key role in all of these mechanisms. Under colonialism, education was the principal means for gaining access to public service and has subsequently 'assumed a decisive role now that the mastery of western knowledge also conditions mastery of the State and the economy' (Bayart, 1993, p. 75). Then and now, access to education, particularly at the secondary and tertiary levels is one of the major resources that those in public service can access for themselves, their children, relatives and friends. Bayart also argues that education is a key mechanism in the reciprocal assimilation of elites precisely because it is an important resource and because of its power to form an *esprit de corps* amongst the emerging elite. Extending Bayart's analysis somewhat, the reciprocal assimilation of elites also provides an explanatory mechanism for the relationship between the state and civil society in the provision of education. This is because it has provided an important bargaining counter between those parts of civil society that have governed and funded education in colonial times (especially religious bodies) and those who have controlled the state.

Finally, policies towards the access of different groups to educational opportunities have also depended on the accumulation strategy and accompanying ideology adopted, i.e. whether capitalist or socialist. Thus although Tanzania and Kenya have both pursued a similar hegemonic project of 'social revolution' in the post-independence phase, they were wedded to socialist and capitalist growth paths respectively with differing implications for education policy (see Cooksey et al., 1994). In Tanzania's case, the dogged pursuit of Nyrere's philosophy of socialist self-reliance (in which the expansion of educational opportunities played a significant part) can be seen as a valiant attempt to resist the growing forces of economic globalisation in the contemporary period.

Tanzania's eventual capitulation to IMF conditional lending in the late 1980s also serves to demonstrate, however, a further feature of the post-colonial African state, namely its fragility in the context of international relations (Clapham, 1996). This is because, in the great majority of cases states have been 'created by international action in the form of European colonialism, and have been left with state frontiers that rarely correspond to pre-colonial social or geographical identities' (p. 4). This, together with the weakness of African economies has meant that the very survival of the state has become a key motive for international action for African governments and elites whose own survival is tied in with that of the state. The fragility of the state and of the postcolonial status quo has ensured that most African states are much more susceptible to global forces than those of wealthier countries. This susceptibility provided the conditions for the imposition from the early 1980s of a new neo-liberal orthodoxy in the economy and politics that has disrupted indigenous post-colonial hegemonic projects and accumulation strategies. As we have seen, this orthodoxy has been severe in its implications for all areas of social welfare including education and has served to exacerbate social stratification. Rather than a subtle 'repositioning' of the state (as in the UK and elsewhere), what has occurred has been nothing short of a full frontal attack on state provision (whilst maintaining support for elites).

It is important, however, not to be overly deterministic with respect to the impact of structural adjustment policies. Despite the fragility of the African State, some countries—notably Eritrea and South Africa—have, for different reasons, been able to resist structural adjustment loans and the conditionalities that accompany them. In the case of Eritrea this has been due to a conscious policy adopted by the revolutionary government. In South Africa's case it is because of its relatively strong economic and political position compared to other African states. Both of these countries have ostensibly pursued their own educational agendas, albeit within the confines of economic austerity and self-imposed restrictions on spending. Further, whereas structural adjustment policies have affected the way that education is governed, they have not impacted (in any direct way) on the content of education. Here, colonial forms have in some cases been superseded by newer approaches linked to the hegemonic projects of postcolonial governments and innovations supported by donor and multilateral funding.

In relation to this last point, it is also important to recognise a range of political mechanisms by which global forces have influenced education policy. Dale (1999) has identified several mechanisms that are relevant for African education. For example, he describes processes of *harmonisation* of policy between countries within a region such as within the post-Mastricht European Union. In a much more limited way, regional organizations such as the Organisation of African Unity (OAU) and the Southern African Development Community (SADEC) have sponsored research aimed at policy harmonisation. He also describes the mechanism of *dissemination* associated, for instance with the setting of policy agendas, indicators and targets in African education by supra-national organisations such as the World Bank. His third mechanism, that of *standardistion* refers to the observed spread of a particular form of Western education throughout the world (manifested in a universal structure of schooling and of the curriculum), which has persisted in the postcolonial era. The fourth mechanism, *installing interdependence* refers to the spread of environmental, human rights and peace issues (amongst others) by the new 'global civil society' and non-governmental organisations. The final mechanism is that of *imposition* and is exemplified by the imposition of structural adjustment policies in education by the World Bank and the IMF as an aspect of structural adjustment lending.

The last two mechanisms draw attention to another feature of the relationship between globalisation and the politics of education in Africa, namely, the often contradictory agendas of different global agencies. Jones (1998) and Mundy (1999) have both drawn attention, for example, to the quite different agendas of the World Bank on the one hand and

UNESCO on the other. To an extent then, education policy can be seen as the outcome of an attempt on the part of the fragile state to negotiate the policy agendas of more than one global agency.

Finally, what of the future of educational politics in Africa in the era of contemporary globalisation? It has been an argument of this section that education in Africa has been profoundly linked to the politics of the postcolonial state. This is likely to remain the case in the foreseeable future. It should be recalled that education systems emerged in Europe over more than a century and as an aspect of a long and painful process of state formation (Green, 1997; Archer, 1984). In the newly industrialised countries of the Pacific Rim, educational advancement in the postcolonial era has been driven by a strong developmentalist state. If education is going to play a part in the development of an African postcolonial block (which it must), then the state needs to play a prominent role. As in other parts of the world, the state is the only indigenous body that is capable of funding an enterprise such as mass education. It is also through the state playing a leading role in education policy that education can be harnessed to indigenous hegemonic projects and accumulation strategies.

A key concept in such an endeavour, however, ought to be that of 'partnership' (Bray, 2000). This is to acknowledge that the state alone cannot ensure universal primary education and must continue to rely on international support as well as support from civil society and communities themselves. Partnership does not just mean sharing the costs of education, however. Partnership must also mean an inclusive approach to policy making that ensures that indigenous social movements in particular have a voice in educational reconstruction and policy is not simply driven by the imperatives of elites. Mechanisms need to be put in place to ensure that marginalised constituencies such as women and youth, the rural poor and the workers have a say in the governance of education and can reign in the elites. The sub-continent is rich with examples of mechanisms at the local level of inclusive governance structures (although these take a plurality of forms from 'traditional' village councils and development committees to 'modern' local government). The same is true at the regional, provincial and national levels. These structures have strengths and weaknesses and vary in the extent to which they provide a forum for marginalised groups to have their say. The point though is that there is much that Africa can learn from Africa in relation to good education governance and there is a role for organisations such as the OAU and SADEC in fostering intra-continental learning and exchanges.

As far as the international community is concerned, the emergence of indigenous governance structures needs to be supported. The effect of structural adjustment policies has been to undermine rather than support the state and civil society and so there is a need for a policy reversal in this respect. Recent developments in the way that donors fund education, such as sector investment policies, are at least an improvement on past practice because they cede greater control of spending in the education sector to the state. Support also needs to be given, however, to emerging governance structures at the local level as it is here that effective civil society can be built.

*Race, Culture and the Globalisation of Education in Africa*
Mention has already been made of the importance of education in spreading Western cultural forms during the colonial era. It has been argued that this provided an important mechanism for the consolidation of Western hegemony during the period of contemporary globalisation. As some commentators have pointed out, however, one of the effects of contempo-

rary globalisation is to reshape cultural identities in new ways. Hall (1992, 1996) and Hoogvelt (1997), for example, have commented on how processes of migration, diaspora formation and cultural hybridisation have transformed individual and group identities and created 'new ethnicities' based on fluid rather than fixed identities. In the African context these processes appear contradictory and partial in their effects. War, famine and poverty on the sub-continent have led to a growing number of refugees and have accelerated processes of migration between countries and between rural and urban areas. This has inevitably entailed the development of cultural melting pots, particularly in the urban areas.

The African diaspora in the USA and elsewhere has also influenced the development of youth culture on the sub-continent. Social movements and forms of resistance in education and politics have also been shaped by political movements and ideas (e.g. such Pan Africanism) that have evolved across the African diaspora (Tikly, 1999).

These 'new ethnicities' have also emerged, however, at the same time as there has been a reassertion of more conservative and essentialised identities and an escalation in ethnic conflict. Writers such as Amin (1997) have argued that the growth in the number and intensity of these conflicts must be seen as an aspect of the colonial legacy which destabilized ethnic relations, the demise of uniting ideologies by which the nation state could secure the basis for national unity and growing poverty and inequality associated with economic globalisation and financial mismanagement. Carnoy (1999) sees the assertion of cultural identities in the contemporary period as 'an antidote to the complexity and harshness of the global market' and to 'the globalised bureaucratic state' (p. 78). Given Africa's increasingly marginal position in relation to global economic and political forces, coupled with growing inequalities, the dynamics giving rise to ethnic conflicts have been writ large on the subcontinent.

In sub-Saharan Africa education continues to play a key role in relation to culture and ethnic politics. This is because schools and other educational institutions are a significant (although by no means the sole) locus where different cultural forms interact. In the post colonial period, many governments have used education as a means of forging national unity through curricular interventions, language policies, ceremonial activities and such like. As some writers have pointed out, however, the challenges of changing cultural identities and the emergence of culturally defined social movements pose new challenges for educational planners and policy makers who must find new ways of working with diversity and difference in the curriculum. Because of education's role in relation to elite formation (see above) and entry to labour markets, access to educational opportunities can often also become the content of ethnic conflict as in countries such as Rwanda, Burundi, Nigeria and South Africa. In some of these countries, decentralisation has provided one mechanism for ensuring a greater say for communities whether defined in cultural, geographical, linguistic or religious terms. As Carnoy (1999) and others (see, for example, Bray & Lillis, 1988) have pointed out, however, the central government still has a key role to play within decentralised systems in 'levelling the playing fields' in terms of opportunities afforded to different groups.

In relation to language planning in particular, Rasool (1998) has described the issues surrounding linguistic human rights in the context of mass migration of peoples and the 'hybridisation' of indigenous cultures. On the one hand, she describes the tremendous possibilities opened up for language choice for migrant and formerly colonised groups of people in relation to ever-changing geographical demographies. On the other hand, she points to the difficulties of language planning in relation to these groups. She demonstrates how the issue of language choice for specific communities in former colonised countries is heavily contingent on a number of factors including their social status within the country in question. Once again this draws attention to the limits of educational reform if it is divorced from wider questions of cultural politics, power, poverty alleviation and democratic governance.

Language planning must also contend with the ambiguous role of colonial languages in relation to globalisation and cultural politics. Pennycook (1995) describes how the spread of English, partly through education has had contradictory effects. On the one hand, it has contributed to Western hegemony. On the other hand, Pennycook argues that this phenomenon can act counter-hegemonically as counter-hegemonic discourses can be 'formed in English' (p. 72) and that access to English can mean access to global networks.

Negotiating issues of language, identity and power is critical in the African context. It links directly with economic globalisation and is deeply implicated in the maintenance of support, and resistance to emerging hegemonic projects. Once again, however, Africa provides rich examples of policies concerned at negotiating language rights in the era of contemporary globalisation as exemplified by the Swahili experiment in Tanzania, the official languages policy in South Africa and the trilingual approach adopted by Camaroon.

Finally, European racism continues to exert an influence on the trajectory of educational reform in sub-Saharan Africa. Hoogvelt (1997) argues that the implementation of structural adjustment policies has been very much tied in with the spread of the 'new racism' which 'has come to underpin popular explanations for the growing political instability and intercommunal conflicts in the marginal areas of the global economy' (p. 179). This new racism, based on cultural explanations of difference, has come to replace biologically driven notions of racial superiority in the Western psyche. In many European constructions of the African 'Other', Africa's malaise is seen to be rooted in Africa itself. International school effectiveness studies, supported by global agencies such as the World Bank can feed into and support such views. Largely based on research, rationalities and an underlying epistemology developed elsewhere, school effectiveness studies lay the 'blame' for school failure at the local level. Understood in discursive terms, as an example of knowledge/power in operation, school effectiveness can be understood as a 'disciplinary technology', i. e. as an important tool for 'managing crisis' and apportioning blame (Morley & Rasool, 1999; Tikly, 1999; Harber & Davies, 1997; Samoff, 1994).

Ndoye (1997) makes the point that the effect of structural adjustment programmes has also been to still indigenous African responses to educational crisis. This is because they have undermined governance structures and have emphasised policies such as user fees. Whereas in the past, many African communities have been successful at intervening in crises through collective action, user fees lay the responsibility at the doorstep of individual parents and families and support a Western, individualistic and entrepreneurial model. Clearly there are dangers in Ndoye's argument of romanticising a collective African past and of presenting an essentialised and homogenous view of African cultures. Nonetheless it is true that the concepts of 'self help' and community provision of education do have a long pedigree on the sub-continent and often have a cultural basis (as in the 'harambee' movement in Kenya or the idea of 'tirisano' which is currently being used by the South African government to mobilise support behind educational reconstruction).

## Conclusion: Education and the African Renaissance

In conclusion, it is worth revisiting the notion of the African Renaissance which has been popularised most recently by the President of South Africa, Thabo Mbeki (1999). In important respects this idea provides a unifying framework that brings together many of the themes explored in this essay. In Mbeki's view the idea of the African renaissance involves a struggle against Africa's marginalisation in economic and political terms as much as it involves a celebration and development of African cultures. In this respect it fits with the Gramscian notion of the formation of a post-colonial historical bloc. For both Mbeki and Gramsci, development has economic, political and cultural dimensions and involves a 'battle on many fronts'. Political and cultural development relies on economic growth but conversely, economic success is contingent on cultural renewal and innovation and on the maintenance of political stability.

It has been the argument of this article that educational change in Africa has been profoundly shaped by global forces both in the contemporary and modern periods. It has also been argued that education can play a crucial role in Africa's renewal because of its central importance for economic, political and cultural development. In this respect, education is a *sine qua non* for the African renaissance. There are, however, many obstacles and vested interests in the way of education playing such a role. Educational change will only begin to play a significant part in development if it is adequately funded and access widened at all levels. More information is also needed about the skills required for development in the global era. Further, policy making also needs to be democratised and vested interests challenged. Finally, policy makers need to find new ways to work with and manage cultural diversity. In meeting these challenges Africa itself provides a rich source of policy options and alternatives to the status quo. Crucially, however, education cannot succeed alone and if educational reform is to be successful it must articulate with broader processes and struggles for change at the global, regional, national and local levels.

## References

Altbach, P. & Kelly, G. (1978) *Colonialism and Education* (London, Longman).

Amin, S. (1997) *Capitalism in the Age of Globalization* (London, Zed).

Archer, M. (1984) *Social Origins of Educational Systems* (London, Sage).

Ball, S. (1990) *Politics and Policy Making in Education* (London, Routledge).

Ball, S. (1998) *Big Policies/Small World: An Introduction to International Perspectives in Education Policy. Comparative Education*, 34 (2), pp. 119-130.

Bayart, J. (1993) *The State in Africa: The Politics of the Belly* (London, Longman).

Blackmore, J. (1999) *Localization/Globalization and the Mid-wife State: Strategic Dilemmas for State Feminists in Education. Journal of Education Policy*, 14, pp. 33-54.

Boyer, R. & Drache, D. (eds.) (1996) *States Against Markets* (London, Routledge).

Bray, M. (2000) *Partnerships in Education. Paper Presented to the Education for All Conference*, Dakar, April.

Bray, M. & Lillis, K. (1988) *Community Financing of Education*

(London, Commonwealth Secretariat).

Brown, P. & Lauder, H. (1997) Education, *Globalization and Economic Development*, in: A. Halsey, H. Lauder, P. Brown & A. Wells (eds.) *Education, Culture, Economy, Society* (Oxford, Oxford University Press).

Carnoy, M. (1999) *Globalization and Educational Reform: What Planners Need to Know* (Paris: UNESCO).

Carter, D. & O'neil, M. (1995) *International Perspectives on Educational Reform and Policy Implementation* (Brighton, Falmer).

Carton, M. & Tawil, S. (1997) *Introduction to the Open. le. Prospects*, 27, pp. 19-25.

Castells, M. (1993) *Economy and the New International Division of Labour*, in: M. Carnoy, M. Astells, S. S. Cohen & F. H. Cordoso (eds) *The New Global Economy in the Information* (London, Macmillan).

Castells, M. (1996) *The Rise of the Network Society* (Oxford, Balckwell).

Chossudovsky, M. (1997) *The Globalization of Poverty* (Penang, Third World Network).

Clapham, C. (1996) *Africa and the International System: The Politics of State Survival* (Cambridge, Cambridge University Press).

Colclough, C. & Manor, J. (eds.) (1991) *States or Markets? Neo-liberalism and the Development Policy Debate* (Oxford, Clarendon Press).

Cooksey, B., Court, D. & Makau, B. (1994) *Education for Self-reliance and Harambee*, in: J. Barkan (ed.) *Beyond Capitalism Versus Socialism in Kenya and Tanzania* (London, Lynne Reinner).

Cowen, R. (1996) *Last Past the Post: Comparative Education, Modernity and Perhaps Post-modernity. Comparative Education*, 32 (2), pp. 151-170.

Crossley, M. (1999) *Reconceptualising Comparative and International Education. Compare*, 29, pp. 249-267.

Dale, R. (1999) *Specifying Globalization Effects on National Policy: A Focus on the Mechanisms. Journal of Education Policy*, 14, pp. 1-17.

Donald, J. (1992) *Sentimental Education* (London, Verso).

Dore, R. (1997) *The Diploma Disease: Education, Qualification and Development* (London, Institute of Education, University of London).

Edwards, R. (1994) *From a distance? Globalization, Space-Time Compression and Distance Education. Journal of Open Learning*, 9, pp. 9-17.

Fritzell, C. (1987) *On the Concept of Relative Autonomy in Educational Theory. British Journal of Sociology of Education*, 8, pp. 23-36.

Giddens, A. (1990) *The Consequences of Modernity* (Cambridge, Cambridge Polity Press).

Green, A. (1997) *Education, Globalization and the Nation State* (Basingstoke, Macmillan).

Green, A. (1999) *Education and Globalization in Europe and East Asia: Convergent and Divergent Trends. Journal of Education Policy*, 14, pp. 55-71.

Hall, S. (1992) *New Ethnicities*, in: J. Donald & A. Rattansi (eds) *'Race', Culture and Difference* (London, Sage).

Hall, S. (1996) *'When Was the Post-colonial'? Thinking at the Limit*, in: I. Chamber, & L. Curtis, (eds) *The Post-colonial Question: Common Skies, Divided Horizons* (London, Routledge).

Harber, C & Davies, L. (1997) *School Management and Effectiveness in Developing Countries* (London, Cassell).

Held, D, Mcgrew, A. Goldblatt, D. & Perraton, J. (1999) *Global Transformations: Politics, Economics, Culture* (Cambridge, Polity).

Henry, M., Lingard, B., Rizvi, F. & Taylor, S. (1999) *Working with/against Globalization in Education*. Journal of Education Policy, 14, pp. 85-97.

Hirst, P. & Thompson, G. (1996) *Globalization in Question: The International Economy and the Possibilities of Governance* (Cambridge, Cambridge Polity Press).

Hoogvelt, A. (1997) *Globalisation and the Postcolonial World: The New Political Economy of Development* (Basingstoke, Macmillan).

Ilon, L. (1994) *Structural Adjustment and Education: Adapting to a Growing Global Market*. International Journal of Educational Development, 14, pp. 95-108. International Journal of Educational Development (1996) 16 (4).

Jones, P. (1998) *Globalisation and Internationalism: Democratic Prospects for World Education*. Comparative Education, 34 (2), pp. 143-155.

Kenway, J. (1996) *The Information Super-highway and Post-modernity: the Social Promise and The Social Price*. Comparative Education, 32, pp. 217-232.

Kress, G. (1996) *Internationalisation and Globalisation: Rethinking a Curriculum of Communication*. Comparative Education, 32 (2), pp. 185-196.

Marais, H. (1997) *South Africa: Limits to Change: The Political Economy of Transformation* (London, Zed).

Marginson, S. (1999) *After Globalization: Emerging Politics of Education*. Journal of Education Policy, 14, pp. 19-31.

Mazrui, A. (1978) *Political Values and the Educated Class in Africa* (Berkeley, University of California Press).

Mbeki, T. (1999) *Speech to Launch the African Renaissance Institute* (Pretoria, African Renaissance Institute).

Mkandawire, T. (1996) *The State, Human Rights and Academic Freedom in Africa*, in: J. Turner (ed.) *The State and the School: An International Perspective*, pp. 18-36 (London, Falmer).

Morley, L & Rassool, N. (1999) *School Effectiveness: Fracturing the Discourse* (London, Falmer).

Mundy, K. (1999) *Educational Multilateralism in a Changing World Order: Unesco and the Limits of the Possible*. International Journal of Educational Development, 19, pp. 27-52.

Ndoye, M. (1997) *Globalization, Endogenous Development and Education in Africa*. Prospects, 27, pp. 79-84.

Ohmae, K. (1995) *The End of the Nation State* (New York, Free Press).

Pennycook, A. (1995) *English in the World/the World in English*, in: J. Tollefson (ed.) *Power and Inequality in Language Education*, pp. 34-58 (Cambridge, Cambridge University Press).

Philipson, R. (1998) *Globalizing English: Are Linguistic Human Rights an Alternative to Linguistic Imperialism?* Language Sciences, 20, pp. 101-112.

Rasool, N. (1998) *Postmodernity, Cultural Pluralism and the Nation-state: Problems of Language Rights, Human Rights, Identity and Power*. Language Sciences, 20, pp. 89-99.

Riddell, A. (1996) *Globalization: Emasculation or Opportunity for Educational Planning?* World Development, 24, pp. 1357-1372.

Samoff, J. (ed.) (1994) *Coping with Crisis: Austerity, Adjustment and Human Resources* (London, Cassell).

Stewart, F. (1996) *Globalisation and Education*. International Journal of Educational Development, 16, pp. 327-333.

Strange, S. (1996) *The Retreat of the State: The Diffusion of Power in the World Economy* (Cambridge, Cambridge University Press).

Tikly, L. (1994) *Education Policy in South Africa Since 1947*. PhD

Thesis, University of Glasgow.

Tikly, L. (1997) *Changing South Africa's schools: An Analysis and Critique of Post-election Government Policy. Journal of Education Policy*, 12, pp. 177-188.

Tikly, L. (1999) *Postcolonialism and Comparative Education. International Review of Education*, 45, pp. 603-621.

Tilak, J. (1997) *The Effects of Adjustment on Education: A Review of the Asian Experience. Prospects*, 27, pp. 85-108.

Usher, R. & Edwards, R. (1994) *Postmodernism and Education: Different Voices, Different Worlds* (London, Routledge).

White, B. W. (1996) *Talk about School: Education and the Colonial Project in French and British West Africa. Comparative Education*, 29 (1), pp. 9-25.

World Bank. (1999) *World Development Indicators* (Washington DC, World Bank).

[From *Comparative Education* Volume 37, No. 2, 2001, pp. 151-171]

# 导读：国际化与后殖民主义社会教育：理论构架与设想

## 1. 引言

本文介绍全球化与低收入、后殖民主义国家教育之间的关系，主要讨论撒哈拉沙漠周围的非洲国家的教育问题。目前的诸多文献大多是论述全球化与西方发达国家或者新兴起的工业化国家（如东南亚四小龙）教育之间的关系，对落后贫穷的后殖民主义非洲国家教育问题关注不足。因此，作者从目前关于非洲国家政治经济发展的文献出发，描绘了一个新的理论框架来了解后殖民主义背景下非洲国家教育问题与全球化的关系。

## 2. 后殖民主义

在教育研究上，后殖民主义也提供了多元社会中公平性种族观念的开展，对西方殖民政权或主流政权，利用教育机制对曾被殖民国家或边缘民族控制的批判与讨论，以及这些曾被殖民的国家如何重新塑造自己的课程、文化或语言模式，朝着各种族教育公平及均等的目标进行。所以后殖民主义主要是以被殖民者的角度，对于西方或主流文化殖民的不当措施及理念进行反省、批判并建构一种以被殖民者为主体的文化的意识形态（张立波，2001；陶东风，2000）。

后殖民主义（postcolonialism）可以理解成是后殖民民族国家独立后，殖民主义并没有因此而终结，从而显示出殖民后果的持久性、延续性及反殖民斗争的艰巨性。在理论研究方法上，后殖民主义理论研究具有多元性，包含政治、经济、社会、文化等多领域的共同研究，从研究对象上来说，也从过去研究殖民文化为主转而以被殖民者为主体的研究。

## 3. 全球化与教育的关系

目前众多有关全球化的意义及影响的争论大致可以分为三大论述：肯定论（the hyperglobalist approach），怀疑论（the sceptical approach）和修正论（the transformationist approach）。作者结合这三种论述分别来评定其在对于理解低收入、后殖民主义国家教育问题上的相关性。

（1）肯定论者认为以全球为单位强调全球化是市场经济与信息社会发展的必然趋势，这类观点主要是延续自由主义主张世界贸易应自由往来的全球主义者，论述主要集中在市场、通信与直接触及全球化的环境生态与心理价值等外部性的讨论，主张政府职能的逐渐消亡。

这种观点被引用到教育文献当中，一些学者认为信息高速公路以及信息与国际市场的相互作用将导致传统教育模式的衰亡。另外,一些学者(如,Green,1997)认为这种观点言过其实,民族政府在教育问题上仍然是最主要的责任承担者,并且,信息技术相比与传统教学而言,仍然发展不够成熟,即使是富裕的国家的学校教育也不可能被虚拟教学所取代。在后殖民主义背景下,对于欠发达的非洲国家而言,作者认为,这种论述更加不能让人信服。后殖民主义国家在转向民主和国家自由的进程中,教育是作为国家最主要的工具来加强团结,因此,政府在教育问题上不仅没有放松,反而比过去更加紧迫。另外,利用信息高速公路资源对于非洲大多数人而言是不现实的,仅仅只有一些精英可以有条件享用。

(2)怀疑论者认为国家仍是国际社会主要行为者,全球化只是国际化的延续或是一种表征。国家的角色不但没有受到侵蚀,反而为了应付全球化所带来的冲击和危机而显得更加重要。同时,资本主义在全球的实行加速了两极分化。

在教育文献当中,Green 表示到目前为止还没有出现任何一种有意义的教育全球化现象,并且,尽管国家教育在某种程度上表现出了相似性,但还没有任何迹象显示国家教育制度正在消失,国家对教育失去了控制。Green 认为目前存在的只是相当温和的一些变化,例如学生和教师的国际流动、广泛的教育政策的互相借鉴等。

怀疑论中关于两极分化的论述与非洲贫穷国家的教育是十分相关的。非洲国家的结构调整和紧缩以及人口的不断增加使得学生入学率下降。根据世界银行1999年的统计,超过4千万的学生辍学,非洲地区的入学率居于世界末位。

(3)修正论者强调国家虽是国际社会最主要的成员,但新兴的全球化风潮确实对传统上以国家为主体的国际社会造成了新的差异和调整。国际社会涵盖领域包括种族、国家、科技、金融、文化与意识形态等多种不同面向,导致了大众强烈需求新理论概念及新治理模式来处理日益复杂的、传统理论无法应对的新的情况和新的全球风险。

修正论者的论述在教育文献中主要可以归结为:教育如今不仅是全球化影响和作用的对象,同时还作为全球化势力的主要工具来影响国民的日常生活。

修正论者的观点在教育领域的应用，其中的一个优势就是可以从全球化的多个角度来探讨其在教育之间的关系，国家和地方社会对于全球化势力的调解，以及关于文化、语言和身份的一系列问题。另外，一些主张修正论的学者还尝试将全球化分工与世界范围内的社会分化问题与教育政策的制定联系起来。然而，修正论者在种族、文化、阶级和性别领域没有更深挖掘其分化对于教育的启示，另外，他们也没能把握住全球化的早期表现，尤其是欧洲殖民主义的持续影响和作用。

### 4. 新框架的理论

由于过去的理论基础都或多或少存在一定不足，本文作者建立了一套新的理论框架来探讨全球化在后殖民主义背景下对教育政策的影响。分析是建立在先前的一些模式的优点基础上，同时尽量避免以前模式的弱点。作者主要从下面几个方面进行探讨：

（1）全球化

首先作者引用 Held 等人（1999 年）对全球化所下的定义，说明其对全球化的理解发展了修正论者的观点。Held 等人把对全球化的理解建立在对一系列"过程"的理解而不是对一种"状态"的理解。这些过程包含了在政治、军事、经济和文化等领域的作用和网络，并且不是呈线形发展的，是不平行的，包含很多复杂的政治和经济关系。

（2）全球化的早期形式对于教育的意义

为了超越修正者论，Held 等人对不同时期和不同形式的全球化作了描述。他们提供了一个丰富的框架作为起始来探讨后殖民背景下的教育与全球化的关系。关于早现代时期的全球物流和网络如何在非洲教育制度上留下印记的例子数不胜数。全球宗教的传播，尤其是伊斯兰教和基督教的传播带来了各自的教育方式和学校制度。

（3）不同全球势力对教育的影响

由于全球化是多方面的，全球化与教育的关系就不应仅仅局限于经济层面,而是应该包含全球化中政治、文化等其他层面对教育的影响。事实上,只有全球化的所有层面都被予以考虑和分析,才能更好揭示非洲教育悲剧的原因。

(4) 经济全球化和教育

为了解经济全球化对于教育在后殖民主义背景下的意义,首先要了解后殖民经济在全球化经济网络中的位置。经济全球化对于非洲而言所产生的具体影响主要表现在:按照世界银行和国际基金组织所说的那样,结构调整政策在非洲广大国家已实行。结构调整旨在使国家通过降低成本来增强国家竞争力并且吸引外资。然而,结构调整给非洲国家带来的仅仅是灾难,如Chossudovsky(1997)所描述的那样"贫穷的全球化"。

在这种景况下的非洲教育又是一番怎样景象呢?相关的教育文献论述主要集中在两个方面:首先是经济全球化对教育的启示,然后是教育、技术培训和全球劳工市场的关系。前者主要谈论的是结构调整政策对于入学率和教育质量的负面影响,后者一方面主要是讲述结构调整对教育的负面作用,另一方面是讲述为了增加全球竞争力而在人力资源领域增加投资的必要性。

(5) 全球化与教育政治

修正论者认为,由于全球化的政治因素,国家的角色在教育问题上被重新定义,被认为是"旨在全球经济当中使国家更具有竞争力"。这种观点对于低收入国家而言,具有一定积极意义,因为它允许不同国家对于全球化势力做出的教育反应可以是不同的,同时也使得全球化的不利影响可以在国家层次上得到抵制甚至修正成为可能。

在谈到非洲目前的状况与全球化与教育政策的关系的时候,作者从Bray(2000)的观点入手,谈到应该把非洲看成是自后殖民时代开始以来政治斗争和发展的结果。这也正解释了非洲国家的多样化特点。其中在保持领导权的两个集团中,他们所存在的共同点就是对"精英的吸收",通过给予精英们一定的社会地位和财富。而教育在这种机制中发挥关键的作用。同时,作者也谈到了其他一系列政治机制对教育政策产生影响。

(6) 种族、文化与非洲的教育全球化

前面谈到了殖民时期教育对于传播西方文化的重要性，在当前全球化时期，教育作为一种重要工具巩固了西方的霸权主义。然而，一些学者指出，当前全球化的任务之一是重新构建文化身份。

在非洲，教育在文化和种族政治方面发挥关键的作用，因为教育一向都是多种文化交合的地方。在后殖民时代，很多政府都利用教育作为加强国家团结的方式，尤其是通过课程、语言政策等。然而，正如一些学者所说的那样，变化着的文化身份和具有文化特色的社会运动的出现给教育政策制定者提出了新的挑战。

## 5. 结束语

本文探讨了现代和当代的全球化势力对非洲教育的转变所产生的重大影响。作者认为因为教育在经济、政治、文化发展中占有中心地位，因此教育在非洲的复兴当中可以扮演非常重要的角色。然而教育的发展面临重重阻力，只有教育得到充分的资助，各个阶层的人都能享受到教育的权利，教育才能在国家发展中发挥一定的作用。另外，政策的制定需要更加民主和考虑到边缘群体的利益，政策制定者需要发现新的途径来发展文化多元性。最重要的是，教育必须站在更高更广的角度，努力从当地、国家、地区乃至全球的范围内寻求转变。

**Questions for reflection**:

1. What's the characteristics of postcolonial studies?
2. What's the implication of the three existing broad approaches of globalization for education?
3. What's the weakness of the current account of contemporary globalization concerning the low-income countries?
4. According to the author, what role does structure adjustment play in education in low-income, postcolonial countries?

5. What's the impact of globalization on education politics in Africa?

# Internationalisation and Globalisation: Rethinking a Curriculum of Communication

Gunther Kress

*ABSTRACT*: *The article describes the changed conditions of communication due to the two factors of globalisation and internationalisation. It looks at four factors in particular: issues of genre; literariness and national cultures; new modes and forms of communication; and the impacts on curricula of communication. It places these issues into the contexts of economic and social futures, and makes suggestions about the necessary relations between these and forms of the curricula of communication.*

## Contexts

The last 15 years or so have seen increasingly insistent demands by governments in Anglo-phone countries for institutionalised education to become more responsive to the needs of local ('national') economies. At times and in certain places these calls have also included demands that the education system should 'deliver' certain cultural and social values: around national identity, morality or whatever. The two demands are connected; they represent attempts to solve problems of increasing uncertainty through one of the few remaining institutions over which national governments still seem to have effective powers. In no area of the curriculum have these calls been more insistent—or strident—than they have in that of communication, appearing variously in curricula (as 'German' or as 'English') or as a curriculum of 'literacy' in the Anglo-phone countries.

Here I will examine the challenges which they face and the possibilities which are actually open to curricula in this area, which I call, broadly, communication. My own field of interest is communication and representation and I will illustrate my argument occasionally by reference to the situation in Australia, England and Germany. Some elements of a comparative approach seem to me to be particularly relevant and even essential, given that so much of the current debate—whether practically focused or theoretical—remains too bound to specific localities, from where vast generalisations are launched.

While such generalisation may be in keeping with some aspects and characteristics of the current state of theorising, it is, nevertheless, not conducive to producing insight. Take as an example the notion of 'fragmentation'. Fragmentation is a fact when viewed from one specific locality. From there it does appear that social institutions are fragmenting, whether those of the family, the neighbourhood, the nation, the church, aspects of the state and of the economy. Seen from a global perspective, the very opposite may be thought to be occurring. So where, for instance, in one locality it may seem that the institutions of the mass media are coming into crisis (issues of local versus transnational media ownership, for instance), from a global perspective the impression and perhaps the reality is one of increasing consolidation, integration, in any case the very opposite of fragmentation. What has fragmented in this situation is the identification of nation with culture—which was of course never an unproblematic reality in any case (Coulby & Jones, 1995; Lyotard, 1984).

In all of this debate the question about the shape and the purposes of curricula remain, in relation to their function and role in a specific locality, whether that is the nation-state—England has now had a National Curriculum for the last 6 years or so—or a part of a state, as for instance in the Lander in Germany or the 'States' of the Commonwealth of Australia or, indeed, a part of, perhaps, much smaller, regional or other entities.

I will consider some of the issues which affect the curricula of communication from four different perspectives: from the point of view of genre, of 'literariness' and national cultures, of modes and media of communication and from the point of view of a local curriculum in a globalising environment.

First a brief word on each of these, to provide some framing to my argument. Although the category does not really reach into the common sense of educators, knowledge of the generic form of texts (Cope & Kalantzis, 1993) is foundational to the possibilities of coherent communication. The category of genre therefore becomes central in times when the possibilities of communication undergo severe change. Similarly, the pre-eminence of language as the mode of communication is coming under increasing challenge, on the one hand, initially through theoretical attacks on 'logocentrism' by groups who had felt oppressed in relation to powerful groups in particular social configurations, but increasingly, on the other hand, over the last two decades or so, through actual changes in the semiotic landscape, the landscape of public communication, which is remaking not only that broad landscape, but, in doing so, is remaking the place and characteristics of written language in it (Kress & Van Leeuwen, 1996). In as far as curricula of communication are curricula of texts which have potency in the society in which the curricula operate, that issue has been settled in the past via the category of aesthetics—a political matter presented as a question of transcendental value. As political structures are challenged, so aesthetics may—for a time at any rate—become less useful as a device for providing shape and coherence for a curriculum of communication. Lastly, the main issue, the curriculum. In the era of the nation-state, the web of structures of control gave value, coherence and integrity to curricula. One element of the web supported every other element in a seamless structure. With globalisation all the purposes of the curriculum are coming into question, at every point (Kress, 1995).

In my discussion I make use of the currently overused term 'globalisation' and I want to set that against another term, 'internationalisation'. Their effects often seem the same, though the structures through which they operate or which they produce, are distinctly different and are distinctly different in different places. The dynamics which they set in train are, similarly, quite distinct. By globalisation I mean the increasing tendency for the globe to constitute the effective domain of action and of thinking, in relation to a specific issue. Financial markets are global. The media are becoming globalised, as is communication generally and, consequently, many aspects of culture are becoming globalised also. Increasingly, production is becoming global as sites of production are shifted at short notice to low-wage environments. Consequently, the labour market is becoming globalised in every locality even though no one person actually might be moving. Where in the nineteenth century and in the early part of this century sites of production were fixed so that the labour force had to migrate to those sites, now it is sites of production which are flexible and moveable leaving the labour force in its original locality. Hence, patterns (and causes) of population movements are now distinctly different from older ideas of immigration and are likely to remain so.

The consequences of these changed forms of population movement for educational thinking and policy have perhaps not been fully appreciated, particularly in relation to pluri- (or multi-) culturalism. In my view that is a fundamental issue and the conclusions at this stage are at best somewhat paradoxical. Take the three cases of Australia, the UK and Germany, in relation to this one factor. Australia has been a (so-called) country of immigration over the last five decades, with an active (if changing) policy of encouraging immigration. It did this for economic (and military) reasons, promising to produce employment in new sites of production where there might initially have been none available. The Snowy Mountains Scheme was one such undertaking, as were the expansion of mining and steel-making activities. The immigrants who went to Australia were invited there as future citizens, with a stake in the country's future Germany, like several other north-western European nations, recruited labour from a variety of areas of southern and south-eastern Europe (leaving aside the question of Europeanness for the moment as it arises with workers going to Germany from Turkey, for instance). These 'guest workers' went to existing sites of production in response to boom conditions in the economy. There was no question and therefore no sense of creating jobs on the part of the host country, no sense of immigration, with its implication of future citizenship. The fact that the people who went to a variety of countries demanded a stake in that place, once they had established themselves there, produced initial surprise and a consequent set of political and social problems. The UK by contrast has not at any time in recent history seen itself as a country of immigration, nor did it actively invite labour to come. The fact that this did happen, initially, was a consequence of the breakup of the empire and of consequent post-imperial, post-colonial dynamics. The people who came to Britain in the immediate post-war decades were already citizens or, more precisely, subjects of the British Crown. They, as much as their increasingly reluctant hosts, could assume—even if this turned out to be too superficial an assumption—that they were 'the same', all part of the one's family. However, if they were the same, as they were already politically the same at least in superficial form and status as subjects of the British Crown, then no special requirements needed to be met in order for them to be a part of this new place.

The older forms of population movement—emigration and immigration—demanded a particular response from the immigrant, namely adaptation to the social conditions of the (new) locality, the new site of production; hence there were, broadly, policies of assimilation, 'integration', and then 'mainstreaming' in the various countries of immigration as an initial response. This made particular kinds of demands on the education systems in these countries. Countries which recruited guest workers had no initial expectation in these areas and therefore no initial (psychological and) social structures to deal with this situation. Britain simply received other members of the same—if somewhat large and diverse—'family'.

Thus, it is essential to recognise that current conditions—of multiculturalism, for instance—which may seem, on the surface, to be quite similar from one place to another, actually rest on fundamentally different histories, which in their turn have led to fundamentally different political and educational responses— 'naturally'. Thus, paradoxically, in Australia, a country of immigration, which expected 'assimilation' in its various forms, the fact of the initial invitation to the newcomers to be citizens ('New Australians') could and did lead after a period of some three decades to some reassessment of the rights of these new and different citizens and a valuation of that difference quite unlike that in either Germany or the UK. This has had important consequences for public policies on communication. Australia developed, in the early to mid-1980s, a National Languages Policy (eventually changed to a National Language Policy) which acknowledged the existence of the multiplicity of languages spoken in Australia and gave to English—implicitly if not explicitly—the status of a lingua franca. Clearly this has had and will continue to have significant consequences for the curricula of communication.

If the expected response to immigration (movement of labour to sites of production) was assimilation, the response required of/by that labour to the relocation of sites of production is fundamentally different. It is predictably the subject of intense ideological debate, which ranges from attempts to introduce the structures of low-wage environments in existing 'developed' countries, to restructuring of various kinds, including the restructuring of the 'skills base' of the labour force. Globalisation of production demands an 'internal' reconstruction of labour and of individual subjectivities (Senge, 1991), so that labour can respond to the demands of globalising production and to the requirements of a globalised employment market. The current common sense of neo-liberal, monetarist, share-holder capitalism is to demand a driving down of labour costs and the dismantling of structural costs, whether of health, unemployment support or pensions (Hutton, 1995). An alternative response sees a way forward by a restructuring of labour in the direction of innovation, flexibility and creativity, as the basis for new economic structures.

Clearly, institutionalised and non-institutional education has the most far-reaching involvement and role in this debate and in the future directions of economies in particular localities. While the pairing of immigration and assimilation left existing educational structures intact—that, after all, was what assimilation was to achieve— the new pairing of relocation of sites of production and reconstitution /restructuring of labour demands a fundamentally changed form of education, a quite different response. This is intensified by the fact that the forms of production which existed in the age of immigration were largely Fordist, with their specific requirements from the education system in terms of the preparation of the labour force. The new age of the movement of production sites and the consequent globalisation of labour is taking place in an environment characterised by non-Fordist forms of production, even if Fordist modes of production continue in very many places. The necessary 'internal remaking' of the labour force and the question of requisite, appropriate, necessary subjectivities pose entirely new questions for education systems and for their curricula. In these, the curricula of communication have central importance, particularly given the new conjunctions of information-based production and globalisation.

Contemporary population movements, which are as large-scale as any in human history and likely (or 'threatening') to be far larger, have to fit, at the moment at any rate, into these new structures. In 'countries of immigration' these structures are no longer simply those of assimilation: in countries which recruited (or received) guest workers, questions of the rights of citizenship have come to the fore; in a post-imperial, post-colonial country such as Britain the uncertainties engendered by that condition cloud over the attitudes to pluriculturalism and its local histories.

All countries have to deal with the effects of globalisation in the contexts of their histories. They are also subject to the effects of internationalisation, a term by which I want to name the cultural, political and economic influences from somewhere outside a particular locality on the value structures, practices and forms of social organisation of that locality.

These are making themselves felt increasingly and although internationalisation is by no means a new phenomenon in this century (or in fact before), the effects of the new technologies of transport and of electronic modes of communication are changing the levels of intensity with which these effects are experienced and the social and cultural transformations which are wrought by them. Food and dress are obvious if perhaps relatively superficial examples. For the former, internationalisation suspends the effects of seasonality, of climate and of ethnic custom for those who are affluent, while the latter suspends the effects of locality for very many—think of the ubiquity of jeans and T-shirts as a uniform for the young and not-so-young in diverse, cultural and geographic parts of the globe.

The cultural effects of internationalisation on culture and communication and its consequent effects on the curricula of representation and communication cannot be overestimated. The internationalisation of the mass media is producing dislocating, locally fragmenting and homogenising cultural effects at the same time as the globalising effects of the media of information and communication—the world wide web, for instance—are producing new, superficially coherent interest-based communities. In these contexts, the questions of genre have been newly topical over the last 30 years or so, with an intensification of that interest since the very late 1970s.

## Genre

Jacques Derrida's 'La loi du genre' (1978) may stand as an iconic marker of this recent intense period of interest (Derrida, 1978). The category of genre itself goes back to Aristotle's *Poetics* and has had a continuous history of use, in the last two or three centuries particularly in relation to literary, aesthetically valued texts. In my own use of the term, the generic form of a text is an effect of the social conditions of its occasion of production. That is, the participants in a particular occasion of interaction have aims, goals and responsibilities and they stand in particular social relations to each other. They enact all these in that situation and they use language (among other modes) to do so. The resultant linguistic text encodes, realises and represents these aims and purposes, the relations of the participants and the unfolding enactment of that situation. The text which results from the interaction is a map of the social occasion in which it was produced.

Thus, for instance, an interview—say, a job interview—is a social occasion in which people come together for particular purposes, with specific aims, in particular 'roles', with their duties, responsibilities and rights ('Are you comfortable?', 'Would you like to ask us some questions now?'). In 'Western' societies this kind of occasion occurs frequently (though it is essential to be clear about significant cultural differences even within that broad label 'Western'), and although there are recognisable historical shifts in the structures of these occasions, from the point of view of any one interviewer or interviewee the regularity and repeatability of the form of the interview gives the text an appearance of fixedness, of stability. It is a form which can be known and understood; therefore it can be consciously acted within or against, that is mimicked, caricatured and parodied. The important aspect is that the (seeming) stability of the form of the text reflects a (seeming) stability of the social occasions; conversely, forms of texts are understood because the corresponding forms of social organization are understood—whether through experience or through an analysis of the text-form based on a knowledge of the social semiotic system of that group. Systems of texts guarantee, as a parallel structure, systems of social practice and texts are understood and re-enacted in that way.

The multiplicity of textual forms, of genres, thus acts as a semiotic, social and cultural mesh which reveals the meanings of that society to its members and allows them to act conventionally or against convention.

The conditions of globalisation and internationalization—as well as other factors—are producing deep challenges to these (seemingly) stable systems of (seemingly) stable textual forms. Internationalisation means that the generic forms— and with these, the social values and forms of organization—travel without let or hindrance from one cultural place to another totally different place. Media-commentators have wondered about the effects of beaming *Dallas* from a geostationary satellite down to dishes and viewers in the New Guinea Highlands or the islands of Melanesia. However, one does not need to travel that far from home to see fierce responses to this phenomenon. In Germany the showing of North American programmes such as *Power-Rangers* caused hostile comment, over worries about the effects of the habitual viewing of violence on young viewers. When a German television company decided to reschedule its *World Wrestling Federation* series from a later evening slot (at 21:30 hours) to a Saturday and Sunday afternoon slot, a veritable storm of hostile comment from media commentators, church groups and parents' associations broke out over this move. The station had, in part, been responding to the fact—documented by its voluminous mailbag—that a very large number of young viewers, from 4 years of age upwards, watched this programme regularly and they and their parents had wanted it moved to an earlier spot.

The television company had prepared—at some considerable cost—a whole series of framing programmes which attempted to demystify the highly staged performances of these 'shows', the first instance, to my knowledge, of serious critical media education being undertaken by a television broadcasting company. That notwithstanding, the company was taken to court, where it was ordered to stop showing the programme during these hours and it lost the case on appeal to the highest court.

The case is instructive in a number of ways: what was at issue was the transposition of a genre from one society to another. The social relations coded in the genre were unacceptable in the society in which it was rebroadcast—but only to one group, educators by and large, both in formal and informal institutional settings. In the originating society, the social relations portrayed in the programmes—communication through (seemingly violent) bodily, physical, interaction—had a broad context and a historical embedding which enabled viewers to 'see them for what they are'. And, it has to be said, that society has developed means to understand physicality and certain forms of masculinity in socially framed ways, which lead to readings of a kind in which those forms of physicality and masculinity can be made sense of in other than violent ways. In the receiving community, by complete contrast, the portrayal of social relations through physical, bodily interaction—with their surface appearance of extreme violence—was not readily acceptable to a generation which has spent 40 years coming to terms with violence of the most enormous magnitude and was witnessing at that time the resurgence of violence from groups of youths towards ethnic minorities.

The young viewers had entirely different readings of these programmes, judging from the letters and drawings which they wrote in their thousands every week to the programme. For them, the issues were about their own fears and anxieties, about families and how they do or do not manage to get on and about fairness and the observance of rules. They had what seemed to me on reading their letters and looking at their images a subtle understanding, which made them respond to the overt portrayal of violence quite differently from their elders' responses.

The point is that internationalisation willy-nilly introduces the generic/social structures of one place to another, whether that place has the means to cope with them or not. The readings that are produced in the new place are relatively unpredictable: neither of the two German responses is, I imagine, like any among a range of typical American readings. In Britain, the same programmes have been shown in the middle of the day or late at night, without causing comment in either case. However, the appearance of entirely new, different generic forms in a social group will lead to an unravelling of the system of generic forms in one place and its reforming in quite different ways.

The education system can ignore this issue and proceed as though national boundaries remain intact and with them the set of value systems and social relations which had characterised a particular society. The young people who are in that education system are constantly engaging with texts of the most diverse generic forms, which never make a fully legitimated appearance in the school, even in media studies. In Britain, rock videos, with their deeply anti-narrative, anti-rationalist formal structures, may be the object of study, but would not appear as a genre of text to be produced in the mainstream curriculum of communication. Some teachers, in some schools, might permit or encourage this; it is not a practice supported by the National Curriculum, by forms of assessment or by official common sense. And so a deep uncertainty develops, not only or even particularly in relation to mass media texts, but in relation to all texts. Producing that uncertainty are, as well as internationalisation, also the facts of cultural diversity in classrooms, the texts of youth cultures read and used by students and, not least, the uncertainties which beset the adult social world of the teacher. Further, as another instance, the politics of gender have meant that certain generic forms have come under the severest critique, as underpinning structures of patriarchy and of oppression. In this context it is difficult to know what a productive curricular response should be. I return to this question briefly at the end of this paper.

## Literariness and National Cultures: The Politics of Aesthetics

At the very moment when the system of genre is coming under attack from a variety of directions, one of the sheet anchors of that system has itself come adrift. In schools in Anglo-phone countries, the curriculum had been able to rely on a canon of literary texts which represented 'the best' in a culture's history of literary production. This worked differently in different places, but it served as the gold standard to which the whole system could be tied. In its terms, forms of writing could be assessed, valued and disvalued and, consequently, in terms of it, human subjects could be formed in relation to 'good taste' a quality which could, while the system was in full working order, be seen as a natural quality, beyond challenge or critique.

There had been critiques of the 'canon' from time to time, but these were not of a fundamental kind. Marxists, for instance, were on the whole content to subject figures and texts in the canon to their re-readings but by and large left it intact and in many ways left it stronger than before, having described the reasons why we should actually be reading Donne, Marlowe or Milton. Feminists have added women writers to the list—slightly more contentiously from the point of view of school curricula. However, both left in place the idea of good writing, the core of the canon and a broad notion of the function of literature. The cultural aspirations and claims of a dominant group had not been challenged: the claims had been somewhat extended and so had the membership of that dominant group.

The challenge which has been most unsettling and is potentially the greatest threat and test both for the canon and for the school curriculum, is that of multi-culturalism. Two instances may serve to define the problem. The first is an incident in Australia, the second concerns the issue of set texts in the English (and Welsh) National Curriculum. The first arises from the fact that in Australia—as in other countries of immigration—writers from groups whose first language is not English have begun to write in English. In some cases there is a conscious attempt to use 'broken English', in the case I am describing, 'Polish Australian' as an aesthetic medium to express the feelings of immigrant women in their new country. The language is crude, and often vulgar and the literary effect is shocking. It is also highly effective as an expressive medium. In the second case a Vietnamese writer, who had arrived as one of the 'boat people', was awarded a literary prize for a short story written in his own, quite rudimentary form of English. This provoked a comment from the editor of a book programme on the Australian Broadcasting Corporation on the aesthetic qualities of the piece, which he condemned as being in no sense 'literary'. Predictably enough, a furore ensued, an argument conducted in bitter and often personal terms, which in the end, equally predictably, was inconclusive.

Not inconclusive, however, in one sense: the argument unsettled, in Australia at least for the near future, the previously settled notions of 'good' or 'best writing' and of literariness. The politics of aesthetics had appeared, as they usually do not do quite so overtly, on the surface, and in the fiercest form. The old owners of the canon asserted their claim, though not as successfully as they might have wished.

A struggle of a somewhat similar kind erupted in England in 1992-1993 over the conservative government's attempt to prescribe what kinds of texts should be taught in the English curriculum. Here the issue did not focus on literariness in the form of aesthetics, rather it focused on the fact that a version of the literary canon was to be used for a different political purpose, to define a certain version of 'Englishness'. That is, aesthetics as literariness was to be used in the service of a reactionary, nostalgic political project to re-establish a version of an English tradition and of a national identity. Apart from the inevitably ludicrous issues— was Joseph Conrad to be counted as an English writer or not—and the equally predictable attempt to re-install a particular version of the figure of Shakespeare at the centre of that curriculum, there were much more serious issues. They were those of class and, in particular, those of the many writers who use English as their medium, but who do not qualify in terms of birth, nationality or passport as English writers from India, from the West Indies, from Africa, from Australia and so on.

The issue, of course, was a particular definition of 'Englishness', a mythic, nostalgic construct, which did not and does not exist in the writing of many authors who use English as their medium of communication— contemporary English authors included— and therefore makes their texts unusable for such a project. This case shows the complexity of the politics of aesthetics and reveals the many tasks which that category has to meet. However, both cases also show that the system of genres now has to operate without one anchor which had been essential for its smooth operation. The question is what to put in the place of that anchor: should it be the demands of business people for effective forms of communication? Or would that, in its turn, prove to be a quite unusable tool to do this job?

The new conditions of globalisation and internationalisation and the pressures which these are producing, have begun to reveal the identification of nation and aesthetics and of class and aesthetics within a particular national entity. The politics of external forces have begun to reveal the political character of the category of aesthetics and of its sociopolitical functions.

## Modes and Media of Communication: The Passing of Logocentrism

My discussion so far has proceeded on the implicit assumption that written language is the medium of representation and communication. We know that this is not the case now. Children live in a communicational and representational environment which is visual as much as it is spoken and written. The question is: does that affect writing? Or is writing (relatively) insulated from other modes of communication? Will writing continue in its present forms, even if perhaps used less than before? My own answer, speculative and necessarily tentative, is that writing is even now undergoing a transformation of a quite foundational kind and that these changes are likely to continue and probably accelerate in the near future.

Several factors contribute to that dynamic. First, young people are formed and form themselves in the totality of their semiotic environment. If that environment is one in which the modes of writing are less significant than other modes, then that is the environment which we, as curriculum planners, need to consider. Young people, who may be spending long periods with electronic games, developing high levels of visual analytic skills and muscular coordination quite unlike those of writing, are not going to leave these at the school gate and then turn back into the kinds of human subjects which we may want them to be: formed around the logics and rationalities of writing. Second, through a multiplicity of factors—in which technological ones are not, I think, causal—many texts are becoming multimodal in a pronounced way, using visual and verbal elements in quite new ways. A glance at any tabloid newspaper will illustrate what I mean, though we need to do some quite serious historical excavation to remember that even 25 years ago these very same newspapers were covered in print and used no or very few images.

Textbooks are increasingly now visual rather than verbal objects (leaving aside the quite other question of the changed uses of books in this new environment). However, is it the case that written language is merely being pushed aside, occupying less of the page of the tabloid and of the textbook than it used to? Or is it changing in its function? Or is writing actually changing in its formal, material characteristics, as an effect of these changes? Comparison is helpful here and so I wish briefly to compare two bits of language from two science textbooks, one from the 1930s and one from the 1980s.

1930s Text
The principle of the electric motor
The simple electric motor consists of a coil pivoted between the poles of a permanent magnet (see Fig. 63). When the current is passed through the coil in the direction indicated in the figure we can show, by applying Fleming's left-hand rule, that the left-hand side of the coil will tend to move down and the right-hand side to move up. (Remember that the direction of the field due to the permanent magnet is from the N. to the S. pole.) Thus the coil will rotate in a counter-clockwise direction to a vertical position.

1980s Text
Circuits
In your first circuits you used torch bulbs joined with wires. Modern electrical equipment uses the same basic ideas. But if you look inside a computer there are not many wires or torch bulbs. The wires and bulbs have been replaced by electronic devices like transistors, chips and light-emitting bodies.

The difference in the form of language is obvious and so I will not comment on it in great detail here. One is what we might still regard as characteristic of scientific writing, the other is no longer so. Both textbooks were written for an age group of 14 year olds: one asks these readers to make the move to the written forms of science, while the other uses forms of writing which make the move from science-like writing to forms which are nearer everyday spoken language. One is impersonal (depersonalised), while the other is personalised and so on. There are deeper questions here about the kinds of syntactic complexity and form of cognition, but I will leave these. Generically speaking, we can see a clear difference in the forms of social relation which each text projects and we can see the pedagogic effects implicit in each form.

Several points which are not apparent from a look at the written language alone are crucial. Each of the pages from which these extracts come has images. In the earlier text they function as illustrations. That is, the verbal text has said what a magnetic field is and there is then the illustration which provides a 'visual version'. In the recent text, images do not function as illustrations, they function informationally. The text proceeds differently: the written text gives some information, then the image gives some information, then the written text, then the image and so on. The image does not restate in visual form what the written text has previously done; it does not provide a visual version of the written text.

This is a fundamental change. Where before written language was the medium of information, in many texts there is now a new code at work which consists of both verbal and visual elements, which are used in specialised ways. In the page that I have in mind, the written elements of the text are used to recount actions—whether past or present—while the visual elements of the text are used to display information of a different kind; they indicate what are the relevant elements in the world and what are the relations between them. This specialisation of modes of communication has far-reaching effects and not in relation to writing alone. What it does is to leave the representation of narrative and of action with the written mode (which is there in the extract from the 1930s 'a current is passed through the coil' and 'We can show that') but removes the need for writing to represent 'what is there' and the relations between elements ('the simple electric motor consists of that' and 'a coil pivoted between the poles'). In the newer text that information is expressed visually. It is impossible to know what the effects of this change on writing will be.

Writing is changing and being changed by other, related factors: electronic technologies are unmaking some of the social conditions which gave writing certain of its features; an economy based on information may in any case have much greater need of the different representational and communicational potentials of visual modes. The spatial semiotic of visual images may be able to deal with large amounts of information much more effectively than writing can do. Images are highly effective at displaying complex relations between elements of visually represented information, quite likely more effective in aiding the handling of this information by a reader/viewer. In a globalising economic environment, post-

Fordist economies will need to rely on information-based forms of production, in which the visual may come to be an essential mode of representation and information. At the same time, markets for any one developed economy are now global (or at any rate no longer solely national); visual communication may prove more effective in that context than language can ever be.

## A Local Curriculum in a Globalising Environment

The economic, political, cultural and social conditions of the next few decades will continue to be transformed and shaped by the forces of globalisation and internationalisation. Their local effects will include, among others, greater degrees of multi-or pluriculturalism in very many places, that is the co-presence in one place of groups of diverse ethnic and cultural origin or constitution. It will include fundamental changes to forms and possibilities of production and therefore of work and to the shape of local economies. It will continue to attenuate, if not to abolish, the nation-state in its nineteenth-century form—even though this is likely to happen unevenly and with periods of (no doubt often violent) reaction. The state's response is difficult to predict and will vary from place to place, in line with local histories and cultural dispositions towards issues of social responsibilities.

It is not clear whether the state will continue to see it as one of its responsibilities—assuming it continues to exist—to offer the provision of education (or of other social services) for its 'citizens' or 'subjects' as in the case of Britain. Certainly in Britain at the moment, one can discern a deliberate attempt by the state to withdraw from responsibilities in these area as shown in the question of 'vouchers' for nursery and other schools, for instance and in continuing moves to privatise functions of the state from health care to prisons.

While some voices maintain that the state will want to keep schools because of their function—at the crudest level—of maintaining social order ('keeping kids off the street' even if not of 'socialisation'), there has to be, nevertheless, a question mark given the radical disengagement discernible in some forms of right-wing polemic. It is here that cultural traditions will play their role, in assisting or in resisting such tendencies.

The issue of what the relevant sites of education will be is in that regard a separate one. Workplace-based education has been an ancient tradition in many areas of work, in many cultures. And even though the traditions of apprenticeship, for instance, may be waning or disappearing, other forms emerge. In Australia workplace training is now seen as a duty of employers, who have to set aside a certain percentage of the cost of their payroll for that purpose. Other, less formal, sites are emerging. Most children under the age of 15 years have probably had their (only or most effective) training in new technologies outside of formal schooling.

However, on the assumption that the state continues to exist and accepts responsibility for the education of the younger population, the question of relevant, necessary, productive curricula emerges in stark form. How a locality (whether as nation-state or as regional authority) responds to the effects and pressures of globalisation and internationalisation is an open question. The possibilities range from reactionary retreat into cultural nostalgia, to progressive attempts to turn local cultural values into productive resources in an engagement with these challenges.

A curriculum of communication cannot escape the demands of a globalising environment, in at least two ways—unless the decision is made to put reaction, nostalgia and decline as the priorities of the curriculum.

First, those responsible for its design have to ask, in searching ways, what the forms and modes of communication are which will be essential during the period of the next decades. Essential both for purposes of communication, locally and globally and essential for social, cultural and economic purposes locally. Second, the question arises ever-more insistently, whether current theories of communication—whether of language, of the visual or of multimodal communication—need fundamental rethinking.

Internationalisation and globalisation of communication will demand quite new kinds of dispositions, attitudes and skills, which go beyond the relatively simple issue of learning a number of languages, though that is an important aspect. If genres and forms of writing, as much as forms of speaking, reflect and encode, enact the social structures and values of one place, then a curriculum will have to make available to its students the resources for communication which reflect global requirements: Utopian forms, literally. Locally, the demands of multicultural environments will, similarly, require responses which go beyond mere insistence on the forms of one, the dominant, group. Harmonious, productive engagement with different cultures in one's own locality will demand attention to communication in quite new ways. Economic demands are presently defined in exceedingly narrow and, in the end, not highly useful terms: spelling, sentence construction and so on.

The demands of the coming decades require, in my view, a move from the learning of specific forms—business communication, Japanese for tourism, etc. —though these will be needed. At the moment curricula of communication still rest on the twin pillars of 'competent use' — 'proper command of English', for instance—and of critical awareness either as 'Milton was of the devil's party without knowing it. Discuss' or as 'Show the relation between forms of text and kinds of audience in game-shows on television.' Future curricula of communication will need to go beyond such goals and aim to give young people the productive skills of design to make texts which fully match and express their needs and conceptions. The education system will need to focus on the quite different requirement of design. This will rest on a realisation that individuals need the fullest competence in the use of resources and the confidence to develop, with these, their own designs in relation to constantly changing demands. The task of the education system will be to make available the requisite resources and the skills, aptitudes and dispositions, an orientation towards design.

This move goes entirely beyond presently advocated notions of competent language use; it sees each individual as creative and innovative in their transformation of existing semiotic resources in relation to their perceived needs, expressed in their designs.

My second point goes to the theoretical centre of this necessary move. At the moment our theories of meaning making, of semiosis in whatever medium, are founded on the late nineteenth-century notion (as it afterwards appeared in the writings of Durkheim and of de Saussure) of stable social systems and their abstract reified formal appearance. In Saussurean linguistics this became, through the agency of his interpreters, the idea of an abstracted, stable system, reflecting a social achievement (*langue*), knowable and usable by individuals, but not subject to their active change in their use (*parole*) of the system. Its effect is to treat the individual as a language user and not as a language maker. It produces dispositions inclined towards an allegiance to and adherence to abstract, autonomous, authoritative systems and their roles. This may have been useful and even essential in the age of Fordist production. It will not be useful in an age in which 'Western' post-industrial societies will need to construct new forms of information-based economies founded on the productive resources of cultural difference, change and innovation. For that, a new mode of thinking about meaning and semiosis will be essential, one in which individuals constantly remake their systems of representation and communication, in productive interaction with the challenges of multiple forms of difference. Writing will have its part in that, but in dynamic interrelation with a web of social factors and a complex system of other modes of representation. In that dynamic, writing will undergo transformations which are not at the moment fully knowable.

Perhaps a curriculum of communication founded on the principle of design will exhibit the constitutive principles of post-modernity.

## References

Cope, B. & Kalantzis, M. (eds.) (1993) *The Power of Literacy: A Genre Approach to Teaching Writing* (Lewes, Falmer Press).

Coulby, D. & Jones, C. (1995) *Postmodernity & European Educational Systems* (Stoke-on-Trent, Trentham Books).

Derrida, J. (1978) La loi du genre, *Glyph*, 28, pp 48-64.

Hutton, W. (1995) *The State We're In* (London, Jonathan Cape).

Kress, G. R. (1995) *Writing the Future: English and the Making of a Culture of Innovation* (Sheffield, National Association of Teachers of English).

Kress, G. R. & Van Leeuwen, T. (1996) *Reading Images: The Grammar of Graphic Design* (London, Routledge).

Lyotard, J. F. (1984) *The Postmodern Condition: A Report on Knowledge* (Manchester, Manchester University Press).

Senge, P. M. (1991) *The Fifth Discipline: The Art and Practice of the Learning Organization* (New York, Doubleday).

(From: *Comparative Education*, Volume 32, No. 2, 1996, pp. 185-196)

# 导读：国际化与全球化：交流与传播课程的再思考

## 1. 引言

本文介绍了全球化和国际化给文化的交流与传播带来的一些变化。这些变化主要从四方面展开：类型问题，美学政治，新型文化交流，对文化交流课程的影响。作者将这些问题置于社会经济的背景下，提出了这些变化与文化交流课程的必要关系。

## 2. 全球化、国际化对文化交流的影响

过去15年中，以英语为本土语的国家政府要求已经制度化和系统化的教育要更加积极应对民族经济发展的需要，并且应该能够传达某些特定的以国民身份、道德等为中心的文化和社会价值观。这些要求尤其体现在文化交流课程中。作者在文中主要以澳大利亚、英国和德国的情形为例分析目前所面临的挑战和文化交流课程所面临的多种可能性。

首先作者从四个方面探讨了影响文化交流课程的有关问题：类型问题，美学政治（文学与民族文化），交流模式与媒体，全球化环境下的地方（民族）交流课程体系等。交流课程的规定内容其实也是传递什么类型内容的问题，这个问题过去一直都是从美学政治角度决定的。由于政治结构目前受到新挑战，美学对于规范文化交流的作用大打折扣。在大国家时代，国家的控制网络为课程提供指引。在如今的全球化时代，过去的课程所要达到的目的则遇到了困难和挑战。

（1）全球化对文化交流的影响

作者认为，全球化带来了经济的全球化和媒体的全球化，同样也带来了文化交流的全球化；文化本身的方方面面也在经历全球化过程。人员的流动也不再等同于过去的移民。这种变化在多元文化的社会里对于教育的思考和教育政策的制定是很有意义的，然而在

过去却一直没有得到充分的重视。

过去的移民由于需要适应新的社会环境和新的工作地点,一些国家往往制定"同化政策"、"主流化政策"作为最初反应。这也就意味着这些国家的教育制度要承担巨大的责任。然而,在如今的多元化社会里,从表面上看,移民仍然是从一个地方移到另外一个地方。但实际上,这种移居是建立在多元化基础上的。这也导致了在政治和教育上所采用的一种顺应自然的方法。在澳大利亚这个移民国家里,尽管政府希望各种形式的同化,但是其国家语言政策却承认所有的语言的地位,英语仅仅是作为通用语。

因此,从某种意义上说,全球化时代的人员流动符合一种新的结构。这种新的结构已经不再是简单的同化了。公民的权利问题首当其冲成为了最主要的问题。

(2) 国际化对文化交流的影响

所有国家不仅受到全球化的影响,同时也受到国际化所带来的冲击。作者认为,国际化指的是某个特定地点以外地区的文化、政治、经济对该地点在价值观、行为和组织形式方面的影响。

国际化并不是一个新出现的现象。然而,随着新的交通工具和电子通信方式的出现,国际化的影响程度将会加深,也会加速社会和文化的转变。

国际化对于文化交流在文化方面的影响不能过高估计。大众传媒的国际化制造了一种混乱、同质的文化效果,而信息媒体的全球化却带来了一种新型的、表面联系紧密、但却是以利益为基础的社会。

## 3. 文化交流的变革

下面,我们从四个方面对全球化环境中文化交流的变革作简要的介绍:

(1) 类型

作者认为,内容的大致分类是其产出场合对社会情形的作用,也就是说,在某种特定场合下,谈话者有自己的目的,并且互相之间存在一定的社会关系。谈话者把所有这些都带入情景中,运用语言来达到自己的目的。随后的语言也就是他们说话的目的、社会关系的体现和表征。

在过去的时代，这种表现形式相对固定和稳定，因此能够为人所理解，并且人可以利用这种类型的表现来表达对传统的顺应或是叛逆。这种稳定状态也反映出社会场合的稳定性。反过来说，类型表现之所以能够为人所理解正是因为所对应的社会组织形式能够为人所理解。

然而，全球化和国际化对这种稳定的状态提出了挑战。国际化也就意味着某种类型形式，伴随着相应的社会价值观和社会组织形式从一个地区传播到另外一个文化迥异的地区。德国播放北美的节目"Power Rangers"导致了国内一片反对之声。人们担心观看这种暴力节目会对年轻的观众带来不利影响。这个事件就是一个典型的类型互换的例子。在这种暴力类型片中所体现的社会关系在另外一个社会被认为是不可接受的。在北美社会，在节目中所体现的社会关系，即那些通过身体的互相接触和互相作用而传递的信息，具有一个非常大的背景和历史渊源。在观众看来，这是力量的体现而不是暴力。相反，在德国社会，这种通过身体接触，尤其是表面暴力的身体接触所表现的社会关系是不太容易被观众所接受的。

因此，全球化与国际化带来了诸多不确定性，不光是在大众媒体内容中，同样也出现在所有形式的情景中。

(2) 文学读本与国家文化：美学政治

在以英语为本土语的国家中，课程往往依托于大量的能够体现文学历史最高水平的文学作品。尽管各地的具体方法不尽相同，但这仍然是所有教育制度的黄金法则。人们认为，好的文学作品能够提升人的品位。这种素质超脱于挑战和评论。

然而，随着文化多元化的出现，也给这种黄金法则提出了新挑战。在澳大利亚，由于很多母语不是英语的移民也开始用英语写作，并且在某些场合故意使用一些不符合语法甚至粗俗，简单原始的英语来表达一种特定的情感或者目的。这无疑带来了一系列的争论，譬如关于规范的争论，但都无果而终。

这些由于全球化和国际化所带来的新的现象揭示了国家的特征和美学观，同时外部势力的政治学也逐渐向我们揭示了美学类型的政治特点和其社会政治功能。

（3）交流模式和媒体

过去人们普遍认为书面文字是表征和交流的媒介。如今的事实已不再如此。人们生活的环境不再仅仅是口头语言和文字，还加入了一种新元素，那就是视觉信息。不仅如此，视觉信息的地位相比于从前也有了质的改变。在过去的课本中，图片仅仅以插图的形式出现，从属于文字。而如今，图片作为另外一个信息来源，已经不再隶属于文字麾下，而是发挥自身高效传递信息的功能，逐渐成为了信息时代传递信息的必要模式，视觉交际模式在这种背景下将比语言交际更加迅速和高效。

（4）全球环境下的地方教育

今后的几十年，全球化和国际化将继续对经济、政治、文化和社会产生影响。对于这种影响，国家所做出的反应将很难预测，将根据各地的历史和文化以及社会责任来决定。其中一个问题就是政府是否还会继续其支持教育的职责。在英国，人们可以感觉到政府通过一些措施，例如私有化来解除在资助教育问题上的部分责任。然而，一些人认为，政府应当继续其教育方面的责任来维持社会秩序。

那么，在全球化的环境里，政府如何应对国际化和全球化所带来的压力和挑战仍然悬而未决。政府要么退回到对自己文化的怀旧情节上，要么就是积极把地方文化价值观转化为一种创造的源泉参与到挑战中。

文化交流课程不能逃离全球化环境对其的要求，至少是从两个方面：如果不是迎头进取，而是怀旧和退缩，那么作为课程的设计者来说，在后面几十年，交流课程采用何种形式和模式是所要面对的问题；另一方面，目前的交际理论，不论是关于语言，还是视觉或是多模式交际的理论，是否需要反思。

全球化和国际化条件下的交流需要一些新形式的态度和能力，而不仅仅是学习一些语言。根据作者的观点，随后的教育应该从学习某些特定的形式转向教育青年人一些设计方面的技巧使所学知识更加切合他们的需要并能够表达他们的观点。

## 4. 结束语

作者通过论述全球化和国际化背景下对教育的反思，提出了交流课程的更高要求，不仅需要掌握语言，同时还需要把个体看成具有创造力的人，在教授知识的同时，还需要教会学生如何把现有的符号资源根据他们的实际需要进行转化，并在设计中体现出来。这种观点对于我们目前的英语教学是很有启发性的，在全球化背景下，学习语言不是最终目的，学习如何利用资源进行发展、转化才是更高层次的目标。

**Questions for reflection：**
1. What's the characteristics of current population movement compared with the older ideas of immigration?
2. What's the implication of multiculturalism for education?
3. What problem does transposition of a genre from one society to another cause? And why?
4. What challenge does multiculturalism pose for the school curriculum?
5. What's the author's suggestion on curriculum of communication?

# Post-modernity, Cultural Pluralism and the Nation-state: Problems of Language Rights, Human Rights, Identity and Power

Naz Rassool

## Introduction

Whilst language is a carrier of culture it is also a signifier of cultural 'belonging'. As such, it has potent cultural and symbolic power. Moreover, as a communication practice grounded in the everyday lives of people and institutions language is not only functional but also has potent political and economic currency, and, as such, it has an exchange value. This then is to argue that language provides not only a central identity variable but also constitutes a key means by which people can either gain access to power or, conversely, be excluded from the right to exercise control over their lives. Language is therefore fundamentally constituted in multilevelled power relations. A fundamental tenet of this paper is the argument that if language is materially and culturally rooted, it follows that issues related to the language rights of specific groups of people—differentially situated within the social structure—cannot be addressed realistically outside a general theory of society and, de facto, a view of social policy. In this regard, the paper takes account of the view expressed by Tollefson (1991) that discussions about language policy need to be related to broader sociopolitical changes and the political economy of language planning.

## Pluralist Dilemmas

I use as my starting point, first, Lewis' (1980) argument that national language policy lies at the very heart of the state-and, secondly, Poulantzas' (1975) contention that the construction of a national language cannot be reduced to only its political and social usage, or to the destruction of dominated languages, since national linguistic demands are inherent in the structuring of the state itself. In order to clarify the concept of linguistic/cultural pluralism I draw on Haugen's (1985:4) view that 'when we speak of 'pluralism', we imply not a state of affairs, but a goal that may make it possible for diverse language groups to live together. It is a more subjective term, implying a policy of deliberate planning and official action, which may or may not be desirable.

National language policy can thus be viewed as constituting an act of governance which legitimizes specific economic, cultural and political projects of particular interest groups within the arena of the state. Viewed as such, national language policy can be seen as a deliberate intervention and therefore embodies a concrete expression of power. Whilst in some societies the nature of this intervention is overt and even coercive, in others it becomes part of a more covert and subtle legitimating discourse. However, whether coercive or hegemonic, official discourses on language choice and language rights are not neutral; they are grounded in (unequal) power relations. Articulated from sites of power these discourses influence definitions of legitimate, high status forms of knowledge and ways of knowing. Thus it is that not all languages have parity; some are favoured above others; some have more economic and policy currency than others. (I will discuss the duality, ambiguity and contradictions inherent in the issue of language choice later.) Language also provides an important site of struggle for control over social and cultural resources within and between linguistic minority groups. Collectively then these arguments highlight the fact that societal language relations cannot be conceptualized outside a consideration of the speakers of different languages, their lived experience and their place within society. Neither can the question or language rights of different groups of people be analyzed without taking account of the dynamic and multi-layered interactions between history, culture, politics and ideology. That is to say, societal language relations cannot be analyzed meaningfully without taking account of what Kristeva (1967) refers to as 'intertextuality' and Bakhtin (1981) terms 'dialogism'. Taking these factors into account, the following section explores the shaping of language relations within pluralist nation-states that have had previous links with colonialism.

# Language Rights and Colonial Hegemony

Since language mediates reality, it circumscribes the frame of reference within which the conceptualization of the world can take place. It also provides the categories available through which both the personal and social world can be interpreted. Thus, language provides a potent means through which the world is defined in social consciousness and, historically, has served a key means by which social inequalities and different forms of cultural oppression have been hegemonized. Colonialist expansionism, as an integral part of the project of modernity, took place largely through a systematic extension of economic boundaries through trade and the domestication of the colonized. The latter was a key variable in structuring both individual and collective subjectivities in terms of relations of domination and subordination. This was achieved to a large extent during different periods and phases of colonialism through multi-levelled forms of separatism, subjugation and exclusion that were reinforced by social divisions created through language, religion, ethnicity and caste (Rassool, 1997). Indeed, as is argued by Ngugi, (1993: 442) with regard to British colonialism, the most important area of domination was:

> the mental universe of the colonised, the control, through culture, of how people perceived themselves and their relationship to the world... To control a people's culture is to control their tools of self-definition in relationship with others (...) The domination of a people's language by the languages of the colonising nations was crucial to the domination of the mental universe of the colonised.

The imposition of the imperial 'mother tongue' as official language relegated indigenous languages in many colonized societies to an inferior position—thus allowing the subordination of indigenous cultures and the refraction of national imaginings to be secured. Representation through language and literature also played a key role in structuring commonsense understandings of cultural inferiority and social 'Otherness'. As is argued by Hall (1993:396) —again in relation to the British colonial experience:

> The ways in which black people, black experiences, were positioned and subjected in the dominant regimes of representation were the effects of a critical exercises of cultural power and normalisation. Not only (...) were we constructed as different and other within the categories of knowledge of the West by those regimes. They had the power to make us see and experience ourselves as 'Other'.

Although the boundaries of the nation-state were maintained, colonialism within the time-frame contributed very powerfully to the fractionalization of colonized cultures. Indigenous languages were substituted by colonial 'mother tongues' through which the cultural consciousness of a 'motherland' could be hegemonized. Structured into the education systems of various countries, the imposed languages became the primary vehicle for the development of selected forms of 'high status' literacies—and, subliminally, the assimilation of a particular worldview.

Another example of the suppression of local languages as part of colonialist hegemony was evident also in Stalin's 'russification' project pursued as part of his five-year modernizing programmes (Shorish, 1984). In this instance minority languages such as Chuvash and the different indigenous languages, East of the Ural mountains were relegated to a domain-specific use; that is, in the home and immediate community. Since these languages had little or no political or economic currency their social marginalization effectively contributed to the cultural disenfranchisement of large, previously cohesive, groups of people. In many colonized societies, the relegation of politically, economically and culturally disempowered groups of people to the periphery of their societies became systematized social practices—and for many, the issue of language rights thus became integrally linked with human rights. Limited language rights of diverse groups of people, sanctioned by the colonialist state, can then be seen as having served primarily in the interest of a political economy. That is to say, they served to shape the awarenesses, expectations, dreams and aspirations of discrete groups of people in terms of the hegemony of the colonizing state. Whilst for some of the elite groups within these societies ways of life were transformed. The disenfranchized could only wait at the margins to be 'given' a space and 'allocated' a place in society.

During periods of crisis this destabilization of cultural communities, invariably stimulated mass migration and the creation of diasporas which, in turn, contributed to the development of 'sub-nations' within the framework of 'host' nation-states. Collectively, these issues raise questions about the theorization of linguistic diversity and cultural pluralism in relation to language planning and social policy within these societies.

## Pluralist Paradigm Problematics

I want to argue here that the linearity of traditional forms of discourse, by limiting analysis to the language relations of the 'pluralist' nation-state, in many instances provided further legitimacy to social inequality. Within this (dominant) framework, minority languages have historically been presented as posing 'dilemmas' in terms of differential levels of integration of specific minority language groups into the dominant culture. The quest of minority groups for their linguistic franchise invariably became interpreted as constituting a 'minority problem', a threat to the dominant culture. As is argued earlier, this representation of minority group interests often resulted in the subjugation of literacies and literary practices in their 'mother tongues'. Indeed, as can be seen later, in both British Colonial and Apartheid South Africa; as well as in Communist Bulgaria the languages of minority groups became the means par excellence through which the binary of 'insider-outsider'; the 'alien wedge' within (Hall, 1983) could be hegemonized in the dominant discourse. Linguistic diversity represented and re-positioned in this way as linguistic difference became a primary variable in the structuring of cultural and social 'Otherness' in social, political and academic discourse.

Such analytical perspectives are often grounded in a simplistic and unproblematic view of cultural pluralism without recourse to the specific power interests operating within particular societies—and, within some societies, the imposition of official (colonial) languages. With dominant languages provided as 'givens' in such analyses, the issue of language rights would thus remain discussed within the parameters of what were, and in some instances, continue to be, in essence, only nominally pluralist nation-states. Many of these socially constructed linguistic 'dilemmas', for example, the case of Bahasa Malaysia vis a vis the Chinese population group in Malaysia or the status of Kurdish speakers in Iraq are still unresolved because the political basis of their existence has remained unaltered. Forming an integral part of specific hegemonic projects of the state, the imposition of dominant languages can serve to perpetuate the divide-and-rule principles of colonialism, or in these instances, neo-colonialism. Thus, it can be argued that it is the unresolved nature of political issues that create 'problems' of social disequilibrium rather than the question of language per se. Contrast this reality of conflict in terms of the complex relationship between language and power with Haugen's unproblematic analysis of colonial relations and the dilemmas of the metropolitan pluralist nation-state. Haugen (1985:5) argues that:

> Today it would actually be hard to point out a single European nation that does not have a minority problem (sic), in the sense of having within its borders a population speaking some language that cannot be regarded as just a dialect of the national tongue. Those nations that have been strong enough to extend their power beyond their European borders into overseas lands have not hesitated to incorporate into their empires populations of different languages and ethnicities. The results are rampant today in the form of internal conflicts at home and colonial collapse abroad.

This perspective clearly lacks a consideration of domination and control which were central elements in colonial policy. It also ignores an analysis of the economic and political project of modernity that underscored linguistic and cultural imperialism during this period of colonial expansion. Indeed, this epoch of globalization restructured not only the social relations of colonized countries but also transformed European states internally. According to Smith (1992:255):

> the emergence of the great colonial empires was accompanied by several significant trends in domestic statehood: the growth of bureaucracy and military organization, the expansion of government budgets, the development of corporate commercial organization and the consolidation of the technological and scientific base for state activity.

That is to say, there were material benefits to be had from colonial policy and practice. Whilst, on the one hand, transnational capital flow contributed to the infrastructural reinforcement of the colonial nation-state, at the same time it also contributed to uneven development in the colonized world which brought about 'profoundly unequal benefits to different classes and nations' (Smith, 1992:264). As argued earlier, for many peoples this included the loss or subjugation of their own languages and culture. Transnational capital thus secured the economic basis of an external nation-state at the expense of material and other social unequalities within the colonized countries. Clearly then, this materiality of social and economic oppression needs to be made concrete in analyses of the language rights of particular groups of people within different societies—and account needs to be taken of the particular set of historical (power) relations that gave rise to these situations. These discursive factors highlight the fact that we cannot have a homogenized discourse on language rights.

## Post-colonial Conundrums

The validity of this argument is borne out in the fact that the incorporation of colonial languages into the meaning-structure of social processes and institutions has increasingly presented complex problems with regard to equity and social justice for linguistic minority groups in postcolonial societies. Of significance here are the practical dilemmas being presented to language planning in post Apartheid South Africa, which was previously a bilingual society with two official (colonial and neocolonial) languages, English and Afrikaans. This 'elitist' policy approach relegated minority languages to the status of domain-specific 'tribal' languages. The adoption of colonial 'mother tongues' within this context arrested the development of minority languages such as Xhosa, Sotho and Zulu in South Africa. This was achieved, to a large extent, by reducing languages of majority cultural groups to the position of minority, predominantly oral languages or with a limited written repertoire. Within the context of the Bantu Education Act (1953), the bilingual/mother tongue education policy adopted by the state had no educational, political or economic currency for the speakers of these 'mother tongues'. And thus the policy was rejected so resoundingly by the Black youth throughout the country in 1976. With the new political dispensation, the country has adopted eleven official languages with each province having to opt for its own selection of official languages suitable to its population/linguistic groupings. Underlying this is the drive to re-instate previously subjugated minority languages as a means of cultural reparation and empowerment. In relation to this, the New South African Constitution defines language as a basic human right stating that 'every person shall have the right to use the language of his or her choice' (Section 31): Section 8 provides for equality for all in terms of the law and states that 'no person shall be unfairly discriminated against, directly or indirectly, on the grounds of 'language'. Section 32 states that 'each person has the right to instruction in the language of his or her choice where this is reasonably practicable' (Government Gazette, June 1995). Although all these principles provide for social justice and equity, they nevertheless contain many dilemmas with regard to equitable provision for the different linguistic minority groups. Although Afrikaans has been reduced greatly within state institutions such as the mass media because of its previous association with oppression, its overall position as the main language of a large constituent group in the Western Cape remains problematic. The issue of English as a previous colonial language is even more problematic in relation to South Africa's location as a participant in the international economic and political arena. The latter situation raises fundamental questions about the relative equity of status and currency of the different languages in real terms within the country as well as with regard to literacy for empowerment within the global terrain. Moreover, with demographic changes in a constant state of flux as a result of continuing rural-urban and north—south migration—the outcomes of uneven development under the previous regime—it would be reasonable to assume that the language map of South Africa will not stabilize enough to be meaningful in terms of a coherent language policy-in-practice within the near future. At the same time, the very real problem of the arrested development of indigenous languages, and, by that fact, the development of a national cultural tradition through literacy and mass communication practices remains.

The issue of language within postcolonial societies is complex also in relation to the migration and subsequent settlement of large groups of colonial peoples within the erstwhile 'mother country'. In an interview with representatives from different ethnic minority communities in Britain conducted as part of another research project (Rassool, 1995), a variety of views emerged on the issue of minority language rights. The representatives from the Urdu and Panjabi immigrant communities both stated that some degree of overall language shift had already started to take place within their communities and both were keen for their children to integrate into British culture. In contrast to this, the representative from the Hindi-speaking community expressed the need to 'relieve the burden on parents to maintain the mother tongue in a formal way with their children since many parents do not have the educational background or expertise to undertake this responsibility'. He argued that language maintenance we enhance the educational potential of bilingual students would ultimately have a positive impact on achievement of GCSE/A Levels. This view was echoed by the Chinese representative who stated that as long as there is no maintenance of the mother tongue in school, English would persist to be a difficultly for Chinese speakers. The Bangladeshi community leader also stressed the importance of developing literacy skills in the students' first language (Bangla) 'in order to bridge the educational gap which currently exists'. Underlying this was the concern that in the absence of adequate linguistic resources students' mother tongue would remain unsupported educationally and a shift to monoliteracy would develop. If this happens, he argued that the chances were that their mother tongue would become relegated to the status of domain-specific language, namely, the home and community. However, the case of Bangla is more problematic in relation to Sylheti speakers. The issue of literacy and language teaching of Sylheti speakers in British schools is a complex one which relates to the national language policy of Bangladesh post-1972 when it became an independent state. Smith (1985) in his study of Sylheti speakers in the London Borough of Tower Hamlets reports that in Bangladesh, the imposition of Bangla displaces the commonly spoken language of the region of Sylheti. Sylheti is generally not taught in schools in Bangladesh, and according to Smith (1985:22):

> .... writing in Sylheti is not taught, and the fact that a tradition of writing Sylheti in the Nagri script exists is withheld from many Sylheti speakers. Sylheti is looked down on by many local teachers, as well as by Benga vernacular speakers from other districts, and this low evaluation is often internalised by Sylheti speaking children.

In this case then, their illiteracy in their 'mother tongue' relates, in the first instance, directly to the specific language policy adopted in their country of origin. Secondly, it also relates to their marginalized position within the social structure in Bangladesh since many of these children came from peasant communities in rural areas. These factors highlight the fact that the linguistic needs of Sylheti speakers are distinct from those of Bengali speakers. Subsequently in a 'mother tongue' teaching programme the issue of teaching Sylheti speakers to become biliterate in their national and cultural group language would cause considerable difficulties with regard to both language choice and provision.

Collectively, these different views highlight some of the complexities that surround the concept of language rights in the postcolonial situation. They underscore the fact that patterns of language shift and language maintenance amongst immigrants also depend on a variety of other factors. These relate to, inter alia, whether the linguistic minority groups consider immigration to the permanent, whether they maintain their religion through their language, the relative isolation between members within the group (e. g. women), their emotional attachment to their language, the degree of national pride in their cultural heritage, the social mobility of the group as well as the attitudes of the host country to their languages (Grosjean, 1982). Language relations in postcolonial societies then, on this evidence, are intrinsically linked with power structures on the one hand, and on the other, with the everyday lives of diverse and highly differentiated groups of people with different lifestyles, aspirations and expectations—and therefore, different levels of lives in society. These are aspects that deserve to be explored further empirically in research.

## Postmodern Possibilities and Problems

Whilst many of these tensions remain in both colonial and postcolonial societies, they have even made more complex by broader events during the past two decades. Globalization, defined as the interlocking of social relations across time and space (Massey, 1994), has fundamentally, altered the way the world is perceived and experienced on an everyday level. Within the Western world, the hegemony of the nation-state has been fractured by and refracted through the emergence of new globalizing social and cultural processes. Facilitated, in the first instance by microelectronics technology, the restructuring of global economic relations and the reshaping of cultural relations are grounded in transnational interactions that are more organic than the previous phase of globalization. Second, the 1990s have turned into the decade of mass migration as the result of a variety of factors including wars, poverty, political destabilization and, also, free travel related to modern lifestyles in the more affluent West. Of primary significance to the discussion here are the implications of continued mass migration for the conceptualization of the language rights of discrete groups of people often living itinerant lives within the margins of different societies. Migration over time and space brings together dissonant narratives, new sets of social relations and new events to fracture previous certainties.

Indeed, we live in a shifting ethnoscape in which tourists, immigrants, refugees, exiles, guestworkers and other moving groups and persons constitute an essential feature of the world and appear to affect the politics of (and between) nations to a hitherto unprecedented degree (Appadurai, 1993:329). These factors have fractured the rigidity and monolithic structure of the nation-state, and, in terms of this, the homogeneity of national cultures is increasingly being challenged by the large scale social displacement of large groups of people across the world. The resultant cultural and social fractionalization, and the dynamic reconstitution of group and individual identities in temporary or more permanent immigrant settlements can therefore be seen as serving to refract the imagined worlds of cohesive nations. Arguing within the analytical framework of postmodernism Homi Bhabha (1994:1) suggests that:

> Our existence today is marked by a tenebrous sense of survival, living on the borderlines of the 'present' (....) we find ourselves in the moment of transit where space and time cross to produce complex figures of difference and identity, past and present, inside and outside, inclusion and exclusion...

Offering a means for people to make sense of this shifting arena, Bhabha argues for the need to give voice to what he terms 'border lives' and hybridized identities within the context of their own experience. Within this framework, self-othering is intrinsic to the reflexive process of self-definition. The latter describes the affective process of critical engagement, negotiation, self-affirmation and validation in relation to particular experiences in everyday life (Rassool 1997). It is in the 'emergence of interstices—the overlap and displacement of domains of difference', Bhabha suggests, that cultural difference needs to be addressed in terms of the possibilities that it provides for the articulation of new identities and cultural value. (Some aspects of this were reflected in the views expressed by the different community representative above.) Postmodernity, according to Bhabha, thus represents alternative realities articulated within a plurality of narratives and voices. This foregrounding of flexible and multiple identities in postmodernist discourse certainly does suggest the opening up of possibilities also for an exploration of the two-edged nature of language, and by that fact, a conceptualization of language rights within a constantly changing ethnic/linguistic landscape. For example, whilst some languages can be domesticating ideologically within one context, in another, they may have the potential to empower and transform. Similarly, as a signifier of identity and cultural belonging, language often exists in conflict, contradictions and ambiguity in relation to the expectations and demands of living within society as a whole. This is related to the choice of lifestyles and multiple identities adopted by individuals or groups of people living in different societies as part of the process of self-definition. In terms of this, the postmodernist analytical framework opens up possibilities for exploring further the polysemic nature of language as the relative value attached to different languages are therefore always provisional; they are subject to change. Theoretically then language choice for specific groups of people would become more flexible in relation to ever-changing geographical demographics.

However, these potentially liberating possibilities have to be balanced against the fact that whilst this constant flow of people across the world has its own dynamic, the spatiality implicit in the new globalizing processes is not free and unbounded. Freedom of movement, access and the right to define is evidently limited to those in the developed world (Massey, 1996). For ultimately, the current phase of mass migration has to be seen within the context of a shrinking labour market internationally, the global restructuring of the manufacturing base as well as the restructuring of economic relations within the global arena. Collectively, these factors have contributed to the intensification of the economic divide between the developed and under-developed world and have contributed to increasing levels of rural-urban and transnational migration. This, in turn, has resulted in a more rapid dislocation of many previously ethnically and linguistically 'stable' nations. If we locate the speakers of minority languages within this discursive terrain it can then be argued that language rights, identity and human rights are dialogically interrelated. In relation to this, the struggle for language rights amongst Hispanic communities in California cannot be viewed without consideration also of the unequal trade relations that underscore the NAFTA agreements. And even here, according to Massey (ibid.) we need to engage a double imagination in light of the fact that what is now California was previously (before it was colonized by the US) part of Mexico. Nor can the uninvited refugee status conferred on Somalian migrants—and, de facto, their complex linguistic and social needs in the inner cities of the metropolitan would be addressed outside a consideration of the stringent forms of control inherent in the structural adjustment programmes of IMF and World Bank policies. The re-adjustment of the internal market in terms of structured export demands in these countries contributes to poverty. Thus language rights counterpose with human rights. If we take these factors into account, it can be argued that in contesting universalist principles of equity and social justice the new globalizing processes have altered the nature as well as the whole terrain of struggle. For, in a general sense, there is clearly a tension between the free movement of the powerful and those existing at the margins; that is, the refugees, guest workers and asylum seekers. Appadurai argues that 'as international capital shifts its needs, as production and technology generate different needs, as nation-states shift their policies on refugee populations, these moving groups can never afford to let their imaginings rest too long, even if they wish to'. In terms of this, their linguistic needs are ever contingent.

Elsewhere, within the context of the European Union the situation regarding language rights of minority groups also cannot be separated from a discussion about human rights. Exclusionary meanings are already inscribed into EU discussions where it has been stated that controls are being strengthened as external frontiers as a means of screening out terrorists, drug dealers and illegal immigrants. Moreover, spot-checks are to be carried out inside the territory of member states and the 'conditions' for granting asylum to political refugees will be tightened to make it more difficult for so-called 'economic' migrants to settle in the EC (CEC, 1993:8). These meanings coincide with those structured within new right discourses in some member countries. In the UK, for example, the debate about educational provision for ethnic/linguistic minority pupils has become a discredited discourse. As a result, funding under Section 11 of the Local Government Act which has since the 1960s provided for the education of children from immigrant groups has been fundamentally restructured and curtailed (Rassool, 1995). Again, minority groups cannot be discussed in relation to cultural identity without also addressing social experience of specific groups of people and specific interest groups within the frame of the state. This refers to their civil, human and political rights as well as their social state citizens (Rassool, 1995). As is argued by Bhabha (1994:175), 'the language of rights, obligations, so central to the modern myth of a people, must be questioned on the basis of anomalous and discriminatory legal and cultural status assigned to migrant, diasporic refugee populations'. As I argue elsewhere (Rassool, 1995), on the face of it, the consolide of the North-South divide does not bode well for displaced refugee or migrant grown Europe at the moment.

## Language Rights and the New Nationalisms

Elsewhere in broader Europe and parts of Africa, however, this transnational exchange identities and futures, as well as the hegemony of the nation-state, is also being contested very powerful way by the reassertion of ethnic nationalisms that are articulated with racialized discourse of language, ethnic 'purity' and religion. Forms of ethnic and linguistic 'self-determination' are evident, for example, in the political opportunism and power revealed in the ethnic cleansing policies of Bosnia and Rwanda and Burundi. 'Self-othering politically dominant ethnic groups within these contexts presents a rather different view to be ascribed to the process within the postmodern framework. Here the process of self-other once again forms an integral part of a destructive nationalism that is divisive and oppressive minority groups. Within many of these contexts, mass migration is the result of his linguistic, political and religious persecutions as is evidenced, for example, in the cultural fractionalization within previous power blocs in Eastern Europe. According to a recent United Nations report more than 9 million former Soviet citizens, one in 30 of the population, had been on the move since the collapse of the communist system (Bennett-Jones, 1996). Movement is in consequence to ethnic disputes in Georgia, Armenia, Azerbaijan, Mold Tadijikistan and, more recently, from Chechenia. Whilst the bulk of these people are set within the Russian Federation, there are those who are filtering to other countries. In linguistic terms, this movement of people to Russia would pose few problems with regard to language rights as most of them are already literate in Russian—others would, in all likelihood, integrate into their countries of adoption. Again, this situation contrasts sharply with that of Chuvash who are now faced with the task of recapturing their language after years of having imposed Russian 'mother tongue'. Similarly, in the case of Bulgarian nationalism during the late 1980s and throughout its long history of colonial oppression, it has been a question not of language maintenance/language rights for the different minority groups. Issues of language also combined very powerfully with sporadic identity changes reflected in the Slavic 'the change' and ethnic expulsion policies pursued against ethnic Turks and the Roman popular group—at least since the late 1940s—and in a more concentrated form during the 1950s. Although the language rights of the Turkish population group have been restored since Bulgaria still regards itself as a uni-nation—and the national status of Slavic Muslims ethnic Turks remain unresolved.

Yet another constituency whose needs have not been addressed in this paper is emergence of religious fundamentalism—especially Islamic fundamentalism and the effect of this on the literacy rights of women in countries such as Afghanistan—and the threats pose women in Algeria, Egypt and Iran.

## Conclusion

This paper has positioned the issue of language rights within two different historical time Frames—each yielding different yet inter-related sets of problems. These resolve around the geopolitics of globalization resulting in flexible and multiple identities and its contestation by postcolonial nationhood in some contexts and the entrenchment of rigid old nationalisms in others. Here the fissures, fractures and refractions within and of the nation-state juxtapose with racialized ethnicities and diverse quests for linguistic self-determination to serve either in the struggle for nationhood or nationalism. This discussion highlighted the fact that the stability of the nation-state always resides in tension, with a variety of factors contributing to the disruption of existing cultural and linguistic relations during different historical periods. The issue of language rights often emerges as an arena of struggle for control over meaning during periods of social and cultural upheaval and transformation. What is significant at this moment is the extent to which the diverse struggles within this discursive terrain are being articulated through the growing re-assertion of minority language rights. The multi-levelled changes taking place within this organic context, it has been suggested, highlight the fact that we need to consider a coherent framework and terms of reference in which to theorize the contingency and fluidity of language and cultural identity. These concerns with temporality, the spatiality of power relations and the increasing mass movement of people globally—juxtaposed with arguments for ethnic and linguistic territoriality—highlight the need to reappraise the traditional concept of cultural pluralism as it is theorized traditionally within the context of the nation-state. New sets of economic, cultural and linguistic problems are in the making. How are the language rights of these moving or itinerant groups of disenfranchised people to be conceptualized, let alone be addressed? Can we remain rooted within paradigms that frame language issues to the exclusion of the materiality of changes within the global cultural economy; of social inequalities grounded in uneven development? Similarly, how adequate is the conceptualization of language relations in terms of global interconnectedness when this is constantly in the process of being fractured by the emergence of ethnic enclaves articulating their separatist demands within an exclusionary nationalist discourse on language rights? In a concrete sense, how effectively can the issue of language rights be conceptualized outside a consideration of not only medium of instruction and access to education, but also the realities of sub-and semi-literacy within such a highly literate world—and, in terms of the democratic process, a consideration of censorship and the control over information legitimized in social policy? Finally, in the light of these dynamic changes taking place globally and nationally can the argument for a universalizing discourse on cultural and linguistic pluralism be sustained? Postmodern analyses seemingly do provide the possibility for exploring the plurality of social experiences within the margins of society. However, as we have seen, the abstractness of the discourse avoids addressing the concrete nature of power and domination—and the ways in which they structure the realities of linguistic minority groups. These 'paradigm' issues highlight new areas to be researched.

## References

Appadurai, A. (1993) *Disjuncture and Difference in the Global Cultural Economy*. In Williams P. and Chrisman L. (eds.), *Colonial Discourse and Post-colonial Theory*, pp. 324-339. Harvester Wheatsheaf, New York.

Bakhtin, M. (1981) *The Dialogic Imagination: Four Essays*. University of Texas Press, Austin.

Bennett-Jones, O. (1996) *Millions Cross Ex-Soviet Border*. The Guardian 28 May 1996.

Bhabha, H. (1994) *The Location of Culture*. Routledge, London.

*Government Gazette*, Vol. 360, No. 16494. *Republic of South Africa. Pan South African Language Board Draft Bill*, 28 June 1995.

Grosjean, F. (1982) *Life with Two Languages: An Introduction to Bilingualism*. Harvard University Press, Cambridge, MA.

Hall, S. (1983) *The Great Moving Right Show*. In Hall S. and Jacques

M. (eds.), *The Polities of Thatcherism*, pp. 19-39. Lawrence & Wishart, London.

Hall, S. (1993) *Cultural Identity and Diaspora*. In Williams P. and Chrisman L. (eds.), *Colonial Discourse and Post-colonial Theory*, pp. 392-403. Harvester Wheatsheaf, New York.

Haugen, E. (1985) *The Language of Imperialism: Unity or Pluralism?* In Wolfson N. and Manes L (eds.), *Language of Inequality*, pp. 3-17. Moulton Publishers. Berlin.

Kristeva, J. (1967) *Bakhtine, le mot, le dialogue et le roman*. Critique No. 239, April 1967, 438-465.

Lewis, E. G. (1980) *Bilingualism and Bilingual Education: A Comparative Study*. University of Mexico Press, Mexico.

Massey, D. (1994) *Space, Place and Gender*. Polity Press, Oxford.

Massey, D. (1996) *Imagining Globalization: Time-Space Geometries*. Plenary Speech Given at Annual Conference of British Sociological Association Held at the University of Reading. 1-4 April, 1996.

Ngugi Wa Thiong'o (1993) *The Language of African Literature*. In Williams P. and Chrisman L. (eds.) *Colonial Discourse and Post-colonial Theory*. pp. 435-456. Harvester Wheatsheaf, New York.

Poulantzas, N. (1975) *Political Power and Social Classes*. Verso Press, London.

Rassool, N. (1995) *Language, Cultural Pluralism and the Silencing of Minority Discourses in England and Wales*. Journal of Education Policy, 10, 287-302.

Rassool, N. (1997) *Fractured or Flexible Identities? Life Histories of 'Black' Diasporic Women in Britain*. In Safia Mirza H. (ed.), *Black Feminism: A Reader*, pp. 187-204. Routledge, London.

Shorish, M. (1984) *Planning by Decree: The Soviet Language Policy in Central Asia*. Language Problems and Language Planning, 8, 284-301.

Smith, A. D. (1992) *Nations and Nationalism in a Global Era*. Polity Press, Oxford.

Smith, G. (1985) *Language, Ethnicity, Employment and Research: The Struggle of Sylheti-Speaking People in London*. CLE/LMP *Working Paper* No. 13, University of London Institute of Education.

Tollefson, J. W. (1991) *Planning Language, Planning Inequality: Language Policy in the Community*. Longman, London.

[From: *Language Sciences*. Vol. 20, No. 1, pp. 89-99, 1998.]

# 导读：后现代主义，大国文化与多元文化：语言权与人权

## 1. 引言

本文作者介绍了文化多元化社会里的语言权力和权利问题，谈到殖民时期语言的控制对人的思想产生的影响，以及语言在后现代主义背景下所面临的可能性和各种问题。语言不仅有其交流的作用，还具有强大的政治经济流动性。语言流动性的大小本身就代表了一种多层次的权力关系。语言享有不同权力的现象，导致了弱势族群争取语言权利的斗争。这些对于制定语言政策的启示是：语言计划要放在广阔的社会政治变迁的基础上和政治经济的背景下。

## 2. 权力 VS 权利

权力（power）是一种力量，一般被分为两类：剥削的权力和操纵的权力。以语言而论，语言本身原本并无地位之别，关键在于行使语言的主体。如果一国势力能够在世界上占有很大的影响地位，那么其他国家就有可能在这样的影响下，自觉或不自觉地接受了这样的权力，当然也包含语言的成分在内。

权利（right）是一种资格，一种让人能做出选择的资格，能积极行使、拥有、参与或完成的资格。有了权利，才能依据自己的判

断行事,才可能产生自我主导的力量而不受外界的控制。同样地,在语言使用中,高层阶级语言"向下扩张"或低层阶级语言"向上反攻"时,语言的改变或使得语言的既得利益受到损失。为了保护既得利益,必须争取"语言权"。而争取"语言权"的最重要目的是取得语言平等,因为语言平等是社会平等的基础,没有语言平等,就不会有政治平等、经济平等、文化平等,更谈不上民族平等和尊重人权。

## 3. 主体的语言权力 VS 客体的语言权利

英美文化在国际上产生了主导作用。各国非英美文化的人民可以感受到这样的力量。没人能够忽视或否定携带强势文化的语言力量。美国承袭了昔日的大英帝国,而成为全球的超级强权,全球超级大国。在这种"力"的支撑下,其语言也自然取得强势的地位。

其他国家人民对于英语的强大势力所做出的回应不一。但是不得不承认,在这样的语言霸权情形下,自己成为"他者"或"弱势"。虽然他们急欲在这种语言权力关系中,争得一席之地,但终究不敌社会文化对英语的渴慕。因此在这种危机意识下,语言政策的制定就显得更为重要。语言权认为,每个公民在公开或是私人场合有使用自己语言的权利,不可因此遭到不公平的排斥或是限制。

语言权(language right)、语言的权利(linguistic right)和语言人权(linguistic human right)这三个词常被视为同义词。语言权和语言的权利指政府在多族群的构架下,制定语言在大众场所、学校机关、宗教等各领域的使用。语言人权的观念则尝试把语言和人权联系在一起,从人权的构建出发,讨论语言权利的议题,以提升语言公平(linguistic justice)。近代的一些社会政治现象以及世界各地族群语言流失严重都促使语言人权的发展。弱势族群为了族语的存活,纷纷争取语言权的立法,以保证其语言的生存权利。对弱势族群而言,语言权的目的就是在于要求族语在社会生活使用的权利,借以维持、发扬族群的语言和文化。

## 4. 语言权和殖民统治

由于语言不仅代表一国文化,也象征一个社会的思想意识;在学习语言的过程中,学习的不仅是语言本身,也间接吸收语言团体的文化背景思想模式。在殖民时期,殖民者正是利用语言的这种特点来控制被殖民人民的思想意识。殖民国家把本国语言强加于被殖民国家,并定为官方语言,使得被殖民国家语言降级为劣势语言或边缘化语言,从而文化也随之降为劣势文化。这些时候,对于弱势群体而言,语言权自然与人权联系在了一起。

## 5. 后现代主义与语言权

后现代主义没有切断与现代主义的联系,是从现代意识的母腹中成长发展起来的。它一方面发展了现代主义出现的一些新风格的萌芽,另一方面又是对现代主义的反叛。后现代主义的关键要素是一种对多元主义及相异性的容忍和尊重,导致矛盾按较少固定的主观状态出现。从后现代的观点而言,中心的观点并不是事先形成或自然存在的,而是一种文化构建的方式,即语言的意义系统及语言系统的使用。语言及论述的建构力量将会使它们定位在后现代,因为语言及语言的组织或是意义脉络并非偶然发生,而是存在于后现代的不确定性,于是形成语言的建构。现代主义的意义建构是清楚的,是真实的意象;而后现代主义认为所有的意象不再只有一个固定的答案。

文章谈到了20世纪90年代的大规模移民现象对不同族群的语言权利观的影响。事实上,我们目前生活在一个人员流动加速的社会,旅游者、移民、难民、劳工等的不断涌入构成了目前世界的一个主要特征,迅速改变了过去一元化的局面,进入了文化多元化的时代。文化的多元性为新的身份和文化价值观的表达提供了新的可能性。后现代主义所代表的正是在多元阐释和论断中的可能性。在这种情形下,一些涌入的语言可能融入当地语言中,也可能反客为主,成为主导的语言。因此,某些族群的人选择语言的权利将更加灵活。

然而，这些看上去自由的可能性也不是绝对自由的，还要受到一些因素的制约。由于全球化的原因，发达国家与发展中国家的差距、城乡差距的不断扩大，跨国移民的加速扩展，这也因过去在种族和语言问题上十分稳定的国家，例如在美国加州西班牙裔族群要求语言权不能不使人联想到不平等的贸易关系。

## 6. 结束语

Garcia 曾以语言花园比喻语言存活的重要性。如果世界各地的花朵都长得一模一样，只有一种颜色的话，那么人生是黑白的！同样的理论也适用于世界的语言花园。语言多样化带来更加丰富、有趣、多姿多彩的世界。弱势语言就像珍稀花朵一样需要精心呵护，加以保护，才有继续存活的机会。

语言人权与语言保存息息相关。语言人权教育的一个重要目的就是提升权利意识，捍卫语言使用的权利，以促进语言公平和语言保存。以过去的语言教学为负担的教育体制将可能会造成教育和社会问题，因此，在政策上独尊一种语言，压制其他语言，将造成族群语言严重流失。政府应把弱势语言视为重要的国家资产及人民的基本人权，根据族群平等的原则，赋予弱势语言生存发展所需要的语言权，立法加以保护和推广。在世界上所有地方，学校一直是，目前仍然是主流文化和主流语言同化其他语言和文化的主要手段，也就是说，教育一方面可能成为剥夺语言人权的手段。将语言人权融入课程教学，可以让我们重新将母语定义为权利和资源。语言权利和语言保存有极为密切的关系，推广语言人权教育将有助于语言的保存与发展。

**Questions for reflection：**

1. Why does the author say "national language policy embodies a concrete expression of power"?
2. What impact does the imposition of imperial "mother tongue" have on

the indigenous language in terms of human right?
3. Why does the author say "language relation in postcolonial society is linked with power structure and people's daily life"?
4. According to the author, what are the potentially liberating possibilities? Is there any problem?
5. In this article, what perspective does the author take to discuss language planning?

# Language, Society and Identity

## Language Society and Identity

J. Edwards

### Introduction

Questions of language and identity are extremely complex. The essence of the terms themselves is open to discussion and, consequently, consideration of their relationship is fraught with difficulties. This is not to say that treatments of the theme are few; indeed, the relationship has been dealt with in a number of disciplines. This in fact is part of the difficulty—there has been much isolated discussion, and some reinventing of the wheel too. Naturally, different perspectives present things in different lights, often for quite understandable reasons, but this can mean a less than complete overall picture. So, one finds that historians, sociologists, psychologists, linguists, educators and others have all attended to the language-identity link in some form or other, usually without much consideration of potentially relevant work in neighbouring disciplines.

An example of this can be found in the way in which ethnicity or ethnic-group identity has been treated. As Connor (1978) has pointed out, the term itself has proved a problematic one; but, however it is defined, there would seem to be a connection between it and the concept of nationalism. Yet one sees very little mention of nationalism in treatments of ethnicity, especially within social science, and, conversely, those dealing centrally with nationalism often ignore ethnicity. One may or may not want to agree with Connor that 'A nation is a self-aware ethnic group' (p. 388), but it is difficult to disagree with his rather inelegant statement that 'The student of nationalism and the student of ethnicity seldom cross-fertilize' (p. 387).

Even though Mead (1934/1959) stressed the importance of language 50 years ago, sociologists have largely ignored it in their work. It is also true that studies of political, economic and social history have seldom attended to linguistic matters (see e. g. Schlossman, 1983a). Seton-Watson (1977), in an excellent study of nationalism, has pointed out how undesirable this is, and how the neglect vitiates the discussion of historical processes—especially, of course, those relating to his own field. More recently, he has reiterated the point: 'The history of language is not just a subject for philologists, but forms a very important part of social history, and one which seems to me to be relatively neglected by most historians' (Seton-Watson, 1981, p. 2). There are signs that this neglect is lessening, however. Seton-Watson's own work shows this and, outside the realm of nationalism per se, other social historians have begun to integrate language into the story. A good example here is Brown's (1981) recent social history of Ireland from 1922, in which Irish language and literature are part of the general thread.

Another apparently obvious link in which ethnicity figures, but which has not been adequately explored, is that between group identity and bilingual education. I shall be looking in some detail at bilingual education in chapter 5; for present purposes, we can simply note that some varieties of this educational approach are supported precisely because they are seen to be important for ethnic identity retention. It seems rather strange, therefore, that Fishman (1977a) has recently called for the investigation of the ethnicity-bilingual education link, an exercise seen to be 'rewarding'. Surely the analysis of such a link is vital, not only for its own sake but also for the light it might shed upon each of the constituents (see Edwards, 1981a, 1983a). There have been many assumptions about relationships between bilingual education and identity retention, but these have not been adequately tested nor even, in many cases, stated. Related to this has been a lack of due regard for the social context in which educational programmes operate. Fishman (1977a, p. 45) thus noted that 'The only aspect of bilingual education that has been even less researched than student attitudes and interests is that of parental attitudes and interests.' Again, I shall turn to these matters later. Here we need only observe, with some amazement perhaps, that programmes intended to bolster identity have not considered the existing parameters of that very phenomenon.

A more general difficulty, one which extends beyond the educational scene to include many aspects of linguistic identity, is the highly charged and often polemical writing which passes for disinterested social analysis. Identity's of course a subject of much emotional power and it has been dealt with in a personal and subjective way for a very long time; within modern times, at least since the writings of the linguistic nationalists of the early nineteenth century. Indeed, there is nothing wrong with treatises of an advocatory nature. The difficulty arises when such writing is disguised in the appropriate scientific language of the day. In short, it can be a difficult and tedious exercise to try and tease out a more or less dispassionate assessment of language, identity and their concomitants from less objective outbreaks of special pleading.

The task, therefore, is to attempt an investigation of language and group identity which draws together relevant threads from a diversity of sources, avoids as much as possible the traps and snares of intrusive value judgement and, therefore, provides a useful synthesis of descriptive information. This, in the main, is necessarily a pre-theoretical effort, although some introductory theoretical conclusions may perhaps be advanced. At the least, however, it should be possible to present some testable hypotheses, which will be based upon a broader and further foundation than is usually provided. As well, this study of language and identity might incorporate and make more illuminating some of the existing empirical and theoretical studies, by giving them a richer and more realistic context. There is, in other words, a possible fusion of 'macro' and 'micro' perspectives which, if at all successful, can only be of benefit to both.

This broadly conceived analysis is, it must be admitted, a daunting exercise and, some might be inclined to say, a foolhardy one. It necessitates, for example, thought and selection in a variety of topics—many of them fully-fledged in their own right—outside one's own particular field of focus. I shall not be surprised, therefore, if this book evokes critical reaction from those into whose areas of expertise I trespass. This is a risk I think is well worth taking, since an integrative consideration of the topic is, I am convinced, much needed. I can only hope that there are few particularly egregious errors, should also be pointed out, unnecessarily perhaps, that this can be looked upon very much as an introductory effort at synthesis. Much of whatever value the work possesses resides in summarising and ground-clearing and this, I hope, will serve some heuristic purposes.

## Sociolinguistics and Identity

It can be seen straight away that there exist a multitude of markers of group identity (age, sex, social class, geography, religion, etc.) of which language is but one. While I hope that the particular relevance of language will become evident in the chapters to follow, it is important not to lose sight of its non-unique status as a marker, nor to succumb to the sort of tunnel vision which often affects workers considering broad matters from narrow perspectives.

It is clear, however, that the link between language and identity is a reasonable one to study and, as we shall see, many have considered that the possession of a given language is well-nigh essential to the maintenance of group identity. In a broader sense, language has increasingly been investigated as an integral part of human social life, within areas of linguistics, sociology and psychology. It seems remarkable, perhaps, that language could ever not have been so regarded, but an examination of main trends of research in the fields just noted reveals that, until quite recently, the social aspects of language (i. e. those matters lying outside the bounds of linguistics) have not been given due attention. Within social psychology, for example, Giles (1979a) notes the rather conspicuous absence of language studies. Similarly, what now appear to be obvious over-lapping interests between linguistics and sociology were underdeveloped for many years. Thus, Giglioli (1973) points out that language has been neglected within sociology and that linguistics, for its part, has ignored the social context within which language occurs.

The emergence of sociolinguistics reflects a desire to reform this situation and to acknowledge a renewed interest in context. It seems to me that, implicit in this, is a concern for group and individual identity, i. e. sociolinguistics (the sociology of language or the social psychology of language: see below) is essentially about identity, its formation, presentation and maintenance. This being so, it is important to consider very briefly the growth and development of this hybrid discipline.

In 1953, Hertzler wrote a paper entitled "Toward a sociology of language" in which he advocated that more attention be paid to the interaction of language and social situation. In 1965 he published a book on the topic and, in 1966, Bright edited the proceedings of a sociolinguistics conference held in California. Since the early 1960s then, developments have accelerated rapidly.

There has been some debate over whether sociolinguistics or the sociology of language is the best title for the approach or, indeed, if the two terms represent different emphases altogether. Fishman (1971a) has noted that, generally, the latter term implies a broader field of interest, the emphasis being upon social behaviour as can be elucidated through the study of language. Sociolinguistics, on the other hand, tends to stress the linguistic variation presented in different contexts. Perhaps the terms are best viewed as reflecting two sides of the one coin. However, the distinction just noted is not necessarily endorsed by all who use the terms, and some (like Fishman) have alternated in their usage, while carrying on with the same sort of work. Fishman (1971a, p. 8) points out that, after all 'Both are concerned with the interpenetration between societally patterned variation in language usage and variation in other societally patterned behavior, whether viewed in intra-communal or inter-communal perspective.' Fishman also makes another possible distinction. Sociolinguistics may have within it the seeds of its own demise, since it represents what many feel to be a necessary broadening of the larger field of linguistics. Once it is accepted that there can be no meaningful linguistics without attention to context, then sociolinguistics may be absorbed. This 'self-liquidation', as Fishman calls it, obviously does not apply to a field termed the sociology of language, which may be seen as a new, enduring and autonomous sub-topic of sociology. As A. Edwards (1976, p. 9) notes, the sociology of language is a relatively loose conception 'falling easily into the growing company of sociologies of this and that'.

Fishman suggests, in fact, that the sociology of language logically encloses the narrower field of sociolinguistics. This follows from the fact that his 'fundamental bias [is] to view society as being broader than language and, therefore, as providing the context in which all language behavior must ultimately be viewed. It seems to me that the concept "sociology of language" more fully implies this bias than does the term "sociolinguistics", which implies quite the opposite bias' (1968, p. 6).

So, the two terms may be different in emphasis and in degree of autonomy, and with regard to the relative importance placed upon language and context. As well, the terms are used loosely and sometimes interchangeably. In any event, there is a mingling of context and language, and it is possible to see that both terms might be more or less accurately used within the same investigation. One might, for example, use social situational information to comment upon linguistic forms produced or linguistic usage might be studied in order to better understand the context. As Herman (1961) has noted, context can influence linguistic choice, and linguistic choice can serve as an index to perceptions of situation.

The intertwining of these terms in real-life contexts is particularly apposite in studies of linguistic identity. Language revival efforts, for example, are often interpreted as being in the service of a renewed or resuscitated social identity. Yet, it is also true that altered perceptions of group identity-based upon many social factors—may lead to desires for language shift. It is, in fact, an interesting exercise in studies of linguistic nationalism to try to disentangle such chicken-and-egg relationships. Even at this early stage, however, it can be appreciated that such an exercise may be rather pointless. A 'packet' of tightly related factors, linguistic and other, often proves singularly resistant to attempts at such disentanglement. Nonetheless, bearing Fishman's quotation in mind, we might want to opt, for present purposes, for a scenario in which the overall social context is perforce larger than any of its constituent parts, language included. This simple observation has some interesting implications which I shall attempt to deal with later. It also rather implies that the sociology of language is a more accurate description, when considering the language-identity link, than is sociolinguistics. Yet the simple difficulty of deriving an adjectival term from the former will account for the continued use of the latter.

## Ethnic Identity

Connor (1978) has discussed, in a useful article, the great confusion surrounding the concept of ethnicity:

> With nationalism pre-empted, authorities have had difficulty agreeing on a term to describe the loyalty of segments of a state's population to their particular nation. Ethnicity, primordialism, pluralism, tribalism, regionalism, communalism, and parochialism are among the most commonly encountered. This varied vocabulary further impedes an understanding of nationalism by creating the impression that each is describing a separate phenomenon. (p. 386)

Not only does this comment illustrate something of the terminological confusion in the area, it also indicates the close relationship between ethnicity and nationalism. Nationalism has, in fact, been seen as an extension of ethnicity or, as Baron (1947) put it, organised ethnocultural solidarity. Francis (1947, 1976) has referred to ethnicity as nationalism which is not completely self-aware and Weber (1968), on the same theme, noted that the presence of ethnic solidarity does not in itself constitute a sense of 'nation'. This presents the possibility of what Connor discusses as 'pre-national' groups or 'potential nations', and leads him to endorse Barker's (1927) view that a nation is essentially a self-aware ethnic group. Thus, 'while an ethnic group may be other-defined, the nation must be self-defined' (Connor, 1978, p. 388).

But, what are the necessary and sufficient conditions for ethnic or pre-national groups, and how important is the question of self-versus other definition? At a very simple level, ethnicity can be thought of as a 'sense of group identity deriving from real or perceived common bonds such as language, race or religion' (Edwards, 1977a, p. 254). But, although true, this definition is very general and invites more questions than it answers. What, for example, are the most important common bonds? Are some more central than others? become essential? And why exactly is the phrase 'real or perceived' necessary? If we turn to the extensive literature on ethnic identity, attempting to resolve these matters, we find that we have opened 'Pandora's box'. Isajiw (1980) examined 65 studies of ethnicity, and found that 52 of them gave no explicit definition of ethnicity, accepting, by default as it were, the sort of general view cited above. Isajiw also considered theoretical treatments of the subject, assessing 27 definitions. A fairly broad range of opinion thus was evaluated and, although there was a great deal of variation, several themes recurred. It is an examination of these that promises to lead to a comprehensive definition of identity.

First, there is the often-expressed equation of ethnic group with minority group, or with a social subgroup. This is found more often among those treating ethnicity in a North American, immigrant-group context. Theodorson and Theodorson (1969) define an ethnic group as a subgroup within a larger society, as does Gordon (1964). Yet even the most casual observer can see that all people are members of some ethnic group or other; in fact ethnos is a Greek word for nation, where this signifies a common-descent group. Intrinsically, therefore, there is no need to associate ethnic with minority. However, and especially perhaps in immigrant societies, the politics of power ensure that, as Royce (1982, p. 3) says 'dominant groups rarely define themselves as ethnics.' My point here is simply that the ethnic-minority link is not a necessary one, but rather one reflecting power and status relationships.

The situation is clarified somewhat if we move from the immigrant context to one in which indigenous groups are involved. Isajiw (1980) notes that European sociological definitions of ethnicity, for example, do not make the ethnic group-subgroup association. On the one hand, terms like 'nation' or 'nationality' are used because of the homogeneity of societies existing as states. On the other hand, 'national minority' is often used to refer to groups within heterogeneous societies—and this, as Isajiw rightly notes, does tend to avoid the connotations of sub-groups which the term 'ethnic minority' sometimes possesses.

In any event, a combination of European, American and other experiences does usefully demonstrate the logical fallacy of thinking of ethnicity as a minority phenomenon. While dominant groups in mixed societies may not usually consider themselves in ethnic terms, they clearly can be conceived of in this way. Indeed, ethnic communities can not only be majority ones within a given society, they may also cross political boundaries, as contemporary and historical pan-ethnic groupings indicate. All of this Isajiw takes as evidence for an abstract-specific distinction in definitions of ethnic identity, in which the geographical context of ethnicity determines, at least in part, its constitution, thus, the relevance of majority-minority considerations. It seems to me, however, that the distinction is not so much between abstract and specific approaches to ethnicity as between different specific ones. As we have seen, definitions of ethnicity which assume or do not assume minority status differ along contextual lines rather than varying in degrees of abstractness or specificity. The important first point in the argument, then, is just that ethnic identity should not be taken to imply, necessarily, minority-group identity.

A second factor in the discussion is the importance of emphasising group boundaries or group content. Barth (1969) is perhaps the most influential of contemporary scholars who have stressed that the essential focal point is the boundary between groups. His reasoning is that the cultures which boundaries enclose may change—indeed, we should stress that they do change, since all groups are dynamic—but the continuation of boundaries themselves is more longstanding. This emphasis has the attraction of illuminating group maintenance across generations; for example, third-and fourth-generation immigrants in the United States are generally quite unlike their first-generation forebears yet, to the extent to which they recognise links here (and differences from other groups), the concept and utility of group boundary has significance. In some ways, too, Barth's emphasis came as a relief from earlier approaches which focused on group cultural content since, as Royce (1982) points out, these often proved little more than lists of alleged ethnic traits.

Nevertheless, I think we can agree with Royce that the received notion in some quarters, after Barth, that boundaries were 'in' and content was 'out' is not completely justified. The fact that group culture may have been less than adequately dealt with is not, a good reason for neglecting it altogether. Both perspectives are important. I shall be suggesting later some ways of looking at group cultural markers which might bring together both content and boundary approaches. An examination of traits which disappear (or become less visible) versus those which show more longevity, for example, would not only clarify content change over time, but would also elucidate the ways in which boundaries are maintained in the face of changing circumstances. As a more specific instance, we might consider that the decline of an original group language may represent a change in cultural content—the loss of that language as a regular communicative instrument, and the adoption of another. But, to the extent to which language remains as a valued symbolic feature of group life, it may yet contribute to the maintenance of boundaries.

A third major feature of ethnic identity has to do with objective versus subjective definitions (cf. Royce's material-ideological dichotomy). As Isajiw (1980) has noted, this distinction reflects that between structural and phenomenological approaches, especially within sociology. On the one hand, we can consider definitions of ethnicity which include objective characteristics (linguistic, racial, geographical, religious, ancestral, etc.). From such a perspective, ethnicity is 'given', an inheritance which is an immutable historical fact. Such an 'involuntary' approach to group membership can be further understood as emphasising common ties of socialisation. It thus allows us to conceptually differentiate between ethnic groups and other forms of association, like clubs and societies, membership of which is not involuntary and does not depend upon common socialisation patterns (although it may do, of course, if the organisations persist over generations). To this point, then, we might tentatively view ethnicity as an involuntary state in which members share common socialisation practices or culture.

However, this objective approach has some serious difficulties. Indeed, Isajiw (1980) notes that only one definition in his sample made explicit reference to the purely objective approach: Breton and Pinard (1960) asserted that ethnic group membership is not a matter of choice, but rather an accident of birth. It is true that they also mention emotional and symbolic relationships among group members but these, no less than more visible entities like language and ancestry, are seen to be basically related to socialisation. The main difficulty here is that the objective or involuntary approach—useful as it first appears as a quick means of categorisation—does not adequately explain the persistence of ethnicity across generation, within rapidly changing social contexts. The obvious example here is the North American immigrant experience. As noted above, continuity of group boundaries may outlive that of specific cultural content; a sense of 'groupness' may persist long after visible or tangible links with earlier generations have disappeared. On what basis is this maintained?

It is at this point that the 'subjective' perspective is useful. An example is provided by Shibutani and Kwan (1965) who note that 'an ethnic group consists of people who conceive of themselves as being of a kind..., united by emotional bonds'; although they may share a common heritage, 'far more important, however, is their belief that they are of common descent' (pp. 40-41). Or, consider Weber (1968): 'We shall call "ethnic groups" those human groups that entertain a subjective belief in their common descent.., it does not matter whether or not an objective blood relationship exists. Ethnic membership, differs from the kinship group precisely by being a presumed identity' (p. 389; my italics). Ethnicity, then, is seen above all as a matter of belief. We find in

Isajiw's (1980) survey that attributes cited include such things as 'sense of peoplehood' and shared values. Further, where the studies surveyed gave no definition of ethnicity, the implicit definition often seemed to be something as loose as 'any group of people who identify themselves or are in any way identified as Italians, Germans, Indians, Ukrainians, etc.' (p. 14). Yet it is very important to understand, as Isajiw notes (and as is implied in the subjective approaches cited above), that the subjectivity here is not completely arbitrary but is, like the more material or objective perspective, based upon ancestors. There must be some real linkage, however much change groups and individuals have undergone, between past and present. It is in this sense, perhaps that the terms 'objective' and 'subjective' are best seen as reflections on the perceived immutability or mutability of ethnic group markers (see Fishman, 1977b).

It seems clear that some combination of objective and subjective perspectives is necessary in understanding ethnic identification. If this appears at first to require a paradoxical mingling of mutable and immutable elements, recall the distinction between group content and group boundaries. Cultural content is, of course, mutable—ethnic groups are dynamic entities, particularly when they exist as minorities within heterogeneous and developing (or highly developed) societies—but boundaries are less so. Indeed, when boundaries disappear, when even the most subjectively or symbolically sustained group markers vanish, then the ethnic group itself has ceased as a viable concept. This usually takes a very long time, and those who are now members of a large homogeneous group, e.g. English speakers in England, will have to delve deep into history to rediscover boundaries.

The final factor I want to discuss here comprises questions of ethnicity as myth, and what Gans has referred to as 'symbolic ethnicity' (1979;

see also chapter 4). Steinberg (1981) has considered the current American interest in ethnicity—the 'new ethnicity', as some have termed it—as representing the dying gasp of ethnic vitality. For Steinberg, economic and social-class approaches are now far more explanatory in understanding groups and group behaviour than is ethnic-group membership. The 'myth', then, is that ethnicity per se is a continuingly useful concept. Steinberg notes that ethnicity is willingly set aside for socioeconomic advance: 'ethnic groups, have been all too willing to trample over ethnic boundaries, in the pursuit of economic and social advantage' (1981, p. 256). The myth of ethnicity resides in the attempt to artificially sustain it beyond limits of usefulness and meaningfulness. Steinberg's final sentence adverts to the mistaken belief that a continued association with symbols of the past can realistically protect group members from contemporary discontents. Patterson (1977), too, has reacted against the rhetoric of current ethnicity. It is, for him, a chauvinistic impulse, a retrogressive longing for boundaries now very much out of place and, indeed, destructive (see also Vallee, 1981, on 'ethnicity as anachronism' and Porter, 1975, on 'ethnicity as atavism'). The major feature of revivalist ethnicity is, for Patterson, the adherence to 'empty symbols'.

I shall have more to say about ethnic revival, its progress and proponents, and value judgements of pluralism; here I simply want to consider the notion. of ethnic symbols. Both Steinberg and Patterson see these as essentially meaningless, or empty and unworthy longings for a past that is unrecapturable. If, however, we can conceive of ethnicity, e. g. among American immigrants, as a real and continuing force, and one which is genuinely felt, then perhaps the idea of symbols is important. I have already alluded to the continuation of boundaries among some groups in which cultural content has altered dramatically over generations, and it is perhaps to these groups that we should look in order to see the power of ethnic symbols.

Here, Gans (1979) has clarified the situation. He notes, first of all, that there has been no ethnic revival in the United States, and that assimilation and acculturation have continued. Nevertheless, there has been a 'new kind of ethnic involvement... which emphasizes concern with identity' (p.1). This apparent paradox is resolved, Gans claims, when one understands that this new involvement is a minimal one, does not require traditional ethnic culture or institutions, but does give importance to symbols. Like many critics of the 'new ethnicity', Gans acknowledges that this symbolic ethnicity is 'an ethnicity of the last resort' (p.1) but, unlike them, does not feel that this is perforce a negative quality nor one doomed to imminent demise; it is something which might persist for a long time. Presumably this reflects the fact that when ethnicity has altered to symbolic status only, it is no longer any sort of barrier to social advance and, as such, can be maintained indefinitely without cost. The ethnic revival, in Gans's terms, is a misnomer; what is actually occurring is symbolic ethnicity which, because of upward mobility, is a visible quantity. Some of the forms that symbolic ethnicity can take include religious rites de passage and holidays, ethnic foods, and ethnic characters in the mass media. This last is particularly interesting because, as Gans aptly points out, although 'films and television programs with ethnic characters are on the increase', these characters do not engage in very 'ethnic' behaviour and 'may only have ethnic names'; thus, 'they are not very different from the ethnic audiences who watch them' (p.10).

Bearing these four factors in mind, we may now attempt a definition of ethnic identity. Such a definition must take into account: (a) the fact that ethnic identity need not be a minority phenomenon; (b) the continuation of perceived group boundaries, across generations which are likely to show significant changes in the cultural 'stuff' of their lives; (c) that objective, material trait descriptions do not fully encompass the phenomenon; and (d) the power of so-called 'symbolic' ethnicity, which can be too easily discounted.

On the basis of his analyses, Isajiw (1980) concluded that 'ethnicity refers to an involuntary group of people who share the same culture or to descendants of such people who identify themselves and/or are identified by others as belonging to the same involuntary group' (p. 24). As a minimal statement, Isajiw's is unexceptionable; it certainly accords with the features discussed here. On the other hand, it defines by excluding non-essential or non-contributory aspects. I suggest, therefore, that the following might be of slightly greater value: Ethnic identity is allegiance to a group large or small, socially dominant or sub-ordinate—with which one has ancestral links. There is no necessity for a continuation, over generations, of the same socialisation or cultural patterns, but some sense of a group boundary must persist. This can be sustained by shared objective characteristics (language, religion, etc.), or by more subjective contributions to a sense of 'groupness', or by some combination of both. Symbolic or subjective attachments must relate, at however distant a remove, to an observably real past.

## Nationalism

I have already discussed some general views which suggest a connection between ethnicity and nationalism, e.g. nationalism as self-aware ethnicity, ethnicity as a state of 'pre-nationalism', nationalism as 'organised ethnocultural solidarity', etc. There is obviously a link between the two concepts, and many of the notes (above) on criteria for ethnic identity apply, at a broader level, to national identity. For this reason I can perhaps be briefer here than I would have to be otherwise. Nonetheless, nationalism is a large and complicated topic, has received a great deal of attention from many quarters, and must be given at least a cursory treatment here.

Royce (1982) points out that, although nationalism and ethnicity share much in common, most importantly the sense of 'groupness' or 'peoplehood', they are not identical. The obvious difference, however, is not one of principle but of scale. Nationalism is an extension of ethnicity in that it adds to the belief in shared characteristics a desire for political autonomy, the feeling that the 'only legitimate type of government is national self-government' (Kedourie, 1961, p. 9).

Nationalism is often seen as a modern phenomenon. Kohn (1961) has traced in great detail the progress of the concept, and it is clear that early uses of the term nation do not accord with contemporary views. It is a fairly recent perspective which associates nation with common sympathies, sentiments, aims and will, a perspective which dates to the beginning of the last century. Kedourie (1961), for example, describes nationalism as a doctrine invented in Europe at that time. It makes three major assumptions: (a) that there is a natural division of humanity into nations; (b) that these nations have identifiable characteristics; and (c) that (as noted above) their only legitimate form of government is self-government. The linguistic criterion is the most important here in marking one nation from another: 'A group speaking the same language is known as a nation, and a nation ought to constitute a state' (Kedourie, 1961, p. 68). In linking language centrally to nationalism, Kedourie claims that there are no substantive distinctions between linguistic and (say) racial nationalism, that there is simply a conception of nationalism which may embrace various features (language, race, religion, etc.). This may have, incidentally, the effect of heightening the importance of language for ethnicity too, if we accept that nationalism is 'organised' ethnicity. On the other hand, perhaps the increase in scale from ethnicity to nationalism, and the concomitant requirement for large organising principles, may raise language from a marker to the marker. In any event, Kedourie's own view is that nationalism is a pernicious doctrine, particularly with regard to its emphasis upon linguistic unity; possession of the same language should not entitle people to governmental autonomy. More generally, political matters should not be based upon cultural criteria.

Smith (1971) has criticised Kedourie's analysis of nationalism, largely on the grounds that it emphasises negative aspects and language. There are instances in which language is not so important for nationalistic sentiment as are other markers; Smith claims that, in Africa, national identity is rarely associated with language per se since this could lead to 'balkanisation' and that, in countries like Greece, Burma and Pakistan, religion has been the pre-eminent 'self-definer'. Thus, 'in general, the linguistic criterion has been of sociological importance only in Europe and the Middle East (to some extent)' (pp. 18-19).

Smith essentially endorses Kedourie's basic description of nationalism (see the three assumptions above), but rejects his emphasis on language. In fact, Smith claims that Kedourie's error is to outline the naked doctrine of nationalism, then add the linguistic criterion (which is applicable only in some instances and based, Smith tells us, on the 'German romantic version'), and then, finally, to amalgamate these two features. It is on this basis that Kedourie's criticism of the overall concept is misguided. Smith expands upon Kedourie's basic assumptions underlying nationalism when he outlines what he calls the 'core nationalist doctrine'. It holds that humanity is divided naturally into nations having particular characteristics. Freedom and self-realisation depend upon identification with the nation, the source of political power, and loyalty to the nation-state overrides all other allegiances. There is, thus, a need for nations and states to coincide, and the strengthening of this natural nation-state is the sine qua non for freedom and peace for all. Smith thus provides an easy conceptual link between ethnicity and nationalism. He notes, for example, that the core doctrine does not define the characteristics of perceived nationhood; supporting theories are required for this. Surely this is exactly the point at which we can insert, as it were, the previously defined concept of ethnicity. Nationalism can indeed be seen as ethnicity writ large, ethnicity with a desire for self-government (total or partial) added. Just as ethnicity does not inevitably require language (or any other specific feature) as a component, neither does nationalism.

We should give some brief further consideration to the notion that nationalism is a recent phenomenon. I have already noted Kohn's (1961) point that the idea of a nation being erected upon common sympathies and aims is a modern one. Before the nineteenth century, in feudal, dynastic and essentially socially immobile societies, the idea of a common consciousness can hardly be said to have characterised even those groups sharing certain sociocultural traits. Thus, Rustow (1968), for example, connects modernisation with nationalistic feeling. But what elements of modernisation led to national consciousness or 'corporate will'? Two important factors were the French Revolution, with its ideals of a popular sovereignty, and the growth of romanticism (especially in Germany: see below). Kohn (1967) thus details the beginnings of the ideas of nationalism and nation-state in a book entitled *Prelude to nation-states*: The

French and German experience 1789 – 1815; earlier, he had made the often-quoted statement that 'before the [French] Revolution there had been states and governments, after it there emerged nations and peoples' (1961, p. 573).

Yet these very elements of 'modernisation' refute the idea that nationalism was a concept which somehow sprung, fully formed and independent, from the social philosopher's mind or a radically altered social context. Both the French Revolution and the romantic reaction to rationalism sit firmly embedded in historical context. In this sense, Kedourie's description of nationalism as an 'invented' doctrine may have misleading connotations; indeed, his own subsequent discussion of revolution, reaction and romanticism underlines the unfortunate nature of his choice of the word. Smith's (1971) analysis of a gradual evolution from a 'pre-modern age' to a 'post-revolutionary' one is surely more accurate. Here, Orridge (1981) makes the useful observation that nationalism, like other political phenomena, is an emergent process; its roots go deep. Thus, the 'first and most influential kind of nationalism has been that of the nation-states of Western Europe... the prototypes of modern nationalism' (p. 42). It is of course possible to say that units like England, France and Denmark were never completely nation-states, but that they developed into larger homogeneous entities: 'at their core lay a sizeable population with a degree of initial cultural similarity that increased as time went on' (p. 42).

Further to this matter, we might agree with Barker (1927). He accepts that national self-consciousness dates from the nineteenth century and, in this sense, the nation is a modern invention. But, 'nations were already there; they had indeed been there for centuries' (p. 173). The apparent paradox here is perhaps resolved if we acknowledge that pre-nineteenth century 'nations' were waiting, as it were, for the spark of consciousness which brought them alive. Groups possessing ethnic solidarity but lacking the final feature—the desire for some degree of autonomy—may be thought of as pre-national groups or potential nations (Connor, 1978). Barker goes on to say that 'a nation must be an idea as well as a fact before it can become a dynamic force' (p. 173). However, perhaps on balance it would be clearer to think of potential nations (i. e. ethnic groups) becoming nations rather than to speak of the nation as a group first lacking, and then acquiring, this vital consciousness, i. e. while we should accept that nations do not materialise suddenly (and, in that sense, are hardly 'inventions') they are not, strictly speaking, nations before the 'idea' has occurred; the transition is thus from ethnic group to nation, and is made possible by the self-conscious desire for autonomy. The 'idea' here relates primarily to the imagined possibilities of autonomy. As regards this, Connor's (1978) comment upon Barker's idea is a bit misleading. He claims that Barker's meaning is that 'a nation is a self-aware ethnic group, while an ethnic group may, therefore, be other-defined, the nation must be self-defined' (p. 388). But, both ethnic group and nation are self-defined; the difference between them resides in the nation's possession of the additional 'idea', the conscious wish for self-control. It is in this sense that both Gellner (1964), when he speaks of nationalism inventing nations, and Anderson (1983), when he defines the nation as an imagined political community, are correct.

I cannot delve further here into the historical forces bearing upon nationalism; many useful treatments may be found (e. g. Kohn, 1961, 1967; Seton-Watson, 1977; Smith, 1971, 1979b). Suffice it to say that it was in the rhetoric surrounding 1789 that nationalism, national loyalty, the notion of the 'fatherland' and, above all, the belief in unity and autonomy first found forceful expression. It was in the German romanticism that the notion of a yolk and the almost mystical connection between nation and language were expounded so fervently in modern times. In 1807, Fichte stressed as absolutely crucial the linguistic criterion of nationhood (in his famous Addresses to the German nation, 1922/1968). Indeed, Fichte not only emphasised the importance of his own language, he actively deprecated that of others, thus foreshadowing much of the negative rhetoric of nationalism. For example, he pointed out that 'the German speaks a language which has been alive ever since it first issued from the force of nature, whereas the other Teutonic races speak a language which has movement on the surface only but is dead at the root (1968, pp. 58-59). From a linguistic standpoint this sentiment is absurd, yet it illustrates the essentially irrational (or, to be less pejorative, non-rational) power and appeal of linguistic nationalism.

It is from these roots that our modern understanding of nationalism has sprung. Connor (1978) points out that the very term nationalism seems first to have appeared around the end of the eighteenth century. Although it did not find a permanent place in dictionaries until almost a hundred years later—and the term nationality apparently received its contemporary launching from Lord Acton in 1862 (1907)—these were the beginnings. From then on, many important commentators discussed national consciousness and the 'corporate will' of a people, Disraeli, John Stuart Mill and Renan among them (see Royce, 1982; Smith, 1971). I shall have more to say about assessments of nationalism in the next chapter.

The final points to be made here have to do with recurring problems of definition and confusion. Nationalism, to reiterate, can be understood as ethnic sentiment expanded to include desires for at least some degree of self-government, for group boundaries to coincide with those of governmental units, and for the preservation, strengthening and dignity of the group. It is in the relationship between nation and state that confusion often occurs. Nation, after all, is commonly used in referring to countries, political units which may or may not be ethnically homogeneous, which are more properly termed states. States are easily defined. Nations, on the other hand, are more elusive; we have seen here that nationalism, like ethnicity, has both objective and subjective aspects. While we can attempt to list characteristics of nations, no particular tangible traits are essential to the definition. A psychological bond, a sense of community residing in affective ties, these are the common and necessary conditions for nationalistic sentiment. Thus, as Seton-Watson (1977) notes, no scientific definition of the notion can be devised. Self-awareness and self-consciousness are the marks of nationalism, and objective features like religion and language 'are significant to the notion only to the degree to which they contribute to this notion or sense of the group's self-identity and uniqueness' (Connor, 1978, p. 389). It will thus be understood that nations can alter or lose characteristics without losing the necessary self-consciousness. Tangible features are, of course, necessary as rallying-points, and they are needed to give the all-important national consciousness a visible form, but none is essential per se (see e. g. Smith's arguments against identifying nations with language groups, 1971).

The state, then, is a political and territorial unit; the nation involves more subjective elements, being essentially an 'imagined' community in Anderson's sense (1983). Connor (1978) suggests that the earliest uses of the term nationalism did not confuse nation and state; but, latterly, nationalism has been used to indicate loyalty not to the nation, properly conceived, but to the state. Indeed, we commonly refer to the 'nations of the world' and the 'United Nations', even though these uses are clearly incorrect.

Loyalties can interact and overlap, of course. Loyalty to nation can coincide, indeed, with state loyalty, but only when the unit in question is a nation-state, a political entity comprising a homogeneous national group. Turning again to Connor (1978), we see that the true nation-state is a rare bird. Surveying the 132 states existing in 1971, he found that only 12 (9.1 percent) were nation-states. Another 50 (37.9 percent) contained a major ethnic group comprising more than three-quarters of the total population. Of the remaining 70 states, 31 (23.5 percent) had a majority ethnic group accounting for between half and three-quarters of the population, while in 39 more (29.5 percent) the largest single ethnic community formed less than half of the total population. So, while in many countries there is a large, often numerically dominant, ethnic group, there are few indeed for whom we could assume that national and state loyalties coincide. Elsewhere (in a review of Patterson, 1977), Connor discusses continuing confusion. Patterson correctly notes that Great Britain, the United States and Canada are not nation-states, but claims that Ireland, France and most other European states are. A case might be made for Ireland, but France and other continental countries are clearly not nation-states, containing as they do many groups. Connor (1980) mentions, by way of illustration, that France contains groups of Alsatians, Basques, Bretons, Corsicans, etc. Even Royce (1982), in her useful work on ethnic identity, seems to confuse nation and state, and to muddy the relationship between ethnicity and nationalism. Thus, 'one does not have to give up allegiances based on primary ties such as ethnic group membership in order to function within a unit such as a nation, which operates on the basis of civil ties' (p. 107). Of course, 'civil ties' are not absent in nations, but Royce seems to refer here to what should more properly be called a state.

In summary, nationalism can indeed be thought of, in Baron's terms (1947), as 'organised ethnocultural solidarity', so long as we recognise that the organising has to do with a desire for self-control. The definition of ethnicity, then, can be expanded in this way to become one of nationalism. It is important to realise that both notions rest upon a sense of community which can have many different tangible manifestations, none of which is indispensable for the continuation of the sense itself. The visible 'content' of both ethnicity and nationalism is eminently mutable; what is immutable is the feeling of groupness. When this disappears then boundaries disappear. Any analysis of nationalism which concentrates solely upon objective characteristics misses the essential point. On the other hand, it must be remembered that the subjective fidelity which is so important is not itself arbitrary; a sense of solidarity must ultimately depend upon 'real' communalities, however diluted or altered over time. The continuing power of ethnicity and nationalism resides exactly in that intangible bond which, by definition, can survive the loss of visible markers of group distinctiveness.

## Language and Dialect

If we are to consider the relationship of language and identity, we should clarify our conceptions of language itself. This may seem an obvious and unnecessary excursion, yet, since there have been almost as many definitions of language as writers on the topic, some brief attention is necessary. As well, I want to introduce here a note on two broad types of language function which are not immediately self-evident. Similarly, we should ensure that we understand what is meant by dialect.

# Language

In 1921, Sapir noted that 'language is a purely human and non-instinctive method of communicating ideas, emotions, and desires by means of a system of voluntarily produced symbols' (p. 7). Morris (1946) described language as composed of arbitrary symbols possessing an agreed-upon significance within a community. Furthermore, these symbols are independent of immediate context, and are connected in rule-governed ways. First, then, language is a system—this implies regularity and rules of order. Second, the system is arbitrary inasmuch as the particular units employed have meaning only because of users' agreement and convention. Third, language is used for communicative purposes by a group of people who constitute the speech or language community.

Implicit here is the idea that languages differ from one another in terms of just how they assign meaning to sounds and symbols. Not wishing to deal at all with the question of how different speech communities evolved, or the origin of language (s), I will only make the obvious statement that there exist numerous language communities in the world, whose patterns of communication are not mutually intelligible (although many, of course, are related in language 'families'? e. g. Indo-European, Semitic, Finno-Ugric).

It is of some interest that, in the face of the obvious pragmatic advantages of a reduction in the number of distinct languages, thousands of varieties continue to flourish. Some have seen the reason for this as the human desire to stake particular linguistic claims to the world, to create unique perspectives on reality and to protect group distinctiveness. Thus, Steiner (1975) speaks of separate languages enabling groups to keep secret the 'inherited, singular springs of their identity' (p. 232).

Language can be seen as a vehicle for concealment, secrecy and fiction. This idea is not Steiner's alone, of course. Popper has suggested that what is most characteristic of human language is the possibility of storytelling, and Wittgenstein in the Tractatus refers to language disguising thought (see Edwards, 1979a). Further, Jespersen (1946) reminds us of TaUeyrand's famous observation that language exists to hide one's thoughts, and also relates Kierkegaard's extension of this, that language is used by some to hide their lack of thought! The idea of language as concealment may seem contrary to that of language as communication, but the communication is a within-group phenomenon and the concealment an attempt, through language, to maintain inviolate the group's own grasp of the world. The historical equation, traduttore-traditore, suggests a disinclination to see 'hoarded dreams, patents of life..., taken across the frontier' (Steiner, 1975, p. 233).

This speculation may be overstatement, but it seems clear enough that there has been, and continues to be, a strong resistance to the abandoning of a particular language, even for the practical attractions of a lingua franca (see chapter 2), and a desire at most for an instrumental bilingualism in which the original variety is retained (often, however, within ever-decreasing domains). This suggests that there can be a distinction, within a language, between what I have called communicative and symbolic functions (Edwards, 1977a, 1984a). The basic distinction here is between language in its ordinarily understood sense as a tool of communication, and language as an emblem of groupness, as a symbol, a rallying-point. We have already seen that language can be important in ethnic and nationalist sentiment because of its powerful and visible symbolism, quite apart from the revived communicative aspect which is often desired within minority groups. However, we need not look at self-conscious group movements to apprehend that power of language which extends beyond the communicative function. For any speech community in which the language of use is also the ancestral language, the intangible symbolic relevance is tied up with the instrumental function. Steiner (1975) has pointed out, for example, that communication inevitably involves translation and interpretation; this is true for communication within a language, as well as for the obvious translation needed across languages. Steiner simply means that the symbolic value of language, the historical and cultural associations which it accumulates and the 'natural semantics of remembrance' (p. 470) all add to the basic message a rich underpinning of shared connotations. It is in this way that we translate when we communicate, and this ability to read between the lines, as it were, depends upon a cultural continuity in which language is embedded, and which is not open to all. Only those who grow up within the community can, perhaps, participate fully in this expanded communicative interaction. Steiner notes, indeed, that 'we possess civilization because we have learnt to translate out of time' (p. 31).

The complicated interweaving of language and culture which depends upon a fusion of pragmatic linguistic skills and the more intangible associations carried by language is not always immediately apparent to native speakers within a majority-speech community. The ordinary English-speaker in Great Britain, for example, uses the language in all regular domains; as well, it is the language of the past in which tradition and culture are expressed. However, the two aspects of language are separable—the communicative from the symbolic—and it is possible for the latter to retain importance in the absence of the former. This is most clearly seen when we examine language use and attitudes among minority groups undergoing (or having undergone) language shift within majority, other-language-speaking populations or, indeed, among any group where a shift has occurred in the fairly recent past. Ireland is an example here.

A 1975 research study (Committee on Irish Language Attitudes Research) sampled some 3,000 respondents, when investigating Irish language use, ability and attitudes. Only about three per cent of the overall population now use the language in any regular way, there is little interest in Irish restoration, and many are pessimistic about the maintenance of the little Irish still used. Yet, there does remain a value for Irish in the symbolic sense, and it can be argued that Irish continues to occupy some place in the constitution of current Irish identity (see Edwards, 1984b; and chapter 3).

The continuing symbolic role of language can also be observed among immigrant groups in the United States. Eastman (1984) discusses the notion of an 'associated' language—one which group members no longer use, or even know, but which continues to be part of their heritage (see also Eastman & Reese, 1981; Edwards, 1984c). When language operates only as a symbol, it may be argued that it is no longer really language. Certainly, the symbolic function of language which co-exists with the communicative (as discussed by Steiner) is not quite the same thing as the more purely symbolic entity which is divorced from the communicative (e.g. Irish for most Irish people, Polish for most fourth generation Polish-Americans, etc.). Still, it should be remembered that language, unlike other purely emblematic markers, is itself a complex system, capable (at least theoretically) of being resuscitated to instrumental status. I shall return to these matters again. Here, I simply note that the two functions of language, as outlined above, are separable—even if they are usually joined—and that ignorance of the distinction between them can lead to lack of clarity and, indeed, misdirection of effort among linguistic nationalists.

A common distinction drawn between language and dialect is that dialects are mutually intelligible varieties of one language (see next section), while languages are mutually unintelligible. It is obvious that speakers of French, for example, cannot understand German; the two languages are different. However, is it the case that one language can be seen, in some sense or other, as better, more logical or more expressive than another? This question has proved a controversial one, although it is perhaps a more reasonable one to ask, in the minds of many, if the languages being compared are not relatively close to each other (e. g. French and German) but are, rather, somewhat farther apart (e. g. French and Yup'ik). Is one somehow more primitive or less developed than the other? The idea has appealed to many in the past and has contemporary adherents too (see Edwards, 1983b; Honey, 1983). However, on purely linguistic grounds, it is quite clear that no language can be described as better or worse than another. Given that language is an arbitrary system in which communication rests upon agreement among members of the speech community, it follows that the only 'logic' of language is to be found in its grammar (i. e. a logic of convention). What is grammatical in French (e. g. the use of two elements to express verbal negation) is not in English (where only one is used), but this surely says nothing about the relative quality of the two systems. And, even if we compare the language of a technologically advanced society with that of an 'undeveloped' one, we find the same different, but not deficient, relationship. Gleitman and Gleitman (1970) have noted that there are no 'primitive' languages, and Lenneberg (1967, p. 364) puts it this way: 'Could it be that some languages require "less mature cognition" than others, perhaps because they are still more primitive? In recent years this notion has been thoroughly discredited by virtually all students of language.'

Languages are best seen as different systems reflecting different varieties of the human condition. Although they may be unequal in complexity at given points, this does not imply that some have, overall, greater expressive power. Environments differ and, therefore, the things that must be detailed in language differ. The shop-worn example of Eskimos using many different words to refer to various types of what English speakers simply term snow does not reflect a capability constitutionally denied to non-Eskimos. It does reflect the fact that different environments evoke, in habitual ways, different linguistic behaviour. However, to continue with the example, English-speakers could learn to differentiate among types of snow if they were transplanted to an Arctic setting and, indeed, English-speaking skiers concerned with snow conditions have demonstrated this in more realistic contexts. The general point here is that a language can be seen as 'better' than another only with regard to certain specified intellectual tasks, which are not themselves comparable across environments (see also Langacker, 1972; Trudgill, 1974a).

Further to this, we can note that ideas of languages decaying are not well-founded. Languages change, certainly—adapting to new conditions and requirements—but they do not do so in terms of linguistic purity. Thus, 'at any stage, a language is fully adequate to its purpose, the idea of a "pure" language is illusory' (Langacker, 1972, p.100). To remake the point, this does not mean that all languages contain the same capabilities; different social, geographical and other conditions determine what elements will be needed and, therefore, developed. All are, however, potentially functionally equivalent. Hymes (1974) has noted that languages differ in many aspects of complexity—lexical, grammatical, phonological—and that bilingual speakers will often prefer one language to another for specific purposes. But, the question of overall language 'goodness' is spurious, unless we were willing to define, compare and judge the goodness of situations, contexts and milieus.

## Dialect

A dialect is a variety of a language which differs from other varieties in terms of vocabulary, grammar and pronunciation (accent). Dialects are often distinguished from languages on the basis that, unlike the latter, they are mutually intelligible, e. g. Yorkshire dialect and Cockney dialect are varieties of English and (perhaps with some difficulty) speakers of one can understand the other. However, the nature of dialects is not without problems, and Petyt (1980) provides a useful discussion. He notes that if we consider dialects as different forms of the same language, how fine-grained do we admit these differences to be? It is certainly the case that, within an accepted dialect, there can be found a number of sub-varieties. Trudgill (1974a) thus points out that, within Norfolk dialect, one can speak of East Norfolk and South Norfolk. Continuing subdivisions would ultimately lead us to idiolect, or the speech of one person. It is simply a matter of convention that we usually stop the analysis at some group level, having decided beforehand, perhaps, how much detail we require. Petyt (1980, p. 12) states: 'Sometimes we speak of "Yorkshire dialect", thus implying that the features shared by all Yorkshire speakers in contrast to outsiders are important..., at other times we speak of "Dentdal dialect" with the "essential" features being much more detailed.'

The notion of mutual intelligibility as a criterion of dialect (as opposed to language) falters on two points. First, there are degrees of intelligibility, such that some dialect speakers may understand each other very well, while others may have considerable difficulty. Second, the existence of dialect continua means that 'adjacent' forms may be mutually understood, but non-adjacent ones may not. Trudgill (1974a) reminds us that the idea of a clear and sharp Linguistic discontinuity between dia-

lect speakers is invalid. Consider four dialects, A, B, C and D. As Petyt (1980, p. 14) says: 'if A can just understand C, but cannot really be said to understand D, does the language division come between C and D? But C and D may understand each other quite well.'

These difficulties lead Petyt to the conclusion that criteria supplementary to the intelligibility notion must be provided. He suggests two. The first has to do with the existence of a written language: if groups who differ in speech patterns share a common written form, they may be said to speak different dialects. The second involves political allegiances. Cantonese and Mandarin speakers, despite a lack of mutual intelligibility, are both considered to have dialects of Chinese, not only because they use the same written form but also because they are both members of the Chinese state. Norwegian and Danish speakers, although they can understand one another well, are seen to speak different languages because of different sociopolitical allegiances. A further example here is provided by Wolff (1959), who describes how the concept of intelligibility itself may be subject to social pressure. Among the Urhobo dialects of south-western Nigeria, mutual intelligibility was generally considered quite high, until speakers of Isoko began to claim that their 'language' was different from the rest, a claim coinciding with their demands for increased political autonomy. Another group, speakers of the Okpe dialect which is almost identical to Isoko, were not making such nationalistic claims and continued to perceive mutual intelligibility (see also Heine, 1979). (See Maurud, 1976, for related findings on reciprocal comprehension among Danes, Norwegians and Swedes.)

As with languages, dialects cannot be seen, linguistically, in terms of better or worse. However, while there may be relatively few people who would want to argue that French is better than English, the idea that Oxford English is better than Cockney remains of wider appeal. Dialect has long been used, of course, to denote a substandard deviation from some prestigious variety or standard form. Dictionary definitions have supported this view; e. g. the Oxford English Dictionary has considered a dialect as 'one of the subordinate forms or varieties of a language arising from local peculiarities'. In a sense this is correct, but it is incorrect to assume that the subordinate status of some dialects has any inherent linguistic basis (see e. g. Trudgill, 1975a). Neither should it be thought, as some have done (e. g. Wyld, 1934), that some varieties simply sound better than others or are more aesthetically pleasing. Studies by Giles and his colleagues have shown that listeners unfamiliar with language varieties (of French in one study, and of Greek in another), asked to judge them in terms of pleasantness, were unable to single out the more standard forms as more aesthetic (Giles et al., 1974, 1979). In each case the standard dialects of these two languages were, within their own speech communities, routinely accorded higher aesthetic and prestige status. The studies demonstrate that, shorn of their usual associations (familiar to speakers within the communities), non-standard dialects were not perceived as less pleasant than others.

If we rule out inherent linguistic and aesthetic qualities, on what basis can dialects be judged superior or inferior? It must surely be on the basis of the social prestige and power of their speakers. I used the term non-standard above, and this non-pejorative label should be taken to mean that some dialects have not received the social imprimatur given to others. This is not to say that such varieties are substandard in any substantive way. In many societies particular dialects rise to the top, as it were, with the fortunes of their speakers. The process is one of historical movement and accident. Thus, Standard English may be considered the dialect most often used by educated members of society; it is the form employed in official pronouncements, public records, writing and (often) the broadcast media. But, there is nothing of a linguistic or aesthetic nature which confers special status upon the standard. It is solely because of its widespread social acceptance that it has become primus inter pares. Thus, it is understandable that not all languages possess standard dialects, and in some a case can be made for several standards, each of which may hold sway in a given context or region.

We should also note that there exists more than a simple dichotomy between standard and non-standard dialect; there are often status hierarchies, e. g. Trudgill (1975a) has suggested that in Great Britain, urban non-standard forms are generally viewed as more unpleasant than rural ones. The explanation again resides in the real or perceived social characteristics of speakers. And, finally, the obvious point should be made that the language-dialect distinction is, in addition to the complexities noted above, also subject to change over time. The Romance languages were once dialects of Latin which, under the influence of time and geography, came to achieve language status.

The fact that there is no linguistic or aesthetic basis for the superiority or inferiority of dialects—standard or non-standard—makes it easier to understand how important any variety can be as part of individual or group identity. Still, it is quite clear that some dialects attract negative evaluations, and can be seen as socially deficient; even so, they are maintained, and speakers can have pride in them. Group solidarity can be expressed through low-prestige varieties (see e. g. Ryan, 1979). As well, dialects lacking in social status often evoke high ratings on dimensions relating to interpersonal warmth and integrity (Edwards, 1982a).

## Summary

In this opening chapter I have presented some basic ideas and brief descriptions. I have, for example, attempted to clarify ethnicity, nationalism, and the relationship between them. For each of these powerful elements of group identity, the most important ingredients are the subjective sense of groupness and the continuation of group boundaries. Indeed, these two are related; given that specific aspects of group culture are always subject to change, it seems obvious that a continuing identity must depend upon elements which transcend any purely objective markers. This is not to say, of course, that visible markers are dispensable, but rather that the presence of any particular marker is not essential. Thus, although we can say that language can be an extremely important feature of identity, we cannot endorse the view that a given language is essential for identity maintenance. We shall see, however, that many have considered language an essential pillar—this point of view, of course, is part of the justification for discussing the language-identity link in this book. The perception of identity in its relationship to certain objective markers, particularly language, and analyses of the history and future of group identity are the social and psychological elements which give the subject its compelling interest. Renan (1882/1947, p. 892) touched upon this in observing: 'l'essence d'une nation est que tous les individus aient beaucoup de choses en commun, et aussi que tous aient oublibien des choses.' Selective historical awareness, as we shall observe later, is a potent weapon in the arsenal of group consciousness.

My introductory remarks on language and dialect were also intended to clear the ground. All varieties, prestigious or not, have the capability to carry identity. Even when language has receded to a purely symbolic role it can still have an important place. The relationship between group identity and language is always interesting and often powerful and, in the remainder of this book, I shall try to demonstrate some of the complexities of the relationship.

[From: Edwards, J. 1985, *Language, Society and Identity*. Oxford: Blackwell. Chap 1. Pages: 1-22]

## 导读：语言、社会和身份的一些基本概念

### 社会语言学和身份

群体身份的标志是多种多样的，语言就是其中的一种。当我们研究人的身份时，往往会考虑语言和身份之间的理性关系。从广义的角度来看，对语言的调查研究是因为语言是社会生活中不可缺少的一部分。社会语言学的出现反应了对一定情景下的语言的认识和兴趣，其中隐含有对群体和个体身份的形成、展现和保持的关注。

和社会语言学对应的有语言社会学，两者有各自不同的侧重点，它们既有联系又有区别的。Fishman (1971) 指出，语言社会学是一个更为广泛的研究领域，重点在通过语言研究来阐述社会行为；而社会语言学强调的是在不同的环境下的语言变体。在现实生活中两个概念是相互交织的，但在讨论语言的特征时，却是不同的。对保留语言所做出的努力常常被看成是为了某个社会身份的复活。但是如果由于多种社会因素我们对群体身份的看法有所改变，也会导致人们产生改变语言的愿望。

### 民族身份

民族和种族之间关系密切，Baron (1947) 指出，民族实际上是种族的延伸，与种族文化休戚相关，种族是民族的初始形式。Barker (1927) 把民族视为一个有基本的自我意识的种族群体。关于种族群体，Edwards (1977) 说，从一个简单的层面上来看，可

以看成为一个由语言、人种和宗教联结起来的实体。但是这种定义过于笼统,对民族身份我们应该有一个更为全面综合的认识。

首先,把种族看成是少数民族的对等物是一种谬误。虽然少数民族的特点引人注意,但是社会不仅可以是同质的也可以是异质的。种族应该是跨越政治历史界限的,不仅指少数民族群体也指社会主要的民族群体。

第二,在讨论种族身份时,强调群体界限和内容相当重要。Barth(1969)认为,尽管边界内的文化会发生变化,因为所有的群体都是动态的,但是界限持续是长期的。在 Barth 以后,研究者不那么关心种族群体的内容,种族界限开始成为当时的关注点。

种族身份的第三个主要特点是必须要处理主观定义和客观定义之间的问题。一方面,我们可以考虑包含种族身份的客观特点的定义,从这样一个视角,种族是一种不可变更的历史遗传。从主观上来看待种族也是有必要的。Shibutani & Kwan(1965)称,民族的成员是那些自认为是同类的人,他们由情感纽带联系在一起;尽管他们可能有共同的传统,但是更重要的是他们来自共同祖先的信仰。

有关种族的最后一个因素是象征种族的神话。神话是指形成一个种族的理想和信念;种族本身是一个连续的有用的概念。种族神话也起着维持民族的意义界限的作用。

根据这四个方面的因素当我们定义种族身份时就应该考虑到如下几个方面:1. 种族身份未必一定就是少数民族。2. 群体界限的持续,很可能就是显示了这个种族文化上的重要变化。3. 对种族的客观的、实际的特点的描述不完全包括所有的种族现象。4. 象征性的种族特点的力量,这一点常常为人所低估。

## 民族特点

前文已经提到了种族和民族两个概念及其之间的联系。比如说民族是种族的延伸,种族是民族的前身,等等。显然,民族和种族之间的联系非常紧密,很多适用于种族的标准也同样适用于民族。

但是，民族特点是一个更为复杂的概念。

　　Royce（1982）指出，虽然民族和种族都包含"群体"和"人们"这些相同的概念，但是他们并非同一。虽然区别很明显，但是只是程度上而不是原则上的区别。民族主义是出现在现代的一个概念。Kedourie（1961）就把民族主义描述成欧洲发明的一个学说。这种说法包含了三个假定：1. 自然的人类分为不同的民族；2. 这些民族各有自己的特点；3. 他们惟一合法的政府对该民族进行自治。Smith（1971）批判了 Kedourie 对民族主义或民族特征的分析，认为他过于强调民族的负面性和民族语言。他虽然赞同 Kedourie 对民族主义的一些基本的描述，但是在语言方面，Smith 持否定的态度。

　　Rustow（1968）把民族主义和现代主义联系在一起，但是现代主义的一些成分驳斥了民族主义完全来源于社会哲学家的思想和根本变革的社会环境的观点。Barker（1927）接受来源于19世纪的民族的自我意识的观点，在这个意义上，民族是现代的一个发明创造。但是民族是在很多世纪以前就早已存在的，Barker 进一步说明，民族在它成为一个动力之前就是一个存在的概念和事实。民族在概念出现之前就已经存在。Connor（1978）把民族当成一个自我意识的种族群体。Connor 认为民族必须自我界定，而种族由他人界定的这种看法有些误导。他认为不管是民族还是种族都是自我界定的，区别是民族有自我控制的意识。

　　此外对民族的认识还要和国家区分开来。国家是和政治相连的实体，可以是单质的，也可以是多民族的。国家比较容易界定，而民族既有客观方面又有主观方面，界定更难一些。民族的一些特征不那么容易把握，心理纽带和群体的感情联系等都是民族情感的必要条件。自我认识和自我意识是民族主义的标准。民族的客观特征如宗教和语言在构筑民族身份时显得相当重要。所以我们可以说国家是一个和政治、土地单位而民族涉及更多的主观因素，民族是一个有组织的种族文化统一体。

## 语言和方言

在考虑语言和方言的关系时，首先得区分语言和方言两个不同的概念。1921年，Sapir 把语言定义为一个人类独有的自创的符号系统、进行思想情感和愿望方面的交流系统。Morris（1946）把语言描述为在一个社区内具有共同意义的任意的符号系统。首先，语言是一个系统，它具有一定的顺序规则。其次，语言是一个任意的系统。语言的意义是使用者约定俗成的。第三，语言是一定的语言社区内的成员进行交流的工具。由此可以看出，语言的不同是因为他们在把意义分配到声音和符号的方式不一样。

语言被视做交流的工具的同时，Steiner（1975）认为说不同语言的人保存着他们独有身份的秘密。语言可视为隐藏、保密和杜撰的工具。语言的这种功能正好和作为交流工具的功能相反。交流是群体内的现象而隐藏是为了保持群体对世界的掌握不受侵犯。

在作为交流工具上，语言之间的区别是它是一个群体、符号和团结的象征。语言和文化紧密相连，在功能上体现在它的象征功能上。当语言不用于交流时它的象征功能仍保持着重要意义。语言的象征功能可以从美国的移民中体现出来。Eastman（1984）说即使一个群体的成员移民后不再使用原来的语言，但是这种语言还是他们的精神遗产。当语言只具有象征功能时，它便不再是一种真正的语言。

对于语言和方言的区别，人们一般认为，方言之间是可以相互理解，而不同语言之间是不可理解的。当然尽管有一定道理，但是这仍然是一个有争议的说法。人们对于语言有很多的探讨，语言之间的关系应该是平等的，没有高低贵贱之分。但是语言可以视为是反映社会情况的不同的系统。尽管它们可能在复杂程度上并不完全一致。

方言是语言的变体，不同的方言在词汇语法上和发音上有一定的区别。把能否相互理解作为方言的标准的说法并不完全正确，我们还需考虑到以下两点：1. 在理解上有一个程度问题，有些方言之间很好理解，而有些方言之间的交流会有一定的困难。2. 方言之间存在连续体，往往邻近的方言之间更为易懂，而距离较远的方言之间却并不一定。Petyt（1980）对方言的标准进行了补充：第一我们要考虑书面语形式，如果群体之间所说的语言的语音模式不同而书面形式相同，我们可以说他们说的是不同的方言。第二方面涉及政治上的忠贞。中国的普通话和广东话尽管彼此都听不懂，仍属于同一语言的方言。

和语言一样，方言也不应该有好坏之分。有些人认为，标准方言更有美感，让人感觉更愉悦。其实有试验证明这种说法只是个人的主观看法。如果排除内在的语言和美学上的特点，方言还是被人们视为有优劣之分，这种说法是基于方言的社会声望和操该方言的说话者的权势。标准方言往往用于学校教育、官方文件、公开刊物和新闻广播等大众传媒。

**Questions for reflection**：
1. What are the similarities and differences between sociolinguistics and sociology of language?
2. What is the relationship between identity and national identity?
3. What is the difference between language and dialect?

# Educational Language Planning and Linguistic Identity

Peter Sutton

*ABSTRACT: There are cases in which a 'high', form of a language is taught and used in formal situations, but linguistic variation is also caused by geography, ethnicity and socioeconomic class. Certain variants are regarded as inferior and restricted in expressive capacity, and are disadvantageous. The paper suggests that it is possible to map each person's linguistic identity in two dimensions: the number of languages spoken, and the situation-specific variants of each language. Further, it is argued that the distance between a "low" variant and a "high" standard form of a language may present to the "low" learner of a standardized mother tongue a barrier just as great as that posed by the learning of a related foreign language to a speaker of the high variant. It is proposed that greater tolerance be exercised in acceptance of variation and in recognition of linguistic identity, so that this can be built on in the necessary and desirable expansion of linguistic competence, rather than being devalued. The relevance of the communicative approach to language teaching is touched on.*

Zusammenfassung—Es gibt Famille, in denen eine "hohe" Form einer Sprache gelehrt und in formellen Situationen gebraucht wird, aber linguistische Verifiende-rungen werden auch durchGeographie, ethnische Identitat und sozialkonomische Klassen hervorgerufen. Gewisse Varianten gelten hinsichtlich ihres Ausdrucksver-mogens als unterlegen und restriktiv und sind unvorteilhaft. In dem Artikel wird vorgeschlagen, die linguistische Identitat jedes Einzelnen in zwei Dimensionen darzustellen: die Anzahl der gesprochenen Sprachen und die situations spezifische Variante jeder Sprache. Weiterhin wird argumentiert, dab die Distanz zwischen ciner 'niedrigen' Variante und einer "hohen" Standardform einer Sprache fur den "niedrigen" Lernenden einer standardisierten Muttersprache ebenso schwierig ist wie das Erlernen einer verwandten auslandischen Sprache fur denjenigen, der die "robe" Form spricht. Es wird vorgeschlagen, groBere Toleranz durch Akzeptieren der Variation und Anerkennung der linguistischen Identitat zu fiben, so dab man darauf die notwendige und wfinschenswerte Erweiterung der linguistischen Fahig-keit aufbauen kann anstatt sie zu entwerten. Die Relevanz des kommunikativen Ansatzes zum Unterrichten einer Sprache wird kurz behandelt.

Resume—Il existe des cas ou une "haute" forme d'une langue est enseignee et utilisee dans des situations formelles, mais la differentiation est causee egalement par la geographie, l'ethnicite et la classe socioeonomique. Certaines variants sont considerees inferieures, d'une capacite expressive limitee, et sont desavan-tageuses. L'article suggere qu'il est possible de tracer l'identite linguistique de chacun dans deux dimensions: le hombre de langues parlees, et les variantes de chaque langue reliees a des situations speifiques. En plus, on raisonne que la distance entre une variante "basse" d'une langue et la "haute' forme standard peut ( International Review of Education—Internationale Zeitschrifi fiir Erziehungswissenschaf—Revue Internationale de Pgdagogie 37 (1): 133—147, 1991—1991 Unesco Institute for Education and Kluwer Academic Publishers. Printed in the Netherlands.) presenter a l'apprenant, ayant la forme "basse" d'une langue maternelle standardisee, une barriere aussi grande que celle qui se dresse devant celui qui parle la variante haute et qui apprend une langue etrangere apparentee. On propose done qu'une tolerance plus large soit exercee en acceptant la variation et en reconnais-sant l'identitd linguistique, afin que cette derniere serve de fondation pour l'elar-gissement necessaire et souhaitable des competences linguistiques, plutot que d'etre devalorisee. La relevance de l'approche communicative a l'enseignement des langues est mentionnee.

Learners in all educational institutions have previous language experience: as soon as a baby hears its first words, it is unconsciously making its own language map, and no two maps are entirely identical. Speakers of what is known as the same language grow up using different variants of it, but while the existence of geographical and some ethnic variants may be generally, recognized, awareness of the crucial importance of sociolects, and certainly tolerance of them, is not as widespread in educational establishments. In extreme cases, a "high" version of the language, quite unlike the vernacular of even higher socio-economic classes, is taught for formal, written educational use. Where this is not the case, the school sociolect may appear to children of lower SECs to be equally "high" and unrelated to their reality.

## Variants of Language

It is customary to think of a language as having various dialects. Works such as *the Dictionary of American Regional English* (Cassidy 1985) or *the Atlas Linguistique de l'Afrique Centrale* (Dieu 1983) record dialect words peculiar to certain districts, and chart the lines (isoglosses) between languages and dialects. However, there are other "lects" which may be overlooked in language planning. There are well-documented cases of diglossia, where a prestigious (high) form of a language used for formal purposes co-exists with a situationally inferior (low) form used for mundane interchange, for example where "the difference between the colloquial vernacular which the child will hear and speak before entering school and the classical Arabic which is there taught to him..., extends to phonology, vocabulary and grammar" (Malhas 1972:191; compare, for example, the situation of Tamil: Sugathapala de Silva 1975:18).

Even where there is no diglossia, there will be dialectal and sociolectal variation. A recent study in Germany (Kallmeyer 1989) shows that speakers of German are themselves very conscious of the linguistic differences within the one language between their own "sociolect" and those of people they regard as superior or inferior: the distinctions were made plain when lower-class speakers were quoting and thereby imitating the speech of persons they held to be of higher or lower social status.
Differentiation is also caused by geographical location and ethnicity. For

example, the uniformity of the structural base of the Philadelphia dialect... is used only by the white population. The 38% of the Philadelphia population that is black does not share in the underlying system of categories and does not participate in the ongoing changes. (Labov 1987:140)

To sociolect and dialect we can thus add "ethnolect". In the American context, distinctions can be drawn not only between black and white speech, but also within the white English-speaking population:

> a very common type of English used in Buffalo are varieties of ethnic dialects, which we call "ethnolects" (cf. Wolck 1983). They are used by third or later generation descendants of the three major continental European immigrant groups, i. e. , by German, Polish and Italian Americans who have "lost" their ancestral language but retain in their (monolingual) English traces that are diagnostic of their family's linguistic heritage. (Wolck 1989:23)

It is therefore possible to view oneself as ethnically or culturally Polish or Italian, etc., while speaking English.

## Disadvantaged Variants

Academic disadvantage frequently attaches to socioeconomic variants, and in particular to lower class speech which deviates from received pronunciation and grammatical rules. Goffinet and Van Damme (1990), for instance, report in a study of functional illiteracy in Belgium that adults who had dropped out from school claim they did so because the teachers made fun of their lower-class accents.

Speakers of geographically distinct dialects may also be at a disadvantage in the educational context. Gadler (1989) refers to research by Maierhofer in which interviews conducted in a regional non-standard variant of German elicited lively responses from adolescent pupils, while those conducted in standard "high" German produced monosyllabic replies or silence. In the same volume Harris (1989) gives examples of school pupils speaking Irish English giving "wrong" answers to questions posed in standard English because of a difference in the conventional use of tenses. In Irish usage, the influence of the structure of the Gaelic language is strongly felt in English, even though Gaelic itself may be unknown to the speaker.

The perceived social status of geographical dialects and socially determined sociolects varies. In urban societies a rural variant is often regarded by speakers of the received standard with an amused tolerance which they do not accord to an urban variant. Despite such bucolic romanticism, the gap in communication may be just as great.

## Mapping Linguistic Identity

It can thus be seen that a person's mother tongue or preferred language of customary use (and the two concepts are not interchangeable) does not embrace all variants of a given language, and may be limited to a sociolect; dialect or ethnolect which is considered inferior to the standard of "educated" speech. It is also apparent, from the frequency of the use of a language other than the learners' mother tongue as the medium of instruction in education, that some form of bilingualism is common. As migration increases and monocultural nation-states become obsolete, cultural identity becomes more complex, less tied to a geographical location, more individualized, and less static.

That bilingualism is not an absolute term has long been recognized (Mackey 1970; Paulston 1978). Nor is it possible to determine a point at which a dialect should be considered a separate language, but it is expedient to distinguish between whole languages on the one hand, and subsystems on the other, notably sociolects and the various registers of language used in particular situations, identified by the degree of formality and the presence of transaction-specific cant or jargon. Fluency in the range of sociolects and registers varies greatly between speakers and writers of the same language, according to familiarity with the relevant situations, level of education, breadth of reading, etc.

We can therefore suggest that each person, teacher and pupil, road mender and high court judge, inhabits a linguistic space which has two dimensions. This is indicated in Fig. 1, where the horizontal plane represents fluency in sociolects, ergolects (professional jargon) and registers of language appropriate to and derived from a range of situations, while the vertical represents the simpler measure of number of languages known in oral and/or written forms. The "home base" of each speaker is situated at the point of intersection, and competence extends in both dimensions in a fluid manner throughout life. If one were to shade the horizontal squares on the "linguistic map" of the figure, the resulting pattern would be different for each language on the vertical scale. In certain circumstances a speaker is able to communicate satisfactorily and with confidence in one language, while in other situations he or she may be obliged to use another, may indeed be able to choose between two or more, or may fail in all.

Sociocultural and political conditions limit the number of situations in which a language—even a language used elsewhere in all possible contexts—can in fact be used. A study of German-speaking minorities in 27 countries, for example, shows the importance of churches, local newspapers and social gatherings for the maintenance of the language among emigrant communities living in countries which demand quite different languages for communication with public authorities and for schooling (Born and Dickgiesser 1989).

## Codes

There is a view that any language or variants of language, whether dialect, sociolect, ethnolect, ergolect, chthonolect (mother tongue), demolect (community language), politolect (official language), or indeed any other sublect or register, should be termed a "code". It is convenient to use this neutral term to indicate that the use of two and more variants of language is not restricted to bilinguals and even occurs within one language. The derived term code-switching makes plain that we do switch from one register to another in everyday life (high, low, working jargon, etc.) according to the social context. If we are literate, we also switch between written and spoken codes. In terms of Fig. 1, each square for each language is therefore arguably its own code; some will be primarily or exclusively oral, others exclusively written. Written standard languages do not orthographically accommodate all geographical, ethnic or social variants. Transcription can be used for the texts of theatrical performances, for example, using approximate spellings to represent non-standard pronunciation, but it is not just considered inappropriate to write academic texts in every dialect of a language: it is also practically impossible.

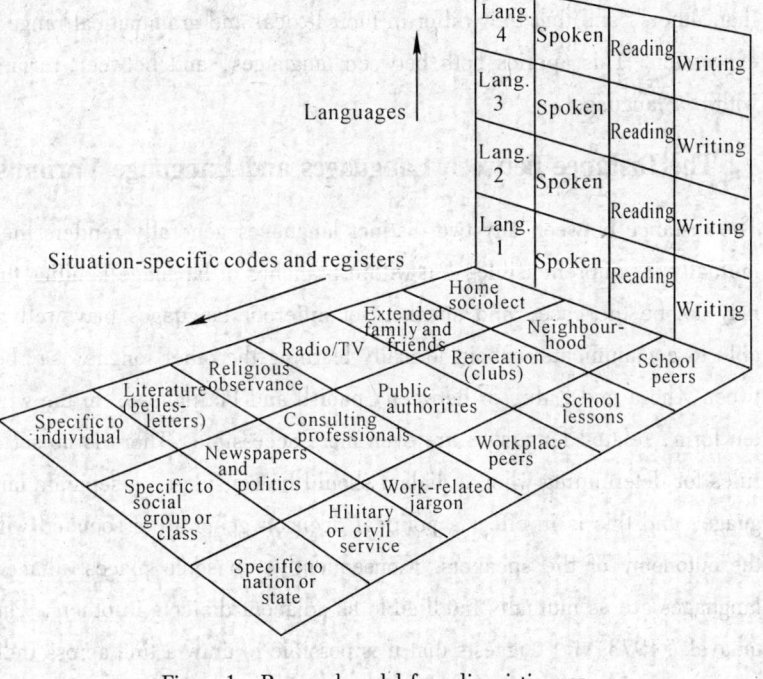

Figure 1  Proposed model for a linguistic map

Bernstein (1971) distinguishes between restricted and elaborated codes. Whether this perception can be accepted depends on how the language is divided up. If, say, a "high" standard language is held to include many situation-related registers and subject-specific jargons, then it is clearly further elaborated than a "lower" variant which uses simple rather than compound sentences and a lexis limited to informal everyday contacts within a narrow socio-economic band. All living codes are in a state of continual change and elaboration, and even those which are restricted in their actual use can potentially be elaborated very swiftly by the incorporation of related variants or vocabulary borrowed from languages conventionally used in other situations. One can nonetheless agree that at any given time and place, some codes are used in a wider range of contexts than others, and that they differ in their lexical and grammatical range of expression. This applies both between languages, and between variants within a language.

## The Distance between Languages and Language Variants

The distance between any two distinct languages generally renders them mutually incomprehensible, but within branches of language families this may not be the case, and speakers of different languages may well be able to communicate without formally learning the other tongue, say between Xhosa and Zulu, or between Spanish and Portuguese. In the written form, related languages are even more accessible. There is no set of rules for determining when a dialect should be considered a separate language, and this is in effect a political decision generally associated with the autonomy of the speakers. Consequently, in some places adjacent languages are as mutually intelligible as adjacent dialects in others. Pattanayak (1973:vii) suggests that it is possible to draw a line across India, and to discover that each dialect spoken along the line is intelligible to its neighbours, while intelligibility between one end of the line and the other is nil. Although one may not subscribe to the view that there can be no language contact without conflict, a proposition treated in the Plurilingua series edited by Nelde (1983-date), it is clear that the propinquity of speakers of languages and variants other than one's own affects every person's linguistic map without any intervention by formal or nonformal educational institutions.

It is therefore possible to suggest that the distance between a variant of a language and the standard, received form of that language, can be as great a barrier to communication and to educational advance as is the distance between one language and another. We may argue that a child speaking a rural or lower-class urban "restricted" sociolect faces a greater difficulty by being expected to function on entry into school in a version of his language which uses unfamiliar grammar, vocabulary and syntax, than does the child from a background where the "high" form is spoken and read, when he learns the familiar grammar and syntax, but unfamiliar vocabulary of a related foreign language. Strength is lent to the hypothesis by the findings of a Canadian study that:

> the cultural or national origin of the parents was far less important than their social class in explaining their differences in values. Thus, the rules governing the education of children of middle-class Portuguese parents were more similar to those for parents of the same social background from Greece, France, the United States, etc., than they were for Portuguese parents of the working class.
> (Lambert 1985:93 original French)

Figure 2 sets out the question schematically. As already indicated, the precise delimitation of sublects is usually unclear. Their number, and their distance: both from each other, from variants of other standards,

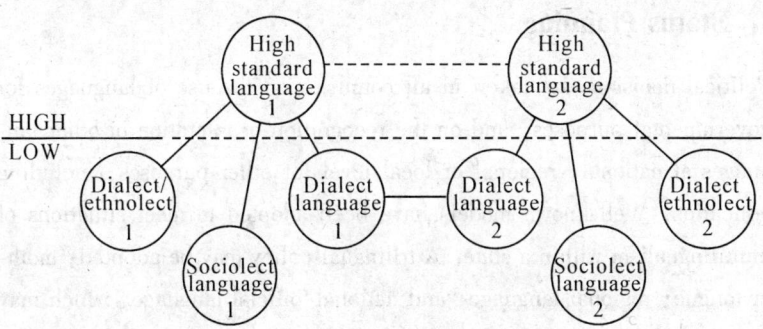

Figure 2  Example of distances between languages and language variants

and from their own notional standard language, will vary. Nonetheless, it may reasonably be speculated that the child is worst off who speaks a "low" variant but is expected to learn a "high" second or foreign language. Corson points to research which indicates that:

> the ability that most children have to pick up everyday uses of a language quickly and easily can be misleading when making judgments about their language proficiency .... Bilingual minority children ... may still have serious problems when they have to carry out the more academic classroom tasks. (Corson 1990: 172)

## The Implications of Code Variation

If we accept that a language is not an indivisible entity, that bilingualism and multilingualism are becoming increasingly common, and that linguistic diversity should be recognized in planning educational activities, then there are implications for decisions on the role to be accorded to each language and sublect (status planning), for attempts to change the vocabulary and structures of languages (corpus planning), and for the teaching of mother tongues, second and foreign languages.

## Status Planning

Political decisions are taken in all countries on the use of languages for governmental purposes, and on the recognition or toleration of other languages at national, regional or local level for other purposes, including education. Well-known models have been adopted to meet situations of multilingualism within a state. A trilingual policy may be adopted: mother tongue, regional language, and national/official language, which may be a residual colonial language (now sometimes replaced by English). In countries with no immediate colonial background, the use of English, in particular, may be necessary in scientific and commercial fields, and it may arguably be taught as a second rather than as a foreign language. That is to say, the classroom may not be the only source of the language, with consequent effects on the methodology that can be used. Where the decision is taken to permit instruction through a medium other than the national or official language, the mother tongue may be used for economically viable or vociferous groups up to a certain grade, or throughout the system, while the amount of coverage given to a second language will vary.

What is of equal importance to these high-level decisions, and is perhaps even more important for those affected, is the status accorded to the variants discussed above. However, whatever decisions on the acceptability of variants are taken at a high level, they are also taken in the classroom and the surrounding society, where teachers, examiners and employers cannot help expressing preference, knowingly or not, for certain forms of a given language, usually closest to their own usage.

Certain squares of language use in the horizontal plane of Fig. 1 have often been blocked off for some members of a society by their perceived or real lack of access to the respective social or employment positions on account of racial prejudice, in which the lack of acceptability of a particular ethnolect plays a major role, as well as on grounds of socio-economic class. The levels of social and linguistic status, and of literacy and educational achievement form a vicious circle:

> the problems experienced by the minorities in acquiring literacy and in academic performance generally are a function of their adaptation to the limited opportunity historically open to them for jobs and other positions in adult life requiring literacy, and where literacy pays off. (Ogbu 1987:151)

There is no easy pedagogical way out of this deadlock, as the answer is also sociopolitical. A helpful approach may be to extend toleration, and a status of acceptability, to a wider range of sublects than has been the case to date. This is not to say that educators should rest content with forms of expression limited in their precision and range by a restricted code, but that each code should be recognized as one of a set of variants which cannot be abolished, ignored or wished away. It has therefore to serve as the starting point for the acquisition of related variants and other languages, and is not "abnormal" or "wrong" in its home context.

## Corpus Planning

Decisions on the use of languages for specific purposes, including government administration, legal proceedings, political debate, journalism or the teaching of natural science, are inextricably related to the ability to express the relevant content in the languages under consideration, both orally and in writing. Major investment may therefore be needed to provide a language hitherto used for other cultural purposes with the vocabulary, and the writing system, of planned new roles. In questions of standardization, the width of the tolerated band of variation is of crucial importance. It is no coincidence that "tolerance" is an engineering term highly relevant to what we may call "language engineering".

Whether efforts at linguistic recovery, reconstruction and expansion will succeed depends not only on their being written down and acquiring new lexis, but also on the usefulness which their speakers perceive them to have. New studies of language loss are being made, which indicate that preservation cannot be guaranteed (Dorian 1987; Weltens et al. 1987). It may also be that alien vocabulary and morphology will be imported into the vernacular, while government lexicographers prefer locally invented terms drawn from the roots of the local language, resulting in another form of diglossia and the widening of the gap between the language of official documents and that of the majority of their readers.

A wider tolerance with regard to the acceptance of alien loan words and dialectal variance may shorten the process, reduce investment needs, expand the vocabulary and accommodate the inevitable. (It should not be forgotten in this context that users of English plundered Latin, Greek and other, non-European languages in the fifteenth and sixteenth centuries to meet the needs for new scientific and trading concepts.)

## Language Teaching

In language policy-making, individuals' competence is seldom regarded: what is thought of is the group identified by language, culture or ethnicity, and the needs of the group or the state for acquisition of second and foreign languages.

Teachers are not provided with linguistic maps of students' knowledge, or of their own, but nonetheless have to function with a class of individual students, and should therefore ideally start from where the learners are, rather than from somewhere different in the hope that their students will catch up before they have gone too far. This applies both to the teaching of a language, and to teaching of other subject matter through the medium of a given language.

## Mother Tongue: the Learners' Home Base

We may imagine learners, individually or in groups, to be familiar with certain streets of a city (their linguistic home base). In order to introduce them to the remainder of the city, the teacher has to go into those streets to guide them, rather than standing in the main square and shouting. Some learners will hear the voice and be curious, while some will ignore it because it is undecipherable. Of the former, some will find the way to the starting point in the square, while others will become confused, discouraged and lost.

To pursue the image further, it is difficult for a teacher to be in two places at once, as when learners start from streets wide apart: this is the case in multilingual, multicultural, and indeed "multisocial" classes. The best that can then be achieved is the sympathetic use of a standardized language by the teacher, the broadcasting of educational messages in the languages and sociolects of the streets by the media and "street workers", and the toleration of variants in educational environments, in order to allow all learners to express themselves until they have enlarged their linguistic maps to include the ability to use the agreed standard language in the appropriate contexts. Even if the generally advocated policy of teaching at least initial literacy and basic education through the medium of the mother tongue is followed, this cannot be successful unless the learner's variant of the mother tongue is accepted as a means of internalizing and recalling what has been learnt.

Although we have been likening the landscape of a language to that of a city in a figurative sense, it is clear that there is frequently some literal truth in the image. Teachers do travel across cities, from middle-class housing to working-class neighbourhoods, and do teach speakers of quite different languages and dialects. Somehow they need to communicate, in other words to develop their own language policy which takes account of the linguistic identity of the learners, and recognizes their own identity too.

If we accept that the distance between "high" and "low" variants can be as great as that between two distinct languages, it begins to appear necessary to teach the standard form of a language almost as a second or foreign language. This is to acknowledge, and even to stress, the distinctions between the variants rather than to pretend that they are essentially the same.

## Second and Foreign Language Teaching

The model of a linguistic map proposed in Figure 1 is not only derived from a simplified view of sociolinguistics, but also owes much to the concept of communicative foreign language teaching adumbrated in the publications arising out of Council of Europe research. It used to be thought that a language should be taught by reference to its grammar, through a series of encoding and decoding exercises. The revolutionary work of Van Ek (1978), Wilkins (1976, 1985) and their associates divides language into quite different categories. It no longer prescribes what is correct, but examines the application of language for functional purposes. Typically, a syllabus is no longer expressed only in parts of speech, tenses, etc., but in functions, and topics or situations:

| Simple | More advanced |
| --- | --- |
| Greeting someone | Telephoning |
| Taking leave | Making compliments |
| Expressing thanks | Giving evasive answers |
| Apologising | Employment interview |
| Asking for something | Conversation: politics |
| etc. | etc. |

There are problems in this approach. Not only has the teacher to take into account the likely situations in which varied learners will apply the language being taught, but also to present the grammatical structures in some kind of order which allows for reinforcement, internalization and transferability of a coherent body of competences. On the other hand, a communicative approach recognizes that grammar is not immutable, that a language is what its users make it, and that it is a tool for the expression of its content rather than an abstract set of rules learnt for their own sake.

Even though the new linguistics of foreign language teaching has been acclaimed in Europe, achievement lags behind what might be expected. This may be on account of inadequate training (Freudenstein 1987), but it is also attributable to the conservatism of language teachers (Byram 1989) and the pull of examination syllabuses.

There is arguably also a sociocultural factor, as indicated above under "Disadvantaged Variants". Whereas languages were taught, and in many places still are taught, by the grammatical method, using situational exemplars from middle-class life which were familiar to the teacher but a barrier to many learners, what has supplanted this is the teaching and testing of a selection of simple exchanges thought to represent the realistic use of language by a larger number of the population. However, this can result in another untypical and restricted set of items:

> All our efforts to create classroom conditions conducive to foreign or intercultural communication seem to be doomed from the start: there is simply no plausible reason for anybody to take part in such fabricated and make-believe language interactions. Foreign language teaching can thus be seen to prevent any true access to life and the world around. Pupils may even be hindered in their personal involvement and expression, in their fantasy and creativity. (Buttjes 1990:54)

It may be that the problem of relevance is particular to the learning of foreign languages and "high" formal dialects, as there are many linguistic stimuli other than the school classroom for those learning to expand their competence in their mother tongue, and usually for those learning a second language.

In addition to the communicative approach, there has also been a move to meet the needs of learners, particularly in multilingual environments, by teaching about language as a phenomenon, rather than plunging straight into the acquisition of any one language. (cf. Pomphrey 1986; Sutton 1989). This teaching of "language awareness" holds some hope of using the multiple home bases of learners as starting points, and may be particularly valuable when it is impossible to use the teaching of a mother tongue for the same purpose of language exploration in a homogeneous, monolingual, monosocial class.

## Conclusion: The Enlarging of Linguistic Identity

The foregoing summary of aspects of linguistic identity indicate that the adoption of a policy on mother tongues, second and foreign languages leads to many other contingent decisions. A main consideration is what variants of a language should be taught, used, tolerated or encouraged. This depends in part on the roles allocated to the language: is it to be used for administration in the interests of national unity, as a regional or local vernacular, as a co-equal with an official language in certain public domains, for scientific research, in cultural performances, or as a purely foreign language with no application within the state? If the last, what uses will realistically be made of it by learners, and is it being taught as a way of conveying cultural information about the speakers of the language, or as a method of giving insight into the phenomenon of language?

It is not possible to teach all of a language, either as mother tongue, second or foreign language. No native speaker can truly claim to be totally fluent, as there will always be professional jargons, slangs, and references which call, if one is honest, for the use of a dictionary. The most that can be hoped for in any language policy is therefore that learners, and incidentally teachers, will be helped to move about the chess board of their linguistic map (see Fig. 1) to the most necessary squares in each relevant language.

The methods chosen for the expansion of learners' linguistic maps must therefore vary, using communicative approaches as well as explication of grammar and language awareness, but the implementation of language policy needs to recognize the existence of individual linguistic identity as well as that of the group. The enlarging of linguistic identity is a part of general education and is very closely related to success in basic and continuing education. Despite all the research in sociolinguistics and language teaching methodology, it is still true, as Paulston said in the last Special Issue of the International Review of Education devoted to language policy in 1978, that "elitist education has never been a problem, and upper and middle class children do perfectly well whether they are schooled in the mother tongue or in the L2 [second language] although we don't really know why" (p. 311). Perhaps it is because they do not have to overcome the double obstacle of climbing from a low to a high linguistic code as well as crossing the bridge to a different language.

## References

BernStein. B. 1971. *Class, Codes and Control.: Theoretical Studies towards a Sociology of Language.* London: Routledge and Kegan Paul.

Born, J. and Dickgiesser, S. 1989. *Deutschsprachige Minderheiten. Ein Uberblick uber den Stand der Forschung fur 27 Lander.* Mannheim: Institut fur deutsche Sprache.

Buttjes, D. 1990. *Teaching Foreign Language and Culture: Social Impact and Political Significance. Language Learning Journal* (September 1990): pp. 53 – 57.

Byram, M. 1989. *Politics and Language Teaching. Curriculum*, 10: pp. 45-50.

Cassidv. F. G. , ed. 1985. *Dictionary of American Regional English.* Vol. 1 (A—C.). Cambridge. MA: Harvard University Press.

Corson, D. 1990. *Language Policy across the Curriculum.* Clevedon (UK): Multilingual Matters.

Dieu, M. Renaud, P. Tadadjen, M. and Breton, R. 1983. *Altas Linguistique de L'Afrique Centrale (ALA C): Structures et Methodes.* Paris: ACCT/CERDOTOLA.

Dorian, N. C. 1987. *Investigating Obsolescence: Studies in Language Contraction and Death.* Cambridge: Cambridge University Press.

Freudenstein, R. 1987. *General Survey of Aspects of Foreign Language Teacher Training.* Paris: Unesco, ref. ED - 87/WS/13.

Gadler. H. 1989. Osterreich. *Soziolinguistica* 3: pp. 85 - 95.

Goffinet. S. and Van Damme, D. 1990. *Functional Illiteracy in Belgium.* Hamburg: Unesco Institute for Education.

Harris. J. 1989. Ireland. *Soziolinguistica* 3: pp. 54 - 60.

Kallmeyer. W. 1989. *Wir und die anderen. Sprachliche Symbolisierung sozialer Identiat und soziale Segmentierung.* In: Nelde. P. H. ed. , *Plurilingua VII: Urban Language Conflict* (pp. 31 - 46). Bonn: Dummler.

Labov. W. 1987. *The Community as Educator.* In: Langer, J. ed. , *Language, Literacy and Culture: Issues of Society and Schooling* (pp. 128 - 146). Norwood NJ: Ablex.

Lambert. W. E. 1985. *Le role du langage dans la formation de l'identite et les relations intergroupes.* In: APLV, *Colloque de Cerisy: Le citoyen de demain et les langues* (pp. 92 - 101). Paris: APLV.

Mackev. W. F. 1970. *The Description of Bilingualism.* In Fishman, J. ed. , *Readings in the Sociology of Language* (pp. 554 - 571). The Hague: Mouton.

Malhas. A. F. 1972. Jordan. In: Opitz. K. ed. . *Mother Tongue Practice in the Schools* (pp. 181–198). Hamburg: Unesco Institute for Education.

Nelde. P. H. , ed. 1983—1989. *Plurilingua. Bonn: Dummler and Brussels: Research Centre on Multilingualism.*

Ogbu. J. O. 1987. *Opportunity Structure. Cultural Boundaries, and Literacy.* In Langer. J. , ed. , *Language Literacy and Culture: Issues of Society and Schooling* (pp. 149–177). Norwood NJ: Ablex.

Pattanayak, D. P. 1973. *Distribution of Languages in India in States and Union Territories.* Mysore: Central Institute of Indian Languages.

Paulston, C. B. 1978. *Education in a Bi/Multicultural Setting. International Review of Education* 24 (3): pp. 309–328.

Pomphrey, C. 1986. *Language Awareness at Hampstead.* ILEA Languages Centre Bulletin (London). Autumn 1986: pp. 17–21.

Sugathapala de Silva, M. W. 1976. *Diglossia and Literacy.* Mysore: Central Institute of Indian Languages.

Sutton. P. 1989. *Language Awareness for Adults.* Adult Education (UK) 61 (4): pp. 319–322.

Van Ek, J. 1978. *The Threshold Level for Modern Language Learning in Schools.* London: Longman.

Weltens, B. , de Bot, K. and van Els. T. eds. , *Language Attrition in Progress.* Dordrecht: Foris

Wikins, D. A. 1976. Notional Syllabuses. Oxford: Oxford University Press.

—1985. *Linguistics in Language Teaching.* London: Edward Arnold.

Wolck. W. 1989. *The Linguistic Resolution of Urban Ethnic Conflict.* In: Nelde, P. H. , ed. , *Plurilingua VII: Urban Language Conflict* (pp. 21–29). Bonn: Dummler.

—1983. *The Role of Language in Defining Ethnic Minorities.* In: Nelde, P. H. , ed. , *Plurilingua I: Current Trends in Contact Linguis-*

tics (pp. 189 – 202). Bonn: Dummler.
[From: Sutton, P. 1991, *International Review of Education*. Vol. 37, No.1, pp. 133 – 147]

## 导读：语言教育计划和语言身份

一般语言都有多个方言，不同的方言具有不同的社会地位。在双语社会里，用于交流的语言有正式和非正式之分。正式的语言具有较高的社会声望。即使是在非双语的社会，不同的方言也常被人视为有优劣之分。方言可以从社会经济角度来进行区分，下层方言常偏离社会中规范的发音和语法系统。地域方言和社会方言之间存在相当大的差别，所以在交流上也会出现障碍。

语言变体：不管是方言、社会变体、种族方言、母语、社区方言、政治方言等任何一种次语言和语域都可以称为语码。语码是一个中性的说法。人们在交流中根据不同的情景选择不同的语域，在必要时进行语码转换。语码转换就是指说话者或写作者从一种语言或语言变体转用另一种语言或语言变体的现象。

两种不同的语言之间互相不可理解，但是同一家系的语言之间的交流则会比较顺畅，这就涉及语言还是方言的问题。前文提到区分语言还是方言，能否相互理解只是一个方面并不是惟一的标准，此外还和政治文化等有密切关系。一些邻近的语言之间也能顺利地进行交流，但它们并不是同一语言的方言。一种语言的某个变体和标准方言之间的距离有时可以大到影响交流和教育的程度。

在语言的使用上，每个国家根据自己的目的比如说教育而制定相应的语言政策。在一个国家里采纳人们所熟知的模式来满足多语社会的需要。在选择语言模式上，一般有三种语言政策：母语，地域方言和民族/官方语言。究竟哪种语言在较量中占优势地位取决于一个国家的社会政治。对于不同方言的容忍和接受也是现在所关注的问题，但是这并不是说教育者以一种限定的语码来传达教育内容。任何一个语码都不可能被人为地消除和忽视。

在语言教育上，如果学生来自不同的方言区，教师则必须使用一种较标准的通用语言来进行教学，同时也应该考虑和尊重学生的语言身份。如果一个社会地位较高的和较低的方言之间的差别太大,两种方言之间的距离可以和两种不同的语言相比时,就有必要教授该语言的标准形式。

**Questions for reflection:**
1. Name some variants of language.
2. Do you agree with the idea that some variants of language are disadvantaged? If not, why?
3. What does second and foreign language teaching focus on at present?
4. How could language variants and code variation influence educational language planning and linguistic identity?

# Socialisation and Classification: Understanding Japanese Society

J. Hendry

## Introduction

Having looked at the ideological position of the family in Japanese society in general, we shall now focus on the very heart of the home to look at the world which is first presented to a Japanese child. Socialisation is the means by which an essentially biological being is converted into a social one, able to communicate with other members of the particular society to which it belongs. A child learns to perceive the world through language, spoken and unspoken, through ritual enacted, and through the total symbolic system which structures and constrains that world. Through socialisation a child learns to classify the world in which it lives, and to impose a system of values upon it.

Much social learning of this sort happens so early that culturally relative

categories are often thought to be 'natural' and 'normal' until a person moves out of his or her society of upbringing. Even then, there is a tendency to describe foreigners as 'strange', 'dirty' or even 'stupid', since their assumptions about the world are different. During the Second World War, for example, the Japanese were described as 'pathologically clean' by their enemies in the United States. It is thus interesting to look at the early training of children in a particular society to try and identify important categories being imparted to them. An understanding of these categories can pave the way for a deeper understanding of relations in later life, and headings found in this chapter cover aspects of Japanese interpersonal relations which are also described elsewhere for adult behaviour.

In Japan, the early period is particularly interesting because mothers and other caretakers of small children are quite assiduous in their efforts to train children in the way they regard as fit and proper to do things. 'The soul of the three-year-old lasts till a hundred', a saying runs, and it is up to the adults around to mould that soul. There is also a high degree of consistency amongst the adults involved in many of their ideas about how children should be trained. There are, of course, regional variations and differences based on social status and occupation, but there are also certain features which seem to be common throughout Japan, no doubt aided by the almost universal influence of television, newspapers and magazines. In this chapter the most important of these common features have been picked out and their role in shaping the child for its membership in society will be discussed.

The socialising role of the kindergarten will also be presented in some detail. Nearly all children are sent to a kindergarten or day nursery for a period of a year or more before they enter school, and this seems to be regarded as an important part of their early education, although it is not compulsory. It is particularly the introduction it provides to interaction with the peer group which is considered important, and thought best to take place before school entry. Various aspects of relations within this group are quite clearly defined and again appear under headings which could also apply to adult interaction. Many of the principles of the approach used in the family are shared by teachers at this early stage, which provides some continuity in introducing the new experience of life in a large group.

## Uchi and Soto

Some of the earliest acquired ideas which are most difficult to dislodge in any society are those associated with dirt and cleanliness. It is all very well to have an understanding at a theoretical level about different kinds of upbringing, but it is much harder to accept behaviour which one's own early training has presented as revolting or disgusting. It seems likely, therefore, that a system of classification associated with notions of dirt and cleanliness is held rather deeply, as Mary Douglas (1970) has pointed out. In Japanese society the distinction between uchi and soto is an example of such a deeply held part of the system of classification.

Uchi and soto translate roughly as 'inside' and 'outside' respectively, and they are probably first learnt by a child in association with the inside and outside of the house in which it lives. They, or parallel words, are also applied to members of one's house as opposed to members of the outside world, and to members of a person's wider groups, such as the community, school or place of work, as opposed to other people outside those groups. The importance of this distinction, and its association with dirt and cleanliness, is illustrated by looking at the ways it is used in training small children.

First of all, uchi and soto are associated with the clean inside of the house, and the dirty outside world, respectively. Japanese houses almost always have an entrance hall where shoes, polluted with this outside dirt, are removed, and it is one of the few inflexible rules enforced by Japanese adults that small children learn to change their shoes every time they go in and out of the house. The anthropologist, Emiko Ohnuki Tierncy, has discussed this practice in some detail (1984: Chap. 2) in terms of the notions of hygiene involved, and she explains that outside is regarded as dirty because that is where germs are thought to be located. This 'outside' is anywhere where there are other people, or other people have been, and the concept is succinctly expressed, she argues, in the term hitogomi, literally 'people-dirt', a word used to refer to crowds.

Moreover, this distinction between the physical inside and outside of the house is reinforced by the use of ritualised phrases of greeting or parting which are uttered when one crosses the threshold, or by those remaining behind to greet or see off others who are coming or going. These phrases are fixed and invariable, and adults take special care to pronounce them carefully with small children, who soon learn to copy them at the appropriate time. Further associations with the supposed pollution of the outside world are expressed in the way children are encouraged when they come into wash, change, and in some houses, even to gargle, again to eliminate the germs they may have encountered while out in the country, children are sometimes held out over the verandah at the side of the house to urinate, and once over the threshold of the front door, anywhere seems to be appropriate for the urine of a small child, even directly in front of the entrance. The toilets of a country house are often physically quite separate from the other rooms, and in most houses a special pair of toilet slippers is provided, which again distinguishes this 'dirty' area from the main part of the house. In the country, too, the gaping hole of the old-fashioned Loo is a real danger to children, as is the steep drop often found at the entrance of the house. Thus, an approach too close in either of these directions will elicit negative response from caretakers, and associate the outside with a danger of falling as well as with possible infection. A similar association will be made in a city house, but for practical reasons more likely to be concerned with traffic and the anonymity of the city streets.

Figure 1: A porch for removing shoes is found at the entrance of every Japanese home. It marks clearly the distinction between uchi and soto worlds.

Figure 1

This association of the outside with danger and fear is actually encouraged in some families, especially by older people, perhaps partly because it seems to work as an effective means of keeping a child close at hand. It is opposed to another association which is consciously built up of security with the inside of the home. Parents take trouble to anticipate the needs of babies and small children, to give them in the early years the abundant attention which they see as necessary to create security and trust in a child, and also to elicit co-operation in following the directives of themselves and other adults. Punishments are avoided where possible, but if their use is necessary, they are often associated with the outside world, rather than with members of the inside of the home. Thus threats may be made about demons, policemen and passing strangers, and a severe punishment is to put a child out of the house altogether.

## Tatemae and Honne

Another way in which the distinction between uchi and soto is made clear to a child is in the way the behaviour of adults varies depending on whether they are inside or outside the house. Put rather simply, this difference in behaviour corresponds to the difference between tatemae or public behaviour, and honne, or one's real feelings. In fact, this association is by no means clear-cut, because members of the family will have close relationships outside the home, and will behave 'publicly' if outsiders are invited into the house. However, the initial physical distinction is applied gradually to the circle of people with whom the child comes into contact, and it will learn to recognize the uchi and soto relations of its family, by participating in changes of behaviour in appropriate circumstances.

The participation is gradually, but firmly encouraged by adults, who will adjust their own levels of politeness according to the situation, and instruct the child about how to adjust his or her level, too. Japanese language has quite clear speech levels, which are chosen according to the relationship between the people involved in a conversation, as well as the context in which they find themselves. The use of polite language also makes possible the maintenance of a certain distance between the conversants, therefore protecting the 'inner feelings' from the probings of an outsider. Other distinctions in Japanese which correspond to that between tatenae and Iwnne, can be translated as 'front' and 'rear', 'face' and 'heart', 'mouth' and 'stomach', and the ability to distinguish between them is regarded as a measure of maturity.

It should be clear, however, that the distinctions are dichotomies only at an ideological level. In practice, there is a range of levels of politeness which varies depending on situations and a variety of relationships, and there are various degrees of closeness as well. A child probably first learns the distinction between the immediate family and the outside world, but will gradually come to recognize wider uchi groups, such as relatives, close neighbours, age-mates and so on, as his or her experience broadens. Even for each of these 'inside' groups, a slightly different type of behaviour will be appropriate.

The importance of these distinctions cannot be overemphasized in explaining features of Japanese society, as will be shown in later chapters, for it is in choosing the appropriate 'face' for a particular occasion that one is able successfully to fulfil one's social role in the world. The 'inner self' is recognised, and children are taught to understand their own selves so that they can project this understanding and devise behaviour which will consider the inner feelings of others. The conscious awareness of different sorts of tatemae behaviour is only learnt gradually, and it is associated with the emphasis placed on another important aspect of Japanese social relations, namely harmony.

## Harmony: Reciprocity and Hierarchy

The concern of adults to create a secure and attentive environment for a small child is part of this wider emphasis in Japanese society on harmony in social relations. It is, of course, an ideal which may or may not be achieved in practice, but much of an adult's training of children is based on the assumption that one should work towards this ideal. Thus, from the very beginning, one should try to maintain a congenial atmosphere with a small child, teaching it the proper way to behave for the sake of behaving properly, rather than for praise or to avoid punishment. An ideal child is a 'bright', cheerful child (akarui, meiro), and, once past the baby stage, a crying child is described as 'strange' or 'peculiar' (Okashii).

This emphasis on harmony also applies to relations between the child and others with whom it may come into contact, and adults take pains to help children playing together to avoid situations of dispute. If a fight does break out, some time will be spent establishing what happened, and who should apologise, with full consultation of the children involved themselves. An apology must then be made clearly, and accepted by the injured party, so that play can resume happily. Two important principles are drawn upon in establishing guilt in such a case, and the same principles are used in pursuit of the aim of establishing and maintaining harmonious relations. They are the principles of hierarchy and reciprocity.

## Reciprocity

Reciprocity is called upon constantly in the way adults teach children to think of others before they act. Essentially it is the principle of 'do as you would be done by' which is being invoked here. Thus a child is exhorted to think of how it would feel if another child were to do to it what it is doing to another child, how it would like it if another child refused to lend a toy when it wanted to borrow one, how it would feel it another child snatched its toy ... and so on. A child must be trained out of its natural selfishness—the word used the selfish, wagarnama, is made up of waga (self) and mama (as it is)—rather implying an untrained state. This is part of a wider general encouragement of children to try and put themselves in the shoes of others before acting.

## Hierarchy

It is of course asking a lot to expect very small children to project themselves in such a way, and the other important principle, that of hierarchy, helps to resolve this problem. Children are made aware of their relative ages from a very early stage, and in case of dispute, an older child is encouraged to give in to a younger child who is not yet old enough to understand. Such encouragement seems to emphasise the long-term advantages of being older, despite temporary deprival, and it seems to be rather a successful method of solving sibling rivalry, as well as quarrels within the neighbourhood. It has the incidental effect of emphasising the superior role, and the responsibility and benevolence associated with it, before the inferior role. This order of learning must be somewhat more palatable than the reverse.

In the family, older children are addressed by younger ones with a term meaning 'older sister' or 'older brother', sometimes as a suffix to their names, and adults make use of this form of address when eliciting 'good' behaviour, perhaps as a demonstration to a younger child. Similar distinctions are made in the wider circle of children in the neighbourhood, for example, and new children entering the group will always be asked for their ages before play can proceed. When adults ask children to play with babies or their younger siblings, they may use a form of request which can be translated as 'do the favour of...', projecting onto the older child a verb which is used for action from a superior to an inferior, and smaller children will learn to ask an older child to play using the converse of this form, used from an inferior to a superior.

These verbs, and terms of address, form part of the system of speech levels mentioned above, and it can be seen that the beginnings of such distinctions are being learned very young. The hierarchical distinctions within a house are sometimes thought appropriate ones to emphasise in teaching a child to use polite language, especially where there are three or more generations living together, but the distinction between uchi and soto may override these differences, so that children will be taught to address the grandparents outside the home more politely than those inside. Speech levels themselves vary greatly with social background, but the general principle of using hierarchy as a means of trying to achieve harmony is widespread.

## Kindergarten: Equality

For a period varying between one and several years before children enter school they will attend a kindergarten or day nursery, which is said, among other things, to introduce them to 'group life' in preparation for school. The class will form a new 'inside' group for a child, a new uchi, to be opposed to the outside world, and various ritual procedures emphasise the nature of the group. Again, children must remove their outside shoes when they come into the classroom, usually changing into special indoor shoes, and they may also have to change their clothes. As the day begins there will usually be some routine activity which the children learn and go through together, involving elements such as songs, chants, movements in time to music, and the reading of the register. There will be a similar routine at the end of the day as the group breaks up.

In contrast to the basically hierarchical relations found in the home and neighbourhood, when children enter kindergarten the emphasis within the class is on the essential equality of members of the group. The children wear uniform, or at least smocks or aprons to make them alike, and they have identical sets of equipment for their activities. The other children in the class are all referred to as 'friends'. These are not special buddies chosen by each child, but up to 39 other children with whom any one child is now to pass a substantial proportion of each day. Of course, any child will form special attachments, and children will also know their relative ages, strengths and so on, but members of the class are regarded as symbolically equal, and this equality is expressed in several ways.

Duties and privileges, for example, are shared out equally by means of a rota system. Thus children take it in turns to be on duty for break and lunch service, which probably involves handing out food and drinks, and also perhaps seeing that the other children are sitting properly before they give the signal to start eating. The children on duty may also be responsible for lining their classmates up for a trip to the hall, and they will probably also take any roles of privilege for the day, like presenting flowers to the altar in an institution with a religious foundation. In this way roles which could, taken out of context, be interpreted as hierarchical, like service, authority and privilege, are equally distributed among all the members of the class. As will be seen elsewhere in Japanese society, apparent hierarchy is often contextual rather than based on any inherent differences in status.

Again, there is much emphasis on creating and maintaining a congenial environment for small children, anti before a child even enters kindergarten much is made of the 'fun' it will have there. This is another part of the emphasis on harmony as an ideal in social relations. Any quarrels are investigated and apologies made. Children are expected to be happy, and anyone who is not, like the crying child, is classed as 'strange' or 'peculiar'. A child who shows reluctance to participate is encouraged to join in, but, if it refuses, will simply be ignored, as the teacher goes about the business of making life 'fun' for all the other children.

This form of classification sets apart a child who appears to be unhappy, by moving it out of the main group and emphasising its difference from the other children. Taken together with the association already established of security with uchi, and fear with soto, and the emphasis on equality of members of the group, this form of ostracism is usually rather effective in encouraging participation. The threat of removal from the group is also used as an effective sanction when an individual child fails to comply with the teacher's directives. A small child at this stage is keen to be just like its mates, and teachers take advantage of and encourage this propensity, making it unattractive to be 'different'.

## Peer Group Pressure

Teachers also take advantage of the propensity of children to impose rules upon themselves (cf. Piaget, 1932), allowing much of the discipline of the group to be generated by the pressure of the peer group. Thus, for example, at the beginning of the day, the routine in which the children participate is initiated by a tune on the piano or organ, played continuously by the teacher until all the children are sitting, or standing in their positions, ready to begin. Those who are slow hold up the whole group, and they are urged by their classmates to hurry up. The same principle is put into practice before break and lunchtime, when the added incentive of hunger ensures rapid co-operation.

In a similar way quarrels are resolved by asking children who witness a dispute to pass judgement on the situation, and decide who was at fault and should therefore apologise. Teachers also appeal to the whole class when pointing out the recalcitrant behaviour of one of their number, asking whether such behaviour is acceptable, and if not, what kind of behaviour is. The personalised collective term mina-san is used to address and refer to the whole group and its needs, and an individual whose behaviour is to the detriment of mina-san is made to feel most uncomfortable. The children are also encouraged to take care of the kindergarten property in the name of its corporate owners, mina-san.

## Cooperation

In general, cooperation is also encouraged in a number of other positive ways. Classroom walls are invariably decorated with cooperative creations to which each child has contributed, like nets full of individually fashioned fishes, or woods full of trees. Marching in formation is another co-operative activity practised in some kindergartens, as are orchestras or choirs. The kindergarten where I worked in Chiba prefecture had an 80-piece orchestra, largely composed of six year olds, which played tolerable renderings of popular Mozart and Vivaldi pieces. The annual sports day usually emphasises cooperation over individual competition, and children are encouraged to exert themselves for the sake of the class, or the area where they live, rather than for their own glory. Popular events include the tug-of-war and the three, or five or seven-legged races, where cooperation is essential for success.

Stories and plays presented to or put on by the children also tend to emphasise the advantages of cooperation over individual endeavour, and a

Japanese version of *The Three Little Pigs*, for example, usually has the first two little pigs escape the attacks of *The Big Bad Wolf* so that they can join the third pig and cooperate in their efforts to entice him down the chimney into the cooking pot. The more usual version found in England, the home of the story, has the first two little pigs being eaten up for their lack of foresight, whereas the third pig uses his individual cunning and cleverness to defeat the wolf. Television programmes for children often reiterate this theme, as a single hero tries unsuccessfully to defeat the monster, or other alien force, until he gains the cooperation of other victims of the danger.

## Self-development

It should be emphasised that the development of the individual child is not neglected in all this collective activity. In the home, the child is, of course, given much individual attention, and one of the first things it is taught as a baby is to respond politely, with the term 'hai', to hearing its own name being called. Parents fill in detailed forms about their children's personal attributes, faults, friends, likes and dislikes, on entering them into kindergarten, and the teachers come to know their charges very well. They pick out individual children for praise or reprimand, and they seek to find ways of dealing with any individual problems they may have. They also maintain close communication with the parents of each child, and in public kindergartens, they visit each child's home at least once a year.

Each child has its own property to take care of in the kindergarten or day nursery, albeit identical to the property of other children, but it must be responsible for its own personal set. It also has personal property at home, and early training includes the specific encouragement to attend to the maintenance and care of these items. Some of the aims of early training, shared by parents and teachers alike, are to develop personal qualities such as perseverance, concentration, effort, independence and self-reliance. Indeed, one of the aims stated by parents in sending their children to pre-school educational establishments is to help them to develop these qualities.

Another often stated aim is that children should learn to think for themselves and understand themselves in order to understand others. By understanding their own needs they are thought to be able to understand the needs of others, and so to work out appropriate behaviour in any situation. They need, parents say, to understand the limits imposed on their self-interest by the needs of others, and the collective needs of the wider group which they join in educational establishments. Thus, a child will gradually learn to exercise self-control in the interest of harmonious social relations.

## Self in the World

In fact, an individual child usually learns to enjoy the advantages of its new identity as a member of a collective group, and sees that it is in fact in its own interest in certain circumstances to put self-interest second. This principle is important throughout school life, and indeed, for many Japanese, on into adult life in relations at work or in the local community. The success of the company, for example, is seen to depend on the co-operation of its individual members, and the success of the members is seen as directly dependent on the success of the company to which they belong. Individuals may also express satisfaction in being part of a greater entity such as this.

Several writers have discussed the Japanese concept of self. Some have suggested that the self as an isolable entity is non-existent, since Japanese people are always defining themselves in reference to other people, or to some group. Others discuss the importance of dependence as a quality of human relations in Japan and oppose this with the independence for which we are supposed to strive in Western societies. Some of the arguments are summarised in Smith (1983:Chap. 3), who continues with an excellent alternative discussion of the issue in terms of social interaction and use of language. Lebra (1976:Chap. 8) discusses various ways in which the concept of 'self' is used in Japanese, and argues that individuality is achieved through introspection.

One of the problems is that 'individualism' and 'individuality' have been associated with 'democracy' and other apparently positively valued aspects of westernisation which were used in the drafting of the 1947 Constitution and new educational tenets. The Japanese words which translate the concepts have quite different connotations, however. The word for individualism (kojinshugi) is seen as little different from that for 'selfishness', which, as we have seen, implies an undesirable, untrained state. The word for 'individuality' (kosei), on the other hand, has become an ideal, and is sought in the pursuit of personal interests and achievements, perfectly acceptable as long as they don't interfere with one's obligations to others. Brian Moeran (1984B) has discussed the 'problem' of individualism in Japanese society in terms of an internal cultural debate.

To return to the child in kindergarten, there is probably little choice. Except for extraordinary cases, like that described in footnote three below, individualism is not really an option. One can either be cooperative or be left out, either be happy or laughed at as 'strange' and 'peculiar'. But this cooperative individual is not losing its individuality or individual identity by participating in group activities. It is merely demonstrating one of the 'faces' it learns to have for different situations. This 'face' is part of the tatemae or "public" behaviour appropriate in this particular context, and an individual will have several such 'faces' for different situations.

These different 'faces' are reflected in different speech forms used on different occasions, and none of them negates the existence of a complete sell using them all. Just as tatemae is distinguished from honne, one's real feelings or intention, behaviour in the group context may be distinguished from the individual who is acting out a role as member of the group. A child who falls down in front of his or her playmates will make every effort to avoid crying and being called 'strange', despite considerable pain. In another context perhaps with a kind-hearted grandmother— the tears may be adjudged appropriate to gain sympathy and special treatment. The same fall, when a child was entirely alone, may be more quickly overcome. These different 'faces' are recognisable in other societies, but they form an integral part of the system of classification in Japan.

## Conclusion

By looking at the early training of a small child we have in fact only touched upon subjects which other studies have discussed in much greater detail as important 'keys' to understanding Japanese people and their ways of thinking. We have, however, isolated some very important indigenous concepts which will recur in the chapters which follow. By seeing how they are first introduced in childhood, we can, I hope, get a feel for how they are acquired by a native speaker. Armed with this 'feel', we can proceed to venture out into the wider world outside the family.

## Notes

1. In reference to groups of people the terms miuchi and tanin oryoso no hito are often used for 'inside' groups and 'outside' people respectively.

2. Omote and ufa, kao and kokoro, kuchi and hara.

3. One exception to this rule is the protagonist of the well-known autobiographical story of Totto-chan (Kuroyanagi, 1981/2), now a popular TV personality in Japan. The book, which is subtitled in English. The little girl at the window, tells the story of a child who never managed to fit in to her class at school, and she was eventually moved to another rather special school.

4. The best known work on this subject is by the psychiatrist Doi Takeo (1973). The essence of the arguement is that the concept amae, which he translates as 'passive love' or 'dependence' is uniquely Japanese and therefore provides a key to understanding. Japanese behaviour. The concept is certainly found elsewhere (e. g. Spanish minar is close), even if there is no easy translation in English, and I have not found the argument particularly helpful from a social point of view. However, a reader with a psychological training might find it useful to follow up.

## References

Doi, TAkeo, *The Anatomy of Dependence* (Trans. by John Bester, Kodansha International, Tokyo, 1973)

Douglas, Mary, *Purity & Danger* (Harmmidsworth, Penguin Books, 1970)

Kuroyanagi, Tetsuko, *Madogiwa no Tottoo-chan* (Kodansha, Tokyo, 1981); Trans. by D. Britten as Totto-chan: *The Little Girl at the Window* (Kodansha, 1982)

Lebra, Takie Sugiyama, *Japanese Patterns of Behaviour* (University Press of Hawaii, Honolulu, 1976) Chapter 8

Moeran, Brian, *Individual, Group and Seishin: Japan's Internal Cultural Debate*, Man, Vol. 19, No. 2 (1984B), pp. 252-266

Ohnuki-Tierney, Emiko, *Illness & Culture in Contemporary Japan* (Cambridge University Press, Cambridge, 1984)

Piaget, J. *The Moral Judgement of the Child* (Routledge & Kegan Paul, London, 1932)

Smith, Robert J., *Japanese Society: Tradition, Self and the Social Order* (Cambridge University Press, Cambridge, 1983)

## Reading

Bachnik, Jane, *Time, Space and Person in Japanese Relationships in Joy Hendry and Jonathan Webber* (eds.) *Interpreting Japanese Society* (Journal of the Anthropological Society of Oxford Occasional Publication, no. 5, Oxford, 1986), pp. 49-75

Benedict, Ruth, *The Chrysanthemum and the Sword* (Routledge & Kegan Paul, London, 1977), Chapter. 12

Hendry, Joy, *Shoes, The Tarly Learning of an Important Distinction in Japanese Society*, in Gordon Daniels (ed.), *Europe Interprets Japan* (Paul Norbury Publications, Tenterden, Kent, 1984)

—Becoming Japanese. *The World of the Pre-school Child* (Manchester University Press, Manchester, 1986)

Koschmann, J. Victor, *The Idioms of Contemporary Japan viii: Tatemae to Honne*, The Japan Interpreter, 9 (1974): pp. 98-104

Maretzki, Thomas W. & Hatsumi, Taira, *An Okinawan Village in Beatrice Whiting* (ed.) *Six Cultures* (John Wiley & Sons, New York, 1963)

Wagatsuma, Hiroshi and George A. De Vos, *Heritage of Endurance:*

*Family Patterns and Delinquency Formation in Urban Japan* (University of California Press, Berkeley 1984)

**Related novel**

Lshiguru, Kazuo, *Pale View of Hills* (Penguin, Harmondsworth, 1983)
[From: Hendry, J. 1987, *Understanding Japanese Society*. London: Croom Helm. Chapter 3, pp. 38-52]

## 导读：社会化与分类：了解日本社会文化

社会化是人由生物个体转化为社会个体，能够和他所在的特定社会其他成员进行交流的过程。我们考察日本家庭的意识形态时，应把视线集中在对孩子的教育和成长过程上。小孩通过语言、礼仪和构成及制约这个世界的符号系统来理解和感知世界。通过社会化，小孩学会对世界进行分类，学会给世界赋予一定的价值体系。

在日本，孩子的成长早期是一个重要的、令人感兴趣的阶段。因为在这个阶段，孩子的母亲和其他抚养人极其卖力地对孩子进行行为规范方面的教育。他们认为"三岁的思想会持续到百年"。父母对孩子的教育一般持有相似的观点，尽管因地位和身份不同而有一定的差异。孩子的早期教育是从幼儿园开始，然后一直持续到成年。

### 内和外

在日本，人们从小就从社会内明白对肮脏和洁净两个不同的概念的区分。人们很难去掉从小就获得的思想。对于"内"和"外"的概念，小孩是和屋里屋外联系起来的。同时，他们也明白屋里人和屋外人的区别。最初，"内"和"外"的概念和屋里的洁净和屋外的肮脏联系在一起。人们进屋要把鞋子脱掉，因为上面沾了外面的灰尘和脏物。此外，"内""外"的概念还指内外不同的礼仪和语言。同时，在他们看来外面的世界总是和危险与害怕联系在一起，而屋内则安全得多。父母总是有意识地建立一种家庭内的安全感,也积极参与小孩的生活,给予他们较多的注意。

与"内、外"相联系的还有:小孩在家庭内外的不同行为有明显的区分,因为家庭成员之间有着更为密切的关系。孩子必须学会在不同的场合表现不同的行为和使用不同的语言和礼仪。父母也积极参与社会活动以指导和教育小孩来适应社会。人们会针对不同的社会关系和不同的社会环境采取不同的礼貌措施;孩子也逐渐学会区分亲朋好友之间的亲疏关系;同时家庭内成员也极力保持一种和谐的相互关系。

当然,日本的家庭也有很明确的等级关系,家庭成员、兄弟姐妹之间长幼有序。对彼此的称呼也因家庭地位的不同而不一样,也由于这样的原因,人们教育孩子要使用礼貌的语言,尤其是当几代人聚在一起的时候。

小孩在上学前一般会去幼儿园读上一两年时间的书,小孩在幼儿园的每个班里形成了自己的内圈。在这个圈子里面,成员平等是极为重要的一个方面。小孩年龄相当,在幼儿园穿统一的服装,轮流值日,以平等的身份参与班里的事务。同时,幼儿园强调小孩以主人翁的态度来对待园里的生活,创造一个和谐宜人的环境,建立同学之间的良好的人际关系。幼儿园的老师也利用小孩的性格特点制订一定的规则和纪律来规范他们的行为。如果发现有孩子顽皮和犯错,老师会让全班同学来进行判断和评价,指出这个孩子的错误所在,并督促其改正。此外,孩子的合作精神也是幼儿园所重视培养的一个重要方面。幼儿园的教室是由小孩自己动手布置的,园里成立的合唱团和管弦乐队也是培养孩子的团队精神的重要活动。每年幼儿园还会举行运动会,其中的拔河比赛和其他游戏性的体育运动,这些活动既需要孩子的个人努力又强调他们的团结合作精神和集体荣誉感。

应该指出的是所有这些集体活动并不忽视孩子的自我发展。教师不仅对小孩在家庭里所受到的教育和得到的关注比较清楚,还了解他们的父母或监护人的情况,并和家长保持着密切的联系。幼儿园要求小孩必须保管好自己的物品,培养他们的独立的性格,并对个人品格进行必要的训练。训练的另外一个目的是学会思考自己和理解自己以便理解别人。通过了解自己的需要，学会替别人着想并了解别人的需要。幼儿园同时也训练他们在不同的情况下表现恰当的行为，逐渐学会对自己的行为进行自控。

当小孩进入幼儿园开始集体生活时，一般会感到集体生活的快乐，也能认识到自己的身份，把自己真正当成集体的一员。小孩从小就懂得自己生活在一个集体当中，应该把集体的利益放在第一位，而个人利益应该置于其次。日本人在界定自己时总是以他人或群体作为参照。尽管在西方，个人主义和个性是和民主联系起来的，但是在日本，个人主义却有不同的含义。在他们眼里，个人主义和自私没有多少区别；而个性则是他们的理想和追求的目的。在他们看来，人们要么合作要么被淘汰出局，要么开心地和人们相处要么被嘲讽为陌生人或异类。他们也非常注重面子，主张在不同的情景下做出适当的行为。

通过对日本孩子的早期教育的研究，我们可以从侧面了解日本人和他们的思维方式。

**Questions for reflection：**
1. What is the difference between "uchi" and "soto"; "tatemae" and "honne" to a Japanese child?
2. How is a Japanese child educated in a kindergarten?
3. What is the relationship between self-identity and social identity for a Japanese child?

# National and Other Identities

A. D. Smith

The year 429 marked a turning-point for Athens. In that year Pericles, after thirty years as the Athenian leader, succumbed to the plague that ravaged Athens. From that moment Athens' power visibly declined.

In the same year Sophocles staged what many consider to be his greatest tragedy, Oedipus Tyrannos (Oedipus the King). It is sometimes seen as the playwright's warning to his countrymen about the perils of pride and power, but its central theme is the problem of identity.

The play opens with a plague. But this one ravages Thebes, not Athens. We soon learn that it has been sent by the gods because of an unsolved murder long ago, that of the Theban King, Laius. Shortly after that murder on the road to Delphi Oedipus arrived in Thebes and freed the city from the terror of the Sphinx by correctly answering her riddles. Oedipus became king, married the widowed queen, Jocasta, and had with her four children, two boys and two girls.

At the beginning of the play Oedipus promises that he will discover the unclean presence that has brought the plague and must be banished. He sends for the blind seer, Teiresias; but Teiresias only answers darkly that he, Oedipus, is the unclean presence who must be sent into exile. Oedipus suspects that Teiresias has been put up to such an accusation by Jocasta's scheming brother Creon. But Jocasta heals their quarrel and reveals that her former husband, Laius, was murdered by robbers at a place 'where three roads meet'. This stirs Oedipus' memory of a moment when he killed some strangers. One man, however, survived, and on his return to Thebes begged to be sent away to the pastures. Oedipus sends for him. He must find out what happened to Laius.

A messenger arrives from Corinth and brings the news that Polybus, the king of that city and Oedipus' father, has died. This prompts Oedipus to reveal why he left Corinth long ago, never to return. It was because of an oracle from Delphi, which said that he would kill his father and marry his mother. Even now he cannot return to Corinth for fear of marrying his mother, Merope.

But the Corinthian messenger has a surprise for Oedipus. He is not, after all, the son of the king and queen of Corinth. He was a foundling given to the royal couple because they were childless, and he was given to them by none other than the messenger himself long ago when he was a shepherd on Mount Cithaeron. If the messenger had not received him from his counterpart, the Theban shepherd, Oedipus would have died of exposure, his little feet swollen from the thongs that pierced them: hence his name, Oedipus (Swollen-foot). Who is this Theban shepherd, and where did he get the child with the pierced feet? Jocasta has realized the terrible truth and begs Oedipus to desist. He refuses. He must find out 'who he is'. Jocasta rushes out and hangs herself. Oedipus exults:

> Let all come out, however vile! However base it be,
> I must unlock the secret of my birth. The woman,
> With more than woman's pride, is shamed by my low origin.
> I am the Child of Fortune, the giver of good,
> And I shall not be shamed. She is my mother;
> My sisters are the Seasons; my rising and my falling
> March with theirs. Born thus, I ask to be no other man
> Than that I am, and will know who I am.

The Theban shepherd is now brought in. He turns out to be the same man who fled when Laius was murdered, and the very man who gave the baby to the Corinthian messenger on Mount Cithaeron long ago, rather than let it die of exposure. Reluctantly at first, in mounting terror later, the Theban shepherd reveals the truth: he was the trusted servant of Laius and Jocasta; they gave him the baby to expose on Mount Cithaeron; it was because of an oracle; the baby was the child of Laius and Jocasta...

Oedipus rushes out, finds Jocasta hanging from the ceiling and blinds himself. The rest of his life becomes one long quest, first in Thebes, thenin exile with Antigone, for the meaning of his strange destiny; until, in the grove of the Eumenides in Colonus outside Athens, the earth itself swallows him up, and by that act he hallows Athens for ever. That was the poet's last thought, in 406 BC, at the end of his long life.

## Multiple Identities

There are many motifs, and more than one level, in Sophocles' play. But the question of identity, collective as well as individual, broods over the action. 'I will know who I am': the discovery of self is the play's motor and the action's inner meaning, but each 'self' that Oedipus uncovers is also a social self, a category and a role, even when it proves to be erroneous for Oedipus. Only after the shattering revelation of 'who he is' does he begin to glimpse the meaning of his destiny. He is not a successful ruler, a normal husband and father, or saviour of his city. In turn, he becomes a defiling presence, a murderer, a low-born slave, a foreigner, a child of Fortune. Only at the end does he see what, though sighted, he was unable to 'see and what only Teiresias, the blind seer, could see, he will become another Teiresias, another blind seer, with the power to heal and save through his suffering and his unique fate.

In Sophocles' drama Oedipus traverses a series of categories and roles. These roles and categories are at the same time so many collective identities, well known to fifth century Greeks. Even if they had no experience of kingship or murder, ancient Greeks were well acquainted with the symbolic and mythical significance of such subjects. The very strangeness of Oedipus' ultimate fate made the false roles he consecutively 'put on' seem familiar and easily intelligible.

Oedipus, like the other heroes whose exploits were, dramatized by the Athenian tragedians, represented the normal person placed in unusual circumstances and set apart by a unique fate. He is normal in so far as the roles he occupied before the revelation of his 'origins represent so many collective identities' and 'locations'. Like others, Oedipus has a series of such role-identities-father, husband, king, even hero. His individual identity is, in large part, made up of these social roles and cultural categories or so it would appear until the moment of truth; then his world is turned upside down, and his former identities are shown to be hollow.

The tale of Oedipus throws into sharp relief, the problem of identity. It reveals the way in which the self is composed of multiple identities and roles—familial, territorial, class, religious, ethnic and gender. It also reveals how each of these identities is based on social classifications that may be modified or even abolished. The revelation of Oedipus' birth teaches us that another, unseen world touches our material world, turns its social categories upside down and destroys all familiar identities.

What are these categories and roles of which each individual self is normally composed?

Most obviously and fundamentally, the category of gender. If not immutable, gender classifications are universal and pervasive. They also stand at the origin of other differences and subordinations. We are in many subtle as well as overt ways defined by our gender, as are many of our opportunities and rewards in life. At the same time the very universality and all-encompassing nature of gender differentiation makes it a less cohesive and potent base for collective identification and mobilization. Despite the rise of feminism in specific countries, gender identity, which spans the globe, is inevitably more attenuated and taken for granted than other kinds of collective identity in the modern world. Geographically separated, divided by class and ethnically fragmented, gender cleavages must ally themselves to other, more cohesive identities if they are to inspire collective consciousness and action.

Second, the category of space or territory. Local and regional identity is equally widespread, particularly in pre-modern eras. Localism and regionalism also appear to possess the cohesive quality that gender differentiation generally lacks. But the appearance often proves to be deceptive. Regions easily fragment into localities, and localities may easily disintegrate into separate settlements. Only rarely do we meet a powerful and cohesive regional movement, as in the Vendae during the French Revolution; but, as in this case, its unity is likely to derive as much from ideology as from ecology. In most other cases 'regionalism' is unable to sustain the mobilization of its populations with their separate grievances and unique problems. Besides, regions are geographically difficult to define; their centres are often multiple and their boundaries ragged.

A third type of collective identity is socioeconomic, the category of social class. Oedipus fear that he prove to be 'slave-born' mirrors the ancient Greek fears of slavery and poverty—fears that have often provided the motors of political action; even when slavery was replaced by serfdom. In Marx's sociology class is the supreme; indeed the only relevant, collective identity and the sole motor of history. Certain kinds of social class—aristocracies of various kinds, bourgeoisies, proletariats—have sometimes provided bases for decisive political and military action. Sometimes: not always, not even frequently. United action by an 'aristocracy' is less common than factional conflicts within aristocracies. Conflicts of sectors and fractions of a national bourgeoisie are not uncommon, starting with the French Revolution itself, let alone conflict between the bourgeoisies of different nations. As for the working class, while the myth of the international brotherhood of the proletariat is widely accepted, that of the unity of workers: within a given nation is equally prevalent and important, as workers divide into industrial sectors and along skill levels. Workers' revolutions are almost as rare as peasant ones; in both cases, sporadic, localized revolts have been the norm.

The difficulty with treating social class as a basis for an 'enduring collective identity is its limited emotional appeal and lack of ' cultural depth. Whether we define 'class', with Marx, as a relationship to the means of production or, with Weber, as an aggregate of those with identical life-chances in the market, there are clear limits to any attempt to use class as a basis for a sense of identity and community. Classes, like gender divisions, are often territorially dispersed. They are also largely categories of economic interest, and are hence likely to subdivide according to differences in income and skill levels. Besides, economic factors are subject to rapid fluctuations over time; hence the chances of retaining different economic: groups within a class-based community are likely to be slim. Economic self-interest is not usually the stuff of stable collective identities.

There is a further aspect of class identity that both favours and militates against the formation of a stable community: 'Class' signifies a social relationship. There are always two or more classes in a given social formation in conflict, which helps to sharpen class differences, and hence identities, as studies of working-class culture in Britain have revealed. At the same time, by definition, only part of a given territorially bounded population will be included in such class identities. If a more inclusive collective identity covering the whole population in that territory were to emerge, it would necessarily be of quite a different kind from an identity based on class and economic interests. Such wider collective identities might even challenge more restricted class identities, and perhaps undermine or divide them through an appeal to quite different criteria of categorization.

This is just what has often happened. Both religious and ethnic identities have striven to include more than one class within the communities created on their bases. Religious communities, where they aspire to be Churches, have appealed to all sectors of a given population or even across ethnic boundaries. Their message is either national or universal. It is never addressed to a particular class as such, even when in practice the religion is reserved for, or primarily aimed at, a particular class. Fifth-century Mazdakism in Sassanid Persia was undoubtedly a movement of social justice for the lower classes, but its message was, in principle, universal. Similarly, Anglicanism in eighteenth-century England was largely an upper-class and middle-class preserve, although in principle open to any Englishman. Many different forms of 'class religion' noted by Weber suggest the close links between class and religious identities and the frequent 'sliding' from one to the other.

Nevertheless, 'religious identity' is based on quite different criteria from those of 'social class' and emerges from quite different spheres of human need and action. Whereas class identities emerge from the sphere of production and exchange, religious identities derive from the spheres of communication and socialization. They are based on alignments of culture and its elements—values, symbols, myths and traditions, often codified in custom and ritual. They have therefore tended to join in a single community of the faithful all those who feel they share certain symbolic codes, value systems and traditions of belief and ritual, including references to a supra-empirical reality, however impersonal, and imprints of specialized organizations, however tenuous.

Religious communities are often closely related to ethnic identities. While the 'world religions' sought to overstep, and abolish, ethnic boundaries, most religious communities coincided with ethnic groups. The Armenians, Jews and Monophysite Amhara offer classic instances of this coincidence, as did the Copt before the Arab conquest of Egypt. The relationship can be even closer. What began as a purely religious community may end up as an exclusive ethnic community. The Druse, a schismatic Muslim sect founded in Egypt but persecuted there, removed to the fastnesses of Mount Lebanon, where they welcomed Persians and Kurds as well as Arabs into their ranks for about ten years in the early eleventh century. But, with the death of their last great teacher, Baha'al Din (AD1031), proselytization ceased. Membership of the community became fixed, largely because of fear of religious foes outside. Entry to, and exit from, the community of the faithful was no longer permitted. Soon the Druse became as much a community of descent and territory. To be a Druse today, therefore, is to belong to an 'ethno-religious' community.

Even now many ethnic minorities retain strong religious bond and emblems. Catholics and Protestants in Northern Ireland, Poles, Serbs and Croats, Maronites, Sikhs, Sinhalese, Karen and Shi'i Persians are among the many ethnic communities whose identity is based on religious criteria of differentiation. Here, too, as John Armstrong demonstrates, it is easy to 'slide' from one type of identity to another, and overlap is frequent. For the greater part of human history the twin circles of religious and ethnic identity have been very close, if not identical. Each people in antiquity possessed its own gods, sacred texts, rituals, priesthoods and temples, even where minority or peasant groups might also share in the dominant religious culture of their rulers. Even in early medieval Europe and the Middle East the world religions of Islam and Christianity sometimes subdivided into ethnically demarcated Churches or sects, as with the Armenians and Copts and, later, the Persian Shi'ites. Though one cannot argue conclusively for ethnic causation, there are enough circumstantial cases to suggest strong links between forms of religious identity, even within world religions, and ethnic cleavages and communities.

Nevertheless, analytically the two kinds of cultural collective identity must be clearly distinguished. Religious community may, after all, divide an ethno-linguistic population, as happened among the Swiss or Germans and in Egypt. For a long time religious cleavages prevented the emergence of a strong and enduring ethnic consciousness among these populations—until the era of nationalism succeeded in uniting the community on a new, political basis. Similarly, though world religions like Buddhism and Christianity may be adapted to pre-existing ethnic communities that they in turn reinforce, as in Sri Lanka and Burma, they may equally help to erode ethnic differences, as happened to several barbarian peoples when they converted to Christianity and merged with neighbouring peoples, as was the case with Angles, Saxons and Jutes in England.

In the next chapter I shall explore the particular features of ethnic identity that mark it off from other, including religious identities. For the moment the similarities between religious and ethnic identity need to be stressed. Both stem from similar cultural criteria of classification. They frequently overlap and reinforce one another. And singly or together, they can mobilize and sustain strong communities.

# The Elements of 'National' Identity

One kind of collective identity, so important and widespread today, is barely mentioned in Sophocles' Theban plays. Though they sometimes hinge on conflict between cities, they never raise the question of 'national' identity. Oedipus' identities are multiple, but being 'foreign' (i.e. non-Greek) is never one of them. Collective conflicts are, at most, wars between Greek city-states and their rulers. Did this not, in fact, mirror the state of ancient Greece in the fifth century BC?

It was Friedrich Meinecke who in 1908 distinguished the Kultur-nation, the largely passive cultural community, from the Staatsnation, the active, self-determining political nation. We may dissent from his use of these terms, indeed from the terms themselves; but the distinction itself is valid and relevant. Politically, there was no 'nation' in ancient Greece, only a collection of city-states, each jealous of its sovereignty. Culturally, however, there existed an ancient Greek community, Hellas, that could be invoked, for example by Pericles, in the political realm— usually for Athenian purposes. In other words we can speak of a Greek cultural and ethnic community but not of an ancient Greek nation.

This suggests that whatever else it may be. What we mean by national identity involves some sense of political community; however tenuous. A political community in turn implies at least, some common institutions and a single code of rights and duties for all the members of the community. It also suggests a definite social space, a fairly well demarcated and bounded territory, with which the members identify and to which they feel they belong. This was very much what the philosophies had in mind when they defined a nation as a community of people obeying, the same laws and institutions within a given territory.

This is, of course, a peculiarly Western conception of the nation. But then the Western experience has exerted a powerful, indeed the leading, influence on our conception of the unit we call the nation. A new kind of policy—the rational state—and a new kind of community—the territorial nation—first emerged in the West, in close conjunction with each other. They left their imprint on subsequent non-Western conceptions, even when the latter diverged from their norms.

It is worth spelling out this Western or 'civic' model of the nation in more detail. It is, in the first place, a predominantly spatial or territorial conception. According to this view, nations must possess compact, well-defined territories. People and territory must, as it were, belong to each other, in the way that the early Dutch, for example, saw themselves as formed by the high seas and as forging (literally) the earth they possessed and made their own. But the earth in question cannot be just anywhere; it is not any stretch of land. It is, and must be, the 'historic' land, the 'homeland', the 'cradle' of our people, even where, as with the Turks, it is not the land of ultimate origin. A 'historic land' is one where terrain and people have exerted mutual and beneficial influence over several generations. The homeland becomes a repository of historic memories and associations, the place where 'our' sages, saints and heroes lived, worked, prayed and fought. All this makes the homeland unique. Its rivers, coasts, lakes, mountains and cities become 'sacred' places of veneration and exaltation whose inner meanings can be fathomed only by the initiated, that is, the self-aware members of the nation. The land's resources also become exclusive to the people; they are not for 'alien' use and exploitation. The national territory must become self-sufficient. Autarchy is as much a defence of sacred-homelands as of economic interests.

A second element is the idea of a patria, a community of laws and institutions with a single political will. This entails as least some common regulating institutions that will give expression to common political sentiments and purposes. Sometimes, indeed, the patria is expressed through highly centralized and unitary institutions and laws, as in post-Revolutionary France, though even there the various regions retained their local identities into the early twentieth century. At the other extreme we find unions of separate colonies, provinces and city-states, whose federal institutions and laws are designed as much to protect local or provincial liberties as to express a common will and common political sentiments. Both the United States of America and the United Provinces of the Netherlands offer well-documented cases of such national unions. In many ways the primary purpose of the Union of Utrecht in 1579 and of the Netherlands' States General was to protect the ancient liberties and privileges of the constituent provinces, which had been so rudely assailed by Habsburg policies of centralization under Charles V and Philip II. Nevertheless, the ferocity and duration of the war against Spain soon bred a sense of common purpose and identity (quite apart from Calvinist influence) that expressed a growing Dutch. National political community, albeit incomplete, is concurrent with the growth of a sense of legal and political community we may trace a sense of legal equality among the members of that community. Its full expression is the various kinds of 'citizenship' that sociologists have enumerated, including civil and legal rights, political rights and duties, and socioeconomic rights. Here it is legal and political rights that the Western conception considers integral to its model of a nation. That implies a minimum of reciprocal rights and obligations among members and the correlative exclusion of outsiders from those rights and duties. It also implies a common code flaws over and above local laws, together with agencies for their enforcement, courts of final appeal and the like. As important is the acceptance that, in principle, all members of the nation are legally equal and that the rich and powerful are bound by the laws of the patria.

Finally, the legal equality of members of a political community in its demarcated homeland was felt to presuppose a measure of common values and traditions among the population or at any: rate its 'core' community. In other words, nations must have a measure of common culture and a civic ideology, a set of common understandings and aspirations, sentiments and ideas that bind the population together in their homeland. The task of ensuring a common public, mass culture has been handed over to the agencies of popular socialization, notably the public system of education and the mass media. In the Western model of national identity nations were seen as culture communities, whose members were united, if not made homogeneous, by common historical memories, myths, symbols and traditions. Even where new, immigrant communities equipped with their own historic cultures have been admitted by the state, it has taken several generations before their descendants have been admitted (in so far as they have been) into the circle of the 'nation' and its historic culture through the national agencies of mass socialisation.

Historic territory, legal-political community, legal political equality of members, and common civic culture and ideology; these are the components of the standard, Western model of the nation. Given the influence of the West in the modern world, they have remained vital elements, albeit in somewhat altered form, in most non-Western conceptions of national identity. At the same time a rather different model of the nation sprang up outside the West, notably in Eastern Europe and Asia. Historically, it challenged the dominance of the Western model and added significant new elements, more attuned to the very different circumstances and trajectories of non-Western communities.

We can term this non-Western model an 'ethnic' conception of the nation. Its distinguishing feature is its emphasis on a community of birth and native culture. Whereas the Western concept laid down that an individual had to belong to some nation but could choose to which he or she belonged, the non-Western or ethnic Concept allowed no such latitude. Whether you stayed off your community or emigrated to another, you remained ineluctably, organically, a member of the community of your birth and were forever stamped by it. A nation, in other words, was first and foremost a community of common descent.

This ethnic model also has a number of facets. First, obviously, is the stress on descent—or rather, presumed descent—rather than territory. The nation is seen as a fictive 'super-family', and it boasts pedigrees and genealogies to back up its claims, often tracked down by native intellectuals, particularly in East European and Middle Eastern countries. The point here is that, in this conception, the nation can trace its roots to an imputed common ancestry and that therefore its members are brothers and sisters, or at least cousins, differentiated by family ties from outsiders.

This emphasis on presumed family ties helps to explain the strong popular or demotic element in the ethnic conception of the nation. Of course, the 'people' figure in the Western model too. But there they are seen as a political community subject to common laws and institutions. In the ethnic model the people, even where they are not actually mobilized for political action, nevertheless provide the object of nationalist aspirations and the final rhetorical court of appeal. Leaders can justify their actions and unite disparate classes and groups only through an appeal to the 'will of the people', and this makes the ethnic concept more obviously 'inter-class' and 'populist' in tone, even when the intelligentsia has little intention of summoning the masses into the political arena. Popular mobilization therefore plays an important moral and rhetorical, if not an actual, role in the ethnic conception.

Similarly, the lace of law in the Western civic model is taken by vernacular culture, usually languages and customs in the ethnic model. That is why lexicographers, philologists and folklorists have played a central role in the early nationalisms of Eastern Europe and Asia. Their linguistic and ethnographic research into the past and present culture of the 'folk' provided the materials for a blueprint of the 'nation-to-be', even where specific linguistic revivals failed. By creating a widespread awareness of the myths, history and linguistic traditions of the community, they succeeded in substantiating and crystallizing the idea of an ethnic nation in the minds of most members, even when, as in Ireland and Norway, the ancient languages declined.

Genealogy and presumed descent ties, popular mobilization, vernacular languages, customs and traditions: these are the elements of the very different route of nation formation; traveled by many communities in Eastern Europe and Asia and one that constituted a dynamic political challenge. It is, as we shall see a challenge that is repeated to this day in many parts of the world, and it reflects the profound dualism at the heart of every nationalism. In fact every nationalism contains civic and ethnic elements: in varying degrees and different forms. Sometimes civic and territorial elements pre-dominate; at other times it is the ethnic and vernacular components that are emphasized. Under the Jacobins, for example, French nationalism was essentially civic and territorial; it preached the unity of the republican patrie and the fraternity of its citizens in political-legal community. At the same time a linguistic nationalism emerged, reflecting pride in the purity and civilizing mission of a hegemonic French culture preached by Barlre and the Abbe Gregoire. In the early nineteenth century French cultural nationalism began to reflect more ethnic conceptions of the nation, whether Frankish or Gallic; later these became validating charters for radically different ideals of France. The clerical-monarchist: Right was particularly wedded to genealogical and vernacular conceptions of an 'organic' nation, which it opposed to the republican territorial and civic model, notably during the Dreyfus Affair.

Nevertheless, even during the most severe conflicts mirroring opposed models of the nation certain fundamental assumptions, tied the warring parties together through a common nationalist discourse. In the French example just cited both republicans and monarchists accepted the idea of France's 'natural' and historic territory (including Alsace). Similarly, there was no real dispute about the need to inculcate national ideals and history through a mass; public education system, only about some of its content (notably the Catholic dimension). Devotion to the French language was also universal. Similarly, nobody questioned the individuality of France and the French as such; differences arose only over the historical content of that uniqueness and hence the lessons to be drawn from that experience.

This suggests that behind the rival models of the nation, stand certain common beliefs about what constitutes a nation as opposed to any other kind of collective, cultural identity. They include the idea that nations are territorially bounded units of population and that they must have their own homelands; that their members share a common mass culture and common historical myths and memories; that members—have reciprocal legal rights and duties under a common legal system; and that nations possess a common division of labour and system of production with mobility across the territory for members. These are assumptions, and demands, common to all nationalists and widely accepted even by their critics, who may then go on to deplore the ensuing global divisions and conflicts created by the existence of such nations.

The existence of these common assumptions allows us to list the fundamental features of national identity as follows:
1. a historic territory, or homeland
2. common myths and historical memories
3. a common, mass public culture
4. common legal fights and duties for all members
5. a common economy with territorial mobility for members.

A nation can therefore be defined as a named human population sharing a historic territory, common myths and historical memories, a mass, public culture, a common economy and common legal rights and duties for all members.

Such a provisional working definition reveals the complex and abstract nature of national identity. The nation, in fact, draws on elements of other kinds of collective identity, which accounts not only for the way in which national identity can be combined with these other types of identity-class, religious or ethnic—but also for the chameleon—like permutations of nationalism, the ideology, with other ideologies like liberalism, fascism and communism. A national identity is fundamentally multi-dimensional; it can never be reduced to a single element, even by particular factions of nationalists, nor can it be easily or swiftly induced in a population by artificial means.

Such a definition of national identity also sets it clearly apart from any conception of the state. The latter refers exclusively to public institutions, differentiated from, and autonomous of, other social institutions and exercising a monopoly of coercion and extraction within a given territory. The nation, on the other hand, signifies a cultural and political bond, uniting in a single political community all who share an historic culture and homeland. This is not to deny some overlap between the two concepts, given their common reference to an historic territory and (in democratic states) their appeal to the sovereignty of the people. But, while modern states must legitimate themselves in national and popular terms as the states of particular nations, their content and focus are quite different.

This lack of congruence between the state and the nation is exemplified in the many 'plural' states today. Indeed, Walker Connor's estimate in the early 1970s showed that only about 10 percent of states could claim to be true 'nation-states', in the sense that the state's boundaries coincide with the nation's and that the total population of the state share a single ethnic culture. While most states aspire to become nation-states in this sense, they tend to limit their claims to legitimacy to an aspiration for poetical unity and popular sovereignty that, even in old-established Western states, risks being challenged by ethnic communities within their borders. These cases, and there are many of them, illustrate the profound gulf between the concepts of the state and the nation, a gulf that the historical material to be discussed shortly underlines.

## Some Functions and Problems of National Identity

Let me recapitulate. National identity and the nation are complex constructs composed of a number of interrelated components ethnic, cultural, territorial, economic and legal-political. They signify bonds of solidarity among members of communities united by shared memories, myths and traditions that may or may not find expression in states of their own but are entirely, different from the purely legal and bureaucratic ties of the state. Conceptually, the nation has come to blend two sets of dimensions, the one civic and territorial, the other, ethnic and genealogical, in varying proportions in particular cases. It is this very multi-dimensionality that has made national identity such a flexible and persistent force in modern life and politics, and allowed it to combine effectively with other powerful ideologies and movements, without losing its character.

We can illustrate this multi-faceted power of national identity by looking at some of the functions it fulfils for groups and individuals. In line with the dimensions listed above, we can conveniently divide these functions into 'external' and 'internal' objective consequences.

The external functions are territorial, economic and political nations, first, define a definite social space within which members must live and work, and demarcate an historic territory that locates a community in time and space. They also provide individuals with 'sacred centres', objects of spiritual and historical pilgrimage, that reveal the uniqueness of their nation's 'moral geography'.

Economically, nations underwrite the quest for control over territorial resources, including manpower. They also elaborate a single division of labour, and encourage mobility of goods and labour, as well as the allocation of resources between members within the homeland. By defining the membership, the boundaries and the resources, national identity provides the rationale for ideals of national autarchy.

Politically, too, national identity underpins the state and its organs, or their pre-political equivalents in nations that lack their own states. The selection of political personnel, the regulation of political conduct and the election of governments are grounded in criteria of national interest, which is presumed to reflect the national will and national identity of the inclusive population.

But perhaps the most salient political function of national identity is its legitimation of common legal rights and duties of legal institutions, which define the peculiar values and character of the nation and reflect the age-old customs and mores of the people. The appeal to national identity has become the main legitimation for social order and solidarity today.
National identities also fulfil more intimate, internal functions for individuals in communities. The most obvious is the socialization of the members as nationals and ' citizens '. Today this is achieved through compulsory, standardized, public mass education systems, through which state authorities hope to inculcate national devotion and a distinctive, homogeneous culture, an activity that most regimes pursue with considerable energy under the influence of nationalist ideals of cultural authenticity and unity?

The nation is also called upon to provide a social bond between individuals and classes by providing repertoires of shared values, symbols and traditions. By the use of symbols flags, coinage, anthems, uniforms, monuments and ceremonies members are reminded of their common heritage and cultural kinship, and feel strengthened and exalted by their sense of common identity and belonging. The nation becomes a ' faith-achievement' group, able to surmount obstacles and hardships.

Finally, a sense of national identity provides a powerful : means of defining and locating individual selves in the world, through the prism of the collective personality and its distinctive culture. It is through a shared, unique culture that we are enabled to know 'who we are' in the contemporary world. By rediscovering that culture we 'rediscover' ourselves, the authentic self, or so it has appeared to many divided and disoriented individuals who have had, to contend with the vast changes and uncertainties of the modern world.

This process of self-definition and location is in many ways the key to national identity, but it is also the element that has attracted most doubt and scepticism. Given the wide range of human attitudes and perceptions, it is hardly surprising if nationalists, their critics and the rest of us have been unable to agree on the criteria for national self-definition and location. The quest for the national self and the individual's relationship to it remains the most baffling, element in the nationalist project.

These doubts are both philosophical and political. Because of the many kinds of national self that present themselves in practice (a natural result of the multifaceted nature of the nation), nationalist doctrine has been attacked as logically contradictory or incoherent. The indeterminacy of national criterion and their vague, shifting, often arbitrary character in the writings of nationalists have undermined the ideology's credibility, even where respect has been accorded to individual nationalist propositions such as the idea of cultural diversity. At best the idea of the nation has appeared sketchy and elusive, at worst absurd and contradictory.

Intellectual scepticism is paralleled by moral condemnation. In the name of 'national identity' people have allegedly been willing to surrender their own liberties and curtail those of others. They have been prepared to trample on the civil and religious rights of ethnic, racial and religious minorities whom the nation could not absorb. International, or more accurately inter-state, relations have similarly suffered. The ideal of the nation, transplanted across the globe from its Western heartlands, has brought with it confusion, instability, strife and terror, particularly in areas of mixed ethnic and religious character. Nationalism, the doctrine that makes the nation the object of every political endeavour and national identity the measure of every human value, has since the French Revolution challenged the whole idea of a single humanity, of a world community and its moral unity. Instead nationalism offers a narrow, conflict-laden legitimation for political community, which inevitably pits culture communities against each other and, given the sheer number and variety of cultural differences, can only drag humanity into a political Charybdis.

This is a familiar indictment, and its scope and intensity proclaim the emotional and political power of the ideal that it so utterly condemns. But an ideal and an identity that can fulfil so many functions, collective and individual, are bound to have the most varied social and political consequences, given the variety of circumstances in which nationalists must operate. We could, equally, catalogue the benign effects of nationalism: its defence of minority cultures; its rescue of 'lost' histories and literatures; its inspiration for cultural renascences; its resolution of 'identity crisis'; its legitimation of community and social solidarity; its inspiration to resist tyranny; its ideal of popular sovereignty and collective mobilization; even the motivation of self-sustaining economic growth. Each of these effects could, with as much plausibility, be attributed to nationalist ideologies as the baneful consequences listed by critics. No more striking, or revealing, testimony could be offered to the ambiguous power of national identity and nationalism or to their profound relevance, for good or ill, to most people in most areas of the world today.

Why this should be so, and what the deeper roots of the power exerted

today by national identities are, we must now explore.
[From: Smith, A. D. 1991, *National Identity*. Harmondsworth: Penguin. Chap 1. pp. 1-18]

## 导读：民族身份与多重其他身份

　　本篇文章从古希腊悲剧家索福克勒斯的著名悲剧《俄狄普斯王》开始，讨论人的身份的复杂性。索福克勒斯的《俄狄普斯王》主题丰富，不限于一个层面，但是对于身份的探讨，不管是集体的还是个人的，始终是该剧关注的一点。"我将知道我是谁"：自我发现是这部戏剧的原动力和行为的内在意义。俄狄普斯所发现的自我也是一种社会性的自我，一种类属和一种角色。只有当他粉碎对自我身份的发现时他才考虑自己命运的意义。他不是一个成功的统治者、一个合格的丈夫和父亲，也不是他所在的城市的拯救者，相反，他以一个肮脏的形象出现：谋杀者、出身卑微的奴隶、外国人、命运女神之子。

　　在索福克勒斯的悲剧中，俄狄普斯王对自己所属的类别和充当的一系列的角色进行了全面的考察，这些类别和角色是许多身份的共同集合体。这一点为当时的5世纪的希腊人所熟知。索福克勒斯笔下所描述的俄狄普斯王代表了不寻常的环境下的普通人，只是他的命运特殊而已。在别的方面他和普通人没什么两样，他的身份也是由社会角色和文化范畴组成的。只是在有关他身份的真相揭露之后他的世界才发生彻底的变化，而他原来的身份开始变得空洞。

　　俄狄普斯王的故事展示了作为人的自我是由多重身份和角色组成的：家庭、领地、阶级、民族、宗教和性别。同时也说明了人的每一种身份都是基于可以改变或消除的社会分类。俄狄普斯的身份的揭示也让我们明白那些看不见的世界会影响我们的现实世界，会使我们的社会类属发生颠倒，也会破坏我们的家庭身份。那么每个人所属的范畴和角色一般是由什么组成的呢？

　　首先，最明显和最基本的范畴是人的性别。对于人的性别的划分是最为普遍的，而性别也是人的其他方面差异的根源。尽管女权主义在一些国家兴起，但是性别身份在全球范围内要比其他的社会身份更为想当然。性别身份，不管人们的地域分布有多广，阶级和民族身份有多么不同，人们都可以因为性别而联合起来，性别身份是一种更能激起人们的集体意识和行为的身份。

其次，是空间和地域范畴。地方主义和乡土观念具有性别身份所没有的凝聚力。但是这一点有时候又具有一定的欺骗性。地区常常被分为一些小的区域，而这些区域又分为更小的居住地。此外，对地区在地理上的界定也有一定的困难。

人的另外一个重要的身份是社会经济的集体身份，社会阶级范畴。俄狄浦斯害怕自己被证实为奴隶出身，说明古希腊人害怕奴隶身份和贫穷。在马克思的社会学里，阶级是高于一切的，是和历史发展相关的惟一的动力。把社会阶级作为一种持续的集体身份的困难是有限的情感感染力和文化深度的不足。阶级身份还可以对一个社团的形成产生有利或不利的影响。阶级标志着一种社会关系，在一个特定的社会中总有两个或更多的阶级处于矛盾斗争之中。

宗教身份与社会阶级所基于的标准不同，阶级身份源于生产和交换，而宗教身份源自交流和社会化。宗教身份基于相似的文化和文化成分——价值观、象征、神话和传统，这些以习俗和礼仪的社会形式存在。人们常会加入一个他们拥有共同的象征准则、价值体系和信念传统的社团。

宗教团体往往与民族身份紧密相关，世界宗教总会跨越、消除民族界限。许多宗教团体正巧与民族团体重合，这样的关系会更为紧密。有些由宗教开始的团体最后发展成了民族社团。

## 民族身份的要素

索福克勒斯的戏剧里没有提到的一个重要的、广泛的集体身份便是民族身份。民族身份包括了政治实体的某些意义。反过来一个政治实体至少又包括了对全体成员的一些共同机构和对权利义务的单一标准。它也暗含着有让它的成员有归属感的一定的社会空间和一定界限的领土。在西方的观念中,民族最突出的是空间和领土的概念。根据这种观点,民族必须有自己较为密集而疆域分明的领土。人们和领土之间有着相互归属的关系。而人们的领土概念包括了历史的土地,家乡的土地、人们的出生地。

民族身份的第二个要素是国家或故土(patria),即有单个的政治意志的法律和制度的实体。它至少包含了一些共同的规章制度以表达共同的情感和目的。随着法律和政治社团意义的发展,我们开始寻求社团内成员的法律平等。这种平等主要表现为多种"公民权利",如民事的法律权利,政治权利和义务,社会经济权利。在西方的观念中法律权利和政治权利是民族权利中不可分割的整体。

最后,在一定疆域的政治实体内,在任何情况下法律平等都是全体成员的共同价值观和传统的前提。也就是说民族必须有一套共同的文化和意识形态的标准和尺度,有共同的认识、目标、情感和观念使得人们在他们共同的土地上结合在一起。历史上的领土,法律政治社团,成员在法律政治上的平等,共同的文化和意识形态,这些都是西方民族模式的标准。

把民族身份的基本特点归纳起来有如下五点:
1. 历史上的领土,或者家园
2. 共同的神话和历史记忆
3. 共同的大众文化
4. 所有成员的共同的法律权利和义务
5. 有随着领土流动的成员的共同经济

因此民族可以定义为具有共同历史领土、共同神话、历史记忆、大众文化、共同经济和共同的法律权利义务的一类人。这种定义显示了民族身份的复杂性。

## 民族身份的功能和问题

民族身份具有多个维面,在功能方面也是多元的,我们可以把民族身份的功能分为"外在的"和"内在的"两个方面。

外在的功能指的是领土、经济和政治方面。首先民族身份界定了民族成员生活和工作的社会区域，划分了历史上民族存在的土地，也为每个成员提供了一个精神和宗教信仰的"神圣"中心。经济上，民族控制着土地和人力资源。他们对劳动力进行分工，鼓励商品和劳动力的流动，并对资源进行配置。政治上民族身份巩固国家及其机构，或者在还没有成立国家之前做前期的努力。民族身份最为显著的政治功能是使法律机构所确立的共同的法律权利和义务合法化。

民族身份还为社团成员执行一些内部的功能。最为显然的是使成员的国民和公民身份社会化。现在民族身份的这种功能主要通过义务的、标准的、全民教育来实现，政府也通过这种途径来灌输民族忠诚的思想和民族独有的文化。民族身份也通过共有的价值观、象征意义和传统来连接社会个体和各个阶层。最后民族身份还通过民族集体的品格和独有的文化为个体在世界中进行自我界定和寻求自身定位的方法。

自我界定和自我定位的过程在许多方面对民族身份来说是非常重要的，但是其中的一些因素也引起了诸多质疑。考虑到人的态度和感知的不同，民族主义者、批评家和普通民众会对民族的自我界定和自我定位持不同的标准。对自我界定和自我定位的怀疑主要在于哲学和政治两个方面。

**Questions for reflection：**
1. What are the multiple identities of the individual self?
2. What elements does national identity include?
3. Point out some functions and problems of national identity?

# Ethnic Groups and Boundaries

Fredrik Barth

This collection of essays addresses itself to the problems of ethnic groups and their persistence. This is a theme of great, but neglected, importance to social anthropology. Practically all anthropological reasoning rests on the premise that cultural variation is discontinuous: that there are aggregates of people who essentially share a common culture, and interconnected differences that distinguish each such discrete culture from all others. Since culture is nothing but a way to describe human behaviour, it would follow that there are discrete groups of people, i. e. ethnic units, to correspond to each culture. The differences between cultures, and their historic boundaries and connections, have been given much attention; the constitution of ethnic groups, and the nature of the boundaries between them, have not been correspondingly investigated. Social anthropologists have largely avoided these problems by using a highly abstracted concept of society to represent the encompassing social system within which smaller, concrete groups and units may be analysed. But this leaves untouched the empirical characteristics and boundaries of ethnic groups, and the important theoretical issues which an investigation of them raises.

Though the naive assumption that each tribe and people has maintained its culture through a bellicose ignorance of its neighbours is no longer entertained, the simplistic view that geographical and social isolation have been the critical factors in sustaining cultural diversity persists. An empirical investigation of the character of ethnic boundaries, as documented in the following essays, produces two discoveries which are hardly unexpected, but which demonstrate the inadequacy of this view. First, it is clear that boundaries persist despite a flow of personnel across them. In other words, categorical ethnic distinctions do not depend on an absence of mobility, contact and information, but to entail social processes of exclusion and incorporation whereby discrete categories are maintained despite changing participation and membership in the course of individual life histories. Second, one finds that stable, persisting, and often vitally important social relations are maintained across such boundaries, and are frequently based precisely on the dichotomized ethnic statuses. In other words, ethnic distinctions do not depend on an absence of social interaction and acceptance, but are quite to the contrary, often the very foundations on which embracing social systems are built, interaction in such a social system does not lead to its liquidation through change and acculturation; cultural differences can persist despite inter-ethnic contact and interdependence.

## General Approach

There is clearly an important field here in need of rethinking. What is required is a combined theoretical and empirical attack: we need to investigate closely the empirical facts of a variety of cases, and fit our concepts to these empirical facts so that they elucidate them as simply and adequately as possible, and allow us to explore their implications. In the following essays, each author takes up a case with which he is intimately familiar from his own fieldwork, and tries to apply a common set of concepts to its analysis. The main theoretical departure consists of several interconnected parts. First, we give primary emphasis to the fact that ethnic groups are categories of ascription and identification by the actors themselves, and thus have the characteristic of organizing interaction between people. We attempt to relate other characteristics of ethnic groups to this primary feature. Second, the essays all apply a generative viewpoint to the analysis: rather than working through a typology of forms of ethnic groups and relations, we attempt to explore the different processes that seem to be involved in generating and maintaining ethnic groups. Third, to observe these processes we shift the focus of investigation from internal constitution and history of separate groups to ethnic boundaries and boundary maintenance. Each of these points needs some elaboration.

## Ethnic Group Defined

The term ethnic group is generally understood in anthropological literature (Narroll 1964) to designate a population which:
1. is largely biologically self-perpetuating
2. shares fundamental cultural values, realized in overt unity in cultural forms
3. makes up a field of communication and interaction
4. has a membership which identifies itself, and is identified by others, as constituting a category distinguishable from other categories of the same order.

This ideal type definition is not so far removed in content from the traditional proposition that a race = a culture = a language and that a society = a unit which rejects or discriminates against others. Yet, in its modified form it is close enough to many empirical ethnographic situations, at least as they appear and have been reported, so that this meaning continues to serve the purposes of most anthropologists. My quarrel is not so much with the substance of these characteristics, though as I shall show we can profit from a certain change of emphasis; my main objection is that such a formulation prevents us from under-society and culture. This is because it begs all the critical questions: standing the phenomenon of ethnic groups and their place in human while purporting to give an ideal type model of a recurring empirical form, it implies a preconceived view of what are the significant factors in the genesis, structure, and function of such groups.

Most critically, it allows to assume that boundary maintenance is unproblematical and follows from the isolation which the itemized characteristics imply racial difference, cultural difference, social separation and language barriers, spontaneous and organized enmity. This also limits the range of factors that we use to explain cultural diversity: we are led to imagine each group developing its cultural and social form in relative isolation, mainly in response to local ecologic factors, through a history of adaptation by invention and selective borrowing. This history has produced a world of separate peoples, each with their culture and each organized in a society which can legitimately be isolated for description as an island to itself.

## Ethnic Groups as Culture-bearing Units

Rather than discussing the adequacy of this version of culture history for other than pelagic islands, let us look at some of the logical flaws in the viewpoint. Among the characteristics listed above, the sharing of a common culture is generally given central importance. In my view, much can be gained by, regarding this very important feature as an implication or result, rather than a primary and definitional characteristic of ethnic group organization. If one chooses to regard the bearing aspect of ethnic groups as their primary characteristic this has far-reaching implications. One is led to identify and distinguish ethnic groups by the morphological characteristics of the cultures of which they are the bearers. This entails a prejudged viewpoint both on (1) the nature of continuity in time of such units, and (2) the locus of the factors which determine the form of the units.

1. Given the emphasis on the culture-bearing aspect, the classification of persons and local groups as members of an ethnic group must depend on their exhibiting the particular traits of the culture. This is something that can be judged objectively by the ethnographic observer, in the culture-area tradition, regardless of the categories and prejudices of the actors. Differences between groups become differences in trait inventories;

the attention is drawn to the analysis of cultures, not of ethnic organization. The dynamic relationship between groups will then be depicted in acculturation studies of the kind that have been attracting decreasing interest in anthropology, though their theoretical inadequacies have never been seriously discussed. Since the historical provenance of any assemblage of culture traits is diverse, the viewpoint also gives scope for an ethnohistory which chronicles cultural accretion and change, and seeks to explain why certain items were borrowed. However, what is the unit whose continuity in time is depicted in such studies? Paradoxically, it must include cultures in the past which would clearly be excluded in the present because of differences in form—differences of precisely the kind that are diagnostic in synchronic differentiation of ethnic units. The interconnection between 'ethnic group' and 'culture' is certainly not clarified through this confusion.

2. The overt cultural forms which can be itemized as traits exhibit the effects of ecology. By this I do not mean to refer to one fact that they reflect a history of adaptation to environment; in a more immediate way they also reflect the external circumstances to which actors must accommodate themselves. The same group of people, with unchanged values and ideas, would surely pursue different patterns of life and institutionalize different forms of behaviour when faced with the different opportunities offered in different environments? Likewise, we must expect to find that one ethnic group, spread over a territory with varying ecologic circumstances, will exhibit regional diversities of overt institutionalized behaviour which do not reflect differences in cultural orientation. How should they then be classified if overt institutional forms are diagnostic? A case in point is the distributions and diversity of Pathan local social systems, discussed below: ( p. 117 ff. ). By basic Pathan values, a Southern Pathan from the homogeneous, lineage-organized mountain

areas, can only find the behaviour of Pathans in Swat so different from, and reprehensible in terms of, their own values that they declare their northern brothers no longer Pathan. Indeed, by 'objective' criteria, their overt pattern of organization seems much closer to that of Panjabis. But I found it possible, by explaining the circumstances in the north, to make Southern Pathans agree that these were indeed Pathans too, and grudgingly to admit that under those circumstances they might indeed themselves act in the same way. It is thus inadequate to regard overt institutional forms as constituting the cultural features which at any time distinguish an ethnic group—these overt forms are determined by ecology as well as by transmitted culture. Nor can it be claimed that every such diversification within a group represents a first step in the direction of subdivision and multiplication of units. We have well-known documented cases of one ethnic group, also at a relatively simple level of economic organization, occupying several different ecologic niches and yet retaining basic cultural and ethnic unity over long periods [cf., e.g., inland and coastal Chuckchee (Bogoras 1904 – 1909) or reindeer, river, and coast Lapps (Gjessing, 1954)].

In one of the following essays, Blom (p. 74 ff.) argues cogently on this point with reference to central Norwegian mountain farmers. He shows how their participation and self-evaluation in terms of general Norwegian values secures them continued membership in the larger ethnic group, despite the highly characteristic and deviant patterns of activity which the local ecology imposes on them. To analyse such cases, we need a viewpoint that does not confuse the effects of ecologic circumstances on behaviour with those of cultural tradition, but which makes it possible to separate these factors and investigate the non-ecological cultural and social components creating diversity.

## Ethnic Groups as an Organizational Type

By concentrating on what is socially effective, ethnic groups are seen as a form of social organization. The critical feature then becomes item (4) in the list on p. 11 the characteristic of self-ascription and ascription by others. A categorical ascription is an ethnic ascription when it classifies a person in terms of his basic, most general identity, presumptively determined by his origin and background. To the extent that actors use ethnic identities to categorize themselves and others for purposes of interaction, they form ethnic groups in this organizational sense.

It is important to recognize that although ethnic categories take cultural differences into account, we can assume no simple one-to-one relationship between ethnic units and cultural similarities and differences. The features that are taken into account are not the sum of 'objective' differences, but only those which the actors themselves regard as significant. Not only do ecologic variations mark and exaggerate differences; some cultural features are used by the actors as signals and emblems of differences, others are ignored, and in some relationships radical differences are played down and denied. The cultural contents of ethnic dichotomies would seem analytically to be of two orders: (i) overt signals or signs, the diacritical features that people look for and exhibit to show identity, often such features as dress, language, house-form, or general style of life, and (ii) basic value orientations: the standards of morality and excellence by which performance is judged. Since belonging to an ethnic category implies being a certain kind of person, having that basic identity, it also implies a claim to be judged, and to judge oneself, by those standards that are relevant to that identity. Neither of these kinds of cultural 'contents' follows from a descriptive list of cultural features or cultural differences; one cannot predict from first principles which features will be emphasized and made organizationally relevant by the actors. In other words, ethnic categories provide an organizational vessel that may be given varying amounts and forms of content in different socio-cultural systems. They may be of great relevance to behaviour, but they need not be; they may pervade all social life, or they may be relevant only in limited sectors of activity. Where is thus an obvious scope for ethnographic and comparative descriptions of different forms of ethnic organization.

The emphasis on ascription as the critical feature of ethnic groups also solves the two conceptual difficulties that were discussed above.

1. When defined as an ascriptive and exclusive group, the nature of continuity of ethnic units is clear: it depends on the maintenance of a boundary. The cultural features that signal the boundary may change, and the cultural characteristics of the members may likewise be transformed, indeed, even the organizational form of the group may change—yet the fact of continuing dichotomization between members and outsiders allows us to specify the nature of continuity, and investigate the changing cultural form and content.

2. Socially relevant factors alone become diagnostic for membership, not the overt, 'objective' differences which are generated by other factors. It makes no difference how dissimilar members may be in their overt behaviour—if they say they are A, in contrast to another cognate category B, they are willing to be treated and let their own behaviour be interpreted and judged as A's and not as B's; in other words, they declare their allegiance to the shared culture of A's. The effects of this, as compared to other factors influencing actual behaviour, can then be made the object of investigation.

## The Boundaries of Ethnic Groups

The critical focus of investigation from this point of view becomes the ethnic boundary that defines the group, not the cultural stuff that it encloses. The boundaries to which we must give our attention are of course social boundaries, though they may have territorial counterparts. If a group maintains its identity when members interact with others, this entails criteria for determining membership and ways of signalling membership and exclusion. Ethnic groups are not merely or necessarily based on the occupation of exclusive territories; and the different ways in which they are maintained, not only by a once-and-for-all recruitment but by continual expression and validation, need to be analysed.

What is more, the ethnic boundary canalizes social life—it entails a frequently quite complex organization of behaviour and social relations. The identification of another person as a fellow member of an ethnic group implies a sharing of criteria for evaluation and judgement. It thus entails the assumption that the two are fundamentally 'playing the same game', and this means that there is between them a potential for diversification and expansion of their social relationship to cover eventually all different sectors and domains of activity. On the other hand, a dichotomization of others—as strangers, as members of another ethnic group, implies a recognition of limitations on shared understandings, differences in criteria for judgement of value and performance, and a restriction of interaction to sectors of assumed common understanding and mutual interest.

This makes it possible to understand one final form of boundary maintenance whereby cultural units and boundaries persist. Entailed in ethnic boundary maintenance are also situations of social contact between persons of different cultures: ethnic groups only persist as significant units if they imply marked difference in behaviour, i. e. persisting cultural differences. Yet where persons of different culture interact, one would expect these differences to be reduced, since interaction both requires and generates a congruence of codes and values—in other words, a similarity or community of culture (cf. Barth 1966, for my argumentation on this point). Thus the persistence of ethnic groups in contact implies not only criteria and signals for identification, but also a structuring of interaction which allows the persistence of cultural differences. The organizational feature which, I would argue, must be general for all inter-ethnic relations is a systematic set of rules governing inter-ethnic social encounters. In all organized social life, what can be made relevant to interaction in any particular social situation is prescribed (Goffman 1959). If people agree about these prescriptions, their agreement on codes and values need not extend beyond that which is relevant to the social situations in which they interact. Stable inter-ethnic relations presuppose such a structuring of interaction: a set of prescriptions governing situations of contact, and allowing for articulation in some sectors or domains of activity, and a set of proscriptions on social situations preventing inter-ethnic interaction in other sectors, and thus insulating parts of the cultures from confrontation and modification.

## Poly-ethnic Social Systems

This of course is what Furnivall (1944) so clearly depicted in his analysis of plural society: a poly-ethnic society integrated in the market place, under the control of a state system dominated by one of the groups, but leaving large areas of cultural diversity in the religious and domestic sectors of activity.

What has not been adequately appreciated by later anthropologists is the possible variety of sectors of articulation and separation, and the variety of poly-ethnic systems which this entails. We know of some of the Melanesian trade systems in objects belonging to the high-prestige sphere of the economy, and even some of the etiquette and prescriptions governing the exchange situation and insulating it from other activities. We have information on various traditional polycentric systems from S. E. Asia (discussed below, Izikowitz p. 135 ff.) integrated both in the prestige trade sphere and in quasi-feudal political structures. Some regions of S. W. Asia show forms based on a more fully monetized market economy, while political integration is polycentric in character. There is also the ritual and productive cooperation and political integration of the Indian caste system to be considered, where perhaps only kinship and domestic life remain as a prescribed sector and a wellspring for cultural diversity. Nothing can be gained by lumping these various systems under the increasingly vague label of 'plural' society, whereas an investigation of the varieties of structure can shed a great deal of light on social and cultural forms.

What can be referred to as articulation and separation on the macro-level corresponds to systematic sets of role constraints on the micro-level. Common to all these systems is the principle that ethnic identity implies a series of constraints on the kinds of roles an individual is allowed to play, and the partners he may choose for different kinds of transactions. In other words, regarded as a status, ethnic identity is superordinate to most other statuses, and defines the permissible constellations of statuses, or social personalities, which an individual with that identity may assume. In this respect ethnic identity is similar to sex and rank, in that it constrains the incumbent in all his activities, not only in some defined social situations. One might thus also say that it is imperative, in that it cannot be disregarded and temporarily set aside by other definitions of the situation. The constraints on a person's behaviour which spring from his ethnic identity thus tend to be absolute and, in complex poly-ethnic societies, quite comprehensive; and the component moral and social conventions are made further resistant to change by being joined in stereotyped clusters as characteristics of one single identity.

## The Associations of Identities and Value Standards

The analysis of interactional and organizational features of inter-ethnic relations has suffered from a lack of attention to problems of boundary maintenance. This is perhaps because anthropologists have reasoned from a misleading idea of the prototype inter-ethnic situation. One has tended to think in terms of different peoples, with different histories and cultures, coming together and accommodating themselves to each other, generally in a colonial setting. To visualize the basic requirements for the coexistence of ethnic diversity, I would suggest that we rather ask ourselves what is needed to make ethnic distinctions emerge in an area. The organizational requirements are clearly, first, a categorization of population sectors in exclusive and imperative status categories, and second, an acceptance of the principle that standards applied to one such category can be different from that applied to another. Though this alone does not explain why cultural differences emerge, it does allow us to see how they persist. Each category can then be associated with a separate range of value standards. The greater the differences between these value orientations are, the more constraints on inter-ethnic interaction do they entail the statuses and situations in the total social system involving behaviour which is discrepant with a person's value orientations must be avoided, since such behaviour on his part will be negatively sanctioned. Moreover, because identities are signalled as well as embraced, new forms of behaviour will tend to be dichotomized: one would expect the role constraints to operate in such a way that persons would be reluctant to act in new ways from a fear that such behaviour might be inappropriate for a person of their identity, and swift to classify forms of activity as associated with one or another cluster of ethnic characteristics. Just as dichotomizations of male versus female work seem to proliferate in some societies, so also the existence of basic ethnic categories would seem to be a factor encouraging the proliferation of cultural differentiae.

In such systems, the sanctions producing adherence to group-specific values are not only exercised by those who share the identity. Again, other imperative statuses afford a parallel: just as both sexes ridicule the male who is feminine, and all classes punish the proletarian who puts on airs, so also can members of all ethnic groups in a poly-ethnic society act to maintain dichotomies and differences. Where social identities are organized and allocated by such principles, there will thus be a tendency towards canalization and standardization of interaction and the emergence of boundaries which maintain and generate ethnic diversity within larger, encompassing social systems.

## Interdependence of Ethnic Groups

The positive bond that connects several ethnic groups in an encompassing social system depends on the complementarity of the groups with respect to some of their characteristic cultural features. Such complementarity can give rise to interdependence or symbiosis, and constitutes the areas of articulation referred to above; while in the fields where there is no complementarity there can be no basis for organization on ethnic lines— there will either be no interaction, or interaction without reference to ethnic identity.

Social systems differ greatly in the extent to which ethnic identity, as an imperative status, constrains the person in the variety of statuses and roles he may assume. Where the distinguishing values connected with ethnic identity are relevant only to a few kinds of activities, the social organizations based on it will be similarly limited. Complex polyethnic systems, on the other hand, clearly entails the existence of extensively relevant value differences and multiple constraints on status combinations and social participation, in such systems, the boundary maintaining mechanisms must be highly effective, for the following reasons: (i) the complexity is based on the existence of important, complementary cultural differences; (ii) these differences must be generally standardized within the ethnic group—i. e. the status cluster, or social person, of every member of a group must be highly stereotyped—so that inter-ethnic interaction can be based on ethnic identities; and (iii) the cultural characteristics of each ethnic group must be stable, so that the complementary differences on which the systems rest can persist in the face of close inter-ethnic contact. Where these conditions obtain, ethnic groups can make stable and symbiotic adaptations to each other: other ethnic groups in the region become a part of the natural environment; the sectors of articulation provide areas that can be exploited, while the other sectors of activity of other groups are largely irrelevant from the point of view of members of any one group.

## Ecologic Perspective

Such interdependences can partly be analysed from the point of view of cultural ecology, and the sectors of activity where other populations with other cultures articulate may be thought of as niches to which the group is adapted. This ecologic interdependence may take several different forms, for which one may construct a rough typology. Where two or more ethnic groups are in contact, their adaptations may entail the following forms:

(1) They may occupy clearly distinct niches in the natural environment

and be in minimal competition for resources. In this case their interdependence will be limited despite co-residence in the area, and the articulation will tend to be mainly through trade, and perhaps in a ceremonial ritual sector.

(2) They may monopolize separate territories, in which case they are in competition for resources and their articulation will involve politics along the border, and possibly other sectors.

(3) They may provide important goods and services for each other, i. e. occupy reciprocal and therefore different niches but in close interdependence. If they do not articulate very closely in the political sector, this entails a classical symbiotic situation and a variety of possible fields of articulation. If they also compete and accommodate through differential monopolization of the means of production, this entails a close political and economic articulation, with open possibilities for other forms of interdependence as well.

These alternatives refer to stable situations. But very commonly, one will also find a fourth main form: where two or more interspersed groups are in fact in at least partial competition within the same niche. With time one would expect one such group to displace the other, or an accommodation involving an increasing complementarity and interdependence to develop.

From the anthropological literature one can doubtless think of type cases for most of these situations. However, if one looks carefully at most empirical cases, one will find fairly mixed situations obtaining, and only quite gross simplifications can reduce them to simple types. I have tried elsewhere (Barth 1964b) to illustrate this for an area of Baluchistan, and expect that it is generally true that an ethnic group, on the different boundaries of its distribution and in its different accommodations, exhibits several of these forms in its relations to other groups.

## Demographic Perspective

These variables, however, only go part of the way in describing the adaptation of a group. While showing the qualitative, (and ideally quantitative) structure of the niches occupied by a group, one cannot ignore the problems of number and balance in its adaptation. Whenever a population is dependent on its exploitation of a niche in nature, this implies an upper limit on the size it may attain corresponding to the carrying capacity of that niche; and any stable adaptation entails a control on population size. If, on the other hand, two populations are ecologically interdependent, as two ethnic groups in a symbiotic relationship, this means that any variation in the size of one must have important effects on the other. In the analysis of any poly-ethnic system for which we assert any degree of time depth, we must therefore be able to explain the processes whereby the sizes of the interdependent ethnic groups are balanced. The demographic balances involved are thus quite complex, since a group's adaptation to a niche in nature is affected by its absolute size, while a group's adaptation to a niche constituted by another ethnic group is affected by its relative size.

The demographic problems in an analysis of ethnic inter-relations in a region thus centre on the forms of recruitment to ethnic groups and the question of how, if at all, their rates are sensitive to pressures on the different niches which each group exploits. These factors are highly critical for the stability of any poly-ethnic system, and it might look as if any population change would prove destructive. This does not necessarily seem to follow, as documented, e. g. in the essay by Siverts (pp. 101 ff.), but in most situations the poly-ethnic systems we observe do entail quite complex processes of population movement and adjustment. It becomes clear that a number of factors other than human fertility and mortality affect the balance of numbers. From the point of view of any one territory, there are the factors of individual and group movements: emigration that relieves pressure, immigration that maintains one or several co-resident groups as outpost settlements of larger population reservoirs elsewhere. Migration and conquest play an intermittent role in redistributing populations and changing their relations. But the most interesting and often critical role is played by another set of processes that effect changes of the identity of individuals and groups. After all, the human material that is organized in an ethnic group is not immutable, and though the social mechanisms discussed so far tend to maintain dichotomies and boundaries, they do not imply 'stasis' for the human material they organize: boundaries may persist despite what may figuratively be called the 'osmosis' of personnel through them.

This perspective leads to an important clarification of the conditions for complex poly-ethnic systems. Though the emergence and persistence of such systems would seem to depend on a relatively high stability in the cultural features associated with ethnic groups — i.e. a high degree or rigidity in the interactional boundaries—they do not imply a similar rigidity in the patterns of recruitment or ascription to ethnic groups: on the contrary, the ethnic inter-relations that we observe frequently entail a variety of processes which effect change of individual and group identity and modify the other demographic factors that obtain in the situation. Examples of stable and persisting ethnic boundaries that are crossed by a flow of personnel are clearly far more common than the ethnographic literature would lead us to believe. Different processes of such crossing are exemplified in these essays, and the conditions which cause them are shown to be various. We may look briefly at some of them.

# Factors in Identity Change

The Yao described by Kamdre (1967b) are one of the many hill peoples on the southern fringe of the Chinese area. The Yao are organized for productive purposes in extended family households, aligned in clans and in villages. Household leadership is very clear, while community and region are autochthonously acephalous, and variously tied to poly-ethnic political domains. Identity and distinctions are expressed in complex ritual idioms, prominently involving ancestor worship. Yet this group shows the drastic incorporation rate of 10% non-Yao becoming Yao in each generation (Kandre 1967a: 594). Change of membership takes place individually, mostly with children, where it involves purchase of the person by a Yao houseleader, adoption to kinship status, and full ritual assimilation. Occasionally, change of ethnic membership is also achieved by men through uxorilocal marriage; Chinese men are the acceptable parties to such arrangements.

The conditions for this form of assimilation are clearly twofold: first, the presence of cultural mechanisms to implement the incorporation, including ideas of obligations to ancestors, compensation by payment, etc.; and second, the incentive of obvious advantages to the assimilating household and leader. These have to do with the role of households as productive units and agro-managerial techniques that imply an optimal size of 6-8 working persons, and the pattern of intra-community competition between household leaders in the field of wealth and influence.

Movements across the southern and northern boundaries of the Pathan area (cf. p. 123 ff.) illustrate quite other forms and conditions. Southern Pathans become Baluch and not vice versa; this transformation can take place with individuals but more readily with whole households or small groups of households; it involves loss of position in the rigid genealogical and territorial segmentary system of Pathans and incorporation through clientage contract into the hierarchical, centralized system of the Baluch. Acceptance in the receiving group is conditional on the ambition and opportunism of Baluch political leaders. On the other hand, Pathans in the north have, after an analogous loss of position in their native system, settled in and often conquered new territories in Kohistan. The effect in due course has been a reclassification of the settling communities among the congeries of locally diverse Kohistani tribes and groups.

Perhaps the most striking case is that from Darfur provided by Haaland (p. 58 ff.), which shows members of the hoe-agricultural Fur of the Sudan changing their identity to that of nomadic cattle Arabs. This process is conditional on a very specific economic circumstance: the absence of investment opportunities for capital in the village economy of the Fur in contrast to the possibilities among the nomads. Accumulated capital, and the opportunities for its management and increase, provide the incentive for Fur households to abandon their fields and villages and change to the life of the neighbouring Baggara, incidentally also joining one of the loose but nominally centralized Baggara political units if the change has been economically completely successful.

These processes that induce a flow of personnel across ethnic boundaries will of necessity affect the demographic balance between different ethnic groups. Whether they are such that they contribute to stability in this balance is an entirely different question. To do so, they would have to be sensitive to changes in the pressure on ecologic niches in a feed-back pattern. This does not regularly seem to be the case. The assimilation of non-Yao seems further to increase the rate of Yao growth and expansion at the expense of other groups, and can be recognized as one, albeit minor, factor furthering the progressive Sinization process whereby cultural and ethnic diversity has steadily been reduced over vast areas. The rate of assimilation of Pathans by Baluch tribes is no doubt sensitive to population pressure in Pathan areas, but simultaneously sustains an imbalance whereby Baluch tribes spread northward despite higher population pressures in the northern areas. Kohistani assimilation relieves population pressure in Pathan area while maintaining a geographically stable boundary. Nomadization of the Fur replenishes the Baggara, who are elsewhere becoming sedentarized. The rate, however, does not correlate with pressure on Fur lands—since nomadization is conditional on accumulated wealth, its rate probably decreases as Fur population pressure increases. The Fur case also demonstrates the inherent instability of some of these processes, and how limited changes can have drastic results: with the agricultural innovation of orchards over the last ten years, new investment opportunities are provided which will probably greatly reduce, or perhaps for a while even reverse, the nomadization process.

Thus, though the processes that induce change of identity are important to the understanding of most cases of ethnic interdependence, they need not be conducive to population stability. In general, however, one can argue that whenever ethnic relations are stable over long periods, and particularly where the interdependence is close, one can expect to find an approximate demographic balance. The analysis of the different factors involved in this balance is an important part of the analysis of the ethnic inter-relations in the area.

## The Persistence of Cultural Boundaries

In the preceding discussion of ethnic boundary maintenance and interchange of personnel, there is one very important problem that I have left aside. We have seen various examples of how individuals and small groups, because of specific economic and political circumstances in their former position and among the assimilating group, may change their locality, their subsistence pattern, their political allegiance and form, or their household membership. This still does not fully explain why such changes lead to categorical changes of ethnic identity, leaving the dichotomized ethnic groups unaffected (other than in numbers) by the interchange of personnel. In the case of adoption and incorporation of mostly immature and in any case isolated single individuals into pre-established households, as among the Yao, such complete cultural assimilation is understandable: here every new person becomes totally immersed in a Yao pattern of relationships and expectations. In the other examples, it is less clear why this total change of identity takes place. One cannot argue that it follows from a universally imputable rule of cultural integration, so that the practice of the politics of one group or the assumption of its pattern of ecologic adaptation in subsistence and economy, entails the adoption also of its other parts and forms. Indeed, the Pathan case (Ferdinand 1967) directly falsifies this argument, in that the boundaries of the Pathan ethnic group cross-cuts ecologic and political units. Using self-identification as the critical criterion of ethnic identity, it should thus be perfectly possible for a small group of Pathans to assume the political obligations of membership in a Baluch tribe, or the agricultural and husbandry practices of Kohistanis, and yet continue to call themselves Pathans. By the same token one might expect nomadization among the Fur to lead to the emergence of a nomadic section of the Fur, similar in subsistence to the Baggara but different from them in other cultural features, and in ethnic label.

Quite clearly, this is precisely what has happened in many historical situations. In cases where it does not happen, we see the organizing and canalizing effects of ethnic distinctions. To explore the factors responsible for the difference, let us first look at the specific explanations for the changes of identity that have been advanced in the examples discussed above.

In the case of Pathan borderlands, influence and security in the segmentary and anarchic societies of this region derive from a man's previous actions, or rather from the respect that he obtains from these acts as judged by accepted standards of evaluation. The main fora for exhibiting Pathan virtues are the tribal council, and stages for the display of hospitality. But the villager in Kohistan has a standard of living where the hospitality he can provide can hardly compete with that of the conquered serfs of neighbouring Pathans, while the client of a Baluch leader cannot speak in any tribal council. To maintain Pathan identity in these situations, to declare oneself in the running as a competitor by Pathan value standards, is to condemn oneself in advance to utter failure in performance. By assuming Kohistani or Baluch identity, however, a man may, by the same performance, score quite high on the scales that then become relevant. The incentives to a change in identity are thus inherent in the change in circumstances.

Different circumstances obviously favour different performances. Since ethnic identity is associated with a culturally specific set of value standards, it follows that there are circumstances where such an identity can be moderately successfully realized, and limits beyond which such success is precluded. I will argue that ethnic identities will not be retained beyond these limits, because allegiance to basic value standards will not be sustained where one's own comparative performance is utterly inadequate. The two components in this relative measure of success are, first, the performance of others and, second, the alternatives open to oneself. I am not making an appeal to ecologic adaptation. Ecologic feasibility, and fitness in relation to the natural environment, matter only in so far as they set a limit in terms of sheer physical survival, which is very rarely approached by ethnic groups. What matters is how well the others, with whom one interacts and to whom one is compared, manage to perform, and what alternative identities and sets of standards are available to the individual.

## Ethnic Identity and Tangible Assets

The boundary-maintaining factors in the Fur are not immediately illuminated by this argument. Haaland (p. 65) discusses the evaluation of the nomad's life by Fur standards and finds the balance between advantages and disadvantages inconclusive. To ascertain the comparability of this case, we need to look more generally at all the factors that affect the behaviour in question. The materials derive from grossly different ethnographic contexts and so a number of factors are varied simultaneously.

The individual's relation to productive resources stands out as the significant contrast between the two regions. In the Middle East, the means of production are conventionally held as private or corporate, defined and transferable property. A man can obtain them through a specific and restricted transaction, such as purchase or lease; even in conquest the rights that are obtained are standard, delimited rights. In Darfur, on the other hand, as in much of the Sudanic belt, the prevailing conventions are different. Land for cultivation is allocated, as needed, to members of a local community. The distinction between owner and cultivator, so important in the social structure of most Middle Eastern communities, cannot be made because ownership does not involve separable, absolute, and transferable rights. Access to the means of production in a Fur village is therefore conditional only on inclusion in the village community—i. e. on Fur ethnic identity. Similarly, grazing rights are not allocated and monopolized, even as between Baggara tribes. Though groups and tribes tend to use the same routes and areas every year, and may at times try in an ad hoc way to keep out others from an area they wish to use, they normally intermix and have no defined and absolute prerogatives. Access to grazing is thus an automatic aspect of practising husbandry, and entails being a Baggara.

The gross mechanisms of boundary maintenance in Darfur are thus quite simple: a man has access to the critical means of production by virtue of practising a certain subsistence; this entails a whole style of life, and all these characteristics are subsumed under the ethnic labels Fur and Baggara. In the Middle East, on the other hand, men can obtain control over means of production through a transaction that does not involve their other activities; ethnic identity is then not necessarily affected and this opens the way for diversification. Thus nomad, peasant, and city dweller can belong to the same ethnic group in the Middle East; where ethnic boundaries persist they depend on more subtle and specific mechanisms, mainly connected with the unfeasibility of certain status and role combinations.

## Ethnic Groups and Stratification

Where one ethnic group has control of the means of production utilized by another group, a relationship of inequality and stratification obtains. Thus Fur and Baggara do not make up a stratified system, since they utilize different niches and have access to them independently of each other, whereas in some parts of the Pathan area one finds stratification based on the control of land, Pathans being landowners, and other groups cultivating as serfs. In more general terms, one may say that stratified poly-ethnic systems exist where groups are characterized by differential control of assets that are valued by all groups in the system. The cultures of the component ethnic groups in such systems are thus integrated in a special way: they share certain general value orientations and scales, on the basis of which they can arrive at judgements of hierarchy.

Obversely, a system of stratification does not entail the existence of ethnic groups. Leach (1967) argues convincingly that social classes are distinguished by different sub-cultures, indeed, that this is a more basic characteristic than their hierarchical ordering. However, in many systems of stratification we are not dealing with bounded strata at all: the stratification is based simply on the notion of scales and the recognition of an ego-centered level of people who are just like us versus those more select and those more vulgar. In such systems, cultural differences, whatever they are, grade into each other, and nothing like a social organization of ethnic groups emerges. Second, most systems of stratification allow, or indeed entail, mobility based on evaluation by the scales that define the hierarchy. Thus a moderate failure in the 'B' sector of the hierarchy makes you a 'C', etc. Ethnic groups are not open to this kind of penetration: the ascription of ethnic identity is based on other and more restrictive criteria. This is most clearly illustrated by Knutsson's analysis of the Galla in the context of Ethiopian society (p. 86 ff.)—a social system where whole ethnic groups are stratified with respect to their positions of privilege and disability within the state. Yet the attainment of a governorship does not make an Amhara of a Galla, nor does estrangement as an outlaw entail loss of Galla identity.

From this perspective, the Indian caste system would appear to be a special case of a stratified poly-ethnic system. The boundaries of castes are defined by ethnic criteria: thus individual failures in performance lead to out-casting and not to down-casting. The process whereby the hierarchical system incorporates new ethnic groups is demonstrated in the sanscritization of tribals: their acceptance of the critical value scales defining their position in the hierarchy of ritual purity and pollution is the only change of values that is necessary for a people to become an Indian caste. An analysis of the different processes of boundary maintenance involved in different inter-caste relations and in different regional variants of the caste system would, I believe, illuminate many features of this system.

The preceding discussion has brought out a somewhat anomalous general feature of ethnic identity as a status: ascription is not conditional on the control of any specific assets, but rests on criteria of origin and commitment; whereas performance in the status, the adequate acting out of the roles required to realize the identity, it: many systems does require such assets. By contrast, in a bureaucratic office the incumbent is provided with those assets that are required for the performance of the role; while kinship positions, which are ascribed without reference to a person's assets, likewise are not conditional on performance—you remain a father even if you fail to feed your child.

Thus where ethnic groups are interrelated in a stratified system, this requires the presence of special processes that maintain differential control of assets. To schematize: a basic premise of ethnic group organization is that every A can act roles, 1, 2 and 3. If actors agree on this, the premise is self-fulfilling, unless acting in these roles requires assets that are distributed in a discrepant pattern. If these assets are obtained or lost in ways independent of being an A, and sought and avoided without reference to one's identity as an A, the premise will be falsified: some A's become unable to act in the expected roles. Most systems of stratification are maintained by the solution that in such cases, the person is no longer an A. In the case of ethnic identity, the solution on the contrary is the recognition that every A no longer can or will act in roles 1 and 2. The persistence of stratified poly-ethnic systems thus entails the presence of factors that generate and maintain a categorically different distribution of assets: state controls, as in some modern plural and racist systems; marked differences in evaluation that canalize the efforts of actors in different directions, as in systems with polluting occupations; or differences in culture that generate marked differences in political organization, economic organization, or individual skills.

## The problem of variation

Despite such processes, however, the ethnic label subsumes a number of simultaneous characteristics which no doubt cluster statistically, but which are not absolutely interdependent and connected. Thus there will be variations between members, some showing many and some showing few characteristics. Particularly where people change their identity, this creates ambiguity since ethnic membership is at once a question of source of origin as well as of current identity. Indeed, Haaland was taken out to see 'Fur who live in nomad camps', and I have heard members of Baluch tribal sections explain that they are 'really Pathan'. What is then left of the boundary maintenance and the categorical dichotomy, when the actual distinctions are blurred in this way? Rather than despair at the failure of typological schematism, one can legitimately note that people do employ ethnic labels and that there are in many parts of the world most spectacular differences whereby forms of behaviour cluster so that whole actors tend to fall into such categories in terms of their objective behaviour. What is surprising is not the existence of some actors that fall between these categories, and of some regions in the world where whole persons do not tend to sort themselves out in this way, but the fact that variations tend to cluster at all. We can then be concerned not to perfect a typology, but to discover the processes that bring about such clustering.

An alternative mode of approach in anthropology has been to dichotomize the ethnographic material in terms of ideal versus actual or conceptual versus empirical, and then concentrate on the consistencies (the 'structure') of the ideal, conceptual part of the data, employing some vague notion of norms and individual deviance to account for the actual, statistical patterns. It is of course perfectly feasible to distinguish between a people's model of their social system and their aggregate pattern of pragmatic behaviour, and indeed quite necessary not to confuse the two. But the fertile problems in social anthropology are concerned with how the two are interconnected, and it does not follow that this is best elucidated by dichotomizing and confronting them as total systems. In these essays we have tried to build the analysis on a lower level of interconnection between status and behaviour. I would argue that people's categories are for acting, and are significantly affected by interaction rather than contemplation. In showing the connection between ethnic labels and the maintenance of cultural diversity, I am therefore concerned primarily to show how, under varying circumstances, certain constellations of categorization and value orientation have a self-fulfilling character, how others will tend to be falsified by experience, while others again are incapable of consummation in interaction. Ethnic boundaries can emerge and persist only in the former situation, whereas they should dissolve or be absent in the latter situations. With such a feedback from people's experiences to the categories they employ, simple ethnic dichotomies can be retained, and their stereotyped behavioural differential reinforced, despite a considerable objective variation. This is so because actors struggle to maintain conventional definitions of the situation in social encounters through selective perception, tact, and sanctions, and because of difficulties in finding other, more adequate codifications of experience. Revision only takes place where the categorization is grossly inadequate—not merely because it is untrue in any objective sense, but because it is consistently unrewarding to act upon, within the domain where the actor makes it relevant. So the dichotomy of Fur villagers and Baggara nomads is maintained despite the patent presence of a nomadic camp of Fur in the neighbourhood: the fact that those nomads speak Fur and have kinship connections with villagers somewhere does not change the social situation in which the villager interacts with them—it simply makes the standard transactions of buying milk, allocating camp sites, or obtaining manure, which one would have with other Baggara, flow a bit more smoothly; but a dichotomy between Pathan landowners and non-Pathan labourers can no longer be maintained where non-Pathans obtain land and embarrass Pathans by refusing to respond with the respect which their imputed position as would have sanctioned.

## Minorities, Pariahs, and Organizational Characteristics of the Periphery

In some social systems, ethnic groups co-reside though no major aspect of structure is based on ethnic inter-relations. These are generally referred to as societies with minorities, and the analysis of the minority situation involves a special variant of inter-ethnic relations. I think in most cases, such situations have come about as a result of external historical events; the cultural differentiae have not sprung from the local organizational context—rather, a pre-established cultural contrast is brought into conjunction with a pre-established social system, and is made relevant to life there in a diversity of ways.

An extreme form of minority position, illustrating some but not all features of minorities, is that of pariah groups. These are groups actively rejected by the host population because of behaviour or actively rejected by characteristics positively condemned, though often useful in some specific, practical way. European pariah groups of recent centuries (executioners, dealers in horseflesh and leather, collectors of night-soil, gypsies, etc.) exemplify most features: as breakers of basic taboos they were rejected by the larger society. Their identity imposed a definition on social situations which gave very little scope for interaction with persons in the majority population, and simultaneously as an imperative status represented an inescapable disability that prevented them from assuming the normal statuses involved in other definitions of the situation of interaction. Despite these formidable barriers, such groups do not seem to have developed the internal complexity that would lead us to regard them as full-fledged ethnic groups; only the culturally foreign gypsies clearly constitute such a group.

The boundaries of pariah groups are most strongly maintained by the excluding host population, and they are often forced to make use of easily noticeable diacritica to advertise their identity (though since this identity is often the basis for a highly insecure livelihood, such over-communication may sometimes also serve the pariah individual's competitive interests). Where pariahs attempt to pass into the larger society, the culture of the host population is generally well-known; thus the problem is reduced to a question of escaping the stigmata of disability by dissociating with the pariah community and faking another origin.

Many minority situations have a trace of this active rejection by the host population. But the general feature of all minority situations lies in the organization of activities and interaction: In the total social system, all sectors of activity are organized by statuses open to members of the majority group, while the status system of the minority has only relevance to relations within the minority and only to some sectors of activity, and does not provide a basis for action in other sectors, equally valued in the minority culture. There is thus a disparity between values and organizational facilities: prized goals are outside the field organized by the minority's culture and categories. Though such systems contain several ethnic groups, interaction between members of the different groups of this kind does not spring from the complementarity of ethnic identities; it takes place entirely within the framework of the dominant, majority group's statuses and institutions, where identity as a minority member gives no basis for action, though it may in varying degrees represent a disability in assuming the operative statuses. Eidheim's paper gives a very clear analysis of this situation, as it obtains among Coast Lapps.

But in a different way, one may say that in such a poly-ethnic system, the contrastive cultural characteristics of the component groups are located in the non-articulating sectors of life. For the minority, these sectors constitute a backstage where the characteristics that are stigmatic in terms of the dominant majority culture can covertly be made the objects of transaction.

The present-day minority situation of Lapps has been brought about by recent external circumstances. Formerly, the important context of interaction was the local situation, where two ethnic groups with sufficient knowledge of each other's culture maintained a relatively limited, partly symbiotic relationship based in their respective identities. With the fuller integration of Norwegian society, bringing the northern periphery into the nation-wide system, the rate of cultural change increased drastically. The population of Northern Norway became increasingly dependent on the institutional system of the larger society, and social life among Norwegians in Northern Norway was increasingly organized to pursue activities and obtain benefits within the wider system. This system has not, until very recently, taken ethnic identity into account in its structure, and until a decade ago there was practically no place in it where one could participate as a Lapp. Lapps as Norwegian citizens, on the other hand, are perfectly free to participate, though under the dual disability of peripheral location and inadequate command of Norwegian language and culture. This situation has elsewhere, in the inland regions of Finnmark, given scope for Lappish innovators with a political program based on the ideal of ethnic pluralism (cf. Eidheim 1967), but they have gained no following in the Coast Lapp area here discussed by Eidheim. For these Lapps, rather, the relevance of Lappish statuses and conventions decreases in sector after sector (cf. Eidhelm 1966), while the relative inadequacy of performance in the widest system brings about frustrations and a crisis of identity.

## Culture Contact and Change

This is a very widespread process under present conditions as dependence on the products and institutions of industrial societies spreads in all parts of the world. The important thing to recognize is that a drastic reduction of cultural differences between ethnic groups does not correlate in any simple way with a reduction in the relevance of ethnic identities, or a breakdown in boundary-maintaining processes. This is demonstrated in much of the case material.

We can best analyse the interconnection by looking at the agents of change: what strategies are open and attractive to them, and what are the organizational implications of different choices on their part. The agents in this case are the persons normally referred to somewhat ethnocentrically as the new elites: the persons in the less industrialized groups with greater contact and more dependence on the goods and organizations of industrialized societies. In their pursuit of participation in wider social systems to obtain new forms of value, they can choose between the following basic strategies: (i) they may attempt to pass and become incorporated in the pre-established industrial society and cultural group; (ii) they may accept a 'minority' status, accommodate to and seek to reduce their minority disabilities by encapsulating all cultural differentiae in sectors of non-articulation, while participating in the larger system of the industrialized group in the other sectors of activity; (iii) they may choose to emphasize ethnic identity, using it to develop new positions and patterns to organize activities in those sectors formerly not found in their society, or inadequately developed for the new purposes. If the cultural innovators are successful in the first strategy, their ethnic group will be denuded of its source of internal diversification and will probably remain as a culturally conservative, low-articulating ethnic group with low rank in the larger social system. A general acceptance of the second strategy will prevent the emergence of a clearly dichotomizing poly-ethnic organization, and in view of the diversity of industrial society and consequent variation and multiplicity of fields of articulation probably lead to an eventual assimilation of the minority. The third strategy generates many of the interesting movements that can be observed today, from nativism to new states.

I am unable to review the variables that affect which basic strategy will be adopted, which concrete form it may take, and what its degree of success and cumulative implications may be. Such factors range from the number of ethnic groups in the system to features of the ecologic regime and details of the constituent cultures, and are illustrated in most of the concrete analyses of the following essays. It may be of interest to note some of the forms in which ethnic identity is made organizationally relevant to new sectors in the current situation.

Firstly, the innovators may choose to emphasize one level of identity among the several provided by the traditional social organization. Tribe, caste, language group, region or state all have features that make them a potentially adequate primary ethnic identity for group reference, and the outcome will depend on the readiness with which others can be led to embrace these identities, and the cold tactical facts. Thus, though tribalism may rally the broadest support in many African areas, the resultant groups seem unable to stand up against the sanctioning apparatus even of a relatively rudimentary state organization.

Secondly, the mode of organization of the ethnic group varies, as does the inter-ethnic articulation that is sought. The fact that contemporary forms are prominently political does not make them any less ethnic in character. Such political movements constitute new ways of making cultural differences organizationally relevant (Kleivan 1967), and new ways of articulating the dichotomized ethnic groups. The proliferation of ethnically based pressure groups, political parties, and visions of independent statehood, as well as the multitude of sub-political advancement associations (Sommerfelt 1967) show the importance of these new forms. In other areas, cult-movements or mission-introduced sects are used to dichotomize and articulate groups in new ways. It is striking that these new patterns are so rarely concerned with the economic sector of activities, which is so major a factor in the culture contact situation, apart from the forms of state socialism adopted by some of the new nations. By contrast, the traditional complex poly-ethnic systems have been prominently based on articulation in this sector, through occupational differentiation and articulation at the market place in many regions of Asia and Middle America, or most elaborately, through agrarian production in South Asia. Today, contending ethnic groups not infrequently become differentiated with respect to educational level and attempt to control or monopolize educational facilities for this purpose (Sommerfelt 1967), but this is not so much with a view to occupational differentiation as because of the obvious connection between bureaucratic competence and opportunities for political advancement. One may speculate that an articulation entailing complex differentiation of skills, and sanctioned by the constant dependence on livelihood, will have far greater strength and stability than one based on revocable political affiliation and sanctioned by the exercise of force and political fiat, and that these new forms of poly-ethnic systems are probably inherently more turbulent and unstable than the older forms.

When political groups articulate their opposition in terms of ethnic criteria, the direction of cultural change is also affected. A political confrontation can only be implemented by making the groups similar and thereby comparable, and this will have effect on every new sector of activity which is made politically relevant. Opposed parties thus tend to become structurally similar, and differentiated only by a few clear diacritica. Where ethnic groups are organized in political confrontation in this way, the process of opposition will therefore lead to a reduction of the cultural differences between them.

For this reason, much of the activity of political innovators is concerned with the codification of idioms: the selection of signals for identity and the assertion of value for these, cultural diacritica, and the suppression or denial of relevance for other differentiae. The issue as to which new cultural forms are compatible with the native ethnic identity is often hotly contended, but is generally settled in favour of syncretism for the reasons noted above. But a great amount of attention may be paid to the revival of select traditional culture traits, and to the establishment of historical traditions to justify and glorify the idioms and the identity.

The interconnection between the diacritica that are chosen for emphasis, the boundaries that are defined, and the differentiating values that are espoused, constitute a fascinating field for study. Clearly, a number of factors are relevant. Idioms vary in their appropriateness for different kinds of units. They are unequally adequate for the innovator's purposes, both as means to mobilize support and as supports in the strategy of confrontation with other groups. Their stratificational implications both within and between groups are important: they entail different sources and distributions of influence within the group, and different claims to recognition from other groups through suppression or glorification of different forms of social stigmata. Clearly, there is no simple connection between the ideological basis of a movement and the idioms chosen; yet both have implications for subsequent boundary maintenance, and the course of further change.

## Variations in the Setting for Ethnic Relations

These modern variants for poly-ethnic organization emerge in a world of bureaucratic administration, developed communications, and progressive urbanization. Clearly, under radically different circumstances, the critical factors in the definition and maintenance of ethnic boundaries would be different. In basing ourselves on limited and contemporary data, we are faced with difficulties in generalising about ethnic processes, since major variables may be ignored because they are not exhibited in the cases at our disposal. There can be little doubt that social anthropologists have tended to regard the rather special situation of colonial peace and external administration, which has formed the backdrop of most of the influential monographs, as if this were representative of conditions at most times and places. This may have biased the interpretation both of pre-colonial systems and of contemporary, emergent forms. The attempt in these essays to cover regionally very diverse cases is not alone an adequate defence against such bias, and the issue needs to be faced directly.

Colonial regimes are quite extreme in the extent to which the administration and its rules are divorced from locally based social life. Under such a regime, individuals hold certain rights to protection uniformly through large population aggregates and regions, far beyond the reach of their own social relationships and institutions. This allows physical proximity and opportunities for contact between persons of different ethnic groups regardless of the absence of shared understandings between them, and thus clearly removes one of the constraints that normally operate on inter-ethnic relations. In such situations, interaction can develop and proliferate—indeed, only those forms of interaction that are directly inhibited by other factors will be absent and remain as sectors of non-articulation. Thus ethnic boundaries in such situations represent a positive organization of social relations around differentiated and complementary values, and cultural differences will tend to be reduced with time and approach the required minimum.

In most political regimes, however, where there is less security and people live under a greater threat of arbitrariness and violence outside their primary community, the insecurity itself acts as a constraint on inter-ethnic contacts. In this situation, many forms of interaction between members of different ethnic groups may fail to develop, even though a potential complementarity of interests obtains. Forms of interaction may be blocked because of a lack of trust or a lack of opportunities to consummate transactions. What is more, there are also internal sanctions in such communities which tend to enhance overt conformity within and cultural differences between communities. If a person is dependent for his security on the voluntary and spontaneous support of his own community, self-identification as a member of this community needs to be explicitly expressed and confirmed; and any behaviour which is deviant from the standard may be interpreted as a weakening of the identity, and thereby of the bases of security. In such situations, fortuitous historical differences in culture between different communities will tend to perpetuate themselves without any positive organizational basis; many of the observable cultural differentiae may thus be of very limited relevance to the ethnic organization.

The processes whereby ethnic units maintain themselves are thus clearly affected, but not fundamentally changed, by the variable of regional security. This can also be shown by an inspection of the cases analysed in these essays, which represent a fair range from the colonial to the polycentric, up to relatively anarchic situations. It is important, however, to recognize that this background variable may change very rapidly with time, and in the projection of long-range processes this is a serious difficulty. Thus in the Fur case, we observe a situation of externally maintained peace and very small-scale local political activity, and can form a picture of inter-ethnic processes and even rates in this setting. But we know that over the last few generations, the situation has varied from one of Baggara-Fur confrontation under an expansive Fur sultanate to a nearly total anarchy in Turkish and Mahdi times; and it is very difficult to estimate the effects of these variations on the processes of nomadization and assimilation, and arrive at any long-range projection of rates and trends.

## Ethnic Groups and Cultural Evolution

The perspective and analysis presented here have relevance to the theme of cultural evolution. No doubt human history is a story of the development of emergent forms, both of cultures and societies. The issue in anthropology has been how this history can best be depicted, and what kinds of analyses are adequate to discover general principles in the courses of change. Evolutionary analysis in the rigorous sense of the biological fields has based its method on the construction of phyletic lines. This method presumes the existence of units where the boundaries and the boundary-maintaining processes can be described, and thus where the continuity can be specified. Concretely, phyletic lines are meaningful because specific boundaries prevent the inter-change of genetic material; and so one can insist that the reproductive isolate is the unit, and that it has maintained an identity undisturbed by the changes in the morphological characteristics of the species.

I have argued that boundaries are also maintained between ethnic units, and that consequently it is possible to specify the nature of continuity and persistence of such units. These essays try to show that ethnic boundaries are maintained in each case by a limited set of cultural features. The persistence of the unit then depends on the persistence of these cultural differentiae, while continuity can also be specified through the changes of the unit brought about by changes in the boundary-defining cultural differentiae.

However, most of the cultural matter that at any time is associated with a human population is not constrained by this boundary: it can vary, be learnt, and change without any critical relation to the boundary maintenance of the ethnic group. So when one traces the history of an ethnic group through time, one is not simultaneously, in the same sense, tracing the history of a culture: the elements of the present culture of that ethnic group have not sprung from the particular set that constituted the group's culture at a previous time, whereas the group has a continual organizational existence with boundaries (criteria of membership) that despite modifications have marked off a continuing unit.

Without being able to specify the boundaries of cultures, it is not possible to construct phyletic lines in the more rigorous evolutionary sense. But from the analysis that has been argued here, it should be possible to do so for ethnic groups, and thus in a sense for those aspects of culture which have this organizational anchoring.

**Notes:**

1. The emphatic ideological denial of the primacy of ethnic identity (and rank) which characteristics the universal religions that have arisen in the Middle East is understandable in this perspective, since practically any movement for social or ethical reform in the poly-ethnic societies of that region would clash with conventions and standards of ethnic character.

2. The difference between ethnic groups and social strata, which seems problematical at this stage of the argument, will be taken up below.

3. I am here concerned only with individual failure to maintain identity, where most members do so successfully, and not with the broader questions of cultural vitality and anomie.

4. As opposed to presumptive classification in passing social encounters—I am thinking of the person in his normal social context where others have a considerable amount of previous information about him, not of the possibilities afforded occasionally for mispresenting one's identity towards strangers.

5. The condemned behaviour which gives pariah position to the gypsies is compound, but rests prominently on their wandering life, originally in contrast to the serf bondage of Europe. Later in their flagrant violation of puritan ethics of responsibility, toil and morality.

6. To my knowledge, Mitchell's essay on the Kalela dance (Mitchell 1956) is the first and still the most penetrating study on this topic.
[From: Barth, F. (ed.) 1969, *Ethnic Groups and Boundaries*, London: Allen and Unwin. Introduction. Pages: 9-38]

## 导读：种族群体和界限

本文主要从文化的角度来探讨种族群体的问题。这属于人类学研究的领域，但是其重要性值得跨文化研究人员和外语学习者进一步思考。在研究方法和理论基础上我们坚持：首先强调把种族群体本身作为一个活动参与者的身份来考察种族的身份符合归属范畴；其次，采用一种生成的观点来看待问题，试图探究种族群体的产生和保持的不同过程；第三，在观察这些过程时，观察的焦点从种族群体的内在结构和不同种族的历史分化转移到种族界限和界限的保持。

### 种族群体的界定

Narroll（1964）把种族群体定义为几个方面特征的群体：1. 生物上能自身永存；2. 共享基本的价值观，在文化形式上以一个整体存在；3. 组建一个可以进行相互交流的场所；4. 有能力识别自我和他人身份的成员。这种理想的定义与传统命题中把种族等同于文化并等同于语言、社会等同于拒绝和歧视他人的理解在内容上没有实质性的区别。

### 种族群体作为文化的载体

种族身份中相对其他特征而言最重要的就是共享文化。这种观点意味着种族具有连续性的本质以及文化是决定其他形式的关键因素。强调对文化的承载，那么对其成员的分类就主要依靠他们的文化特征。群体之间的差异变成了群体习性的差异，人们的关注点就会转移到文化分析上。群体之间的动态关系也被描述成了文化适应。

种族群体中归类为公开的文化形式展示了其生态效果。也就是说，文化反应了一个种族群体对环境的适应，也以一种直接的方式反映了他们所适应的外在环境。对一个种族群体光看它文化特征的外在机构的形式是不够的，这些外在的公开形式不仅由传承的文化而且也由生态所决定。

## 种族群体作为组织类型

在集中考察社会效果时，种族群体常被视为一种社会组织形式。人的一般身份总是由他的出身和背景决定的，人们也利用这种身份把自己和他人分成不同的类别，然后形成组织意义上的种族群体。尽管种族范畴常常把文化差异考虑在内，但是对我们来说假定种族单元和文化的异同并没有一对一的关系是很重要的。那些被考虑的种族特征并不是所有的客观的文化差异，而是种族活动参与者所认为有意义的那部分。有些差异被认为是种族特征的标准而有些被忽略和否定了。这种两分的文化内容包括那些公开的象征和符号以及基本的价值定位。

## 种族群体的界限

考察种族界限时，尽管有领土界限的存在，但我们必须更多注意的是社会界限。当一个种族群体的成员与其他人进行交往时，一个群体还保持着他的身份，那么这种身份就包含着决定成员身份的标准和标志。种族群体不只是也不一定建立在对领土的占有上。此外，种族界限引导着社会生活，它需要行为和社会关系的持续的复杂的组织关系。把他人认同为自己群体的成员说明他们有共同的评价和判断标准。另一方面，把他人区分为陌生人或其他群体的成员，暗示着对共有知识不足、判断标准的差异和相互交流的局限性的认识。种族身份的保持也存在于来自不同文化的个体间的交流。因此在相互交流中维持自己的种族身份意味着存在允许文化差异存在的区分的标准和相互交流的结构。

## 多种族社会系统

根据 Furnivall（1944）的分析，多种族社会在市场上进行统一，主要由其中一个群体控制，但是仍保留着文化和宗教的多样性。人类学家发现，在多种族社会系统里，多个种族进行结合和分离。宏观层面的结合和分离对应在微观层面上的对角色的系统控制。与所有这些系统相同的是种族身份暗含对各种每个人所允许扮演的角色的控制的原则，合作者会选用不同的方式进行交流。

## 身份和价值标准之间的联系

对跨种族关系的交流和组织特征的分析往往因为没有充分注意到种族界限的问题而受到影响。这可能是因为人类学家错误地看待了跨种族关系。

## 种族群体之间的相互依存

在一个多种族的社会里，把几个民族群体联系起来的积极因素主要是因为各个种族文化特征的互补性。这种互补导致了依存与共生。社会系统的不同在很大程度上是由于处于支配地位的种族决定的。另一方面复杂的多种族系统也明显包含了相关的价值差异和对参与社会活动限制的存在。由于以下几种原因，维持种族群体之间相互依存的机制的界限应该是非常有效的：第一是社会的复杂性是基于那些重要的互补的文化差异的存在；第二是这些差异必须在一个种族群体内被标准化；第三是种族群体的文化特征必须是稳定的，以致在种族之间的密切接触中仍能保持这种互补性的差异。

## 生态视角

对种族之间相互依存的分析一部分是源于文化生态学的观点，这种生态上相互依存以几种不同的形式出现，只要有种族群体之间的相互接触的存在就会出现如下几种形式的相互适应：

1. 他们在自然环境里分别占据着不同的生态龛并为有限的资

源进行竞争。
2. 他们各自垄断着一些独立的土地，既在资源上竞争又在政治上合作。
3. 他们为各自提供着重要的商品和服务，尽管处于不同的生态龛但同时相互依存。

## 种族群体和社会分层

一旦有某个种族群体控制其他的群体的生产方式时，种族之间的不平等的关系和社会分层就会出现。一般说来，分层的多种族社会系统存在于一个种族对社会其他种族的财产的掌控。这种社会的各个种族的文化以一种特殊的方式结合起来，他们共享一套价值定位和尺度系统，在此基础上达到不同阶层上的平衡。相应的是社会分层系统并不一定要求不同种族的存在。Leech（1967）认为社会阶层是由不同的次文化进行区分的，而这些文化是比社会阶层更为基本的种族特征。在许多分层的社会制度中，我们并未关注这些有明显界限的社会等级，而这些分层仅仅基于以自我为中心层面上的认识和概念。

**Questions for reflection:**
1. How does the author define ethnic groups?
2. Point out some boundaries of the ethnic groups?
3. What is the relationship between ethnic groups and stratifications?

# The Stranger

G. Simmel

If wandering, considered as a state of detachment from every given point in space, is the conceptual opposite of attachment to any point, then the sociological form of "the stranger" presents the synthesis, as it were, of both of these properties. (This is another indication that spatial relations not only are determining conditions of relationships among men, but are also symbolic of those relationships.) The stranger will thus not be considered here in the usual sense of the term, as the wanderer who comes today and goes tomorrow, but rather as the man who comes today and stays tomorrow—the potential wanderer, so to speak, who, although he has gone no further, has not quite got over the freedom of coming and going. He is fixed within a certain spatial circle—or within a group whose boundaries are analogous to spatial boundaries—but his position within it is fundamentally affected by the fact that he does not belong in it initially and that he brings qualities into it that are not, and cannot be, indigenous to it.

In the case of the stranger, the union of closeness and remoteness involved in every human relationship is patterned in a way that may be succinctly formulated as follows: the distance within this relation indicates that one who is close by is remote, but his strangeness indicates that one who is remote is near. The state of being a stranger is of course a completely positive relation; it is a specific form of interaction. The inhabitants of Sirius are not exactly strangers to us, at least not in the sociological sense of the word as we are considering it. In that sense they do not exist for us at all; they are beyond being far and near. The stranger is an element of the group itself, not unlike the poor and sundry "innerenemies" —an element whose membership within the group involves both being outside it and confronting it.

The following statements about the stranger are intended to suggest how factors of repulsion and distance work to create a form of being together, a form of union based on interaction.

In the whole history of economic activity the stranger makes his appearance everywhere as a trader, and the trader makes his as a stranger. As long as production for one's own needs is the general rule, or products are exchanged within a relatively small circle, there is no need for a middleman within the group. A trader is required only for goods produced outside the group. Unless there are people who wander out into foreign lands to buy these necessities, in which case they are themselves "strange" merchants in this other region, the trader must be a stranger; there is no opportunity for anyone else to make a living at it.

This position of the stranger stands out more sharply if, instead of leaving the place of his activity, he settles down there. In innumerable cases even this is possible only if he can live by trade as a middleman. Any closed economic group where land and handicrafts have been apportioned in a way that satisfies local demands will still support a livelihood for the trader. For trade alone makes possible unlimited combinations, and through it intelligence is constantly extended and applied in new areas, something that is much harder for the primary producer with his more limited mobility and his dependence on a circle of customers that can be expanded only very slowly. Trade can always absorb more men than can primary production. It is therefore the most suitable activity for the stranger, who intrudes as a supernumerary, so to speak, into a group in which all the economic positions are already occupied. The classic example of this is the history of European Jews. The stranger is by his very nature no owner of land—land not only in the physical sense but also metaphorically as a vital substance which is fixed, if not in space, then at least in an ideal position within the social environment.

Although in the sphere of intimate personal relations the stranger may be attractive and meaningful in many ways, so long as he is regarded as a stranger he is no "landowner" in the eyes of the other. Restriction to intermediary trade and often (as though sublimated from it) to pure finance gives the stranger the specific character of mobility. The appearance of this mobility within a bounded group occasions that synthesis of nearness and remoteness which constitutes the formal position of the stranger. The purely mobile person comes incidentally into contact with every single element but is not bound up organically, through established ties of kinship, locality, or occupation, with any single one.

Another expression of this constellation is to be found in the objectivity of the stranger. Because he is not bound by roots to the particular constituents and partisan dispositions of the group, he confronts all of these with a distinctly "objective" attitude, an attitude that does not signify mere detachment and nonparticipation, but is a distinct structure composed of remoteness and nearness, indifference and involvement. I refer to my analysis of the dominating positions gained by aliens, in the discussion of superordination and subordination, typified by the practice in certain Italian cities of recruiting their judges from outside, because no native was free from entanglement in family interests and factionalism.

Connected with the characteristic of objectivity is a phenomenon that is found chiefly, though not exclusively, in the stranger who moves on. This is that he often receives the most surprising revelations and confidences, at times reminiscent of a confessional, about matters which are kept carefully hidden from everybody with whom one is close. Objectivity is by no means nonparticipation, a condition that is altogether outside the distinction between subjective and objective orientations. It is rather a positive and definite kind of participation, in the same way that the objectivity of a theoretical observation clearly does not mean that the mind is a passive tabula rasa on which things inscribe their qualities, but rather signifies the full activity of a mind working according to its own laws, under conditions that exclude accidental distortions and emphases whose individual and subjective differences would produce quite different pictures of the same object.

Objectivity can also be defined as freedom. The objective man is not bound by ties which could prejudice his perception, his understanding, and his assessment of data. This freedom, which permits the stranger to experience and treat even his close relationships as though from a bird's eye view, contains many dangerous possibilities. From earliest times, in uprisings of all sorts the attacked party has claimed that there has been incitement from the outside, by foreign emissaries and agitators. Insofar as this has happened, it represents an exaggeration of the specific role of the stranger: he is the freer man, practically and theoretically; he examines conditions with less prejudice; he assesses them against standards that are more general and more objective; and his actions are not confined by custom, piety, or precedent.

Finally, the proportion of nearness and remoteness which gives the stranger the character of objectivity also finds practical expression in the more abstract nature of the relation to him. That is, with the stranger one has only certain more general qualities in common, whereas the relation with organically connected persons is based on the similarity of just those specific traits which differentiate them from the merely universal. In fact, all personal relations whatsoever can be analyzed in terms of this scheme. They are not determined only by the existence of certain common characteristics which the individuals share in addition to their individual differences, which either influence the relationship or remain outside of it. Rather, the kind of effect which that commonality has on the relation essentially depends on whether it exists only among the participants themselves, and thus, although general within the relation, is specific and incomparable with respect to all those on the outside, or whether the participants feel that what they have in common is so only because it is common to a group, a type, or mankind in general. In the latter case, the effect of the common features becomes attenuated in proportion to the size of the group bearing the same characteristics. The commonality provides a basis for unifying the members, to be sure; but it does not specifically direct these particular persons to one another. A similarity so widely shared could just as easily unite each person with every possible other. This, too, is evidently a way in which a relationship includes both nearness and remoteness simultaneously. To the extent to which the similarities assume a universal nature, the warmth of the connection based on them will acquire an element of coolness, a sense of the contingent nature of precisely this relation the connecting forces have lost their specific, centripetal character.

In relation to the stranger, it seems to me, this constellation assumes an extraordinary preponderance in principle over the individual elements peculiar to the relation in question. The stranger is close to us insofar as we feel between him and ourselves similarities of nationality or social position, of occupation or of general human nature. He is far from us insofar as these similarities extend beyond him and us, and connect us only because they connect a great many people.

A trace of strangeness in this sense easily enters even the most intimate relationships. In the stage of first passion, erotic relations strongly reject any thought of generalization. A love such as this has never existed before; there is nothing to compare either with the person one loves or with our feelings for that person. An estrangement is wont to set in (whether as cause or effect is hard to decide) at the moment when this feeling of uniqueness disappears from the relationship. A skepticism regarding the intrinsic value of the relationship and its value for us adheres to the very thought that in this relation, after all, one is only fulfilling a general human destiny, that one has had an experience that has occurred a thousand times before, and that, if one had not accidentally met this precise person, someone else would have acquired the same meaning for us.

Something of this feeling is probably not absent in any relation. Be it ever so close, because that which is common to two is perhaps never common only to them but belongs to a general conception which includes much else besides many possibilities of similarities. No matter how few of these possibilities are realized and how often we may forget about them, here and there, nevertheless, the crowd in like shadows between men, like a mist eluding every designation, which must congeal into solid corporeality for it to be called jealousy. Perhaps this is in many cases a more general, at least more insurmountable, strangeness than that due to differences and obscurities. It is strangeness caused by the fact that similarity, harmony, and closeness are accompanied by the feeling that they are actually not the exclusive property of this particular relation, but stem from a more general one a relation that potentially includes us and an indeterminate number of others, and therefore prevents that relation which alone was experienced from having an inner and exclusive necessity.

On the other hand, there is a sort of "strangeness" in which this very connection on the basis of a general quality embracing the parties is precluded. The relation of the Greeks to the barbarians is a typical example so are all the cases in which the general characteristics one takes as peculiarly and merely human are disallowed to the other. But here the expression "the stranger" no longer has any positive meaning. The relation with him is a non-relation; he is not what we have been discussing here the stranger as a member of the group itself.

As such, the stranger is near and far at the same time, as in any relationship based on merely universal human similarities. Between these two factors of nearness and distance, however, a peculiar tension arises, since the consciousness of having only the absolutely general in common has exactly the effect of putting a special emphasis on that which is not common. For a stranger to the country, the city, the race, and so on, what is stressed is again nothing individual, but alien origin, a quality which he has, or could have, in common with many other strangers. For this reason strangers are not really perceived as individuals, but as strangers or a certain type. Their remoteness is no less general than their nearness.

This form appears, for example, in so special a case as the tax levied on Jews in Frankfurt and elsewhere during the Middle Ages. Whereas the tax paid by Christian citizens varied according to their wealth at any given time, for every single Jew the tax was fixed once and for all. This amount was fixed because the Jew had his social position as a Jew, not as the bearer of certain objective contents. With respect to taxes every other citizen was regarded as possessor of a certain amount of wealth, and his tax could follow the fluctuations of his fortune. But the Jew as taxpayer was first of all a Jew, and thus his fiscal position contained an invariable element. This appears most forcefully, of course, once the differing circumstances of individual Jews are no longer considered, limited though this consideration is by fixed assessments, and all strangers pay exactly the same head tax.

Despite his being inorganically appended to it, the stranger is still an organic member of the group. Its unified life includes the specific conditioning of this element. Only we do not know how to designate the characteristic unity of this position otherwise than by saying that it is put together of certain amounts of nearness and of remoteness. Although both these qualities are found to some extent in all relationships, a special proportion and reciprocal tension between them produce the specific form of the relation to the "stranger."

**Notes**

1. From "Der Fremde," in *Soziologie* (Munich and Leipzig: Duncker & Humblot, 1908), pp. 685-691. Translated by Donald N. Levine.
2. Simmel refers here to a passage which may be found in *The Sociology of Georg Simmel*, pp. 216-221.
3. Where the attacked parties make such an assertion falsely, they do so because those in higher positions tend to exculpate inferiors who previously have been in a close, solidary relationship with them. By introducing the fiction that the rebels were not really guilty, but only instigated, so they did not actually start the rebellion, they exonerate themselves by denying that there were any real grounds for the uprising.

[From: Simmel, G. 1908/1971, **The Stranger.** *On Individuality and Social Forms. Selected Writings.* (edited by D. N. Levine), Chicago: University of Chicago Press. pp. 143-149]

## 导读：陌生人

本文讨论的"陌生人"不是通常意义上的今天来明天走的概念而是今天来明天留的这种潜在的逗留者。虽然他们不再继续前行，但无法掌控自己的去留；他们被固定在某个一定的区域内或类似有空间界限群体内，但是同时他们又不属于这一群体，从而与其他本土成员的身份和地位不同。

对于陌生人来说，人际间的亲疏关系主要指以下几个方面：人际间的疏远表现为"咫尺天涯",而陌生正好相反表现为"天涯咫尺"。作为陌生人的状态其实是一种完全明确的关系,同时也是一种交流的特定形式。文章主要阐述了对陌生人的排斥和距离及如何创立一种相处的形式,一种基于相互交流的统一。

在经济活动的历史上,陌生人常常以商人的身份出现在世界各地,也正是由于对圈外人的产品的需求,使得商人的存在成为必须,而商人也只可能是其他地区的陌生人。如果不定居的话,陌生人的地位显得格外突出。在很多情况下,他们以贸易中间人的身份存在。因为生产者不具有流动性,他们只能依靠商人来联系更多的消费者,所以历史上的陌生人,即商人,作为编外人员出现主要是经济上的考虑。陌生人没有自己的土地,一方面是指具体的实际意义上的土地,另一方面也是指他们居无定所,没有固定的社会环境。尽管他们可能和其他人有亲近的关系,但是只要被视为陌生人,在他人眼里他们永远都不是土地的所有者。所以这些陌生人具有流动性。他们在一个群体内流动,体现了距离上的"远"和"近"的结合。

陌生人的特殊地位还可以从他们的客观性上体现出来。因为陌生人不受任何特定群体的约束,所以当他们面对这些群体的某些特征时便会有一种明显的客观态度。这种态度显示地并不是他们对这些群体的不参与和相对独立,而是陌生人与群体间既远又近的距离,既冷漠又关切的特殊状态。陌生人的客观性常与他们的不停的迁移紧密相关,同时又有积极肯定的参与。正因为陌生人的处境不同,所以在看待同一事物时会有不同的观点。客观性也可以定义为自由:一个客观的人是指他不受任何固有的观念、习俗和偏见束缚;有了这种自由,他们能居高临下鸟瞰一切;最后这种赋予他们客观性的又远又近的距离在关系本质上也有体现。

在对陌生人的关系上,作者看来,这主要是个人因素在起作用。人们觉得与陌生人的距离还是因为他们在民族和社会地位、职业或人的本性方面有相似之处。同时又觉得陌生人遥远是因为他们之间的相似处过于普遍,而且陌生人是因为接触许多人才接近他们。这种陌生的痕迹很容易侵入人类最亲近的关系，比如说爱情。陌生感在人际关系中是无处不在的。不管人们是否意识到它的存在，或人们如何经常忘记这种感觉。事实上它像影子一样存在于人与人之间。另一方面，"陌生"也是与参与双方的一般特点相联的。就因为这是人普遍存在的共性，陌生人显得既近又远。正是由于"远"和"近"两个因素的存在，人们会过于关注差异而忽视共性，从而产生了一种特殊的紧张。当陌生人进入另一个国家、城市、种族群体时，人们看重的不是他作为个体的存在，而是和其他陌生人一样的来源。正因为这个原因，陌生人实际上并不被视为某一个体，而是某一类型或陌生群体，因而距离比亲近更为普遍。尽管陌生人并不附属于某一群体，但事实上还是构成群体这一有机整体的成员。他们之间的距离可近可远正是这种距离所产生的紧张形成了这种陌生关系。

**Questions for reflection:**
1. What is the meaning of the "stranger" in the article?
2. Why does the author think that the stranger possesses objectivity?
3. What is the relationship between the stranger and economic activity?
4. What does nearness and remoteness mean in the author's mind?

# Stereotype and Prejudice

## The Nature of Prejudice

G. W. Allport

### Chapter 1: What Is the Problem?

Two Cases—Definition—Is Prejudice a Value Concept? —Functional Significance—Attitudes and Beliefs Acting Out Prejudice

> *For myself, earth-bound and fettered to the scene of my activities, I confess that I do feel the differences of mankind, national and individual....*
> *I am, in plainer words, a bundle of prejudices made up of likings and dislikings—the veriest thrall to sympathies, apathies, antipathies.*
>
> —Charles Lamb

In Rhodesia a white truck driver passed a group of idle natives and muttered, "They're lazy brutes." A few hours later he saw natives heaving two-hundred pound sacks of grain onto a truck singing in rhythm to their work. "Savages," he grumbled. "What do you expect?"

In one of the West Indies it was customary at one time for natives to hold their noses conspicuously whenever they passed an American on the street. And in England, during the war, it was said, "The only trouble with the Yanks is that they are over-paid, over-sexed, and over here."

Polish people often called the Ukrainians "reptiles" to express their contempt for a group they regarded as ungrateful, revengeful, wily, and treacherous. At the same time Germans called their neighbors to the east "Polish cattle." The Poles retaliated with "Prussian swine" a jibe at the presumed uncouthness and lack of honor of the Germans.

In South Africa, the English, it is said, are against the Afrikaner; both are against the Jews; all three are opposed to the Indians; while all four conspire against the native black.

In Boston, a dignitary of the Roman Catholic Church was driving along a lonesome road on the outskirts of the city. Seeing a small Negro boy trudging along, the dignitary told his chauffeur to stop and give the boy a lift. Seated together in the back of the limousine, the cleric, to make conversation, asked, "Little Boy, are you a Catholic?" Wide-eyed with alarm, the boy replied, "No sir, it's bad enough being colored without being one of those things."

Pressed to tell what Chinese people really think of Americans, a Chinese student reluctantly replied, "Well, we think they are the best of the foreign devils." This incident occurred before the Communist revolution in China. Today's youth in China are trained to think of Americans as the worst of the foreign devils.

In Hungary, the saying is, "An anti-Semite is a person who hates the Jews more than is absolutely necessary."

No corner of the world is free from group scorn. Being fettered to our respective cultures, we, like Charles Lamb, are bundles of prejudice.

## Two Cases

An anthropologist in his middle thirties had two young children, Susan and Tom. His work required him to live for a year with a tribe of American Indians in the home of a hospitable Indian family. He insisted, however, that his own family live in a community of white people several miles distant from the Indian reservation. Seldom would he allow Tom and Susan to come to the tribal village, though they pleaded for the privilege. And on rare occasions when they made the visit, he sternly refused to allow them to play with the friendly Indian children.

Some people, including a few of the Indians, complained that the anthropologist was untrue to the code of his profession that he was displaying race prejudice.

The truth is otherwise. This scientist knew that tuberculosis was rife in the tribal village, and that four of the children in the household where he lived had already died of the disease. The probability of infection for his own children, if they came much in contact with the natives, was high. His better judgment told him that he should not take the risk. In this case, his ethnic avoidance was based on rational and realistic grounds. There was no feeling of antagonism involved. The anthropologist had no generally negative attitude toward the Indians. In fact he liked them very much.

Since this case fails to illustrate what we mean by racial or ethnic prejudice, let us turn to another.

In the early summer season two Toronto newspapers carried between them holiday advertisements from approximately 100 different resorts. A Canadian social scientist, S. L. Wax, undertook an interesting experiment. To each of these hotels and resorts he wrote two letters, mailing them at the same time, and asking for room reservations for exactly the same dates. One letter he signed with the name "Mr. Greenberg", the other with the name "Mr. Lockwood". Here are the results:

To "Mr. Greenberg":
  52 percent of the resorts replied;
  36 percent offered him accommodations.
To "Mr. Lockwood":
  95 percent of the resorts replied;
  93 percent offered him accommodations.

Thus, nearly all of the resorts in question welcomed Mr. Lockwood as a correspondent and as a guest; but nearly half of them failed to give Mr. Greenberg the courtesy of a reply, and only slightly more than a third were willing to receive him as a guest.

None of the hotels knew "Mr. Lockwood" or "Mr. Greenberg." For all they knew "Mr. Greenberg" might be a quiet, orderly gentleman, and "Mr. Lockwood" rowdy and drunk. The decision was obviously made not on the merits of the individual, but on "Mr. Greenberg's" supposed membership in a group. He suffered discourtesy and exclusion solely because of his name, which aroused a prejudgment of his desirability in the eyes of the hotel managers.

Unlike our first case, this incident contains the two essential ingredients of ethnic prejudice. (1) There is definite hostility and rejection. The majority of the hotels wanted nothing to do with "Mr. Greenberg". (2) The basis of the rejection was categorical. "Mr. Greenberg" was not evaluated as an individual. Rather, he was condemned on the basis of his presumed group membership.

A close reasoner might at this point ask the question: what basic difference exists between the cases of the anthropologist and the hotels in the matter of "categorical rejection"? Did not the anthropologist reason from the high probability of infection that it would be safer not to risk contact between his children and the Indians? And did not the hotelkeepers reason from a high probability that Mr. Greenberg's ethnic membership would in fact bring them an undesirable guest? The anthropologist knew that tubercular contagion was rampant; did not the innkeepers know that "Jewish vices" were rampant and not to be risked?

This question is legitimate. If the innkeepers were basing their rejection on facts (more accurately, on a high probability that a given Jew will have undesirable traits), their action would be as rational and defensible as the anthropologist's. But we can be sure that such is not the case.

Some managers may never have had any unpleasant experiences with Jewish guests a situation that seems likely in view of the fact that in many cases Jewish guests had never been admitted to the hotels. Or, if they have had such experiences, they have not kept a record of their frequency in comparison with objectionable non-Jewish guests. Certainly they have not consulted scientific studies concerning the relative frequency of desirable and undesirable traits in Jews and non-Jews. If they sought such evidence, they would, as we shall learn in Chapter 6, find no support for their policy of rejection.

It is, of course, possible that the manager himself was free from personal prejudice, but, if so, he was reflecting the anti-Semitism of his gentile guests. In either event our point is made.

## Definition

The word prejudice, derived from the Latin noun praejudicium, has, like most words, undergone a change of meaning since classical times. There are three stages in the transformation

(1) To the ancients, praejudicium meant a precedent—a judgment based on previous decisions and experiences.

(2) Later, the term, in English, acquired the meaning of a judgment formed before due examination and consideration of the facts—a premature or hasty judgment.

(3) Finally the term acquired also its present emotional flavor of favorableness or unfavorableness that accompanies such a prior and unsupported judgment.

Perhaps the briefest of all definitions of prejudice is: thinking ill of others without sufficient warrant. This crisp phrasing contains the two essential ingredients of all definitions—reference to unfounded judgment and to a feelingtone. It is, however, too brief for complete clarity.

In the first place, it refers only to negative prejudice. People may be prejudiced in favor of others; they may think well of them without sufficient warrant. The wording offered by the New English Dictionary recognizes positive as well as negative prejudice:

*A feeling, favorable or unfavorable, toward a person or thing, prior to, or not based on, actual experience.*

While it is important to bear in mind that biases may be pro as well as con, it is none the less true that ethnic prejudice is mostly negative. A group of students was asked to describe their attitudes toward ethnic groups. No suggestion was made that might lead them toward negative reports. Even so, they reported eight times as many antagonistic attitudes as favorable attitudes. In this volume, accordingly, we shall be concerned chiefly with prejudice against, not with prejudice in favor of, ethnic groups.

The phrase "thinking ill of others" is obviously an elliptical expression that must be understood to include feelings of scorn or dislike, of fear and aversion, as well as various forms of antipathetic conduct: such as talking against people, discriminating against them, or attacking them with violence.

Similarly, we need to expand the phrase "without sufficient warrant." A judgment is unwarranted whenever it lacks basis in fact. A wit defined prejudice as "being down on something you're not upon."

It is not easy to say how much fact is required in order to justify a judgment. A prejudiced person will almost certainly claim that he has sufficient warrant [or his views]. He will tell of bitter experiences he has had with refugees, Catholics, or Orientals. But, in most cases, it is evident that his facts are scanty and strained. He resorts to a selective sorting of his own few memories, mixes them up with hearsay, and overgeneralizes. No one can possibly know all refugees, Catholics, or Orientals. Hence any negative judgment of these groups as a whole is, strictly speaking, an instance of thinking ill without sufficient warrant.

Sometimes, the ill-thinker has no first-hand experience on which to base his judgment. A few years ago most Americans thought exceedingly ill of Turks—but very few had ever seen a Turk nor did they know any person who had seen one. Their warrant lay exclusively in what they had heard of the Armenian massacres and of the legendary crusades. On such evidence they presumed to condemn all members of a nation.

Ordinarily, prejudice manifests itself in dealing with individual members of rejected groups. But in avoiding a Negro neighbor, or in answering "Mr. Greenberg's" application for a room, we frame our action to accord with our categorical generalization of the group as a whole. We pay little or no attention to individual differences, and overlook the important fact that Negro X, our neighbor, is not Negro Y, whom we dislike for good and sufficient reason; that Mr. Greenberg, who may be a fine gentleman, is not Mr. Bloom, whom we have good reason to dislike.

So common is this process that we might define prejudice as:
an avertive or hostile attitude toward a person who belongs to a group, simply because he belongs to that group, and is therefore presumed to have the objectionable qualities ascribed to the group.

This definition stresses the fact that while ethnic prejudice in daily life is ordinarily a matter of dealing with individual people it also entails an unwarranted idea concerning a group as a whole.

Returning to the question of "sufficient warrant", we must grant that few if any human judgments are based on absolute certainty. We can be reasonably, but not absolutely, sure that the sun will rise tomorrow, and that death and taxes will finally overtake us. The sufficient warrant for any judgment is always a matter of probabilities. Ordinarily our judgments of natural happenings are based on firmer and higher probabilities than our judgments of people. Only rarely do our categorical judgments of nations or ethnic groups have a foundation in high probability.

Take the hostile view of Nazi leaders held by most Americans during World War II. Was it prejudiced? The answer is No, because there was abundant available evidence regarding the evil policies and practices accepted as the official code of the party. True, there may have been good individuals in the party who at heart rejected the abominable program; but the probability was so high that the Nazi group constituted an actual menace to world peace and to humane values that a realistic and justified conflict resulted. The high probability of danger removes an antagonism from the domain of prejudice into that of realistic social conflict.

In the case of gangsters, our antagonism is not a matter of prejudice, for the evidence of their antisocial conduct is conclusive. But soon the line becomes hard to draw. How about an ex-convict? It is notoriously difficult for an ex-convict to obtain a steady job where he can be self-supporting and self-respecting. Employers naturally are suspicious if they know the man's past record. But often they are more suspicious than the facts warrant. If they looked further they might find evidence that the man who stands before them is genuinely reformed, or even that he was unjustly accused in the first place. To shut the door merely because a man has a criminal record has some probability in its favor, for many prisoners are never reformed; but there is also an element of unwarranted prejudgment involved. We have here a true borderline instance.

We can never hope to draw a hard and fast line between "sufficient" and "insufficient" warrant. For this reason we cannot always be sure whether we are dealing with a case of prejudice or nonprejudice. Yet no one will deny that often we form judgments on the basis of scant, even nonexistent, probabilities.

Overcategorization is perhaps the commonest trick of the human mind. Given a thimbleful of facts we rush to make generalizations as large as a tub. One young boy developed the idea that all Norwegians were giants because he was impressed by the gigantic stature of Ymir in the saga, and for years was fearful lest he meet a living Norwegian. A certain man happened to know three Englishmen personally and proceeded to declare that the whole English race had the common attributes that he observed in these three.

There is a natural basis for this tendency. Life is so short, and the demands upon us for practical adjustments so great, that we cannot let our ignorance detain us in our daily transactions. We have to decide whether objects are good or bad by classes. We cannot weigh each object in the world by itself. Rough and ready rubrics, however coarse and broad, have to suffice.

Not every overblown generalization is a prejudice. Some are simply misconceptions, wherein we organize wrong information. One child had the idea that all people living in Minneapolis were "monopolists." And from his father he had learned that monopolists were evil folk. When in later years he discovered the confusion, his dislike of dwellers in Minneapolis vanished.

Here we have the test to help us distinguish between ordinary errors of prejudgment and prejudice. If a person is capable of rectifying his erroneous judgments in the light of new evidence he is not prejudiced. Prejudgments become prejudices only if they are not reversible when exposed to new knowledge. A prejudice, unlike a simple misconception, is actively resistant to all evidence that would unseat it. We tend to grow emotional when a prejudice is threatened with contradiction. Thus the difference between ordinary prejudgments and prejudice is that one can discuss and rectify a prejudgment without emotional resistance.

Taking these various considerations into account, we may now attempt a final definition of negative ethnic prejudice one that will serve us throughout this book. Each phrase in the definition represents a considerable condensation of the points we have been discussing:

> Ethnic prejudice is an antipathy based upon a faulty and inflexible generalization. It may be felt or expressed. It may be directed toward a group as a whole, or toward an individual because he is a member of that group.

The net effect of prejudice, thus defined, is to place the object of prejudice at some disadvantage not merited by his own misconduct.

## Is Prejudice a Value Concept?

Some authors have introduced an additional ingredient into their definitions of prejudice. They claim that attitudes are prejudiced only if they violate some important norms or values accepted in a culture. They insist that prejudice is only that type of prejudgment that is ethically disapproved in a society.

> One experiment shows that common usage of the term has this flavor. Several adult judges were asked to take statements made by ninth-grade children and sort them into piles according to the degree of "prejudice" represented. It turned out that whatever a boy may have said against girls as a group was not judged to be prejudice, for it is regarded as normal for an early adolescent to heap scorn on the opposite sex. Nor were statements made against teachers considered examples of prejudice. This antagonism, too, seemed natural to this age, and so-

cially unimportant. But when the children expressed animosity toward labor unions, toward social classes, races or nationalities, more judgments of "prejudice" were given.

In brief, the social importance of an unfair attitude entered into the judges' view of its prejudiced character. A fifteen-year-old boy who is "off" girls is not considered as biased as one who is "off" nationalities other than his own.

If we use the term in this sense we should have to say that the older caste system in India—which is now breaking down involved no prejudice. It was simply a convenient, stratification in the social structure, acceptable to nearly all citizens because it clarified the division of labor and defined social prerogatives. It was for centuries acceptable even to the untouchables because the religious doctrine of reincarnation made the arrangement seem entirely just. An untouchable was ostracized because in previous existences he failed to merit promotions to a higher caste or to a supermortal existence. He now has his just desserts and likewise art opportunity through an obedient and spiritually directed life to win advancement in future reincarnations. Assuming that this account of a happy caste system really marked Hindu society at one time, was there then no question of prejudice?

Or take the Ghetto system. Through long stretches of history Jews have been segregated in certain residential zones, sometimes with a chain around the region. Only inside were they allowed to move freely. The method had the merit of preventing unpleasant conflict, and the Jew, knowing his place, could plan his life with a certain definiteness and comfort. It could be argued that his lot was much more secure and predictable than in the modern world. There were periods in history when neither the Jew nor gentile felt particularly outraged by the system. Was prejudice then absent?

Were the ancient Greeks (or early American plantation owners) prejudiced against their hereditary class of slaves? To be sure, they looked down upon them, and undoubtedly held fallacious theories concerning their inherent inferiority and "animal-like" mentality; but so natural did it all seem, so good, so proper, that there was no moral dilemma.

Even today, in certain states, a modus vivendi has been worked out between white and colored people. A ritual of relations is established, and most people abide unthinkingly by the realities of social structure. Since they merely follow the folkways they deny that they are prejudiced. The Negro simply knows his place, and white people know theirs. Shall we then say, as some writers have, that prejudice exists only when actions are more condescending, more negative, than the accepted culture itself prescribes? Is prejudice to be regarded merely as deviance from common practice?

Among Navaho Indians, as in many societies on earth, there is belief in witchcraft. Whoever is accused of being a witch is earnestly avoided or soundly punished on the basis of the prevailing erroneous conceptions concerning the dark powers of witches. Here, as in our preceding illustrations, all the terms of our definition of prejudice are met but few members of the Navaho society make a moral issue of the matter. Since the rejection of witches is an accepted custom, not socially disapproved, can it be called prejudice?

What shall we say about this line of argument? It has impressed some critics so much that they hold the whole problem of prejudice to be nothing more than a value-judgment invented by "liberal intellectuals."

When liberals do not approve of a folkway they arbitrarily call it prejudice. What they should do is to follow not their own sense of moral outrage, but consult the ethos of a culture. If the culture itself is in conflict, holding up a higher standard of conduct than many of its members practice, then we may speak of prejudice existing within the culture. Prejudice is the moral evaluation placed by a culture on some of its own practices. It is a designation of attitudes that are disapproved.

These critics, it would seem, confuse two separate and distinct problems. Prejudice in the simple psychological sense of negative, overgeneralized judgment exists just as surely in caste societies, slave societies, or countries believing in witchcraft as in ethically more sensitive societies. The second problem whether prejudice is or is not attended by a sense of moral outrage is a separate issue altogether.

To be sure, countries with a Christian and democratic tradition view ethnic prejudice with disfavor more often than do countries without this ethical tradition. And it is also probably true that "liberal intellectuals" are more likely than most people to become emotionally aroused by the problem.

Even so, there is not the slightest justification for confusing the objective facts of prejudice with cultural or ethical judgment of these facts. The unpleasant flavor of a word should not mislead us into believing that it stands only for a value-judgment. Take the word epidemic. It suggests something disagreeable. No doubt Pasteur, the great conqueror of epidemics, hated them. But his value-judgment did not affect in the slightest degree the objective facts with which he dealt so successfully. Syphilis is a term flavored with opprobrium in our culture. But the emotional tinge has no bearing whatever upon the operations of the spirochete within the human frame.

Some cultures, like our own, abjure prejudice; some do not; but the fundamental psychological analysis of prejudice is the same whether we are talking about Hindus, Navahos, the Greeks of antiquity, or Middletown, USA. Whenever a negative attitude toward persons is sustained by a spurious overgeneralization we encounter the syndrome of prejudice. It is not essential that people deplore this syndrome. It has existed in all ages in every country. It constitutes a bona fide psychological problem. The degree of moral indignation engendered is irrelevant.

## Functional Significance

Certain definitions of prejudice include one additional ingredient. The following is an example:

> Prejudice is a pattern of hostility in interpersonal relations which is directed against an entire group, or against its individual members; it fulfills a specific irrational function for its bearer.

The final phrase of this definition implies that negative attitudes are not prejudices unless they serve a private, self-gratifying purpose for the person who has them.

It will become abundantly clear in later chapters that much prejudice is indeed fashioned and sustained by self-gratifying considerations. In most cases prejudice seems to have some "functional significance" for the bearer. Yet this is not always the case. Much prejudice is a matter of blind conformity with prevailing folkways. Some of it, as Chapter 17 will show, has no important relation to the life-economy of the individual. For this reason, it seems unwise to insist that the "irrational function" of prejudice be included in our basic definition.

# Attitudes and Beliefs

We have said that an adequate definition of prejudice contains two essential ingredients. There must be an attitude of favor or disfavor; and it must be related to an overgeneralized (and therefore erroneous) belief. Prejudiced statements sometimes express the attitudinal factor, sometimes the belief factor. In the following series the first item expresses attitude, the second, belief:

> I can't abide Negroes.
> Negroes are smelly.
> I wouldn't live in an apartment house with Jews.
> There are a few exceptions, but in general all Jews are pretty much alike.
> I don't want Japanese-Americans in my town.
> Japanese-Americans are sly and tricky.

Is it important to distinguish between the attitudinal and belief aspects of prejudice? For some purposes, no. When we find one, we usually find the other. Without some generalized beliefs concerning a group as a whole, a hostile attitude could not long be sustained. In modern researches it turns out that people who express a high degree of antagonistic attitudes on a test for prejudice, also show that they believe to a high degree that the groups they are prejudiced against have a large number of objectionable qualities.

But for some purposes it is useful to distinguish attitude from belief. For example, we shall see in Chapter 30 that certain programs designed to reduce prejudice succeed in altering beliefs but not in changing attitudes. Beliefs, to some extent, can be rationally attacked and altered. Usually, however, they have the slippery propensity of accommodating themselves somehow to the negative attitude which is much harder to change. The following dialogue illustrates the point:

Mr. X: The trouble with the Jews is that they only take care of their own group.
Mr. Y: But the record of the Community Chest campaign shows that they give more generously, in proportion to their numbers, to the general charities of the community, than do non-Jews.
Mr. X: That shows they are always trying to buy favor and intrude into Christian affairs. They think of nothing but money; that is why there are so many Jewish bankers.
Mr. Y: But a recent study shows that the percentage of Jews in the banking business is negligible, far smaller than the percentage of non-Jews.
Mr. X: That's just it; they don't go in for respectable business; they are only in the movie business or run night clubs.

Thus the belief system has a way of slithering around to justify the more permanent attitude. The process is one of rationalization—of the accommodation of beliefs to attitudes.

It is well to keep these two aspects of prejudice in mind, for in our subsequent discussions we shall have occasion to make use of the distinction. But wherever the term prejudice is used without specifying these aspects, the reader may assume that both attitude and belief are intended.

## Acting Out Prejudice

What people actually do in relation to groups they dislike is not always directly related to what they think or feel about them. Two employers, for example, may dislike Jews to an equal degree. One may keep his feelings to himself and may hire Jews on the same basis as any workers perhaps because he wants to gain goodwill for his factory or store in the Jewish community. The other may translate his dislike into his employment policy, and refuse to hire Jews. Both men are prejudiced, but only one of them practices discrimination. As a rule discrimination has more immediate and serious social consequences than has prejudice.

It is true that any negative attitude tends somehow, somewhere, to express itself in action. Few people keep their antipathies entirely to themselves. The more intense the attitude, the more likely it is to result in vigorously hostile action.

We may venture to distinguish certain degrees of negative action from the least energetic to the most.

1. Antilocution. Most people who have prejudices talk about them. With like-minded friends, occasionally with strangers, they may express their antagonism freely. But many people never go beyond this mild degree of antipathetic action.
2. Avoidance. If the prejudice is more intense, it leads the individual to avoid members of the disliked group, even perhaps at the cost of considerable inconvenience. In this case, the bearer of prejudice does not directly inflict harm upon the group he dislikes. He takes the burden of accommodation and withdrawal entirely upon himself.
3. Discrimination. Here the prejudiced person makes detrimental distinctions of an active sort. He undertakes to exclude all members of the group in question from certain types of employment, from residential housing, political rights, educational or recreational opportunities, churches, hospitals, or from some other social privileges. Segregation is an institutionalized form of discrimination, enforced legally or by common custom.
4. Physical attach. Under conditions of heightened emotion prejudice may lead to acts of violence or semiviolence. An unwanted Negro family may be forcibly ejected from a neighborhood, or so severely threatened that it leaves in fear. Gravestones in Jewish cemeteries may be desecrated. The Northside's Italian gang may lie in wait for the Southside's Irish gang.
5. Extermination. Lynchings, pogroms, massacres, and the Hitlerian program of genocide mark the ultimate degree of violent expression of prejudice.

This five-point scale is not mathematically constructed, but it serves to call attention to the enormous range of activities that may issue from prejudiced attitudes and beliefs. While many people would never move from antilocution to avoidance, or from avoidance to active discrimination, or higher on the scale, still it is true that activity on one level makes transition to a more intense level easier. It was Hitler's antilocution that led Germans to avoid their Jewish neighbors and erstwhile friends. This preparation made it easier to enact the Nfirnberg laws of discrimination which, in turn; made the subsequent burning of synagogues and street attacks upon Jews seem natural. The final step in the macabre progression was the ovens at Auschwitz.

From the point of view of social consequences much "polite prejudice" is harmless enough—being confined to idle chatter. But unfortunately, the fateful progression is, in this century, growing in frequency. The resulting disruption in the human family is menacing. And as the peoples of the earth grow ever more interdependent, they can tolerate less well the mounting friction.

## Notes and References

1. S. L. WAX. A Survey of Restrictive Advertising and Discrimination by Summer Resorts in the Province of Ontario. Canadian Jewish Congress: Information and comment, 1948, 7, pp. 10-13.
2. Cf. *A New English Dictionary*. (Sir James A. H. Murry, ed. ) Oxford: Clarendon Press, 1909, Vol. Ⅶ, Pt. Ⅱ, 1275.
3. This Definition Is Derived from *the Thomistic Moralists Who Regard Prejudice As "Rash Judgment."* The Author Is Indebted to the Rev. J. H. Fichter, S. J. , for Calling This Treatment to His Attention. The *Definition Is More Fully Discussed* by the Rev. John Lafarge, S. J. , in *The Race Question and the Negro*, New York: Longmans,

Green, 1945, p. 174 ff.
4. Cf. R. M. WmLXAMS, JR. *The Reduction of Intergroup Tension*, New York: Social Science Research Council, 1947, Bulletin 57, 37.
5. H. S. DYER. The Usability of the Concept of "Prejudice." *Psychometrika*, 1945, 10, pp. 219-224.
6. The following definition is written from this relativistic point of view: "A prejudice is a generalized anti-attitude, and/or an anti-attitude toward any distinct category or group of people, when either the attitude or the action or both are judged by the community in which they are found to be less favorable to the given people than the normally accepted standard of that community." P. Black and R. D. Atkins conformity versus prejudice as exemplified in *white-Negro relations in the South: some methodological considerations. Journal of Psychology*, 1950, 30, pp. 109-121.
7. N. W. Ackerman and Marie Jahoda. *Anti-Semitism and Emotional Disorder*. New York: Harper, 1950, p. 4.
8. Not all scales for measuring prejudice include items that reflect the attitudes and beliefs. Those that do so report correlations between the two types of items of the order of . 80. Cf. Babette Samelson. *The Patterning of Attitudes and Belifs Regarding the American Negro Unpublished.*) Radcliffe College Library, 1945. Also, A. Rose, Studie in reduction of prejudice. (Mimeograph.) Chicago: American Counciil on Race Relations, 1947, pp. 11-14.
9. Aware of the world-wide problem of discrimination, the Commission on Human Rights of the United Nations has prepared a thorough analysis of the main types and causes of discrimination. United Nations Publications, 1949, XIV, p. 3.

## Chapter 2: The Normality of Prejudgment

Separation of Human Groups—Process of Categorization—When Categories Conflict with Evidence—Personal Values as Categories—Personal Values and Prejudice—Summary

Why do human beings slip so easily into ethnic prejudice? They do so because the two essential ingredients that we have discussed erroneous generalization and hostility are natural and common capacities of the human mind. For the time being we shall leave hostility and its related problems out of account. Let us consider only those basic conditions of human living and thinking that lead naturally to the formation of erroneous and categorical prejudgement and which therefore deposit us on the very threshold of ethnic and group antagonism.

The reader is warned that the full story of prejudice cannot be told in this or in any other single chapter of this book. Each chapter, taken by itself, is one-sided. This is the inevitable defect of any analytical treatment of the subject. The problem as a whole is many-sided, and the reader is asked, while examining one facet, to hold in mind the simultaneous existence of many other facets.

Thus, the present chapter presents a somewhat "cognitive" view of prejudgment. For the time being, many ego-involved, emotional, cultural, and personal factors that are, simultaneously operating are, of necessity, held in suspense.

### The Separation of Human Groups

Everywhere on earth we find a condition of separateness among groups. People mate with their own kind. They eat, play, reside in homogeneous clusters. They visit with their own kind and prefer to worship together. Much of this automatic cohesion is due to nothing more than convenience. There is no need to turn to out-groups for companionship. With plenty of people at hand to choose from, why create for ourselves, the trouble of adjusting to new languages, new foods, new cultures, or to people of a different educational level? it requires less effort to deal with people who have similar presuppositions. One reason for the gaiety and joy of college class reunions is that all members are the same age, have the same cultural reminiscences (even to the old popular songs they all love), and have essentially the same educational history.

Thus most of the business of life can go on with less effort if we stick together with our own kind. Foreigners are a strain. So too are people of a higher or lower social and economic class than our own. We don't play bridge with the janitor. Why? Perhaps he prefers poker; almost certainly he would not grasp the type of jests and chatter that we and our friends enjoy; there would be a certain awkwardness in blending our differing manners. It is not that we have class prejudice, but only that we find comfort and ease in our own class. And normally there are plenty of people of our own class, or race, or religion to play, live, and eat with, and to marry.

In occupational situations we are much more likely to have to deal with members of out-groups. In a stratified industry or business, management must deal with workers, executives with janitors, and salesmen with clerks. At machines, differing ethnic clusters may work side by side, though they almost certainly take their recreation in their own more comfortable groups. Contact at work is seldom sufficient to overcome psychological separateness. Sometimes the contact is so stratified that the sense of separateness is intensified. The Mexican worker may grow jealous of the greater ease of life enjoyed by his Anglo employer. The white workman may fear that the Negro helper stands ready and eager to advance and take the white man's job. Foreign groups have been imported into an industrial level to do menial work, only to arouse fear and jealousy in the majority group when they start to rise in the occupational and social ladder.

It is not always the dominant majority that forces minority groups to remain separate. They often prefer to keep their identity, so that they need not strain to speak a foreign language or to watch their manners. Like the old grads at a college reunion, they can "let down" with those who share their traditions and presuppositions.

> One enlightening study shows that high school students representing American minorities—display even greater ethnocentrism than do native white Americans. Negro, Chinese, and Japanese young people, for example, are much more insistent upon choosing their friends, their work companions, and their "dates" from their own group than are white students. It is true that they do not select "leaders" from their own group, but prefer the non Jewish white majority. But while agreeing that class leaders should come from the dominant group, they then seek the greater comfort of confining their intimate relations to their own kind.

The initial fact, therefore, is that human groups, tend to stay apart. We need not ascribe this tendency to a gregarious instinct to a "consciousness of kind," or to prejudice. The fact is adequately explained by the principles of ease, least effort, congeniality, and pride in one's own culture.

Once this separatism exists, however, the ground is laid for all sorts of psychological elaboration. People who stay separate have few channels, of communication. They easily exaggerate the degree of difference between groups, and readily misunderstand the grounds for it. And, perhaps most important of all, the separateness may lead to genuine conflicts of interests, as well as to many imaginary conflicts.

Let us take one example. The Mexican worker in Texas is sharply set off from the Anglo employer. He lives apart, speaks a different language, has a totally different tradition, and attends a different church. His children, very likely, do not attend the same school as do the employer's children; nor do they play together. All the employer knows is that Juan comes to work, takes his money, and departs. He notes that Juan is irregular in his work, seems indolent and uncommunicative. Nothing is easier than for the employer to assume that this behavior is characteristic of Juan's entire group. He develops a stereotype concerning the laziness, improvidence, and undependability of the Mexicans. Then if the employer finds himself inconvenienced economically by Juan's irregularity, he has grounds for hostility—especially if he believes that his high taxes or financial troubles are due to the Mexican population.

Juan's employer now thinks "all Mexicans are lazy." When he meets a new Mexican he will have this conviction in mind. The prejudgment is erroneous because (1) not all Mexicans are alike; (2) Juan was not really lazy but had many private values that caused him to behave the way he did. He liked to be with his children; he observed religious holy days; he had repairs to make on his own house. The employer is ignorant of all these facts. Instead of saying, as he logically ought, "I do not know the reasons for Juan's behavior because I do not know either him as a person or his culture," the employer disposed of a complex problem in an oversimplified way, attributing to Juan and his nation an attribute of "laziness."

Yet the employer's stereotype grew up out of a "kernel of truth." It was a fact that Juan was a Mexican and was irregular at his work. It may also have been a fact that the employer had had similar experience with other Mexican workmen.

The distinction between a well-founded generalization and an erroneous generalization is very hard to draw, particularly by the individual who himself harbors the generalization. Let us examine this issue more closely.

## The Process of Categorization

The human mind must think with the aid of categories (the term is equivalent here to generalizations). Once formed, categories are the basis for normal prejudgment. We cannot possibly avoid this process. Orderly living depends upon it.

We may say that the process of categorization has five important characteristics.

(1) It forms large classes and clusters for guiding our daily adjustments. We spend most of our waking life calling upon preformed categories for this purpose. When the sky darkens and the barometer falls we prejudge that rain will fall. We adjust to this cluster of happenings by taking along an umbrella. When an angry looking dog charges down the street, we categorize him as a "mad dog" and avoid him. When we go to a physician with an ailment, we expect him to behave in a certain way toward us. On these, and countless other occasions, we "type" a single event, place it within a familiar rubric, and act accordingly. Sometimes we are mistaken: the event does not fit the category. It does not rain; the dog is not mad; the physician behaves unprofessionally. Yet our behavior was

rational. It was based on high probability. Though we used the wrong category, we did the best we could.

What all this means is that our experience in life tends to form itself into clusters (concepts, categories), and while we may call on the right cluster at the wrong time, or the wrong cluster at the right time, still the process in question dominates our entire mental life. A million events befall us every day. We cannot handle so many events. If we think of them at all, we type them.

Open-mindedness is considered to be a virtue. But, strictly speaking, it cannot occur. A new experience must be redacted into old categories. We cannot handle each event freshly in its own right. If we did so, of what use would past experience be? Bertrand Russell, the philosopher, has summed up the matter in a phrase, "a mind perpetually open will be a mind perpetually vacant."

(2) Categorization assimilates as much as it can to the cluster. There is a curious inertia in our thinking. We like to solve problems easily. We can do so best if we can fit them rapidly into a satisfactory category and use this category as a means of prejudging the solution. The story is told of the pharmacist's mate in the Navy who had only two categories into which he fitted every ailment that came to his attention on sick call if you can see it put iodine on it; if you can't, give the patient a dose of salts. Life was simple for this pharmacist's mate; he ran his whole professional life with the aid of only two categories.

The point may be stated in this way: the mind tends to categorize environmental events in the "grossest" manner compatible with the need for action. If the pharmacist's mate in our story were called to task for his overcrude practice of medicine, he might then mend his ways and learn to employ more discriminated categories. But so long as we can "get away" with coarse overgeneralizations we tend to do so. (Why? Well, it takes less effort, and effort, except in the area of our most intense interests, is disagreeable.)

The bearing of this tendency on our problem is clear. It costs the Anglo employer less effort to guide his daily behavior by the generalization "Mexicans are lazy," than to individualize his workmen and learn the real reasons for their conduct. If I can lump thirteen million of my fellow citizens under a simple formula, "Negroes are stupid, dirty, and inferior," I simplify my life enormously. I simply avoid them one and all. What could be easier?

(3) The category enables us quickly to identify a related object. Every event has certain marks that serve as a cue to bring the category of prejudgment into action. When we see a red-breasted bird, we say to ourselves "robin." When we see a crazily swaying automobile, we think, "drunken driver," and act accordingly. A person with dark brown skin will activate whatever concept of Negro is dominant in our mind. If the dominant category is one composed of negative attitudes and beliefs we will automatically avoid him, or adopt whichever habit of rejection (Chapter 1) is most available to us.

Thus categories have a close and immediate tie with what we see, how we judge, and what we do. In fact, their whole purpose seems to be to facilitate perception and conduct in other words, to make our adjustment to life speedy, smooth, and consistent. This principle holds even though we often make mistakes in fitting events to categories and thus get ourselves into trouble.

(4) The category saturates all that it contains with the same ideational and emotional flavor. Some categories are almost purely intellectual. Such categories we call concepts. Tree is a concept made up of our experience with hundreds of kinds of trees and with thousands of individual trees, and yet it has essentially one ideational meaning. But many of our concepts (even tree) have in addition to a "meaning" also a characteristic "feeling." We not only know what tree is but we like trees. And so it is with ethnic categories. Not only do we know what Chinese, Mexican, Londoner mean, but we may have a feeling tone of favor or disfavor accompanying the concept.

(5) Categories may be more or less rational. We have said that generally a category starts to grow up from a "kernel of truth." A rational category does so, and enlarges and solidifies itself through the increment of relevant experience. Scientific laws are examples of rational categories. They are backed up by experience. Every event to which they pertain turns out in a certain way. Even if the laws are not 100 percent perfect, we consider them rational if they have a high probability of predicting a happening.

Some of our ethnic categories are quite rational. It is probable a Negro will have dark skin (though this is not always true). It is probable that a Frenchman will speak French better than German (though here, too, are exceptions). But is it true that the Negro will be superstitious, or that the Frenchman will be morally lax? Here the probability is much less, perhaps even zero in significance if we compare these groups with other ethnic groups. Yet our minds seem to make no distinction in category formation: irrational categories are formed as easily as rational.

To make a rational prejudgment of members of a group requires considerable knowledge of the characteristics of the group. It is unlikely that anyone has sound evidence that Scots are more penurious than Norwegians, or that Orientals are more wily than Caucasians, yet these beliefs grow as readily as do more rational beliefs.

> In a certain Guatemalan community there is fierce hatred of the Jews. No resident has ever seen a Jew. How did the Jew-is-to-be-hated category grow up? In the first place, the community was strongly Catholic. Teachers had told the residents that the Jews were Christ-killers. It also so happened that in the local culture was an old pagan myth about a devil who killed a god. Thus two powerfully emotional ideas converged and created a hostile prejudgment of Jews.

We have said that irrational categories are formed as easily as rational categories. Probably they are formed more easily, for intense emotional feelings have a property of acting like sponges. Ideas, engulfed by an overpowering emotion, are more likely to conform to the emotion than to objective evidence.

An irrational category is one formed without adequate evidence. It may be that the person is simply ignorant of the evidence, in which case a misconception is formed, as defined in Chapter 1. Many concepts depend on hearsay, on second-hand accounts, and for this reason category-misinformation is often inevitable. A child in school is required to form some general conception of, say, the Tibetan people. He can take into consideration only what his teacher and textbook tell him. The resultant picture may be erroneous, but the child has done the best he can.

Much deeper and more baffling is the type of irrational prejudgment that disregards the evidence. There is the story of an Oxford student who once remarked, "I despise all Americans, but have never met one I didn't like." In this case the categorization went against even his first-hand experience. Holding to a prejudgment when we know better is one of the strangest features of prejudice. Theologians tell us that in prejudgments based on ignorance there is no question of sin; but that in prejudgments held in deliberate disregard of evidence, sin is involved.

## When Categories Conflict with Evidence

For our purposes it is important to understand what happens when categories conflict with evidence. It is a striking fact that in most instances categories are stubborn and resist change. After all, we-have-fashioned our generalizations as we have because they have worked fairly well. Why change them to accommodate every new bit of evidence? If we are accustomed to one make of automobile and are satisfied, why admit the merits of another make? To do so would only disturb our satisfactory set of habits.

We selectively admit new evidence to a category if it confirms us in our previous belief. A Scotsman who is penurious delights us because he vindicates our prejudgment. It is pleasant to say, "I told you so." But if we find evidence that is contradictory to our preconception, we are likely to grow resistant.

There is a common mental device that permits people to hold to prejudgments even in the face of much contradictory evidence. It is the device of admitting exceptions. "There are nice Negroes but..." or "Some of my best friends are Jews but..." This is a disarming device. By excluding a few favored cases, the negative rubric is kept intact for all other cases. In short, contrary evidence is not admitted and allowed to modify the generalization; rather it is perfunctorily acknowledged but excluded.

Let us call this the "re-fencing" device. When a fact cannot fit into a mental field, the exception is acknowledged, but the field is hastily fenced in again and not allowed to remain dangerously open.

A curious instance of re-fencing takes place in many discussions concerning the Negro. When a person with a strong anti-Negro bias is confronted with evidence favorable to the Negro he frequently pops up with the well-known matrimonial question: "Would you want your sister to marry a Negro?" This re-fencing is adroit. As soon as the interlocutor says, "No," or hesitates in his reply, the biased person can say in effect, "See, there just is something different and impossible about the Negro," or, "I was right all along—for the Negro has an objectionable essence in his nature."

There are two conditions under which a person will not strive to re-fence his mental field in such a way as to maintain the generalization. The first of these is the somewhat rare condition of habitual open-mindedness. There are people who seem to go through life with relatively little of the rubricizing tendency. They are suspicious of all labels, of categories, of sweeping statements. They habitually insist on knowing the evidence for each and every broad generalization. Realizing the complexity and variety in human nature, they are especially chary of ethnic generalizations. If they hold to any at all it is in a highly tentative way, and every contrary experience is allowed to modify the pre-existing ethnic concept.

The other occasion that makes for modification of concepts is plain self-interest. A person may learn from bitter failure that his categories are erroneous and must be revised. For example, he may not have known the right classification for edible mushrooms and thus find himself poisoned by toadstools. He will not make the same mistake again; his category will be corrected. Or he may think that Italians are primitive, ignorant, and loud until he falls in love with an Italian girl of a cultured family. Then he finds it greatly to his self-interest to modify his previous generalization and act thereafter on the more correct assumption that there are many, many kinds of Italians.

Usually, however, there are good reasons for maintaining the grounds of prejudgment intact. It takes less effort to do so. What is more, we find our prejudgments approved and supported by our friends and associates. It would not be polite for a suburbanite to disagree with his neighbors about admitting Jews to the local country club. It is comforting to find that our categories are similar to those of our neighbors, upon whose goodwill our own sense of status depends. How pointless for me to be perpetually reconsidering all my convictions, especially those that form the groundwork of my life, so long as that groundwork is satisfactory to me and to my neighbors.

## Personal Values as Categories

We have been arguing that rubrics are essential to mental life, and that their operation results inevitably in prejudgments which in turn may shade into prejudice.

The most important categories a man has are his own personal set of values. He lives by and for his values. Seldom does he think about them or weigh them; rather he feels, affirms, and defends them. So important are the value categories that evidence and reason are ordinarily forced to conform to them. A farmer in a dusty area of the country listened to a visitor complain against the dust-bowl character of the region. The farmer evaded this attack on the place he loved by saying, "You know I like the dust; it sort of purifies the air." His reasoning was poor, but it served to defend his values.

As partisans of our own way of life we cannot help thinking in a partisan manner. Only a small portion of our reasoning is what psychologists have called "directed thinking," that is, controlled exclusively by outer evidence and focused upon the solution of objective problems. Whenever feeling, sentiment, values enter we are prone to engage in "free," "wishful," or "fantasy" thinking. Such partisan thinking is entirely natural, for our job in this world is to live in an integrated way as value-seekers. Prejudgments stemming from these values enable us to do so.

## Personal Values and Prejudice

It is obvious, then, that the very act of affirming our way of life often leads us to the brink of prejudice. The philosopher Spinoza has defined what he calls "love-prejudice." It consists, he says, "in feeling about anyone through love more than is right." The lover overgeneralizes the virtues of his beloved. Her every act is seen as perfect. The partisan of a church, a club, a nation may also feel about these objects "through love more than is right."

Now there is a good reason to believe that this love-prejudice is far more basic to human lira than is its opposite, hate-prejudice (which Spinoza says "consists in feeling about anyone through hate less than is right"). One must first overestimate the things one loves before one can underestimate their contraries. Fences are built primarily for the protection of what we cherish.

Positive attachments are essential to life. The young child could not exist without his dependent relationship on a nurturant person. He must love and identify himself with someone or something before he can learn what to hate. Young children must have family and friendship circles before they can define the "out-groups" which are a menace to them.

Why is it that we hear so little about love-prejudice: the tendency to overgeneralize our categories of attachment and affection? One reason is that prejudices of this sort create no social problem. If I am grossly partisan toward my own children, no one will object unless at the same time it leads me, as it sometimes does, to manifest antagonism toward the neighbor's children. When a person is defending a categorical value of his own, he may do so at the expense of other people's interests or safety. If so, then we note his hate-prejudice, not realizing that it springs from a reciprocal love-prejudice underneath.

Take an example from anti-American prejudice. It has been a longstanding condition among many cultivated Europeans. As long ago as 1854 one of them described the United States with contempt as "a grand bedlam, a rendezvous of European scamps and vagabonds." The abuse was so common that in 1869 James Russell Lowell was moved to chide the European critics in an essay entitled "On a certain condescension in foreigners." But the same type of criticism is still current.

What lies at its root? In the first place, we can be sure that before there was criticism there was self-love a patriotism, a pride of ancestry and culture, representing the positive values by which the European critics live. Coming to this country they sense a vague threat to their own position. By disparaging America they can feel more secure. It is not that initially they hate America, but that they initially love themselves and their way of life. The formula holds equally well for Americans traveling abroad.

A student in Massachusetts, an avowed apostle of tolerance—so he thought—wrote, "The Negro question will never be solved until those dumb white Southerners get something through their ivory skulls." The student's positive values were idealistic. But ironically enough, his militant "tolerance" brought about a prejudiced condemnation of a portion of the population which he perceived as a threat to his tolerance-value.

Somewhat similar is the case of the lady who said, "Of course I have no prejudice. I had a dear old colored mammy for a nurse. Having grown up in the South and having lived here all my life I understand the problem. The Negroes are much happier if they are just allowed to stay in their place. Northern troublemakers just don't understand the Negro." This lady in her little speech was (psychologically speaking) defending her own privileges, her position, and her cosy way of life. It was not so much that she disliked. Negroes or northerners, but she loved the status quo.

It is convenient to believe, if one can, that all of one category is good, all of the other evil. A popular workman in a factory was offered a job in the office by the management of the company. A union official said to him, "Don't take a management job or you'll become a bastard like all the rest of them." Only two classes existed in this official's mind: the workmen and the "bastards."

These instances argue that negative prejudice is a reflex of one's own system of values. We prize our own mode of existence and correspondingly underprize (or actively attack) what seems to us to threaten it. The thought has been expressed by Sigmund Freud: "In the undisguised antipathies and aversion which people feel towards strangers with whom they have to do, we recognize the expression of self-love, of narcissism."

The process is especially clear in time of war. When an enemy threatens all or nearly all of our positive values we stiffen our resistance and exaggerate the merits of our cause. We feel and this is an instance of overgeneralization that we are wholly right. (If we did not believe this we could not marshall all our energies for our defense.) And if we are wholly right then the enemy must be wholly wrong. Since he is wholly wrong, we should not hesitate to exterminate him. But even in this wartime example it is clear that our basic love-prejudice is primary and that the hate-prejudice is a derivative phenomenon.

While there may be such things as "just wars," in the sense that threats to one's values are genuine and must be resisted, yet war always entails some degree of prejudice. The very existence of a severe threat causes one to perceive the enemy country as wholly evil, and every citizen therein as a menace. Balance and discrimination become impossible,

## Summary

This chapter has argued that man has a propensity to prejudice. This propensity lies in his normal and natural tendency to form generalizations, concepts, categories, whose content represents an oversimplification of his world of experience. His rational categories keep close to firsthand experience, but he is able to form irrational categories just as readily. In these even kernel of truth may be lacking, for they can be composed wholly of hearsay evidence, emotional projections, and fantasy.

One type of categorization that predisposes us especially to make unwarranted prejudgments is our personal values. These values, the basis of all human existence, lead easily to love-prejudices. Hate-prejudices are secondary developments, but they may, and often do, arise as a reflex of positive values.

In order to understand better the nature of love-prejudice, which at bottom is responsible for hate-prejudice, we turn our attention next to the formation of in-group loyalties.

**Notes and References**

1. A Lundberg and Leonore Dickkson. Selective Association Among Ethnic Groups in a High School Population. *American Sociological Review*, 1952, 17, pp. 23-34.
2. In the science of psychology the processes of "directed thinking" and "free thinking" have in the past been kept quite separate. The "experimentalists," traditionally so-called, have studied the former, and the "dynamic psychologists" (e.g., the Freudians) the latter. A readable book in the former tradition is George Humphrey, Directed Thinking, New York: Dodd, Mead, 1948; in the latter tradition, Sigmund Freud, *The Psychopathology of Everyday Life*. New York: Macmillan, Transl. 1914.

    In recent years there is a tendency for "experimentalists" and "dynamicists" to draw together in their research and in their theory. (See Chapter 10 of this volume.) It is a good sign, for prejudiced thinking is not, after all, something abnormal and disordered. Directed thinking and wishful thinking fuse.
3. See G. W. Ali. Port, A Psychological Approach to Love and Hate.

Chapter 5 in P. A. Sorokin (ed.), *Explorations in Altruistic Love and Behavior*. Boston: Beacon Press, 1950. Also, M. F. ASHLZY-MONTAGU, *On Being Human*. New York: Henry Schumann, 1950.
4. Merle Curti, The Reputation of America Overseas (1776-1860). *American Quarterly*, 1949, 1, pp. 58-82.
5. Important relations between war and prejudice are discussed in H. Cantril (ed.), *Tensions That Cause Wars*. Urbana: Univ. of Illinois Press, 1950.

## Chapter 17: Conforming

Conformity and Functional Significance—Social Entrance—Ticket the Neurosis of Extreme Conformity—Ethno-centric Pivots in Culture—Basic Psychology of Conformity—Conflict and Rebellion

Someone has defined culture as that which gives ready-made answers to the problems of life. So far as life's problems have to do with group relations, the answers are likely to be ethnocentric in tone. This is natural enough. Each ethnic group tends to strengthen its inner ties, to keep bright the legend of its own golden age, and to declare (or imply) that other groups are less worthy. Such ready-made answers make for self-esteem and for group survival. This ethnocentric habit of thought is much like grandmother's furniture. Sometimes it is revered and prized, more usually just taken for granted. Occasionally it is modernized. But for the most part, it is used generation after generation. It serves a purpose. It is homelike and therefore good.

### Conformity and Functional Significance

Now the important problem we face is this: Is conforming a superficial phenomenon or has it deep functional significance for the person who conforms? Is it skin-deep or marrow-deep?

The answer is that our obedience to cultural ways has all gradations of depth. Sometimes we follow customs almost unconsciously or with only a surface interest (e. g., keeping to the right side of the street); sometimes we find a cultural pattern of great significance to ourselves (for example, the right to own property); sometimes a culturally transmitted way of life is particularly precious (belonging to a certain church). Psychologically, we may say that people find all degrees of ego-involvement in their habits of conformity.

The following study illustrates nicely two different degrees of ego-involvement in conforming with an ethnocentric folkway. It is taken from *The American Soldier*.

During the war a large number of Air Force enlisted men were asked two questions: (1) Do you think white soldiers and Negro soldiers in the Air Force should be in the same or in separate ground crews? About tour-fifths voted for separate, i. e., segregated, ground crews. (2) Would you have any personal objection to working in the same ground crew with Negro soldiers? Roughly, one-third of the Northern white and two-thirds of the Southern whites had "personal objections." Allowing for the proportions of Northern and Southern soldiers in the sample, we may safely say that apparently half of the soldiers who favored the segregated policy had no personal objection to working with Negroes. If this result is representative of ethnocentrism as a whole, we might then guess that about a half of all prejudiced attitudes are based only on the need to conform to custom, to let well enough alone, to maintain the cultural pattern.

But the other half are not based on conformity alone. Deeper motives are apparently at work motives with a functional significance for the individu-

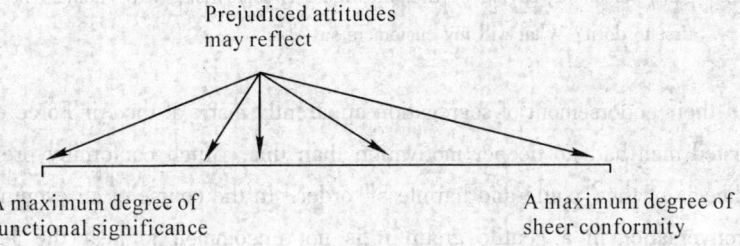

Figure 1: The continuum of ego-relevance in prejudiced attitudes

al. He has "personal objections" to working with Negroes. For him the status quo is more than an arbitrary custom. The sheer conformist says, in effect, "Why should I be the one to buck the situation?" Whereas the functional bigot says, in effect, "This custom of segregation is essential to the economy of my life."

It would be wrong, of course, to imply that every case of prejudice can be classified clearly as "sheer conformity" or as "functionally significant." There may be a degree of mixture, as Figure 1 suggests. The situation should be regarded as a continuum. A given case of prejudice may fall anywhere between the pole of surface conformity and the pole of extreme functional relevance.

## Social Entrance Ticket

Many conformists have no deeper motive than to avoid a scene. Finding themselves with prejudiced people, they string along. Why be rude? Why challenge the community pattern? Only the headstrong idealists make a nuisance of themselves. Better to parrot a folkway than to be a bore.

> An employer with a penchant for peace (and profits) refused to hire Negro sales personnel, saying, "After all, there is some risk. Why should I be the first to do it? What will my customers say?"

In their endorsement of segregation apparently many of the Air Force enlisted men had no deeper motivation than this. Much conformity prejudice is of the "polite and harmless" order. In the course of an evening's conversation in a gentile group it is not uncommon to hear the Jews blamed once or twice for some current evil. Everyone nods a head and goes on to the next subject. A group of Republicans might find the same conversational cement in abusing the Democratic administration, or vice versa. And a dig at Irish politicians is in many cities a safe adhesive to apply to a faltering conversation. The abuse is often as hollow as that we heap upon the weather.

Such chatter—if indeed there is little behind it—can be called phatic discourse—the words meaning nothing excepting as a device to avoid silence and signify social solidarity.

Sometimes, of course, there is somewhat more at stake in the act of conforming.

> A girl with very little money entered a private school, attended chiefly by girls from homes of wealth. In order to become accepted by the students "who were somebody" she found herself aping their prejudiced talk concerning the one or two Jewish girls in the school. In this case, the need for greater personal security underlay the conformity.

No one, least of all an adolescent, wants to be excluded from the dominant group. Even a tone of voice may bring him into line. A college student reports a memory of his first day at prep school:

One of the older boys remarked about a schoolmate, "Don't you know that Harry is a Jew?" I had never met a Jewish boy before, and personally didn't care whether or not Harry who seemed a likable fellow was a Jew. But the older boy's tone of voice was enough to convince me that I had better not make Harry my friend. Thereafter I avoided Harry. And, although I could not understand why we should dislike Jews, I gradually accepted the prejudice. It seems strange that a feeling of antagonism toward Harry should grow up in me. But it did. Personally, I had no unpleasant experience with him or with any other Jew I ever met.

This case is particularly interesting because the writer goes on to show how little personal ground (how little functional significance) the prejudice seemed to have for any of the boys at school.

The boys concerned were all secure economically. They were all seventeen or under and had few worries about social prestige. They received as good grades as did Harry. There were no marked frustrations that made them look for a scapegoat. These boys simply had a fixed, irrational prejudice which they could neither explain nor discard. Of course they brought the attitude from home, but why? What earthly good did it do them?

Why a child should take on a ready-made prejudice without its having specific functional significance for him as an individual is a subject that will soon engage our attention? First, however, let us consider a case of extreme cultural obedience with manifestly high functional significance.

## The Neurosis of Extreme Conformity

It is still difficult for us to believe the story of the Auschwitz Concentration Camp. The tale is the zenith of horror. Between the summer of 1941 and the end of World War II, two and a half million men, women, and children were murdered there. The gas chambers and ovens, working 24 hours a day, exterminated as many as 10,000 human beings daily. The victims were mostly Jews, and the deliberate genocide represented what Hitler had called the "final solution" of the Jewish problem. Gold from their teeth and their rings was melted down and sent to the Keichsbank. Hair from the women's heads was salvaged for commercial purposes.

A forty-six-year-old colonel of the German Army, Rudolf Hoess, was commandant of the camp, and when testifying at the Nürnberg trials, readily admitted these facts. He said he had received orders in the summer of 1941 when Himmler called for him and explained, "The Fuhrer has ordered the final solution of the Jewish question and we have to carry out this task. For reasons of transportation and isolation, I have picked Auschwitz for this. You now have the hard job of carrying this out."

Asked how he felt when receiving such grim orders, Hoess denied any feeling. He had answered, "Jawohl," to Himmler and set about obediently to carry through the endless murders, just because two superior officers, first Hitler and then Himmler, had told him to do so. When pressed to say whether the Jews whom he murdered deserved such a fate, he complained that such questions didn't mean anything. "Don't you see, we men were not supposed to think about these things; it never even occurred to us." And besides, it was something already taken for granted; he said, "We just never heard anything else... It was not only newspapers like the Sturmer, but it was everything we ever heard. Even our military and ideological training took for granted that we had to protect Germany from the Jews. It only started to occur to me after the collapse that maybe it was not quite right, after I had heard what everybody was saying."

Hoess had put obedience to his superior officer above everything else above the Ten Commandments, above sympathy, above logic. "You can be sure that it was not always a pleasure to see those mountains of corpses and smell the continual burning. But Himmler had ordered it and had even explained the necessity and I really never gave much thought to whether it was wrong. It just seemed a necessity."

The case of Hoess demonstrates a neurotic degree of conformity. The loyalty and obedience involved were prepotent over every rational and humane impulse. The frenzy of conformity to a Nazi folk-belief and to the Fuhrer's orders was a vital factor in the personality of Hoess a compulsive obedience. Yet, one cannot suppose Hoess to be a madman; there were too many other guards who would have done the same thing with as little remorse. We can only learn from this case that a fanatic ideology may engender conformity of incredible tenacity.

## Ethnocentric Pivots in Culture

Less extreme, but more widespread, is the deliberate attempt to maintain a chosen ethnocentric creed as a vital part of a culture. Anyone exposed to this creed is bound to be affected by it in some degree. The doctrine of "white supremacy" in various parts of the world is such a pivotal theme.

More than a century ago de Tocqueville discussed this feature of the culture of the southern portion of the United States. He reported that a cheaply won pride seemed characteristic of the dominant group:

> In the South there are no families so poor as not to have slaves. The citizen of the Southern states becomes a sort of domestic dictator from infancy; the first notion he acquires in life is that he is born to command, and the first habit which he contracts is that of ruling without resistance. His education tends,

then, to give him the character of a haughty and hasty man, irascible, violent, ardent in his desires, impatient of obstacles, but easily discouraged if he cannot succeed in the first attempt.

Writing on this same subject more than a century later, Lillian Smith tells how child training in many Southern families is still directed toward the theme of white supremacy.

> I do not remember how or when, but by the time I had learned that God is love, that Jesus is His Son and came to give us more abundant life, that all men are brothers with a common Father, I also knew that I was better than a Negro, that all black folks have their place and must be kept in it, that sex has its place and must be kept in it, that a terrifying disaster would befall the South if ever I treated a Negro as my social equal...

Child training is not the only focus of self-conscious ethnocentrism. The following incident shows how solidarity may be maintained even in the halls of justice:

> In 1947, in the state of South Carolina, 28 white men were charged with the lynching of a Negro. The counsel for the defense faced the task of persuading the jury to disregard the confessions of several of the prisoners. It proved to be a not difficult task. Although under the stern eye of the judge the counsel was prevented from injecting the race issue directly, he contrived to appeal to white southerners to stick together in their crusade to maintain white supremacy. Leaning on the jury box, and speaking softly, he said, "I know that you are all good citizens of South Carolina." "We understand each other," he coaxed. "Not a soul in South Carolina would criticize you if you turn these boys loose. You are not expected to convict them." The jury acquitted the defendants. One more Negro was lynched with impunity.

Self-conscious maintenance of in-group superiority is by no means confined to the United States. A Chinese student indicates how parents and teachers cooperate to instil in-groupism into the children of that land:

> Why can China still survive when the country has had numerous times of national crisis? It is thoroughly believed by the Chinese that the great philosophy of our ancestral teachers has saved the nation. The culture and civilization of China were, are, and will be always the light of the Orient. When the boy Sun Yat-Sen (the founder of the Chinese Republic) refused to kneel down before an ancestral wooden tablet, he was fiercely condemned by his schoolteacher, who later stirred up the whole village mob to drive Sun Yat-Sen out of that locality even though his father was one of the elders of the town.

The writer of this analysis reports that the total atmosphere of her upbringing gave her a strong prejudice against American missionaries. Why should they try to impose their ways upon an older and superior civilization?

> My hatred of American missionaries has carried over, even to this country. When some American friends tell me excitedly that they had missionary relatives or acquaintances in China, my response is always a very discouraging,

"Oh?" She reports that fences are formed, not only to exclude other races or nationalities, but to exclude regions and classes.

> The education of northern China, we were taught, was better than that of the southern Chinese. So we in Shanghai looked down upon Canton. Also, we learned the old Chinese saying of some educated sage, "Our people are masters of the servant class, because there is an unremovable feeling of prestige and superiority existing among educated people." Since educated people live mostly in the city, we hired our servants from the country, and looked down upon them for their rural upbringing.

Deliberate teaching thus established prejudice against other Orientals, western nations, southern Chinese, rural Chinese, and less-educated Chinese. The communist suzerainty has no doubt complicated and perhaps modified all this. But the case is instructive because it has been said that China is a land relatively free from prejudice !

## Basic Psychology of Conformity

As we pointed out in Chapter 3, there is no society on earth where the children are not thought to belong to the ethnic and religious group of their parents. By virtue of kinship, the child is expected to take on the prejudices of his parents, also to become the victim of whatever prejudice is directed against his parents.

It is because of this fact that prejudice looks as though it were inherited, linked somehow to biological descent. Since children are identical with their parents in respect to memberships, we must expect ethnic attitudes to be handed down from parent to child. So universal and automatic is it that somehow heredity seems to be involved.

Actually, the course of transmission is one of teaching and learning, not heredity. As we have seen, parents sometimes deliberately inculcate ethnocentrism, but more often they are unaware of doing so. The following excerpt shows how the process appears to a child:

> In my earliest childhood I recall that I felt strong antagonism toward anyone who opposed the views and feelings of my parents. They would often talk about such people at the supper table. I think it was the confident tone of voice in which my parents aired their convictions and condemned their opponents that affected me, and assured me of their omnipotent wisdom.

A young child is likely to regard his parents as omnipotent (for they seem to be able to do all the things that the child fumbles with and fails to do). Why should not their judgments be his judgments?

Sometimes the family circle includes other omnipotent and omniscient relatives:

> When I was about six, my great-grandfather lived in our home. He was especially rabid against Southerners and against Irish Catholics. After hearing him condemn both these groups repeatedly, I became convinced that they must be obnoxious indeed.

Sometimes the parental view contains mixtures of tolerance and intolerance, and both are adopted:

> My father was a minister. One of the ideas I acquired from him was that one never hates a person, but only some vice in a person, such as conceit. Yet he taught me that certain vices—superstitiousness, for example—were more likely to be found in Catholics.

In the following case the teaching is less complicated:

> My prejudice against Jews arose through my parents' attitude toward Jews. In my father's business, he had encountered certain Jews with whom his transactions had been unfortunate, and he was, and still is, very bitter on the subject. I also avoided Catholic girls because I heard my parents talk of what an awful mess the world would come to if everyone turned Catholic.

Tolerance too can be learned from family and neighborhood mores:

> Every child has a need for conforming to his group in order to be accepted by the group. In the community in which I grew up, and in our family, conformity

did not involve antagonism toward other groups. Therefore, I did not acquire prejudice.

If we take a Darwinian view of the matter, we may say that all this conforming has "survival value." The young child is helpless unless, in matters of basic value, he strings along with his parents. His only possible pattern for survival is their pattern. If their design for living is tolerant, so too is his; if they are hostile toward certain groups, so too is he.

We must not imply that the young child is consciously aware of his imitativeness. Certainly he does not say to himself, "I must conform to my family ways in order to survive." Psychologically there are more subtle ways of acquiring family attitudes.

The process most often named in this connection is identification. The term is broad and ill-defined, but it serves to convey the sense of emotional merging of oneself with others. One form of identification is indistinguishable from love and affection. A child who loves his parents will readily become depersonalized from himself and "repersonalized" in them. Their signs of feeling are eagerly scanned and mirrored in the child, who is alert to all cues coming from them. Whether in play or in seriousness, the parental model is acted out. The young son, firmly attached to his father, mimics him from morning until night. Not only are the outer acts cues for mimicry, but so too the thoughts expressed including the hostilities and rejections. It is almost impossible to describe the subtlety of the process involved. Learning through identification seems basically to involve a type of muscle strain or postural imitation. Supposing the child, hypersensitive to parental cues, senses a tightness or rigidity when his parents are talking about the Italian family that has moved in next door. In the very act of perceiving these parental cues, the child himself grows tight and rigid. (His perceptions tend to take a motor form acting out what he perceives.) This strain in the child becomes conditioned by the words his parents are speaking. After this associated experience, he may tend, ever so slightly, to feel a tenseness (an incipient anxiety) whenever he hears (or thinks) of Italians. The process is infinitely subtle.

It is not only affection for the parent that may lead to identification. Even in a family where power is dominant over love, the child has no other model for strength, for success in life, than his parents. By imitating their conduct and mirroring their attitudes, he often can gain approval and reward from the parent. Even if reward is not forthcoming, he can, as it were, gain assurance by simulating their adulthood. Strutting, scolding, hating like his father makes the youngster feel grown-up.

One of the areas where identification may most easily take place is that of social values and attitudes. The child has none of his own to start with. Topics that are beyond his comprehension leave him no alternative but to absorb the pronouncements of others. Sometimes a child who confronts a social issue for the first time will ask his parent what attitude he should hold. Thus he may say, "Daddy, what are we? Are we Jews or gentiles; Protestants or Catholics; Republicans or Democrats?" When told what "we" are, the child is fully satisfied. From then on, he will accept his membership and the ready-made attitudes that go with it.

## Conflict and Rebellion

Although conformity with the home atmosphere is undoubtedly the most important single source of prejudice, it must not be thought that the child grows up to be a mirror image of his parents' attitudes. Nor is it true that the parents' attitudes are always in conformity with the prejudices, prevailing in their community.

What the father and mother transmit to their offspring is their own personal version of cultural traditions. They may be skeptical concerning the stereotypes current in their community, and pass their skepticism on to the children. They may have a few pet prejudices of their own that are not represented in their cultural group. Unless the child picks up outside the home the standard attitudes of the community, his pattern of prejudice will reflect whatever idiosyncrasies the parents have imposed.

And the child himself is sometimes selective. While he lacks the experience and strength to counter his parents' value-attitudes in his earliest years, he sometimes develops early skepticism regarding them. The case of the six-year-old who absorbed anti-Southern and anti-Irish prejudices from his great-grandfather was even at that age complicated by conflict.

> One day I was playing with my uncle, and I said, with foolish patter, "Well, anyway, we wouldn't let you and your old Irishmen live on our street." Later, with a sick feeling, I heard that my good-natured uncle was Irish. I then and there decided that my great-grandfather must be mistaken. If anyone as nice as Uncle Bill was Irish, it must be a very fine national group.

A similar conflict occurred in a little girl, likewise six years old:
> My mother told me not to play with girls on the next street, who were of a lower social class. She said she wanted me to grow up to be a "lady." I remember feeling distinctly guilty that I had not, up to then, been ladylike. Yet I was fond of my playmates and felt guilty ever after for avoiding them.

What we learn from such cases is that even a young child may be skeptical concerning the grounds for parental prejudice. Even while conforming, they may have their doubts. Later they may reject the parental model altogether.

Sometimes the rejection takes the form of open rebellion in adolescence:
> At the age of fifteen I revolted, not only against my parents, but against the whole system of living in our town that had led me through so much misery as a boy. If the custom was to hate Negroes, I would cultivate them as friends. I shocked my parents by bringing the janitor's son into our house to play cards and listen to the radio.

Often the process of outgrowing parental prejudice, taken over second-hand, occurs first in college years:
> My parents were much prejudiced against Roman Catholics. They told me the church was treacherous, had too much political power, kept firearms, and practised immorality in the convents. During college I rethought my religious position. I came to know Roman Catholic clergy and to understand their position. Closer contact with the group led me to see that my previous fears were groundless. Now I laugh at my parents' fixed ideas.

Another college student writes:
> Inwardly I rebelled. I finally broke loose from my chains—from my father's ideas of class prejudice that I had acquired from him. For a time I went to the other extreme and compulsively associated with all sorts of people of all races, creeds, religions, and classes.

We do not know what proportion of children grow into adulthood without modifying the second-hand ethnocentrism taken over initially from the parents. Probably for every rebel who reverses his value-attitudes, there are several conformists who merely modify slightly the parental teaching to accord with their own functional needs in later life. Certain it is that in spite of rebels ethnocentrism continues generation after generation. While it may be slightly re-tailored, it is not often discarded.

Since the home is the chief and earliest source of prejudiced attitudes, we should not expect too much from programs of intercultural education in the schools. For one thing, schools scarcely dare to countermand parental teachings. They would get into trouble if they did so. And not all teachers are themselves free from prejudice. Nor can the church or the state for all their official creeds of equality easily cancel out the earlier and more intimate influence of the family.

The primacy of the family does not mean, of course, that school, church, and state should cease practising or teaching the principles of democratic living. Together, their influence may establish at least a secondary model for the child to follow. If they succeed in making him question his system of values, the chances for a maturer resolution of the conflict are greater than if such questioning never takes place. Some effects from school, church, and state may be expected, and their cumulative influence may affect the next generation of parents. We recall in this connection that college students are today much more reluctant to ascribe stereotyped judgements to national out-groups than were students twenty years ago (p. 202). Why should this be so, unless extra-familial influences are gradually working upon students or upon the parents, or upon both?

## Notes and References
1. S. A. Stouffer, et al. *The American Soldier: Adjustment During Army Life*. Princeton: Princeton Univ. Press, 1949, Vol. 1, p. 579.
2. A similar conclusion is offered by Van Til and Denmark on the basis of their survey of a wide variety of investigations. These authors

write, "There are two major sources of prejudice and discrimination toward minority groups: (a) frustration and (b) cultural learning." In our terms frustration is one (but not the only) important factor making for functional significance. Cultural learning refers to conformity. W. Van Til and G. W. Denmark. Intercultural education. *Review of Educational Research*, 1950, 20, pp. 274-286.
3. Reproduced from G. W. Allport, Prejudice: a problem in psychological and social causation. *Journal of Social Issues*, 1950, Supplement Series, No. 4, p. 16.
4. This account is derived from G. M. Gilbert. *Nuremberg Diary*. New York: Farrar, Straus, 1947, pp. 250 and 259 ff.
5. A. De Tocquzville, *Democracy in America*. New York: George Dearborn, 1838, 374.
6. Lillian Smith, *Killers of the Dream*. New York: W. W. Norton, 1949, p. 18.

[From: G. W. Allport, 1954, *The Nature of Prejudice*. Cambridge, Mass: Addison-Wesley. Chapters 1-2 pp.3-28; Chapter 17. pp. 285-296]

# 导读：偏见的本质

在本文中，作者通过对两个案例的分析和对定义的阐述，逐步将"偏见（prejudice）"这个我们既熟悉又陌生的概念一层一层地展示给我们读者。并且，作者对于偏见产生的原因和本质也分别进行了阐释。

在文章中，作者列举了很多事例说明不同国家的人对于其他民族和国家的人存在很多的偏见。接着，作者列出了两个案例。首先谈到的是一个人类学家，他的工作要求他与一个部落的印第安土著人住在一起，却要求他的两个孩子住在一个离印第安部落几英里的白人社区，甚至不准他的两个孩子接近土著人部落。很多人，包括一些印第安人都认为这位人类学家违反了他的职业道德,因为他表现出种族偏见。事实上并非如此。这位人类学家了解到在这个部落里,肺结核病十分盛行,他寄居的那个印第安家庭的四个孩子就是死于肺结核。为了避免感染,所以他不希望他的孩子来到这个部落,与这里的孩子一起玩耍。

另一个例子是关于一个有趣的实验。一个加拿大社会学家给报纸上列出的100多家度假胜地分别发出了两封不同的信件,一封署名为"Mr Greenburg",另一封署名为"Mr Lockwood"。两封信同时发出,要求预订的是同一天的房间,可是受到的待遇却是大相径庭。大部分的度假胜地回复并且欢迎 Mr Lockwood 前去度假,但也有一半的度假胜地没有回复"Mr Greenburg",并且三分之一的度假胜地愿意为"Mr Greenburg"提供住宿。"Mr Greenburg"之所以没有受到礼遇就是因为名字的缘故。

我们不禁要问,那么这两个案例之间的区别是什么呢?事实上,人类学家所做出的行为完全是基于事实,而度假胜地所做出的反应只是基于自己主观的对名字所做出的判断,而不是基于事实。从而引出了对"prejudice(偏见)"的定义,那就是"一种不是基于事实的,对于人或事的一种正面或负面的情绪。"事实上,偏见所针对的对象往往不是个人,而是一个群体,这往往是人们对过去经验加以延伸和扩大化的结果。一个美国人可能根据与一个中国人交往的经历来得出对所有中国人的一个判断,而这个判断不一定适用于所有中国人。

其他一些学者给"偏见"加入了其他一些因素,他们认为只有在人们的态度违反了文化中一些重要的规则和价值观的时候才能被称为是"偏见",也就是说,只有在一个社会里违反道德的判断才是"偏见"。

另外，还有一些学者认为，只有在负面的态度具有能够自我满足私人的目的的时候才能成为是"偏见"。在很多情况下，确实很多态度是具有这种特点，但是并非所有的情况。因此，作者认为，如果把这点加入到"偏见"的基本定义中是不明智的。

当然，很多学者还认为，"偏见"中包含态度和信仰两个不同的方面。这种意见对我们的启示是我们需要把两者之间的区别铭记在心，因为在有些时候，它们的区别将会发挥作用。

在本文中，作者还列举出了几种"偏见"的表现形式，表示强度从弱到强。首先是负面评论，当人们存有偏见时，往往首先是谈论。接着，如果偏见表示的程度更强，可能会导致个人避开某个群体的人。如果程度进一步加深，就会导致歧视。进一步发展就会导致身体接触，最后就是灭绝性行动，例如大屠杀，这就是偏见的终极表现。

然而，人们不禁要问，为什么人类这么容易陷入到种族偏见当中呢？作者认为，过度概括和敌意是人类思想中自然而常见的两种因素。

在人类社会中，我们随处可见不同群体。人们与同群体的人一起生活。不同群体之间的人往往缺乏足够的交流。他们很容易夸大自己与其他群体之间的区别，因此也很容易产生误解。更为重要的是，这种不同群体的划分会导致利益的冲突，甚至是很多无须有的冲突。

现在我们就来谈谈人们脑中概括的观念是如何形成的，这个过程包括五个特点：
(1) 它形成概念块来指导我们日常判断。
(2) 当我们碰到困难的时候，我们迅速把它归类，并用现成的概念作为解决问题的方式。

(3) 概括出来的想法使我们很快联想到相关的事物。
(4) 人的大脑里不仅存在事物概念还包含对事物的好恶。
(5) 概括的概念具有一定的理性因素。

大家都知道，这些概括的概念在很多时候是很固执，不容易改变的。但是，一旦这些想法与现实证据冲突的时候会发生什么呢？在大多数情况下，即使碰到现实情况与我们的想法相左，我们依然坚持我们自己的想法。只有在遭遇痛苦的失败时，或是在性格中具有怀疑精神的时候，我们会对形成的偏见做出一些改变。

对于偏见的产生，很多人提出了另外一种想法，他们认为，偏见很大程度上是由于人们遵从传统。当然，并不是说，任何一次的偏见的产生都完全是由于"顺从"某种传统。这其中包含一种程度，应该被认为是一种渐变的过程。文章中列举出纳粹集中营的军官对于犹太人的迫害出于遵从上级命令而不是十诫或是同情或是理性。最后文中谈到家庭教育对于偏见形成的影响。

**Questions for reflection:**
1. According to the author, what's the difference between the two cases?
2. Why do some authors claim that attitudes are prejudiced only if they violate some important norms or values in a culture? Do you agree with it? Why and why not?
3. What role does categorization play in the formation of prejudice?
4. What has happened when categories conflict with evidence?
5. What role does conformity play in the formation of prejudice?

# Prejudice and Intergroup Conflict

James Vivian and Rupert Brown

Prejudice as a feature of

Relative deprivation

individual psychology
The prejudiced personality
Belief similarity as an
  explanation of prejudice
Frustration, aggression, and
  prejudice
Individual cognitive processes
  underlying prejudice
Prejudice as a result of
  intergroup relationships

Realistic conflict theory
Prejudice as an aspect of group
  membership
Social identity theory
Reducing prejudice
Conclusion
Further reading
References

Although there has been little discernible improvement in social relations across the globe, there have been considerable advances in our understanding of the causes of prejudice and intergroup conflict. In analysing the major contributions of social psychology to this topic it is possible to distinguish between three approaches: there are those that locate the cause of prejudice in the psychological make-up of the individual; there are approaches that emphasise the role that external or environmental factors play; and finally, there are approaches in which group membership itself is seen as critically important. Each of these different perspectives may be important to a full understanding of the causes of intergroup conflict and prejudice and the best strategies for their reduction.

By prejudice we mean the derogatory attitudes that members of one group may hold about another, and the discriminatory behaviour that is often associated with this. Although prejudice and intergroup conflict are conceptually distinct, they often coexist; wherever we find prejudice, we also find conflict, if only dormant. Prejudice, then, can be thought of as a special case of intergroup conflict.

Intergroup conflict occurs when people think or behave antagonistically towards another group or its members in terms of their group memberships and seem motivated by concerns relating to those groups (Sherif, 1966; Tajfel & Turner, 1986). Conversely, conflict is "interpersonal" to the extent that no reference to membership is made, and the issues dividing the participants are specific to those particular individuals. The distinction between these levels of social interaction is critical as behaviour is often qualitatively different between intergroup and interpersonal contexts. In spite of this dichotomy, most social relationships are recognized to be a mixture of both interpersonal and intergroup components, the relative importance of which may fluctuate over time and across situations.

## Prejudice as a Feature of Individual Psychology

### The prejudiced personality

Some psychologists believe that people who display prejudice differ in personality from non-prejudiced people. This notion was popularized by Adorno, Frenkel-Brunswick, Levinson, and Sanford (1950) in their analysis of the "authoritarian personality". These authors argued that a particularly strict upbringing by parents overly concerned with convention and conformity gives rise to an authoritarian personality, which is thought to predispose certain people to prejudice. According to this theory, the hostility felt towards such parents is repressed by the child, who then idealizes the parents and who subsequently displays a deferential and submissive attitude towards authority figures in general (who are presumed to symbolize the parents). Following from a presumed need to discharge the psychic energy that has accumulated from repression, the pent-up hostility is displaced on to less threatening, lower status targets who are normally other groups (e.g., foreigners, minority groups).

These are seen as inherently defective or flawed in character and therefore deserving of contempt.

To measure authoritarianism, Adorno et al. (1950) developed the F-scale (tendency towards Fascism scale). Through detailed clinical interviews and projective tests of personality, Adorno and his colleagues were able to examine the relationships between F-scale responses, patterns of personality, and upbringing. Consistent with their theorizing, results seemed to indicate that highly authoritarian individuals tended to hold more ethnocentric (e. g., anti-Semitic, racist) attitudes and tended also to be those who had been subjected to stricter child-rearing practices than their less authoritarian counterparts.

Following its publication, critics pointed to methodological flaws associated with the F-scale and the clinical interviews used to validate it (Brown, 1965). The major problem with the F-scale is that the items are coded in such a way that agreement with statements always implies an authoritarian attitude of one form or another (see Table 1). As a result, it is unclear whether those who score highly on the F-scale are actually more authoritarian than others or whether they are simply more inclined towards acquiescence with statements in general. Further, the clinical interviews used to validate the F-scale as a measure of authoritarianism were flawed because the interviewers were aware of the prior F-scale responses of their interviewees, thus possibly contaminating the interview in subtle ways.

But perhaps a more damning criticism of the theory relates to the problems associated with an "individual differences" (i.e., personality) approach to explaining prejudice and intergroup behaviour (Billig, 1976). The problem, very simply, is that an analysis of individual personalities cannot account for the large-scale social behaviour that normally characterizes prejudice and intergroup conflict more generally. If it were true that prejudice derived from a disorder in personality, then we would expect the expression of prejudice or discrimination within groups to vary as much as the personalities of members comprising the group. But in fact the evidence seems to indicate that prejudice within groups is often remarkably uniform. For example, Pettigrew (1958), while studying prejudice in South Africa and the United States, found that levels of prejudice between the countries differed markedly while levels of authoritarianism did not. As a result, he concluded that rather than seeing the prejudice as an expression of a personality disorder, it was more likely to be a result of the norms prevailing in society. The fact that all members are exposed to such cultural norms may thus account for the oftobserved uniformity of prejudice.

**Table 1  Sample Items from the F-scale**
1. Obedience and respect for authority are the most important virtues that children should learn.
2. Young people sometimes get rebellious ideas, but as they grow up they ought to get over them and settle down.
3. What the youth needs most is strict discipline, rugged determination, and the will to work and fight for family and country.
4. An insult to our honour should always be punished.
5. Sex crimes, such as rape and attacks on children, deserve more than mere imprisonment; such criminals ought to be publicly whipped, or worse.
6. A person who has bad manners, habits, and breeding can hardly expect to get along with decent people.
7. Most of our social problems would be solved if we could somehow get rid of the immoral, crooked, and feeble-minded people.

8. If people would talk less and work more, everybody would be better off.
9. People can be divided into two distinct classes: the weak and the strong.
10. Human nature being what it is, there will always be war and conflict.
(Source: Adorno, Frenkel-Brunswick, Levinson, and Sanford, 1950, pp. 255-257)

Additionally, if prejudice is rooted in individual personalities, which are, by definition, enduring characteristics, then one would expect consistency over time in the expression of prejudice. But the historical evidence seems to reveal patterns of prejudice that suddenly appear and disappear, depending on the relations between the groups in question. Thus, for example, the prejudice displayed by Americans during the Second World War that eventually led to the internment of thousands of Japanese living in the United States cannot plausibly be explained by the individual personalities of Americans suddenly becoming more authoritarian in the 1940s. It seems more likely that the rise in prejudice directed specifically at the Japanese was related to the change in the objective relations between the groups that followed the bombing of Pearl Harbor.

## Belief Similarity as an Explanation of Prejudice

As an alternative to a "personality explanation" of prejudice, Rokeach (1960) offered an account that emphasized the role of belief systems. He proposed that similarity or "congruence" of individuals' beliefs determine, in large part, their attitudes towards one another. Specifically, he reasoned that we are generally more attracted to those who share our beliefs and opinions because they validate and legitimize our own. Those who disagree with us, on the other hand, are less attractive because they invalidate our beliefs.

Rokeach made a direct application of these ideas to racial prejudice. According to belief congruence theory, racial prejudice is seen as an outcome of perceived differences in belief (belief incongruence) between members of different racial groups and, further, that these belief differences are ultimately more important than the differences in group membership. Thus, according to Rokeach, we are more likely to discriminate against someone in our own ethnic group who disagrees with us than against someone in another group with whom we concur.

In order to test the theory, Rokeach, Smith, and Evans (1960) developed what has come to be called the "Race-belief" paradigm whereby individual subjects are presented with "stimulus persons" who vary in terms of their attitudinal and ethnic similarity to the subject. With few exceptions, studies utilizing this paradigm have generally established that belief influences subjects' reported attitudes more than race. Thus, white subjects are usually more attracted to a black person with similar beliefs than a white person with different beliefs (Insko, Nacoste, & Moe, 1983). Field research has also provided results generally supportive of belief congruence theory. Other researchers, working in different cultural contexts, report relatively strong correlations between perceived cultural or linguistic similarity and attraction to different ethnic groups (e. g. , Berry, Kalin, & Taylor, 1977; Brewer & Campbell, 1976).

As a further test of the hypothesized connection between similarity and intergroup attitudes, a number of experimental investigations have been conducted using methods that do not pit belief similarity directly against group membership. The evidence on this front is somewhat mixed. While certain studies offer support for the idea that similar outgroups are treated better than dissimilar ones (e. g. , Brown, 1984), others do not (Diehl, 1988). In fact, there is some experimental evidence that actually contradicts belief congruence theory. Under certain conditions, such as where there is strong attitudinal consensus in the ingroup, unstable status discrepancies, or competition between groups, more discrimination can be found against a similar out-group (Brown, 1984). These latter experimental findings thus challenge some of Rokeach's original claims.

How can these disparate results be accounted for? One explanation is offered by Brown and Turner (1981), who caution against the direct application of ideas developed to explain interpersonal behaviour to the realm of intergroup relations which are controlled, they argue, by different psychological processes. In a reconsideration of the race-belief literature, for example, they suggest that race may have had little impact because of the explicitly interpersonal, as opposed to intergroup, nature of the encounter. When race is made salient, they argue, the findings can be reversed, with race influencing judgements more than similarity. This argument has been supported by an experiment in which either interpersonal or intergroup similarity was made the main focus of people's attention (Diehl, 1988). As expected, in the former case, less discrimination was observed while the latter condition led to an increase in ingroup favouritism.

As a complete explanation of intergroup prejudice, then, belief-congruence theory is probably inadequate in its original form. In fact, Rokeach himself recognized the limitations of the theory and limited his claims to situations where prejudice or racism is not institutionalized as it was in South Africa under apartheid or where there is not significant social support for their expression (e. g. , in certain areas in the southern United States).

# Frustration, Aggression, and Prejudice

Predating both the authoritarian personality and belief-similarity theories was an ambitious attempt by Dollard, Doob, Miller, Mowrer, and Sears (1939) to explain aggressive behaviour between individuals and groups in society. Combining insights from traditional psychoanalytic and learning theories, Dollard et al. proposed that frustration, deriving from the blocking of basic needs, produces a "build-up of psychic energy" or an "instigation to aggress". Following a hydraulic model of human personality, such mounting pressure is alleged to be experienced as an aversive state of arousal that must eventually be relieved. Release of this energy restores balance or equilibrium and is thereby experienced as pleasurable or "cathartic". According to the theory, the release of such mounting tension normally takes the form of explicit or implicit acts of aggression that may be directed at the original source of the frustration or at alternative targets. Dollard and colleagues point out that the source of the frustration is often seen as relatively powerful or threatening (e.g., parents) and is sometimes difficult to identify at all, as when the impoverished consider the causes of their unfortunate position. Borrowing another psychoanalytic concept, Dollard et al. suggested that in cases like these, the aggression is displaced on to alternative targets who either share some surface similarity to the threatening source or are simply convenient scapegoats.

Dollard et al. (1939) used these ideas to explain prejudice, believing that they could account for both the pervasive character of prejudice and its apparent historical specificity. Prejudice is pervasive, they argued, because frustration is pervasive. In every culture at any point in time, most individuals are not having all of their needs met to their satisfaction. They may feel economically disadvantaged or unhappy with work or family life, but because almost nobody is perfectly contented, there exists at all times and places a certain "baseline" level of frustration and, consequently, of aggression. And because the sources of such frustration endemic to social life cannot be easily identified, the associated aggression is thereby displaced on to convenient targets, the targets of prejudice who are normally relatively powerless minority groups. Historical fluctuations can be explained, according to the theory, in terms of the frustrations associated with changing economic conditions (e. g., the rise of anti-Semitism in Germany following the First World War may have been due to the collapse of the German economy at this time). Evidence in support of this idea was offered by Hovland and Sears (1940) among others, who showed that lynchings of blacks in the southern United States in the late nineteenth and early twentieth centuries were related to the price of cotton, a major industry in this region during that time. As the economic standing of many declined along with the price of cotton, the number of lynchings increased. Presumably, the bleak economy produced feelings of frustration in those affected who vented their frustration in a particularly savage way on the convenient scapegoats of the day, the blacks. Some experimental studies have lent further support to the theory (e. g., Miller & Bugelski, 1948).

Despite its attractive simplicity and its empirical support, frustration-aggression theory may still be limited in its ability to explain intergroup prejudice. As with personality, the level of frustration experienced may vary from individual to individual and thus one would expect more variation in the expression of aggression or prejudice than is normally observed. Another major limitation relates to the choice of particular outgroups as targets of prejudice. Why, for example, did whites in the United States select blacks for lynchings rather than other disadvantaged minority groups? Finally, it has been established that frustration was neither necessary nor sufficient to produce aggression leading to a reformulation of the original theory (Berkowitz, 1962). However, even this revised version, based as it is on individual motivational states, is subject to some of the same criticisms that applied to the original theory offered by Dollard et al. (1939).

## Individual Cognitive Processes Underlying Prejudice

Some theories of prejudice emphasize the role of cognitive processes in the formation and maintenance of negative group stereotypes. Stereotypes are preconceived ideas about entire classes of people and are thought to derive more from limitations in the ability to process information than from a disordered personality or individual needs or motivations. According to Tajfel (1959), we need to simplify the extraordinarily complex physical and social world that we inhabit by placing objects, events, and people (including the self) into various categories. Following from such categorical differentiation, Tajfel further showed that diffe-rences between separate categories of physical stimuli are overestimated (Tajfel & Wilkes, 1963). Similar effects have been obtained with social stimuli (people). Using children from Switzerland as subjects, Doise, Deschamps, and Meyer (1978) demonstrated how groups of boys and girls perceived greater differences between photographs of unknown boys and girls when the gender distinction was made explicit than when it was not. Further, the photographs of boys alone and girls alone were judged to be more similar under these same conditions. These results were repeated in a second study which involved judgements of Swiss linguistic groups. Thus, Doise et al. (1987) showed that both differences between and similarities within social categories are accentuated when intergroup categorizations are clear.

It is important to note, however, that the effects of social categorization are not symmetrical. While it appears that categorical distinctions tend to enhance the perception of within-category similarity, this effect is normally more pronounced for the outgroup which is seen as more internally homogeneous than the ingroup (e. g. , Quattrone, 1986). For example, Jones, Wood, and Quattrone (1981) found when they asked members of university clubs to estimate the variability (of personalities) of members belonging to different clubs, that club members consistently perceived other clubs as more homogeneous than their own. With some important exceptions (e. g. , Simon & Brown, 1987), similar results have been obtained in diverse contexts generally confirming the idea that group members tend to believe while "they" are all the same, "we" are different.

The cognitive process of social categorization may also lie at the heart of stereotype formation. It has been shown that when two distinctive (unusual) events co-occur, people come to believe that there is a correlation between them and that they go together (Chapman & Chapman, 1967). Hamilton and Gifford (1976) extended this notion to stereotypes by arguing, for example, that whites might perceive a correlation between criminality and black skin colour because the two events are unusual and therefore distinctive. To demonstrate this, they presented subjects with scenarios depicting desirable and undesirable actions of members of hypothetical groups. While one of the groups was twice as large as the other and, overall, there were more desirable than undesirable acts depicted, the proportion of desirable to undesirable behaviour within each group was held constant. So, for example, although there were twice as many undesirable acts emanating from the larger group, there were also twice as many people in that group, so there was no actual correlation between the nature of the act (desirable or undesirable) and group membership. Nevertheless, when asked to indicate which acts came from the larger and smaller groups, subjects overestimated the number of undesirable (less common) behaviours in the smaller (minority) group (see Table 2). Consistent with Hamilton's reasoning on the impact of distinctive stimuli, subjects thus perceived an "illusory correlation" between the possession of undesirable traits and minority group membership. This research provides some support, then, for the notion that distinctiveness explains why minorities are seen as having undesirable traits.

Although there is some evidence that people hold fewer derogatory stereotypes about traditionally oppressed groups than before (e. g., Campbell, 1971) later evidence seems to suggest that stereotypes persist even among liberally minded people. When more subtle measures are used (Crosby, Bromley, & Saxe, 1980) or when discriminatory attitudes cannot be unambiguously attributed to prejudice (Gaertner & Dovidio, 1986), a surprising number of seemingly non-prejudiced people behave in characteristically prejudiced ways. Why is it that stereotypes are so resistant to change? One possibility is that people selectively attend to information that confirms their stereotypes. Thus, for example, Howard and Rothbart (1980) showed that even when ingroup and outgroup speakers make the same number of favourable and unfavourable remarks, subjects recall more unfavourable remarks coming from the outgroup. This selective memory together with the fact that unfavourable stereotypes are generally easier to acquire but more difficult to lose than favourable ones, probably contributes to the persistence of unflattering stereotypes of minority groups (Rothbart & Park, 1986).

### Table 2 Distinctive (infrequent) events as a source of illusory correlation

| | Group | |
|---|---|---|
| | A (majority) | B (minority) |
| Actual distribution of behaviours between two groups | | |

| | | |
|---|---|---|
| Desirable | 18 (67%) | 9 (33%) |
| Undesirable | 8 (67%) | 4 (33%) |
| Distribution of behaviours between two groups as perceived by subjects | | |
| Desirable | 17.5 (65%) | 9.5 (35%) |
| Undesirable | 5.8 (48%) | 6.2 (52%) |

[Source: Hamilton and Gifford, 1976, Table 1

Note: Subjects overestimate the amount of undesirable behaviour emanating from the smaller (minority) group (Group B)]

Additionally, there is reason to believe that many of these cognitive processes may be outside of conscious control. Devine (1989) has proposed that most people share a knowledge of stereotypes and that this knowledge can affect, quite unconsciously, the processing of information. In one study Devine showed that a hypothetical person was viewed as more hostile (black stereotype) by subjects (both prejudiced and non-prejudiced) who had been previously exposed to stereotype-relevant words flashed so quickly that subjects could not recall their content. Presumably, the presentation of the stereotype-associated words activated the cultural stereotype which then had unconscious effects on subjects' assessments of the hypothetical person.

Although there is good reason to believe that individual cognitive processes play a role in the formation and maintenance of stereotypes, there is still reason to doubt that they can account for all of the stereotypes that we hold. If it were true, for example, that people tend to exaggerate the correlation between unusual events that sometimes co-occur, then minority groups should have as part of their stereotype both undesirable and unusually desirable traits (e.g., geniuses). Clearly, this is not the case as stereotypes of minority groups are normally derogatory. This fact highlights one of the important limitations of the purely cognitive explanation of prejudice phenomena: it cannot explain why categorical differentiation normally takes on an asymmetry that either favours the ingroup or derogates the outgroup. In addition, cognitive explanations are still individualistic in nature and thus have difficulty explaining widespread, collective behaviour which, it can be argued, are controlled by processes that differ from those operating at the individual psychological level.

## Prejudice as a Result of Intergroup Relationships

### Relative Deprivation

Frustration-aggression theory subsequently evolved into a form which was more explicitly "intergroup" in focus and thus overcame some of the difficulties associated with the earlier version. Following Berkowitz's (1962) lead in emphasizing the subjective nature of frustration, others have argued that it is precisely when people feel deprived of something that they feel entitled to that they experience frustration. The discrepancy between our actual attainments (e. g. , position in life) and our expectations (e. g. , the position we feel we deserve) is referred to as "relative deprivation". Two types of relative deprivation can be distinguished (Runciman, 1966). One is "egoistic" relative deprivation which derives from comparisons made with other individuals who are seen as similar to oneself. Thus, if colleagues or peers are considerably better off in terms of wages or standard of living, one would be expected to feel deprived relative to these similar others. In "fraternalistic" relative deprivation, on the other hand, feelings of deprivation are thought to derive from comparisons between groups such as when members of particular ethnic or minority groups consider their standard of living in comparison to the dominant majority.

Runciman's discovery that intergroup comparisons could lead to relative deprivation has been confirmed in a number of studies. Vanneman and Pettigrew (1972) found that racist political attitudes were related to feelings of relative deprivation generally and that the most racist attitudes were found among those who reported being fraternally deprived. Further demonstrating the utility of distinguishing between egoistic and fraternalistic deprivation, Abeles (1976) and Walker and Mann (1987) have shown that blacks in the United States and unemployed workers in Australia were more likely to engage in social action when they felt that their group as a whole has not attained what they justly deserved relative to other groups. Abeles also points out that levels of militancy appear to be highest among blacks with higher socio-economic and educational status. This is consistent with Runciman's observation that leaders of collective movements are usually the least deprived members of their groups in an objective sense. Following from an understanding of frustration as a subjective phenomenon, it is likely that these individuals have higher expectations both for themselves and for their group and thus experience the perceived deprivation more acutely.

Relative deprivation theory is thus quite helpful in explaining when hostility will emerge between groups. When members of a given social group perceive a discrepancy between what they believe their group deserves and what they have actually attained, members share a sense of deprivation and a sense of injustice. Because notions of justice are socially determined in the sense that they reflect norms and values of a given culture, they are thought to apply equally across all members of the group. The shared sense of injustice then helps explain the uniformity of behaviour that normally characterizes intergroup relations generally and prejudice in particular.

## Realistic Conflict Theory

Social scientists in various disciplines have long recognized that in addition to the needs, desires, or personalities of individual members, the goals or interests of groups are potent influences of behaviour. Thus, when members believe that another group can satisfy its desires only at their own group's expense (and vice versa), hostility develops between the groups along with the discriminatory and prejudiced behaviour that is commonly associated with such antagonistic intergroup relationships. According to this view, the attitudes and actions of members of different groups reflect the goal relations between those groups. This approach to intergroup relations is known as realistic conflict theory, as real (or perceived) conflicts of interest are presumed to underlie much of the prejudice and hostility often observed between groups.

The best known proponents of this approach have been Muzafer Sherif and his colleagues, who conducted some of the earliest empirical investigations of intergroup conflict. In these studies, they noted the relative ease with which groups of otherwise healthy, well-adjusted boys could be induced to display marked ingroup favouritism and openly hostile behaviour towards other groups of boys, simply as a result of introducing a competition between them (Sherif, 1966). Furthermore, they were able to reduce the tension by replacing the competitive arrangement, whereby one group succeeded at the other's expense, with a cooperative one, where both groups' success was contingent on cooperation between the groups. Based on these and other observations, Sherif suggested that conflict between groups, and the associated intergroup biases, develops through competition and can be reduced through intergroup cooperation in pursuit of superordinate goals.

Results similar to Sherif's have also been obtained among groups of adult managers in human relations workshops and among members of different cultures (e.g., Blake & Mouton, 1962; Diab, 1970). Nevertheless, subsequently, findings have begun to accumulate which suggest that while competition may be sufficient for the emergence of intergroup bias, it may not be necessary. In a series of what have come to be called "minimal group" experiments, where distinctions between groups are trivial (e.g., presumed aesthetic preferences) and members remain anonymous, the tendency to favour the ingroup either in evaluative judgements or the distribution of rewards has been clearly demonstrated (Rabbie & Horwitz, 1969; Tajfel, Flament, Billig, & Bundy, 1971). Additionally, though cooperative contact between groups in pursuit of "superordinate" goals generally improves relations between them, there are important exceptions when this is apparently not the case. For example, later research found that in order for the superordinate goals strategy to be effective, the cooperative effort must be successful and members of the groups must be able to preserve distinctive identities rather than being absorbed into a common culture (Brown & Wade, 1987; Worchel, Andreoli, & Folger, 1977). Otherwise, there is reason to believe that such contact can exacerbate rather than alleviate hostility.

## Prejudice as an Aspect of Group Membership

### Social Identity Theory

How can the "incipient hostility" that appears to emerge between groups even in the absence of explicit competition or conflicts of interest be explained? Further, why are comparisons between groups' material outcomes apparently so important in generating resentment and hostility? One influential theory which has been offered to explain these phenomena is one that emphasizes the role of cognitive and motivational processes in prejudice and intergroup relations; this explanation is now commonly known as social identity theory (Tajfel, 1978; Tajfel & Turner, 1986).

This theory starts with the assumption that the desire to understand and to evaluate oneself constitutes a primary motive underlying much of social behaviour. Joining two traditions in psychology, it proposes that we satisfy this desire through social categorization and social comparison. With social categorization, as noted, the complex social world is simplified by placing people, including the self, into various categories (e. g., gender, race, nationality, or political ideology). It is this process of self-categorization that defines what Tajfel called the social identity. Social identity theory hypothesizes that people are strongly motivated to understand and evaluate these group-based identities and, echoing an earlier theory (Festinger, 1954), it holds that this evaluative activity is primarily carried out through comparisons with other groups.

However, along with a need for self-evaluation and understanding, there may be a need for "self-enhancement". This added feature is necessary because while the dual processes of social categorization and social comparison can account for the tendency to compare and contrast groups, they cannot easily explain why, when the self is involved, the differentiation normally takes on an asymmetry that favours the groups to which one belongs (the ingroup). With this added concern for self-enhancement, it is argued that individuals are motivated not only by the desire to know and evaluate themselves, but also to evaluate themselves favourably relative to others. Comparisons between groups therefore often have the objective of attaining some distinctiveness from other groups in order to achieve or maintain a positive social identity. From this perspective, then, prejudice may be an expression of a basic motivation for a positive identity which is accomplished, in part, by positively distinguishing an ingroup from an outgroup.

There is abundant research evidence supporting the general claims of social identity theory. It is clear from the literature that intergroup bias (the tendency to favour the group to which one belongs over other groups) is an extraordinarily robust phenomenon which occurs in diverse contexts across a variety of group tasks (see Brewer, 1979). Consistent with the notion that people are motivated to attain positive social identities through intergroup comparisons, the evidence indicates that once groups are perceived to be meaningfully distinct from one another, intergroup bias often ensues in the form of discriminatory reward allocations, trait evaluations, or performance evaluations. In minimal group experiments especially, where the basis for group categorization is trivial, the results reveal a consistent pattern of ingroup favouritism in the allocation of financial rewards that supports social identity theory. Even when alternative allocation strategies would have yielded higher profits for an anonymous ingroup member, participants in these experiments tended to prefer strategies that maximized the difference between the groups' outcomes in favour of the ingroup (Tajfel et al., 1971; see also Figure 1). Similar results were obtained in a field setting where Brown (1978) noted factory-workers' desire to maintain wage differentials between their own and other departments even at the expense of their own absolute wage levels.

Central to social identity theory is the idea that group members discriminate against outsiders in the service of the need to achieve, maintain, or enhance self-esteem. The evidence that relates to this hypothesis is mixed. Consistent with this idea, Oakes and Turner (1980) found that group members who were given the opportunity to discriminate reported higher levels of self-esteem afterwards than those who could not discriminate. Nevertheless, other evidence on this front indicates that the relationship between self-esteem and intergroup behaviour is not as straightforward as social identity theory would predict. In some cases, higher levels of self-esteem are associated with intergroup discrimination while in others, discrimination is actually associated with lower levels of self-esteem (Abrams & Hogg, 1988). Another problem for the theory stems from the supposed link between the strength of group identification and the amount of intergroup bias. While many studies report a consistent relationship between identification and intergroup bias, the magnitude of the relationships are relatively weak, and, in some cases, they are actually negative (see Hinkle & Brown, 1990). Additionally, it is clear that in certain cases, people favour the out-group. It is commonly found, for example, that members of low-status groups exhibit outgroup favouritism to high-status outgroups (Mullen, Brown & Smith, 1992). This does not fit simply with the theory's view that group members are attempting to create positive social identities by always engaging in ingroup-favouring behaviour.

| Ingroup member | 7 | 8 | 9 | 10 | 11 | 12 | 13 | 14 | 15 | 16 | 17 | 18 | 19 |
|---|---|---|---|---|---|---|---|---|---|---|---|---|---|
| Outgroup Member | 1 | 3 | 5 | 7 | 9 | 11 | 13 | 15 | 17 | 19 | 21 | 23 | 25 |

(Figure 1 Sample matrix used in Tajfel et al. (1971). Subjects were instructed to allocate points (representing money) to anonymous members of their own and another group. Average responses were slightly to the left of the centre column (13, 13) suggesting that subjects were interes-ted in allocating more money to the ingroup than to the outgroup member even at the expense of absolute profit for the ingroup member.)

Finally, and perhaps most importantly, it is not entirely clear whether social identity theory can account for intergroup prejudice if prejudice is defined as derogatory attitudes or behaviour directed at members of another group. Where the data are available, the majority of empirical studies concerned with intergroup bias report that differences in evaluations of ingroup and outgroup typically result from elevated ratings of the ingroup (Brewer, 1979). So while it is clear that members of groups often show favouritism to the group to which they belong, there is actually very little evidence that they derogate outgroups in the way that is characteristic of prejudice.

## Reducing Prejudice

The various approaches discussed above have direct implications for the reduction of prejudice and the resolution of conflict. The majority of programmes aimed at fostering harmonious relations between previously conflictual groups have operated under assumptions embodied in what has come to be known as the "contact hypothesis" (Allport, 1954). This hypothesis asserts attitudes and behaviour towards outgroups will become more positive after interaction with them. Although many studies conducted in diverse contexts support this idea, because many others were less encouraging, several qualifications to the original hypothesis were required. Thus, the effects of contact are greatly enhanced if it is sanctioned by institutional supports (e. g., law, custom), takes place between participants on an equal status footing in pursuit of common goals, and provided it is of a sort that leads to the perception of communality between the two groups (Amir, 1969).

In spite of the early awareness that these moderating conditions were necessary for the success of intergroup contact, many integration policies in the United States and elsewhere have gone forward somewhat blindly, ignoring the recommendations of social scientists. Contact between black and white children in US public (state) schools is a case in point. Early legislative action imposing desegregation was largely ineffective in the reduction of prejudice between these children probably because the interracial contact in the school setting did not satisfy the criteria necessary for successful intergroup contact. The contact was mostly involuntary and of a superficial nature between groups of markedly different statuses in communities which were often unsupportive of the contact to begin with (Schofield, 1986). Another interesting example of an attempt to reduce ethnic prejudice was described by Schwarzwald and Amir (1984). This study is concerned with efforts in Israel to deal with inter-ethnic tensions between those of middle eastern (North African and Asian) and western (European and American) descent; it documents an "asymmetry" in the patterns of acceptance and rejection between members of these two cultural groups. When asked to indicate social preferences, for example, westerners of all ages tended to accept and prefer other westerners over their eastern counterparts. At the same time, those of eastern descent appear also to prefer westerners, devaluing their own cultural heritage and social standing. This situation is not unlike some encounters between black and white Americans where it has been established that sometimes the minority group (blacks) adopt the majority evaluation of their group and consider themselves less worthy (Clark & Clark, 1947). As in the United States, the results of imposed ethnic integration within the Israeli schools were not very encouraging primarily because policy was rarely guided by scientific knowledge. Because the schools continued to "track" (i. e. , to stream) their students, the clear status differentials remained, leaving a disproportionate number of middle easterners in the lower tracks (Schwarzwald & Amir, 1984).

These examples in the United States and Israel strongly suggest that contact itself is largely ineffective at reducing prejudice between cultural groups. More recent theoretical work has built on the original contact hypothesis in specifying additional conditions under which contact will successfully reduce prejudice and thereby improve relations between groups. It is generally agreed that intergroup contact is successful to the extent that diverse groups can coexist peacefully while maintaining distinctive identities. Such integration is the goal in any truly pluralistic society and should be distinguished from assimilation, another possible outcome of contact which is said to have occurred when previously differentiated groups are reduced into a common culture. In spite of efforts in numerous experimental and societal contexts, however, it remains to be seen how best to realize the goal of true integration.

To this end, two seemingly divergent positions have been advanced, both of which claim to offer the optimal strategy for facilitating integration between groups (Brewer and Miller, 1984; Hewstone & Brown, 1986). In their model of "de-categorization", Brewer and Miller propose that the goal of contact is "non-category-based" interaction. The major symptoms of category-based interaction, which prevents integration, include the depersonalization of outgroup members, who are treated as if they are part of a homogeneous or undifferentiated category. In order to achieve more harmonious relations, it follows that respective group memberships need to be made less salient during contact, the boundaries between groups less rigid, and social relations more interpersonally oriented. The assumption is that repeated interpersonal contact with members of the disliked group will produce stereotype-disconfirming experiences which encourage truly inter-personal as opposed to intergroup interactions. Miller, Brewer, and Edwards (1985) have provided some experimental evidence in favour of this approach. They found that cooperative group interactions which emphasized interpersonal (rather than task) aspects of the situation generated more favourable intergroup attitudes and less discriminatory reward allocations.

Consistent with this view, several educational interventions have been developed which attempt to structure intergroup contact in a way that will weaken boundaries between groups by providing members with cooperative interpersonal experiences with members of a disliked group. One application of this strategy was offered by Aronson and his colleagues in their work with school-aged children of varying ethnic backgrounds in the United States (Aronson, Blaney, Stephan, Sikes, & Snapp, 1978). They devised a cooperative learning strategy referred to as the "jigsaw classroom". Classrooms employing this technique are comprised of racially mixed groups of students who are each responsible for mastering separate portions of material and for teaching this material to others in their group. Members thus depend on one another to achieve the common or superordinate goal of getting good marks in the class. Evidence indicates that students in jigsaw classes report liking classmates of other races more after the technique has been introduced than before. More generally, curricula which emphasize cooperative learning strategies seem to be effective in reducing intergroup tensions (Slavin, 1983).

The problem with many of these strategies that draw attention away from group memberships is that positive attitude changes are often restricted to the situation that produced them and to the members present in the original contact situation. Although the contact may provide stereotype-disconfirming experiences, the individuals present can be considered atypical or exceptions to the rule with respect to the group as a whole. As a result, attitudinal and behavioural changes achieved in the contact situation are often short-lived.

Hewstone and Brown (1986) addressed this problem of the lack of generalization associated with many intergroup contact efforts. Their model is based on the distinction between interpersonal and intergroup behaviour. Because the two levels of interaction may be controlled by different psychological processes, they argue that contact will produce generalized attitude change beyond the contact setting only when the interaction is construed as intergroup in nature, when members are seen as represen-tative of their respective groups. In an experimental context, Wilder (1984) provided evidence in favour of this model. By varying the level of "prototypicality" of an outgroup member, he found that significant improvements in the evaluation of the outgroup as a whole, in this case a rival college, occurred only when there was a pleasant encounter with what was perceived to be a typical member of the outgroup (see Figure

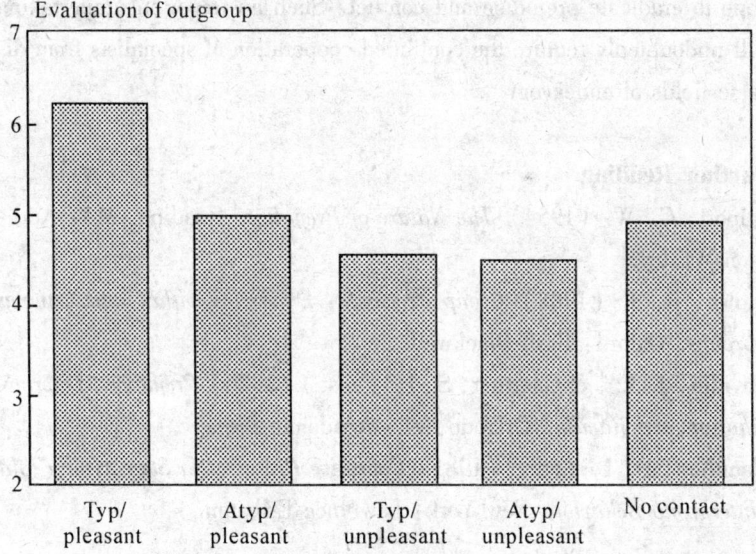

(Figure 2 Evaluation of an outgroup after contact with a typical or atypical outgroup member who behaved in either a pleasant or unpleasant manner. Source: Adapted from Wilder, 1984, Table 1)

2). In this case, a stereotype-confirming, yet pleasant experience with a typical outgroup member improved perceptions of rival groups.

## Conclusion

In this chapter several theories of prejudice and intergroup conflict have been reviewed. It is clear that while each theory contributes to our understanding of these phenomena, there are, nevertheless, important limitations to each. It would thus appear that a complete understanding of prejudice and intergroup conflict requires multiple perspectives including those that focus on the individual, those that focus on the group, and those that focus on the relations between groups in society. It is also clear from this review that only under very specific conditions can we hope to eradicate prejudice and conflict. Such an important undertaking will undoubtedly require the continued cooperation of specialists from diverse fields of endeavour.

**Further Reading**

Allport, G. W. (1954) *The Nature of Prejudice*. Reading, MA: Addison Wesley.

Brown, R. J. (1988) *Group Processes: Dynamics within and between Groups*. Oxford: Basil Blackwell.

Dovidio, J. F., & Gaertner, S. L. (eds.) (1986) *Prejudice, Discrimination and Racism*. Orlando, FL: Academic Press.

Hamilton, D. L. (ed.) (1981) *Cognitive Processes in Stereotyping and Intergroup Behavior*. New York: Lawrence Erlbaum.

**References**

Abeles, R. P. (1976) Relative Deprivation, Rising Expectations and Black Militancy. *Journal of Social Issues*, 32, pp. 119-137.

Abrams, D., & Hogg, M. A. (1988) Comments on the Motivational

Status of Self-esteem in Social Identity and Intergroup Discrimination. *European Journal of Social Psychology*, 18, pp. 317-334.

Adorno, T. W., Frenkel-Brunswick, E., Levinson, D. J., & Sanford, R. N. (1950) *The Authoritarian Personality*. New York: Harper.

Allport, G. W. (1954) *The Nature of Prejudice*. Reading, MA: Addison Wesley.

Amir, Y. (1969) Contact Hypothesis in Ethnic Relations. *Psychological Bulletin*, 71, pp. 319-342.

Aronson, E., Blaney, N., Stephan, C., Sikes, J., & Snapp, M. (1978) *The Jigsaw Classroom*. London: Sage.

Berkowitz, L. (1962) *Aggression. A Social Psychological Analysis*. New York: McGraw-Hill.

Berry, J. W., Kalin, R., & Taylor, D. M. (1977) *Multiculturalism and Ethnic Attitudes in Canada*. Ottawa: Supply and Services Canada.

Billig, M. G. (1976) *Social Psychology and Intergroup Relations*. London: Academic Press.

Blake, R. R., & Mouton, J. S. (1962) Overevaluation of Own Group's Product in Intergroup Competition. *Journal of Abnormal and Social Psychology*, 64, pp. 237-238.

Brewer, M. B. (1979) In-group Bias in the Minimal Intergroup Situation: A Cognitive-Motivational Analysis. *Psychological Bulletin*, 86, pp. 307-324.

Brewer, M. B., & Campbell, D. T. (1976) *Ethnocentrism and Intergroup Attitudes. East African Evidence*. New York: Sage.

Brewer, M. B., & Miller, N. (1984) Beyond the Contact Hypothesis: Theoretical Perspectives on Desegregation. In N. Miller & M. B. Brewer (eds.) *Groups in Contact. The Psychology of Desegregation* (pp. 281-302). Orlando, FL: Academic Press.

Brown, R. (1965) *Social Psychology*. New York: Macmillan.

Brown, R. J. (1978) Divided We Fall: An Analysis of Relations between Sections of a Factory Work-force. In H. Tajfel (ed.) *Differentiation between Social Groups. Studies in the Social Psychology of Intergroup Relations* (pp. 395-429). London: Academic Press.

Brown, R. J. (1984) The Role of Similarity in Intergroup Relations. In H. Tajfel (ed.) *The Social Dimension: European Developments in Social Psychology* (pp. 603-623). Cambridge: Cambridge University Press.

Brown, R. J., & Abrams, D. (1986) The Effects of Intergroup Similarity and Goal Interdependence on Intergroup Attitudes and Task Performance. *Journal of Experimental Social Psychology*, 22, pp. 78-92.

Brown, R. J., & Turner, J. C. (1981) Interpersonal and Intergroup Behaviour. In J. C. Turner & H. Giles feds) *Intergroup Behaviour* (pp. 33-65). Oxford: Basil Blackwell.

Brown, R. J., & Wade, G. S. (1987) Superordinate Goals and Intergroup Behaviour: The Effects of Role Ambiguity and Status on Intergroup Attitudes and Task Performance. *European Journal of Social Psychology*, 17, pp. 131-142.

Campbell, A. (1971) *White Attitudes Towards Black People*. Ann Arbor, MI: Institute for Social Research.

Chapman, L. J., & Chapman, J. P. (1967) Genesis of Popular but Erroneous Diagnostic Observations. *Journal of Abnormal Psychology*, 72, pp. 193-204.

Clark, K. B., & Clark, M. P. (1947) Racial Identification and Preference in Negro Children. In T. M. Newcomb & E. L. Hartley (eds) *Readings in Social Psychology* (pp. 169-178). New York: Holt, Rinehart & Winston.

Crosby, F., Bromley, S., & Saxe, L. (1980) Recent Unobtrusive

Studies of Black and White Discrimination and Prejudice: A Literature Review. *Psychological Bulletin*, 87, pp. 546-563.

Devine, P. (1989) Stereotypes and Prejudice: Their Automatic and Controlled Components. *Journal of Personality and Social Psychology*, 56, pp. 5-18.

Diab, L. N. (1970) A Study of Intragroup and Intergroup Relations among Experimentally Produced Small Groups. *Genetic Psychology Monographs*, 82, pp. 49-82.

Diehl, M. (1988) Social Identity and Minimal Groups: The Effects of Interpersonal and Intergroup Attitudinal Similarity on Intergroup Discrimination. *British Journal of Social Psychology*, 27, pp. 289-300.

Doise, W., Deschamps, J. C., & Meyer, G. (1978) The Accentuation of Intracategory Similarities. In H. Tajfel (ed.) *Differentiation between Social Groups. Studies in the Social Psychology of Intergroup Relations* (pp. 159-168) London: Academic Press.

Dollard, J., Doob, L. W., Miller, N. E., Mowrer, O. H., & Sears, R. R. (1939) *Frustration and Aggression*, New Haven, CT: Yale University Press.

Festinger, L. (1954) A Theory of Social Comparison Processes. *Human Relations*, 7, pp. 117-140.

Gaertner, S. L., & Dovidio, J. F. (1986) The Aversive form of Racism. In J. F. Dovidio & S. L. Gaertner (eds.) *Prejudice, Discrimination and Racism* (pp. 61-89) Orlando, FL: Academic Press.

Hamilton, D. L. (1981) Illusory Correlation as a Basis for Stereotyping. In D. L. Hamilton (ed.) *Cognitive Processes in Stereotyping and Intergroup Behaviour* (pp. 115-144) New York: Lawrence Erlbaum.

Hamilton, D. L., & Gifford, R. K. (1976) Illusory Correlation in Interpersonal Perception: A Cognitive Basis of Stereotypic Judgements. *Journal of Experimental Social Psychology*, 12, pp. 392-407.

Hewstone, M. R. C., & Brown, R. J. (1986) Contact Is Not Enough: An Intergroup Perspective on the Contact Hypothesis. In M. R. C. Hewstone & R. J. Brown (eds.) *Contact and Conflict in Intergroup Encounters* (pp. 1-44). Oxford: Basil Blackwell.

Hinkle, S., & Brown, R. (1990) Intergroup Comparisons and Social Identity: Some Links and Lacunae. In D. Abrams & M. Hogg (Eds) *Social Identity Theory. Constructive and Critical Advances* (pp. 48-70). Hemel Hempstead: Harvester-Wheatsheaf.

Holland, C., & Sears, R. R. (1940) Minor Studies in Aggression: VI. Correlation of Lynchings with Economic Indices. *Journal of Psychology*, 9, pp. 301-310.

Howard, J. W., & Rothbart, M. (1980) Social Categorization and Memory for Ingroup and Outgroup Behavior. *Journal of Personality and Social Psychology*, 38, pp. 301-310.

Insko, C. A., Nacoste, R. W., & Moe, I. L. (1983) Belief Congruence and Racial Discrimination: Review of the Evidence and Critical Evaluation. *European Journal of Social Psychology*, 13, pp. 153-174.

Jones, E. E., Wood, G. C., & Quattrone, G. A. (1981) Perceived Variability of Personal Characteristics in Ingroups and Outgroups: The Role of Knowledge and Evaluation. *Personality and Social Psychology Bulletin*, 7, pp. 523-528.

Miller, N., & Brewer, M. B. (eds.) (1984) *Groups in Contact. The Psychology of Desegregation.* New York: Academic Press.

Miller, N., Brewer, M. B., & Edwards, K. (1985) Cooperative Interaction in Desegregated Settings: A Laboratory Analogue. *Journal of Social Issues*, 41, pp. 63-79.

Miller, N. E., & Bugelski, R. (1948) Minor Studies in Aggression:

The Influence of Frustrations Imposed by the Ingroup on Attitudes toward Outgroups. *Journal of Psychology*, 25, pp. 437-442.

Mullen, B., Brown, R., & Smith, C. (1992) Ingroup Bias as a Function of Salience, Relevance, and Status: An Integration. *European Journal of Social Psychology*, 22, pp. 103-122.

Oakes, P. J., & Turner, J. C. (1980) Social Categorization and Intergroup Behaviour: Does Minimal Intergroup Discrimination Make Social Identity More Positive? *European Journal of Social Psychology*, 10, 295-302.

Pettigrew, T. F. (1958) Personality and Sociocultural Factors in Intergroup Attitudes: A Cross-national Comparison. *Journal of Conflict Resolution*, 2, pp. 29-42.

Quattrone, G. A. (1986) On the Perception of a Group's Variability. In S. Worchel & W. Austin (eds). *The Social Psychology of Intergroup Relations* (2nd edn, pp. 25-48), Chicago, IL: Nelson Hall.

Rabbie, J. M., & Horwitz, M. (1969) Arousal of Ingroup-outgroup Bias by a Chance Win or Loss. *Journal of Personality and Social Psychology*, 13, pp. 269-277.

Rokeach, M. (ed.) (1960) *The Open and Closed Mind*. New York: Basic Books.

Rokeach, M., Smith, P. W., & Evans, R. I. (1960) Two Kinds of Prejudice or One? In M. Rokeach (ed.). *The Open and Closed Mind* (pp. 132-168). New York: Basic Books.

Rothbart, M., & Park, B. (1986) On the Confirmability and Disconfirmability of Trait Concepts. *Journal of Personality and Social Psychology*, 50, pp. 131-142.

Runciman, W. G. (1966) *Relative Deprivation and Social Justice*. London: Routledge & Kegan Paul.

Schofield, J. W. (1986) Black-white Contact in Desegregated Schools. In M. Hewstone & R. J. Brown (eds.) *Contact and Conflict in In-*

tergroup Encounters (pp. 79-92). Oxford: Basil Blackwell.

Schwarzwald, J., & Amir, Y. (1984) Interethnic Relations and Education: An Israeli Perspective. In N. Miller & M. Brewer (eds) *Groups in Contact. The Psychology of Desegregation* (pp. 53-76). Orlando, FL: Academic Press.

Sherif, M. (1966). *Group Conflict and Cooperation.* London: Routledge & Kegan Paul.

Simon, B., & Brown, R. J. (1987) Perceived Intragroup Homogeneity in Minority-majority contexts. *Journal of Personality and Social Psychology*, 53, pp. 703-711.

Slavin, R. E. (1983) When Does Cooperative Learning Increase Student Achievement? *Psychological Bulletin*, 94, pp. 429-445.

Tajfel, H. (1959) The Anchoring Effects of Value in a Scale of Judgements. *British Journal of Psychology*, 50, pp. 294-304.

Tajfel, H. (ed.) (1978) *Differentiation between Social Groups. Studies in the Social Psychology of Intergroup Relations.* London: Academic Press.

Tajfel, H., & Turner, J. C. (1986) The Social Identity Theory of Intergroup Behavior. In S. Worchel & W. Austin (eds.). *Psychology of Intergroup Relations* (pp. 7-24). Chicago: Nelson-Hall.

Tajfel, H., & Wilkes, A. L. (1963) Classification and Quantitative Judgement. *British Journal of Psychology*, 54, pp. 101-114.

Tajfel, H., Flament, C., Billig, M. G., & Bundy, R. P. (1971) Social Categorization and Intergroup Behaviour. *European Journal of Social Psychology*, 1, pp. 149-178.

Vanneman, R. D., & Pettigrew, T. F. (1972) Race and Relative Deprivation in the Urban United States. *Race*, 13, pp. 461-486.

Walker, L., & Mann, L. (1987) Unemployment, Relative Deprivation, and Social Protest. *Personality and Social Psychology Bulletin*, 13, pp. 275-283.

Wilder, D. A. (1984) Intergroup Contact: The Typical Member and the Exception to the Rule. *Journal of Experimental Social Psychology*, 20, pp. 177-194.

Worchel, S., Andreoli, V. A., & Folger, R. (1977) Intergroup Co-operation and Intergroup Attraction: The Effect of Previous Interaction and Outcome of Combined Effort. *Journal of Experimental Social Psychology*, 13, pp. 131-140.

[From: Argyle, M. and Colman, A. M, 1995, *Social Psychology*. London: Longman. pp. 57-77]

## 导读：偏见与群体冲突

本文主要从心理学的角度来研究偏见和群体间的冲突。尽管这两个概念之间存在很大区别，但是它们经常是共存的。当我们发现偏见的时候，往往也能看到冲突。因此，偏见可以被看成是群体间冲突的特殊表现。很多心理学家提出，表现出偏见的人群与不怎么表现出偏见的人群在性格上存在着差异。这种观点在 Adorno, Frenkel-Brunswick, Levinson & Sanford (1995) 对"权威式性格"的剖析当中得到了普及。这些学者们认为对于过分关注常规和服从的家庭教育方式来说很容易导致"权威式性格"，据说这种性格容易使人产生偏见。

为了测量这种"权威性"的程度，Adorno et al 设计出了 F-量表来检测法西斯倾向。经过细致的临床访问和性格检测，结果显示出具有高度权威性格的人更加具有种族中心主义。成果发表之后，评论者对其 F-量表和临床访问提出质疑，同时更为重要的质疑是针对个体差异相关的问题。这个问题也就是对于个体性格差异的研究无法解释大规模的社会行为，例如偏见和群体冲突。如果偏见是由于性格的不同造成的，那么在一个群体内部偏见和歧视的表现也应该是不同的，但是事实的情况是，群体内部的偏见往往是十分一致的。因此，Petteigrew（1958）认为偏见不应该被认为是个性的表达，而应该是社会规范的表现。

除了"性格说"以外，Rokeach（1960）提出了"信仰说"。他认为个人信仰的相似性在很大程度上决定了对他人的态度。他认为，我们往往对接受自身信仰和观点的人情感上更加亲密，Rokeach 把这个理论应用到种族偏见问题上。他认为，种族偏见是不同种族群体的成员感到信仰差异的结果。为了检验这个理论，Rokeach, Smith & Evans 设计出了一种"种族信仰"范例。通过测试，他们发现信仰比种族因素更加能够影响态度，也就是说，一个白人与一个具有共同信仰的黑人要比这个白人与不同信仰的白人走得更近。尽管如此，还是有很多后来的实验显示出与 Rokeach 的信仰说不符的事例。那么如何来解释这些例外呢？有些学者对此提供了解释，他们认为应该在把人际交往行为的理论应用到群体关系领域中时需要谨慎。作为对群体间偏见地解释，信仰说可能确实存在不足。事实上，Rokeach 也认识到理论的局限性。

另外一些学者，例如 Dollard 等学者提出了一种新的解释，那就是"压抑—敌对行为"理论。他们的基本观点是，很多个人和群体间的敌对行为是由于压抑情绪造成的，这种压抑情绪的来源往往是那些相对富有和有势力的人或群体，有时也是很难确定。很多人和群体在情绪受到挫折和压抑的时候，通过敌对的进攻行为来宣泄自己的情绪。尽管这种理论看上去简洁，具有吸引力，并且还有实证支持，这种理论在解释群体间冲突的时候还是存在着一定的局限性。

下面我们要谈到的是偏见后面所隐含的人们的心理过程。根据一些学者的说法，我们人类为了简化我们所居住的身边的复杂的人或者事物，因此往往对他们进行分类。对一个人来说，想要毫无偏见地认识所有与之交往的人，是件很不容易的事。换言之，会耗费大量时间和精力，这就说明偏见的第一个功能。是在尽量保留人们对同类事物的判断力的同时，节省人们对每件具体事物的认识成本。值得注意的是，这些社会分类的人际效应并不是对称的。人们往往认为自身群体成员是不同的，而其他群体的成员之间是相似的。在许多事物上都持有同一偏见的人往往属于同一族群，偏见在人与人的斗争中，对划分敌友有极大帮助，减少了与"异类"的认同感，促进人把思想和行为推向极端，它是一种原始的战争动员准备，与人类的利他本能互相制衡。

这些社会分类的心理过程也许就是思维定势（stereotype）形成的原因。尽管有足够理由相信个人心理过程在思维定势形成过程中的作用，但是仍然有理由怀疑说个人心理过程是否在所有思维定势形成中都发挥了作用。因此，完全从心理的角度来看待偏见的形成也是存在缺陷的。

前面所提到的压抑—敌对行为理论后来逐步演化为"相对剥夺理论"。Berkowitz从压抑的主观特点出发，认为压抑是相对的，它只是相对于人们的期望而产生的压抑，也就是说当特定群体的人感到他们认为他们应该得到的和实际得到的有差距的时候，他们会感到一种被剥夺和不公平的感觉。这种共同的不公平感也就解释了代表群体关系和群体偏见的一致行为。后面还相继提出了一些其他具有代表性的理论如现实冲突理论和社会身份理论等有意义的理论，值得大家去体味。

文章的最后还提到了如何减少偏见现象的发生。为了取得更和谐的关系，各群体在交往中应当弱化成员身份，放松群体间差异的标准，使社会关系更加人性化。很多教育机构也采取措施来增加来自不同种族的儿童的合作。

**Questions for reflection：**
1. What's the "authoritarian personality" and what's its relationship

with prejudice?
2. How do you explain the counter examples of belief congruence theory?
3. What are the limitations of "frustration-aggression theory"?
4. Why does the author say the effects of social categorization are not symmetrical?
5. What are the effective ways to reduce prejudice?

# Intercultural Communication and Intercultural Education

## Cross-cultural Adaptation: Axioms

Y. Y. Kim

The problem of human adaptation could he presented as a dialectic between permanency and change.

Rene Dubos

Individuals enter an unfamiliar culture with the cultural communication competence that they have internalised in their home country. The internalised cultural imprinting that governs individuals' identity and behavior remains largely unrecognised, unquestioned, and unchallenged until they encounter people with different cultural attributes. As Boulding (1956/1977) stated, the human nervous system is structured in such a way that 'the patterns that govern behavior and perception come into consciousness only when there is a deviation from the familiar'. (p. 13)

### Strangers Adapting

Intercultural encounters provide such situations of deviation from the familiar, assumed, and taken-for-granted, as individuals are faced with things that do not follow their unconscious cultural program. They now need to learn and acquire a new system of communication patterns acceptable in the host society. As strangers in the new land, they are subject to a greater or lesser necessity to conform to the communication patterns of the host society. Permanent immigrants or long-term settlers generally have a greater need to conform than temporary sojourners, yet no one is completely free from having to understand, and manage, the various communication patterns sanctioned and operating in the host culture.

## Acculturation and Deculturation

This process of learning and acquiring the elements of the host culture is called acculturation (cf. Shibutani & Kwan, 1965:470). Specifically, acculturation of strangers involves the cultural patterns established in the host society at large and regarded by the majority of people as the 'standard' for that society. In many ethnically diverse societies, the standard cultural patterns refer mainly to those of the dominant culture. In the United States, for example, the standard cultural patterns refer mainly to those of the Anglo-white Americans. Although acquiring minority cultural patterns is a part of the overall adaptation process of newcomers, the most compelling pressure to conform comes from the dominant elements of the host society.

In this process, strangers are re-enculturated, only this time into the host society. This second-time enculturation does not occur so smoothly as their childhood enculturation, because of the distinct cultural identity and communication patterns internalised in their childhood. As acculturation occurs in the strangers, unlearning (or undoing) of at least some of the old cultural patterns occurs (at least in the sense that new responses are adopted in situations that previously would have evoked old ones). The cost of acquiring something new is inevitably the 'losing' of something old in much the same way as 'being someone requires the forfeiture of being someone else' (Thayer, 1975:240).

This cultural discontinuity in strangers' internal cultural identity and attributes has been recognized by a number of investigators as desocialisation or deculturation (Bar-Yosef, 1968; Eisenstadt, 1954). These two phenomena are not necessarily observable in a direct one-on-one basis. Acquiring knowledge and skill in the host language may not necessarily result in the unlearning of the corresponding amount of knowledge and skill in the original language, as has been indicated in studies of bilingual children (e.g., Arnberg, 1987; Beardsmore, 1986; Phinney & Rotheram, 1987). As we consider the make-up of strangers after a given time in the host milieu, however, we will note that their internal attributes are no longer the same as they once were before being exposed to the host culture.

In this dynamic interplay of acculturation and deculturation, strangers gradually undergo an adaptive transformation in their communication system. Ultimately the new cultural patterns replace many of the old patterns and the overall transformation of strangers becomes noticeable, particularly to others. (See Figure 1.)

## Stress-adaptation-growth Dynamics

As discussed previously, human systems are characteristically homeostatic attempting to hold constant a variety of variables in our internal structure so as to achieve an ordered whole. When individuals receive messages that disrupt their existing internal order, they experience disequilibrium. In this state of disequilibrium, stress confronts the individual. As such, strangers inevitably experience acute stress as they go through the experiences of acculturation and deculturation. They lack 'intersubjective understanding' (Schuetz, 1944:499) of the social world inhabited

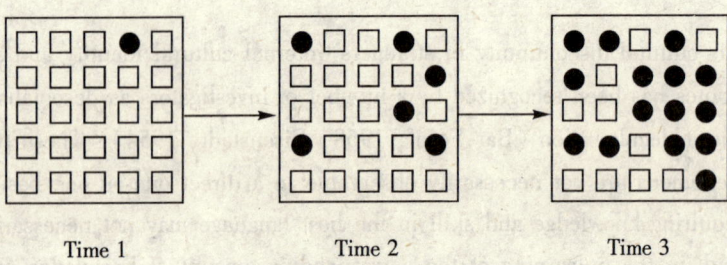

Time 1    Time 2    Time 3

□ Original cultural elements in strangers
● Host cultural elements in strangers

Figure 1  Deculturation and acculturation in the adaptation process

by the members of the host society. As Parrillo (1966) observed:

> For the natives, then, every social situation is the coming together not only of roles and identities, but also of shared realities—the intersubjective structure of consciousness. What is taken for granted by the native is problematic for the stranger. In a familiar world, people live through the day by responding to daily routine without questioning or reflection. To strangers, however, every situation is new and is therefore experienced as a crisis. (p.3)

As long as there are discrepancies between the demands of the host environment and the capacities of the strangers' internal communication to meet those demands, the strangers must adjust and readjust themselves to better function in the host society. Everyone requires on-going validation of his or her 'place' in a given environment, and the inability to meet this basic human need can lead to symptoms of mental, emotional, and physical disturbance (Berger & Kellner, 1970). The shifting of the self-world relationship brings about a heightened level of consciousness through an increased awareness of the split between inner, subjective experiences and external, objective circumstances.

When experiencing internal stress or disequilibrium, strangers 'instinctively' react to maintain or restore their inner balance and stability. Through various psychological maneuvers, they temporarily escape from the necessity of having to deal with stressful conditions. Often the 'problem-solving' approach is not used by strangers when they are under high stress, but, instead, more primitive, rigid, and less adequate attempts are made to protect feelings or master the situation. Consequently, strangers may become more aggressive or hostile toward the new country, attacking its values, customs, food, climate, and so on. As coping mechanisms, they may yearn for home, become dependent on others, be excessively concerned with unimportant details, rationalise their inabilities, or simply avoid problematic situations by ignoring them (cf. Lazarus, 1966).

Unfortunately, these defensive reactions do not facilitate learning about a new environment. Although defensive reactions to stressful situations may temporarily reduce inner tension and anxiety, strangers cannot avoid the necessity to 'face' and cope with the host environment if they are to perform satisfactorily in it. Although internal protective reactions are frequently necessary for strangers, such reactions are generally temporary. Sooner or later, the strangers must stop protective reactions that merely postpone dealing with the impending problems of adaptation. As long as they remain in the host society, and as long as the quality of their performance in the host society depends on how well they can communicate with host nationals, they eventually must acquire the information that will improve their functional relationship with the host environment.

To acquire the necessary communication competence of the host society means going through many stressful emotional 'lows'. Strangers must weather internal conflicts—conflicts between their original cultural patterns and the host cultural patterns—through active communication participation in the host society. In this process, stress is inevitably present: it is 'part-and-parcel of the stress-adaptation cycle' (Ruben, 1983:143). The psychological movements of individuals' internal systems into new dimensions of perception and experience often produce forms of temporary personality disintegration, or even 'breakdown' in some extreme cases. Stress, in the present context, can be viewed as the internal resistance of the human organism against its own cultural evolution.

As strangers face the demands of the host environment and cope with the accompanying stress, parts of their internal organisation undergo small changes. The interior organisation of strangers is in flux as they continue to communicate with and adapt to the host environment. The periods of 'crisis' will be temporary as the strangers work out new ways of handling problems through sources of strength in themselves and in their social environment. A crisis, once managed by the strangers, presents an opportunity to strengthen their coping abilities and potential for adaptive changes. Stress, then, is responsible not only for suffering, frustration, and anxiety, but also for providing the impetus for adaptive personal transformation and growth—the learning and creative responses to manage new cultural circumstances.

Stress, adaptation, and growth, together, define the internal dynamics of strangers' cross-cultural experiences in a 'draw-back-to-leap' pattern similar to the movement of a wheel. (See Figure 2.) Each stressful experience is responded to by strangers with a 'draw back', which then activates their adaptive energy to help them reorganise themselves and 'leap forward'. This stress-adaptation-growth cycle involves communication activities that shift between out-looking, information-seeking behavior and tension-reducing, defensive retreat, and the resultant capacity to see a situation 'with new eyes'. The break-up of the old internal conditions usually results not in chaos or breakdown, but in the creation of a whole new internal structure that is better adapted to the host environment.

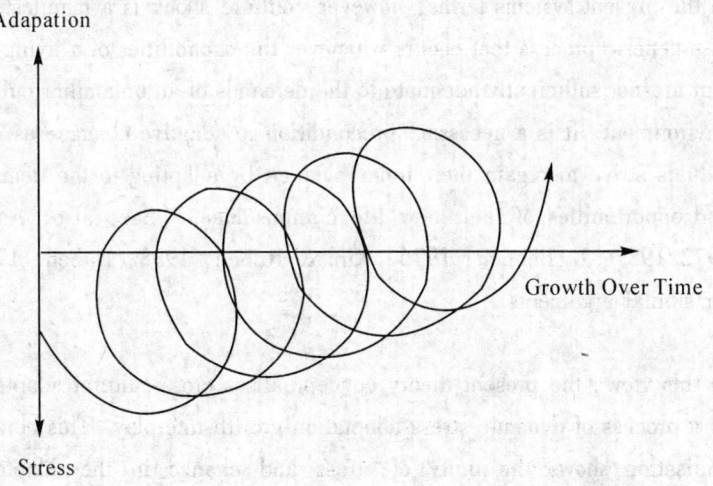

Figure 2   Stress-adaptation-growth dynamics of adaptive transformation

The adaptation process, thus, is not a smooth, linear process, but a transformation of individuals through the successive interplay of degeneration and regeneration. The stress, adaptation, and resultant internal growth essentially characterise the strangers' conscious and unconscious movement forward and upward in the direction of greater success in meeting the demands of the host environment. The resolution of stressful difficulties promises the qualitative transformation of strangers toward a greater internal capacity to cope with varied environmental conditions. The increased internal capacity, in turn, facilitates the subsequent handling of stress and adaptation, learning and unlearning, acculturation and deculturation, crisis and resolution.

At this point, recall from Chapter 2 that many studies of the culture shock phenomenon have focused on these initial-phase stress reactions of strangers, these studies have typically viewed culture shock as a negative, problematic, and undesirable phenomenon to be avoided. Viewed in the present systems terms, however, culture shock is a manifestation of a generic process that occurs whenever the capabilities of a living system are not sufficiently adequate to the demands of an unfamiliar cultural environment. It is a necessary precondition to adaptive change, as individuals strive to regain their inner balance by adapting to the demands and opportunities of their new life circumstance. (See, also, Adler, 1972/1987; J. Bennett, 1976; Kim & Ruben, 1988; Ruben, 1983, for similar arguments.)

In this view, the present theory conceptualises cross-cultural adaptation as a process of dynamic stress-adaptation-growth interplay. This conceptualisation shows the unity of stress and change in the adaptation process: neither occurs without the other and each occurs because of the other. To the extent that stress is said to be responsible for suffering, frustration, and anxiety, it also must be credited as an impetus for learning, growth and creativity for the individual. Temporary disintegration is thus viewed as the very basis for a subsequent increase in the awareness of life conditions and ways to deal with them.

Empirical research has provided some supportive indication, although indirect and rudimentary, that the stress of meeting with new cultural elements lays the groundwork for subsequent adaptation. For example, Eaton & Lasry (1978) reported that the stress level of more upwardly mobile immigrants was greater than those who were less upwardly mobile. Among Japanese-Americans (Marmot & Syme, 1976) and Mexican-American women (Miranda & Castro, 1977), the better adapted immigrants had a somewhat greater frequency of stress-related symptoms (such as anxiety and need for psychotherapy) than the less adapted group. Additionally, Ruben & Kealcy (1979) suggested that the Canadians in Kenya who would ultimately be the most effective in adapting to the new culture underwent the most intense culture shock during the transition period. Other acculturation studies of immigrants and foreign students in the United States have shown that, once the initial phase has been successfully managed, individuals demonstrate an increased cognitive complexity, a positive orientation toward the host environment and toward themselves, and behavioral capacities to communicate with the natives (cf. Coelho, 1958; Y. Kim, 1976, 1978a, b, 1980). (See, also, Gullahorn & Gullahorn, 1963; Torbiorn, 1982; for further discussions on the stress and adaptation phenomena).

The stress-adaptation-growth dynamics of strangers' cross-cultural experiences speak of profound human pliability, resilience and potential for growth. Except for a small portion of strangers who are unable, or unwilling, to cope with the stress or cross-cultural adaptation, most strangers in foreign cultures have demonstrated an impressive capacity to manage their cross-cultural encounters successfully and without damaging their overall psychological health. This observation can be extended to individuals under even more extreme life conditions, such as those in concentration camps and prisons who have shown repeatedly that humans are capable of coping with severely stressful situations by adaptively transforming themselves.

It must be pointed out that not all individuals are equally successful in making transitions toward adaptation. Certain individuals, although in the minority, may strongly resist such change, thereby increasing the stress level and making the stress-adaptation-growth cycle intensely difficult. Some may not be able to cope with intense stress experiences due to lack of psychological resilience. Others may find themselves in situations that present too severe a challenge to manage. Most individuals in most circumstances, however, undergo the stress-adaptation-change cycle and achieve at least a minimum functional effectiveness in the host environment.

## Strangers Communicating

As strangers accumulate adaptive experiences, they cultivate the capability to code and decode verbal and non-verbal messages so that the messages will be recognised, accepted, and responded to. Through prolonged and varied communication experiences, strangers gradually acquire the coping mechanisms that help discern and deal with the dynamics of the host environment. Once acquired, communication capabilities function as an instrumental, interpretive, and expressive means of coming to terms with the host environment, and of feeling more at ease and less stressed.

Indeed, communication is at the heart of cross-cultural adaptation as it is in the enculturation process of native-born children. The cross-cultural adaptation process is essentially a process of achieving the communication capacities necessary for strangers to be functional in the host society. In the continuous process of message encoding and decoding, up-to-date information about the self, the host environment, and the relationship of the self to the host environment leads to the acquisition of appropriate techniques, and eventually increases the individual's mastery of life. Through effective communication, strangers are able to gradually increase their control over the environment and over life itself—just as the capacity of a balloon expands with the increased amount of incoming air.

Conversely, the development of adaptive communication capacity occurs through countless acts of communication. Communication activities of strangers serve to develop their internal communication capacities: one learns to communicate by communicating. Furthermore, the acquired host communication competence has a direct bearing on the overall cross-cultural adaptation of strangers, serving as their primary means of utilizing the resources of the host environment. It also functions as a set of adaptive tools assisting strangers to further participate in the communication processes of the host society, and to attempt to meet their personal and social needs. Through communication, they adapt to and relate to the new environment, and acquire membership and a sense of belonging in the various social groups of the host society on which they depend.

## Dimensions of Communication

In understanding the complex process of communication between strangers and the host cultural environment, Ruben's (1975) parameter of human communication provides a useful and comprehensive framework. In this parameter, each person's communication activity is conceptualized in two closely interrelated, inseparable communication processes— personal (or intrapersonal) and social.

Personal communication refers to the 'private symbolisation' (Ruben, 1975) activities of individuals all the internal mental activities that occur in individuals that dispose and prepare them to act and react in certain ways in actual social situations. Geyer (1980) refers to this process as 'off-line functions', that is, 'internal information exchange within the

system' of individuals when
(1) no inputs are received from the environment,
(2) no outputs are given to the environment, or
(3) there are 'outputs' but the system directs these back into itself as 'inputs' as when a conclusion of a thinking process is not transmitted to anybody else but is used as an element in a further line of thought (p. 32).

Personal communication is linked to social communication when two or more individuals interact with one another, knowingly or not. Social communication is the process underlying "intersubjectivisation", a phenomenon that occurs as a consequence of 'public symbolisation' (Ruben, 1975). According to Geyer, these externalized communication processes of individuals are referred to as 'on-line functions' of human systems. The actual interface of individuals with their environment occurs through their on-line input-output transactions of messages.

Social communication activities occur in many different contexts—from communication in the macro-level society via newspapers, television and movies, to communication within the micro-level environment such as family, neighborhood, museum, workplace, bank, classroom, and friends. Social communication occurs when strangers make simple, passing observations of people on the street, when they listen to a newly released record album, or when they engage in serious dialogue with close friends. These and numerous other aspects of social communication activities can be grouped into two dimensions: (1) interpersonal communication and (2) mass communication.

Interpersonal communication of strangers refers to their social engagements through people in their immediate micro-level environment. Much of their adaptive learning takes place in the context of interpersonal communication. Mass communication, on the other hand, includes all other social processes that occur within larger, societal contexts. Through mass media communication experiences (such as radio, television, magazines, newspaper, movies, museums) and other forms of indirect communication (such as lectures, posters, and computerised networks), individuals participate in 'para-social' activities substituting for, or in conjunction with, direct person-to-person encounters. Mass communication, thus, is a more generalised, public form of communication by which individuals interact with their larger societal environment without involvement in any relationships with specific persons.

Along this line of systems thinking, the present theory focuses on host communication competence in examining personal (or 'off-line') communication processes of strangers. To understand social (or 'on-line') communication processes, we will examine the strangers' participation in the host society in general (host social communication) and in their ethnic community (ethnic social communication). Each of these two communication processes is explained below in relation to cross-cultural adaptation.

## Personal Communication: Host Communication Competence

The successful adaptation of strangers is realised only when their internal communication systems sufficiently overlap with those of the natives. This internal capacity enables strangers to organise themselves in and with their sociocultural milieu, developing ways of seeing, hearing, understanding, and responding to the environment appropriately. As they become more competent in the host communication system, they are better able to discern the similarities and differences between their original home culture and the host culture and are able to act accordingly.

For the natives, such internal communication capacity has been acquired from so early in life and has been so completely internalised into their personal communication system that, by and large, it operates automatically and unconsciously. For immigrants or sojourners, however, the interpretive frames need to be learned and internalised (acculturation) and, at the same time, some of their original cultural communication patterns must be unlearned (deculturation). Through trial and error, with frequently accompanying stress and despair, they are able to gradually transform their personal communication patterns and achieve an increasing level of host communication competence. Until the strangers have acquired a sufficient level of host communication competence, they are handicapped in their ability to appropriately and effectively receive and transmit messages and retain information, and to perform operations in such a way that they may contribute to furthering their physical, psychological and social fulfilment in the host society.

In a way, strangers become more 'mature' members of the host society through acquiring host communication competence. They become less reliant on others for protection and correction of their behaviors in managing their daily activities, and feel a greater sense of belonging to the host society. Strangers' host communication competence, thus, facilitates the process of achieving the ultimate goal and outcome of cross-cultural adaptation—increased functional fitness and decreased cross-cultural stress. As Ruesch & Bateson (1951/1968) stated, 'the ability to communicate successfully becomes synonymous with being mentally healthy'. (p. 87)

Host communication competence as presently conceptualised, then, is a continuum, on which different strangers can be plotted and analysed. At the lowest end of this continuum is a hypothetical 'zero competence', that is, a complete inability to communicate in a new cultural environment. At the highest end, we can theoretically place those individuals whose capability to communicate is at the highest possible attainment.

## Host Social Communication

Strangers actually participate in the reality of the host environment through social communication. Through such participation, they become actively 'engaged' in the host society and develop a functional relationship with it, and are given the opportunity to learn and enhance their host communication competence (cf. Cooley, 1909; Dewey, 1916; Duncan, 1967).

The critical importance of host social communication as a cross-cultural adaptation medium has been shown in numerous empirical studies, although findings are still scattered across several human science disciplines. Typically, the group-level anthropological studies of cultural contacts and change have taken communication as a 'given' condition that facilitates the adaptation flow between two or more contacting cultures (cf. Herskovits, 1958), and thus, little scientific attention has been placed on the communication process itself. In sociological studies, strangers' communication behaviors have been included as part of the indexes of 'social integration' or as a factor that is positively associated with the 'majority-minority' relations among ethnic groups within societies (cf. Gordon, 1964; Marden & Meyer, 1968; Pool, 1965).

Like interpersonal communication activities, mass communication activities (particularly the use of mass media) have been observed to promote adaptation of strangers. Gordon (1964) stated, for example, that the mass media (along with public schools) exert 'overwhelming acculturation powers' over immigrants' children (pp. 244-245). Shibutani & Kwan (1965) also supported this view indicating that

> the extent to which members of a minority group become acculturated to the way of life of the dominant group depends upon the extent of their participation in the communication channels of their rulers. (p. 573)

The underlying assumption is that access to, exposure to, and use of the mass media of the dominant group influences ethnics and migrants in their processes of learning about and taking part in the dominant society (Subervi-Velez, 1986).

Recently, a few communication researchers have begun to pay closer attention to the communication patterns of immigrants. Nagata (1969), for example, made a first conceptualisation of the immigrant adaptation process based on various communication variables (such as interpersonal communication relations, mass media behavior, and perceptual and attitudinal orientations). In his study of Chicago area Japanese-Americans, Nagata observed a progressive increase in such communication variables. (See also Chang, 1972, for a similar study.) Ryu's study (1976) suggested the positive role of mass media in the adaptation of Korean immigrants in the United States. Other studies of sojourners and immigrants have repeatedly shown that individuals who are more active in interpersonal communication with members of the host society are better adjusted psychologically as well as financially (cf. Y. Kim, 1976, 1978a, 1980; Selitiz et al., 1963).

Strangers themselves are also keenly aware of the vital role that communication plays in their overall functioning in the host society. The majority of the Indochinese refugees in the United States, for example, expressed a strong need for communication training and general cultural orientation. A similar view was expressed by the social and educational service agencies and organisations serving refugee resettlement and adaptation. The agencies considered cultural and communication barriers one of the most serious problems impairing their service delivery to refugee clients (Y. Kim, 1980).

Indeed, the critical importance of the host communication activities of strangers cannot be over-emphasised. Adaptive transformation occurs in and through such communication activities, which, in turn, facilitate learning of all other aspects of the host culture including its economic, social, political and aesthetic dimensions.

## Ethnic Social Communication

Along with host interpersonal and mass communication activities, strangers in many societies today have access to individuals of the same national or ethnic origin. Whether we speak of British compounds in India, American military posts in West Germany, Puerto Rican barrios in New York City, Chinatown in Tokyo, or a Japanese student association in a Canadian university, there are ethnic communities that provide strangers with opportunities to interact with fellow countrymen (women). In large cities in countries like Australia, Canada, England, Germany, and the United States, where there has been a large influx of immigrants, many immigrant groups have organised some form of 'mutual aid' or 'self-help' ethnic community group. Such ethnic organisations render assistance to those who need material, informational, emotional, and other forms of social support (De Cocq, 1976). In many larger immigrant groups, ethnic media (including newspapers, radio stations, and television programs) perform various informational, educational, and entertainment services for their members.

These ethnic support systems serve adaptation-facilitating functions for new immigrants and sojourners during the initial phase of their adaptation process. Because many strangers initially lack host communication competence and other resources to be self-reliant in the new environment, they tend to rely on ethnic sources of support,' compensating for the lack of support from host nationals. In the long run, however, heavy reliance on ethnic sources for their social activities would contribute to the sustenance of ethnic identity (Burgess, 1978), and deter the development of strangers' host communication competence. Because of the relatively 'easy' communication experiences in dealing with ethnic individuals and media, strangers are likely to delay or avoid confronting the stressful experiences of host social communication that are essential for adaptation. The relatively stress-free ethnic communication activities offer temporary relief and refuge, but in doing so discourage the long-term development of host communication competence and participation in the host social processes.

Strangers, therefore, cannot remain rigidly ethnic and also become highly adapted to the host culture. The longer strangers avoid or only minimally interact with the host communication environment, the longer it will take for them to acquire host communication competence. To the extent that strangers participate in ethnic communication channels, they are likely to maintain perspectives different from the normative patterns of the host culture and will experience difficulty in understanding and relating to the host environment.

In sum, the personal and social communication processes are functionally interrelated by a reciprocal causal relationship. (See Figure 3) Strangers' host communication competence promotes their social engagements with the host environment. Their participation in host social communication processes, in turn, facilitates their host communication competence. This reciprocal and mutually defining relationship between host communication competence and social communication activities is analogous to computer operations in which the former is comparable to the capabilities of a software program and the latter to the actual application of the software for a specific purpose. Added to this interaction of host communication competence and participation in host social communication activities are ethnic social communication activities. Initially, ethnic social communication serves the adaptive process by compensating for the lack of host communication competence and host social communication activities. In time, ethnic social communication is likely to inhibit

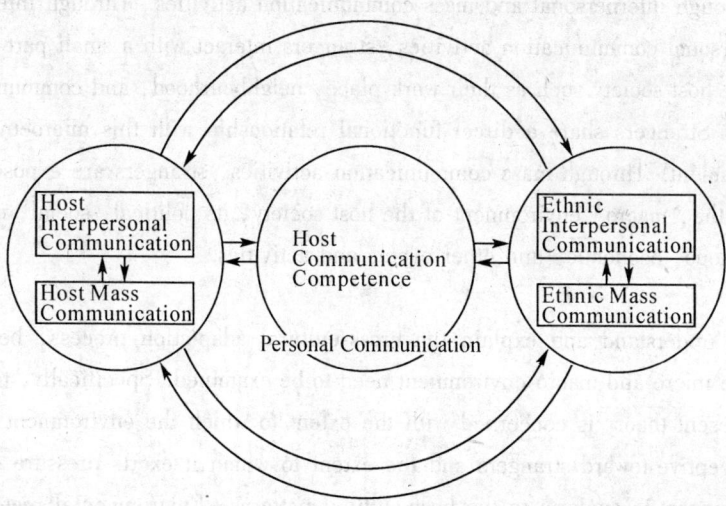

Figure 3  Interrelated processes of host communication competence, ethnic social communication, and host social communication

strangers' development of host communication competence and social participation.

## Host Environment and Predisposition

The personal and social (interpersonal mass) communication processes of strangers cannot he fully understood in isolation from the host environment or without understanding their individualised backgrounds. By adding these dimensions to the present discussion of communication and adaptation, we can address issues concerning the observed differences among individual strangers in their adaptation patterns.

## Host Environment: Receptivity and Conformity Pressure

Host environment refers to the social milieu that strangers encounter through interpersonal and mass communication activities. Through interpersonal communication activities, strangers interact with a small part of the host society such as their work place, neighbourhood, and community. Strangers share a direct functional relationship with this microenvironment. Through mass communication activities, strangers are exposed to the 'macro' environment of the host society, its political, social, religious, economic, and other events and activities.

To understand and explain the cross-cultural adaptation process, both the micro-and macro-environment need to be examined. Specifically, the present theory is concerned with the extent to which the environment is receptive toward strangers and the extent to which it exerts pressure on strangers to conform to the host cultural patterns. Environmental receptivity refers to the opportunities offered to strangers to participate in ongoing social activities. Other terms such as 'interaction potential' (Y. Kim, 1979a) or 'acquaintance potential' (Cook, 1962) have been used for environmental receptivity in relation to strangers' interpersonal communication activities. For instance, United States military personnel who live in a remote military camp have limited access to local people in their daily activities. On the other hand, Peace Corps volunteers who live primarily with natives in local residences have greater access to the host social processes.

The 'conformity pressure' (Zajonc, 1952) of the host environment refers to the extent to which the environment challenges strangers to adopt the normative patterns of the host culture and its communication system. Although very few systematic studies have examined the role of environmental pressure in cross-cultural adaptation, societies and sub-societies clearly show different levels of tolerance (or rigidity) for strangers and their different cultural attributes. Generally, heterogeneous and 'free' societies such as the United States tend to exert less conformity pressure on strangers than homogeneous and 'rigid' societies such as the Soviet Union.

The above two environmental factors—receptivity and conformity pressure—help define the relative level of encouragement and challenge that a given environment offers to strangers. A society offering an optimal influence on strangers' adaptation would be one in which receptivity and conformity pressure are in an optimal balance.

## Predisposition: Adaptive Potential

All additional dimension in explaining strangers' communication adaptation is the nature of their experiential backgrounds prior to migrating to the host society. Strangers' predispositional factors precede the actual adaptation process, and set the tone for subsequent stranger-host communication encounters. The present analysis focuses on three predispositional factors that have direct bearing on strangers' communication-adaptation

processes:
(1) cultural and racial background,
(2) personality attributes, and
(3) preparedness for change.

These predispositional factors collectively characterise the strangers' overall adaptive potential.

Clearly, strangers from a culture similar to the host culture would begin their adaptation process with a greater advantage, compared to those who must bridge a more substantial cultural gap. A similar advantage is found among strangers whose racial/physical make-up closely resembles that of the natives. These cultural and racial similarities equip strangers with a greater potential for successful adaptation in the host environment. Strangers themselves also contribute to their own adaptive potential with differential personality attributes. Those who are more open-minded and receptive toward the host culture and who are stronger and more resilient under stressful circumstances are likely to be better able to manage the uncertainties and challenges of the host environment. In addition, strangers' adaptive potential is influenced by the degree of their preparedness for change. Those who are better educated and better informed about the host culture (through training and other forms of learning) begin their adaptation process with a greater adaptive potential.

## Cross-cultural Adaptation Outcomes

In time, changes take place within strangers as a cumulative result of prolonged communication and adaptation experiences with the host environment. Such adaptive changes in strangers have been examined in numerous aspects—from tastes for different foods, dress habits, and leisure activities, to religious practices, social values, and attitudes toward host culture and home culture. In the present theory, three interrelated aspects—functional fitness, psychological health, and intercultural identity are examined as the most direct and critical changes that are likely to be observed in strangers.

## Functional Fitness

Strangers conduct continuous 'experiments' in the host society. They try and fail, they try and fail less disastrously, they try another alternative and partially succeed. Learning some of the host culture and unlearning some of the original culture gradually brings about an internal transformation in strangers. In time, we see them deviate from the accepted patterns of their original culture and acquire the new patterns of the host culture. A natural outcome of this stress-adaptation-growth process in an increased functional fitness, that is, a greater congruence and compatibility between the strangers' internal conditions and the conditions of the host environment. This notion of person-environment fit implies an interactive systems perspective that, unlike assessments based solely in terms of individual traits, regards human behavior as a function of both the person and the environment (cf. Caplan, 1979; French, Rodger & Cobb, 1974; Murray, 1938; Pervin, 1968). Functional fitness, further, requires some 'compromise' in the internal structure of a person in the face of pressure from the host environment.

As such, the increased functional fitness of strangers promotes their life chances in the host society. Successfully adapted strangers have the desired level of appropriate and effective ways of communicating with the host environment. As they achieve an increasing level of fitness in the host culture, they are better able to meet their basic survival needs and social necessities (e.g., friendship, occupation, and status), as well as philosophical drives (e.g., creativity, actualisation and fulfilment). The increased functional fitness further enhances the potential effectiveness of the strangers' performance and control in the host environment.

## Psychological Health

An increase in functional fitness will, in turn, reduce the stranger's overall cross-cultural stress, as well as defensive reactions to stress such as withdrawal, denial and hostility. As strangers achieve a greater functional fitness in the host environment with increased communication competence, their experience of internal stress due to cross-cultural challenges will decrease.

Issues of mental health (or illness) have been a subject of great interest among researchers, as well as practitioners. Culture shock studies have been mainly concerned with this psychological-health aspect of sojourn experiences, as was reviewed previously. Immigrant studies have also been conducted in psychology and psychiatry examining the issues of mental illnesses (e.g., Williams & Westermeyer, 1986). In the present theoretical framework, the psychological health (or illness) of strangers is viewed as a direct outcome of their communication-adaptation experiences and as directly related to the level of functional fitness achieved in the host environment.

## Intercultural Identity

Another related aspect of the cross-cultural adaptation outcome is the development of an intercultural identity. Strangers are capable of adapting to the host environment and of growing and developing through the process. The psychological movements of strangers into new dimensions of perception and experience produce 'boundary-ambiguity syndromes' (Hall, 1976:227), in which the original cultural identity begins to lose its definiteness and rigidity and the emergent identity shows an increasing 'interculturalness'.

From the present systems perspective, intercultural identity, like cultural identity (cf. Chapter 3), refers to the complex process of interpretive activity inside a stranger and the resultant self-conception in relation to a cultural group. As strangers undergo adaptive transformation, their internal attributes and self-identification change from being cultural to being increasingly intercultural, and their emotional adherence to the culture of their childhood weakens, while accommodating the host culture into their self-conception. In other words, a stranger's cultural identity becomes increasingly flexible—no longer rigidly bound by membership to the original culture, or to the host culture—and begins to take on a more fluid intercultural identity (Adler, 1982; Gudykunst & Kim, 1984; Kim & Ruben, 1988).

Such an intercultural identity is likely to have the cognitive, affective, and behavioral flexibility to adapt to the situation and to creatively manage or avoid conflicts that could result from inappropriate switching between cultures. As pointed out earlier, the cross-cultural adaptation experiences of strangers contribute to the expansion of their internal capacity beyond the cultural parameters of the original culture. Through the dynamic and continuous process of stress-adaptation-transformation, strangers' internal conditions gradually transform toward becoming increasingly intercultural.

So far in this chapter, the process, and outcomes of cross-cultural adaptation has been theoretically based on the General Systems perspective, focusing on strangers' communication experiences. The adaptation process has been described as a communication process in which strangers learn and acquire dominant communication patterns of the host society. Just as native-born individuals acquire their cultural communication patterns through interaction with their significant others, strangers, acquire the cultural communication patterns of the host society and develop relationships with the new social environment through communication. Influencing this communication-adaptation process are the adaptive predisposition of strangers and the characteristics of the host environment. Three aspects of strangers' adaptive change increased functional fitness, psychological health, and intercultural identityhave been identified as direct consequences of prolonged communication-adaptation experiences in the host society. These theoretical principles of the process and outcome of cross-cultural adaptation can be summarised into the axioms shown opposite.

# Axioms

Axiom 1: Cross-cultural adaptation occurs in and through communication.

Axiom 2: Cross-cultural adaptation necessitates at least a minimum level of acculturation of the host culture and a minimum level of deculturation of the childhood culture.

Axiom 3: Individuals continually undergo the internal dynamics of stress-adaptation-growth vis-a-vis the host environment, maintaining their overall integrity.

Axiom 4: Host communication competence and host social (interpersonal, mass) communication interactively and collectively facilitate cross cultural adaptation.

Axiom 5: Ethnic social (interpersonal, mass) communication indirectly facilitates the initial short-term cross-cultural adaptation, compensating for the lack of host communication competence and host social (interpersonal mass) communication.

Axiom 6: Ethnic (interpersonal, mass) communication indirectly deters the subsequent cross-cultural adaptation by discouraging the long-term development of host communication competence and host social (interpersonal, mass) communication.

Axiom 7: Receptivity and conformity pressure of the host environment facilitates the development of host communication competence and host social (interpersonal, mass) communication.

Axiom 8: Adaptive predisposition facilitates the development of host communication competence and host social (interpersonal, mass) communication.

Axiom 9: Achieved outcomes of cross-cultural adaptation experiences. at a given time include increased functional fitness, psychological health, and intercultural identity.

Axiom 10: The increased functional fitness, psychological health, and intercultural identity, in turn, facilitate subsequent development of host communication competence and host social (interpersonal, mass) communication.

[From: Kim, Y. Y. 1988, *Communication and Cross-Cultural Adaptation: An Integrative Theory*. Clevedon: Multilingual Matters. Chapter 4, Pages: 52-71]

# 跨文化适应：原理篇

文章主要论及了跨文化调适过程中的十大原理或规律，指出文化适应是一个紧张－适应－成长的动态过程。文章分别从交流的不同层面：陌生人之间的交流、交流的维度、人际交流、东道社会交流、种族社会交流等各个方面阐述了跨文化适应中的普遍规律，并从跨文化代言者的角度分析了东道环境给个体造成的压力，个体的适应潜能，跨文化适应结果和个体在跨文化适应过程中的心理健康问题。

跨文化适应的十大原理：

**原理1**：跨文化适应出现在交流过程中。

原理 2：跨文化适应需要至少对东道文化进行最低程度的适应和对原有的文化进行解构。

原理 3：个体面临东道文化环境时会持续地经历一个紧张-适应-成长的动态过程，并保持自身的全面完整。

原理 4：东道交流能力和东道社会（人际，大众）交流相互作用一起促进跨文化适应。

原理 5：种族社会交流间接地促进了最初的短期的跨文化适应，补充了当时东道交流能力和东道社会交流的不足。

原理 6：种族社会交流由于并不鼓励东道交流能力和东道社会交流而间接阻碍了随后的跨文化适应。

原理 7：接受和遵循东道文化的压力促进了东道交流能力和东道社会交流的发展。

原理 8：跨文化的适应性倾向有助于东道交流能力和东道社会交流的发展。

原理 9：特定时间的跨文化适应经历的结果包含增强的功能适应、心理健康和跨文化身份。

原理 10：增强的功能适应、心理健康和跨文化身份反过来又能促进随后的东道交流能力和东道社会交流的发展。

**Questions for reflection:**

1. Why can we say that cross-cultural adaptation is a dynamic process?
2. What are the outcomes of cross-cultural adaptation? And how to understand them?
3. What is the difference between acculturation and deculturation?
4. What are the implications you could draw from reading the intercultural axioms?
5. What are the two dimensions of communication and could you illustrate the difference?

# Toleration and Recognition

Susan Mendus

The question which informs this paper is 'How, in multicultural and democratic societies, can we educate children in a way which both acknowledges their cultural identity and instills democratic values in them?' To answer this question we need first to understand why there might be a tension between democratic values and the recognition of ethnic or cultural identity. Two writers have recently drawn attention to areas in which conflict can arise. In Market, State and Community David Miller notes that the loyalties required for active citizenship in a democratic society such as Britain may conflict with loyalty to an ethnic or cultural group, and he argues that when that happens 'political education must try to shape cultural identities in the direction of common citizenship. It must try to present an interpretation of, let us say, Indian culture, which makes it possible for members of the Indian community to feel at home in and loyal to, the British state. In so far as there are elements in Indian culture which are at odds with such a reconciliation, the interpretation must be selective or, if you like, biased'.

So expressed, Miller's formulation is puzzlingly abstract, and it is difficult to know what exactly he has in mind here. His main argument is that specifically national identity, in this case British identity, must take priority over cultural loyalty, but in saying this he gestures towards the more general problem of reconciling the values of cultural communities with the values of democratic citizenship, for we must suppose that part of what is involved in being British is having at least some commitment to the kinds of democratic processes characteristic of a Western liberal society. And there are some cultural communities which lack this commitment, or at any rate are reluctant to extend it to all members of the community. For example, in some cultures the role and status accorded to women is such as to render problematic their education for active citizenship in a democratic state: it is, or may be, thought fitting for women to display the virtue of obedience, but a highly developed sense of obedience, a willingness to accept the word of those in authority, fits ill with being an active citizen in a democratic society such as Britain. Where such conflict occurs, Miller argues, cultural loyalty must take second place to citizen loyalty, and the values of the cultural community must be 'reinterpreted' in a way which lessens the tension between it and citizen identity. For Miller, then, citizen identity trumps cultural identity, and insofar as multicultural education was attention to values which are at odds with the development of citizen identity (values such as unquestioning obedience), it is to be treated with great attention.

A second approach is to be found in Charles Taylor's book, Multiculturalism and the Politics of Recognition. Taylor is concerned with the content rather than the aim of education, and his central question is whether, in a multicultural society, the syllabus ought to be enlarged beyond the traditional 'canon' of great works so as to develop, for example, Afrocentric curricula for mainly black schools. He argues (with some reservations) that it should, and his reason is that it is only by such a strategy that hitherto excluded groups may be given due recognition: 'dominant groups tend to entrench their hegemony by inculcating an image of inferiority in the subjugated. The struggle for freedom and equality must therefore pass through a revision of these images. Multicultural curricula are meant to help in the process of revision'.

So where Miller sees cultural loyalty as a potential threat to common citizenship, Taylor sees it as an important step in the development of self-respect among members of minority groups: a step without which they are doomed to remain inferior in their own eyes and unacknowledged in the eyes of others. Put differently, where Miller sees cultural loyalty as potentially disabling for citizens of a democratic society, Taylor sees cultural recognition as the precondition of a society in which the democratic ideal of equality can be realised.

It would be unwise to exaggerate the differences between these two writers: Miller is no ruthless suppressor of cultural identity. On the contrary, he is anxious to enable members of minority groups to retain a sense of their own cultural identity, but (and it is a big 'but') only insofar as that does not conflict with the requirements of common citizenship. Similarly, Taylor is no naive evangelist for multiculturalism. Recognising the difficulties inherent in supposing that all cultures deserve equal respect, he urges that this be accepted only as a 'presumption', and one which itself has homogenising and colonising tendencies, since it implies that we already have the standards by which to judge that 'their' culture is as good as ours. Nevertheless, their different responses highlight the problems inherent in answering the practical question which forms the topic of this paper: how can we educate people, in a way which both respects their cultural identity and fits them for citizenship in a democratic society? Crudely put, the problem is to say how we can acknowledge cultural identity without condoning cultural immurement, or, from the other direction, how we can assert the value of citizen loyalty without driving out cultural loyalty.

In what follows I shall suggest that these problems may be less acute than they at first appear, but solving (or dissolving) them depends upon adopting an understanding of educational aims which is both clearer than and different from the aims implied by Miller and Taylor. So I will try to show that if we understand the purposes of education aright, we need not be forced to choose between citizen identity and cultural loyalty. Or, at least, that those hard choices will be far less frequent than is often supposed.

## The Aims of Education

I begin with Taylor. His preference for an enlarged canon springs from his belief that self-recognition is a sine qua non of flourishing in modern society. But self-recognition includes receiving recognition from others and this, he says, cannot be attained where the excluded culture remains excluded. Thus the reason for these proposed changes is not, or not mainly, that all students may be missing something important through the exclusion of a certain gender or certain races, or certain cultures, but rather that women and students from the excluded group are given, either directly or by omission, a demeaning picture of themselves, as though all creativity and worth inhered in males of European provenance. Enlarging and changing the curriculum is therefore essential not so much in the name of a broader culture for everyone as in order to give recognition to the hitherto excluded.

This argument contains some important assumptions about the aims of education and it is worth dwelling on it for a little while. In the first place, Taylor is not making claims about the objective importance of works currently excluded from the canon. They may or may not be great literature or great works of art, but their inclusion is to be justified not by their inherent worth, but by appeal to the needs of the (hitherto) excluded. Of course, and as Taylor himself points out, there is a potential problem here: members of excluded groups may interpret his strategy as at root patronising, as equivalent to saying your culture contains nothing to equal ours, but we will change the curriculum in order that your culture, inferior though it is, may nevertheless be represented. To guard against this, he proposes that we work with a 'presumption of equal worth' among cultures. This presumption will allow for the recognition of previously excluded groups without degenerating either into cultural relativism or condescension. As a presumption of equal worth, it gives recognition to others, but as merely a presumption of equal worth it does not imply cultural relativism and the complete rejection of standards. Thus it constitutes a mid-point between cultural immurement and cultural imperialism.

One thing, however, which the account omits is any statement of how an enlarged canon may benefit members of the majority as well as members of the excluded group. As Taylor presents the matter, we are faced with a choice between the claim that enlargement is justified as a pragmatic device for enabling the minority to obtain recognition, and the claim that enlargement is justified by the objective worth of what was previously excluded. But there is a third possibility, which is that enlargement is justified as a means of facilitating recognition in both the minority group and the majority group—in both the hitherto excluded and the hitherto included. If enlargement enables the excluded to understand and value themselves, it should also enable the included to understand and value themselves by comparison with the excluded. My suggestion therefore is that we should see education as, quite generally, a means of enabling all students to understand themselves. There is nothing particularly new (indeed nothing new at all) in this suggestion, but it does require careful application if it is to do the philosophical work I require of it, so I turn now to some interpretations of the claim.

On one, very familiar, interpretation of the claim, education enables us to understand ourselves by encouraging and facilitating the development of individual autonomy. We come to understand ourselves by recognising what we as individuals want and value, as distinct from what those around us (our parents, our friends, our colleagues) want and value. This is most eloquently expressed by Saul Bellow in his preface to Allan Bloom's cult book, *The Closing of the American Mind*. Bellow writes:

> As a mid-Westerner, the son of immigrant parents, I recognised at an early age that I was called upon to decide for myself to what extent my Jewish origins, my surroundings (the accidental circumstances of Chicago), my schooling, were to be allowed to determine the course of my life. I did not intend to be wholly dependent on history and culture. Full dependency must mean that I was done for. The commonest teaching of the civilised world in our time can be stated simply: 'Tell me where you come from and I will tell you what you are.'

On this view, education can enable students to understand themselves by facilitating the development of autonomy and the critical assessment of social and cultural circumstances. It is a view which has great currency in modern philosophy of education, but it is not obviously conducive to solving problem of education in multicultural societies because it renders problematic our attitude to those groups and cultural communities which do not themselves value autonomy. Thus, for example, Joseph Raz urges that 'in an autonomy-supporting environment there is no choice but to be autonomous' and therefore members of such minority cultures must be brought 'humanely and decently' to placing value on the condition of autonomy. Because autonomy is of great practical importance in democratic societies, non-autonomy valuing groups will not flourish unless they cultivate it. The development of autonomy is therefore not so much a moral as a practical necessity which must, if needs be, over-ride considerations of cultural loyalty. So this interpretation of 'understanding ourselves' is one which threatens to drive out cultural loyalties, particularly loyalties to cultures which give priority to virtues such as obedience or humility rather than self-determination or autonomy. Certainly this seems to be the slightly uneasy conclusion of Raz's argument, and it also, I think, lies behind Miller's suspicion of multicultural education, since it provides a definite context within which the claims of cultural loyalty and the claims of citizen identity will conflict.

There are, however, two other ways of interpreting the claim that education should enable us to understand ourselves. One, which is emphasised by Susan Wolf in her commentary on Taylor, is that education should enable us to understand and reflect upon our cultural heritage. She writes: 'we may think of education not merely as a way of acquainting students with what is best, but also as learning to understand ourselves, our history, our environment, our language'. And she goes on to argue for the inclusion of African, Asian, Latin American and East European story books in public libraries; this, she says, has enabled Americans to see themselves as essentially multicultural. 'The most significant good is not that our stock of legends is now better or more comprehensive than before. It is, rather, that by having these books and by reading them, we come to recognize ourselves as a multicultural community and so to recognize and respect the members of that community in all our diversity'.

I do not wish to take issue either with the sentiment or with the strategy which lies behind this conclusion. It does seem to me, however, to be a strategy which is available only on certain assumptions, most notably on the assumption that the stories from other lands really do tell us something about ourselves. In the United States, which is through its history essentially multicultural, this may be a plausible account, but it is far less readily conceded in Britain, where the disputed issue is precisely whether it is true that these 'other' cultures are in any way part of 'us', or we part of them. One commentator has suggested, that 'this polyphony of voices, this constant eddying of claims to identity, is one of the things that makes America America', but for better or worse it is implausible to say the same about Britain, or about many other multicultural societies.

However, what I want to concentrate on here is a slightly different, though connected, implication of Wolf's account. By emphasising the importance of all these different stories to our community, she implies that there is, in the end, no significant distinction between the cultural heritage of African-Americans, Italian-Americans, Irish-Americans and so on. American identity transcends and includes all these different and diverse origins. Understanding ourselves therefore involves understanding all these different and diverse backgrounds understanding them as all and equally ours. In this, I think, there may be both mistake and loss. The mistake lies in supposing that all such identities are correctly represented as 'hyphenated', but as Amy Gutmann has pointed out 'because of the systematic social injustice against African-Americans that persists over time, the identity of a significant proportion of African-Americans is not comfortably hyphenated (as the name African-American might suggest) but rather conflictually divided (African versus American) . . . without this added sense of suffering from systematic injustice, African-American identity would be similar in form (but not in content) to that of Irish-Americans, Korean-Americans, Jewish-Americans, and many other hyphenated-American identities'. The mistake therefore is to suppose that each hyphenated group bears the same relation to the transcendent community of Americans. It is to suppose that the members of these groups

feel no pressure to choose between the different component parts of their identity. And in some cases that assumption is false.

However, in addition to this mistake, there is also, I believe, the potential for loss inherent in the very desire to render all identities hyphenated in the way Wolf proposes, and I shall now attempt to say why I think there is loss and how a third interpretation of 'understanding ourselves' might serve to minimise that loss.

My third interpretation takes its cue from a recent book by Bernard Williams. In Shame and Necessity, Williams asks why we should study the texts of the ancient Greeks, and he answers that we should do so at least partly in order to understand ourselves. However, for Williams, 'understanding ourselves' does not simply mean 'understanding our cultural heritage' (seeing where we have come from), nor does it mean 'developing autonomy' (critically evaluating where we have come from). It also means seeing ourselves as autonomy valuers and recognising the merits and defects of that position by comparison with others. Thus he writes: 'when the ancients speak, they do not merely tell us about themselves. They tell us about us. They do that in every case in which they can be made to speak, because they tell us who we are. That is, of course, the most general point of our attempts to make them speak. They can tell us not just who we are, but who we are not: they can denounce the falsity or the partiality or the limitations of our images of ourselves'. It is, I think, for this reason that we should reject both Wolf's attempt to make out culture include all other cultures, and Raz's attempt to make other cultures subservient to our culture. The pretence that our culture includes all others is just that—a pretence; and, as Gutmann points out, a damaging one in some cases. On the other hand, the insistence on the practical priority of our culture is, somewhat paradoxically, uncritical about the importance we attach to critical evaluation.

I shall try to elucidate this last claim by appeal to two examples, one taken from Williams himself, the other from Norvin Richards' discussion of humility. In the chapter of his book titled 'Shame and Autonomy' Williams draws attention to the ancient Greek concept of shame and its relationship to the modern concept of guilt. It is often argued that the ancient Greeks had a shame culture whereas we have a guilt culture, and this distinction is also obliquely referred to by Taylor when he notes the move in modernity from an ethic of honour to an ethic of dignity. Indeed, in Taylor's eyes it is precisely this move which generates the problem of recognition that lies at the centre of his discussion:

> in those earlier societies, what we would now call identity was largely fixed by one's social position..., the birth of a democratic society doesn't by itself do away with this phenomenon, because people can still define themselves by their social roles. What does decisively undermine this socially derived identification, however, is the ideal of authenticity itself. As this emerges, for instance, with Herder, it calls on me to discover my own original way of being. By definition, this way cannot be socially derived, but must be inwardly generated.

The crucial move which Taylor alludes to here is the move from a culture in which identity is determined, from without to a culture—a democratic culture — in which identity is determined (or is thought to be determined): from within the individual. The rejection of social determination was a natural concomitant of the decline of hierarchy, but with it came a wholly implausible view of the possibility of dispensing entirely with recognition by 'significant others' as an important component in the construction of identity. Thus, by placing too much emphasis on ourselves as self-evaluators, we run the risk of ignoring the extent to which even 'we moderns' require recognition by others 'we define our identity always in dialogue with, sometimes in struggle against the things our significant others want to see in us. Even after we outgrow some of these others—our parents, for instance—and they disappear from our lives, the conversation with them continues within us as long as we live'.

Similarly, in Williams' account, the distinction between the ancient Greek understanding and our own is that the Greeks gave centrality to shame understood as a feeling about ourselves generated by others' views of us whereas we give centrality to guilt, understood as an inward recognition of what it is that we have done. Thus Williams notes that shame is often explicated by analogies of sight, and particularly by analogies of nakedness in the eyes of others. To experience shame is to be seen by others in a certain way, and (crucially) to know that one is the way they perceive one as being. In Sophocles' play, Ajax asks:

> What countenance can I show my father Telamon?
> How will he bear the sight of me
> If I come before him naked, without any glory,
> When he himself had a great crown of men's praise?
> It is not something to be borne.

It is tempting, as Williams notes, to interpret the emphasis on shame as indicative of a culture which lacks any understanding of the moral in a Kantian sense. The heroes of Greek tragedy appear to be concerned not with what they have done, but with how they are perceived. They live not in their own estimation of themselves, but in the eyes of others. And this, of course, is quite contrary to modern (specifically Kantian) morality: 'in the Kantian scheme of oppositions, shame is on the bad side of all the lines'. However, to dismiss shame as an ignoble concern with and dependence upon the views of others is misleading both with respect to the Greeks and with respect to ourselves. It is misleading with respect to ourselves because, as Taylor points out, we cannot both reject shame and yet acknowledge that 'a person or group of people can suffer real damage, real distortion, if the people or society around them mirror back to them a confining or demeaning or contemptible picture of themselves'. We do still, and always, live partly in the eyes of others and even if their picture of us is distorted or unfair, it may still be a picture which influences our own views of who we are. In this sense, the concept of shame is not entirely alien to us.

Nevertheless, shame is less central to modern conceptions of morality than it was for the ancient Greeks. But this difference also may enable us the better to understand ourselves and the limitations of our moral world. If, following Williams, we take guilt to be centrally concerned with what we have done, and shame to be centrally concerned with what we are, then the modern emphasis on guilt leads in the direction of making reparation to those who have been wronged, but it does not, in itself, lead in the direction of rebuilding oneself. By making guilt central, therefore, we foreclose on the kind of moral understanding which demands a reconstruction of ourselves in the light of others' opinions of us. And this is not, or not always, indicative of a noble refusal to live in the reflection of others' opinions. It is also symptomatic of an inability to move beyond an acknowledgement of what we have done to an acknowledgement of what we should be. Here, then, is a second sense in which other cultures—this time the culture of the ancient Greeks—may enable us the better to understand ourselves. If Williams' analysis is correct, the ancient Greeks suggest to us that we are the kinds of people who will make recompense for what we have done, but not the kind of people who will be capable of rebuilding ourselves. And the reason for that is precisely because we emphasise the solitary notion of guilt to the near exclusion of the more relational concept of shame.

What I am suggesting here is that understanding ourselves is a central aim of education, but 'understanding ourselves' may have various interpretations. It may mean understanding our cultural heritage, understanding 'where we have come from,' but in that case it is a problematic injunction in cases where the disputed issue is precisely whether members of minority cultures are part of 'us' —whether their identity is hyphenated rather than divided. Alternatively, it may mean developing our autonomy, understanding what are the important values for us as individuals living in a democratic society, but that threatens intolerance and repression of those who are not autonomy-valuing. Finally, it may mean understanding ourselves as autonomy valuers, recognisng that our values are the values of modern, democratic societies. As such, they may simultaneously be both more and less contiguous with the values of other cultures than we are inclined to imagine.

To illustrate this point further, I shall introduce a second example, taken from Norvin Richards' book, Humility. Richards asks: how can humility count as a virtue in modern Western society? And he answers that it can so count if we understand it not as 'holding oneself in low esteem', but rather as 'having oneself in proper perspective'. The humble person is not someone who puts a low value on his own talents. Rather, he is someone who makes a proper assessment of those talents. Moreover, this account of humility is one which, according to Richards, can transcend considerations of time and place : members of other cultures may value themselves more harshly than we do, but they can all concur in the analysis of humility as understanding oneself aright. Richards, then, is inclined to see our culture as transcending and including other cultures.

When we study those other cultures, we will see that they are at root very much like ours. And in order to substantiate his claim he draws attention to the Old Order Amish and their renunciation of personal ambition as inconsistent with proper humility. Richards argues that ambition need not be inconsistent with humility either for the Amish or for us, since humility (properly understood) requires only that we not take undue pride in what we achieve. It does not require the rejection of personal achievement or ambition.

I give this example because it seems to me to ignore the important sense in which enlarging the canon, or studying other cultures, may enable us to understand ourselves. In Amish culture, at least as it is portrayed in the literature, what is most important is to be forgetful of oneself, to give oneself up to the community, or to 'disappear rather than stand out'. As one writer puts it: 'the size and number of mirrors in a society indicate the cultural importance attached to the self. Thus it is not surprising that the mirrors found in Amish houses are smaller and fewer than those found in modern ones.' What this suggests to me is not that both we and the Amish share a concept of humility as 'having oneself in proper perspective'. What it suggests is that for the Amish, but not for us, any concern for 'proper perspective' is itself a threat to humility. Interpreting humility as 'understanding oneself aright' can be acceptable only to people who think that understanding oneself aright is a legitimate and important aim. But it is at least arguable that the Amish do not think that and therefore, for them, humility has both a different meaning and a different significance. They would interpret the very desire to 'understand oneself aright' as a desire which sprang from an inappropriate, indeed morally reprehensible, concern with oneself and one's own moral standing.

What we learn from this is indeed something about ourselves: we learn that we are the kind of people for whom self-assessment is morally legitimate. But we also learn that this is something which makes humility a different and more difficult concept for us than it is for the Amish, since we are required to provide an interpretation of humility according to which it is both virtuous and consists in a concern with oneself which borders on the narcissistic. We learn that the price of self-assessment is the loss, or at least the deformation, of humility as it was originally conceived. We learn, in Williams' words, 'the falsity or the partiality or the limitations of our images of ourselves'.

## Conclusion

I have suggested that the fundamental aim of education is to enable students to understand themselves. But this does not mean simply that they should recognise their own cultural heritage, nor yet that they should form their own opinions by critical reflection on that cultural heritage. It also, and crucially, means that they should understand themselves as the kinds of people for whom critical reflection, autonomy and self-fulfilment are central. This, I have argued, is the way in which education can enable us, particularly those of us who belong to the dominant groups in democratic societies, to understand ourselves.

How does this understanding of the aim of education help to answer the question with which I began, namely 'how can we educate people in a way which both respects their cultural identity and fits them for citizenship in a democratic society?' It does so in two ways: first, if we enlarge the canon and deploy it as a means of increasing self-understanding among the majority as well as the minority, one result may be that the majority will revise their own estimation of themselves. To revert to the example used earlier, by understanding Amish values I may come to see my own interest in self-fulfilment as partial, or even as partly misplaced.

I may be more willing, not merely to acknowledge other values, but also to see the constraints of my own value system. If this happens, then the contest between citizen identity and cultural loyalty will become less acute, since cultural loyalty will both inform and transform citizen identity.

In my opening remarks, I referred to David Miller's insistence that 'political education must try to shape cultural identities in the direction of common citizenship. It must try to present an interpretation of Indian culture in Britain which makes it possible for members of the Indian community to feel at home in, and loyal to the British state. In so far as there are elements in Indian culture which are at odds with such a reconciliation, the interpretation must be selective or, if you like, biased'. But this seems to require that the interpretation of Indian culture should be malleable, whereas the interpretation of British citizenship remains fixed. I see no reason, however, why the concept of British citizenship should not also be malleable. Not, of course, in Wolf's sense that being British or being American transcends and includes all these different cultural loyalties, but certainly in the sense that we (the majority) may come to recognise things of value in those other cultures and attempt to incorporate, or at least acknowledge, some of them in our societies and in the construction of our sense of citizenship.

Secondly, and connectedly, by enlarging the canon we may come to see that some problems which are presented as problems of toleration are in fact problems of recognition. Reflecting on the invitation to relativism inherent in his presumption of equal worth, Taylor writes: 'it makes sense to demand as a, matter of right that we approach the study of certain cultures with a presumption of their value..., but it can't make sense to demand as a matter of divine right that we come up with a final concluding judgement that their value is great or equal to others'. But this too invites a false choice: either other cultures are better than ours, or they are worse or we must submit to cultural relativism. The discussion of the Amish and Williams' discussion of the ancient Greeks suggest, however, that there are at least some cases where this simple division does not do justice to the situation. We have gained autonomy, they have retained humility, and there may be no answer to Taylor's question: 'Is their value equal to or greater than ours?' Moreover, to say this is not to submit to a crude cultural relativism. It is merely to suggest that the question is the wrong one to pose. As autonomy-valuers we are prone to identify the oppressive nature of Amish culture, and we may decide to tolerate that oppressiveness. But if we employ, education as a means of understan-ding ourselves, we may also come to see that as autonomy-valuers we lack the moral language with which to provide an explanation of their humility as anything other than oppression. In this way, we learn something about the limitations of our own moral world. We learn that there are virtues which are valuable, yet which cannot properly be accommodated within a moral framework which gives centrality to self-assessment and autonomy.

I began with the question 'how can we educate people in a way which both respects their cultural identity and instils democratic values in them'? My partial and tentative answer is that we should not begin by trying to understand, include or tolerate members of minority groups. Rather, we should begin by trying to understand ourselves and, if it is not too paradoxical, to understand ourselves as the kind of people who may place altogether too much importance on self-understanding.

## Notes and References
1. Miller, D., *Market, State and Community: Theoretical Foundations*

of *Market Socialism*, Oxford: Clarendon Press, 1989, p. 291.
2. Taylor, C., *The Politics of Recognition*, in: A. Gutmann (ed.) *Multiculturalism and the Politics of Recognition*, Princeton: Princeton University Press, 1992, p. 66.
3. Ibid., p. 71.
4. Ibid., p. 65.
5. Ibid., p. 66 ff.
6. Bloom, A., *The Closing of the American Mind*, Harmondsworth: Penguin Books, 1987, p. 13.
7. Raz, J., *The Morality of Freedom*, Oxford: Oxford University Press, 1986, p. 301.
8. Taylor, op. cit., p. 84.
9. Ibid., p. 83.
10. Hughes, R., *Culture of Complaint*, New York: Oxford University Press, 1993, p. 95.
11. Gutmann, A., *The Challenge of Multiculturalism in Political Ethics*, *Philosophy and Public Affairs*, 1993, p. 186.
12. Williams, B., *Shame and Necessity*, University of California Press, 1993, p. 20.
13. Taylor, op. cit., pp. 31-32.
14. Ibid., pp. 32-33.
15. Williams, op. cit., p. 77.
16. Taylor, op. cit., p. 25.
17. Williams, op. cit., p. 94.
18. Richards, N., *Humility*, Philadelphia: Temple University Press, 1992, p. 181.
19. It has been suggested to me that the example of the Amish is problematic in two ways: first, because Amish culture is less self-effacing than is often supposed in the literature, or at least that it lacks

the homogeneity which is usually attributed to it. I owe this point to Amy Gutmann and it is persuasively argued, though in a slightly different context, in her article 'The Challenge of Multiculturalism in Political Ethics', Philosophy and Public Affairs, 1993, pp. 171-206. Secondly, and connectedly, Paul Standish has suggested to me that the people who genuinely embrace the values I refer to here will be anonymous and unsung heroes, not the sorts of people about whom a large body of literature has been written. These are important considerations, but I hope that my general point survives the specific difficulties.

20. Taylor, op. cit., pp. 68-69.

[From: *Journal of Philosophy of Education*. Vol. 29, No. 2, pp. 191-201, 1995]

## 导读：容忍和认同：多元文化社会的教育

本文从"多元文化社会里应该如何教育儿童并使其既认识到自己的文化身份又能对其灌输民主价值观"这一问题入手，引入了 Miller 和 Taylor 两位作者有关民主价值观和种族文化身份之间的矛盾争议。Miller 认为在民主社会首先要保持对国民身份的忠诚，其次才是对文化的忠诚，而 Taylor 主要关心的是教育的内容，而不是教育的目的，他的中心问题是在多元文化社会教学大纲是否应该扩大并超越传统的标准，他认为通过该策略使人们对那些被排除在主流文化之外的群体有一个正确的认识。本文以此来说明多元文化社会的教育的目并且认为对教育目标应该有一个比 Miller 和 Taylor 更为全面清晰的认识：我们并不一定要选择国民身份或文化忠诚两者其一作为我们的教育目的。看来，多元文化社会里教育的根本目的在于使学生充分了解自己。

既然是把"了解自己"作为教育的中心目标，对于"了解自己"的理解又是丰富多样的。它并不仅仅意味着认识自己的文化遗产以及通过批判性的思考形成自己对文化的独到的观念;对个体来说更重要的是应该懂得发展批判性思维,在民主社会里实现自主和自我才是首要的。

其次,文章还论述了对不同文化的容忍事实上就是对不同文化的认同。我们不能忽视文化标准的扩大和对其他文化的研究,因为了解不同文化有助于了解自己。通过对文化正确客观的认识我们不仅能意识到自身世界的局限性也能以一种平等、开明、宽容的态度去对待不同文化。

**Questions for reflection:**
1. The author suggests that understanding ourselves is a central aim of education. Do you agree with his idea and why?
2. How do you understand "understanding ourselves"?
3. What attitudes does the author suggest we should have towards other cultures?

# Describing Intercultural Communication and the Intercultural Speaker

Michael Byram

## Introduction

The following is a description of the competences, additional to linguistic/grammatical competence, needed for successful intercultural communication. It comprises a model of intercultural competence, to which need to be added linguistic and socio-linguistic competence, and some examples of how the model can lead to the formulation of teaching objectives. Elsewhere (Byram, 1997), the model is also proposed as a basis for deciding on curricula and for approaches to assessment.

## Rationale

Whatever a person's linguistic competence in a foreign language, when they interact socially with someone from a different country, they bring to the situation their knowledge of the world which includes in some cases a substantial knowledge of the country in question and in others a minimal knowledge, of its geographical position or its current political climate, for example. They also have knowledge of their own country, although this may be less conscious, and they may not be aware of its significance in the interaction.

Their knowledge of their own country is a part of the social identity which they bring to the situation, and which is crucial for their interlocutor. For it is important to remember that the interaction between two individuals can only be fully understood when the relationship of the 'host' to the 'visitor' is included as well as 'visitor' to 'host'. The mutual perceptions of the social identities of the interlocutors is a determining factor in the interaction. They may share some knowledge of each other's country and they may share one or more of their social identities—their professional identity, for example in the case of diplomats or FL teachers—or they may be almost completely unknown to each other, as in the first visits of groups from one town to its twin town.

It will be evident from this that we cannot describe such an interaction as if there were two 'native-speakers' of the language involved, one of whom is a true native and the other attempting to be so. It is clear that, in a dyadic interaction for example, both interlocutors have different social identities and therefore a different kind of interaction than they would have with someone from their own country speaking the same language. It is for this reason that I shall introduce the concept of the 'intercultural speaker' to describe interlocutors involved in intercultural communication and interaction.

The success of such interaction can be judged in terms of the effective exchange of information, as has been the tendency in much communicative language teaching, but also in terms of the establishing and maintenance of human relationships. The latter in particular depends on attitudinal factors, for example the willingness of the interlocutors to expect problems of communication caused by lack of common ground in their respective knowledge of the world and of each other's country. It may depend on the ability of the interlocutors to accept criticism of the values they share with people in their usual social groups, and of which they may not have been consciously aware. It may also depend on their willingness to accept at least initially that they will be perceived by their interlocutor as a representative of a particular country, its values and its political actions, whatever their own views of these.

Knowledge and attitude factors are preconditions, although I shall argue that they are also modified by the processes of intercultural communication. The nature of the processes is a function of the skills which a person brings to the interaction. These can be divided into two broad and related categories:

—skills of interpretation and establishing relationships between aspects of the two cultures, which involves the ability to analyse data from one's own and from another country and the potential relationships between them;
—skills of discovery and interaction: skill a of discovery of new data and understanding of another country which can be operated in some cir-

cumstances independently of; and in others in combination with skills of interaction; and skills of interaction, of drawing on existing knowledge and attitudes to establish a successful communication and relationship.

## A Model of Intercultural Competence

Based on these preliminary reflections, I propose the following diagram of the factors involved and the relationships among them, which I shall then discuss in more detail:

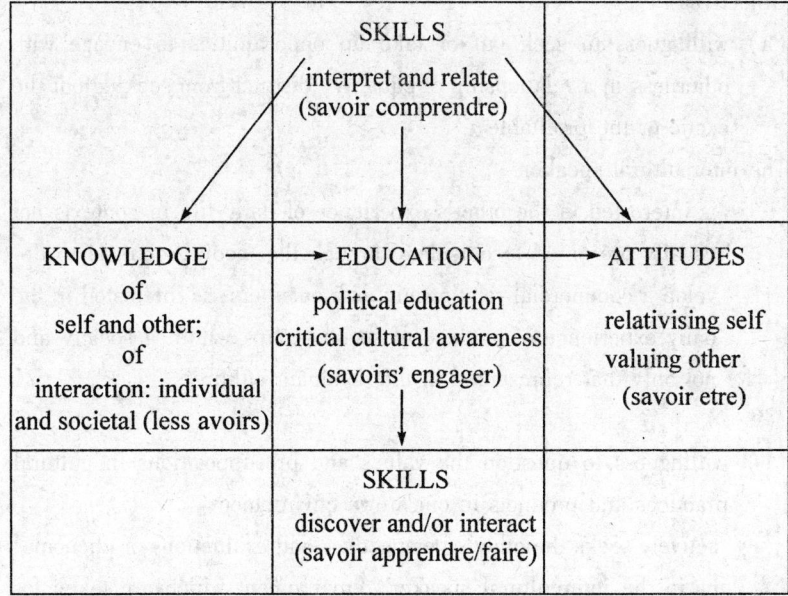

## Attitudes

I am concerned here only with attitudes towards people who are perceived as different in respect of their cultural meanings, beliefs and behaviours. Attitudes which are the pre-condition for successful intercultural interaction need to be not simply positive, but to be attitudes of curiosity and openness, of readiness to suspend disbelief and judgement with respect to others' meanings, beliefs and behaviours. There also needs to be a willingness to suspend belief in one's own meanings and behaviours, and to analyse them from the viewpoint of the others with whom one is engaging.

## Some Specimen Objectives

Attitudes: curiosity and openness, readiness to suspend disbelief about other cultures and belief about one's own

Objectives:

(a) willingness to seek out or take up opportunities to engage with otherness in a relationship of equality, distinct from seeking out the exotic or the profitable

The intercultural speaker

* is interested in the other's experience of daily life in contexts not usually presented to outsiders through the media, or used to develop a commercial relationship with outsiders; is interested in the daily experience of a range of social groups within a society and not only that represented in the dominant culture

(……)

(c) willingness to question the values and presuppositions in cultural practices and products in one's own environment

* actively seeks the other's perspectives and evaluations of phenomena in the intercultural speaker's environment which are taken for granted, and takes up the other's perspectives in order to contrast and compare with the dominant evaluations in their own society

(……)

## Knowledge

The knowledge individuals bring to an interaction with someone from another country can be described in two broad categories:

—knowledge about social groups and their cultures in one's own country, and similar knowledge of the interlocutor's country;
—knowledge of the processes of interaction at individual and societal levels.

Knowledge about other countries, and the identities brought to an interaction by an interlocutor from another country, is usually 'relational', i.e. it is knowledge acquired within socialisation in one's own social groups and often presented in contrast to the significant characteristics of one's national group and identity. For example, knowledge of the history of another country is through the stories from the history of one's own nation-state, and is consequently a different interpretation to the story told within the foreign country. The foreign language teacher needs to supplement this kind of knowledge with an 'insider' perspective on the values, beliefs and behaviours of those who belong to the other country.

Secondly, there is knowledge of the processes of interaction at individual and societal level, which is crucial to success. If an individual knows about the ways in which their social identities have been acquired, how they are a prism through which other members of their group are perceived, and how they are in turn perceive their interlocutors from another group, that awareness provides a basis for successful interaction. This needs to be complemented by procedural knowledge of how to act in specific circumstances.

## Some Specimen Objectives

Knowledge: of social groups and their products and practices in one's own and in one's interlocutor's country, and of the general processes of societal and individual interaction

Objectives (knowledge of/about):
(a) historical and contemporary relationships between one's own and one's interlocutor's countries

The intercultural speaker

* knows about events, significant individuals and diverse interpretations of events which have involved both countries and the traces left in the national memory; and about political and economic factors in the contemporary alliances of each country

(b) the means of achieving contact with interlocutors from another country (at a distance or in proximity), of travel to and from, and the institutions which facilitate contact or help resolve problems

* knows about (and how to use) telecommunications, consular and similar services, modes and means of travel, and public and private organizations which facilitate commercial, cultural/leisure and individual partnerships across frontiers

(c) the types of cause and process of misunderstanding between interlocutors of different cultural origins

* knows about conventions of communication and interaction in their own and the foreign cultures, about the unconscious effects of paralinguistic and non-verbal phenomena, about alternative interpretations of shared concepts, gestures, customs and rituals

(d) the national memory of one's own country and how its events are related to and seen from the perspective of other countries

* knows the events and their emblems (myths, cultural products, sites of significance to the collective memory) which are markers of national identity in one's own country as they are portrayed in public institutions and transmitted through processes of socialisation, particularly those experienced in schools; and is aware of other per-

spectives on those events
(……)

## Skills

An individual coming across a 'document', used in the widest sense, from another country can interpret it with the help of specific information and general frames of knowledge which will allow them to discover the allusions and connotations present in the document. The ability to interpret a document from one country for someone from another, or to identify relationships between documents from different countries, is therefore dependent on knowledge of one's own and the other environment.

## Some Specimen Objectives

Skills of interpreting and relating: ability to interpret a document or event from another culture, to explain it and relate it to documents or events from one's own

Objectives (ability to):
(a) identify ethnocentric perspectives in a document or event and explain their origins

The intercultural speaker
* can 'read' a document or event, analysing its origins/sources—e. g. in the media, in political speech or historical writing—and the meanings and values which arise from a national or other ethnocentric perspective (stereotypes, historical connotations in texts) and which are presupposed and implicit, leading to conclusions which can be challenged from a different perspective

(b) identify areas of misunderstanding and dysfunction in an interaction and explain them in terms of each of the cultural systems present
* can identify causes of misunderstanding (e. g. use of concepts ap-

parently similar but with different meanings or connotations; use of genres in inappropriate situations; introduction of topics inappropriate to a context, etc.) and dysfunctions (e.g. unconscious response to unfamiliar non-verbal behaviour, proxemic and paralanguage phenomena; over-generalisation from examples; mistaken assumptions about representativeness of views expressed); and can explain the errors and their causes by reference to know-ledge of each culture involved

(……)

The skill of discovery comes into play where the individual has no, or only a partial existing knowledge framework. It is the skill of building up specific knowledge as well as an understanding of the beliefs, meanings and behaviours which are inherent in particular phenomena, whether documents or interactions. The knowledge acquired may be 'instrumental' or 'interpretative'. In the first case, the individual might be geographically mobile and needs to discover the ways to gain access to a new society, the institutions giving permissions for travel and residence, the institutions which manage relations between the host country and the country of origin. The skill of discovery is the ability to recognise significant phenomena in a foreign environment and to elicit their meanings and connotations, and their relationship to other phenomena. Although the skill is essentially identical in different environments, it may be more difficult to operate in those which have least in common with the individual's country of origin, the so-called 'exotic' languages and cultures.

One mode of discovery is through social interaction, often face-to-face, even though this adds constraints of time and mutual perceptions and attitudes mentioned earlier. The skill of interaction is above all the ability to manage these constraints in particular circumstances with specific interlocutors. The individual needs to draw upon their existing knowledge, have attitudes which sustain sensitivity to others with sometimes radically different origins and identities, and operate the skills of discovery and interpretation. In particular, the individual needs to manage dysfunctions which arise in the course of interaction, drawing upon knowledge and skills. They may also be called upon not only to establish a relationship between their own social identities and those of their interlocutor, but also to act as mediator between people of different origins and identities. It is this function of establishing relationships, managing dysfunctions and mediating which distinguishes an 'intercultural speaker', and makes them different from a native speaker.

## Some Specimen Objectives

Skills of discovery and interaction: ability to acquire new knowledge of a culture and cultural practices and the ability to operate knowledge, attitudes and skills under the constraints of real-time communication and interaction

Objectives (ability to):
(a) elicit from an interlocutor the concepts and values of documents or events and develop an explanatory system susceptible of application to other phenomena
The intercultural speaker
  * can use a range of questioning techniques to elicit from informants the allusions, connotations and presuppositions of a document or event and their origins/sources, and can develop and test generalisations about shared meanings and values (by using them to interpret another document; by questioning another informant; by consulting appropriate literature) and establish links and relationships

among them (logical relationships of hierarchy, of cause and effect, of conditions and consequence, etc.)

(b) identify significant references within and across cultures and elicit their significance and connotations

* can 'read' a document or event for the implicit references to shared meanings and values (of national memory, of concepts of space, of social distinction, etc.) particular to the culture of their interlocutor, or of international currency (arising for example from the dominance of western satellite television); in the latter case, the intercultural speaker can identify or elicit different interpretations and connotations and establish relationships of similarity and difference between them

(……)

(e) identify contemporary and past relationships between one's own and the other culture and society

* can use sources (e.g. reference books, newspapers, histories, experts, lay informants) to understand both contemporary and historical political, economic and social relationships between cultures and societies and analyse the differing interpretations involved

(……)

(g) use in real-time knowledge, skills and attitudes for mediation between interlocutors of one's own and a foreign culture

* can identify and estimate the significance of misunderstandings and dysfunctions in a particular situation and is able to decide on and carry out appropriate intervention, without disrupting interaction and to the mutual satisfaction of the interlocutors

## Acquiring Intercultural Competence in General Education

Much acquisition of Intercultural Competence is tutored and takes place within an educational setting. Some educational institutions may fulfil functions other than those of general education, i. e. the development of the individual in all their facets to their fullest potential—and focus on vocational skills or short-term objectives. In other cases, institutions and teachers, including FL teachers, have a responsibility to pursue general educational aims together with those of the subject taught. In the model proposed here, there is an element of critical thinking about one's own and other cultures and their taken-for-granted values and practices

## Some Specimen Objectives

Critical cultural awareness/political education: an ability to evaluate, critically and on the basis of explicit criteria, perspectives, practices and products in one's own and other cultures and countries

Objectives (ability to):
(a) identify and interpret explicit or implicit values in documents and events in one's own and other cultures
The intercultural speaker
　　* can use a range of analytical approaches to place a document or event in context (of origins/sources, time, place, other documents or events) and to demonstrate the ideology involved
(b) make an evaluative analysis of the documents and events which refers to an explicit perspective and criteria
　　* is aware of their own ideological perspectives and values ('human rights'; socialist; liberal; Moslem; Christian etc.) and evaluates documents or events with explicit reference to them
(c) interact and mediate in intercultural exchanges in accordance with explicit criteria, negotiating where necessary a degree of acceptance of those exchanges by drawing upon their knowledge, skills and attitudes
　　* is aware of potential conflict between their own and other ideologies

and is able to establish common criteria of evaluation of documents or events, and where this is not possible because of incompatibilities in belief and value systems, is able to negotiate agreement on places of conflict and acceptance of difference

[From: Byram, M. (1997) *Teaching and Assessing Intercultural Communicative Competence*, Clevedon: Multilingual Matters.]

## 导读：描述跨文化交流和跨文化代言者

本篇主要描述了进行成功的跨文化交流除了语言能力外的跨文化代言者所必须的其他能力。文中介绍了跨文化能力的模式主要包括知识、技能、态度和教育等几个方面。

跨文化能力模式图表示如下：

```
                   技能
                （解释和领会）
                    ↓
知识 →             教育→                   态度
（关于自我和他人   （政治教育）         （自我相对化并
的相互关系：       （批判的文化意识）      尊重他人）
个人的和社会的）        ↓
                   技能
               （发现和相互交流）
```

成功的交流主要从信息的有效交流来判断，也从人际关系的建立和保持上来考虑。知识和态度是成功交流的先决条件。交流的成功还取决于在交流过程中所利用的技能。

态度指自我相对化和对他人的评价。此处讨论的主要是对那些在文化意义、信仰和行为方面不同的态度。态度作为成功跨文化交流的先决条件，应该不仅仅只是肯定的态度，还应该包括好奇心、思想开明和对其他文化与自我文化中的意义、信念和行为的判断和怀疑有重新分析和认识的准备或愿望；愿意寻求和利用各种机会并以平等身份接触他国文化，积极地从他人的视角来看待和评价跨文化环境中想当然的各种现象。

知识是指对本国文化和社会群体的了解及与对方主动交流所应具备的相应的知识，还包括对个人和社会层面上的相互交流过程的认识。与对方主动发起交流者所应用到交流中的有关他国和身份的知识常常是相关的，比如说在一定社会群体中所获得的知识常常与该民族整体不同，对他国历史的知识也是从自身历史出发的。其次，有关个人层面和社会层面上交流过程的知识对交流也是至关重要的。

技能则是指个体利用已有的信息和一般的知识框架对外来事物和文献进行理解并发现其内涵的能力。这种对外来文献和事物解释的能力主要依赖于有关自我和他人环境的知识。个体需要利用已有的知识和敏感的态度来发挥自己的发现和解释技能。

**Questions for reflection：**
1. What is the model of intercultural competence Byram raises in his article and what are some of the specific objectives of the model?
2. Illustrate the importance of knowledge and attitude factors in intercultural communication.
3. What are the skills in the intercultural communication?

# Culture Shock: Psychological Reactions to Unfamiliar Environments

A. Furnham & S. Bochner

## Introduction

A convenient starting point from which to begin the study of psychological reactions to unfamiliar environments is to consider what motivates people to travel in the first place. Human motivation as an area of research has attracted psychologists from many different research traditions for a number of years (Weiner, 1980), yet it is not an easy topic to study. Motives are often complex, having biological, psychological and cultural determinants. Furthermore, stressful behaviours may be the result of a host of 'complementary and competing motives, which are often difficult to disentangle.

From a methodological point of view the study of social motives is limited because of the unreliability of self-report (for a review of the literature on the relationship between verbal self-reports and behaviour, see Bochner, 1980). There are numerous reasons why people will not or cannot report on their true motives: there may be memorial or other response biases which distort reports of past behaviour; subjects may be loath to admit to researchers their real reasons and motives for travel, particularly if these conflict with official stated or funded reasons; also, as many clinicians have pointed out, people often cannot, even if they want to, report on their motives for various actions, particularly in the area of social motivation (Atkinson, 1958). Despite these difficulties, researchers have attempted to describe the motives of cultural travellers and link them systematically to different patterns of coping with culture stress.

The motives for travel will be discussed under headings which correspond with various chapters in Part II. The motives of tourists and business people, students and voluntary workers, and migrants, respectively, will now be considered.

## The Motives of Tourists and Business People

According to Pearce (1982a), research into the motives of tourists poses various problems. First, it is wrong to regard tourist motivation as a short-term process isolated from the rest of a person's activities and concerns. People often plan and work for their holidays far in advance of the actual event and apparently derive as much satisfaction from this planning as they do from the travelling itself. Furthermore, the decision to go to a particular place, for a particular time, with particular associates cannot be separated from the wider, long-standing motivation of individuals.

Second, there is the problem associated with whether motives are measured before, during or after travel. There are numerous reasons for supposing that motives recorded before travelling, in order to predict specific reactions to specific places, are rather different from a post hoc descriptive account of travel motivation, which is usually more general. Other difficulties stem from the belief that travel is supposed to be intrinsically satisfying, and hence motivations that are offered are often tautological.

In his analysis Pearce (1982a) draws on several theoretical areas— including the hierarchy of needs, attribution theory and achievement motivation— to account for tourist motivation. For instance, it is suggested that the motives of tourists may be linked to their level on Maslow's (1966) hierarchy of needs. Thus some may travel to fulfil needs for love and belongingness, others to achieve higher self-esteem and still others to 'self-actualize' themselves. Alternatively, one's need for achievement may dictate to what extent travel may be used as pure 'time-out', relaxation or an opportunity to better oneself materially and mentally. Pearce reviews two studies that have used this perspective to account for tourist motivation. Dann (1977) has distinguished between two types of tourists: those wishing to escape and 'get away from it all' in order to reduce the feelings of anomie prevalent in many western cultures, and those primarily in pursuit of 'ego-enhancement'. From data collected in Barbados, he concluded that anomie tourists were married and middle class while ego-enhancers were of lower socio-economic status, female and older. The former, he suggested, needed to feel they belong to a caring, integrated, emotionally rewarding community, while the latter needed an elevated social position and power. Despite obvious problems with this study, it does highlight the very different motives of different groups travelling on holiday to the same place.

Crompton (1979) has offered a fairly comprehensive analysis of the motives for tourism. From both a review of the previous literature and an empirical study, he identified nine motives for a 'pleasure vacation'. Seven of these motives were classified as socio-psychological and included escape from a perceived mundane environment, exploration and evaluation of self, relaxation, prestige, regression, enhancement of kinship relationships and facilitation of social interaction. Two of the motives were labelled cultural and include novelty and education. Whereas the socio-psychological motives were unrelated to attributes of the destination, the cultural motives were related, at least partially. The actual destination served only as a medium through which these various psychological needs could be satisfied. Methodologically, Crompton noted that the interviews caused many of the thirty-nine respondents to confront for the first time their 'real motives' for going on holiday. Crompton noted that his study may have implications for destination promotion and market segmentation.

Cohen (1979) derived various motives for travel after making a distinction between five modes of tourism: recreational, diversionary, experiential, experimental and existential. Each of these is quite different and presupposes different destinations, activities and adaptations. In contrast to market research, a psychological perspective leads to the view that tourists are not motivated by specific factors associated with their destination (beaches, hotel facilities, arranged amusements) but rather by the broad suitability of a place to meet particular psychological needs:

> Conceptualizing holiday destinations, according to their capacity to fit human needs, may produce some strange and novel mental maps of travel destinations. Instead of distance, culture and climate being used to classify destinations, one can envisage clusters of vacation centres which are predominantly self-exploratory, or social interaction, or indeed sexual arousal and excitement. (Pearce, 1982a, p. 65)

The motives for travel are imperfectly understood, complex and manifold. In specific instances, however, where they are known, they may easily account for how and why tourists experience their holiday as fulfilling, pleasant, relaxing; or tiring, disappointing and aggravating. Often no amount or type of travelling can satisfy the desires of some travellers (for self-actualization, enlightenment, etc.) while many holiday destinations make promises of facilities and activities that may appear to, but cannot, fulfil certain needs.

Whereas there is limited psychological research on tourists' travel motives, there is even less on the motives of business people moving from one locale to another. While the reasons for companies posting their employees to foreign places may be fairly easy to understand (Torbiorn, 1982), the motives of individual business persons moving abroad and back again remains relatively unexplored territory. It is generally assumed such moves are simply motivated by economic rewards (Barrel, 1979), yet, as Torbiorn (1982) found in his study of Swedish business people, the motives were much more complex than this. He found both 'push' or negative motives relating to dissatisfaction and 'pull' or positive motives relating to a belief in increased satisfaction being associated with the move. Pull motives included a special interest in the particular host country, increased promotion prospects, wider career opportunities or generally more favourable economic conditions. Torbiorn found some evidence for his thesis that positive rather than negative, and greater rather than lesser freedom in choosing the host country, was associated with higher levels of adaptation and satisfaction.

## Motives of Students and Volunteer Workers

Why do students go abroad to study? There is no dearth of opinion on this topic, but very little empirical evidence. As part of a major study in which sixty-nine returned students were interviewed in their homeland after the completion of their overseas sojourn, Bochner (1973) asked the respondents why they had accepted their respective scholarships and what they had hoped to get out of the experience. The subjects, all of whom had earned a higher degree in the United States, were 27 Thais, 16 Pakistanis and 26 Philippine respondents, and the interviews were conducted in Bangkok, Karachi and Manila, respectively. Several measures of motivation were used, some direct and others indirect. Of special interest in the present context were the responses to the question: What was your main reason for going abroad to study? The answers were coded into four categories: get a degree; gain academic or professional expertise; culture-learning; and personal development. Of the sixty-nine responses, sixty-four (93 percent) fell into the first two categories. Only two of the students said that their main reason was culture-learning, and three (all from the Philippines) listed personal development (e.g. to gain insight, to become better people, to find themselves) as their main purpose. Other questions yielded a similar pattern. More recently, in a study of 2536 foreign students in ten different countries by Klineberg and

Hull (1979), 71 per cent of the respondents said that obtaining a degree or diploma was important, and again the acquisition of qualifications and experience ranked as the single most important reason for going to a foreign university.

Thus there is no doubt that the overwhelming majority of foreign students are primarily interested in getting a degree and/or professional training rather than learning a second culture or achieving personal growth. Uppermost in their minds are concerns about the tangible pay-offs a sojourn might provide in the shape of career advancement, prestige and upward mobility. Indeed, it would be remarkable if this were not the case, given the amount of dislocation and hardship involved in an educational sojourn abroad.

However, as some observers have noted (Bochner, 1979; Bochner, Lin and McLeod, 1979), there is a discrepancy between the motives of the students participating in educational exchange, and the concerns of those persons and organizations which administer, fund and sponsor the participants. Although there are substantial numbers of private students in the system, a great many of the sojourners are sponsored by various governments, foundations and international agencies (Bochner and Wicks, 1972), and even the so-called private students do not fully pay their way, particularly in countries where tertiary students are not charged fees. Thus, since the taxpayer is deeply revolved in contemporary international education, there arose a need to justify it to the public. To that end there has emerged a curious alliance between the idealists who see international education as a way of solving some if not all of the world's ills, and the pragmatic politicians who represent overseas-student programmes as being in the national interest, usually as an extension of foreign policy (Bochner and Wicks, 1972) and who use their advocacy for educational exchange to get themselves re-elected (e.g. Fulbright,

1976). Neither assumption is supported by a great deal of empirical evidence, that is sponsoring foreign students is not a very efficient way of solving the world's problems, nor of conducting foreign policy, but that has not deterred governments from continuing to commit extensive funds to international education; which is just as well, since otherwise a great many young people would have been denied access to higher learning. It is interesting to examine why there is almost unanimous support for educational exchange, despite its somewhat flimsy empirical foundations.

The idealists regard it as self-evident that educational exchange must lead to improved international relations. They take it for granted that cross-cultural contact, particularly among young people, creates mutual understanding, and when these students in the fullness of time assume positions of influence in their societies, this will be reflected in harmonious relations between their respective countries, and thus contribute to world peace. The evidence reviewed elsewhere in this book, both with regard to the contact hypothesis in general (Amir, 1969, 1976; Cook and Selltiz, 1955) as well as its application in the area of host-foreign student relationships, indicates that the connection between inter-group contact and inter-group attitudes is very complex, such that contact may either increase or reduce mutual tolerance and understanding, depending on a very large matrix of interacting variables. Indeed, as we saw, there have been instances where educational exchange has led to a worsening of cross-cultural attitudes (Tajfel and Dawson, 1965), a proposition that many people find difficult to accept and therefore tend to ignore.

The politicians likewise assume that foreign students will return home full of good-will for their erstwhile hosts, thus making them easier targets for subsequent influence. Often too, educational exchange is seen as a part of economic aid (Bochner and Wicks, 1972), the idea being that the skills that the students acquire abroad will be used to further the economic and technical development of their countries, thereby reducing hunger and poverty, creating markets and promoting stability in the regions concerned. Although, no doubt, these objectives have at times been achieved, such results are not inevitable or, for that matter, necessarily desirable (Bochner, 1979). Thus some foreign students return home with an abiding hatred for the country in which they sojourned (Tajfel and Dawson, 1965). Not all students return home, giving rise to the notion of brain drain (Adams, 1968) or the tendency of the brightest students to emigrate, usually to the country where they had studied. Sometimes students return home so imbued with the notion of the superiority of the technology they acquired abroad that they set about applying these techniques, solutions and practices in an unthinking and inappropriate way, making no attempt to adapt what they have brought back with them to conform to local cultural requirements (Alatas, 1972, 1975), sometimes with disastrous results (Boxer, 1969; Mortimer, 1973). Sometimes, also, the students use their overseas qualifications to improve their own conditions at the expense of those who were not able to go abroad; to exploit their countrymen on behalf of foreign interests (Curle, 1970; Wade, 1975); and in extreme instances, perpetuate repressive social systems that lack humanity and equity. None of this should be taken to suggest that we in any way oppose international education. Study abroad can be justified on intrinsic grounds, as increasing humankind's sum total of furnished minds (although whether there are any votes in that idea is debatable). However, there is a need to evaluate the various programmes and describe their actual rather than their assumed or intended effects. Such research is almost non-existent, partly because of the enormous methodological and logistical problems involved, but also because, on the one hand, the benefits of educational exchange are seen to be self-evident and hence not in need of scrutiny and, on the other hand, because many educational exchange programmes have become identified with the conduct of a country's foreign policy, so that investigators in this area have to contend with an uncooperative or hostile establishment. After all, if educational exchange did not exist, governments would have to invent it. How else would they suitably commemorate a visit by a royal personage or a head of state, sweeten a trade treaty, show concern for the poor and disadvantaged of this world or signal an indication of good-will towards a previously ignored or maligned nation? There are literally thousands of fellowships and scholarships which have been conceived under such circumstances, and the authors as well as many people reading this book have or will at some time in the future travel to distant places under their auspices. It is highly unlikely that the motives of the sojourners will coincide fully with the objectives of those who established these schemes. Incidentally, this is another reason why evaluation in this area is so difficult, because the criterion variables shift according to whether the objectives are regarded from the perspective of the donor/sponsor, the incumbent, the recipient nation, the region or the global community. However, such complexities do not preclude making these various considerations explicit, examining their desirability and evaluating the extent to which the various goals are realized. We are not aware of any research which has tackled this problem in such a systematic way.

## The Motivation of Peace Corps Volunteers

An examination of the motives of Peace Corps Volunteers (PCVs) also reveals some complexities and contradictions. In a study of the first four groups of trainees (about 300 individuals) Guthrie (1966) reports that about 80 percent evinced interests closely resembling those of the typical social worker. When interviewed, they freely acknowledged that they had joined the Peace Corps because they wanted to do something significant and because they had not found a satisfying career at home. At the same time, many of these individuals brought with them highly unrealistic notions as to what they could achieve, how quickly they could solve the problems of the region in which they served or what tangible results could be expected from their work.

Although it is customary to refer to the Peace Corps as if it were an entity, it really consisted of three sub-groups, each with its own particular aims, values and standards, not equally shared by each group. In addition to the PCVs in the field, there was the Peace Corps/Washington staff subculture, and the Overseas Representative staff subculture. The primary aim of the Washington organization was to gain and expand domestic political acceptance of the Peace Corps, to administer its day-to-day operations within the framework of a civil-service bureaucracy and to develop effective new overseas programmes. The officials in Washington saw themselves as accountable to the politicians from whom they derived their budgets, authority and power. In contrast, the volunteers in the field regarded themselves to be in the business of communicating and co-operating with the local people and striving for goals consistent with indigenous concerns. The success of the Volunteers was judged according to how well they were able to bridge the gap between their own culture and that of the people whom they were assisting. Finally, the job of the Local Representatives was to establish administrative and communication links between Washington and the Volunteers, and provide logistical and other support for the workers in the field. Local Representatives were in a particularly difficult position, because the standards which Washington used to gauge their performance were sometimes quite different from those employed by the Volunteers. In addition, staff members were usually older, had distinguished themselves in their professions and enjoyed a relatively high income. In contrast, the Volunteers were young, received no salary (they were paid an allowance geared to the cost of living in the host country) and for many of them their transcultural experience was their first adult job. The Washington staffers differed from the Overseas Representatives in being more career orientated, who in turn were much more career orientated than the Volunteers. Nevertheless, according to Textor (1966), despite all these differences, the three subcultures all shared one overriding value, namely that the most important thing that one can do in one's job is to facilitate the success of the Volunteers in the field. Textor suggests that this unifying ethic was one of the major reasons for the success of the Peace Corps programmes. Nevertheless, the tensions in that organization parallel the discrepancies in motives that occur in overseas-student programmes.

The general conclusion to be drawn is that the motives and concerns of sojourners cannot be assumed to coincide with the motives and concerns of those who set up and direct these programmes. Although we have illustrated this proposition with reference to overseas students and PCVs (because there is direct evidence in these two areas to draw on) we suspect that the same tensions occur with respect to most categories of sojourners. Since such conflicts may impede the process of culture-earning and accommodation, this relatively neglected aspect of the sojourn process deserves more attention than is generally accorded to it, both in regard to research concerning its extent and effects, as well as in establishing procedures to contain its impact.

## Motives for Migration

The topic of migration has interested historians, geographers, sociologists and many others for a long time. Peterson (1958) has categorized types of migration, and these are given in Table 3.1.

Despite the voluminous literature in this area, there is little information regarding people's motives to migrate. Most studies have concentrated on the demographic, historical or structural variables of migration and from these have made certain assumptions about motives. Ghosts of economic determinism abound in this literature, yet study after study has shown that although economic factors are important, people are not simply economic maximizers (Lansing and Mueller, 1967).

Taylor (1966) has suggested that one needs to know a number of factors about an individual's subjective perception of his or her home place of residence in order to understand the motives for migration—that is, the degrees of structural 'conductiveness' or strain at the place of origin and the person's evaluation of it; the presence of long- or short-term aspirations; feelings of alienation and dislocation; objective feasibility of migration as a project; and trigger factors which spur a decision. Naamary (1971) has suggested that the predisposition to migrate is a function of the relative deprivation of full employment opportunities, educational facilities, health facilities, social and community ties, housing facilities and climate. Others have also put stress on the idea of place, utility—

Table 1　**Peterson's general typology of migration**

| | Migratory Force | Class of Migration | Type of Migration | |
| --- | --- | --- | --- | --- |
| | | | Conservative | Innovating |
| Nature and Man | Ecological Push | Primitive | Wandering Ranging | Flight from the Land |
| State (or Equivalent) and Man | Migration Policy | Forced Impelled | Displacement Flight | Slave Trade Coolie Trade |
| Man and His Norms | Higher Aspirations | Free | Group | Pioneer |
| Collective Behaviour | Social Momentum | Mass | Settlement | Urbanization |

(Source: W. Peterson, A General Typology of Migration, *American Sociological Review*, 23 (1958), 266.)

subjective evaluations of the composite utilities (goods, services, benefits) derived from alternative (i. e. home versus foreign) places (Wolpert, 1965; Brown and Holmes, 1971). That is, people rationally weigh up the advantages and disadvantages of different places before deciding whether to migrate.

Sociologists and anthropologists, on the other hand, have stressed the importance of kinship ties in migration. In a critical review of the predominantly economic, geographic and sociological literature Shaw (1975) concluded that: just as it is important to consider the socio-demographic and socio-economic elements in questions concerning 'Who are the migrants?' and 'Why did they migrate?', it is important also to consider the influence of culture-systems components (including ideological commitments), personality systems (including the individual's aspirations, identity, integrity, role performance), social-system components (including socialization practices) and levels of stress in the system. (p. 116)

Various attempts have also been made by social psychologists over the years to study the motives of migrants in moving from one country to another. What is perhaps most disappointing about this literature is its simple-minded, a theoretical nature. While it may be that early periods of migration were less complex motivationally than they are today, current studies on migrant motivation still remain too simplistically conceived and executed to capture the complexity of a migrant's motives.

Turner (1949) investigated the attitudes, motives and personal characteristics of migrants in a medium-sized American city. He found that his respondents gave essentially four sets of reasons for their migration: economic or job considerations; the influence of friends or relatives; standard-of-living considerations; and other, miscellaneous reasons, such as to retire.

A number of studies have been done on migration to Australasia (Brown, 1959, 1960; Richardson, 1974). Brown (1960) found immigrants to New Zealand provided five types of explanation for their decision to migrate: personal reasons (a new life, travel experience), the appeal of New Zealand, a dislike of England, job opportunities and other miscellaneous reasons. However, the author did notice some dissonance reduction: 'When a favourable attitude to the destination is formulated, other destinations are systematically undervalued' (p. 173). Richardson (1974) has done an extensive psycho-social study of British immigrants to Australia. He looked at people's decisions to emigrate as well as specific factors which he labelled 'opportunity', 'personality', 'precipitating' and 'bolstering'.

Whereas most studies have looked at the more common experience of migration from less to more developed countries (or between countries of equal development), there have also been studies of why people migrate from more to less developed countries. Berman (1979) followed up Antonovsky and Katz's (1979) study on why North Americans migrate to Israel, and found six major reasons: Zionism (identification as a Zionist); Jewishness (to lead a fuller Jewish religious life); attraction to life in Israel (interesting, less hectic, sense of community); family reasons (for raising children); dissatisfaction with North America (crime, anti-Semitism) and personal reasons. The typical migrants are thus in search of Jewishness and see Israel as a good rich environment for the expression of their and their children's Jewish identity.

Many writers have distinguished between factors that push and pull people to emigrate from one country and immigrate to another (Rossi, 1955). However, most researchers have commented on the problems of this simplified distinction. For instance, Brown (1960) wrote, 'It should be pointed out, however, that this model is an oversimplification because the relationship between pushes and pulls is complex, with each of these forces interacting and having both positive and negative components' (p. 168); and Berman (1979) said:

The difficulty of conceptually separating 'push' and 'pull' motives for migration has been acknowledged in the literature. Motives can reflect both 'push' and 'pull' elements. For example, if poor job opportunities in the country of origin were a reason to move, then better opportunities in the new country would likely be a correlate. (p. 143)

Nearly all of the psychological studies of migration have been concerned with immigrants' reasons or motives for leaving one country (usually the country of their birth) and choosing another country. However, almost no research appears to have been done on the native inhabitants' beliefs about the immigration and emigration. This is surprising given the widespread social and political debate on immigration in Britain and other developed countries. And although immigration is a much discussed topic, emigration is practically ignored even though, for instance, as many people leave Britain as enter it. Thus, between 1961 and 1971 nearly 500,000 more people left Britain than entered, yet this topic has remained very little researched in that country (Sillitoe, 1973).

Furthermore, very little research has been done on the difference between natives' and immigrants' explanations for or beliefs about immigration. Studies from a social-attribution framework in other, but related areas (Furnham, 1982) suggest that different social, cultural or political perspectives lead people to make different attributions for political or economic phenomena. Older people, and those from a more conservative background, are more likely to explain the motives of migrants in negative, selfish terms, while younger, less conservative natives would explain immigration in more positive terms.

Furnham (1986a) has attempted to apply attribution theory to a study of migrants' and non-migrants' explanations for immigration to and emigration from Britain. Not surprisingly, he found striking differences in the explanations native Britons offered for people leaving or coming to Britain as migrants (Table 3.2). People believed that the most important motives for both immigration and emigration were personal advancement and better job opportunities. Overall there seemed to be five factors or types of explanations for both immigration and emigration—four 'pull' factors (destination's culture and values, high standard of living, benefits of the welfare state and improved quality of life) and one 'push' factor (political and economic reasons). Furnham (1986a) has noted that the acceptance of immigrants may depend partly upon whether it is believed that they come for cultural or family reasons rather than to benefit from the welfare state. Thus the study of natives' perceptions of migrants' motives may be as important as the study of the migrants' motives themselves, for an understanding of how, when and why migrant groups do or do not adapt to the native culture.

In summary, research into the motives of migrants needs to take into account three issues. First, it must be recognized that there exist various types of migration, such as internal versus international; voluntary versus forced; legal versus illegal; and permanent versus temporary. To talk of motives for migration in general is misleading as the motives vary with the type of migration. Second, economic determinism and a rational calculus will not suffice to explain motives for migration. People do not, indeed cannot, simply work out a balance sheet between positive and negative economic, political and life-style factors. People decide to migrate for a variety of reasons. For instance, they might be urged into working abroad by a domineering parent; they may feel the need to follow a close family member whose decision to migrate was highly whimsical; there may be powerful religious or political motives for migration which override all other considerations. Third, every country has an immigration policy which may inhibit or encourage particular types of migration. Immigration decisions and policies may be based on population requirements, economic and political considerations or humanitarian principles, all of which would encourage some migrants while making it practically impossible for others. Further, the official policy of government may be quite different from what is actually implemented. Consequently, the motives to migrate are often shaped by others both in the migrants' countries of origin and destination.

Motivation to migrate, therefore, should not be conceived of merely in individualistic terms. The decision to migrate is shaped by many people, including family, friends and employers, their access to information, and the various policies of the countries to which one might migrate.

## Definitions and Typologies

The title of this book *Culture Shock* warrants some discussion. This section sets out to look at how anthropologists, psychologists and sociologists have used the term 'culture shock'. Then the concept of 'mental health', as it appears in the migration and mental-health literature, will be briefly reviewed.

## Culture Shock: the Shock of the New

The culture shock 'hypothesis' or 'concept' implies that the experience of a new culture is an unpleasant surprise or shock, partly because it is unexpected and partly because it may lead to a negative evaluation of one's own culture. Like the related concepts of 'jet-lag' and 'alienation', 'culture shock' is a term used by the lay person to explain, or at least label, some of the more unpleasant consequences of travel. However, like a lot of pseudo-psychological jargon (e. g. 'nervous breakdown'), it is more of a generic expression connoting much and signifying little—a term which in attempting to explain all, fails to explain a great deal.

The anthropologist Oberg (1960) is the first to have used the term. In a brief and largely anecdotal article, he mentions at least six aspects of culture shock:

1. Strain due to the effort required to make necessary psychological adaptations.
2. A sense of loss and feelings of deprivation in regard to friends, status, profession and possessions.
3. Being rejected by/and or rejecting members of the new culture.
4. Confusion in role, role expectations, values, feelings and self-identity.
5. Surprise, anxiety, even disgust and indignation after becoming aware of cultural differences.
6. Feelings of impotence due to not being able to cope with the new environment.

Table 2  **Means and F-levels for the explanations for people either immigrating to or emigrating from Britain**

| Explanations | Immigration | Emigration | F-levels |
| --- | --- | --- | --- |
| There are better job opportunities here/there. | 2.24 | 1.67 | 23.62*** |
| They want to join other members of their family already here/there. | 2.27 | 2.94 | 23.02*** |
| They were suffering from political oppression at home. | 3.39 | 5.59 | 183.90*** |
| Their previous living conditions were very poor. | 2.48 | 4.18 | 115.57*** |
| They believe that there is greater political freedom in— | 2.78 | 4.83 | 159.26*** |
| They admire — values and culture. | 4.81 | 3.50 | 59.95*** |
| They believe that the prospects for personal advancement are better. | 1.93 | 1.77 | 1.91 |
| There are better educational and cultural opportunities here/there. | 2.69 | 3.59 | 31.77*** |
| They want to provide a more secure future for their family. | 2.52 | 2.26 | 3.55 |
| They want to benefit from our social-security system. | 4.22 | 5.50 | 52.03*** |
| They had poor access to places of interest/amusement at home. | 5.02 | 5.00 | 0.02 |
| They will have a much higher standard of living here/there. | 2.93 | 2.00 | 45.67*** |
| They believe that — has a better climate. | 6.02 | 2.54 | 566.78*** |
| They like the tolerant attitude of the — towards foreigners. | 4.96 | 4.18 | 21.54*** |
| Their ancestors come from — originally. | 5.21 | 4.71 | 8.17** |
| They will get free education and health services here/there. | 3.40 | 5.06 | 89.32*** |
| They believe that life is more exciting in — | 4.93 | 2.61 | 233.33*** |
| They prefer to live in less crowded countries. | 5.32 | 3.59 | 99.85*** |

| | | | Continued |
|---|---|---|---|
| Explanations | Immigration | Emigration | F-levels |
| They have been encouraged by advertising to come here/there. | 4.92 | 3.44 | 73.12*** |
| They hope to marry someone from —and acquire citizenship. | 4.66 | 5.35 | 14.90*** |

[ Notes: The numbers represent the mean score on a 7-point important-unimportant scale. The—refers to Britain in the case of immigration and 'another country' in the case of emigration. ***p < .001 **p < .01 *p < .05 Source: A. Furnham, 'Explanations for immigration to and emigration from Britain', *New Community* (1986a) ]

The flavour of Oberg's observations may be gathered from this quote:
Culture shock is precipitated by the anxiety that results from losing all our familiar signs and symbols of social intercourse. These signs or cues include the thousand and one ways in which we orient ourselves to the situations of daily life: when to shake hands and what to say when we meet people, when and how to give tips, how to give orders to servants, how to make purchases, when to accept and when to refuse invitations, when to take statements seriously and when not. Now these cues which may be words, gestures, facial expressions, customs, or norms are acquired by all of us in the course of growing up and are as much a part of our culture as the language we speak or the beliefs we accept. All of us depend for our peace of mind and our efficiency on hundreds of these cues, most of which we are not consciously aware . . . .

Some of the symptoms of culture shock are: excessive washing of the hands; excessive concern over drinking water, food, dishes, and bedding; fear of physical contact with attendants or servants; the absent-minded, far-away stare (sometimes called 'the tropical stare'); a feeling of helplessness and a desire for dependence on long-term residents of one's own nationality; fits of anger over delays and other minor frustrations; delay and outright refusal to learn the language of the host country; excessive fear of being cheated, robbed, or injured; great concern over minor pains and irruptions of the skin; and finally, that terrible longing to be back home, to be able to have a good cup of coffee and a piece of apple pie, to walk into that corner drugstore, to visit one's relatives, and, in general, to talk to people who really make sense. (Oberg, 1960, p. 176)

Cleveland et al. (1960) offered a similar analysis relying heavily on the personal experience of travellers, especially those at two extremes of the adaptation continuum, individuals who act as if they had 'never left home' and those who immediately 'go native'. These two extremes are well described, but the various possible 'intermediate' reactions are not considered.

Researchers since Oberg have seen culture shock as a normal reaction, as part of the routine process of adaptation to cultural stress and the manifestation of a longing for a more predictable, stable and understandable environment.

Others have attempted to improve and extend Oberg's definition and concept of culture shock. Guthrie (1975) has used the term culture fatigue, Smalley (1963) language shock, Byrnes (1966) role shock and Ball-Rokeach (1973) pervasive ambiguity. In doing so, different researchers have simply placed the emphasis on slightly different problems—language, physical irritability, role ambiguity—rather than actually helping to specify how or why or when different people do or do not experience culture shock.

Bock (1970) has described culture shock as primarily an emotional reaction that follows from not being able to understand, control and predict another's behaviour. When customary categories of experience no longer seem relevant or applicable, people's usual behaviour changes to beco-ming 'unusual'. Lack of familiarity with both the physical setting (design of homes, shops, offices) as well as the social environment (etiquette, ritual) have this effect, as do the experiences with and use of time (Hall, 1959). This theme is reiterated by all the writers in the field (e. g. Lundstedt, 1963; Hays, 1972) — culture shock is a stress reaction where salient psychological and physical rewards are generally uncertain and hence difficult to control or predict. Thus a person is anxious, confused and apparently apathetic until he or she has had time to develop a new set of cognitive constructs to understand and enact the appropriate behaviour.

Writers about culture shock have often referred to individuals' lacking points of reference, social norms and rules to guide their actions and understand others' behaviour. This is very similar to the attributes studied under the heading of alienation and anomie, which include powerlessness, meaninglessness, normlessness, self-and social estrangement and social isolation (Seeman, 1959). There appears to be a connection between the concepts of culture shock, alienation and anomie.

In addition, ideas associated with anxiety pervade the culture-shock literature. Observers have pointed to a continuous general 'free-floating' anxiety which affects normal behaviour. Lack of self-confidence, distrust of others and mild psychosomatic complaints are also common (May, 1970). Furthermore, people appear to lose their inventiveness and spontaneity and become obsessively concerned with orderliness (Nash,

1967).

Central to the concept of shock are questions about how people adapt to it, and how they are changed by it. Hence there exists an extensive literature on the U-curve, the W-curve and the inverted U-curve, referring to the adjustment of sojourners over time. Many (e. g. Torbiorn, 1982) are happy to interpret their data in terms of these curves, although there is a debate in the literature about the validity of this approach (Church, 1982).

Most of the investigations of culture shock have been descriptive, in that they have attempted to list the various difficulties that sojourners experience and their typical reactions. Less attention has been paid to explaining who will find the shock more or less intense (e. g. the old or the less educated); what determines which reaction a person is likely to experience; how long they remain in a period of shock, and so forth. The literature suggests that all people will suffer culture shock to some extent, which is always thought of as being unpleasant and stressful. This assumption needs to be empirically supported. In theory some people need not experience any negative aspects of shock; instead they may seek out these experiences for their enjoyment. Sensation-seekers, for instance, might be expected not to suffer any adverse effects but to enjoy the highly arousing stimuli of the unfamiliar (Zuckerman, 1981). However, it is likely that their numbers are very small.

For instance, Adler (1975) and David (1971) have stated that although culture shock is most often associated with negative consequences, it may, in mild doses, be important for self-development and personal growth. Culture shock is seen as a transitional experience which can result in the adoption of new values, attitudes and behaviour patterns:

> In the encounter with another culture the individual gains new experiential knowledge by coming to understand the roots of his or her own ethnocentrism and by gaining new perspectives and outlooks on the nature of culture... Paradoxically, the more one is capable of experiencing new and different dimensions of human diversity, the more one learns of oneself. (Adler, 1975, p. 22)

Thus, although different writers have put emphases on different aspects of culture shock, there is, by and large, agreement that exposure to new cultures is stressful. Fewer researchers have seen the positive side of culture shock either for those individuals who revel in exciting and different environments or for those whose initial discomfiture leads to personal growth.

## Defining 'mental health' as it relates to migration

There are numerous problems both in the definition of mental health and in the definition of migration. Definitional problems are, however, not unique to the social sciences. For instance, studies may not be directly comparable if different definitions, nosologies or measures are used. These differences may account for the numerous contradictory findings in this intriguing but frustrating literature. Indeed, the different definitions may also give a clue as to why mental illness has come to be associated with migration, because sometimes the 'different' behaviour patterns (dress, non-verbal behaviour, food preferences, sense of time, etc.) of migrants compared with natives make them look as if they are mentally disturbed.

To consider the relationship between mental health and migration requires some agreement as to the meaning and measurement of mental health. There is a long-standing debate in psychiatry concerning the effect of culture on mental health and the definition of 'mental health'. On the one extreme are the absolutists who argue that mental illnesses, like physical illnesses, are found in all cultures, though possibly at slightly different rates. This group uses standard western nosologies and cites as evidence studies which have found a similar range and incidence of symptoms in rural Third World countries as in urban western countries (Kapur et al. 1974). On the other hand, there are the relativists who accuse the above of psychiatric imperialism and argue that some mental illnesses which are common in one culture (i. e. depression, schizophrenia) do not exist in the same form (symptoms, language) in others (Marsella, 1979). There is a rich and vigorous debate concerning the relationship between race, culture and mental disorder which cannot be considered here (Yap, 1951; Rack, 1982). This issue is discussed at length by Draguns (1980).

There is an equally extensive and complicated literature on the diagnosis of mental illness. Rack (1982) has considered in some depth the cultural pitfalls in the recognition (diagnosis and hospitalization) of depression and anxiety, mania, schizophrenia, paranoia and hysteria.

Table 3 presents a nosological diagram which attempts to spell out the type and regularity of the diagnoses made in Britain, the evidence suggests that the incidence, cause, diagnosis and treatment of mental health varies significantly across cultures. Hence the measurement of mental health in two different cultures may not be strictly comparable. It is well known, for instance, that the chances of being diagnosed schizophrenic in America are much higher than in Britain (Draguns, 1980).

Table 3　**Rack's nosological diagram for psychiatric diagnosis in Britain**

| | Depression | Excitement | Schizophrenia |
|---|---|---|---|
| Endogenous Biological, genetic factors. Stress not primary cause. | 1 Endogenous depression (psychotic depression). Recognized in all cultures, but symptoms may differ. | 3 'Mania' recognized in all cultures, less common than depression. | 5 'Schizophrenia' probably exists everywhere. |
| Reactive Response to stress, conflict, 'neurotic' rather than 'psychotic'. | 2 Reactive depression. Common in Britain. In other cultures may be regarded as not being a 'medical' problem. | 4 Reactive excitation ('reactive mania') rare among British but well known elsewhere. psychogenic psychoses. | 6 Acute schizophreniform stress reaction. |
| Hysterical motivated, attention-seeking. | 7 (e.g. many cases of 'parasuicide') Common in Britain, rare in some other cultures. | 8 Varieties of 'hysterical madness' (hysterical pseudo-psychosis). Uncommon among British, more common in non-European cultures. | 9 |

(Source: P. Rack, *Race, Culture and Mental Disorder*, London, Tavistock, 1982.)

A great deal of the mental health and migration literature relies on mental hospital admission statistics, which are notably weak. Cochrane (1983) has pointed out the various stages in becoming admitted to a mental hospital. Table 3.4 explains why a (possibly very large) number of people never get admitted to mental hospitals. There are many cross-cultural studies on different patterns of somaticization and help-seeking behaviour in different cultures (Cheung and Lan, 1982). The figures that are available may be misleading because impatient statistics give no clue about the range, amount or type of outpatients; admission is largely dictated by the number of beds available; the data are aggregated and give no idea of degree of distress; many confounding variables are not reported, and so on. It is because of these difficulties that community surveys properly conducted with sensitive instruments and representative random samples present a better picture of the true rate of mental illness. Pope (1983) was particularly interested in the relation between migration and manic-depressive illnesses. His interest arose from the seemingly discrepant findings that pre- and actual schizophrenics migrate more often than others, and yet migration is a stressful and complicated process likely to be avoided by schizophrenics. His conclusion, which was tested in Massachusetts, is that manic-depressives, rather than simple or other schizophrenics, are more likely to migrate. This is because hypomanic indivi-duals may be more likely to migrate than the average individual and experience psychotic depression while in their new country. To test this hypothesis, hospital and other records were examined which showed manic patients were significantly more likely than schizophrenic patients to be foreign-born, and also that 30 per cent of the manics' parents were foreign-born compared to 9.5 per cent of the schizophrenics' and 18.2 per cent of the controls' parents. The birth places of the manics' parents compared to migrant controls showed that no one national or cultural

Table 4  **Stages in becoming admitted to a mental hospital**

| Decisions leading to hospital | Decisions not leading to hospital |
|---|---|
| Occurrence of distress | |
| Acknowledgement that something is wrong | Failure to recognize as a problem or problem masked |
| Conscious recognition as an emotional problem | Defined as physical problem (menopause, etc.) |
| Belief that problem can be overcome | Belief that problem is intractable or inevitable |
| Decision to seek help | Self-medication, antidepressive behaviour, drinking, etc. |
| Going to a doctor | Seeking help from friends, family, other professionals |
| Recognition as psychological problem by doctor | Defined by doctor as physical disorder, minor upset, overwork, etc. |
| Referral to a psychiatrist | Doctor prescribes psychotropic drugs or other treatment |
| Diagnosis of depression made | |
| Admitted to hospital | Outpatient treatment or other care offered |

(Source: R. Cochrane, *The Social Creation of Mental Illness*, London, Longman, 1983.)

group was more represented than others. It seems reasonable to accept the author's conclusion that earlier studies may have diagnosed as schizophrenic, individuals now considered to be manic-depressive.

Suffice to say that there are numerous difficulties in defining and measuring mental health. Crude, biased, confounded statistics are misleading as has already been established. The issue is made more complex by the political overtones of the research which may be seen to be racist or ethnocentric.

Good psychiatric epidemiological research takes time and care because of sampling difficulties and the specification of transcultural measures of distress. Certainly one reason for ambiguities in the literature may be the very different (and often unreliable) measures of mental health.

## Typologies of Migration

Migration occurs when people move within one community/area; from one community/area within the same country to another; or from one community in one country to another in another country. There are therefore two variables which, though often correlated, may also be oblique or orthogonal—that is geographic distance and amount (quality) of change. It is quite possible for people to move a comparatively short distance—in miles/kilometres—but to experience large socio-cultural, economic and political differences, while the opposite may also be true in that people may migrate very great distances to be in a community almost identical to the one they left.

Figure 1 illustrates some of these possible relationships. That one can experience great change by migrating comparatively short distances within a country has been pointed out. Whereas geographic distance is comparatively easy to quantify, quality or quantity of change is much more difficult. Change may range from variations in meteorological and dietary to socio-economic and religious conditions, some of which may be more disturbing than others. Furthermore, change may be experienced very subjectively, depending on the socio-economic status, age and education level of the migrant. Some attempt has been made to get an operational definition by factor-analytic studies, such as those done by Cattell (Cattell et al., 1951, 1979). For instance, in a study of 82 variables (social, economic, educational, behavioural) of 120 nations, Cattell et al. (1979) found 21 clear factors, such as Cosmopolitan Muslim; Nordic-Protestant Industriousness and East-Asian Buddhist. It may therefore be possible to create various linear scales and measure the distance between the country of departure and the country of arrival and then sum them for a crude but objective measurement of change. This has been done with various degrees of success (see Chapters 4, 5 and 8).

A second crucial definition for migration concerns the circumstances or motives under which the change occurs, and the intended length of time spent in the other country. Some immigrants are political refugees or deported people who often involuntarily migrated, many with the hope of eventual return, while others migrate happily with no thought of return.

Figure 2 illustrates a possible relationship between these two variables. Strictly speaking, not all of the categories in Figure 3.2 could be described as migrants (e. g. tourists). However, if the length of stay is for three years and over— which is fairly common for students and diplomats— the experience may have all the characteristics of migration. Again, the length of stay is relatively easy to operationalize, although time may not necessarily be experienced subjectively as linear. Yet, as has been noted, the motives for migration are difficult to specify. The di-

```
Much ↑
         ┌─────────────────┐              ┌─────────────────┐
         │ Short distance  │              │ Far distance    │
         │ Much change     │              │ Much change     │
         └─────────────────┘              └─────────────────┘
         i.e. a few miles across a national   i.e. travelling from one continent
         border; movement from very           to another with different
         rural to urban setting; from         language, climate, religion as
         island to mainland                   well as major social, economic
                                              and political differences

                          ┌─────────────────────┐
                          │ Intermediate distance│
                          │ Intermediate change  │
                          └─────────────────────┘
Amount/                   i.e. movement within a continent
quality of                to an area which shares some
change                    traditions but not others

         ┌─────────────────┐              ┌─────────────────┐
         │ Close distance  │              │ Far distance    │
         │ Little change   │              │ Little change   │
         └─────────────────┘              └─────────────────┘
         i.e. movement within a homoge-    i.e. movement from one close
         neous community                   homogeneous ethnic community
                                           to another (i.e. on another conti-
                                           nent) but with similar traditions;
                                           social, economic and political
                                           institutions
Little
       └──────────┬──────────────────────────────────────────→
                Close                                        Far
                          Geographic Distance
```

Figure 1　A representation of possible patterns of migration based on geographic distance and cultural difference

mension of voluntarily/happily is, of course, very crude, as it itself is of necessity a balance of positive and negative motives. For instance, a business person could always resign his job and in that sense is not forced to live abroad for a number of years. However, various other commitments mean that resignation, although voluntary, may be unwise. To this extent, therefore, the move abroad may be seen to be only partially voluntary.

The placing of the various groups in Figure 3.2 is hypothetical and not

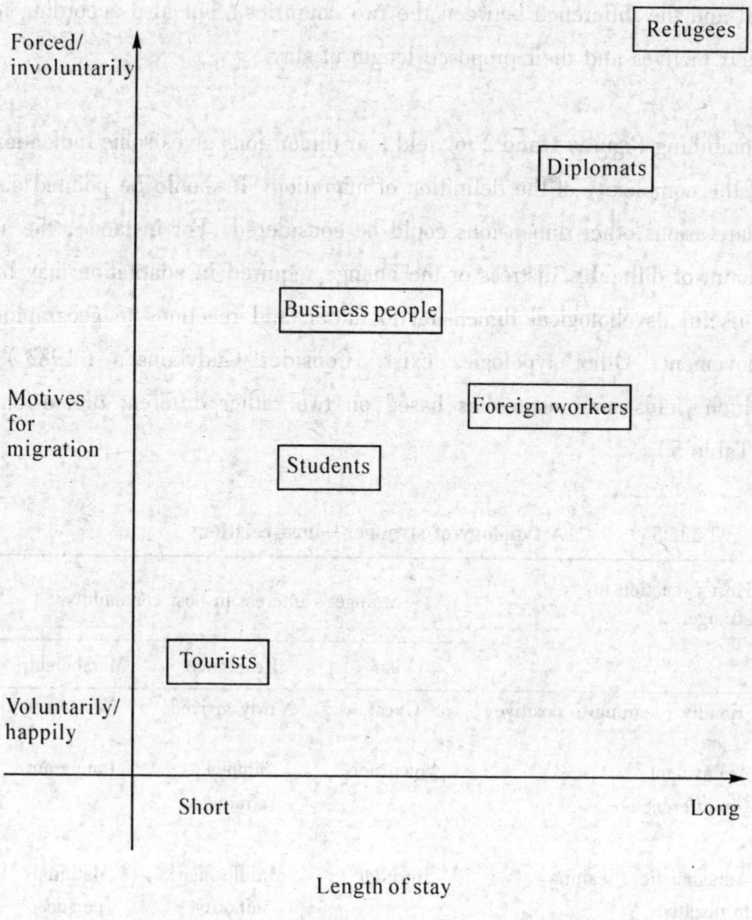

Figure 2  A representation of possible patterns of migration based on proposed length of stay and motives for migration

meant to suggest a positive correlation between the two axes. Indeed, many western developed societies impose severe restrictions to prevent potential immigrants from coming to their countries. What the figure is attempting to illustrate, however, is that migrants differ not only according to their country of origin (its distance from the chosen point of arrival and the difference between the two countries) but also according to their motives and their proposed length of stay.

Combining Figures 1 and 2 to yield four dimensions gives some indication of the complexity of the definition of migration. It should be pointed out that various other dimensions could be considered. For instance, the amount of difficulty/distress or the change required in adaptation may be a useful psychological dimension to understand reactions to geographic movement. Other typologies exist. Consider Gudykunst's (1983), which yields nine categories based on two rather different dimensions (Table 5).

Table 5    **A typology of stranger—host relations**

| Host's reaction to stranger | Stranger's interest in host community | | |
| --- | --- | --- | --- |
| | Visit | Residence | Membership |
| Friendly (leaning to positive) | Guest | Newly arrived | Newcomer |
| Ambivalent (indifference) | Sojourner | Simmel's stranger | Immigrant |
| Antagonistic (leaning to negative) | Intruder | Middle-man minority | Marginal persons |
| General area of research | Sociology of tourism | Intercultural adjustment | Acculturation/ assimilation |

(Source: W. B. Gudykunst, Toward a typology of stranger-host relationships, *International Journal of Intercultural Relations*, 7 (1983), 401-413).

There are therefore many ways to arrange and categorize travellers. The next section in this book considers four groups: migrants, sojourners, tourists and business people. These groups differ according to length of stay, motives for movement and amount of psychological/behavioural adaptation required.

## Chapter Summary

This chapter set out to describe the reasons or motives for geographic movement. The motives of tourists were manifold, though these were classifiable into various groups, such as ego-enhancement and educational. The motives of students and volunteer workers seem more straight-forward education, culturelearning and personal development, but there is often a discrepancy between the motives of students and those persons and organizations which administer, fund and sponsor the participants. Special mention was made of the motives of Peace Corps Volunteers, who were among the first group of sojourners to be studied by psychologists. The chapter also considered general motives for migration, but it was argued that there were various types, of migration (each of which affects motives), that a simple economic calculus is insufficient to understand the complex motives for migration, and that various migration policies of different governments may inhibit or encourage various types of migration.

The chapter also examined the concepts of 'culture shock' and 'mental health' as they relate to migration. Although there are serious definitional problems in this area, various schemes or typologies were proposed based on two sets of two dimensions: geographic distance/amount of change, and motive for migration/amount of time spent in the other country. Various other typologies were also considered.

[From: Furnham, A and Bochner, S. 1986, *Culture Shock*: *Psychological reactions to unfamiliar environments*. London: Routledge. Chapter 3, pp. 35-58]

## 导读：文化休克的动机和定义：地理迁移的原因和结果

本文把地理迁移分为四类：旅行者和商务人员，留学生和志愿者，和平军团以及移民。笔者从动机这一心理学的角度考察了各类人群进行地理迁移的原因和结果并进一步分析了地理迁移中所遭遇的文化休克和移民的类型。动机是一个很复杂的概念，往往有生物的、心理的和文化的决定因素。此外人的紧张行为也可能是一系列互补的、竞争的动机的结果，而处理这些动机也存在一些困难。尽管对动机的调查有着种种困难，研究者们也还是试图对文化旅行者的动机进行描述并把他们的动机和适应文化压力的各种不同模式系统联系起来。

### 1. 旅行者和商务人员的动机

Pearce (1982) 提出了有关旅行者的动机研究的各种问题。首先，他认为把旅行者的动机视为与个人的其他活动和所关心的事情分割开来的短期过程是一种错误的观点。其次，旅行前中后的动机是否得到衡量存在问题。在 Pearce 的分析中，他利用一些理论阐述旅行者的动机。这些理论包括需求层次理论、归因理论和成就动机理论等。Pearce 认为旅行者的动机可能与马斯洛的需求层次理论中的某个层次有关，因此有些旅行者是为了实现爱或归属感的需要，或为了达到自尊和自我实现的需要，而有些人正好相反是为了暂时的休息或放松。此外 Pearce 还介绍了 Crompton，Cohen 等人对旅游动机的分析。其实旅行的动机是复杂多样的，至今尚未为人类所全面了解。

对于商务人员旅行的心理动机的研究也颇为不足，很多人认为他们是受利益所驱。但 Torbiorn（1982）在研究瑞典商人时发现他们的动机比我们想像的要复杂得多。他发现，无论是"推力"即与不满情绪相联系的否定动机还是"拉力"即与满意的信念相联系的肯定动机都与旅行有关。

## 2. 留学生和志愿者的动机

Bochner（1973）就留学生的动机问题进行了调查，所得的答案分为四类：大部分以获得学位，获取学术或职业专长为目的，只有少数学生的动机是文化学习和个人发展。Klineberg & Hull（1979）的调查研究也得出了相似的结论。在留学生当中，大部分为政府出资的公费生，或是国家之间互派的留学生。理想主义者认为教育交流显然会加强国际关系。他们想当然地认为跨文化接触尤其是在年轻人当中跨文化接触会增强共识，促进世界和平。实际上在调查宾—主国留学生之间的关系时显示文化圈之间的接触与态度之间的关系颇为复杂。比如说考虑到相互交流的各种变量，接触可能会加强或减弱共同的宽容和理解，部分留学生定居国外，有些归国学生不再适应国内原有的文化或因处理问题不当而显得格格不入。

对于出国志愿者的调查 Guthrie（1966）在报告中指出 80%的志愿者表示出与社会工作者相同的兴趣，在调查过程中，他们自由地承认加入志愿者队伍是因为他们想做一些有意义的事情，而且他们在国内找不到满意的工作。同时他们当中许多人对于将来的成就和在国外所遇到的问题的处理过于理想化。尽管出国志愿者队伍可以作为一个实体来看待，各自有其特定目的、价值观和标准。他们主要的目的是为了获得和扩大他们的政治认可，发展在国外新的有效项目。对志愿者成功与否的判断主要根据他们是否能在自己的文化和被救助的当地人的文化之间进行理解和沟通并建立交流沟通的纽带。

## 3. 移民的动机

有关移民的动机问题在一些文献里只提到了经济因素的重要性。实际上移民注重的并非只是经济（Lansing & Mueller, 1967）。Taylor（1966）指出要了解移民的动机首先需要知道个体对原来的定居地的感受和评价、他们的长期或短期的愿望以及引起他们决定的刺激因素。Naamary（1971）也指出移民是由于在就业、教育、健康、社会联系、住房和天气等方面感觉不满意而引起的。Shaw（1975）表示在考虑社会经济因素时也应考虑文化系统、人格系统、社会系统以及各个系统层面上的压力的影响。Furnham（1986）试图利用归因理论来研究解释英国的移民现象。在英国，人们认为移民最重要的动机是个人进步和更好的工作机会。对于移民现象存在五大因素这一解释，其中四种是拉力因素（目的地的文化和价值观，较高的生活水平，社会福利，更好生活质量），一种是推力因素（即国内的政治经济原因）。Furnham 还指出研究本地人对移民动机的理解也有利于研究移民的文化适应。

## 4. 文化休克

文化休克的"假设"或"概念"暗含的意义：经历一种新的文化会引起一种不愉快的感受或者冲击，因为这种新的文化出乎人们的意料，而且也因为它会导致对自我文化的否定评价。人类学家 Oberg（1960）最早使用"文化休克"这一概念并指出了"文化休克"的六个方面：由于心理适应所必须付出的努力而引起的紧张；在友谊、社会地位、职业等方面的失落感；拒绝新文化或被新文化所拒绝；角色、价值、情感和个性方面的混淆；意识到文化差异后的惊奇、焦虑甚至厌恶和愤怒；由于不能适应新的环境而产生的无能为力的感觉。在 Oberg 的观察中，文化休克是由于失去原来的熟悉的社会交流符号而产生的焦虑引起的。文化休克的症状主要表现为：类似强迫症的行为，对琐事的过分关注，害怕与人接触，阵怒和挫折感等。

自Oberg之后研究者们已把文化休克视为一种正常的反应，也是作为适应文化压力常规过程的一部分。Bock（1970）认为文化休克是由于不能理解控制和预知他人行为而产生的一种基本的情感反应。在遭遇新的文化时个体失去了指导自身行为和理解他人行为的参照点和社会准则，在这一点上显示出了文化休克、间情法（alienation）、和失范（anomie）三者之间的联系。Adler和David称文化休克虽然常常与负面效应联系在一起，但是程度轻微的文化休克对于自我发展和个人成长是很重要的。我们可以把文化休克视为一种适应新的价值观、态度和行为模式的一个过渡性经验。在遭遇另一种文化时个体通过理解自我民族中心主义的根源和获得看待文化本性新的视角而得到新的经验性的知识，或者说越能经历人类文化的多样性就越能更多地了解自己（见Adler 1975）。

**Questions for reflection:**
1. What is culture shock and what is the effect of culture shock on intercultural adaptation?
2. What are the motives of migration? Discuss the relation between motives of migration and inter-cultural adaptation process?
3. Are there any differences among the motives of students, tourists, business people and immigrants? If there are any, what are they?

# A Survey of Intercultural Communication Courses

A. E. Fantini & E. M. Smith

## Abstract

The last quarter of a century has witnessed rapid development of the intercultural field; and with this, a concomitant growth in Intercultural Communication (ICC) courses in colleges and universities in various parts of the world. Instructors are called upon to design and implement such courses often for the first time and, in so doing, they are helping to define the content and parameters of this subject matter. Often, the context in which they teach, or the department or program in which the course is placed, also further define the scope of the courses.

This survey was designed to learn about the evolving nature of ICC courses, given interest among faculty to learn what their colleagues are doing elsewhere. Through compilation and presentation of the data obtained, this interim report provides a snapshot of SO plus courses in 11 countries between 1992 and 1994. It reveals not only the pursue of these courses, but also their goals and objectives, content areas, and approaches to implementation. It also begins to identify common models, frameworks and schema, useful materials and resources, and assessment procedures. For those who participated in the survey— and for others interested in the questionnaire instrument—it serves also as a self-study guide for examining one's own approach to the task by reviewing the 70 plus questions contained in the survey questionnaire. Copyright, 1997 Elsevier Science Ltd.

## Background

Not too many years ago, Intercultural Communication (ICC) was primarily the province of orientation sessions and workshops designed to prepare individuals for an intercultural sojourn. As the intercultural field grew, however, ICC found its way increasingly into credit-bearing courses in colleges and universities in various parts of the world. In many cases, ICC courses are available as electives; but in more recent years, they are increasingly required in academic programs offering degrees in this or related areas, ranging from undergraduate to postgraduate and doctoral levels. With the increase of ICC offerings in more and more institutions—often for the first time—instructors are contributing to defining aspects of the intercultural field through the design of the courses they develop. They are challenged to conceptualize what they believe to be relevant, to find materials and resources, to consider formal and experiential approaches to instruction, and to seek appropriate ways to gauge the results of their efforts. There is wide curiosity among faculty to learn what colleagues are doing in other institutions and to exchange information about their experiences. What is the appropriate purvue of an ICC course? What models, frameworks and schema are commonly in use? What approaches and techniques are effective for course implementation and delivery? What useful materials and resources are available? And how best to assess results? This survey was designed to investigate these questions, and to learn about ICC courses in general and the various forms they take.

## About the Questionnaire and the Survey

This survey was conducted through use of a rather detailed questionnaire. Besides serving as an information gathering device, the questionnaire was also intended to serve as a self-study guide for respondents and others by increasing awareness of various aspects of course design and delivery. A secondary motive was to encourage development of a network of individuals sharing interest in this area by identifying respondents to each other. This was facilitated through a preliminary report which listed names and addresses of all respondents who participated in the survey. The primary, objective of the survey, however, is to contribute knowledge about ICC courses and our field through dissemination of a compilation of the survey results. This is what this initial report intends to accomplish, while a lengthier report containing all of the data is intended for later publication.

A pilot questionnaire was drafted as the primary instrument for the survey. The draft was sent to twelve individuals located in different parts of the SIETAR world via its three major affiliates in Europe, Japan, and North America. Eight responses were received with suggestions on how to modify the questionnaire to insure relevance and appropriateness from various institutional and cultural perspectives. The revised form was piloted by several individuals teaching ICC courses and further revised.

The survey was announced in publications of SIETAR International (SI), SIETAR Europa, and SIETAR Japan; as well as in the newsletter of TESOL International (Teachers of English to Speakers of Other Languages). Actual questionnaire forms were also included as a center-fold tear-out insert in the Communique, SIETAR International's news-letter (Vol XXII, No 3, April/May 1992). Additional forms were mailed to approximately 100 other individuals whose names were obtained from related sources. In all, announcements about the survey reached about 22,400 individuals, and actual forms provided to approximately 2,100 persons. The purpose of this enormous effort was to obtain extensive coverage and a broad perspective.

## Information from the Completed Survey

Data from completed questionnaires resulted in a compilation of more than 100 pages of information. The present report, then, attempts only to summarize information and to highlight trends on the assumption that this information will be useful to those responsible for the conduct of ICC courses. The form used in the survey addresses nine areas which form the sections which follow.

### Part I. General Information: Respondents

Fifty-three responses were received. Of these, 47 were from university instructors and 6 from other types of institutions. Where applicable, data from all 53 forms are used. Although few in number (given the total targeted population), completed forms were high in terms of the quality of information provided. On the one hand, the length and complexity of the questionnaire (74 questions in addition to general information about the respondent) may have contributed to a low rate of return; on the other, however, those who responded clearly took the task seriously, and most appended related documents such as course syllabi, bibliographies and other information. Stated another way, the data represent a cross-section of ICC courses taught at over 50 institutions in 11 countries between 1992 and 1994. Most responses came from individuals in the United States (38); in addition, others were from individuals in Canada (1), England (1), Ireland (1), Japan (6), Mexico (1), the Netherlands (1), Nigeria (1), Pakistan (1), South Africa (1), and Switzerland (1). Following is a portrait of those who responded.

There were more female respondents than male, although not significantly so. Nearly half are between the ages of 30-50. The other half is divided almost equally between the 20-35 and 51-65 age groups. Exactly the same number of respondents (21) hold doctorates as those who have Master degrees. Two list post-Master level work; very few have only an undergraduate degree. The highest number of respondents has taught in this field for 5 years or less. Beyond that, numbers decline steadily. The longest any respondent has been in the field of intercultural communications is 50 years (1). Sixty-seven percent of respondents have been teaching 5 yrs or less (in fact, 10 people say they have been teaching for only 1 year, and 9 for 2 years—a total of 42% of all respondents). Beyond that, the responses decline sharply in a number of years. The recent beginnings of these courses suggest the relatively young nature of this field.

Most people indicate experience in 5 or fewer cultures (29). However, a significant number list experiences in some 6-10 cultures (11). Three people indicate experience with over 10 cultures, with 16 as the upper limit. The cultures listed are extremely varied. Languages with which respondents are familiar are also extremely varied and the highest number of languages anyone lists is 6. Most evaluate their proficiency at a wide range of levels.

## Part Ⅱ. General Information: Institution, Program & Faculty

The institutions at which respondents teach (Item No. 1) vary in size from very small (5 institutions with 100 students or less) to small (11 with 1,000 students or less) to mid-size (15 with 15,000 students or less) to large (11 with more than 15,000 students up to 42,000 students). All report varying degrees of ethnic composition and/or foreign students from a great variety of countries at their schools. Of the institutions represented in the survey, 17 offer a program in Intercultural Studies; 26 do not (Item No. 5). Of the 17 ICC programs, two are certificate programs, 9 are undergraduate programs, 11 are MA, and 4 are doctoral programs. Twenty-one institutions offer programs in related fields (e.g., International Studies, Communication, Business, TESOL, etc.).

Faculty qualifications for teaching ICC courses (Item No. 9) include mixes of prior intercultural experience, prior teaching experience, knowledge of a second language, and/or an academic degree (usually an MA to PhD), although 3 institutions require only an undergraduate degree and 8 cite no degree requirement at all. The most important factor appears to be prior intercultural experience, although a second language is cited as helpful. Twenty-two programs require experience in all 4 areas. That number drops to 8 institutions requiring 3 areas; 3 for 2 areas, and

6 programs require only 1 of the 4 criteria. In 15 cases, courses are team taught, and involve more than one instructor.

## Part III. General Information: Course

The earliest reporting of an ICC course is listed as 1968 (Item No. 10). By the end of the 1960's two ICC courses were reported; by the end of the 1970's there were 9, and by the end of the 1980's this number more than doubled, producing a total of 20 courses. Thus far into the 1990's, the number has nearly doubled again in only 3-4 years, attesting to a trend (Item No. 12). Many of the courses are not part of a program and are taught under the auspices of various academic departments. In some cases programs were founded at the same time as the first ICC course offered and, in a few cases, the course came first and the program followed.

Class size stands at 30 or under in 25 of the cases (or 71%); the remaining 10 courses (29%) indicate much larger classes with samplings of 35, 40, 50, 90 and 100 students. The minimum class size requirement which is most common is 19 students or less, with 21 out of 28 responses in that range. The highest minimum class size is 40. For maximum class size, the peak varies between 20-39 out of 34 in that range. No one indicates a maximum class size lower than 10, and the highest maximum class size is 69. The most popular course offering configuration is twice per year (either once a semester for two semesters or twice in the same semester). Other institutions also offer ICC courses once a year, or three to four times a year.

Enrollment trends are shown as stable in 16 cases and increasing in 19 others. No enrollment decreases are reported by any institution. Average class sizes generally range from 5 to 32 with only a few exceptions beyond this range. Courses are offered through a variety of departments and in nearly half of the cases, the course is part of an interdisciplinary offering. Courses are cross-listed in another department in only 12 cases and where this occurs, they are most commonly listed under anthropology or sociology.

There is great variation in terms of course length, number and length of sessions, classes per week, credits, etc. (Items No. 18-19). Courses range from a minimum of 50 minute sessions to a high of 4 h sessions with all sorts of combinations in between. Courses also vary from about 10 h in length to a high of 88 h, with the most frequent length at about 40-49 h (18 responses). Credits offered range from none to as many as 5, with the most common credit offering at 3 (15 respondents). The course is generally offered as an elective (22 cases) except when required to satisfy a specific course of study requirement (20 cases) such as intercultural communication, TESOL, an International MBA Program, etc. It is offered at various levels, from introductory (18) to intermediate (10) to advanced (8), and on both undergraduate (22) and graduate (12) levels. Prerequisites (Item No. 23) are cited in only 9 cases, and in 66% of the cases, the course is related to a field experience and is offered either prior to (7), concurrent with (7), or following that experience (3).

The most common reasons students give for taking ICC courses (Item No. 25) are: study or travel abroad, international career, improve knowledge of other people and cultures, required, personal growth, interest in content, the instructor. A great variety of other reasons are also given. Commonly cited "attractive" features of ICC include: interest in other cultures, learning to communicate, contact with individuals from other cultures, reflection and self-awareness, experiential nature, interactive, relevant and practical nature, in addition to various other aspects.

## Part IV. Course Goals & Objectives

ICC courses are known by various names (Item No. 28) although almost all contain the term Intercultural Communication or Cross-Cultural Communication in the title. As stated, goals generally relate to cross-cultural concerns (Item No. 29); however, they vary significantly in terms of focus. (The framework used in the form is A + ASK, an acronym standing for "awareness + attitude/affect, skill and knowledge".) Most course goals fall neatly into one or another of these categories but not necessarily in all four. Most respondents acknowledge the importance of raising awareness while learning about others.

Whereas goals are long-term in nature, not immediately achievable nor measurable within the limitations of a course, objectives are often short-term, achievable, and measurable. Moreover, objectives presumably lead in the direction of goals and directly affect course design and implementation. More than any other item in the questionnaire, the solicitation of course goals and objectives (Items No. 28-29) showcases differences across courses, illustrates wide divergence, a great array of items, no clear distribution of objectives (in terms of A + ASK), and often no clear link between stated goals and clear objectives. It appears that articulating clear goals and objectives, even for college level professors, is an area begging for further refinement; the same statement may be inferred about explicit links between goals and objectives and course implementation and assessment.

A rather lengthy and diverse listing of reported objectives (Item No. 30) is summarized and grouped under several categories, as follows:

ICC and general culture concepts
  * learning about the nature of culture
  * understanding and applying ICC concepts
  * understanding world views and their effect on communication
  * developing general communication concepts and skills

Functioning in ICC situations
  * recognizing and applying methods of ICC
  * being able to enhance ICC relationships
  * developing skills for functioning in ICC situations
  * resolving conflict
  * preparing for study abroad
  * cultural adjustment
  * exploring cross-cultural literature

Self-awareness
  * learning to describe and appreciate one's own culture and self
  * dealing with prejudices

Teaching and management
  * understanding cross-cultural aspects of teaching or managing
  * learning about cross-cultural management and work ethics

Developing other skills
  * English usage
  * learning to do research
  * developing journal writing skills
  * preparing for proposal writing
  * students generate own objectives

In response to Item No. 31, 18 respondents base course design on a needs assessment; 16 do not. In several cases, objectives are organically derived as the course progresses, or determined with input from course participants. Sources on which needs assessments are based include: program context, the students, the teacher, and the field (Item No. 31). All four categories seem equal in popularity; however, only 4 respondents checked all four. Various respondents identified other sources; these include: social and business trends, needs of clients and participants, and objectives provided by the Director of International Education on their campus. With few exceptions among the 55 responses to a question about distribution of objectives in terms of awareness, attitudes, skills and knowledge, most indicate objectives in all four areas, although not always equally. Most courses tend to lean more heavily toward knowledge while attitude receives the least weighting.

## Part V. Curriculum Design

In response to Items No. 33 and 34, the majority of respondents classify their course under "education" (34); many also indicate training (20); while several also include research (7). All but one respondent address both theoretical and applied aspects with the highest number of responses at 50% for each, or equal distribution (10); likewise all but one respondent indicate concern with both content and process, again with the highest number of responses at 50% for each, or equal distribution. The overall learning, however, is toward applied rather than theoretical aspects: 16 indicate a higher percentage under applied, whereas 11 indicate a higher percentage under theoretical (Item No. 34).

Item No. 35 soliciting major course components evoked a wide range of responses. These are grouped into the following subject areas (listed in descending order of popularity) with the number of respondents addressing each indicated in parentheses:

* ICC theory/models/concepts/definitions of culture (23)
* Preparation for an ICC experience or re-entry/culture shock (18)
* Understanding self and other culture (12)
* Attitudes, beliefs and values (10)
* Communication and culture (8)
* Literacy and language issues (8)
* Nonverbal communication (7)
* World view and differences (6)
* Prejudice, discrimination and stereotypes (6)
* Gender, race, ability and class issues (6)
* Management/business issues (5)
* Culture acquisition (4)
* Community involvement (4)
* Conflict resolution (3)
* Second language development (3)
* Research methods (3)
* Designing training programs (3)
* Comparing and contrasting cultures (2)
* Media as a cross-cultural tool (2)

All respondents address culture in a generic sense, although the amount of attention to general culture varies significantly: no course devotes less than 15% of the content to general culture and none has more than 90% of its content in this area. Additionally, all but four also address a specific target culture as part of the coursework. Almost all also deal with communication in a general or generic sense; however, it is noteworthy that more than two-thirds (63%) state that exploring communication through a second language—other than in the tongue of the students—has no bearing on the course. This leaves unaddressed the question of how another tongue mediates the interculture experience.

Item No. 37 seeks to learn what emphasis courses give to intercultural, international and/or interpersonal relations. The emphasis is clearly on intercultural dimensions (not surprising given the course titles); at least 20% of every course focuses on the ICC aspect and in one case as much as 90%. All courses except one also address interpersonal aspects (with about 25 falling in the range of 10% to 33%); whereas international dimensions are least popular overall.

Item No. 38 elicits a variety of what are assumed to be well known models, frameworks or schema in the perspective of those who contributed to designing the form. The list, however, was not intended to limit responses which is why respondents were asked to describe and/or append copies of others they favor (Item No. 39). The following are models, listed in descending order of use (the number of users is in parentheses):

* Hall's High/Low Context Cultures (23)
* Various Communication Models (20)
* Kluckhohn's Model (Variations in Value Orientations) (18)
* Bennett's 6 Stages (18)
* Maslow's Hierarchy of Needs (16)
* Hofstede's Values Framework (16)
* Nichol's Aspects of Cultural Differences (9)
* Kolb's Experiential Learning Cycle (8)
* The Five Culture Questions (8)
* Hall's Map of Culture (8)
* Triandis' Attribution Theory (8)

* Ruben's Facets of Cross-Cultural Competence (5)
* Allport, Amir's Contact Hypothesis (5)
* Kim's System Approach to Adaptation (5)
* Kealey's Overseas Effectiveness Traits (3)
* Fantini's Language and World View Schema (3)
* Lysgaard's Cultural Adaptation Curve (2)
* Gudykunst and Hammer's Quadrant (2)
* Fantini's 7 Stages to Language Development (2)
* Gallois' Communication Accommodation Theory (1)

Aside from the number of respondents who incorporate the above models, considerable variation exists in the amount of hours each teacher spends with each. For example, although Hall's high/low context scheme is cited by the largest number of respondents, no one spends more than 6 h with this model. Conversely, while other models are used by fewer individuals, they often occupy more course time despite use by only one respondent. One teacher, for example, spends 15 h with Hofstede's model, while others sometimes use a model to frame a significant segment of the course.

In addition to models listed above, various respondents also cite 23 others (Item No. 39), including the 18 models listed below:

* Pierre Casse's Adjustment Model
* Katz's Oppression Model
* Teun van Dijk's Discourse Analysis
* AFS' Iceberg Concept of Culture
* Ethnography of Communication Theory
* Perry's Scheme of Intellectual Development
* Yoshikawa's Theory (no further details provided)

* Kohl's Values Continuum
* Stewart's American Cultural Patterns
* Sapir-Whorf Linguistic Relativity Hypothesis
* Charles Moms' Ways to Live
* Fantini's Communicative Competence Framework
* Detweiler's Category Width
* Furnham & Bockner's Social Skills
* Furnham & Westwood's Expectancy Values
* Gudykunst & Hammer's Anxiety & Uncertainty
* Fantini's A + ASK Framework
* Fantini's NAPRI/KEPRA (A Culture Exploration Grid)

While all respondents are already acquainted with a variety of models, they expressed considerable interest in learning about others; many respondents requested information about those they did not already know.

## Part VI. Content

Following are major content areas on the questionnaire (Items No. 40-52) which respondents said they include and address in their courses. Each area is divided into subtopics (listed in descending order of popularity) with the number of responses indicated in parentheses. Since details are not provided concerning the amount of time spent on each topic, one must be careful not to confuse frequency of an item with its weight or importance in terms of relative class time spent with each. In some cases categories are followed by an observational note about this relationship:

Item No. 40/The Field of Intercultural Studies
* History and development (14)
* Current status of the field (16)

Item No. 41/Culture
- * Definitions (40)
- * Components (33)
- * Cultural contrasts/comparisons (29)
- * High/low context cultures (27)
- * Interrelationship of components (26)
- * Specific target cultures (25)
- * Generic cultural concepts (24)
- * Relative power of cultures (political aspects) (18)
- * Maps or grids of culture (16)
- * Etic/emic views of culture (7)
- * Diachronic/synchronic aspects (7)

(Note: This appears to be the most popular topic in the content area with consistently high numbers both in terms of respondents and in hours spent on each.)

Item No. 42/World View
- * Cultural relativity & determinism (22)
- * Culture as paradigm (20)
- * Transcending one's world view (20)
- * Interrelationship of language & culture (19)
- * Definitions of world view (19)
- * Universals & particulars (18)
- * World view as paradigm (12)
- * Language as paradigm (12)
- * Interrelationship of components (11)
- * Language/parole & culture/behavior (11)
- * Linguistic relativity & determinism (11)
- * Paradigms as reality constructs (9)
- * Components (8)

* Confines of self (5)

(Note: This topic elicited a high number of responses, but the number of hours is quite low; a popular topic but not considered very weighty.)

Item No. 43/Intercultural Competence
* Definitions (20)
* Relevant traits (17)
* Components (15)
* Training/developing (11)
* Determining traits (10)
* Assessing individual profiles (7)
* Monitoring & measuring (3)

Item No. 44/Communicative Competence
* Nonverbal aspects (20)
* Definitions (19)
* Verbal aspects (14)
* Sociolinguistic aspects (14)
* Concept of competence vs. performance (12)
* Components (9)

Item No. 45/Interpersonal Processes
* Interpersonal relations (23)
* Conflict resolution (23)
* Discovery of self (17)
* Individual variants vs. regional (15)
* Group dynamics (14)
* Interconnections (13)
* Dyadic systems (8)

Item No. 46/Intercultural Processes
　Processes/phases/end results
　　* Culture shock (26)
　　* Intercultural contact (24)
　　* Assumptions (22)
　　* Stages of cultural entry (17)
　　* Types (15)
　　* Entry options (13)
　　* Results of choices (12)
　　* 2-way process (11)
　　* Internal/external factors (10)
　　* Country shock (9)
　Adjustment
　　* Degrees of adjustment (20)
　　* Factors that help and hinder (18)
　　* Strategies (15)
　　* Indicators (13)
　　* Levels/scale (10)
　Maladjustment
　　* How/why it occurs (15)
　　* Results, solutions, specifications (12)
　　* Over-adjustment (11)
　　* Indicators (10)
　Re-entry/Readjustment
　　* Re-entry process (23)
　　* Impact of IC experience (18)
　　* Returnee as world citizen (11)
　　* Relation to global issues (9)
　　* Relevance to multicultural (5)
　　* Maladaptive re-entry (5)

(Note: Not much time is spent on the various subthemes of this item (Intercultural Processes); however, the number of responses is quite high. It is interesting to note that culture shock is one of the most popular topics. The entire first category in general is addressed a great deal, while adjustment and re-entry run a close second and third. Maladjustment is least frequently addressed.)

Item No. 47/Other Sojourner Concepts
  * Stereotypes (22)
  * Definitions (12)
  * Sojourners' responsibilities (11)
  * Third culture children (9)
  * Dependent variables (6)
  * Expatriate communities (6)
  * Independent variables (5)
  * Defense mechanisms (5)

(Note: On a subjective note, it seemed surprising that this topic is not more popular; however, this may have to do with the fact that not all courses deal with preparing people to go abroad.)

Item No. 48/Language Development
Concepts
  * Variations in language (9)
  * Comparisons between L1 and L2 (6)
  * Idiolect, dialect, speech communities (6)
  * Concepts of "acquisition/learning" (5)
  * Native language acquisition (4)
  * L2 acquisition process (4)
  * Impact of host language on IC experience (4)
  * Interlanguage stage/effects (3)

Second Language Development
- * Attention to L2 development (6)
- * Learner strategies (4)
- * Utilization of resources (3)
- * Actual learning of host language (2)
- * Identification of resources (2)

(Note: Fewer people address this and the following topics in their ICC courses. These appear to be more specialized content areas.)

Item No. 49/Bi-/Multilingualism & Bi-/Multiculturalism
Bi-/Multilingualism
- * Code switching patterns (6)
- * Definitions of bilingualism (5)
- * Style shifting patterns (4)
- * Bilingual behaviors & dual language use (3)
- * Profiles of bilinguals (2)
- * Societal vs. individual bilingualism (1)
- * Developmental patterns (1)
- * Stages & phases (1)
- * Impact, effects (1)
- * Types of bilinguals (1)
- * Linguistic interference/transference (1)
- * Effects of L1, L2, L3, etc. (0)

(Note: The "effects of L1, L2, L3" is the only topic with no responses in Part VI.)

Bi-/Multiculturalism
- * Definitions (9)
- * Societal vs. individual (6)
- * Anomie (5)

* Stages & phases (4)
* Impact, effects (4)
* Bicultural behaviors (4)
* Cultural interference/transference (4)
* Internal/external conflicts (4)
* Developmental patterns (3)
* Types of biculturals (3)
* Effects of C1, C2, C3, etc. (2)

(Note: One respondent added two more topics — monolingualism and issues such as English Only.)

Item No. 50/Ethics. Issues examined, elicited 23 responses of which 20 identified the specific issues which follow:
* Missionary work
* Research in cross-cultural settings
* Impact of exchange students on a host culture
* Role of Peace Corps and teaching English in Pakistan
* Use of the Bennett framework & the "platinum rule" approach
* Merit hiring & promotion vs. traditional culture approaches: nepotism, cultural hierarchies, despised groups, seniority, etc.
* Marxism, functionalism, interpretivism, caring (Gilligan & Noddings), and the contextualization of ethics, metaethical perspectives
* Changing other cultures, harming others, manipulation, deceit
* Mass media & broadcast of people of color on TV news; racism; developing a world bias
* Cultural values conflict
* Rationale for L2 teaching, particularly English as L2
* Management practices

* Larger responsibility to facilitate understanding, especially in a business context
* Personal responsibility/perception and one's impact on others
* Personal choice in a professional context
* Trying to balance issues & learning in areas of cultural studies & politics
* Discussions and readings around political issues of going to Third World societies to study & "help"
* Issues of choice readjustment
* Gender-related or issues of "truth" vs. harmony; group vs. individual; cheating vs. honesty
* Business ethics

Item No. 51/Field Applications
* Strategies for culture exploration (14)
* General field methods and techniques (12)
* Identifying & using resources (12)
* Identifying field objectives (11)
* Monitoring & assessing progress (9)
* Strategies for language acquisition (4)

Item No. 52/Implications of Course Content for the Students' Intercultural Experiences
* Self-selection & evaluation (11)
* Explaining failures/successes (7)
* Identifying relevant traits for success (8)
* Predicting success (3)
* Personnel selection (3)
* Other: Better prepared for diverse workforce (1)

## Part VII. Course Implementation/Delivery

It is evident from the responses that all courses include both theoretical and applied focuses, with allocations between the two ranging from 10% theoretical and 90% applied at one end of the spectrum, to 70% theoretical and 30% at the other. Distribution between both is fairly evenly divided along the continuum with highest concentrations somewhere between 40%-60% theoretical and 60%-40% applied (Item No. 43).

When inductive-deductive approaches and teacher-led vs. student-centered approaches are considered, all respondents favor some combination of both while varying greatly in the emphasis given to each. Only one respondent indicates a 100% teacher-led format. On the whole, instructors use various combinations of lecture, discussion, and experiential activities. It is important to note that those who employ experiential activities use them no more than 65% of the time at one extreme, whereas the largest number uses such activities about 20% of the time. Some of the more popular formats devote equal time to each of the three activity types, or 33% for each. Finally, almost all indicate that they also allow for content to evolve organically to some degree, although the greater portion of instruction in almost all cases is previously planned and follows a syllabus. A syllabus plan seems widely accepted in university settings and a popular way to organize a course; once written, it is followed quite closely.

In Item No. 55, respondents list a great variety of teaching/learning techniques as follows (items are listed in descending order of popularity with the number of responses indicated in parentheses):

* discussions (42)
* lectures (37)
* review of readings (36)

* exercises/activities (33)
* small group tasks (32)
* case studies (24)
* simulations/skits (29)
* observational tasks (28)
* exploration tasks (25)
* collaborative learning activities (20)
* panels (16)
* roleplays (16)
* fishbowls (8)
* other types of field research (8)
* debate (5)

Under the category of "other activities", respondents volunteered: interviews, videos, buzz groups, small group discussion of journals and homework, interaction with an intercultural pal, hot seat participation, summary translation, participation in public lectures, slides, and library research. Additionally, a great variety of outside-of-class activities are also cited. These are classified as:

* interaction/interviews with persons of another culture (e. g. , interviewing native speakers, foreign student partners, community involvement, etc. )
* fieldwork (e. g. , drop-offs, site visits, ethnographies, field trips, etc. )
* writing tasks (e. g. , papers, critical incidents, journals, reflective essays, etc. )
* media and theater tasks (viewing films, reading newspapers, skits, etc. )
* projects (collaborative tasks, oral reports, exploratory tasks, etc. )
* other (research, practicing skills, internships, etc. )

Finally, whereas 16 respondents clearly see implementation of the course related to their goals and objectives, many more did not respond at all (Item No. 58). Several placed question marks or seemed confused by the question. One wonders how well course goals and objectives, course implementation, and evaluation are integrated—not an uncommon challenge in many courses designed by instructors lacking specific background and preparation in the field of education itself.

## Part Ⅷ. Materials & Resources

To Item No. 59 regarding the use of specific course texts, 29 indicate "yes", 9 "no", 3 indicate use of course packets or workbooks, and 2 use xeroxed articles. No single text received a clear or frequent endorsement; however, works cited two or more times are (number of times cited in parentheses):

Archer, C. (1990) *Living with Strangers in the USA*. Englewood Cliffs, NJ: Prentice-Hall. (2)

Damen, L. (1987) *Culture: The Fifth Dimension in the Language Classroom*. Reading MA: Addison-Wesley. (2)

Dodd, C. H. (1991) *Dynamics of Intercultural Communication*. Dubuque, IA: Wm. C. Brown. (4)

Gudykunst, W. B., & KIM, Y. Y. (1984) *Communicating with Strangers: An Approach to Intercultural Communication*. NY: Random House. (3)

Hall, E. T. (1973) *Silent Language*. NY: Doubleday. (2)

Hall, E. T. (1977) *Beyond Culture*. NY: Doubleday. (2)

Kohls, L. R. (1984) *Survival Kit for Overseas Living*. Yarmouth, ME: Intercultural Press. (2)

Samovar, L., & Porter, R. E. (eds.) (1987) *Intercultural Communi-

*cation*: *A Reader* (6th ed.). Belmont CA: Wadsworth. (5)

Other items include books, articles, periodicals, movies, videos, and other resources, filling more than 25 pages and too numerous to list here. Twenty-seven individuals indicate use of multiple works; 34 include audio-visual materials. Forty use their own students as resources and 33 use their institution and/or community in various ways to support their work: speakers, observation tasks, ethnographies, drop-offs, field trips, homestays, tours, and community involvement projects. Nearly half also cite SIETAR International as a resource, and others add: local groups, networking, embassies, local people, movies, etc.

## Part IX. Assessment: Students, Teacher & Course

To the question "are students assessed with reference to course goals and objectives" (Item No. 66), 36 replied "yes," and surprisingly, three individuals also replied "no." The fact that 12 other instructors did not reply at all is intriguing and perplexing. Most instructors seem to utilize various approaches to assessment, e.g.: tests, quizzes, exams (24); essays and written reports (34); and feedback (27). Other assessment techniques cited are: student presentations, demonstrated competencies, portfolios, projects in small groups, field study reports, journals, and poster sessions. However, essays clearly emerge as the most frequent evaluative technique (34).

In addition to direct indicators, many respondents also utilize indirect indicators (Item No. 67), such as attendance (34), participation (37), attitude (18), and quality of performance (27). Only 23 respondents conduct on-going assessment; 16 others report conducting assessment at specific intervals (Item No. 69). Thirty-eight respondents assess the students themselves; in many fewer cases (10), self-assessment by students also forms part of the evaluative process. In 6 cases, students assess each other, and in 3 cases outside evaluators are involved (Item No. 70).

Course results are expressed in letter grades in 29 cases, in number grades in 5 cases, and on a pass/fail basis in 5 cases (Item No. 72). Other ways include: determination of achievement of competencies, narrative evaluations, or reported satisfaction by the client organization. In 38 cases, students evaluate the instructor and in 38 cases students evaluate the course.

## Summary and Conclusions

The last quarter of a century has witnessed rapid development of the intercultural field; and with this, a concomitant growth in Intercultural Communication courses in colleges and universities in various parts of the world. Instructors are called upon to design and implement such courses often for the first time and, in so doing, they are helping to define the content and parameters of this subject matter. Often, the context in which they teach, or the department or program in which the course is placed, also further define the scope of the courses.

This survey was designed to learn about the evolving nature of ICC courses, given interest among faculty to learn what their colleagues are doing elsewhere. Through compilation and presentation of the data obtained, this interim report provides a snapshot of 50 plus courses between 1992 and 1994. It reveals not only the purvue of these courses, but also their goals and objectives, content areas, and approaches to implementation. It also begins to identify common models, frameworks and schema, useful materials and resources, and assessment procedures. For those who participated in the survey—and for others interested in the questionnaire instrument—it serves also as a self-study guide for examining one's own approach, to the task by reviewing the 70 plus questions contained in the survey questionnaire.

## Appendix 1

### Respondents

Archer, Carol M., Instructor, Cross-Cultural Communication, University of Houston, Houston, TX, USA

Asuni, Judith Burdin, Academic Director, College Semester Abroad/Nigeria. School for International Training, Lagos, Nigeria

Baldwin. John R., Graduate Associate, Department of Communication, Arizona State University, Tempe, AZ, USA

Bennhold, Laurette, Director, Graduate Studies. Kingston College, Vienna. VA. USA

Blanchard, Karen, Faculty, Program in Intercultural Management, School for International Training, Brattleboro, VT, USA

Bowen, Doug, ESL Instructor, University of California-Riverside, Riverside, CA, USA

Burry, Harry J., Professor, Baldwin-Wallace College, Berea, OH, USA

Clauss, Leonore, Consultant, Communications International, Toronto, Ontario, Canada

Clifford, Kay, Program Director, International Center, University of Michigan, Ann Arbor, MI, USA

Demartin, Lyn, Faculty, Student Development, Prescott College, Prescott, AZ, USA

Dollahite, Nancy, ESL Instructor, Universidad de Celaya, Celaya, Guanajuato, Mexico

Elder, Gore G., Visiting Professor, University of North Carolina, Chapel Hill, NC, USA

Ellingboe, Brenda J., Visiting Instructor, Inver Hills Community College, Inver Grove Heights, MN, USA

England, Wayne H., Vice President for Academic Affairs and Provost, Salem-Teikyo University, Salem, WV, USA

Gareis, Elisabeth, Public Service Faculty, American Language Program, Georgia Center for Continuing Education, University of Georgia, Athens, GA, USA

Garrott, June Rose, Professor, Seinan Jo Gakuin Junior College for Women, Kita-Ku, Kitakyushu-shi, Japan

Gaston, Brent, Lecturer, International Exchange Office, Fukuoka University, Fukuoka City, Japan

Goodman, Neal R., Professor, Saint Peter's College, Jersey City, NJ, USA

Hayashi, Kichiro, Professor, International Management, Graduate School of International Politics, Economics and Business, Aoyama Gakuin University, Tokyo, Japan

Hinshaw, JoAnn, Visiting Faculty, Maharishi International University, Fairfield, IA, USA

Hubbard, Ann, Study Abroad Advisor, University of St. Thomas, St. Paul, MN, USA

Jilani, Andrew, Consultant, Human Resource Development, Academy for Educational Development, Quetia, Pakistan

Ka, Omar, Assistant Professor, Linguistics & French, University of Maryland, Baltimore, MD, USA

Kennedy, Gwen, Consultant, Kennedy & Associates; Also, Fielding Institute, Anchorage, AK, USA

Lalos, Kathy, Instructor, Bunsai Gakuen Institute of Intercultural Communication, Lincoln, MA, USA

Lynn, Kevin, Trainer, Kobe Steel Inc., Kobe, Japan

McDowell, Elizabeth V., Professor, Pierce College, Philadelphia, PA,

USA

McFarland, S. Diane, Assistant Professor, Youngstown State University, Youngstown, OH, USA

McGroarty, Mary, Associate Professor, Northern Arizona University, Flagstaff, AZ, USA

Metzger, Janet C., Assistant Professor, Communication Studies, Texas Tech University, Lubbock, TX, USA

Monteiro, Basilio, Assistant Professor, New York Institute of Technology, Old Westburs,, NY, USA

Nelson, Gayle, Assistant Professor, Dept. of Applied Linguistics & ESL, Georgia State University, Atlanta, GA, USA

O'Dwyer, Tony, Head of Training & Evaluation, Agency for Personal Service Overseas, Dublin, Ireland

Padro, Came, Houston, TX, USA

Patton, Jane, Faculty/Speech Communication, Mission College, Santa Clara, CA, USA

Peñaranda, Stacy, Field Relations Manager, Au Pair Homestay Program, World Learning, Washington, DC, USA

Pen-in, Shirley J., Teacher, Carriere International Business College, Kyoto, Japan

Poole, Kathleen, Overseas Program Coordinator, Office of International Education & Exchange, University of Oregon, Eugene, OR, USA

Prosser, Michael, Professor, University of Virginia, Charlottesville, VA, USA

Robinson, Stuart D. G., Institute for Cross-Cultural Communication, Zug, Switzerlan J

Rowland, Diana, President, Rowland & Associates, San Diego, CA, USA

Royal, Nick, Coordinator, Merrill College Field Program at UC-Santa Cruz, Santa Cruz, CA, USA

Rubin, Don, Professor, University of Georgia, Athens, GA, USA

Serrie, Hendrick, Prof & Chair., Dept. of International Business, Eckerd College, St. Petersburg, FL, USA

Sinnigen, John, Associate Professor of Spanish, University of Maryland, Baltimore, MD, USA

Sparrow, Lise M., Faculty, Master of Arts in Teaching Program, School for International Training, Brattleboro, VT, USA

Sreberny-Mohammadi, Annabelle, Professor & Director, Centre for Mass Communication Research, University of Leicester, Leicester, England

Tyler, V. Lynn, Director, Intercultural and Outreach Programs, Kennedy Center for International Studies, Brigham Young University, Provo, UT, USA

Ungerteider, John & Ange DiBenedetto, Assistant Professors, World Issues Program & Program in Intercultural Management, School for International Training, Brattleboro, VT, USA

Van der Leye, Frits, Head of Training, Kontakt der Kontinenten (K. D. K.), Soesterberg, The Netherlands

Van Zyc, John A., Professor, School of Dramatic Art, Witwatersrand University, Miweruapcein, South Africa

Watson. Malcolm L., Director, American Language Academy/Baldwin-Wallace College, Berea, OH, USA

Westebbe, Shelly, Lecturer, University of Maryland (Asia-Pacific/US Military camp), Tokyo, Japan Country, MD, USA

# Appendix 2

## Questionnaire
## A Survey of Intercultural Communication Courses

Not so long ago. Intercultural Communication (ICC) was addressed primarily through orientation sessions and workshops preparing individuals for an intercultural sojourn. As the intercultural field has grown, ICC courses are found increasingly in colleges and universities throughout the world. This survey is designed to learn about these courses and the forms they take. The 30-minute questionnaire may serve as a sort of self-study for respondents, increasing awareness about various aspects of course design and delivery. Dissemination of the results will hopefully benefit all involved, strengthening the field.

Because the primary audience is SIETAR International's membership, we seek your help in identifying other individuals' and/or institutions for inclusion in this project. Feel free to copy this form for others in the field, or, if you prefer, send a list of names and addresses to the survey address below. Analysis of the survey will be completed by Summer 1992. Preliminary results will be disseminated to respondents in Fall 1992, and eventually through SIETAR publications.

To insure inclusion of your data in the survey compilation, return this form no later than July 15, 1992. Mail to: Eh Alvino F. Fantini, School for International Training, Brattleboro, Vermont 05302, USA. (Tel: 802-257-7751; Fax: 802-254-6774)
(Please type or print clearly.)

## Part I. General Information: Respondent
Name:        Title or Position:        Institutional Affiliation:
Address:
Country.            Telephone.            Fax
Sex:    Male/Female    Age: 20-35    36-50    51-65    Over 65
Highest degree attained: Undergraduate    Master    Doctorate    Other
Years in this field?    Years teaching this course?
Other cultures with which you are experienced:

Other languages in which you can communicate and proficiency in each on a scale of 0-5 (where 5 = native ability):

## Part II. General Information: Institution, Program & Faculty

How many students are enrolled at your institution?
Describe their ethnic composition using approximate percentages (%) of each:
How many foreign students?　　What % of the total enrollment?
List countries represented:
Do you offer a program in Intercultural Studies?　　Yes　　No
Type of program: Certificate　BA　MA　PhD　Other.
Do you offer a program in a related field? If so, what is it called?
Type of program: Certificate　BA　MA　PhD　Other.
How many total faculty are qualified to teach the ICC course?
How many actually do?
Are any courses team-taught? (i. e. taught by more than one teacher)?
Yes　No　If yes, how many?
What qualifications are needed to teach in this area? (Check all that apply) Prior intercultural experience; Prior teaching experience; A second language; Academic degree (state level: others:)

## Part III. General Information: Course

When was the course first offered?　　Or, the program?
What is the average enrollment?　Per course　Per term　Per year
Enrollment trends: Increasing　Decreasing　Stable
Average class size:　Minimum class size:　Maximum class size:
What is the ethnic make-up of students? (Give %'s)
In what department is the course offered?
Is it also listed in another department?　Yes　No　If yes, in which

department?
Is it an 'interdisciplinary' offering'?
Course configuration: Length in hours: Hours per class session:
Number of sessions:.
Class schedule per week:   Hours of homework expected par session:
Credits/units awarded:
Is the course: Optional    Required; for what course of study?
Is the course needed to satisfy university 'diversity' requirement?
Yes    No
Course levels: Introductory    Intermediate    Advanced
Undergraduate    Graduate
Are there prerequisites?    Yes    No    If yes, please list:
Is the course prior to concurrent with, or following an intercultural field experience?
Reasons students give for taking this course:
Describe successful/attractive features of the course:
Describe challenging/difficult aspects of the course:

## Part Ⅳ. Course Goals & Objectives (append a copy, if available)
Title of course:
List course goals:
List course objectives:
Are the above based on a needs assessment? Yes No If yes, check the basis/source of the needs,
    program    student    teacher    the 'field'    other
What % of the objectives address: Knowledge % Skills % Attitude % Awareness %

## Part Ⅴ. Curriculum Design (append a copy of syllabus, if available)
Do you consider the course: training    education    research    other    ?

What % is: Theoretical    %    Applied    %    What % is:
   Content    %    Process    %
List or group major course, if possible:
What    %    address: General culture    %    A specific target
   culture    %    General communication    %
Communication through a specific language system    %
What    %    addresses the following processes? Interpersonal    %
Intercultural    %    International.    %
Indicate in hours the time spent with any of the following models, frameworks, schema, etc.:
Hammer's Quadrant (The Field of Cross-Cultural Communication)
The 5 Culture Questions (Who am I? Where am I? etc.)
Ruben's Facets of Cross-Cultural Competence
Allport Amir's Contact Hypothesis
Janeway & Gochenour's 7 Stages of Cultural Entry (or other similar frameworks)
Kolb's Experiential Learning Cycle
Kim's System Approach to Adaptation
Gudykunst & Hammer's Quadrant (Classification Scheme for Training Techniques) Lysgaard et al.'s Cultural Adaptation Curve
Hall's Map of Culture
Bennett's 6 Stages (Development of Cultural Sensitivity)
Hall's High/Low Context Cultures
Triandis' Attribution Theory
Fantini's 6 Stages (Process Approach for Language Acquisition)
Nichols' Aspects of Cultural Difference
Communication Models (describing: sender/receiver, input/output; deep/surface strictures, etc.)
Maslow's Hierarchy of Needs    Kealey's Overseas Effectiveness Traits

Gallois et al.'s Communication Accommodation Theory
Hofstedes' Value Framework
Kluckhonn's Model (Variations in Value Orientations)
Fantini's Language & World View Schema
Please describe and/or append copies of other models used:

## Part Ⅵ. Content
Check any of the following content items addressed, indicating how much time (in hours) is spent with each:

**The Field of Intercultural Studies**
history and development    current status of the field

**Culture**
definitions    diachronic/synchronic aspects    specific target cultures    components    high/low context cultures    cultural contrasts/comparisons    interrelationship of components    etic/emic views of culture (political aspects)    relative power of cultures    maps or grids of culture    generic cultural concepts

**World View** (Weltanschauung, Cosmovision, etc.)
definitions of world view    language as paradigm    universals (human) & particulars    components (symbol/semantic/pragmatic)    paradigms as reality constructs    (cultural)    interrelationship of components    interrelationship of language & culture    confines of self    world view as paradigm    cultural relativity & determinism    language/parole&culture behavior    culture as paradigm    linguistic relativity & determinism    transcending one's world view

**Intercultural Competence**
definitions    determining traits for specific    intercultural contexts (needs assessment)    assessing individual profiles    components    training/developing these traits    relevant traits or attributes    monito-

ring and measuring traits

**Communicative competence**
Definitions    components (meaning, form, use/context)    non-verbal aspects (extralinguistic)    concept of competence vs. sociolinguistic aspects (appro-performance contextual variations)

**Interpersonal Processes**
interpersonal relations    conflict resolution    individual variants (idiolect) vs. regional or cultural community    dyadic systems (contextually or culturally based); discovery of self ('looking out' is 'looking in') group dynamics; interconnections: interpersonal to intercultural to international

**Intercultural Processes**
Processes/Phases/End Results:
intercultural contact/encounter; internal/external factors affecting entry; culture shock/stress assumptions/expectations/conditioning; country shock/stress types (integration /assimilation /accommodation /bicultural behaviours, etc); entry options & choices; two-way process: impacts on hosts and sojourners    results or consequences of choices    stages, phases of cultural entry

**Adjustment:**
degrees of adjustment    factors which help and hinder    strategies levels/scale (job/life/community/country); indicators: behaviors, feelings, etc.

**Maladjustment:**
how/why it occurs; results, solutions, specifications; over-adjustment (going 'native,' antipathy toward own culture); indicators

**Re-entry/Re-adjustment:**
the re-entry process, stages, phases; relevance to multicultural movements; returnee as world citizen; impact of an intercultural experience; maladaptive re-entry; relation to global/planetary issues

### Other Sojourner Concepts
Definitions/types of sojourner; independent variables (time/purpose etc); defence mechanisms & indicators; dependent variables (stress/quality/contact/changes in self-concept); expatriate communities; stereotypes (both ways); 'third culture' children; sojourners' responsibilities

### Language Development
**Concepts:**
concepts: 'acquisition' vs. 'learning'; second language acquisition processes; interlanguage stages/effects; native language acquisition processes; idiolect, dialect, speech communities; impact of developing host language on IC experience; comparisons between L1 & L2; variations in language

**Second Language Development:**
attention to L2 Development; learner strategies & techniques; utilization of resources; actual learning of host language; identification of resources
BI-/Multilingualism & BI-/Multiculturalism

**Bi-/Multilingualism:**
definitions of bilingualism; impact, effects; linguistic interference/transference; societal vs. individual bilingualism; types of bilinguals; code switching patterns; developmental patterns; profiles of bilinguals; style shifting patterns; stages and phases; bilingual behaviors & dual language use; effects of L1, L2. L3. etc.

**Bi-/Multiculturalism:**
definitions; impact, effects; anomie; societal vs. individual biculturalism; types of biculturals; internal/external conflicts; developmental patterns; bicultural behaviors; effects of C1. C2. C3. etc.; stages and phases; cultural interference/transference

### Ethics
issues examined:

**Field Applications**

identifying field objectives; strategies for culture exploration; identifying and using resources; general field methods & techniques; strategies for language acquisition; monitoring & assessing progress

**Implications of Course Content for the Students' IC Experiences**

Self selection & evaluation; identifying relevant traits for success; explaining failures/successes; personnel selection for IC experience; predicting success; other.

## Part VII. Course Implementation/Delivery

What % of work is: Theoretical % Applied % Content/information % / Student processing % deductive % /inductive % teacher-led %/ Student-led % lecture % ; Discussion % / Experiential activities %

What % of work follows a structured syllabus? % What % organic (flows with class needs as they arise)? %

Check all of the following teaching/learning techniques you use: lectures discussions review of reading case studies role plays fishbowls panels debate simulations/skits exercises/activities small group tasks collaborative learning activities observational tasks exploration tasks other types of field research other:.

Types of outside-of class activities (include number of hours):

How is the work processed (used in class)?

How is it related to goals and objectives?

## Part VIII. Materials & Resources

Do you use a specific text? Yes No If yes, give bibliographical reference:

Do you use multiple works: Yes No If yes, please append a copy of the bibliography,

Do you use audio-visual materials? Yes No If yes, please list (or append list if available):

Are students used as a resource? Yes No.

Is the institution or community used as a resource? Yes No If yes, how?

Is SIETAR used as a resource? Yes No If yes, how?

Other resources used:

## Part IX. Assessment: Students, Teacher& Course

Are students assessed with reference to course goals and objectives? Yes No

What is assessment based on?

Direct indicators: tests, quizzes, exams; essays, written reports; feedback; other

Indirect indicators: attendance; participation; attitude; quality of performance.

Specific assessment instruments used:

Is assessment ongoing, done at specific intervals; How often is it done?

Who assesses? Teacher assesses students; Students assess themselves; Students assess each other; Outside evaluator assesses.

Summarize your approach to assessment:

How are course results expressed? Letter grades; Number grades; Pass/Fail Other:

Do students evaluate instructor? Yes No.

Do students evaluate the course? Yes No If yes, common comments:

Positive:

Negative:

(Anno E. Fantini. 1992 Brambetoto, VT 05302, USA)
(From: Fantini, A. E. and Smith E. M. 1997, A survey of intercultural communication courses. *International Journal of Intercultural relations*, Vol. 21, No. 1, pp. 125-148.)

# 导读：关于跨文化交际课程的调查

20世纪八九十年代跨文化领域有了快速的发展，与此相伴跨文化交际课程在世界各地的大专院校相继开设。教师们被号召起来进行该课程的设计和实施，并帮助确定该课程的内容和参数。教学环境或者课程所在的项目也进一步确定了课程的范围。本调查就是对跨文化课程的特点进行探索以便给同行们一些有关的信息，通过资料的收集这份报告简要地提供了1992到1994年间的跨文化交际课程的概况，它不仅展示了该课程的范围还介绍了课程的目的与目标、内容、实施方法，以及认识它的一般模式、框架和图式，有用的材料和评估程序。并在文后为感兴趣者附录了调查问卷供自测。

完全调查所获得的信息：

## 1. 一般信息：调查对象

共收回53份答卷，其中47位被调查者是大学教师，6位来自其他机构，所获取的信息来自整个这53份答卷。大部分被调查对象（38人）来自美国，还有其他一些来自另外十个国家。其中女性较男性稍多，21人获取了博士学位，其他均有硕士以上学位，大部分经历过5种以内的文化，其他人为6~10种。

## 2. 一般信息：机构，项目和能力

被试者来自的机构大小规模不一，其中17个提供了跨文化研究项目，26个没有，21个提供了相关领域的项目。教授跨文化课程的能力资质包括预先的跨文化经验、教学经验、第二语言知识、学位等。

### 3. 一般信息：课程

班级学生规模不等，一般在 30 人左右，学生报名上课人数稳中有升。各个学校的课程长度、上课时间和每周课时和学分分配时也各不相同。大部分学校把跨文化交际课程作为选修课程，学校也各自提供了不同层次的教学，有入门的、中级的、高级的，既有本科的也有硕士的。学生修跨文化交际课程的一般原因是：出国学习或旅游、国际企业、增加对他人和文化的了解、个人成长或对课程内容和教师感兴趣。

### 4. 课程目的和目标

课程的一般目的是意识、态度、技能和知识。但各个院校各有侧重。大部分实验对象都意识到在学习不同文化时加强意识的重要性。

课程教育的目标则描述得比较详细，归纳起来包括如下的几个方面：跨文化交际和一般文化概念，跨文化情境的功能与应用、自我意识、教育和管理、发展其他技能。

### 5. 课程设计

多数被调查者把跨文化交际课程归类为"讲授类课程"，许多人也在"训练"类上作了标计，也有一些人认为应该包括研究。在整个的学习过程中，其中一位认为理论和实践应各占 50%，16 位认为应用应该占较大的比例，而 11 位则刚好相反。所有实验对象都认为应该从一般意义上来对待文化，尽管对普遍文化的关注有所不同。其中 4 位认为应该把特定目的文化作为课程的一部分。但是值得注意的是三分之二的人认为通过外语来探索交流与该课程无关。此外作者还调查了有关跨文化的、国际的、人际的关系的重要性，以及课程设计的模式框架和图式。

## 6. 内容

如下主要是问卷中关于课程的内容的几个方面,并把每个方面再细分为一些次主题。内容主要包括以下的内容:

跨文化研究领域,文化,世界观,跨文化能力,交流能力,人际过程,跨文化过程,其他旅居者概念,语言发展,双/多语现象和双/多文化现象,场景应用,课程内容和学生跨文化经历的密切关系。

## 7. 课程实施

很显然从问卷的回答可以看出跨文化所有课程都包括了对理论和应用的强调,只是程度不同而已。此外还调查了在教学中是否该由教师引导还是以学生为中心,所有被调查者都倾向于把两者结合起来,只是对两者赋予了不同程度的重要性。总的说来,教师常常把讲课、讨论和经验性活动结合起来。大多数情况下课程都会遵循教学大纲进行。在大学,教学大纲为大家普遍接受,也是组织课程的普遍方法,一旦设计好教学大纲,就应该比较严格地执行。

## 8. 教材与资料

作者还调查了是否有特定教材,以及其他的资料如书本、论文、电影、电视和其他材料。

## 9. 评估:学生、教师和课程

评估主要根据学生的课堂发言、能力展示、作业、小组活动、实证研究报告和论文等方面进行。

**Questions for reflection**:

1. What are the goals and objectives of intercultural communication

courses in your university?
2. After reading this survey what do you learn about the nature of intercultural communication courses?
3. Do you agree that intercultural communication courses should be based on the teaching of the target culture?
4. If an intercultural communication course focuses on the relationship between language and culture, do you think of it as acceptable?

# Preparing Teachers for an Intercultural Context

Kenneth Cushner

It is often hard to learn from people who are just like you. Too much is taken for granted. Homogeneity is fine in a bottle of milk, but in the classroom it diminishes the curiosity that ignites discovery.

Vivian Gyssin Paley (1979)

In an increasingly global world one need not step out of one's community to experience "culture shock". Many teachers who have grown up in a relatively homogeneous society are now faced with the challenge of educating a heterogeneous group of students. This module not only provides the reader with facts and figures pertaining to the multiethnic reality many educators must face but also introduces strategies to help understand and solve problems that arise from cultural differences. Readers are also provided with exercises that assist in analyzing as well as solving cross-cultural classroom problems.

## Contents

Ⅰ. Self-Assessment Test

Ⅱ. Case Studies: Critical Incidents
Ⅲ. Skill Concepts: Diversity in Education
Ⅳ. Skill Applications
Ⅴ. Field Exercises

## Self-Assessment Test

Read the following list of questions regarding teacher education and the education of children in a diverse society. Grade yourself according to how well you think you could answer the question. A grade of A assumes that you would be able to write a truly excellent, accurate, and comprehensive answer. A grade of F indicates that you would not know where to begin. A grade of B indicates that you would be able to write a good answer. A grade of C means you would be able to respond in an adequate manner. A grade of D means you would write an inadequate answer.

### Questions

1. What percentage of children in schools in your country in the 1990s are children of color?
2. What are the projections for the demographics of cultural diversity in your nation's schools for the year 2025?
3. What percentage of your national teaching force are people of color?
4. What is the percentage of women in the teaching force in your country during the 1990s?
5. What are the projections for the percentage of teachers representing diverse groups as well as the gender balance of your nation's teaching force into the next century?
6. How many Limited English Proficient (LEP) students are in your nation's schools?
7. What percentage of your nation's teachers speak a second language?

8. Characterize the experience of first-generation immigrant or refugee children in the classroom. How do the processes of acculturation and adjustment enter the picture?
9. How might the teacher today, faced with students from so many backgrounds, begin to understand the complexities of the multicultural experience?
10. How do such concepts as assimilation, melting pot, and pluralism affect the education of children in your country?
11. Identify 3 to 5 aspects of your own cultural upbringing that may present obstacles as you learn to interact in a culturally diverse classroom setting.
12. What are some key concepts from the fields of cross-cultural psychology and training that can assist teachers as they respond to the needs of a diverse student population? How are these concepts evident in cross-gender interactions? In able-bodied/disabled interactions?

Score your own paper according to the grades you gave yourself for each item. Each grade of A counts as 3 points, a B counts as 2 points, a C as 1 point, a D as 0 points, and a grade of F counts as —1 point. Determine your grade point average.

## Case Studies: Critical Incidents

The purpose of the following critical incidents is to encourage you to identify and discuss the experiences faced by numerous children and teachers in culturally diverse school settings. You will be presented with a series of situations that have actually occurred in classroom and school settings. These incidents center around many of the themes in the 18-theme culture-general framework proposed by Brislin, Cushner, Cherrie, and Yong (1986), which have been further developed in Cushner, Mc-

Clelland, and Safford (1992). You will be asked to offer your own explanations and suggested resolutions to the proposed incidents, and you should do so both individually as well as in groups. The more diverse your discussion groups can be, both in terms of teachers and students, the more lively and informative your discussion is certain to be.

## The Rural Elementary School

Renata is a 21-year-old Mexican-American student majoring in elementary education at an urban university located a few miles from where she grew up in the Eastern part of the United States. She is about to begin a field experience in a rural elementary school. Having lived in the inner city all of her life and having traveled very little, she is apprehensive and feels unprepared to deal with students from rural backgrounds. After 1 week in the classroom, Renata has encountered many potentially disruptive and unexplained behaviors. For instance, three new students entered her classroom in 1 week. These students are children of migrant farmworkers and they will be living in the community for approximately 1 month. These students have been in 12 schools over the past 3 years. One student missed 3 days of class because one of the work horses was sick. Renata also finds the faculty very low-keyed. She explains it that the faculty display a very "down-home" attitude and are not very wise to the world. And to top things off, one of the parents confronted her after school one day and told Renata that she just doesn't understand the values of the community and that she should "go back to where you belong!" Renata found this especially disturbing because as long as she could remember she had wanted to give all she could to children in school.

Renata met with her university adviser and told her that she wanted to leave the field of education.

## Discussion Questions

1. What is behind Renata's problem? If you were the adviser, what would you suggest?
2. How might a teacher best approach people whose value orientations, expectations of educators, and work style are significantly different from one's own?
3. Who should change? Renata? The faculty?
4. What experiences have you had living and/or working with people different from yourself where you had to contend with significant cultural differences? How did you react to the strong emotions and unexpected stress? How did you cope in such a situation?

## Moving from Hawaii

Alice, a 12-year-old sixth-grade student, had recently moved from Hawaii to a small town in Ohio, about 45 minutes outside of Cleveland. Although she was sad to leave her friends in Hawaii, Alice had grown up in a family that traveled quite frequently, moved relatively often, and prided itself on its ability to make easy adjustments. Alice was born in Australia while her parents had been on a 2-year teaching assignment. Alice anticipated few adjustment difficulties. At the start of the year, Alice went to school with little more than the expected "start-of-the-year" jitters.

Alice's language arts teacher was also new to the community and on the first day of school asked the children to stand, introduce themselves, tell where they were born, and of course to comment on "what they did on their summer vacation." In her turn, Alice stood up, introduced herself, said she was born in Cleveland, and spoke about her recent move from Hawaii. Her response was greeted with a few ooh's and aah's as most of the children in the class had spent their whole life in this small community. Alice appeared happy and content with her first day at school.

## Discussion Questions

1. How would you explain Alice's reluctance to share her actual birthplace with the teacher and students? Can you articulate what her internal dialogue might be during this experience?
2. What instances can you relate where you were treated as an outsider? How did you finally gain the status of insider?
3. In what situations might you find students, teachers, and/or parents in the role of outsider? What impact might this have on relationships within the school setting?
4. What might a teacher and/or school counselor do to help facilitate the emotional needs of new students?

## Eyes on Your Own Paper

Ulrike's parents sent her from Germany to school in the United States with the hope that she would improve her English language skills. Although she had studied English for many years in school and could speak it rather fluently, she did not have a good understanding of the more subtle aspects of the language. This was an area her parents wanted to see more fully developed.

Because of her apparent English language ability, the guidance counselor at her new school placed her with a full academic load. In one case in particular, her biology teacher, Ms. Reynolds, noticed that while taking tests Ulrike seemed to look at her neighbor's paper from time to time. Ms. Reynolds tried to quietly warn Ulrike to keep her eyes on her own paper and that if she needed some help to simply ask and it would be provided. Ulrike, however, never asked for assistance and continued to glance at her neighbor's papers.

Finally, Ms. Reynolds had enough and confronted Ulrike with evidence that she had been cheating. Ulrike responded that she was aware that she looked at a few answers but insisted that she did not cheat on the whole test. She seemed to give the impression that she did not understand why the teacher would be so upset since there are so many tests that she would take. Ms. Reynolds is upset that Ulrike would cheat and feels that she is dishonest and too lazy to study hard.

### Discussion Questions

1. What insights could you provide to Ms. Reynolds that would help shed some light on the situation?
2. In what ways does culture influence the manner in which people learn how to learn? How do these differences in learning styles affect educational gain?
3. What might educators do to accommodate differences in learning styles? In what ways do learning styles affect testing and evaluation?
4. What recovery skills might Ulrike employ to alleviate her current problem?

## Skill Concepts: Diversity in Education

Perhaps the greatest challenge yet to face the educational system of most nations is how best to address issues of equity and excellence within a context of diversity. Coupled with this task is the growing need that schools and nations face as they prepare their citizenry for the kinds of interactions that are becoming apparent as the world becomes increasingly global in nature. This section discusses the changing demographics of children and teachers in the United States as well as in a global context, introduces a culture-general framework useful for understanding and exploring the kinds of experiences both teachers and students are likely to encounter as they interact across cultural boundaries, and highlights some examples of school-based modifications that effectively address such issues.

In the United States alone at the beginning of the 1990s, roughly one third of the school-age population were children of color. This percentage is expected to increase to somewhere between 44% and 48% by the year 2025. Complicating this issue is the fact that relatively few of those in the teaching force represent minority populations. As of the late 1980s, roughly 88% of teachers in the United States represented the majority culture—that is, white, Anglo, and middle class, with about two-thirds of those being women. This figure, too, is expected to increase resulting in approximately 94% of the American teaching force representing a rather homogeneous, privileged, and cross-culturally inexperienced majority. This pattern of increased diversity in the classroom with an increasingly homogeneous teaching force is being mirrored in many nations of the world, including Canada, Australia, Israel, Great Britain, and New Zealand.

The United States has prior experience integrating significant numbers of immigrants, albeit with mixed reaction and success. During the early part of the 20th century, hundreds of thousands of legal immigrants entered the country through Ellis Island in New York. Although the road for new immigrants into the United States (or any country for that matter) has never been an easy one, the majority of the immigrants in the early part of the century having come from Europe could "fit" the human landscape, so to speak, once they learned the English language. The physical features they exhibited were not all that different from those of the majority of the people already here. Assimilationist ideology was easy to defend—people could conceivably "melt" into the greater pot called "America."

Those entering the United States today come from a much greater diversity of nations and backgrounds. Immigrants from the many diverse countries of Central and Latin America, Asia, and the Middle East are not uncommon. Into the schools they bring not only different ways of thinking and behaving but also diverse ways of communicating. Such diverse languages as Vietnamese, Cambodian, Arabic, Spanish, Russian, and Japanese are found in American schools with increasing regularity. In Florida's schools, for instance, at least 84 different languages are spoken—and the schools are actively working to provide educational services in 50 of these. And they are coming into that state in such great numbers that in 1989, as an example, enough children from Nicaragua alone were entering Dade County to support the building of a new elementary school each month. Of course, no such massive building efforts were undertaken, and few of the badly needed teachers were recruited. Increasingly across the country, children are speaking a language other than English at home. Between 30% and 50% of children in such cities as New York, Santa Fe, Hartford, and Providence speak languages other than English (Vobejda, 1992). In Miami, nearly three quarters of the residents speak a language other than English at home, with 67% saying they don't speak English very well. The United States is now the fourth largest Spanish-speaking country in the world! Although bilingualism is increasing among the American population in general (even given the English-as-an-Official-Language movement currently under way)! Only 5% of our nations' teachers are themselves truly bilingual.

The plight many immigrants to the United States face today is far more difficult than that of previous times. The desire by many today is to retain their cultural and linguistic identity and to avoid the push to fit in to some pre-existing mold. But even when the English language is effectively learned; the distinct physical features of many of the immigrants today are quite different from those in the mainstream, thus creating a phenotypic barrier. Physical features have a strong impact on people's attributions and until the greater population becomes more accepting and tolerant will be a tremendous obstacle.

But not only teachers must be prepared to accommodate diversity. Today's young people are growing up in a world significantly different from that of their parents. As such, they, too, must be prepared for the kinds of intercultural interactions they are certain to encounter. Consider some of the following.

The world has become much more technologically oriented in the past 50 years. As such, attention must be paid to the ethical and moral use of such technology as well as to the preparation of all its citizenry for the use of such technologies. It has been proposed that the United States is fast becoming two societies—not black and white or rich and poor, but those who are technologically functional and connected worldwide versus those who are technologically illiterate. Niche-marketing by the smaller, well-connected firms who are able to quickly respond to needs will bring success to such firms in the coming years. The large corporate dinosaurs, such as General Motors, will continue to struggle in today's market and economy.

Coupled with this is the fact that the world has become increasingly nuclear—and our own safety and security as a species may depend on our ability to adequately manage these capabilities. Even though the Iron Curtain has crumbled and communism has essentially dissolved, people are still, if not even more so, quite xenophobic. Recent outbreaks in Germany in response to "guest-workers" and in Los Angeles in the wake of the Rodney King incident, as well as the many nationalist movements around the globe point out the necessity, even more essential now, to firmly face issues of racism, prejudice, and intercultural interaction.

Finally, our dependency on international linkages is also greater than ever before. It is estimated that four out of five new jobs presently created in the United States are the direct result of foreign trade. Add to this the fact that over 6,000 American firms have operations overseas and 6,000 international firms have branch offices in this country. It quickly becomes apparent that young people in today's schools stand a great chance of having significant contacts with individuals from backgrounds quite different from their own—not by themselves living in a foreign country during their career but by foreign nationals spending increasing amounts of time in various American communities.

The focus of multicultural education has often been on curricular addition and expansion. This is important in that historically many groups and perspectives have been ignored or otherwise absent from the knowledge base provided in schools. Today, however, efforts must reach beyond a simple infusion of knowledge. Preparation of educators to deliver instruction from an intercultural or international perspective quickly becomes a double-edged sword. Teachers must be prepared to teach young people from a variety of cultural and linguistic backgrounds. At the same time, the knowledge and skills that teachers themselves are learning must become the content that is taught to young people in order for them to gain the skills necessary to live effectively in a global, interdependent world. This double-edged sword will not be easy to satisfy given what we know about our current population of teachers and the process of culture learning. We must begin to seek out concepts that cut across the various diversities that teachers and students will encounter in the schools. Such concepts must assist one in understanding and accommodating interactions across not only cultural barriers but also gender, age, class, and ability lines.

## Search for a Common Ground

Each of us is socialized within a given culture to believe that certain things are right and good. That, by its very nature, is the manner in which every individual gains an understanding of his or her world, forms an allegiance to a given group, and seeks to transmit those understandings to others of the group. It should not be surprising, then, to consider the school as an institution that has embedded within it certain values and expectations that have been determined by the majority culture-at-large. If such is the case, schools, which inherently operate from one "majority" culture perspective, reward those whose mode of interaction, communication, and manner of learning are congruent with its method of operation. In contrast, a significant number of students are left out of the process, thus feeling alienated and "unreached." Perhaps the concepts of ethnocentrism and culture shock from the field of cross-cultural psychology capture the essence of the dilemma better than any as we begin to consider the experiences of traditionally marginalized groups as they confront the culture of the school.

The 18-theme culture-general framework proposed by Brislin et al.

(1986) forms the essence of many of these problems and provides a context from which to understand relevant issues. This framework suggests that people will encounter similar experiences whenever they interact over a significant period of time with people who have been socialized in a manner different from themselves. Such similar experiences are found to occur regardless of the backgrounds of the actors, regardless of their roles, and regardless of the situation in which they find themselves.

At one level, understanding and accepting the strong emotional responses people will have when involved in intercultural interactions is critical to one's success in this arena. People's emotions will be aroused as they meet with unpredictable behavior on the part of others or when their behavior does not bring about an expected response. This will be true for the student where there is a clash between the culture of the school and that of the child, as well as for the teacher who finds her or himself in a highly diverse context. But in addition to emotional readiness, gaining the perspective of an insider is critical to establishing any functional relationship among teacher, students, and family. The culture-general framework points out that such differences in work styles, value orientations, and roles are common across cultures, as well as among the various subcultures or subgroups that make up a multicultural nation at large. This framework can also help individuals prepare themselves for the kinds of reactions they will have as they encounter differences in the school and community.

The 18 culture-general themes are categorized into three broad areas of concern and potential misunderstanding. When people from different backgrounds come together, it is common (1) for people's emotions to be highly charged and as a result to experience intense feelings; (2) for people to misunderstand and experience conflicts because of their operating from a different knowledge base; and (3) for people to interpret similar stimuli in different ways because of underlying bases of cultural differences. The 18 themes are found within these three major categories. People's Experiences That Engage Their Emotions include anxiety; disconfirmed expectations; the need to belong; ambiguity; and confronting one's own prejudices. The Knowledge Areas That People Find Difficult to Understand include work-related behaviors such as decision-making, problem-solving, and the locus of control; orientation in time and space; verbal and nonverbal language use as well as language learning; role-determined behavior; group versus individual orientation; rituals versus superstitions; social hierarchies of class and status; and value orientation. The Bases of Cultural Differences include the process of categorization; differentiation; the tendency people have to form ingroups and outgroups; differences in learning styles; and the manner in which people make judgments or attributions about others.

It is important at this juncture to stress that this is not the "melting pot" myth presented under another guise. It is possible to identify common ground without diminishing the importance of cultural/individual differences. Both culture-general and culture-specific approaches need to be presented in balance. You might analyze the case studies presented earlier and demonstrate how they imply both general and specific aspects.

Looking at the school context through the lens of the culture-general framework enables us to frame or explain some of the situations encountered almost daily by teachers and students in a variety of contexts while at the same time guiding our goal-setting efforts. Although the entire range of 18 themes cannot be discussed fully here (see Brislin et. al., 1986; and Cushner et al., 1992), a few will be expanded on.

## Belonging and Related Concepts

There is probably nothing more critical in the life of an adolescent than "fitting in." The concept of belonging—the need people have to fill a niche, to feel that they belong and are at home, and to strive to gain the status of insider with a group with which they wish to identify—is of utmost importance to most young people. New teachers, too, as well as new community members, have a need to feel that their contributions, ideas, and efforts are recognized, heard, and perhaps integrated into the existing fabric. People find meaning, security, and identity by belonging to various groups or networks. When excluded from such groups, people may begin to experience such negative responses as loneliness, alienation, a loss of self-esteem, and a decreased sense of direction and purpose.

Related to the need to belong is the tendency people have to form ingroups—defined as those with whom they feel comfortable and are able to discuss concerns with—and outgroups—those generally kept at a distance, both physical as well as emotional. A difficulty faced by newcomers to most situations is that they are entering a context in which people have already formed their ingroups. The newcomer, as Alice was in the second case study above, has left her ingroups behind. It is important to recognize that those in the new context generally do not need newcomers. A good deal of time is often required before new ingroups are established.

The issue of belonging is of critical importance in the intercultural context. Isolation from a group due to cultural or social incompetence, as well as physical separation, may have a similar impact on the individual. In the cross-cultural context, lack of social skills and language competence required to communicate effectively and to develop and maintain interpersonal relationships can likewise lead to isolation.

Cushner et al. (1992) state:

> Whatever the cause of the isolation, psychologists tell us that people tend to react in the same manner; they become more negative, rejecting, self-deprecating, self-absorbed, less responsive, and perhaps hostile.

It is no wonder that people, especially adolescents in schools, strive so very hard to be a part of the groups that appeal to them. What other "groups" may occur in schools in which individuals, both students, teachers, and families, may desire access but for some reasons may feel left out?

## Anxiety

Related to the need to belong is another of the 18 themes—anxiety. Anxiety refers to feelings of discomfort individuals may experience when in an unfamiliar situation. A high degree of anxiety, evident in such school-based settings as test-taking with its accompanying threat of failure as well as with interactions with peers, teachers, and parents, may result in inattention and an inability to operate at higher levels of cognitive processing.

Renata's situation in the first case study demonstrates the link between the knowledge issues of the culture-general framework and people's emotional responses. The migrant students in the school are experiencing significant change—quite regularly, it seems. Their emotional needs must be met if they are to benefit in any educational setting. Billy Davis (1972), who grew up in a family of migrant farmworkers, speaks of the practical experiences teachers assume students bring with them to the classroom from the home experiences, as well as of the resulting anxiety:

> No expert in measurement knows better than I the wishful thinking inherent in the concept of culture-free testing. I have sat with cold, damp hands, holding my breath, hoping the teacher would not call on me... We never had a private bathroom, or a kitchen sink, or an oven. I never owned a tricycle, bicycle, or pets (stray dogs are a separate category). We did not "go on vacations," "have company," "take lessons," or "pack luggage."... For years I owned no toothbrush, nail file, or pajamas. I could go on. In short, the ordinary middle-class world was strange to me and its terms frightened me.

In addition, in the case study, Renata has come into critically close encounters with people who have vastly different values, expectations, and way of life. Overcoming her own immediate emotional reactions and then striving to learn as much as she can about the people with whom she will interact will prove to be critical to her success in this realm.

## Communication Issues

Included in the knowledge areas are issues related to differences in language and communication styles, which seem to cut across the various diversities people will encounter in the schools. Verbal as well as nonverbal messages have significant impact, not only on the interpersonal interactions in the school context but also on the teaching and learning process. Critical to the development of any educational relationship is the degree to which trust and mutual understanding emerge. Because of the extent to which communication differences can result in significant misattributions or misjudgments about the motivations of others, considerable attention should be paid to this area in any teacher training program. Beyond the general cross-cultural communication differences any trainer would be prepared to introduce in a training program, attention to cross-gender communication, as well as communication between able-bodied and disabled individuals, should be stressed.

For instance, communication between able-bodied and disabled individuals often creates a unique set of problems to be addressed. Nonverbal behavior of a disabled person is often misinterpreted and viewed as inappropriate. In a similar manner, the nonverbal behavior of an able-bodied individual may signal discomfort, confusion, or rejection of the disabled individual, thereby further complicating the interaction. As the behavior of one is misjudged, the relationship may be strained, and a cycle of miscommunication may be set up that is difficult to break.

Uncertainty regarding appropriate behavior may result in strained relationships lacking the spontaneity and relaxed tone of more "normal" interactions. Differences in communication patterns between able-bodied and disabled individuals are quite apparent. For instance, able-bodied individuals tend to be more inhibited and nervous when communicating with individuals with disabilities—interpersonal distances are exaggerated, and encounters are characterized by greater anxiety and emotional discomfort. In addition, conflicting messages are often sent, as able-bodied individuals may verbally send positive messages while nonverbally communicating rejection or avoidance. Disabled persons report that their able-bodied communicators tend to glance away from them more frequently, stand farther away, act more nervous, pretend to ignore the disability, and assume that the disabled person is more disabled than he or she actually is. All of these increase the difficulty of communication.

Paul Williams, writing from the perspective of a disabled person, relates a vivid encounter:

When one of us meets one of you, especially if it is for the first time, we are quite likely to lack many of the skills for successful communication. We may not be able to think of anything appropriate to say; or to put it into the right words, or to control our facial expression. But you also will show a great lack of skill. You will be embarrassed, you won't be able to think of anything appropriate to say, you will tend to talk in an inappropriate tone of voice, you will tend to have a wide grin on your face and ask questions without really being interested in the answer. The handicap is a mutual one. Both of us have difficulty in communicating with and forming relationships with the other. The trouble is that you have lots of opportunities to go off and form relationships more easily. We don't. You can deny your handicap. We can't—we live with it all the time (Shearer, 1984)

The stereotypes of differences between male and female communication patterns are also critical to consider in the educational context (Cushner et al., 1992). Folklore tends to perpetuate the perception of certain stereotypical differences in male and female speech, even though empirical research often indicates this to be inaccurate and biased. For instance, the common belief that women speak more than men does not stand up in the research. In fact, in mixed-sex groups, men tend to speak at least twice as much, interrupt more often, and have a tendency to speak in ways that control both the direction of the talk and the overall situation in which people are speaking (Spender, 1981). Other cross-gender communication findings that are of interest: men are more likely to interrupt women than men; men receive more criticism and reprimands in the workplace than do women; women professionals are touched more often than male professionals; women are more likely to reveal personal information than are men; men use more personal space while they are talking than women; and men tend to initiate more conversation with mixed company at work than do women (see Chapter 4 by Bailey in this book; Cushner et al., 1992; Spender, 1981).

Although there is a lack of empirical research on the subject at the moment, it appears that the real differences in communication patterns between males and females may not be as important as the perceived differences or stereotypes. Although categorization or stereotype formation are inevitable and serve necessary and useful functions, when they are used to enforce inequalities of power and influence, their unquestioned use may cause not only miscommunication but also miscarriages of justice.

## Learning Styles

The example of Ulrike above points out numerous issues related to learning styles as well as testing and assessment across cultures. In this particular instance, Ulrike seems to be overwhelmed by the extreme number of tests that American students must complete. In Ulrike's native country, as in many places around the world, most of class time is spent studying, discussing, or otherwise "learning" the specific content of the course with little, if any, time devoted to testing. Testing is simply accomplished at the end of the term with students preparing for one major exam in the field of study to determine if she or he qualifies for the next level. Ulrike may find studying for tests on a weekly (or more) basis too demanding and distracting from the manner in which she is accustomed to learning.

Although slow to change in the minds of some, and slower to change in behavior, it seems that we are beginning to move away from the cultural deficit model that was so often used to explain school failure on the part of some groups. Rather, a cultural difference model is slowly being accepted. This position posits that the cognitive, learning, and motivational styles of many students in our schools are merely different from those most often expected by teachers, administrators, and curriculum developers who, you will recall, in the majority of cases represent the dominant culture. There exists, in a sense, a "culture clash" between the expectations and skills of students and those of teachers. As assimilationist ideology is fading, so too is the expectation that all children should be forced to fit a monocultural school culture that tends to favor white, middle-class values, behavior, and thinking skills.

As learning style preferences are recognized by many to exist within a group, differences are also found across cultures. People learn how to learn in ways that are rather specific to their group. Socialization into one's group not only teaches one what to think and learn but how to think and learn as well. This knowledge, like our knowledge of our own culture, is often tacit. That is, it is not articulated within the culture and is, for the most part, unknown to those outside it. In general then, thinking about differences in learning style suggests that culture significantly influences the manner in which one learns how to learn.

Researchers suggest that individuals tend to fall in distinct categories with regard to the manner in which they prefer to learn and, to a large degree, that these preferences are culturally determined. Some propose that there exist field-dependent versus field-independent learners. That is, field-independent learners are parts-specific, can isolate facts as needed, are rather linear in their thinking and approach to problem solving, and tend to test rather well, given the kinds of assessment practices predominantly in use today. Field-dependent learners, on the contrary, must see the big picture, seek to find personal relevance in the task at hand, and require that some sort of personal relationship is established between teacher and student.

Schools tend to stress the cognitive domain, rather low-level thinking, and the memorization of facts. In order to achieve success at the tasks presented in most schools, students are required to adopt a logical and rather linear approach to problem solving, to be highly task- and rule-oriented, and to function within a rather rigid hierarchy. Field-independent or analytical thinkers tend to be rewarded in the school context.

Field-independence tends to be more often associated with the dominant white middle class than with other groups. As a result, one often finds a majority of children from Mexican-American, African-American, Puerto Rican, and Native American backgrounds to be quite unfamiliar with the preferred learning and teaching style of the school when they first come into contact with the school environment. There appears to be a tendency that field-independent students perform better at school tasks than their field-dependent counterparts. It is incumbent on teachers, then, to develop instructional and assessment strategies that complement those that the students naturally bring with them to school.

Cooperative learning is one instructional strategy that seems promising in its ability to accommodate a variety of learning styles while significantly improving the educational achievement of individuals from traditional minority groups (see Johnson & Johnson, 1985; Slavin, 1985, 1989/1990). Characteristic of well-structured cooperative learning groups is positive goal interdependence; that is, common goals for individual as well as group success are expected. Members of the group are accountable to one another. Considerable evidence exists to suggest that cooperative learning encourages students to help one another learn how to learn; increases achievement for the majority of students; results in more positive feeling toward school; improves intergroup relations in the classroom as well as out of school; and improves student self-esteem, time on task, as well as school attendance.

## Key Factors in Successful Innovation

The analysis of schools that are successfully addressing issues of diversity suggests that there is no formula that can be widely developed and applied to any particular school setting. Successful innovation seems more likely to occur when school personnel make the effort to adapt what is known about effective schools to their own situation and when some form of partnership develops between the school and local community and businesses. And oftentimes the most successful innovations are rather small. The addition of an Italian language course in a community that has many Italians, although a small step, may serve to let others know that their concerns are recognized.

Successful innovation in schools can be looked at in terms of four dimensions.

1. Sociocultural inclusion refers to building a sense of community from within the school. This helps to remove barriers of access to knowledge, to the mainstream society and culture, as well as to one's own identity. Schools that accept and integrate various cultures, languages, and experiences throughout the school context help all students learn to negotiate life in a society characterized by diversity. Dialogue among home, school, and community helps greatly to facilitate this dimension. Understanding that people's values may differ is one thing. Providing the opportunity for people to come together to dialogue about such phenomena is another. An effective school becomes a community of dialogue around critical issues related to the education of children.

2. Curriculum inclusion and expansion suggests that people continue to

ask if a standard, universal curriculum is best for all students and teachers, just what such a standard curriculum would consist of, or if diversification might be more effective. Inclusive curricula focus on all students and integrate the contributions of many different people and groups to the history and experiences of a nation and the world.

3. Modification of pedagogy should occur so that it reflects the living hand of cultural tradition, including culturally specific learning style differences as well as the social, linguistic, and cognitive requirements of a future characterized by change and diversity. Teaching from such a perspective does not mean throwing out the knowledge and understanding necessary for success in the dominant society. Rather, it suggests that all can, as does the multilingual who can function in two (or more) languages, gain the skills necessary to function in a multicultural society.

4. Finally, methods of assessment that consider the complex interrelationships of race, class, ethnicity, religion, gender; culture, and disability in students are characteristic of effective schools. Assessment strategies that consider cultural and other differences provide students and parents with better indicators of student performance. Portfolio assessment, for instance, is proving to be an effective means of gathering a wide range of evaluative information on students (see Means, Chelemer, & Knapp, 1991; Tharp, 1989).

## Skill Applications

The application of many of the concepts from cross-cultural psychology and training to American ethnic groups is proving to be rather fruitful. The following exercise, modified from the Ethnic Literacy Test—A Cultural Perspective prepared by Shirla McClain in 1980, is an attempt to bring some of the culture-general themes to light in terms of major American ethnic groups.

Directions: Caution must be taken to avoid the creation of stereotypes when using specific examples to illustrate certain points. Such is the case here. Although fixed statements cannot be sensitive to individual differences to the complexity or the dynamic conditions of any multicultural context, the following statements have been identified, for the most part, as being true. Either individually or in groups: (1) expand on the content of the sentence, perhaps adding limits or examples that do not fit to generalizations where appropriate; (2) explain why the sentence is true; and (3) explore the possible implications of this knowledge for teaching, learning, and assessment. For what other groups do each of these findings hold true?

## Communication Differences

1. A Mexican-American child may have difficulty in reading words that begin with two consonants.
2. Non-Standard English is a language system that has rules.
3. Many Appalachians form some possessive pronouns by adding n, such as in "his'n" or "her'n".
4. Vietnamese children may experience problems in spelling words that end with a double consonant.
5. Nose wiggling and pointing with the lips are two forms of nonverbal communication used by Puerto Rican Americans.
6. African-Americans may interrupt a speaker with encouraging remarks.
7. Black English is not a synonym for black slang. Rather, it is a form of Standard English that has its own slang.
8. Vietnamese children have great difficulty learning to read polysyllabic

words.
9. Touch between teacher and student can have multiple meanings. It can facilitate learning with children of Hispanic backgrounds while alienating children from some Southeast Asian cultures.
10. For some African-Americans, as well as students of Hispanic descent, to avoid eye contact with people of authority is a sign of respect.

## Value Orientations

11. The Native-American concept of time is significantly different from that of European-Americans.
12. Mexican-American religious beliefs include the concept of fatalism.
13. Native-Americans usually prefer private rather than public recognition.
14. Mexican-American students generally prefer to work in groups rather than as individuals.
15. Appalachians have difficulty adapting well to urban life.
16. Among Native-Americans, the concept of private ownership may not exist.
17. Appalachians have strong kinship bonds.
18. African-Americans have a strong work orientation.
19. African-Americans tend to be deeply religious.

## Family-Related Roles

20. The concept of an extended family is central for many Native-Americans, Asians, and Hispanics.
21. Mexican-American families are patriarchal.
22. Family roles and responsibilities are rather fluid and flexible in the African-American family.
23. For most Native-Americans and Asians, the elderly are honored and revered.

# Field Exercises

## Sensitivity to Diversity

Planning for the needs of a diverse student population requires teachers who are sensitive to a variety of interactions as they occur in the school environment, both in terms of interpersonal interaction as well as in terms of teaching and learning. Developing the ability to make accurate judgments or attributions regarding the behavior of others is critical if one is to facilitate mutual understanding. The 18-theme culture-general framework provides the opportunity for teachers to begin to develop a vocabulary as well as concepts to help explain the cross-cultural interactions in which they are engaged.

This exercise requires participants in a training program to make extended observations in a school or classroom, paying special attention to perceived intercultural problems or issues that arise. Record your observations as precisely as possible; identify any and all of the culture-general themes that you believe apply; and final 135 propose any action that you feel will help resolve or otherwise shed light on this problem. This exercise can be accomplished under a variety of conditions. For instance, participants might conduct one observation session of an hour during their regular "workday" report back to the group, and follow up with a second observation session. Alternatively, participants can go on a "scavenger hunt," seeking evidence of these issues in schools, newspapers and magazines, television, and so forth. Again, the 18 themes include the following:
  * Anxiety
  * Disconfirmed expectations

* The need to belong
* Ambiguity
* Prejudice and ethnocentrism
* Work-related behaviors such as decision making, problem solving, and the onus of control
* Orientation in time and space
* Nonverbal behavior, including the use of time and space
* Language use and language learning
* Role-determined behavior
* Group versus individual orientation
* Rituals versus superstitions
* Social hierarchies of class and status
* Value orientation
* Categorization of information
* Differentiation
* Ingroups and outgroups
* Differences in learning styles
* Attributions formation

A simple observation form might be developed, such as the following:

| Problem as I Perceive It | Culture-General Themes | Proposed Action |
| --- | --- | --- |
| Student does not participate in class discussions. | Role-determined behavior, group vs. individual orientation, and differences in learning styles | Provide all new students an orientation on expected class behavior. Show a film demonstrating "ideal" classroom behavior. |

## Learning and Teaching Styles

The following, taken from C. Grant and C. Sleeter, *Turning on Learn-*

ing (1989), might be used as an introduction to the investigation of learning styles. Below are some items that describe criteria to investigate among individual students. You should decide how best to go about investigating these items. Once sufficient data has been collected, look for patterns based on gender and ethnic backgrounds; but as above, try not to stereotype certain groups as learning in one particular way. Once patterns in student learning styles have been determined, use them as guides for selecting teaching strategies.

Working Alone or Working Together can be investigated by asking a student her or his preference or by observing the student when there is a choice and noting which option is selected most often.

Preferred Learning Modalities refers to the sensory channels or processes the student prefers to use for acquiring new information or ideas, including observation, reading, listening, discussing, experiencing, writing, and so forth. Again, this can be investigated by giving students a choice and recording their preference; recording student success under each condition; or asking individual preference.

Content About People Versus Content About Things can be determined again by asking or by offering a choice (i.e., in story content or math story problems) and noting which is selected most often.

Structured Versus Nonstructured Environment can be observed by noting student preference for a highly structured environment compared to a more open-ended one in which the individual has greater control. Students who seem to get lost or do poorly on open-ended assignments and those who seem bored with structured assignments should be noted.

Details Versus the Whole Picture relates to the distinction between field-dependence and-independence. Student preference for, and success with, detail versus greater comfort with ideas should be noted. For instance, some students may pay great attention to grammar and punctuation when story writing but may have little to say, whereas others may produce good first drafts that are weak in mechanics.

An observation form such as the following may be useful:

## Learning Style Record Sheet

Directions: For each student, record data you collect about each item related to her or his preferred style of learning.

Student's Name

Method of Data Collection    Findings
1. Style of Working
   Alone
   With others
2. Modality
   Watching
   Reading
   Listening
   Discussing
   Touching
   Moving
   Writing
3. Content
   People

Things
4. Need for Structure
   High
   Low
5. Details vs. Generalities

**References**

Brislin, R., Cushner, K., Cherrie, C., & Yong, M. (1986) *Intercultural Interactions: A Practical Guide.* Newbury Park, CA: Sage.

Cushner, K., McClelland, A., & Safford, E. (1992) *Human Diversity in Education: An Integrative Approach.*, New York: McGraw-Hill.

Davis, B. (1972) *The Ripe Harvest: Educating Migrant Children.* Coral Gables, FL: University of Miami Press.

Grant, C. A., & Sleeter, C. E. (1989) *Turning on Learning.* Columbus, OH: Merrill.

Johnson, D., & Johnson, R. (1985) Student-student Interaction: Ignored But Powerful. *Journal of Teacher Education*, 36 (4), pp. 22-26.

McClain, S. (1980) Ethnic Literacy Test: A Cultural Perspective. Unpublished Document, Kent State University, Kent, Ohio.

Means, B., Chelmer, C., & Knapp, M. (eds.) (1991). *Teaching Advanced Skills to At-risk Students.* San Francisco: Jossey-Bass.

Shearer, A. (1984) *Disability: Whose Handicap?* Oxford, UK: Basil Blackwell.

Slavin, R. (1985) Cooperative Learning: Applying Contact Theory in Desegregated Schools. *Journal of Social Issues*, 41 (3), pp. 45-62.

Slavin, R. (1989/1990) Research on Cooperative Learning: Consensus and Controversy. *Educational Leadership*, 47 (4), pp. 52-54.

Spender, D. (1981) *Men's Studies Modified: The Impact of Feminism on the Academic Disciplines.* Oxford, UK: Pergamon Press.

Tharp, R. G. (1989) Psychocultural Variables and Constants: Effects on Teaching and Learning in Schools. *American Psychologist*, 44 (2), pp. 349-359.

Vobejda, B. (1992, April 16) More Americans Are Speaking Little English. *The Beacon Journal*, p. A8.

[From: R. W. Brislin and T. Yoshida (eds.) (1994). *Improving Intercultural Interactions. Modules for Cross-Cultural Training Programmes.* London: Sage. Pages: pp. 109-128]

## 导读：为跨文化情境准备教师

该篇文章主要是为了帮助在单一文化社会成长起来的教师决定该采取什么策略来应对由于文化差异所引起的各种问题，并提供分析和解决跨文化问题的场景练习。因为教师正面临着跨文化的严峻挑战，来自世界各地的不同民族、不同种族的学生的挑战。该篇的主要内容有：自评测试，个案研究，技能概念，教育的多样性，技能应用和场景练习。

在个案研究中作者找出了一些比较关键的事例来鼓励读者识别和讨论在多元文化情境下师生的一些经历。文中提供了在学校和课堂里的真实情境及针对这些事件的思考题。这些关键事件主要以普遍文化为中心，要求读者个人或通过群体讨论给出自己的解释和解决办法。

在世界文化多样性的今天，在教育上应该引入普遍文化框架，并让师生经历各种不同的文化以便使其在跨文化交流中更为有效。特别是在美国这样的移民国家很多人希望保留自己的文化和语言特性，避免遵循现存的模式。即使很好地掌握了英语，移民还是和主流文化有显著的差异，从而产生表现行为上的差异。现代的跨文化教育不只是简单的灌输知识，从国际角度提供跨文化教育很快成了一柄双刃剑。教师必须准备好从多种文化和语言背景来教育年轻人，同时教师自身获得的知识和技能也应成为学生学习的内容以便他们在全球化相互依赖的世界里获得良好生活的有效技能。

Brislin（1986）指出，普遍文化框架形成了许多文化问题的本质，也为理解相关文化事件提供了情境。这一框架暗示人们无论与之相互交往的人们来自多么不同的文化背景，都会遇到一些相似的经历。在一定层面上，从跨文化相互交往中理解和接受强烈的情感反应对交流的成功是至关重要的。当人们遇到他人所表现出来的意外的行为或他们自己的行为没有得到预期反应时，就要唤起他们的情绪。除了情感准备外，获得作为圈内人看问题的视角对建立各种人际间的功能关系也是至关重要的。普遍文化框架指出这些在工作风格、价值定位和角色方面的差异不仅在跨文化还在多元文化国家中的亚文化和亚群体中都是普遍存在的。这种框架可以帮助个体在面对不同反应时做好充分准备。

而归属（belonging）这一概念是指人在一定社会环境中占据某种社会地位的需要，有归属感，觉得自在并为成为自己愿望中的圈内成员而努力。他们希望通过自己的努力、观点和贡献得到认可并能融入现存的总体中去。人们通过归属某些不同的群体或关系网而寻求自己的意义、安全和社会身份。一旦被排除在外，他们便会产生一些负面的反应诸如孤独感、陌生感、丧失自尊、失去人生方向和目标。

在学习风格上，学校开始脱离原有的文化匮乏式的教育而是逐渐接受了文化差异模式。这种立场假定学生的认知方式，学习风格和动机与教师、领导以及课程设置者的期望不一致。从某种意义上来说学生的期望与技能与教师的期望之间存在文化冲突。人们不仅认识到同一圈内的学生具有各自的学习风格的偏好，在跨文化中也发现了这种差异。人们学习他们各自的文化圈的独特的学习方法。圈内社会化既教育学生思考学习的内容又包括思考和学习的方式。而这种知识正如对自己文化的认识一样是潜在的，总的说来，考虑学习风格的差异暗示着文化差异对学习方式的深远影响。研究者们认为，文化决定了他们的学习方式上的不同的倾向，由于学习方式的不同，个体常被区分为两种不同的学习者：场独立性和场依存性。此外合作学习也是有效的教育策略。它能够调节各种不同的学习方法并能使个体从少数文化圈内取得更丰硕的教育成果。

在学校处理文化多样性时并没有一定的模式，但成功的教学改革创新需要从以下四个方面来衡量：社会文化包含，课程内容和扩展，教学法的改变以及评估方法。

文章在最后还提供了一些能力应用方面的知识（交流差异，价值定位），场景练习中对教师所要求的对文化多样性的敏感和教学风格方面的一些概念。

**Questions for reflection:**

1. As a teacher, how do you cope with the multicultural context in school setting?
2. What is the importance of culture-general framework in dealing with the cultural problems?
3. What is the relationship between learning styles and intercultural contexts?

# Intercultural Education at the University Level: Teacher-Student Interaction

Neal R. Goodman

As teacher/student interaction is such an archetypal human phenomenon, and so deeply rooted in the culture of society, cross-cultural learning situations are fundamentally problematic for both parties.

Geert Hofstede (1986)

Too often even those in the field of intercultural communication are oblivious to the differing perceptions of teacher-student interactions. We may lecture about "Low versus High Power Distance" cultures, while insisting on treating our students from High Power Distance cultures as "equals." The assumption that our way of teaching is more "advanced" seems to be a hard one to discard. In this module, Goodman applies Hofstede's five concepts to the actual teaching situation. Readers are given an opportunity to assess their own preferences, orientations, and biases while being exposed to potential cross-cultural problems.

## Contents

I. Self-Assessment Exercise: Instruction Styles
II. Case Studies
III. Skill Concepts
IV. Applications
V. Additional Activities

## Self-Assessment Exercise: Instruction Styles

Instructions: Below there are 46 statements that are clustered in pairs. Circle the statement in each matched pair that you are most comfortable with. There are no wrong answers. Make your choice as spontaneously as possible. You will have 23 items circled at the end of the exercise. (Adapted from Hofstede, 1986.)

1. A positive association in society is with whatever is rooted in tradition.
2. A positive association in society is with whatever is "new."
3. Impersonal "truth" is stressed and can, in principle, be obtained from any competent person.
4. Personal "wisdom" is stressed and is transferred in the relationship

with a particular teacher (guru).

5. A teacher should respect the independence of his or her students.
6. A teacher merits the respect of his or her students.
7. One is never too old to learn; continual education.
8. The young should learn; adults cannot accept a student role.
9. Students expect to learn how to do.
10. Students expect to learn how to learn.
11. Student-centered education (value is placed on student initiative).
12. Teacher-centered education (value is placed on teacher-ordered learning).
13. Students expect teacher to initiate communication.
14. Teacher expects students to initiate communication.
15. Teacher expects students to find their own paths.
16. Students expect teacher to outline paths to follow.
17. Individual students will speak up in class in response to a general invitation by the teacher.
18. Individual students will only speak up in class when called upon personally by the teacher.
19. Individuals will speak up in large groups.
20. Individuals will only speak up in small groups.
21. Large classes are split socially into smaller cohesive subgroups based on particularist criteria (e. g. ethnic affiliation).
22. Subgroupings in class vary from one situation to the next based on universalist criteria (e. g. , the task at hand).
23. Students may speak up spontaneously in class.
24. Students speak up in class only when invited by the teacher.
25. The teacher is seldom contradicted and rarely criticized.
26. Students are allowed to contradict or criticize teacher.
27. Confrontation in learning situations can be beneficial; conflicts can be brought into the open.

28. Formal harmony in learning situations should be maintained.
29. Effectiveness of learning is related to the excellence of the teacher.
30. Effectiveness of learning is related to the amount of two-way communication in class.
31. Neither the teacher nor any student should ever be made to lose face.
32. "Face-saving" is of little importance.
33. Education is a way of improving one's economic worth and self-respect based on ability and competence.
34. Education is a way of gaining prestige in one's social environment and of joining a higher status group.
35. Outside class, teachers are treated as equals to students.
36. Respect for teachers is also shown outside of class.
37. Diploma certificates are important and displayed on walls.
38. Diploma certificates have little importance.
39. In teacher-student conflicts, parents are expected to side with the student.
40. In teacher-student conflicts, parents are expected to side with the teacher.
41. Older teachers are more respected than younger teachers.
42. Younger teachers are more liked than older teachers.
43. Acquiring competence is more important than acquiring certificates.
44. Acquiring certificates is more important than acquiring competence.
45. Teachers are expected to give preferential treatment to some students (e. g. based on ethnic affiliation or on recommendation by an influential person).
46. Teachers are expected to be strictly impartial.

## Scoring

Step 1: On the chart below, circle the numbers corresponding to the numbers circled on your inventory sheet. (For example, if you circled 1 on the inventory, circle it below in the CS category.) Total the circles in each row and place in the blank.

1   8   9   18   20   21   28   31   34   37   44   45
CS = _____
2   7   10   17   19   22   27   32   33   38   43   46
IS = _____
3   5   11   14   15   23   26   30   35   39   42
SP = _____
4   6   12   13   16   24   25   29   36   40   41
LP = _____
(CS + IS + SP + LP should equal 23)     TOTAL = _____

Step 2: Transfer your scores above to the appropriate blanks below and compute totals for Collectivism/Individualism and Power Distance.

CS (   ) – IS (   ) = _____ Collectivism/Individualism Score
SP (   ) – LP (   ) = _____ Power Distance Score

Step 3: Mark your scores below. Collectivism/Individualism is on vertical line; Power Distance is on horizontal line.

```
                High Collectivism
              (Low Individualism)
                      +12
                       +9
                       +6
                       +3
Small                                             Large
Power   +11  +9  +6  +3  0  -3  -6  -9  -11       Power
```

Distance                                              Distance
                        −3
                        −6
                        −9
                       −12
                High Individualism
                (Low Collectivism)

As faculty search for ways to internationalize their courses, they often fail to note that the very nature of how they teach and how students learn is often culture-bound. The self-assessment that you just completed will be used later to examine cross-cultural differences in student-teacher interaction. However, before we examine the self-assessment, let's turn to some illustrative cases.

## Case Studies

### Japan

Recently, a major educational joint venture was established between a prestigious U. S. business school and an equally renowned Japanese university. The purpose of the venture was to establish an American-style MBA program in Japan. Although the vast majority of students in the first year's class were Japanese, the professors and some of the students were from the U. S. school.

As the first semester neared the end, the American and Japanese students had gotten over their initial shyness and were getting along very well. The examination period was approaching and one of the first exams for the year was in finance. The professor had distributed a case that would be the basis for the exam. Each student was to prepare a comprehensive spreadsheet and provide exhibits to be attached to the exam. The students were free to use computers and outside reference books. All preparatory work was to be done individually, guided by the U. S. school's honor code that all students signed pledging their commitment to honesty and integrity in their work at school. While the American students were busy at the library and computer center, their Japanese counter-parts were nowhere to be seen.

While grading the exams, the American professor noted the near uniformity of the answers of the Japanese students. After some further investigation, he learned that nearly every Japanese student had collaborated during their preparation for the exam in clear violation of the specific instructions of the professor and in violation of the honor code they all pledged to follow.

The American professor was dismayed by the betrayal of the students. He was even more upset by the apparent lack of concern shown by the Japanese administration. The American students who quickly learned of the Japanese "conspiracy' were totally disillusioned. They realized that they could no longer trust their Japanese colleagues whom they otherwise admired for their hard work.

## Discussion Questions

How do you explain the behavior of the Japanese students? How do you explain the reaction of the Japanese administration? How should the American professor respond to this situation? How should the American students respond to the situation? A discussion of this case will be presented later in this chapter.

# Nigeria

Charles had been an honors student throughout high school and college. On the advice of his professors at a highly regarded liberal arts college in the Midwest, he decided to take his junior year abroad in Nigeria. Charles was excited about studying in an area where there were few Americans. He was hopeful that he could be integrated into the local student culture. By the fourth month at his host university, Charles was beginning to feel comfortable in his new setting. He had made some friends and he was enjoying his classes. Of all his classes Charles particularly liked a class on Nigerian literature. The professor seemed to be particularly attentive to Charles's presence because he had just returned from a visit to the United States.

One day in class the professor was giving a lecture on comedy. During the lecture the professor mentioned that he was very impressed by an American improvisational group he saw at Second City in Cleveland. Charles, noting that Second City is in Chicago not Cleveland, raised his hand and as soon as he was acknowledged he mentioned the correct location. The professor showed no appreciation for Charles's contribution and continued his lecture. At the end of the lecture the professor asked Charles to remain in the classroom. The professor told Charles that he was not to come to any further classes and that he would receive an incomplete for the course. Charles was shaken and felt that this was some sort of a trick, but the professor was very rigid and gave Charles no explanation or alternative. Finally, in desperation, Charles left the classroom feeling that his whole year was going to be ruined.

# Discussion Questions

How would you explain the professor's action? What could Charles do to remedy the situation? A discussion of this case will be presented later in this chapter.

## Korea

In his early 20s, Harold taught high school history and was an adjunct professor at a nearby community college. When he was 25, he was invited to become an instructor/trainer for a large U. S. corporation based in Chicago. As Harold entered his mid-40s, he was considered to be one of his company's most accomplished instructors.

In fact, he was recently part of a team that developed a new course called "The Qualities of a Master Trainer." Having taught the course several times, Harold had made small changes in the course to get it to the point where he was extremely proud and satisfied with it.

The corporation Harold works for recently opened a subsidiary in Korea and was trying to provide their new Korean employees with the same training opportunities as were provided to its American employees. One of the first courses to be selected for delivery in Korea was "The Qualities of a Master Instructor." This was deemed to be a critically important course because the subsidiary was going to employ a number of new trainers who would be instructing the remaining employees in many courses, including sales, stress management, quality improvement, and career planning.

In light of Harold's seniority, reputation, and experience with the course, Harold was selected to go to Korea to teach the course to the Korean trainers. Harold was indeed a master trainer, although he thought of himself more as a facilitator. His style, which he learned through many years of trial and error, was participatory. He loved to get his trainees involved in his courses. He always projected an informal and easy style in which he was more an equal of his students, not their superior.

Though this was Harold's first business trip abroad, he felt confident in teaching the course he helped to design. Harold's main concern before accepting the assignment was the English language ability of the trainers. He was relieved to learn that they all spoke English fluently.

Harold arrived in Korea on Sunday and tried to stay up to get a regular night's sleep before having to teach the course on Monday morning. When he awoke on Monday he was a bit disoriented but after his third cup of coffee he felt alert and anxious to get to the training center. In the cab on his way to the training center Harold reviewed his notes one final time. He was confident and enthusiastic about meeting his Korean colleagues.

As he entered the training room Harold was pleased to see that the materials were in place, and all the audiovisual equipment was working. He checked out the room carefully and waited the 10 minutes before his students were to arrive. The eight students all arrived together and right on time. He introduced himself and put Harold on the board in big letters so they could practice and remember his name. As he engaged in some small talk with the participants before the program, Harold was concerned that some of the students would speak in Korean to each other before responding to him. Also, some of the students spoke in very halting English. He had been told that they were all fluent in English.

Harold began the class with the usual introductions. He introduced himself, told people to address him by his first name, and told the students about his rural upbringing and his prior teaching experience and his experience with the firm. The students introduced themselves but said little about themselves, with the exception of Kim Park who had been to the United States and loved American movies. Harold proceeded with his usual icebreaker, a brief joke about the company. The joke, which generates a lot of laughter at home, did not seem to work. Harold felt that something might have been lost in the translation as he proceeded with the first part of the class.

Harold asked the class what they hoped to get out of this class on the qualities of a master trainer. The students looked back at him with no response. He then asked the participants to contribute an objective they had for the course. Again there were blank stares. Finally, one of the participants responded, saying, "We want to learn the qualities of a master trainer." That was not the type of individual objective he was looking for but at least he had a response. Harold explained that the response was fine and he then asked the participants to provide him with a list of the qualities of a good trainer. After waiting 5 minutes for the participants to generate their lists, Harold asked for volunteers to present their list of qualities. To his dismay no one raised a hand. None wanted to contribute their ideas. Finally, the same student who spoke earlier raised his hand and in a hushed voice said, "A master trainer must possess great wisdom."

Wisdom was not the response Harold was expecting. He already had a list of "good" and "bad" qualities and in all cases in the past the students could generate a list that identified each one. Harold thought the next best thing to do was to present the list to the students, so he quickly went to the board and wrote the following good and bad qualities:

## Good Instructor

A. Relates to his or her students
B. Shows great enthusiasm
C. Gets and gives feedback
D. Puts students at ease
E. Draws students into discussion
F. Humanizes him- or herself (tells jokes, etc.)
G. Shows flexibility
H. Identifies students' needs and interests
I. Is prepared and knowledgeable
J. Uses a variety of training aids
K. Is him- or herself

## Bad Instructor

A. Monopolizes classroom conversation
B. Is pompous
C. Is dictatorial
D. Speaks too fast or too slow
E. Reads materials to the students
F. Interrupts answers
G. Fakes it
H. Has distracting mannerisms

The trainees quietly wrote down everything Harold put on the board. Once he was finished writing Harold turned to the group and asked, "What items on the board do you agree or disagree with?" Again, there was no response. Exasperated, Harold announced a short break and asked the participants to come back from the break with at least one question. Harold could not generate much discussion about his course during the break. Mostly people wanted to know what he thought about Korea.

The break was over and Harold, fearing no-response again, asked the group for some questions. Again, for a painfully long time, there was silence. Finally the student who had been to the United States raised his hand. Harold excitedly asked, "Yes, what is your question?" The student responded, "Do you know when Sylvester Stallone will make his next movie?"

Harold wanted to get on the next plane to Chicago.

## Discussion Questions

What are some of the causes of Harold's frustration? What could Harold have done differently? A discussion of this case will follow later in this chapter.

## Skill Concepts

## Introduction

In any intercultural encounter, one must distinguish individual differences in personality from group or national characteristics. One of the foremost examinations of national characteristics has been conducted by Geert Hofstede (1980, 1991).

Hofstede is a Dutch social psychologist who designed a massive research study involving the local country employees of subsidiaries of International Business Machines (IBM). The research included a survey of over 116,000 employees at all levels from unskilled workers to top managers.

The research was conducted in over 50 countries and in 20 languages. All the employees worked for the same company and they were otherwise matched for characteristics such as job category, age, and gender. Based on this voluminous amount of data, Hofstede identified four dimensions of national culture that can serve as a basis for comparing the dominant value systems between national cultures.

It is important to note that Hofstede examined the relationship between nationality and mean values scores. Focusing on the relationship between nationality and mean values scores meant that the country, not the individual respondent, became the unit of analysis. Thus, the dimensions that derived from the research were ecological dimensions of collective national cultures and not dimensions of individual personality. However, it is appropriate to think of the dimensions of national culture as examples and measures of the "personality" of each culture.

## The Four Dimensions of National Culture

The Four Dimensions of National Culture that Hofstede identified were these:
1. Power Distance. The degree to which a society accepts the idea that power is to be distributed unequally. The more this is accepted, the higher the country's ranking in power distance.
2. Individualism-Collectivism. The degree to which a society feels that individuals' beliefs and actions should be independent of collective thought and action. The more this idea is accepted, the higher the rank on this measure. Individualism contrasts with collectivism, which is the belief that people should integrate their thoughts and actions with those of a group (e. g. , extended family organizations). In individualistic societies, people are more likely to pursue their own personal goals. In collective societies, people are more likely to in-

tegrate their own goals with those of group members.
3. Uncertainty Avoidance. The degree to which a society feels threatened by ambiguous situations and tries to avoid them by providing rules and refusing to tolerate deviance. The more a society accepts this idea, the higher its ranking in uncertainty avoidance.
4. Masculinity. The degree to which a society focuses on assertiveness, task achievement, and the acquisition of things as opposed to quality of life issues such as caring for others, group solidarity, and helping the less fortunate. The more assertiveness, competitiveness, and ambition are accepted, the higher a country's rank on this measure.

Hofstede found that the more a nation is characterized by masculine values, the greater is the gap between the values espoused by men and women in that nation.

## The Four Dimensions and Teacher/Student Interactions

The relevance of Hofstede's research to educational settings is "based on the assumption that role patterns and value systems in a society are carried forward from the school to the job and back" (Hofstede, 1980, p. 306).

In order to appreciate how the Four Dimensions can impact on student-teacher interactions, we will examine the extreme differences between the dimensions while recognizing that in many countries the situation may be closer to the center. However, by looking at extreme cases we can best identify situations that can create cross-cultural difficulties. For each dimension one extreme will be described, such as High Power Distance, and the opposite extreme can be extrapolated from the former (Low Power Distance).

## Power Distance

High Power Distance societies are characterized by teacher-centered education, in which the teacher transfers wisdom to students. Information flow is from the teacher to the student and students are not expected to initiate communication or speak up unless called upon to do so. In such societies, teachers are respected in and out of class and are not to be publicly contradicted. Age is respected and formal presentations are appreciated. The status of the school is also an important factor in determining the status of a person.

## Individualism-Collectivism

In societies that are strong on Collectivism, there is a strong sense of respect for tradition and the group. Individuals will find more satisfaction working with a group for a collective goal rather than working individually for their own achievement. Students are not expected to call attention to themselves by calling out answers. Thus, group work is preferred when giving assignments. Neither the teacher nor the student should be put into a situation where they might "lose face." The acquisition of diplomas and certificates (even through questionable means) is very highly prized.

## Uncertainty Avoidance

Societies that are high in Uncertainty Avoidance have learning environments characterized by structure. Both the student and the teacher prefer structured learning situations with precise objectives, detailed assignments, and adherence to a schedule set up well in advance. In such an environment, lecturing is most common and there are no interruptions or disagreements with the "all-knowing" teacher. Learning the subject as precisely as possible is more important than learning how to learn.

## Masculinity

In a society characterized as being Masculine, teachers encourage competition and openly praise the success of the "winners." Failure, however, is detrimental to success and leads to low self-esteem. In order to prove themselves, students try to make themselves visible and they choose academic subjects that have clear career paths. In highly masculine societies, there is more gender segregation in careers, so males tend to avoid feminine academic subjects.

## National Differences and Correlations Between the Dimensions

The research findings show that there is a very strong correlation between Power Distance and Individualism/Collectivism (Hofstede, 1980). Societies that are high in Power Distance also tend to be high in Collectivism. This association may be due to the fact that both Low Power Distance and High Individualism correlate with national wealth. When national wealth is controlled for, the correlation disappears.

Countries that are high on Individualism and low in Power Distance include the United States, Australia, Great Britain, The Netherlands, Canada, and New Zealand. These are joined by Denmark, Sweden, Switzerland, Germany, Ireland, Norway and Finland, with Israel and Austria both having scores less individualistic but with less Power Distance.

Countries that are relatively high in Power Distance and high in Individualism are Italy, Belgium, France, South Africa, and Spain (though the latter is less individualistic than the others). Costa Rica was the only country in the study that had low Power Distance and low Individualism.

The countries that were the highest in Power Distance and Collectivism were mostly in South America (Guatemala, Panama, Venezuela, Ecuador). These are followed by countries that were a little less collectivist or that had slightly lower Power Distance scores: Colombia, Indonesia, Pakistan, Peru, Taiwan, Singapore, El Salvador, Korea, Thailand, Chile, The West African Region, Hong Kong, Portugal, Yugoslavia, and Mexico. Malaysia and the Philippines were each very high in Power Distance but only moderately high in Collectivism.

Several countries scored moderately high in both Collectivism and Power Distance. These included Greece, Turkey, Brazil, Arab countries (Egypt, Lebanon, Libya, Kuwait, Iraq, Saudi Arabia, UAE), India, Japan, Argentina, Jamaica, and Uruguay.

Uncertainty Avoidance and Masculinity did not correlate as strongly. Listed are a sample of the countries that scored the highest in Uncertainty Avoidance: Greece, Portugal, Guatemala, Uruguay, El Salvador, Belgium, Peru, Japan, Korea, Panama, Argentina.

Weak Uncertainty Avoidance was found among the following countries (in descending order): Singapore, Jamaica, Denmark, Sweden, Hong Kong, Ireland, Great Britain, Malaysia, India, the United States, Canada, Norway, and The Netherlands.

Countries that were distinctively feminine included Sweden, Norway, Denmark, The Netherlands, Costa Rica, Finland, Yugoslavia, and Chile. Countries that were at the high end of the Masculinity scale include Japan, Austria, Venezuela, Mexico, Switzerland, Ireland, Jamaica, Germany, and Italy.

# The Fifth Dimension: Confucian Dynamism

A fifth dimension called Confucian Dynamism was developed after the first four factors (Chinese Culture Connection, 1987; Hofstede, 1991; Hofstede & Bond, 1988). This dimension was developed as part of an effort to explain the rather sudden economic growth among some Asian countries, notably Japan, South Korea, Taiwan, Hong Kong, and Singapore.

Michael Bond and a group of researchers who refer to themselves as The Chinese Culture Connection set out to examine whether there was a connection between the acceptance of Confucian teachings within a society and the degree of economic growth (Chinese Culture Connection, 1987; Hofstede, 1991; Hofstede & Bond, 1988). The research, which was carried out in 22 countries, showed that rapid economic growth was found in societies that valued and practiced certain significant Confucian values. The "dynamism" aspect of the concept comes from the findings that not all Confucian values were correlated to economic growth to the same degree. Rather, some values were emphasized while others were followed less rigorously.

Confucian values that were emphasized in the societies that experienced economic growth included the following:

a. Persistence and perseverance (if at first you don't succeed, try, try, try again)
b. Observing adherence to status relationships in which there were mutual obligation between the junior and senior members (father-son, ol-

der brother-younger brother, manager- subordinate)
c. Thrift: saving, saving, and more saving
d. Having a sense of shame

The researchers found that although the following Confucian values exist in the economically successful societies, they were de-emphasized:

e. Personal stability
f. Protecting face
g. Adherence to tradition
h. Reciprocal giving of favors and gifts

An analysis of Confucian Dynamism shows that "those countries which emphasize the dynamic aspects involving the future and the importance of hard work have experienced economic growth within recent years" (Brislin, 1993, p. 264).

The de-emphasized values can be seen as factors that could retard growth if practiced too rigidly. For example, too much adherence to tradition would subvert the need for change. Similarly too much personal stability would reduce the likelihood of taking risks necessary for entrepreneurship and business growth. However, do not be misled into thinking that these values are dismissed; they are simply not emphasized to the same degree as the others. The implications for university educators is that professors will appreciate persistent students (Value a above) who stick to their assigned tasks and who respect status relationships, as in the professor-student relationship (Value b above). Professors will also report students who experience shame (Value d) if they do not take their assignments seriously.

# Applications

## Using the Inventory

Now run to the answer sheet from the Self-Assessment Exercise in Part I and look at the scores. Survey your students/trainees to see where they scored. It is best to have students place an X on a large flip chart page or on an overhead transparency so the "norm" for the class can be determined. This can then lead to a discussion of the reason for any differences and/or similarities found in the class. Although it is not a good idea to require those outside the norm to try to provide an explanation, it would certainly be a good idea to invite people to discuss their scores. This exercise could also be done in small group discussions with each group reporting to the entire class. Members of groups can ask: How similar or different are we from our national norms, and why? (The United States, for example, would be found in the quadrant featuring High Individualism and moderately Low Power Distance.)

## Group Exercise

Arrange the students into small groups (3-5). Ask some groups to assume they are from a High Power Distance culture and going abroad to teach students in a Low Power Distance culture. Have the group come up with potential problems, in and out of class, that might be encountered (see Hofstede, 1986, for further guidance in applying these concepts). Have the group come up with possible strategies that might be adopted to avoid the potential problems in and out of class. Have the group discuss any actual similar situations like this that they know about or have experienced.

Have a second set of groups assume they are from a Low Power Distance culture and are going abroad to teach in a High Power Distance culture. Have them conduct the same exercise described above.

Assign additional groups similar tasks reversing High and Low Individualism, High and Low Uncertainty Avoidance, and High and Low Masculinity. Have each group report on the following:

a. The potential problems anticipated in and out of class
b. Strategies they adopted for behaviors in and out of class to allow them to fit in to their new environment
c. Any actual cases like this on their campus

One way to make this exercise more realistic for your students is to invite someone from the office that is responsible for international students on your campus to sit in on the class and address the issues as they relate to experiences at your school. One note of caution: First brief the person you are going to invite in order to be sure they understand what you will be doing and what you expect of them. Make sure they understand the assessment tool, the Four Dimensions of Culture, and the way they will be applied.

## Using the Case Studies

Have your students read the case studies in the second part of this chapter. Ask your students to try to explain what had happened. Next, have the students fill out the self-assessment. Deliver a brief lecture explaining Hofstede's Four Dimensions. After describing the Dimensions, have the students return to the cases and offer alternative explanations using Hofstede's research. An analysis of each of the cases using Hofstede's model is provided below.

# Discussion of Japan Case Study

American society is characterized by a strong sense of individualism. In fact, in Hofstede's research (1980), the United States scored highest in Individualism of all the countries studied. In societies high in Individualism, students are expected to work on their own initiative for their personal achievement, which will be rewarded by the society. Inducements to compete and succeed as individuals permeate the educational systems and the society. American children are taught that individual achievement, hard work, and fair play will lead to success.

In highly Collectivist societies such as Japan, group work is idealized as the preferred method to achieve success. Calling attention to oneself through individual initiative for individual rewards is not the ideal. Working within the group context, whether at home, school, or work, is rewarded and leads to success.

Although teachers are honored for their knowledge, the social order of society is preserved by learning how to be an effective group member. In such societies, it is common for students to collaborate before and sometimes during tests. A student who did not cooperate by not engaging in group preparation for exams or by not letting his or her paper be seen by others would become an outcast and could not succeed within the context of the group. The future assistance of the others would be withdrawn and the stigma of not being a team player would have dramatic consequences. There have been hundreds of recorded incidents of Americans going abroad to study and being shocked by the apparent "cheating/cooperating" found in other more Collectivist societies. Likewise, there have been many cases in which international students coming to the United States to study found themselves quickly ostracized from their American peers because they anticipated greater sharing of information during tests and exams and were labeled as cheaters when they acted on their expectations.

In the description here, the Japanese students were acting in a perfectly appropriate manner for success in Japan. Likewise, the American students were acting as Americans do. The Japanese students had no way of knowing that they had created such a serious violation of trust in the eyes of the Americans.

The American professor should have been prepared for this situation. Granted, he is part of an American institution, but he is operating in Japan and the honor code form is not going to change a custom that the students have been socialized to perform throughout their lives. The American students were outraged by the actions of their Japanese "friends." A deep sense of betrayal destroyed much of the trust that had been developed. Such deep wounds do not heal quickly, if at all.

The educational issue here was not what or whether the students learned but how they learned and how their learning was evaluated. Obviously, in this situation the underlying cultural values of the importance of group versus the importance of the individual destroyed the educational process and the promise of successful intercultural interaction.

## Discussion of Nigerian Case Study

One of the most significant differences between cultures is the degree to which the society views the distribution and display of personal power (Brislin, 1991). There are vast differences in how people are expected to demonstrate power differences in society. Hofstede's research (1986) examines how differences in Power Distance can impact on student-teacher interaction. In Low Power Distance societies, open displays of power are avoided, academic titles are sometimes exchanged for first names, and the give and take of a good intellectual debate in class between the professor and students is often seen as a very desirable outcome. In such societies, class time is often extended into after-class discussions, sometimes over coffee, soft drinks, or beer.

In High Power Distance societies such as Nigeria, there is an expectation that the professor is the expert who deserves significant deference. Academic titles are always used in public and private conversation and communication is mostly in one direction, from the professor to the student. In classroom settings, the students are expected to sit dutifully and respectfully at their desks as they take notes, which they will be expected to repeat back as close as possible to the original. In such societies, students only speak up when invited to do so by the teacher and teachers are never corrected, contradicted, or criticized in public.

The offense of public correction is in effect the public humiliation of a person deserving the utmost of respect for his privileged position. Such an act does more than cause the professor to "lose face;" it violates the shared cultural expectations regarding the distribution and use of power in the society.

In this situation, Charles had made an inexcusable mistake for which he was going to suffer. Charles's attempt to smooth things over immediately after the insulting incident was based on how he might have acted in the United States. In this case, it is entirely likely that Charles is not even aware of the offense. In such situations, it is advisable to consult with a cultural informant, someone who understands the culture and who can interpret the situation for the novice. Because Charles had already established some friendships at the school, his best tactic would be to seek the help and advice of a cultural informant who could explain the situation and provide some guidance as to how to resolve his predicament. In societies in which High Power Distance is common, it is often advisable to use a mutually respected intermediary to help resolve conflicts. In this case, if Charles barges into the administrative offices demanding "fair" treatment, his appeal will fall on deaf ears. The professor has and deserves all the power according to the norms in his country. His authority cannot be questioned. However, if Charles appeals for help from a respected intermediary, there is a good chance of ameliorating the situation.

## Discussion of Korean Case Study

The application of Hofstede's research (1986) to Harold's predicament is multifaceted. The distinction between Individualism and Collectivism is again helpful. In highly individualistic societies, students are expected to speak up in class in response to a general invitation to do so. There is a great emphasis on learning how to learn, teachers are supposed to be fair and impartial, and the need to prevent someone from losing face is weak. In this situation, Harold was approaching his students as if they were Americans. He called out for answers in a situation that might cause someone to lose face if they had a "wrong" answer. More important, Harold expected the trainees to respond as individuals rather than asking them to come up with a group response.

Hofstede's Dimension of Power Distance also helps to explain part of Harold's problem. In High Power Distance societies such as Korea, there is a strong belief in the authority and wisdom of the instructor. The focus of all teaching is from teacher to student. The teacher is there to teach and the students are there to learn. The notion that the students could somehow come up with the objectives of the program is absurd in this context. The instructor must know the objectives and be prepared to dictate these to the students. More important, the very content of the course "The Qualities of a Master Instructor" is something that the American had come thousands of miles to tell the Korean students. In the eyes of the Korean students, this instructor, who asks them to tell him what the qualities are, must be some sort of a fool. He has certainly lost credibility. When Harold finally gets around to providing the students with his "wisdom" by writing the qualities on the board, he becomes even less credible, because many of the qualities of a good instructor that he lists are clearly negative qualities in the Korean context and many of the bad qualities he lists are in fact good qualities in the Korean context.

In addition to the cultural contradictions discussed above, Harold began the class by making two additional mistakes. First, he began the class by telling everyone to call him by his first name. Although this may be the norm in the United States, where an egalitarian situation is preferred, in Korea, Harold should have started with formal titles until he developed a closer relationship with his students.

In addition, Harold followed up his introduction with a joke about the company. Again, although this may work in Chicago, where the clever ridiculing of everyone and everything may earn one some respect, it has the opposite impact in Korea. By beginning the class with a joke about the company, Harold was developing a sense of mistrust among his students. How could someone who is so disloyal to the employer in front of the class be a good teacher?

A final problem for Harold regarding Power Distance was Harold's insensitivity to the distribution of power that existed among his students. In many cases similar to Harold's, there is a senior member of the group to whom the group defers and shows respect. To Harold, all the students were equal. Achievement is based on performance and merit. In the case here, there was a senior person to whom Harold should have shown special attention and respect. However, Harold was not aware of this. Had Harold shown special attention to the senior person, Harold would have earned respect. When Harold asked the group for a response, he was slighting the senior member of the group who would otherwise perform the role of a spokesperson for the group, especially in the early stages of the relationship. By ignoring the importance of the role of power within the group, Harold had fallen through yet another hidden cross-cultural trap door.

One mistake instructors who work with international students often make is to gravitate to those students who have the best command of English. Although it may seem perfectly normal to want to communicate with those who appear to have the best ability to do so, such actions will often ignore the hidden power relationship that permeates the situation. In most cases, it is advisable to seek out the senior person, brief him or her before the program, show them proper respect, and never put them in a situation that might cause them to lose face in front of their group. Be sensitive to the fact that the second-language proficiency of the senior person may not be as good as others in the group.

Uncertainty Avoidance is a third Dimension of Hofstede's research that comes into play here. Compared to the United States, South Korea ranks very high in Uncertainty Avoidance. In the learning environment, the level of Uncertainty Avoidance can clearly shape the nature of student-teacher interactions.

In Low Uncertainty Avoidance environments, students feel comfortable in unstructured learning situations and teachers reward students for their innovative contributions to the class. In Korea, Harold's attempt to engage his students by asking them to supply the objectives for the course created a serious violation of the role he was expected to play. He was supposed to provide a structured course with clear and precise objectives. He was supposed to supply the answers, not them! Harold had created a situation full of uncertainty and ambiguity. This was not a comfortable learning environment for the students.

All organizations that attempt to take intact educational systems or prepackaged courses overseas are bound to be undermined by cultural differences. In many cases, the instructors may not even know that they have failed; in other cases, the failure will be all too obvious. In either event, there is no excuse for organizations to be so blatantly ethnocentric as to expect that what works at home will fit neatly into another corner of the world. All course materials and teaching methods are culture bound. It takes very little effort to review course content and instruction style to make courses more culturally sensitive and therefore effective. All instructors who are going to teach overseas would significantly benefit from cross-cultural training prior to going abroad. As the cases above illustrate, the cost of ignorance and insensitivity can be disastrous.

## Role Plays

An interesting way to use Hofstede's research is to have students/trainees design a role play based on the findings. For example, you could ask one of your participants to prepare a presentation on a topic and employ a style characteristic of Low Power Distance and High Individualism (similar to the United States). You could then have a group of participants play the role of students in a culture that is High Power Distance and

High Collectivism. Similarly, you could make assignments based on any set of combinations of the Dimensions, for example, teacher who is Low Power Distance, Highly Individualistic, Low Uncertainty Avoidance, and Masculine.

## Additional Activities

There are many ways to promote cross-cultural understanding in the classroom. One approach is to use a textbook published in another country. This allows students to learn the subject matter and gain an appreciation of what is important from the perspective of that country. You as the instructor can point out any differences from the standard text you use.

Another idea is to invite an international student or a visiting international scholar to your class to make a presentation on a cross-cultural topic such as differences in education, dating, family relations, and the like. It is important that you select someone who is comfortable with making such a presentation and not make someone feel obligated to do so. In the event that you have no resource people on your campus, the Council for International Exchange of Scholars (CIES), which sponsors the Senior Fulbright Program, prepares a directory of all Fulbright scholars arranged by discipline. CIES will assist in making short-term visits or lectures possible. The address for CIES is 11 Dupont Circle, Suite 300, Washington, DC 20036.

Another resource on campus is the students who have returned from studying overseas. Many of these students are very willing to share their experiences. In addition, there may be teachers or others in the community who have taught abroad.

For faculty who are conducting training programs for other faculty, you may wish to have the faculty create their own critical incidents based on their own experiences. They might then try to apply Hofstede's concepts to explain the incident.

**References**

Brislin, R. (1991) *The Art of Getting Things Done: A Practical Guide to the Use of Power.* New York: Praeger.

Brislin, R. (1993) *Understanding Culture's Influence on Behavior.* Fort Worth, TX: Harcourt, Brace, Jovanovich.

Chinese Culture Connection. (1987) Chinese Values and the Search for Culture-free Dimensions of Culture. *Journal of Cross-Cultural Psychology*, 18, pp. 143-164.

Hofstede, G. (1980) *Culture's: International Differences in Work-related Values.* Beverly Hills, CA: Sage.

Hofstede, G. (1986) Cultural Differences in Teaching and Learning, International, *Journal of Intercultural Relations*, 10, pp. 301-320.

Hofstede, G. (1991) *Cultures and Organizations: Software of the Mind.* London: McGraw-Hill.

Hofstede, G., & Bond, M. H. (1988) Confucius and Economic Growth: New Trends in Culture's Consequences. *Organizational Dynamics*, 16 (4), pp. 4-21.

[From: Brislin, R. W. and Yoshida, T. (eds.) (1994) *Improving Intercultural Interactions. Modules for Cross-Cultural Training Programmes.* London: Sage, Pages: 129-147]

## 导读：大学层次的跨文化教育：师生间的相互交流

本篇文章主要论述了由于文化差异而引起的师生交流上在跨文

化方面存在的问题。作者通过一系列的个案分析对师生间跨文化交流问题的根源进行了探索。

在理论方面作者引用了 Hofstede（1986）的观点，主要从民族文化的角度来阐述师生间交流的问题。民族文化的四个维度：权利距离，个人主义—集体主义，避免不确定性，阳刚之气。高权利距离社会的教育以教师为中心，教师受到尊敬，学生不能公然和教师对抗。集体主义强大的社会崇尚传统和集体。课堂上学生表现为不愿过多吸引注意力，师生都不愿让自己丢脸，获得文凭才是最高奖励。对不确定性的回避主要表现为师生更喜欢进行有计划、目的明确、任务详尽，按部就班地学习。对他们来说学习知识可能比学习方法更为重要。阳刚之气或男性气质突出的社会教师鼓励竞争，公开表扬获得成功的学生。学生为了提高自己，努力使自己显得突出。在事业上也是男女有别。民族文化的这四个维度之间有很强的相关性。文中还提及了民族文化的第五个维度——中国文化中的儒家的力本论。这个方面是从前四个维度发展起来的，最初源于解释亚洲一些国家的经济发展。Michael Bond 和其他研究者认为儒家的教育思想和经济的发展有一定的关系。在孔子的价值观中强调了与经济有关的几个方面：持之以恒，长幼有序，节俭，有羞耻感。

正因为民族文化的这四个方面的差异，导致了师生交流上的障碍。文中分别应用来自日本、尼日利亚、韩国等国家的实际案例来分析和讨论民族文化中四个不同维度在教育上的差异而引发的师生交流的问题。

作者在最后部分还提出了促进跨文化交流中师生的共同理解的建议性的活动。其一是利用国外的教材使学生从不同文化角度看问题；其二是邀请来自国外的学生或访问学者进行跨文化讲座；还可以请本校曾出国过的留学生与其他学生分享他们的出国经历。

**Questions for reflection:**

1. Do the self-assessment exercise and analyze Chinese national culture in education from the four dimensions.

2. Find out and discuss a representative incident of interaction between you and foreign teacher and try to solve the problem of intercultural understanding.
3. Discuss the impact of Confucianism on Chinese students.

# Human Rights and Intercultural Education

Micheline Rey

## Experiencing Human Rights in an Intercultural Context

Human rights are not just those stodgy texts gathering dust under a pile of other documents waiting to be read on your desk. They are also references in the field of individual and collective rights that are as relevant to our own social behaviour as they are to the behaviour of others in far-away places of little concern to us. They are also projects which bear the stamp of the periods when they were formulated and which demand to be critically assessed by us as well as updated, implemented and further developed.

Teachers can teach human rights, but they can also experience human rights with their pupils, in their own environment; they can experience diversity and thwart the mechanisms of domination, inequality, rejection, intolerance and denial; they can overcome the misunderstandings which differences tend to generate; and they can promote the same awareness in others.

Some feel that such concepts as 'interculturalism' and 'human rights' are irrelevant and superfluous in education. What purpose is served by interculturalism and human rights education, they ask, when all education is 'obviously' aimed at the development of all children? They forget that saying is not the same as doing and that our references are not universal. Education is threatened by individual and collective egocentrism as well as by socio- and ethnocentrism. Particular vigilance is necessary.

Accordingly, human rights education is a matter of experience and awareness (which undoubtedly stimulates thinking and knowledge) rather than a question of teaching a 'subject'. And, to my mind, an intercultural approach is essential if human rights education is to transcend ethnocentrism. It should be envisaged in terms of strategies and relationships. The strategies should be aimed at:

* challenging our egocentric certainties;
* modifying the weight attached to different skills, values and cultures, whether or not they are represented in our communities;
* transforming and diversifying balances of power and offering a position of equality to those who have been devalued as well as to their skills and modes of expression;
* fostering desegregation and the recognition of the complexity of relations existing not only between human beings but also between cultures, social classes, institutions, education systems, academic subjects, scientific objects and so on;
* and, finally, developing communication between individuals, groups and communities and ensuring that it is positive and enriching for all concerned.

That was how interculturalism was construed when, upon completing its work, the group of experts set up by the Council of Europe's Council for Cultural Cooperation to study the training of teachers responsible for educating migrants' children stated in its conclusions that the intercultural approach encapsulated the Council of Europe's whole action:

The intercultural approach is recognized not only as worthy of inclusion in the Council of Europe's cultural priorities, but also as a means of recapitulating its whole activity, in the double sense which can be given to this term. On the one hand, the intercultural approach defines and sums up the nature of the efforts made by the Council of Europe since its creation in developing human rights, promoting international understanding and establishing the European Cultural Convention. On the other hand, it constitutes a point of reference, a method and a stimulating theoretical framework for carrying out all its programmes and activities. (Rey, 1986, pp. 7, 8)

Since then the term 'interculturalism' has become more widespread and been the subject of much controversy. I should, however, like to demonstrate that, when all is said and done, an intercultural approach, which covers the social field in its entirety, is essential if human rights education is to go beyond the latent egocentrism, sociocentrism and ethnocentrism which distort our view of the world.

I shall attempt to do this in three different ways: first, by presenting an historical outline of the context in which the intercultural concept developed in the Council of Europe and of the Council's activities in the matter, then by making some terminological remarks, and, finally, by giving some examples of the methods that can be used in human rights education.

# The Migration Phenomenon and the Development of the Intercultural Approach in the Council of Europe

## From Education of Migrants to Human Rights Education

I shall use the term 'migrants' in a generic sense, even though other terms might be more accurate in certain cases, such as 'emigrants', 'immigrants' and 'cultural, linguistic, ethnic or religious groups or minorities', for the choice of words depends on the historical context and the scientific references used.

The intercultural approach in the Council of Europe was first developed in connection with the migration problem, as part of the Council's work on the integration of migrant workers into the industrialized countries of Western Europe. Although it cannot be limited to such a context, the context is nonetheless significant. For one thing, it underlines the attention paid to relationships of domination and to those who are left out of the process of development in the industrialized countries and, secondly, it points the way towards the recognition of others regardless of national, economic, social, ethnic and religious barriers.

What is more, the attitudes of industrialized countries towards migrants, asylum-seekers and refugees is illustrative of their relations with 'others' and of the place they reserve for those who are different. And the attitudes of schools are indicative of the attitudes and choices of the community both in its present circumstances and in its projects for the future. The fluctuations and changes which have occurred over the last 20 years thus reflect how our schools and communities viewed and continue to view human relations and human rights in terms of realities, hopes and disillusions.

Of course, this outline of developments in perceptions of migratory movements and the education of migrant groups and the indigenous population in a migration context will not be an exhaustive one. The choice of aspects covered will be subjective, and particular attention will be paid to the educational field, which is what concerns us here, and to activities in which I myself have taken part, partly because they are what I know best and I am therefore better placed to identify their effects, and partly because this participation illustrates a genuine form of interaction which is common in the Council of Europe and essential in the promotion of social action at international level, namely the network of collaboration between local and national field-workers and the staff of the institutions concerned. But what I am most concerned with and would urge the reader to observe are the changes of outlook brought about by the intercultural approach, in terms of the recognition of others as partners, the joint study of our society's problems, and the sharing of its assets.

These changes of outlook are also to be found in the sphere of human rights. First of all: marginalization of the problem, Manichaeism, attitude of superiority, egocentricity and ethnocentrism ( 'Violations of human rights occur elsewhere, not in our countries'), and shifting of responsibility on to others. Then: thanks to human rights education, a gradual awakening to cultural interactions and to the need to learn intercultural communication, a common questioning which postulates the existence of universal, worldwide responsibility and considers humanity in its diversity and human rights in their spacial and temporal framework ( 'There is room for improvement in human relations and human rights both here and elsewhere. However, such improvement is not a matter of course; it requires time, a particular form of social behaviour and education in solidarity.').

## Some Salient Aspects of the Activities of the Council of Europe and the Council for Cultural Co-operation with Regard to the Education of Migrants and Intercultural Relations

As early as 1965 the Council of Europe concerned itself with the situation of migrant workers. At that time of economic expansion, the industrialized countries of Western Europe were importing manpower on an ostensibly temporary basis to make up for the shortage of local workers. They were little inclined to consider the problems of social integration, family reunification and training. The work of the CAHRS (Special Representative's Advisory Committee for National Refugees and Overpopulation) led to several resolutions being adopted.

1970: Adoption of Resolution (70) 35 (of the Committee of Ministers of the Council of Europe) school education for the children of migrant workers, recommending that member states guarantee the exercise of the right to school education for children of migrant workers and take all necessary steps for their integration (information, assistance with enrolment, academic and medical reports, special classes or lessons whenever appropriate but only for as long as is strictly necessary, supervised study periods, access to pre-school education and leisure activities, participation by parents in the life of the school, teaching of the language and culture of origin, training of teachers, co-operation between immigration and emigration countries, recognition of qualifications and diplomas, courses in the host country for teachers from the country of origin and vice versa, educational reintegration in the event of a return to the country of origin, etc.).

1972: Running of experimental special classes to encourage the implementation of Resolution (70) 35.

Having personally been responsible, in 1974-1975 and 1975-1976, for some of the Council of Europe's experimental classes in Geneva, where reception classes had existed in secondary education since 1968, I was asked in 1978 to assess the methods used to organize and implement the programme of experimental classes (Rey, 1979). Following the proposals put forward in my own report and in subsequent reports (Perotti, 1982; Karagiorges, 1984), the programme was extended and transformed in 1986 into a programme of experiments in intercultural education, conducted both in countries of origin and in host countries under the supervision of a joint group of experts of the CDCC (Council for Cultural Cooperation) and the CDMG (European Committee on Migration, which had replaced the CAHRS).

1973 and 1974: The CDCC took over responsibility for the matter and organized meetings of experts to examine the problems of specialized training for teachers responsible for teaching the children of migrant workers. I took this opportunity to stress the importance of training for all teachers and all educational staff (advisers, etc.) in primary and secondary schooling, not only for those teaching in 'special' classes of migrant children.

1974: Ad hoc conference on the education of migrants.

1977-1983: The CDCC set up a working group to develop its action concerning the training of teachers responsible for teaching the children of migrants. After being appointed to chair the group, I invited its members to adopt an intercultural approach (an expression borrowed from a report on an experiment conducted by the IRFED in Fontenay-sous-Bois in 1975, where exchanges had taken place between migrants and local people on a reciprocal footing). It was on the basis of this programme that the intercultural approach was developed and conceptualized in the Council of Europe (Porcher, 1979; Rey, 1986), while numerous consciousness- raising measures were carried out: reports on the sociocultural situation of migrants and minority groups such as gypsies and nomads, survey of intercultural education schemes, bilateral and multilateral teacher-training seminars and detailed investigation of certain fields (the situation of Muslim children, the education of gypsy children, collaboration with the media, etc.).

Looking back over the ground covered so far, we can see that for a long time in Europe the integration of families of migrant workers into their host countries or upon their return home was not considered a priority concern and that their rights as human beings were not always recognized. Those who did show concern for them (individuals or institutions) were themselves in danger of being ostracized. In view of the magnitude of the educational problems facing not just migrant children but also the children of workers belonging to the disadvantaged social strata, the term handicap was used to describe the difficulties experienced by them (either linguistic or social handicaps). On that basis, various compensatory educational measures were introduced. This approach went hand in hand with a policy of assimilation or integration (for those able to stay on in the host country) requiring one-way adaptation of the migrants to the local community and its standards. These measures came in for considerable criticism: not only did the compensatory education prove inappropriate, increasing the workload without solving the problem, but also the very notion of handicap was misleading, for it implied that responsibility for the difficulties lay with the victims, whereas the causes were in fact external.

Then there was talk of denial, in the form of non-recognition of the skills, references, values, modes of expression needs and sociocultural rights of the populations concerned. Awareness of this denial led to a reverse trend: the host community and schools were asked to adapt to the migrants. It was important to recognize their needs, languages and cultures. But this reaction was also criticized. The highlighting of cultural differences entailed a risk of caricatural folklorization as well as stigmatization and ostracizing of the individuals or groups concerned. It was also pointed out that schools, having long been instruments of conservation and unification, could not suddenly become factors for openness and diversity. And finally it was considered misleading to talk about culture when the causes of the difficulties were social ones. Wherever schools were still grappling with the problem of educating for newly arrived immigrant children with numerous adaptational difficulties (as in Switzerland, for example), this approach was felt to be a luxury rather than an urgent necessity.

The truth of the matter is more complex than is suggested by these two trends in favour of one-way adaptation on the part of the migrants or the host community. It was therefore important not to reject either but to attempt to perceive the links between the different factors involved and combine them in a dialectical approach. The intercultural approach stressed the fundamental importance of interactions and the need to appraise them more fully and act accordingly. Let us not forget (Bordieu, 1977) that people's behaviour with regard to society, education, learning, etc. is influenced by the practical benefit they hope to derive from their linguistic, social or cultural activity. That is the basis on which their personality is forged (confident, hesitant, shy, passive, aggressive, etc.). The recognition- and schools have an important part to play in this respect of migrants' status as human beings and social beings in the first instance, then of their languages, values, cultural references and forms of expression, not forgetting their right to choose their own means of identification, was seen to be an essential condition for breaking out of the vicious circle generating the real difficulties which are perceived as internal ones (handicaps), but whose causes actually lie mainly in social balances of power and in the hierarchization of values. The accent should therefore be placed on mutual respect and interrelations at all levels and between all individuals and groups making up the educational, local and international community.

1984: Recommendation (84) 18 of the Committee of Ministers to member states on the training of teachers in education for intercultural understanding, notably in a context of migration.

1985: Recommendation (84) 9 of the Committee of Ministers to member states on second-generation migrants.

1980-1984: In view of the interest expressed by many member states in the continuation of work on the education of migrants, the Council of Europe set up a broader project with the help of experts from many member states, under the chairmanship of L. Porcher, encompassing the whole educational and cultural field in countries of origin and host countries. The project was known as CDCC Project 7 on the education and cultural development of migrants. It was concerned first and foremost with the integration of second-generation migrants. In order to relate theory to practice, the group of experts made analyses of significant educational and/or cultural experiments in the form of case studies or visits, and prompted various activities in host countries and countries of origin. To elucidate the more difficult aspects, the group conducted studies and held hearings of experts (for example, on the concept of immigrant culture, the effects of migration on the role of women, the economic and political dimensions of migration, sociocultural innovation and the role of associations in member states).

From the conceptual viewpoint, Project 7 confirmed the fundamentally dialectical and dynamic intercultural approach and laid stress on the relations underpinning our societies. Migratory phenomena are made up of the functional interlocking of differences and similarities (Porcher, 1984). Both amongst migrants and between migrants and local citizens the differences are numerous (diversity of ethnic, national or cultural groups, social classes, ages, languages, lifestyles, statuses, needs, etc.), but so are the similarities (living in the same place at the same time, being dependent on the same socioeconomic structures, belonging to the same human species having the same rights, aspiring to the same right of expression, etc.). To understand the reality of the situation is to understand the interactions between these two dimensions.

The reality of the situation is that immigrants have become an integral part of the community. In other words, European societies have become multicultural. They can no longer be defined as consisting of local citizens on the one hand and immigrants on the other. The question of identity arises to the same degree for all. The fact is that values are diverse, identities are multidimensional, affiliations plural and differences shared. Networks of communication and participation need to be developed which both preserve plurality and ensure social cohesion and justice (Porcher et al. 1986; Rey, 1987).

At the end of Project 7 the CDCC handed over the baton to individual member states, leaving it to them to continue on a larger scale what it itself initiated by way of pilot schemes. It did, however, co-operate by cofinancing many activities: conferences, workshops, magazines and competitions designed to develop intercultural education and communication.

The concept of responsibility towards migrants and the intercultural approach were also included in other CDCC projects (modern languages, primary education, etc. ), or taken up, as appropriate, by other sectors of the Council of Europe. The following examples are just three of many:

1983: a symposium on the human rights of foreigners in Europe;
1987: the Parliamentary Assembly's European Days on the theme 'Enjoying our diversity';
The CDMG's current project on intercommunity relations.

Other international organizations, both governmental and non-governmental, also took up the intercultural approach and continued the investigation, not only in the educational field, e. g. UNESCO, the Commission of the European Communities, the World Organization for Early Childhood Education, the Association for Teacher Education in Europe and the International Association for Intercultural Education, but also in the social field in general, at local, national and international level.

While the predominant trend at the end of Project 7 was towards the integration of second-generation migrants and of ethnic and cultural minorities of migrant origin, other responsibilities were emerging and new challenges looming up (Widgren, 1987) in connection, for example, with:

* clandestine migration, which is basically due to the economic imbalance between emigration and immigration countries and which calls for a worldwide effort of North-South co-operation;
* the civic rights of foreigners;
* the combating of xenophobic and racist tendencies;
* the reception of asylum-seekers.

Migratory movements may be changing in nature, but they are still continuing and indeed increasing. The interactions and responsibilities involved have taken on worldwide proportions. Respect for human rights, equality of educational opportunity, social recognition and intercultural communication in the local and international community are all interdependent.

## A Word about Terminology

Regardless of the context in which it is used, the word 'intercultural', precisely because it contains the prefix 'inter', necessarily implies: interaction, exchange, desegregation, reciprocity, interdependence and solidarity. As it also contains the term 'culture', it further denotes in its fullest sense: recognition of the values, lifestyles and symbolic conceptions to which human beings, both as individuals and in groups, refer in their dealings with others and in their vision of the world, as well as recognition of the interactions occurring both between the multiple registers of one and the same culture and between the various cultures, in space and in time.

The intercultural approach has two dimensions:
* Firstly, in terms of facts (objective, descriptive and scientific dimension), the approach means recognizing the dynamics which were set in motion by migratory movements and all forms of contact between individuals, social groups and peoples; as well as recognizing the reality of the interactions which shape and transform our communities and trying to describe how they operate, for dialectics; interaction and intercultural dynamics appear to give a better picture of reality than mere juxtaposition.
* Secondly, in terms of a project (political and educational dimension), the approach means making sure that these interactions contribute to mutual respect and the formation of cohesive commu-

nities rather than accentuating relations of domination and attitudes of exclusion and rejection.

English-speaking countries have often preferred other terms, such as 'multicultural' or 'antiracist', to describe their approach. The intercultural approach does not preclude this, but it goes an important step further by challenging segregation, exclusion and egocentrism. Its strength lies in the fact that, even in the choice of terms, it explicitly affirms the essential role of interactions and of our responsibility towards them in everything concerning human beings and their rights.

And how does intercultural education fit in? It fits in fairly easily, for it is neither more nor less than an acknowledgement of this multiple reality and its interactions applied to a particular environment (schools and educational establishments in general) which uses its own resources (those of intercultural teaching) in a context of mutual comprehension, respect and enrichment.

## Intercultural Education and Human Rights Education: Methodological Approaches and Lines of Action

### A Word about Methodology

It should be made clear first of all that intercultural education is not only aimed at migrants, minority groups or 'others' in general. It is aimed to the same extent and at the same time at 'ourselves', whoever we may be. This is a fundamental principle which, for all of us, underlines any educational activity-from infant schooling to vocational training, university studies and adult education. But it is not an end in itself. It is but a means of better achieving the more general objectives of democratization of education, equality of opportunity, promotion of human rights and learning of solidarity.

It should also be clearly understood that intercultural education does not mean substituting new concerns for the tasks which schools and educational institutions already perform, or adding an extra subject to the curriculum.

But there can be no respect for or promotion of human rights without a reappraisal of the egocentric relations and socio- and ethnocentric standards prevalent in schools, i. e. without a re-examination of schools' criteria.

Of course, nobody perceives the world, life, reality or nature itself in a completely objective, universal manner. We view life through the prisms and systems formed by our culture and social background and inculcated in us by our education. Reality may be said to be a sort of chaos which human beings view through the lenses of their cultures and social experiences, organize by passing it through their filters and manage according to their systems of codes (all these metaphors being suitable for use by educators to help their students to understand diversity). In our multicultural communities it is important to be aware of this. We also know that it is beneficial for the cognitive and relational development of the child to bring him or her into contact with several languages (the 'stereo linguistic' approach). Similarly, he or she can benefit from coming into contact with various cultures and social environments which differ from his or her own. In this way schools can help children to discover and accept diversity, thus enabling them to overcome cultural barriers and misunderstandings and acquire a communication basis which is not distorted by a lack of suitable references for interpreting the behaviour of others.

Every aspect of school life and its relationship with families and the community lends itself, to an intercultural approach and an enquiry into respect for human rights, whether it be the cost of education, the way in which children are selected and classified, the design of school premises, the teaching methods advocated, the training of staff (and of which categories of staff? —Either teachers alone or everybody involved in the educational process, such as psychologists and social workers, librarians, secretaries, caretakers, teacher trainers and health personnel?) or the organization of curricula and timetables. In the same way, all school subjects may provide vehicles and opportunities for (intra-or interdisciplinary) intercultural activities.

However, just as the intercultural dimension is not an end in itself but a means to an end, so intercultural activities are merely tools-necessary ones, it is true, but not sufficient in themselves. As instruments of intercultural teaching, they raise a twofold problem: how to put the guidelines into practice ( 'What can we do?' ) and how to assess the results ( 'What purpose does it serve?' ). In other words, teaching materials and intercultural activities considered as objects are merely residual factors. What really counts is the quality of the relationships they help to develop. They should therefore be designed in terms of strategies and dynamics. What should be assessed, then, is not the intrinsic quality of these media (when the wise man points at the moon, the fool looks at his finger), but rather the efficacy of these strategies— their positive effects, as well as the attendant traps and pitfalls. We must gauge the risks involved and weigh up the probability of failures or adverse side-effects in relation to possible alternative courses of action, so that the risks can be controlled. But this is no easy matter, for such an assessment can only be made in context and over a period of time, taking all the groups concerned into consideration (students, parents, teachers, social community, migrants, indigenous population, etc.), and bearing in mind the multiple nature of these effects (on learning, identities and relationships in schools and in the community).

## Suggestions for Intercultural Activities

How can intercultural activities be discussed out of context when their very purpose is to materialize the intercultural dimension and bring it to life in everyday communication and encourage a committed process of thinking?

The interests and professional activities of readers of this volume will cover various sectors of the educational field; their teaching responsibilities will apply to students of all ages in a variety of institutional structures and in countries whose political systems, laws and terminologies differ, where the range of cultures in contact as well as the history and forms of such contacts differ... How can everybody's expectations be fulfilled in practice? It is impossible to allow for every possible situation or give an account of all the many projects carried out in Europe, particularly with the help of the Council of Europe. I shall therefore merely suggest one or two lines of action that can be followed with students or partners of different ages and statuses, illustrating them with examples from the professional, social, political and linguistic context in which I work. The reader is requested to forgive this ethnocentrism and make the necessary transpositions—and intercultural exercise in itself!

### Line I: Education Experienced 'in Stereo'

From early infancy a stereocultural approach to education is beneficial. Sensory and motor development, expression and communication and relations with the environment are amongst the primary aims of infant education. They can give children an opportunity to discover the diversity of tastes, forms of expression, languages, social organization, lifestyles, rules of behaviour and relationships to life, time, animals and objects, the real and the imaginary, as well as learn to respect the freedom of others. Here are a few ideas:

* Filters, lenses and codes can form the basis of many practical activities designed to stress diversity: drawing what one sees through one's spectacles, inventing communication codes. See, for example, Munter (1973) and UNICEF-UNESCO (1986).
* Rhythms, music, musical instruments and dances of various origins and their transition from one culture to another.
* Nursery rhymes and children's songs in several languages. See, for example, Husler (1987).
* Observing how names vary from one region to another and from one environment to another and how great is the emotional charge they carry.
* Drawing the tree of life, or other subjects calculated to arouse intercultural awareness. See, for example, Berefels et al. (1978).
* Kamishibai theatre.
* Fairy tales and short stories.
* Books, selected and used in accordance with the educational approach adopted.

See, for example, Spier (1981) and Ducamp (1983).

* Inviting teachers and children from other local kindergartens or schools (where a different language is spoken or a different religion practised, for example).
* Inviting parents and preparing for the occasion.
* Meals with dishes from different cultural traditions (educating the senses of smell, colour and taste; the importance of meals and

their preparation in family and social life).
* Festivities, including family celebrations of different geographical or religious origins; if Christmas is celebrated, for example, the act of giving presents and the customs and rituals connected therewith can be studied.
* Pen-friend correspondence, which is possible even for young children through the use of cassettes, photographs, drawings, etc.
* Visits to places of culture (markets, museums, churches, mosques, pagodas, etc.) and participation, according to age, in local events (exhibitions, puppet theatres, films, artistic activities) which offer varying views of the world.

**Line Ⅱ: Intercultural Books, Libraries and Workshops**

The space which school and public libraries allocate to books and audio-visual documents in the languages of the different cultural groups represented in the community, and their selection of documents relating to different cultures and regions of the world, are indicative of the way in which our schools and institutions view community relations. The arguments put forward in defence of egocentric attitudes are often dubious from the human rights point of view: 'Immigrants don't read anyway', 'They ought to become integrated and learn the local language', 'There is not enough room on the shelves', 'Only the local prison ever asks us for books in that language', 'How can we possibly classify books written in alphabets we do not understand?', and so on. What is to be inferred from such answers?

The provision of libraries with a wealth of documentary material representing different cultures and the organization of intercultural activities based on books can prove highly fruitful, particularly in primary education, as well as initiate a change in public opinion.

In the canton of Geneva, 140 nationalities are represented in the schools and more than one-third of all pupils have a mother tongue other than French. All the children from one of the canton's schools take part once a week during school hours in activities run at the intercultural workshop. The activities are based on the reading of a children's book (documentary, short story or fairy tale). The activity inspired by a particular book may take the form of the staging of a play, the making of an object or the learning of a dance, song or some words in a foreign language, often with the collaboration of language teachers or parents from the countries concerned. Other possible activities are a critical study, a research project, a survey, an exhibition, an exchange of documents with schools in other countries or a comparative investigation into living conditions in different places (e.g. the work children do, the games they play, the languages they speak and the occasions they celebrate). Children from every origin and every social background are encouraged to participate. Those of foreign origin feel recognized and show great enthusiasm; little by little, they pluck up the courage to speak about their countries and borrow books in their mother tongues. They gradually learn to share what they know and be tolerant towards others. On the basis of this experience, the workshop leader recently compiled a set of teaching sheets suggesting various activities: reading, writing, oral activities, vocabulary, geography, drawing, music and games (Zurbriggen, 1989).

During holidays, 'street libraries' visit multicultural working-class districts and organize activities based on books, which can be another means of democratizing reading and a source of fruitful cultural exchanges.

Books are undoubtedly an important element in the educational process, but not all texts lend themselves equally well to intercultural use. It is important in teacher training to consider how books should be selected and used. This was done in Geneva, for example, at an intercultural teaching seminar based on a display of 200 books selected by the Bern Declaration (Abdallah-Pretceille, 1984; 'Dis-moi comment ils vivent', 1983).

## Line III: The Intercultural Dimension and Human Rights Education through School Subjects in Secondary Education

All school subjects, be they modern languages, geography, history, civics, science, religious studies, ethics or whatever, can serve as a basis for intercultural practices and thinking, providing an education in human rights without necessarily requiring a departure from the set curriculum (indeed, teachers often have more room for manoeuvre than they realize).

I shall limit myself here to one or two examples.

Language teaching can open doors to other worlds besides the mother-tongue environment. It can provide an opportunity, for example, to discover how phonological 'filters', relations between written and oral codes, links with spelling and morphological and syntactical systems vary from one language to another, how words migrate in various forms from one language to another, and how the rules governing conversation and social intercourse differ from one language or culture to another. Students can also be encouraged to consider the role of their mother tongue as a vehicle of their identity and take an interest in the choice of languages taught at school as well as in linguistic rights (Rey, 1985).

The teaching of languages, including the mother tongue, gives an opportunity to study different cultures and literature. It is often forgotten, for example, that literature in French does not come only from France, Belgium, Switzerland and Canada, but also from the Maghreb countries and the French-speaking countries of Africa.

Supervised reading and literary analysis: although it is stated in curricula that teachers should study texts with their students, the choice of texts is sometimes left to the teachers. So why not choose texts that will make the students think about intercultural communication and human rights? The secondary education orientation cycle in Geneva is in the process of publishing some methodological sheets and packs on intercultural teaching compiled by a number of teachers. Among other things, they contain suggestions concerning Marie Feraud's novel Anne ici, Selima la-bas (ed. Ducolot) and Montesquieu's 30th Persian Letter (Nouveaux Classiques Larousse).

History and geography can provide an opportunity to study migratory movements and the migration of foodstuffs. Gastronomy and exchanges of recipes can be a basis for studying the relationships between climate, agriculture, stock-breeding, fishing, local produce and food (meat, fish, cereals, spices, etc.) in different countries. Preparing meals consisting of traditional dishes from one region or another— an activity often suggested in connection with intercultural education, but which can also be a mere caricature unless it is incorporated into everyday life at school and is not dependent on the unreciprocated goodwill of migrants or minority groups—can be another source of learning and sharing rather than a confirmation of personal prejudices or a mere pandering to a taste for exoticism.

What idea of life in our countries, of international relations and of respect for human rights shall we offer through a study of history, and what civic education shall we provide?

The age of the 'Great Discoveries' is not, of course, viewed by the Swiss in the same way as by the Portuguese. This could offer a pretext for contacts and joint projects with teachers and pupils in classes studying the Portuguese language and culture. And what do non-Europeans think about this?

When students study the history of democratic Athens in the fifth century BC and learn to their surprise that people of mixed parentage did not vote, are they encouraged to think about voting rights and suffrage in our present-day countries, which also have foreigners and second-class citizens?

The bicentenary of the French Revolution and the Declaration of the Rights of Man and the Citizen was a fine opportunity to stimulate thinking about citizenship and the rights of non-citizens and foreigners. What are the disadvantages of non-citizenship and of being a foreigner? At its sitting on 15, March 1989 the European Parliament approved a proposed directive on the voting rights of member states' nationals in municipal elections in the member state of residence. But what rights do immigrants from non-member states enjoy?

There is no doubt that the non-citizens with the fewest rights of all in their country of residence are the increasingly numerous clandestine immigrants as well as seasonal workers. But they too are human beings, and what rights do they enjoy in each of our countries? The question of a right to schooling for clandestine children who cannot always be enrolled at state schools was, for example, recently raised by teachers in Geneva with the support of schoolchildren and members of the local community. Solutions are in preparation. This example illustrates the dynamic dimension of human rights education and the influence that the educational environment can have on the local community (Perregaux and Togni, 1989).

## Line IV: Training of Teachers and Other Categories of Educational Staff

Teacher training should provide:
* conceptual tools (in this case, for the intercultural approach and for human rights and the promotion thereof) that will enable them to cope properly with the situation at local and international level and interpret instances of diversity in an appropriate manner;
* a knowledge of the relevant facts and documents as well as of the interactions between the populations involved, so that teachers may overcome their prejudices and one-sided attitudes;
* a subjective and relational experience that will make teachers aware of the complexity of the feelings and relationships involved in human and intercultural contacts as well as of the potential for mutual enrichment which can be tapped;
* methodological tools that will equip teachers to apply the intercultural approach to their own teaching;
* suitable teaching aids.

One idea seemed to me particularly useful as a means of combining knowledge (of the migration phenomenon) and experience (of the complexity of the resultant relations), i. e. work based on the family trees of the trainees. In Switzerland, as elsewhere, almost every family can show examples of migration and experiences of rejection and curtailment of human rights—but also, when positive relations develop, of mutual enrichment. Realizing that they are personally affected by these matters modifies the trainees' outlook and their attitudes towards others (Rey, unpublished).

## Line V: Transverse Strategies and Setting up of Networks of Intercultural Thinking, Action and Training

One swallow does not make a summer. One intercultural activity does not make an intercultural education; and one discussion on human rights does not make a human rights education. It is important to organize networks of projects that combine various forms of intercultural practice in schools, training of teachers and educators, co-operation between the various levels of the education system, the sensitization of public opinion, the development of a sense of responsibility on the part of education authorities, and so on. The co-ordination of local, national and international activities is also of prime importance, since each of these dimensions can make an invaluable contribution to the others. A knowledge of local problems provides international organizations with the foundation they need, while the wide range of information and research they themselves provide, the recommendations made by them (often as a result of such co-operation) and subsequently disseminated by the media, and the symbolic or financial support they give to various activities constitute an appreciable form of backing for those working in the field, whose efforts are thus lent a certain status and sometimes given a wider impact.

Many things can be done to help to set up such a network. I shall give just one example to illustrate the links we are trying to develop in Switzerland in order to establish a network that will promote the intercultural approach in education. Some of the salient events were as follows:

1. For a year, with the participation of teachers, educational activities were conducted and methodological documents drawn up at local le-

vel; training sessions were then held to enable the teachers who had contributed to these activities to report on their work (this deadline was in itself a stimulus) and pursue their thinking further. The results were then published.
2. A nationwide competition was held, involving descriptions of practical intercultural education activities and projects and prompting contributions from a large number of teachers (including several of those who took part in the previous activity).
3. All those who had submitted projects were invited to discuss the matter in greater depth at a Council of Europe seminar whose proceedings were published (Cesari, et al. 1985).
4. Thanks to the setting up of an intercultural team at national level, the joint committee of the Centro Pedagogico Didattico of the Italian embassy in Bern was able, with the help of education authorities, representatives of emigration countries and the Council of Europe, to publish a magazine entitled: Inter-Dialogos; Idies expdriences, nouvelles pour l'education interculturelle en Suisse.

And so the list goes on. Numerous links have thus been established which are helping to stimulate the thinking of all concerned in their everyday work.

These suggested lines of action are by no means exhaustive. They are just some examples which may be used by others who are working in the same direction, for the march towards education in solidarity and human rights goes on.

**References**

Abdallah-Pretceille, M. (1984) Le livre dans une perspective interculturelle, comment le choisir, comment l'utiliser? in Rey, M. (ed.)

*Une pedagogie interculturelle*: *Actes des journees de formation d'enseignants des 8-10 mai 1984 a Geneve*, Swiss National Committee for UNESCO, Bern, pp. 90-94.

Berefels, G., Lindstrom, S. and Wik-Thorsell, A. L. (1978) *L'arbre de vie*: *Le monde raconte par les enfants*, Radda, Barnen, Sweden.

'Dis-moi comment ils vivent' (1983) *Vers un Developpement Solidaire*, No. 69 November.

Ducamp, J. L. (1983) Les droits de l'homme racontes aux enfants, *Les editions ouvrieres et le Temps apprivoise*, Paris.

Husler, S. (1987) Trois Tristes Tigres. ... Drei Traurige Tiger... Zauberspriiche, Geschichten, Verse, Lieder und Spiele fiir die mehrsprachige Kinder- (Garten) Gruppe, Freiburg im Breisgau, Lambertus.

Karagiorges, A. (1984) Evaluation of the Educational Aspects of the Council of Europe's Experimental Classes for the Academic Years 1981-1982 and 1982-1983, Council of Europe, Strasbourg.

Munter, A. (1973) II mondo negli occhiali, Emme Edizioni. Perotti, A. (1982) *Pedagogical Assessment of the Council of Europe's Experimental Classes from 1978-1979 to 1980-1981*, Council of Europe, Strasbourg.

Porcher, L. (1981) *The Education of the Children of Migrant Workers in Europe*: *Interculturalism and Teacher Training*, Council of Europe, Strasbourg.

Porcher, L. (1984) Education and Cultural Development of Migrants, *Interim Report of the Project Group to the CDCC*, Council of Europe, Strasbourg.

Porcher, L. et al. (1986) DECS/EGT (86) II, Council of Europe, Strasbourg. Contains a List of Documents Published in Connection with the Project.

Rey, M. (1979) CAHRS (72) (79) rev.: Assessment of the Method for Organizing and Running the Experimental Classes of the Council of Europe, Council of Europe, Strasbourg.

Rey, M. (1984) DECS/EGT (84) 84 (Brochure) du 21.9.1984: Education of Migrant Workers' Children — 'The Training of Teachers', Final Report of the Working Group, Council of Europe, Strasbourg.

Rey, M. (1985) Des Cribles Phonologiques Aux Cribles Culturels: Vers Une Communication Interculturelle, *Bulletin Gila*, University of Neuchatel, pp. 44-84.

Rey, M. (1986) Training Teachers in Intercultural Education? The Work of the CDCC (1977-1983), Council of Europe, Strasbourg. Contains a List of Documents Published in Connection with the Programme.

Rey, M. (1987) The Educational and Cultural Development of Migrants, Abstract of the Final Report of the Project Group, Brochure DECS/EGT (87) 19, Council of Europe, Strasbourg. Contains a List of Documents Published in Connection with the Project.

Spier, P. (1981) Quatre Milliards de Visages, *Ecoles des Loisirs*, Paris.

UNICEF-UNESCO (1986) L'etranger vu par l'enfant, *Flammarion*, Paris.

Widgren, J. (1987) International Migration: New Challenges to Europe. Migrants in Western Europe: Present Situation and Future Prospects. Third Conference of European Ministers responsible for Migration Affairs, Council of Europe, Strasbourg.

Zurbriggen, A. (1989) Arc-en-ciel: Activites interculturelles, Departement de I'Instruction Publique, Geneva.

[From: Starkey, H. (ed.) (1991) The Challenge of Human Rights Education. London: Cassell. pp. 135-151]

# 导读:人权和跨文化教育

人权与我们的社会行为息息相关。教师可以在学校对学生进行人权教育,同时也和学生一起在自己的环境中经历人权。人权教育是经历和意识的教育而不仅仅是讲授一门课程的问题。在作者看来,如果人权教育旨在超越民族中心主义,那么跨文化途径是一种必要的方法。人权教育应从策略和关系方面来考虑,策略的目的在于:挑战已有的民族中心主义的自以为是;重新看待不同技能、价值和文化的分量;改变权利平衡赋予平等地位;取消种族歧视,认识人类各种关系的复杂性;发展各个层面的交流。而人权教育的目的也在于超越那些扭曲我们世界观的潜在的自我中心主义、社会中心主义和民族中心主义。文章主要从三个方面来论述跨文化教育途径与人权之间的关系:首先简单介绍在欧洲议会中发展的跨文化概念和议会活动的历史概况,然后进行一些术语评论,最后给出了一些人权教育方法的例子。

## 移民现象和跨文化途径在欧洲议会的发展

在欧洲议会,跨文化途径最初的发展与移民有关。当然它并不局限于移民问题,但移民情况是颇为重要的,因为它首先突出了对统治关系和工业化发展之外的国家的关注,其次它指出了不管民族、经济、社会、种族和宗教障碍认识他人的方法。在过去二十年中,学校和社区对移民的态度经历过波动和变化。在人权领域也同样经历了这些变化,最初是问题轻视、二元论、优越感、自我中心和民族中心主义、把责任转移给他人;后来由于人权教育逐渐对文化交流和学习跨文化交流和人类的共同问题有了一定的觉悟。在此期间欧洲议会也就移民教育和跨文化关系开展了一系列的活动。

## 有关的术语概述

跨文化的精确含义包含两个方面:一方面,"跨"意指相互交往、交流、消除种族歧视、相互关系、互相依存和团结一致。同时它还包括"文化"才传达最完整的意义：不仅对人类还有个人和群体的价值、生活方式、符号概念的认识，以及相同文化内或不同文化间的相互交流的认识。跨文化途径有两个方面：第一，就事实方面而言此方法意味着认识迁移的动态过程和接触的各种形式和相互交流的各个方面。第二，就政治和教育方面而言，此方法意味着确定这些交流是有助于相互尊重和形成有凝聚力的团体。

第三部分给出了有关跨文化活动的建议：路线1，进行多维度的教育。路线2，利用跨文化书籍、图书馆和讲习班。路线3，通过中学和大学的学校课程进行跨文化和人权教育。路线4，对教师和其他教育人员进行培训。路线5，利用横向策略建立跨文化思考、行动和训练网络。

## Questions for reflection:

1. What is the relation between human rights and intercultural education?
2. Why do we use intercultural approach in human rights education?
3. What are the suggestions for intercultural activities the author put forward?
4. How do we try to avoid ethnocentrism?

# Intercultural Understanding and Intercultural Competence

## Becoming an Intercultural Mediator: A Longitudinal Study of Residence Abroad

Geof Alfred & Michael Byram

The focus of the research is twofold: on the acquisition of intercultural competence and the longer term manifestations of this in people's lives, and second on the significance of this major and sometimes only experience of living in another country in their biography.

The central aim is to illuminate the long term value of this substantial part of university education for modern language students, as revealed in their biographies.

Our research questions are:
◇ In what terms do former students give meaning to the experience of living abroad in a European country ten years earlier?
◇ Have they developed careers or ways of life that draw upon what they learned during the YA?
◇ How are the effects of the YA manifest in their lives in terms of the

qualities inherent in intercultural competence.

## Intercultural competence

A working definition of intercultural competence is '*the ability to behave appropriately in intercultural situations, the affective and cognitive capacity to establish and maintain intercultural relationships and the ability to stabilise one's self identity while mediating between cultures*' ①.

The model of intercultural competence used to guide the analysis, to look for evidence of specific attitudes, skills and knowledge, was worked out in detail in an earlier publication② (Byram, 1997). In brief it has five elements:

**Pre-conditions** for (successful) intercultural / interlingual interaction:

—**attitudes**: relativise self and value other; suspend belief in own and disbelief in other's behaviours, beliefs and values (decentre) [savoir être]

—**knowledge**: of own and other's behaviours, beliefs and values; of how each is seen by other (le regard croisé) — comparative methods [savoirs]

**Skills**:

—of **interpreting and relating** ' documents ' / ' texts ' based on existing knowledge and attitudes [savoir comprendre]

---

① A. A. Jensen, K. Jaeger and A. Lorentsen, (eds.) (1995) *Intercultural Competence: A New Challenge for Language Teachers and Trainers in Europe. Vol II: The Adult Learner*. (Aalborg: Aalborg University Press, 1995)

② M. Byram, (1997) *Teaching and Assessing Intercultural Communicative Competence*. (Clevedon: Multilingual Matters, 1997)

—of **discovering** (in own time or in interaction) new behaviours, beliefs and values [savoir apprendre]

—of **interacting** in real time based on other pre-conditions and skills [savoir faire]
(not the only aim for language and culture teaching: savoir faire not always needed by learners)

## AND IN AN EDUCATIONAL SETTING:

—the responsibility of the teacher to develop 'critical cultural awareness' (cf. politische Bildung) [savoirs' engager]

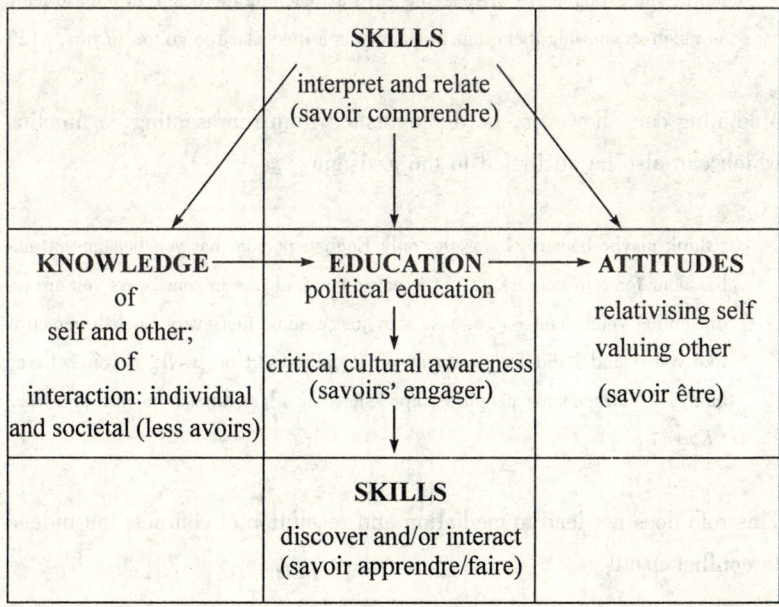

A person with these qualities, in some degree since there is no notion of 'perfection' implied here, we shall call an "intercultural mediator".

## Intercultural mediation during the YA

An intercultural mediator is someone who, drawing upon their savoirs of intercultural competence, is able to perceive the origins of conflicting perspectives and to use that knowledge to explain one in terms of the other and, where possible, resolve the conflict.

It is Lynn who explains the mediating— and motivating— role of the assistant in detail:

> I arrived in my first class, tried to speak to them in English and they didn't understand a single word and I soon realised that I wasn't going to do very much for a year. It was the teaching side, the communicating with the children but not teaching English as in speaking—it was teaching the desire to want to learn as much as showing them that England was a nice place to go to. (*Lynn*, *p*12)

Mediating can, however, be distinguished from representing, a function which can also be attributed to the assistant:

> I think maybe because I was the only English person that you became an ambassador for your country [...] because you feel that in some ways you are representing your country [...] so they just assume that every English person is like you— and I did feel that way of actually, sort of, well, if you behaved badly, it does colour people's impressions of what English people are like. (*Karen*, *p.*4)

This role does not lead to mediation and resolution of conflicts but indeed to conflict itself:

> I did find that sometimes people could be very critical— I was often told that French was the best language in the world— I didn't meet people like that be-

fore—English cooking was dreadful, you know—and you felt like—you had count less arguments with them. (*Karen*, p. 4)

## Continuing mediation

At the time of the interviews, Sylvia, Yvonne, Elizabeth and Carol were teaching, Lynn, Alice and Amanda were considering it. Karen was teaching her own and others' children at home, having been a primary teacher. John was in accountancy, Sarah in a building society, Ann in marketing, Lynn in a law firm and Alice and Amanda were full-time mothers.

It can be argued that teaching foreign languages is one of the jobs which incorporates mediation to the highest degree. The foreign language teacher understands (some of) the foreign language and culture as well as (part of) that of their pupils, and their task is to help their pupils understand that otherness. As we saw earlier, Sylvia does not feel this has to be a part of the task, that it is not even required by the English national curriculum, that what is needed is the ability to "communicate" which she appears to understand as the ability to speak the foreign language for purposes of social transactions without needing to know much of anything about other cultures. This is, in fact, a view which is widely held but particularly striking in that it allows Sylvia to continue to teach French even though she does not like France because she hated her YA.

Yvonne however ensures that classroom language teaching is accompanied by other activities:

> We had an exchange to L [...]. We go in Year 12— we go to Paris and visit, we visit companies really and do a tourist visit—but this year they're going to stay with families so they speak French as well—we found it hard to have,

we used to have a work experience visit but the types of school we were interested in, in France, are very different to our type of schools [...] so we go on a visit now. (*Yvonne*, *p.* 3)

There is also a visit to Japan and Yvonne took lessons with her pupils to accompany them. She is thus still very much the linguist mediating the experience of otherness for pupils. She also keeps direct links between her YA and her work through former pupils:

> I think it would be just terrible if people didn't go— I know, I mean, what I was saying to you on the phone about some of my students have come back to ask me— I've had three students come in the same week to say please can we talk to you about the years abroad— and it was lovely and I was really touched by that, because they left two years ago but they want to be prepared— and they've written to me since being there and, you know, phoned me up at Christmas to say how things went— and, you know, I think they must be going through all the same things I went through. (*Yvonne*, *p.* 18)

She goes on to explain how she persuaded one girl to go despite her fears, ensuring she was met and looked after by using her contacts in France. It is thus evident that the YA is still a significant part of her professional life and her role as mediator. She contrasts this however with the job in retailing which she took on graduating:

> I was so bored and it was all about money, you know, wasn't interesting at all and I just thought, I know I'll be a teacher and I was so lucky because I just immediately enjoyed it. (*Yvonne*, *p.* 10)

Those who are not teachers may not be as aware of their mediating role but there is evidence that it is part of their professional life to differing degrees depending on needs and opportunities. Neither Ann, in marketing, nor Sarah, in a building society, have opportunity to engage with people of substantially different cultural and linguistic origins, but they attribute some of their success to the YA even though it seems distant.

> I mean, I think that the year abroad probably helped me, sort of, take new experiences and, sort of, deal with them as best I could because I think that's perhaps what we had to do in France— so I tend not to get too, sort of, fazed out about things— I tend to, sort of, take things in my stride and I think that probably helped a lot. (*Sarah*, *p.* 19)

This was also how she talked about the YA in the interview on her return, so despite the hesitation here, there is consistency over the ten years. She had re-read her diary immediately before this interview because otherwise it seemed "quite a long way in the past".

Of those who are not teachers, Lynn is the one who has most opportunity to act as mediator. She returned abroad on graduation "as a result of my year abroad in France [...]. I didn't particularly want to stay in England— I didn't want to go into teaching, I didn't want to go into banking or all the other things which seemed to be relevant at the time". (pp. 1-2) So she had a distinction between teaching and other careers, as we saw earlier. However, in the category "abroad" she had no specific idea of "what I wanted to do", so she found a post-graduate course in Brussels and then a job in a law firm, where she still was, at the time of the interview, working as office manager, although, in fact, on maternity leave. The law firm is American, with attorneys and staff of various nationalities, working in a Belgian administrative context. So she describes herself as "very much the middle person trying to placate the two (the attorneys and the staff and she sees her success in this partly in terms of her nationality:

I think of the office managers that I know in Brussels— most of them are Belgian— of the other American law firms— whereas I'm English and I think I work better with the attorneys and partly in terms of age and experience. I find nowadays that as I get older the staff get younger [...] I'm looking after people, listening to people— that sort of quality, there, of being unbiased and there to help one side and to work with the others on the other side. (*Lynn*, p. 3)

She also identifies her knowledge of cultural difference as significant and here her savoir être emerges:

I'm certainly conscious of explaining to others that the Germans are a little bit more abrupt— we did have one case with a Spanish attorney, but she's very easy-going, very nice to get on with, but one person said, she never says please, she never says thank you— and I said I noticed that, I have a Spanish friend, it's sort of a different cultural thing. (*Lynn*, p. 4)

She goes on to tell the person about her own socialisation into saying please and thank you and the effect this has on one's expectations and also the effects of people using English as a lingua franca: "you may all be speaking English, but you're not an English speaker— it may be a Flemish woman I'm talking to—you're not English speaking, she's not English speaking, you know, there's bound to be misunderstandings because you're both using a foreign language" (p. 4) Here then the linguist mediator with an awareness of linguistic and cultural phenomena in intercultural interaction is clearly evident. It is not possible to attribute this capacity for mediation directly to the YA but Lynn does say that, as we saw earlier, she saw her role as an assistant above all in terms of mediation and, when asked what else comes to mind, she says the YA was "the first experience of living with other people with different nationalities, where I first lived with a Spanish friend and a German friend" (p. 13). The reference to Spanish and German again may be just coincidental but it shows that she had from the YA onwards a life with mediation at the centre.

In short, the narratives created in the interviews are precisely that i. e. narratives about their lives, but at the same time they are accounts elicited by the interviewers with a certain number of research questions in mind. In particular we were asking interviewees to recount experiences and events which might provide direct or indirect evidence for intercultural competence, either in the events or in the ways in which they were presented. Similarly we were framing our questions so as to provide opportunity for them to give us evidence that their intercultural competence was related to, perhaps developed through, their YA. These questions were sometimes direct, asking interviewees if they attributed any present competences or interests to the YA. As we have seen, neither they nor we can be entirely sure, and certainly not able to quantify, but there is often strong evidence of the significance of the YA in their lives.

One clear statement comes from Alice:

> I think, having you know, sort of been able to say that you have actually lived in a different country— I always think it when people tell me that they've, you know— I've lived abroad— you think, oh well, you know that, and you respect them, sort of thing— so you know I'm pleased with myself really, you know, glad that I've had that opportunity and, you know— yes, it's this life experience, isn't it, that you draw on— and I can always think back on that time and have really good memories. (*Alice*, p.9)

Elizabeth is quite categorical that the YA has no relationship to her professional life, not in any direct way, "but personally, it was a really wonderful experience for me and I think I, sort of, grew up a hell of a lot in my year abroad" and she still refers to it, recently stimulated by the fact that her younger sister is spending a YA at the moment:

> And I still remember it and I still talk about it— I mean, the trouble is now, it's one of those things, you know, it's actually not credible any more to be talking about my year abroad, 'cause I'm a bit old— it's sort of talking to my sister about it, saying yes I did that— and, you know, I remember and actually it's years ago. (*Elizabeth*, *p.* 4)

Thus, on the specific question of the impact of the YA on intercultural competence, we have argued that it is a confirmation and strengthening of an intercultural competence which is probably incipient from previous school and family learning experiences above all where the YA was enjoyed. Those who enjoyed it tend to follow careers and life-worlds which allow them to be intercultural mediators, but those who did not find themselves in careers and circumstances where being interculturally competent is not a frequent demand. However when, as with Elizabeth (and John), circumstances demand it, the YA becomes a reference point.

The causal relationship between the YA, prior intercultural learning experience and subsequent seeking for a career with an intercultural potential is doubtless multi-directional. It might also be argued that some other factor, such as 'personality' would be more powerful in explaining prior, during and subsequent experiences. This is however not our purpose and we do not have appropriate data for such an approach. What is clear is that the YA can function as a reference point, a sufficiently bounded and identifiably different experience to serve as a lens through which to consider some current experience, as a force which pushed someone in an unexpected direction, as the moment which created an awareness of otherness and how one relates to it. It can also function in a quite different way, as a confirmation of oneself as belonging "at home", rather than among others. In both cases, and neither need be evaluated as better or worse than the other, it is the demanding and consuming nature of the YA which makes it such a powerful reference point.

However, although neither the effect of opening to otherness and becoming a mediator, nor the effect of closing back into oneself need be judged, it is probably the hope of most of those concerned with the YA, administratively or educationally, that the former effect will dominate in the long term. This interpretation of our data shows that this is not necessarily the case. One could speculate on what might be done ......

[From *Journal of Multilingual and Multicultural Development*; 2002, 23, 5, pp. 339-352.]

# 导读：十年后访谈一年海外经历的影响

本文主要通过访谈形式来研究跨文化能力的形成过程和这种能力在人的一生中的长期表现。文章对几位曾经在国外旅居过的学生进行访谈，就旅居国外的经历对后来职业生涯以及生活的影响进行了讨论。

## 跨文化能力

作者在文章中给出了跨文化能力的一个工作定义：在跨文化交流中表现恰当的能力；建立和保持跨文化关系的能力；在文化交流中协调不同文化、同时保持自身文化的能力。

跨文化能力从广义上说可以被定义成一种效果，即在特定语境里采取了合适而有效的行为。合适一般是指没有严重违反已定的关系原则、规范和期望。有效是指重要目标的实现或者相对于付出和替代选择而言的回报。跨文化能力包括一些技巧，主要有处理压力的能力、理解、文化意识、自我实现等。

## 旅居国外时的跨文化调解

跨文化调解是指依据自身的跨文化能力感触到文化间的抵触源头，并用一定的知识来解释这种不一致并试图解决文化冲突。被访者 Lynn 解释说，在任英语助教的过程中，她认识到，教英语重要的不是教语言，而是如何与学生交流，使他们想学英语，并使他们认为英国是个值得去的地方。教语言被认为是把文化调解发挥到最高境界的工作之一。外语教师了解外语及其文化以及其学生的文化，教师的任务就是帮助学生了解其他的文化。然而，很多人认为学习外语不需要了解太多文化方面的知识，只要达到交流的目的就可以了。其中被访谈到的 Sylvia 就是一个例子，她厌恶曾经在法国的生活，因此也不喜欢法国，但是她却一直在从事法语教学工作。同样是作为教师，Yvonne 在教学生语言的同时还经常带学生去游历，接触语言中所包含的文化。Yvonne 还通过她过去在国外的经历帮助学生出国留学。从上面可以看出，Yvonne 过去旅居国外的经历在她后来的职业教师生涯中发挥了重要作用。对于不是从事教师行业的其他几位被访者而言，尽管她们可能没有强烈地感觉到她们所扮演的文化调解者的身份，但是这种文化调解人的身份已经不同程度地渗透到了她们的职业生活当中了。Ann 和 Sarah 虽然在工作中没有机会接触到来自不同文化背景以及与讲母语不同的人群，但是她们都认为她们从国外的生活中获益不少。Lynn 是被访者中除了教师以外的最有可能成为文化调解人的对象，她那时正在一家律师事务所工作，律师和工作人员都是来自于不同的国家。所以她形容自己是一个"中间人"，在律师和工作人员中进行调解。她也同时认为对不同文化的了解十分重要，在这个过程中，她同时也发现了自我。

总之，访谈主要是要求被访者回顾她们过去在国外的生活和经历，从中引出一些跟本文研究相关的内容。她们所说的内容或多或少地与跨文化能力有直接或间接的联系。因此,作者认为国外的经历使在学校已经初步建立起来的跨文化能力得到了进一步的确认和巩固。从上面的访谈中我们也可以发现国外生活与先前的跨文化学习经历和后来的职业关联是比较松散的,是多层面的。但是,很明显的一点是,国外生活可以作为一个参照点,一种不同的经历。她们可以通过这种经历来体验目前的生活经历。

Questions for reflection:

1. How do we define "intercultural competence", what do you think is its most important component?
2. What can be called a mediator?
3. Is the experience of staying abroad a necessary factor to be an intercultural person?
4. Why does Lynn think her knowledge of cultural difference is important?
5. What's the relationship between the year abroad and intercultural mediation?

# Searching for the Intercultural Person

Phyllis Ryan

In Turkish the phrase *örümcek beyin* characterizes the closed-minded person. It provides a negative stereotype of a person as someone who has a spider web covering his or her brain. The metaphor can be extended to someone who is controlled by this invisible web and is often unable to break out of it. Carlos Fuentes, in referring to group cultures, discusses the frailty of a culture that closes itself to outside influence and seeks to maintain a pure culture. In an interview in the Mexican newspaper, he commented that:

Una cultura que se quiere >pura', y cierre sus fronteras a la invasión de otras culturas, es una cultura destinada a perecer. No se encuentra a si misma, no se encuentra su identidad sino en el contacto con el otro. No somos lo que somos sino el conocimiento de lo que no somos (1990b, 13).

(Translated by author: A culture that wants to be pure and closes its borders to the invasion of other cultures is a culture destined to die. It doesn't find itself, it doesn't find its identity except in contact with the other. We are not that which we are without the knowledge of what we are not.)

The search for understanding of what we are, as well as what we are not, takes us, as foreign language learning practitioners, through paths of experience involving languages being learned, cultural identities being formed and the range of attitudes toward contact with other cultures. Autobiographical literature is rich in narrative detail about such life experiences with multiple languages in diverse cultural settings (note the books of Hoffman, 1989, Kristeva, 1997, and Todorov, 1989, to mention a few).

A person who decides to learn a foreign language, becomes involved through language and culture contact in a process that may or may not lead to increasing interculturality and challenging his statues as *örümcek beyin*. I would like to discuss a preliminary look at interculturality from the viewpoint of two women. This may be taken as the first tentative steps of an ethnographic research program. That will lead both to describing an intercultural person and to a way of connecting insights to the goals of the foreign language learner. A problem that often confronts the foreign language learner is that he or she may not have a bank of experiences with languages or direct contact with speakers of such languages.

We will consider first the concept of interculturality, then relate it to the narrative of the two women, and finally consider to what extent the goals of foreign language study, especially English, can incorporate aspects of the intercultural profile.

## Introduction

Interculturality is a term used to refer to a person who has life experiences that bring him or her into contact with people of cultures other than their own. It implies that the person has lived in more than one country for short or long periods of time during his life. It does not specify why these experiences took place, that is whether they were prompted by work, tourism, political asylum, economic advancement, or adventure. Residence in another country does not necessarily produce interculturality.

In foreign language learning settings, the person who is involved in the process of acquiring an intercultural perspective is drawn into contact with the interactive nature of language and culture, often going beyond structuralist views of learning connected with the mastery of grammatical rules and linguistic conventions and the restrictive goals of instrumental learning. The learner is called upon to rely on existing knowledge of the cultures of speakers of the language he is learning to unravel meaning of language and to discover inner resources that lead to refining as well as extending one's knowledge. In the context of student study abroad, where the learner is challenged by the newness of phenomena, Byram (1997) writes that the skill of discovery as an ability calls for recognizing significant phenomena in a foreign environment and eliciting their meanings and connotations and their relationship to other phenomena

(37). In this new context the existing knowledge of the person is called upon when one is involved with documents in the classroom setting or with social interactions with speakers of the language being studied:

> It is through social interaction that the individual draws on existing knowledge, has attitudes which sustain sensitivity to others, and operates skills of discourse and interpretation while managing dysfunctions that arise in interaction with others. They may be called upon to act as a mediator between people of different origins and identities. It is this function of establishing relationships, managing dysfunctions and mediating that distinguishes an intercultural speaker from other speakers and makes him/her different from a native speaker.

Byram (1997; 1998) and colleagues (such as Zarate, in Byram and Zarate, 1997, for example) study the European context where the student is often learning a foreign language as an obligatory academic subject and may experience living abroad for a period of time in another European country related to the language being studied. Byram presented a model representing features of intercultural competence and outlined prescriptive objectives. This model, while it is highly prescriptive in nature, detailing knowledge and skills, also touches on essential chara-cteristics. Several objectives stand out: namely, those in the area of attitudes; for example, a willingness to seek out and take up opportunities to engage with otherness. Such objectives call for an open-mindedness, a curiosity and a readiness to suspend disbelief and judgement with respect to others' meanings, beliefs and behaviors. (1997; 34).

These objectives are deeply involved in the narrative of the two women, Mary and Guadalupe, that follows. It includes perspectives on interculturality, including their vision of the intercultural person, how interculturality functions, as well as its limits, and allows us to outline possible conclusions that will speak to whether interculturality is too ambitious a concept for foreign language learning and to whether it can be appropriately applied to learners and their language goals.

These two women were selected on the basis of the contact they have had with other cultures as they learned or acquired languages. The first woman, Mary, has had experiences with multiple languages, various direct contacts with cultural groups in Eastern Europe and the Middle East as well as Americans and Latin Americans. Her life began in Russia and was affected by events surrounding the Second World War in the European setting. Eventually she emigrated to the United States and ultimately to Mexico. She speaks fluent Russian, Turkish, German, English and Spanish. I would like to propose her for consideration as an intercultural speaker. She was interviewed as a person with a command of languages and strong beliefs about the effect of interculturality on a person.

The other woman, Guadalupe, is an advanced student of English as a foreign language in an urban university in Mexico. Her major is political science, but at the same time she is interested in learning French, Russian, Arabic, and English at her university's center for foreign language study. She has not had any experience living in or visiting countries outside of Mexico, her country of origin.

Both women represent distinct differences in age, nationality, type of culture contact, purpose for learning a foreign language, and linguistic and cultural interests. Their perceptions of what interculturality means vary as they touch upon the areas involved in how a person develops an intercultural person, including its essential features.

We shall address two groups of questions: two related to the intercultural person (questions 1 and 2) and two related to pedagogy (questions 3 and 4):

1. What can be learned from a person who has lived for periods of time in various countries, acquiring the dominant language of the countries? If we call this person intercultural because of these life experiences, what insights can be gained from their perceptions of interculturality and how does this person fit into those views.

2. Without direct cultural contact, is the foreign language learners' vision of the cultures of speakers of this language distorted by indirect contact?

3. The belief that an intercultural speaker must have lived in at least one other country for definite period of time calls for careful consideration when the person has indirect rather than direct contact with other cultures. If a foreign language learner has not had such experiences, how will they become part of the process of eventually gaining interculturality?

4. How can the foreign language student's view of different cultures be amplified through classroom experiences if we accept interculturality as a goal of foreign language learning?

## Mary

Let us start with the perceptions of the woman whose early life was shaped by the historical contexts of various countries at the time of the Second World War. Her adult years included professional work, marriage and children. She defines interculturality as:

... a person that lived, studied or worked in certain countries and learned the language. After living in a country you start to think, act and understand better these people and how they think, so that when you go back to that country after many years you still feel like you are right there at home... like the other cultures you learned after that when you lived in other countries don't exist. They go away from you. You start to act and think again the way of people in that country do.

Was she giving up her culture base to do that? She answered, absolutely not!

> I think your origin stays the way it is. It is just that you become part of that society. You become accepted and in a way you start to think the way they think there. For example, when I am in Russia, when I hear people talking about their problems, about their lives, it feels like I understand them very well. Like I never lived in the United States. I just drifted away from that way of living in the United States. The tempo of the life and thinking... I just go back to Russia again. I kind of become a part of them. I understand them very well. I don't try to rationalize that they are doing this wrong, that they are thinking wrong because in other countries it is considered a different way of thinking. I don't mix it up at all.

Her examples about understanding a different way of thinking start with Russia. Although she was born there and lived there until she was 10 years old, she is a Crimean Tartar and Turkish is her mother tongue. Russian was her school language. She explained how her family lived as a minority group:

> I think that certain minorities in many countries survived only through their families that kept a tight hold on their traditions that they practiced at home. Their children carry on these traditions. So usually this type of minorities survived stronger, they kept on their traditions stronger, than maybe for example the old

country. From my experience when I went to Turkey I found myself much stronger traditionally than Turkish people.

Her life is filled with events of a Turgenev nature in each cultural setting that need to be maintained separately and not compared. An example she pointed out a way of buying food in Russia that stands out as an illustration of this difference:

When they tell me they have to leave their work and they have to go to run to stand in a line to get a certain product to me it seems to be normal. Because if you think in the American way, to leave your work and run and stand in a line to buy yourself meat would be absolutely unheard of. But in Russia that is very normal to do. In fact, you will go and ask your friends if anybody wants meat too. And then you buy meat for the 2 or 3 people that work in your office. And they would do the same way for you. If they have to run and buy some bread, they would ask you, Do you need bread? I am running to get some bread. In the meantime, your friends will cover up your work and they will do your work in the office while you are standing in line. The boss will know but he will close his eyes, because when it is necessary for him to go and buy something he will do the same and you will cover it up for the boss.

I feel that I understand them very well when they do this. For example, if you take an American person, for him it would be absolutely unheard to leave his job and do this kind of thing, and have everyone in the office cover up for him.

Why do I find it [this Russian way] so normal? Why do I go back straight into this type of life? I think understanding of the problems of the country and living with the people many times becomes a part of your nature and it looks to you absolutely normal. Now, when you go to another country and you start to live another type of life in another country you put this behind you; you have to put it behind you otherwise you would be very unhappy. You should never compare, just accept.

She stressed the importance of adjusting to a new country:

> What is done normally and accepted in one country definitely is not accepted in another country. If you start to say, over there it is done like this, you will not be able to live there. Because it will be awfully hard to fight it. You should just learn the way these people live.

> I think that living in a foreign environment, as for example we did as a minority living in Russia, made us naturally have to survive. For this reason, the parents had to be stricter with each of their children, teaching them at home traditions, language, religion, customs, values... the way of living in the house. That is the way I felt in Turkey. We were much more aware of these things than Turkish people that lived in Turkey.

Her opinion was that an intercultural person has to have lived for a period of time in different countries, while at the same time this person needs to be open-minded toward other countries and have curiosity about people there:

> Of course, there is a way of learning a language that people have to learn in school. They learn a foreign language but that is because they need it for work or school. In that way you learn only the grammar and vocabulary of the language unless a person is very open-minded and wants to learn all about the history and the character of the people of the language they are learning. It is kind of hard. Many people that learn Japanese never have a chance to go to Japan and see how they live. They have to then be very, very open-minded to learn and very hard-working people to learn their literature, their way of living, to try to picture what is their character, what makes them tick.

I asked her what she meant by character. She explained that it is what you are born with as well as the way you are brought up. There are many ways to understand the character of people of different cultures. One way she points out is through reading the literature of a country:

> Well, I know many people who did read Russian literature, for example, and they did know very much about Russian character that is kind of sentimental, romantic, kind of pessimistic type of personality that sometimes you meet in Tolstoy's books and Turgenev's. So it is really an old Russia type of character.
>
> So how would you learn a Japanese person's character? You might get an idea reading the books about the way they live, what they think, what their values are. I really don't know if you can really get the feeling of it if you don't live there or if you don't visit. Do you?

Mary recounted many of her life experiences concluding that they fell into five stages or chapters:

> Definitely, I think I became a more interesting person. When I was young, I lived in only one or two countries. All this living in different countries molded me to what I am now. If I had stayed in the same country I would have been completely different.

I asked more precisely about these stages she found her life falling into. She said:

> Well, I take culture from each country. I think of where I was born, Russia. I have a very fond, very romanticized memories. A warm feeling of constantly helping each other to survive. I remember living in a village sitting by the candle light reading books and no other entertainment. It left me with this warm feeling... all children were sitting around the table and reading our books in one room with a stove that was burning, warm, and no radio, no television. It left me with the warm feeling. The feeling of the closeness of the family, of sharing, of loving.

Discipline characterized her second stage:

> And then of course after the war started, trying to survive, also sharing the bread with your mother or your brother. Then, moving to Germany. It taught me that working hard was a type of discipline. That you had to put away other feelings, you had to finish your work, you had to be on time all the time. You had to do things in a certain way. So it was a disciplined type of life. Although in Germany you had the feeling of warmth, like music, getting together, enjoying little things... picnicking with just boiled potato and a piece of bread was the best memories I had... somewhere in the mountains. Germany gave me the feeling of discipline which I don't think I had much of in Russia. I was there until I was 15, so it was a time when you couldn't do anything until you did your homework.

Here the third stage might be called sybaritic, a love of enjoyment, enjoying things, liking to be pampered:

> Then I went to Turkey, the middle east, and what I learned in Turkey was the beauty of the people's expressions. The love of beautiful things, enjoying things. You could go to the Bosporus, sit there for hours seeing the water run. You would have a cup of coffee. In Turkish there is one word. It is **Kaif**. **Kaif** means to enjoy something thoroughly. Now that is something I can't really describe or translate because you can sit and have coffee and look out of the window and having the feeling of enjoying the cup of coffee so thoroughly... having the feeling of **Kaif**.

During her fourth stage, her professional or productive years, she lived in the United States. She calls this her working or productive stage:

> So then I went to the United States. It was a place of discipline, hard work, good friendship... you also enjoyed your life. Your hard work earned money you could spend well. You were able to get things you wanted. I think the US is

very productive, that you are doing something. You feel that you are fulfilled. The US culture is something that gives a person something of fulfillment. Maybe also it was my age that I already understood and appreciated many things. Maybe I had to go through all those stages of my life to get to this, to enjoy it to appreciate it. The US was a country where I appreciated everything. The other cultures prepared me for it.

For the past 30 years she has been in Mexico and this time is her fifth stage or period of reflection:

> I think that in Mexico I ripped off all the wonderful things I learned everywhere else and I finally started to enjoy my life. I definitely did. Here I was not working. I could do things I wanted to do. I was at home I was raising my child, talking about my past. It was becoming more reflective, sorting through all this. Actually having time for myself. I think here finally I had time to think. Before I never had time to think. You have responsibilities.

Mary added one additional comment about her reflections. She asked if I had seen the sun series of paintings by Diego Rivero at a museum in Xochimilco (a section in the south of Mexico City). I said no. The tones, ranging from yellow to dark amber, in the series capture the stages that she is describing here.

Through Mary's account we find her relating her concept of interculturality to specific times and events when she lived in different countries. She closely ties understanding a culture to understanding the character of the people of the culture. Her beliefs about interculturality are so closely tied to her life experiences that she basically finds it impossible for foreign language students to reach these goals except, of course, at a superficial level. Her concept of culture places it separate from her concept of learning a foreign language, since she thinks of the latter as only studying grammar.

# Guadalupe

Guadalupe presents an entirely different perspective on interculturality. Unlike Mary she depended on her institutional foreign language learning experiences as she relates to her concept of interculturality. To understand her perspective on interculturality calls for a pause in this discussion first to look at the role of English as a foreign language in Mexico and second to consider strong negative attitudes toward studying English.

First of all, English stands out in the national setting of Mexico as an international lingua franca used by Mexican speakers of different language backgrounds (both Spanish and indigenous). In professional, academic and social contexts, both urban and rural there is a tendency for Mexicans to find the forces due to the globalization of English intrusive, penetrating their daily lives, a problem that is not unique to Mexico. Kachru and Nelson (1996), as well as Charaudeau et al. (1992), recognize this danger (especially in Third World countries) and tie it to forces of power and dominance. Contrasts appear in this lingua franca setting between the pedagogical positions taken in foreign language learning, whether instrumental or cultural or a combination of both. (See research findings that report on the impact of English as a foreign language on Mexican students: Chasan & Ryan, 1999; Gómez de Mas & Ryan, 1999; Ryan, 1994; Ryan, 1998; Ryan, Byer & Mestre, 1999).

Interest obviously creates a strong force toward rapid acquisition of a foreign language if other factors are positive, but pressure of the sort that a lingua franca creates can take away the free selection of the language one wants to study, creating an impression for some that it is being imposed by outside sources (Gómez de Mas & Ryan, 1999). From the standpoint of foreign language teachers of English in large urban universities in Mexico, a large number of students want to learn English without learning about cultural aspects attached to the language. English is seen by some students as a vehicle for political penetration in their daily lives. One of the teachers points out:

> Many of the students I've had here would like to learn English without learning the culture. I think most of the students who come with that idea are ones who drop out after one or two semesters because they have an idea they can learn English just for instrumental use.

Other teachers talk about imperialism associated with Americans (*Anorteamericanos*):

> I have my own opinions of why they are taking English. I tell them there's a lot of cultural imperialism: US and UK. Most come to (name of institution) because of cultural imperialism. *La llave del éxito*. (Key to success). What keeps them here is that it's so ingrained, no matter how much I tell them, they will still stay here. I tell them that there is a conflict: 'I need to study English and I dislike Americans'.

> When asked to learn other things that can be more identified with the culture of the people, they usually react against that. I heard some student say, 'I don't want to know that. I don't want to know whether in the US you have to be punctual or not. I don't care. I just want to speak English and that's all.'

In effect, in a number of research studies the idea that English is imposed creates a major conflict for urban *universitarios* (university students) and one that needs to be given considerable attention (Chasan & Ryan, 1995; Chasan, Mallén & Ryan, 1998; Francis & Ryan, 1998; Ryan, 1994).

Some *universitarios* talk about a tension that is created over the value of having their culture in contact with other cultures through foreign language study. They are proud of having a flag, a past, traditions, a nation and a language. Others feel good when watching a group of foreigners enjoying a ride, while listening to Mariachi bands, on a *trajinera* (a boat) through the channels of Xochimilco (a section of Mexico City with floating gardens, remnants of the Pre-Columbian period). While they appear to be open to other cultures through language study, they acknowledge that a protective shield develops if their home culture is threatened by the new ways of seeing the world other cultures bring. They express concern about losing one's national pride while learning a new language and about new cultures (Why do people want me to change what I have now, what I am proud of? Do I have to change? If I am seeing the world through a different set of eyes, where does my original point of view go?) (Ryan, Byer & Mestre, 1998). For many *universitarios* they say that their own culture base should not be invaded by learning a foreign language (Don't touch my culture! Don't teach culture! Learning not losing!). Their words capture the desire to protect one's culture from outside threats that learning a foreign language might impose. Their attitudes can be represented graphically along a continuum:

| Defensive: | Neutral: | Non-defensive: |
|---|---|---|
| /_____/_____ | /_____/_____ | /_____/_____ |
| Don't touch my culture. | Learning about culture | I would be interested in studying cultural aspects |
| Don't teach culture | Is a help but not necessary. | |
| We don't allow culture to be imposed. | Culture is not indispensable but useful. | |
| Learning not losing. | | I would like a little more about the US in my English classes. |

Figure 1: Defensiveness reflected in student discourse (Adapted from Ryan, Byer & Mestre, 1998, Reconocimiento de information cultural en la experiencia de aprendizaje del ingles.)

*Universitarios* also recognize existing political, historical and economic relationships between Mexico and the United States and attitudes these relationships provoke. Surveys reveal students react most negatively to the intervention of the United States in foreign countries and in the daily life of Mexicans, to attitudes of the United States toward Mexicans, and to attitudes toward Mexicans working in the United States (Chasan & Ryan, 1995; Ryan, 1998).

Interviews reveal both ambivalent as well as strong negative attitudes toward North Americans as speakers of English (Gómez de Mas & Ryan, 1999; Ryan, 1994; 1998). These attitudes appear as stereotypes in such phrases as Accultural imperialists and Accultural penetrators, observed in studies with Mexican and Canadian foreign language students (Gómez de Mas & Ryan, 1999). Mexican students of French and German and Canadian students of Spanish provide an example of how attitudes toward North Americans appeared spontaneously as secondary to the main purpose of the study. It was observed that Quebecois talked about Mexicans as being warm, cheerful, hospitable, empathetic, poor people. Mexican students described Canadians (Quebecois) as being friendly, cultured, calm people, hard workers. The two groups differed, however, when they talked about images they held of each other. When the Mexicans talked about Canadians, they contrasted them with North Americans, saying that North Americans are not friendly, not cultured, racists, imperialists, people with few values. It is interesting to note that Canadians, however, did not mention North Americans in their descriptions of Mexicans. Figure 2 below represents this phenomena:

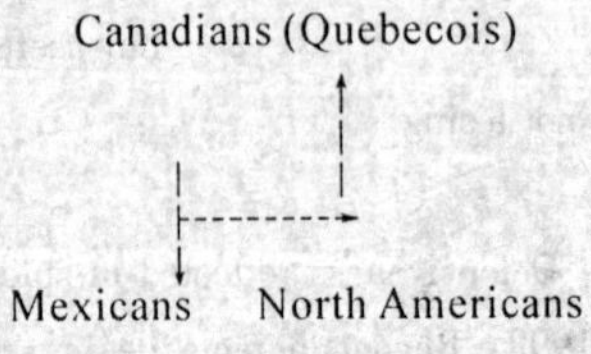

```
          Canadians (Quebecois)
                  ↑
          |       |
          |-------|
          ↓
     Mexicans   North Americans
```

Figure 2: Mexican and Canadian stereotypes.

Tajfel (1981; also Tajfel & Turner, 1986) suggest that oversimplified mental images such as these create 'in-groups' and 'out-groups' out of a need to maintain or enhance the positively valued distinctiveness of the 'in-groups' compared to the 'out-groups'.

Now let us return to Guadalupe, keeping in mind the special case of Mexican students learning English, and follow her views expressed about interculturality and the foreign language learner as part of a process that is beginning for this learner, *una visión más amplia* (a more extensive vision). She defines interculturality as *Aun intercambio entre las dos culturas, entre la cultura de la persona que aprende el lenguaje, y la de la lengua extranjera* (an exchange between the two cultures, between the culture of the person who is learning the language and that of the foreign language). She adds that:

> La persona conoce la cultura extanjera a traves del lenguaje. Hay un intercambio de estas dos culturas y un enriquecimiento. Es como una presentación que se da de la cultura extranjera a través de la lengua. Yo pienso que es un enriquecimiento de la cultura de esta persona que amplia su vision. Entonces tiene una vision > más amplia' de lo que pasa en su país. En su misma cultura lo puede ver desde otro punto de vista, al conocer la otra cultura. Es más amplia la visión de la cultura misma, de la tuya, y de la otra también. Enriquece ambas culturas.

(The person knows a foreign culture by means of the language. There is an exchange of these two cultures and an enrichment. It is like an introduction to the foreign culture by means of the language. I think that it is an enrichment of the culture of this person that extends his vision. Then, he has a more extensive vision of what happens in his country. He can see his own culture from another point of view by knowing the culture of others. The vision of culture itself is more extensive, of yours and of the other also. It enriches both cultures.)

When asked how accurate this vision is, she explained:

> Al principio yo me imagino que es muy general la visión porque no se tiene un conocimiento de cada uno de los puntos que se requieren para conocer bien la otra cultura. Entonces, el estudio de la lengua extranjera nos da una visión más bien general que se puede ir haciendo más precisa en algunos puntos si se sigue estudiando tanto la lengua como otros aspectos de la cultura de ese otro país que pudieran ser la historia, y las manifestaciones culturales, como el día de muertos y costumbres que guarden de otros paises.

> (At the beginning I imagine it is very general because he does not have the knowledge of each of the points that are required to know the other culture well. Then, studying a foreign language gives us a more general vision that can continue being made more precise in some areas if one continues studying both the language and other aspects of culture which could be in the history and cultural manifestations—such as the 'day of the dead'—and customs of other countries.)

## *Una Vision Más Amplia*

I asked Guadalupe in what way a student's vision of a culture changes and becomes as she had mentioned, *Amás amplia* when the student has the opportunity to live in another country.

> Es otra manera de entrar en contacto con otro país. Enriquece más la visión. Algunas personas cuando van al país extranjero se quedan en comunidades de la misma cultura de la que ellos vienen. Lo que pasa es que depende mucho de que la persona quiera conocer más allá, no? de la otra cultura. Porque cuando se va al extranjero es un contacto que quizás no enriquezca mucho, no? Porque son cosas que uno ya conoce. La cuestión sería ampliarlo al convivir con otras personas para comprender la otra cultura desde otro punto de vista.

> (It is another way of entering into contact with another country. It enriches the

vision. Some people, when they go to a foreign country stay in communities of the same culture they themselves came from. What happens depends heavily on the person wanting to know more there, not of the other culture. Because when you go abroad it is a contact that perhaps does not enrich much. Because they are things one already knows. The question would be to increase them by living with people in order to understand the other culture from their point of view.

## Aser Tolerante

What about the learner in the classroom situation? She points out that negative attitudes, such as those previously mentioned, exist toward certain cultures of native speakers of English. Even so she adds that one, nevertheless, needs to understand and be tolerant (*Aser Tolerante*) of these cultures. She refers to North Americans in particular:

> Muchas veces la gente está cerrada a ciertas culturas. Entonces, es cuando yo pienso que se debe ser tolerante con esas culturas. Quizás si no le interésa a uno no tienes que estudiarlas si no le parecen interesantes. Tampoco, está en contra de eso. Hay que ser tolerante para entender estas otras culturas.

> (Many times people are closed to certain cultures. Then when I think that one must be tolerant of these cultures. Perhaps if someone is not interested then he doesn't have to study them, if they don't seem interesting. You have to be tolerant to understand other cultures.)

By avoiding the aspects of culture tied to contexts where English is spoken and focusing on the language instead, instrumental goals may be viable to an extent (such as in the case of reading comprehension in an academic area). Guadalupe accepts this fact but also suggests that everyone should develop an interest in studying English:

> Inglés es como un instrumento para avanzar su carrera. Por ejemplo, como un

químico quién querría leer artículos en inglés y presentarlo en un congreso, pero no importa la cultura de los nativohablantes del idioma. El objetivo de esta persona es muy instrumental cuando no tiene mucha interés en la cultura.

(English is like an instrument for advancing your career. For example, when a chemist would like to read articles in English and present one at a conference, the culture of the native speaker of English is not important. The objective of this person is very instrumental when he obviously does not have much interest in the culture.)

Este es lo que pasa con muchas personas que estudian inglés actualmente en la universidad. En la mayoría de las carreras lo que les piden es como un requisito. Es decir, tengo que estudiar inglés para obtener el título. 'En ese sentido, quizás o si estén de acuerdo con sus objetivos, quizás no haga falta ser más tolerante, no en el sentido de que están aprendiendo la lengua extranjera, no hace falta ser más tolerante porque no les interesa ir más allá en el aspecto de la cultura. Los alumnos dicen que los maestros nos dan la gramática y ya'Quizás falta que a la hora que ellos estudiaran el idioma se les dieran más aspectos de esa cultura extranjera para empezar a despertar el interés, sino que se puede trascender un poco más el nivel académico y ellos por si solos pudieran decir, Ah, mira! la cultura también es interesante!'

(This is what happens with many people who are studying English at the university. In the majority of the majors that they take it is a requirement, that is to say: I have to study English in order to obtain my degree. In this sense, perhaps if they agree with its objectives, it is not necessary to be more tolerant, not in the way that they are learning a foreign language, it is not necessary to be more tolerant because it does not interest them to go into the aspect of culture. Students say to teachers, Give us grammar and that's all! Perhaps what is lacking when they study the language that they be given more cultural aspects in order to awaken their interest, that is they can transcend a little the purely academic level and they themselves could say, Ah, look! Culture is also interesting!)

En el caso de la persona que estudia química, puede decir, Ahora que sé inglés, puedo leer artículos en inglés, entender conferencias acerca de mi carrera, y escribir artículos en inglés pero también puedo leer libros en inglés, periódicos en inglés y tener conversaciones con personas de allá que no necesariamente tienen que ver con la química. Sino que es otro contacto que ya va más por el interés, que por el gusto.

(In the case of the person that studies chemistry, he can say. Now that I know English, I can read articles in English, understand talks in my major and write articles in English, but I also can read books in English, newspapers in English, and carry on conversations with people from abroad that don't necessarily have to do with chemistry. This is another type of contact that comes more through interest, through pleasure.)

## Gaining Interculturality: The Process

The process Guadalupe sees as possible is that of teaching a little culture in a foreign language course to overcome the feeling of being forced to study English (*Tengo que estudiar inglés para obtener el título*) and change negative attitudes toward certain speakers of English such as North Americans by awakening student interest (*Ah, mira! la cultura también es interesante!*) and encouraging the desire to learn more. In this way, the vision of culture becomes *más amplia*.

I wanted to know more about what occurs as one begins to acquire interculturality. Australia was a topic she found that was popular since interest was high in the Olympics for it had just taken place during the summer:

Quizás el profesor no conozca mucho de Australia. Habla inglés pero no ha estado jamás en Australia. Por ejemplo, puede conseguirse libros, periódicos, revistas, noticiarios grabados, programas de televisión, de radio, y transmitirlos aquí y ver cual es la idiosincracia de la gente que habla en aquellos lugares. Ambos, el maestro y los alumnos, están en un proceso de aprendizaje también.

(Perhaps the teacher does not know much about Australia. He speaks English but has never been to Australia. For example, he can get books, newspapers, journals, recorded news, television programs, radio programs, and transmit them here and see what idiosyncracies of speech exist in those places. Both the teacher and the students, are in the process of learning.)

Se puede establecer contacto directo con personas, con hablantes de los otros paises y las otras culturas. El profesor trae personas de California o Inglaterra o habla personalmente con nativohablantes. Ya establece un cambio diferente de los que se ven en los libros o en las revistas, o en programas de televisión. Ellos hablan sobre sus experiencias. Hablan de sus percepciones a nivel de personas.

(They can establish direct contact with people, with speakers of the other countries and other cultures. The professor can bring people from California or England or have the students speak personally with native speakers. This will establish a different way than what is seen in book or magazines on in television programs. They are speaking of their experiences. They speak of their perceptions at the human level.)

Si uno vea un documental de Australia, dice que Australia es un lugar bellísimo y cuando uno habla después con un nativo de Australia dice que pues sí. Entonces, es un enriquecimiento muy diferente porque se entera de las cosas oficiales y las experiencias personales que son las que dan a uno más o menos el parámetro de como es que se vive allá. Por ejemplo, muchas amigas comentan que la gente piensa que francia es un lugar muy bello. No es, porque también hay dificultades, no? Estos tipos de experiencias con contacto directo con personas nativas de aquellos lugares que nos imparten estas experiencias puede hacer más amplia la interculturalidad.

(If one sees a documentary about Australia, it says that Australia is a beautiful place and when one speaks later with a native of Australia and that person says, Well, yes. Then, it is a very different enrichment because one finds out about official things and personal experiences that give one more or less the parameter of how it is that one lives there. For example, many friends comment that the people think France is a beautiful place. It isn't, because there are also difficulties. This type of experiences with direct contact with native people of those places who tell us about their experiences that can make us more intercultural.)

Guadalupe commented on the way other foreign language teachers (Russian, French and Arabic) handled their classes. Her main impression of English in comparison with other foreign languages is that these languages are taught differently, mainly because English is a lingua franca:

El punto es que necesitan conocer inglés y ya. Esto es lo que se hace aquí en el Centro en otros idiomas. Los profesores captan que la gente entra por gusto. Una persona quiere estudiar arabe. En arabe obviamente no tienen solo reglas gramaticales siempre dan aspectos culturales.

(The point is that it is necessary to know English and that's it. This is what is done here at the Center in other languages. The teachers think that people take the course because of interest. A person wants to study Arabic. In Arabic obviously one does not have only grammatical rules, there are always cultural aspects.)

Inglés es un idioma universal que muchas personas aprenden, por ejemplo, en el campo de la química, economía, las finanzas, pero ellos lo ven como un caso separado de la cultura.

(English is a universal language that many people learn, for example, in the fields of chemistry, economics, finance, but they see it as something separate from culture.)

Her observations led to her own experience with other languages and teachers:

Tomé otros idiomas aquí en el Centro, como francés, ruso, e inglés. Una cosa que fue importante, por ejemplo, mis maestras de inglés siempre han sido mexicanos, de francés, mexicanos, pero mi maestra de ruso es rusa. Entonces, es muy diferente porque la maestra de ruso nos platica de las formas de vida en Rusia y de las costumbres de Rusia. Tiene una pronunciación muy diferente porque ella es de allá. Ella toda su vida ha vivido allá. Aquí solo lleva cinco años.

(I took other languages here at the Center, such as French, Russian and English. One thing that was important for example was that my English teachers have always been Mexicans, French teachers, Mexicans, but my Russian teacher is Russian. It is very different because the Russian teacher talks to us about the Russian way of life and the customs in Russia. Her pronunciation is very different because she is from there. She lived there all her life. She has lived here only five years.)

El nivel o grado de contacto al aprender una lengua extranjera depende de quién lo enseñe, porque nuestro maestro de cuarto nivel de inglés, nos presentó algunos amigos inglesas, incluso manejamos un libro inglés. Ella vivió en inglaterray nos platicaba sobre las costumbres de inglaterra. Se aprende por medio de estos contactos.

(The level of contact on learning a foreign language depends on who is teaching it, because our Fourth Level English teacher introduced us to some British friends. She had lived in England and talked to us about English customs. One learns through these contacts.)

Nuestra maestra nos trajo algunos compañeros de California, estudiantes también. Obviamente el nivel es muy diferente. Se conoce bastante la cultura a través de las lecturas, películas, y de todas maneras de expresión cultural que podrían ser la literatura, la danza, la música, la pintura, todas son formas de expresión cultural a través de las cuales también se aprende bastante de la ideología.

(Our teacher brought us some friends of hers from California, also students. Obviously the level is very different. One knows a lot about the culture through reading, films, and all types of cultural expression that could be literature, dance, music, painting, all are forms of cultural expression by means of which one learns a lot about the ideology.)

Guadalupe's vision of *más amplia* required that the student be tolerant of people of other cultures (even though it does not necessarily imply knowledge of a cultural group; perhaps a respect would be more appropriate here). Could this vision, *mas amplia*, and a tolerant attitude be the means of initiating the process of interculturality in the learner? She said, Yes, it can. She admitted that some distortions are inevitable when one doesn't know the other culture: *A Cuando se llega con personas de este pais les plantea sus ideas. Es una distorción porque no conocen aquello. Si tiene conocimiento, puede decir, sí es la verdad.* (When you meet people of this country they tell you their ideas. They are distorted because they don't really know that country. If you have knowledge, you can say, Yes, it's true.) What is important is that the process has begun. Distortions can be clarified and modified later.

## Discussion

This study was begun with the intention of entering, in a limited context, the world of the intercultural speaker and identifying aspects or characteristics that are part of identity and may shed light on the process involved in the initial stages of acquiring interculturality. The interviews enabled the participants to express much of their thinking, assumptions, and beliefs about this phenomenon.

Several questions were raised to initiate the study and several emerged during the interviewing process that caused the participants who had either considerable or no culture contact during their lives to react. The important factor was direct culture contact, and one response was that it was a central requisite of interculturality, the other that it was not necessarily essential, but did enrich one's knowledge. The method of learning through indirect contact (that is, through classroom experiences) drew attention to possible distortions about cultures even when all possible mass media and literary means are used. Mary's life experiences revealed understandings about other cultures that could not have been obtained otherwise. Guadalupe, considering her lack of direct culture contact through experience living abroad, focused on pedagogical concerns ultimately leading to insights about the gradual process of acquiring interculturality. Her position was cognitively oriented in that knowledge was the entry point for her, combined with attitudes of tolerance (or respect) toward speakers of the foreign language being learned. Experiences were also essential to her views about how teachers and students search for both direct and indirect cultural contact. Her primary concern though was for teachers to create a situation where the students' vision of culture becomes more extended (*Amás amplia*).

Questions raised at the beginning of this discussion to guide the case study have begun to be answered, especially Questions 1, 2, and 4. Question 3 particularly has been lightly addressed and remains as the guiding question for further study. It is suggested that including more participants in this type of study with varying degrees of direct culture contact will aid in the attempt to describe more precisely the intercultural person and ultimately lead to describing goals for basic courses in foreign language study that will allow students to think: *Ah*, ! *la cultura también es interesante*!

**References**

Byram, Michael (1989). *Cultural Studies and Foreign Language Education*. Clevedon: Multilingual Matters.

Byram, Michael & Zarate, Genevieve (1997). *Sociocultural Competence in Language Learning and Teaching*. Strasbourg: Council of Europe Publishing

Byram, Michael (1997). *Teaching and Assessing Intercultural Communicative Competence*. Clevedon, UK: Multilingual Matters.

Byram, Michael & Flemming, M. (eds.) (1998) *Language Learning in Intercultural Perspective*. Cambridge University Press.

Charaudeau, P., Gómez de Mas, M. E., Zaslavsky, D. & Chabrol, C. (1992) *Miradas Cruzadas, Percepciones Interculturales Entre Mexico y Francia*. Universidad Nacional Autónoma de México, Instituto Frances de American Latina.

Chasan, M. & Ryan, P. (1995) Un estudio de actitudes de algunos alumnos de inglés hacia las culturas de nativo-hablantes del inglés. *Estudios de Lingüística Aplicada*, número 21/22.

Chasan, M., Mallén, Maria Teresa & Ryan, Phyllis (1998). Students Perceptions of Culture and Language: Open Spaces. En Ortiz Provenzal, A. (ed.), *Antología*, IX Encuentro Nacional de Profesores de Lenguas Extranjeras, UNAM, México, Otoño, ISBN 968-36-6611-6, pp. 223-244.

Francis, N. & Ryan, P. (1998) English as An International Language of Prestige: Conflicting Perspectives and Shifting Ethnolinguistic Loyalties, *Anthropology and Education Quarterly*, 29 (1), pp. 25-43.

Fuentes, Carlos (1990a). *Valiente mundo nuevo*. México, D. F.: Fondo de Cultura Económica.

Fuentes, Carlos (1990b). A Entrevista a Carlos Fuentes por G. Scarpetta: El barroco contra la ortodoxia. Tr. S. González. *El nacional* (México, D. F.), August 21, 1990.

Gomez de Mas, Maria Eugenia & Ryan, Phyllis (1999). Emergencia de estereotipos sobre EUA en la enseñanza de lenguas extranjeras: Un acercamiento psicosocial. *Antología*, 100 *Encuentro Nacional de Professores de Lenguas*, CELE, UNAM, ISBN 968-36-8065-8, pp. 177-194.

Hoffman, Eva (1989). *Lost in Translation, A Life in a New Language*. Penguin Books. New York City: New York.

Kachru, B. & Nelson, C. L. (1996) World Englishes. In S. L McKay & N. H. Hornberger. *Sociolinguistics and Language Tea-ching*. Cambridge University Press, pp. 71-103.

Kristeva, Julia (1997). *Etrangers a Nous-memes*, Francia: Librairie Artheme Fayard.

Kramsch, Claire (1998). The Privilege of the Intercultural Speaker, in Byram, M. & Flemming, M. (eds.) *Language Learning in Intercultural Perspective*. Cambridge University Press.

Ryan, Phyllis (1994). Foreign Language Teachers' Perceptions of Culture and the Classroom. PhD Dissertation. University of Utah. Summarized (1995), in ERIC Clearinghouse on Languages and Linguistics, ERIC Document ED 385, 135, pp. 1-25.

Ryan, Phyllis (1998). Investigaciones sobre el papel de percepciones socioculturales y lingüística en la enseñanza de idiomas. *Estudios en Lingüística Aplicada*, año 16, número 28, diciembre, pp. 101-112.

Ryan, Phyllis (1999). Interculturality and the Emotional Dimension in Foreign Language Learning. In M. S. Byram & Allison Phipps (ed.), *Language for Intercultural Communication and Education*. UK: Multilingual Matters.

Ryan, Phyllis, Byer, Barbara & Mestre, Rafael (1999). Reconocimiento de información cultural en la experiencia de aprendizaje del inglés, *Antología*, 10 *Encuentro Nacional de Profesores de Len-*

guas, CELE, UNAM, ISBN 968-36-8065-8, pp. 177-194.

Todorov, Tzvetan (1989). *Nous et les autres.* Paris, Francis: Editions du seuil.

[From: M. Byram (ed.) (2001). *Developing Intercultural Competence in Practice*, Clevedon: Multilingual Matters]

## 导读：寻找跨文化的代言人

本篇文章主要围绕具有跨文化特征的人进行探讨。作者认为人不应该成为一个思想封闭的人。同样，对于文化而言，也不应为了文化的纯正而把自己封闭起来，因为这样文化注定会走向死亡。只有在与其他文化接触的过程中，文化才能找到自我。只有知道我们不是什么，才是真正意义上的懂得我们是什么。对于学习外语的人而言，通过学习语言和文化，最终可能成为也可能成为不了一个具有跨文化的代言人。作者从两位女士的观点入手来初步探讨有关跨文化性的问题。这是作为人类学研究探索的一个初步尝试。作者在文中将描述什么才称得上是具有跨文化性的人，以及简要谈一谈跨文化性对于外语学习的影响。

### 跨文化性（interculturality）

跨文化性是指一个人具有与其他文化接触的生活经历，也即意味着这个人在一个以上的国家居住或长或短的一段时间。在外语学习的背景下，外语学习者需要接触到语言和文化的交互性，不仅要学习建构主义所提倡的语法规则等知识，还需要依靠现有的文化知识来揭示语言的意义和内在的资源。这种在陌生的异国环境中发现重要的现象并揭示其内涵和意义的能力被认为是十分重要的。

一些学者提出了跨文化能力的模型，描述其中必要的知识和技能，同时也提出了一些必要的特征。其中最重要的主要是态度方面的因素。举例来说，寻找机会或者希望能够有机会去融合到其他文化当中。这些目标需要思想开明，有好奇心。在本文中，作者对两位女士 Mary 和 Guadalupe 进行了访谈。谈论的话题包括跨文化性、对跨文化人的看法、跨文化性如何运作、跨文化性的一些局限等。Mary 通晓多国语言，并与东欧、中东、美洲和拉美国家有直接的接触，作者把她当成是一位跨文化人。而 Guadalupe 是墨西哥一所大学的学生。她主修的是政治科学，但是同时她还对学习法语、俄语、阿拉伯语和英语感兴趣。她没有在墨西哥以外的国家居住或停留。这两位被访谈者在年龄、国籍、文化接触的类型、学习外语的目的等方面均存在着很大差异。作者主要就四个方面的问题展开访谈，两个是关于跨文化人的，两个是关于教学法方面的。

1. 从一个在很多国家居住过，并掌握了每个国家主要语言的人身上可以学到什么？如果我们因为这些生活经历把这类人称为跨文化人，我们可以从他们对跨文化的感触中获取什么？
2. 如果没有直接接触别国文化，那么语言学习者对那个国家文化的理解是否被这种不直接接触扭曲了？
3. 如果外语学习者没有在国外居住的经历，他们如何获取跨文化性这种特质？
4. 如果我们把跨文化性作为学习外语的一个目标，那么如何通过课堂教学来丰富外语学习者对文化的感知？

## Mary

她把跨文化性定义为："一个人在一个国家居住、学习或工作若干年后，就会对当地人的想法和行为了解更深。即使你若干年后再重新回到这个国家，你仍然感到像是家的感觉。你的想法和行为也逐渐变得像这个国家的人一样。"那么是否她就放弃了自己的文化了呢？她的回答是"绝不！"她认为自己的文化还是跟以前一样，不会改变，当她听到俄罗斯人谈论自己的问题时，她不会把美国人的思维带入其中，她十分理解这些俄罗斯人的想法，她不会把文化搅在一起。在谈话中，她还谈到了俄罗斯与美国在工作期间出外买东西这件事上的区别，但她认为在一个国家居住一段时间以后，都会觉得习以为常，因为对这些做法有了很深的了解和体会。在谈话中，Mary 还谈到了迅速适应一个新的国家的重要性。在一个国家普遍接受的行为在另一个国家可能行不通。但是，如果你不接受并与其抗争，结果可能是无法在那个国家生存下去，因此必须学会像当地人那样生活。

在谈到没有条件接触他国文化的情况下如何了解外国的风土人情时，Mary 认为只有头脑非常开明并且非常勤奋的人，通过阅读这个国家大量的文学作品，才能体会出这个国家人的生活方式，他们的性格，等等。即使这样，有时了解的也不是很全面，很多人对俄国过去的文学涉猎很多，但是了解的只是比较古老的一种性格。从 Mary 自身的经历中，她觉得在多国居住的经历把她逐渐塑造成了如今的她，如果没有这些经历，那么今天的她会大不相同。现在的她是个多国文化的混合体。她把自己的生活经历分为五个阶段，分别是：①在俄罗斯出生时亲情的温暖；②在德国的自律阶段；③中东的享受阶段；④在美国的工作期；⑤在墨西哥的反思阶段。

从 Mary 的讲述中，我们可以看出她把对跨文化性的理解跟特定的时间和事件联系在一起。同时，她把对文化的理解当成是对那种文化的人的性格的理解。她把跨文化性同她的人生经历联系起来，因此她认为外语学习者不太可能达到跨文化性这个目标，除非是在很表面的层次上。她认为学习外语仅仅只是学习语法结构而已。

## Guadalupe

Guadalupe 对于跨文化性采用了完全不同的看法。由于没有像 Mary 那样丰富的经历，因此她是依赖于外语学习的经验来理解跨文化性这个概念的。谈到外语学习，首先看看英语在墨西哥的地位和对于学习英语的一种强烈的负面态度。首先英语在墨西哥是作为一种通用语在职业、学术和社会领域里使用。利益的驱动自然就带来了对外语学习的迅速推动。但是，对于一些人来说，就是外界因素把学习英语强加到了他们身上，因此很多学生学习英语只是作为一个工具帮助他们日后的发展，对于学习文化没有太多兴趣。同时,英语的传播所导致的文化霸权也带来了对墨西哥文化的冲击,因此也引起了文化间的紧张场面。

在谈到如何定义跨文化性时,Guadalupe认为是两种文化间的交流,即学习外语的人的文化与外语所在的国家的文化之间的交流。她认为通过学习语言,可以不断了解到语言背后的文化和风俗。当问到一个学生如果去到另外一个国家,他对这个国家文化的见解是如何发生变化时,Guadalupe说这要取决于这个学生了解那里的文化的希望有多强烈。她认为出国一般的接触并不能丰富一个人对于文化的见解,只有了解那里的人如何看待某些问题才能了解文化。

对于课堂中所存在的一些对于某些说英语国家文化的抵触现象,Guadalupe认为要更加包容。如果确实不感兴趣,可以不必学习那种语言。在墨西哥,英语在很多大学都是必修课,只有这样,才能拿到学位。很多学生要求老师只要教语法就足够了。在Guadalupe看来,如果老师能够传达更多文化的东西,或许能唤起学生的兴趣,突然发现文化也是很有趣的。

因此,在课堂上传递一些文化的因素可以帮助学生克服那种被迫学英语的情绪。在教学中,也许教师和学生一样也没有去一些国家亲身体验。但是,可以通过书籍、报刊杂志、电视媒体等获取相关的资料来填充这个空白。老师和学生一样,都需要不断学习。但现实情况却是,很多老师在教英语的同时,把语言和文化分隔开来,认为学生是受利益驱使来学习英语,因此不是很注重文化方面的传授。

从Guadalupe的谈话当中,我们看出,她提倡学生要对其他文化采取一种宽容和接纳的态度,这种态度就是跨文化性培养的开始。在文化接触过程中,对某些文化不可避免地会产生一些扭曲,因而对文化缺乏了解。但是随着了解的加深,这些扭曲的看法会得到不断的修正和改变。

## 结束语

这项研究主要是通过两位被访者的谈话来讨论跨文化人,并且确定在获取跨文化性的过程中初步的一些特征和要素。采访中被访者表达了她们对于这种现象的一些思考、假设和信念。其中一些比较重要的是文化的接触，一个认为它是获取跨文化性的先决要素，一个认为它只是一个必要条件，不是决定性的因素。课堂学习外语条件下的不直接接触文化，尽管有众多的媒体资料可以借鉴，但仍然避免不了对于文化某些方面的曲解。Mary 的人生经历显示出对于文化的理解只有亲身体验才能获得，别无他法，而 Guadalupe 考虑到缺乏与文化的直接接触，因此提出一些教学上的关于促进跨文化性的忧虑。她主要担心的是教师如何创造一个环境来使学生对于文化的理解能够得到延伸和扩展。

**Questions for reflection:**
1. What is interculturality?
2. In the context of student studying abroad, how does Ryan think of the skill of discovery?
3. What is the defining feature of an intercultural person?
4. How does a teacher develop learners' interculturality in the classroom setting?
5. How teachers help students overcome their negative attitude toward otherness?

# Defining and Describing Intercultural Communicative Competence

Michael Byram

## Introduction

The assessment of an individual's ability to communicate and interact across cultural boundaries is facilitated by a detailed description of the process involved and definition of what is expected of the individual. It is an advantage to the assessor but also to both teacher and learner. All three can benefit from clarity and transparency (Council of Europe, 1993:5) and agree upon the aims and purposes of the teaching, learning and assessment processes in which they are involved. It is important to remember, too, that their aims and purposes are determined in part by the societal contexts in which they find themselves— national, international and intra-national and by the preoccupations of institutions, which reflect those of the societies in which they function.

In this first chapter, I shall begin to describe and define Intercultural Communicative Competence (ICC) as it relates to foreign language teaching. This will involve building up a view of ICC from a base in existing FLT theory, and adding to it insights from other disciplines, in order to offer a model of ICC capable of informing discussion of teaching and assessment. I shall however also consider how that model relates to some specific contexts, to illustrate the general need always to define models of ICC according to the requirements of the situations in which learners find themselves.

## Communicating Across Linguistic and Cultural Boundaries

### Communicative competence

The concept 'communicative competence' was developed in the anglophone world by Hymes' critique of Chomsky and in the germanophobe literature by Habermas. Hymes argued that linguists wishing to understand first language acquisition, need to pay attention to the way in which not only grammatical competence but also the ability to use language appropriately is acquired. He thus put emphasis on sociolinguistic competence and this concept was fundamental to the development of communicative language teaching, when Hymes' description of first language acquisition and communication among native speakers was transferred into the description of the aims and objectives of foreign language teaching and learning. I shall argue later that this transfer is misleading because it implicitly suggests that foreign language learners should model themselves on first language speakers, ignoring the significance of the social identities and cultural competence of the learner in any intercultural interaction. In fact, Hymes' argument ought to lead to a greater awareness of the relationship between linguistic and sociocultural competence, since he described linguistic competence as just one kind of cultural competence:

> From a finite experience of speech acts and their interdependence with sociocultural features, (children) develop a general theory of speaking appropriate in their community which they employ, like other forms of tacit cultural knowledge (competence) in conducting and interpreting social life. (my emphasis)
> ...
> From a communicative standpoint, judgements of appropriateness may not be assigned to different spheres, as between the linguistic and the cultural; certainly the spheres of the two will interact. (Hymes, 1972:279, 286)

However, in the following decade, in his major review of language teaching Stern argued that the sociolinguistic might have developed but that the sociocultural had not:

> As a generalisation, one can say that language teaching theory is fast acquiring a sociolinguistic component but still lacks a well-defined socio-cultural emphasis. (Stern, 1983:246)

This was the case in the 1980s and into the 1990s. For example, even in the work of the Council of Europe, the socio-cultural component was not dealt with as thoroughly as the sociolinguistic (Van Ek, 1986) until a new version of the Threshold Level was produced (Van Ek & Trim, 1991) and a Framework of reference for language learning and teaching introduced a more nuanced vision (Council of Europe, 1996).

The reasons for this diversion from cultural knowledge/competence are yet to be clarified but Roberts (1998) has argued that what has happened is that the link with the cultural sphere has been lost because, despite the origins in Hymes, language teaching has been influenced above all by speech act theory and discourse analysis, where the linguistic predominates.

Hymes was not writing for the FLT profession and did not pay specific attention to cross-cultural communication; he was concerned to analyse social interaction and communication within a social group using one language. The interpretation of the concept for FLT was undertaken by others, in North America by Canale & Swain (1980) and in Europe by Van Ek (1986), working independently of each other. The former developed their work from Hymes and others, Van Ek makes no explicit reference to either Hymes or Habermas, but presented his work as part of a developing project under the auspices of the Council of Europe; in fact, Van Ek refers to 'communicative ability'. The work of Canale and Swain and Van Ek and the Council of Europe team has much in common and could be analysed comparatively. I propose here however to take Van Ek's work as a starting point, partly because it is more detailed and partly because it was the origin of the model I shall present later.

Van Ek presents what he calls 'a framework for comprehensive foreign language learning objectives' (1986:33) which is explicitly developed in the context of his view of how FLT must be justified through its contribution to learners' general education. He emphasises that FLT is not just concerned with training in communication skills but also with the personal and social development of the learner as an individual. His framework thus includes reference to 'social competence', 'the promotion of autonomy' and the 'development of social responsibility' which are perhaps inherent in the original discussions of communicative competence but certainly not central and explicit. Nor are they part of the interpretation of communicative competence undertaken by Canale and Swain. Yet, as I suggested earlier, the institutional context in which ICC is taught cannot be ignored, nor can a society's requirements of FL teachers, and I shall follow Van Ek in framing the discussion within a general educational context.

There is no doubt however that the definition of communicative competence and ICC is made more complex by this contextualisation, as are the issues of assessment. For example, the assessment of autonomy or social responsibility might be not only. technically complex but also involve significant ethical issues, concerning the right of an institution and its members to make judgements about an individual's degree of social responsibility, Van Ek was not concerned with assessment — or methodology— but only with objectives and content. It may ultimately be appropriate to assess only part of what we define as ICC.

Van Ek's model of 'communicative ability' (1986:35) comprises six 'competences', together with autonomy and social responsibility. He emphasises that these are not discrete elements, but that they are different aspects of one concept (1986:36). His approach is like someone observing a globe by circling around it and stopping at six points. At any one point, one aspect will be central but others, and their relationship to that aspect, will also be in view. This is an important and positive dimension of his approach. On the other hand there are still omissions and also a tendency to posit the native speaker communicating with other native speakers as the underlying phenomenon which the model has to describe, a tendency to retain the native speaker as a model for the learner, which I shall argue against later. The problem would be rendered even more complex if this were then retained for purposes of assessment too.

Nonetheless the model of six competences is a useful starting point and can be summarised as follows:

* Linguistic competence: the ability to produce and interpret meaningful utterances which are formed in accordance with the rules of the language concerned and bear their conventional meaning ... that meaning which native speakers would normally attach to an utterance when used in isolation (p. 39).
* Sociolinguistic competence: the awareness of ways in which the choice of language forms ... is determined by such conditions as setting, relationship between communication partners, communicative intention, etc., etc .... sociolinguistic competence covers the relation between linguistic signals and their contextual— or situational— meaning (p. 41).
* Discourse competence: the ability to use appropriate strategies in the construction and interpretation of texts (p. 47).
* Strategic competence: when communication is difficult we have to find ways of 'getting our meaning across' or of 'finding out what somebody means'; these are communication strategies, such as rephrasing, asking for clarification (p. 55).
* Socio-cultural competence: every language is situated in a sociocultural context and implies the use of a particular reference frame which is partly different from that of the foreign language learner; socio-cultural competence presupposes a certain degree of familiarity with that context (p. 35).

*Social competence: involves both the will and the skill to interact with others, involving motivation, attitude, self-confidence, empathy and the ability to handle social situations (p. 65).

It is above all in linguistic and sociolinguistic competence that the native speaker as model is implicit in van Ek's definition. He requires learners to speak or write 'in accordance with the rules of the language concerned', without specifying the origins and nature of 'the rules'. He also requires utterances to 'bear their conventional meaning', i.e. 'that meaning which native speakers would normally attach to an utterance when used in isolation'. Even if this concept of 'use in isolation' has to be viewed with some concern— it is not possible to use an utterance isolated from all social contexts, even if the speaker is alone— it might be interpreted as the meanings defined in dictionaries. Yet in both cases the authority and evaluation of a learner's use is vested in the native speaker, not explicitly defined, but perhaps implicitly referring to the educated native speaker. Kramsch (1993, and 1998) has argued for a quite different view, namely that the learner has rights to use a foreign language for their own purposes, and makes the very important point that van Ek's approach places power in social interaction in the hands of the native speaker.

With respect to 'sociocultural competence', there is again a tendency to view the learner as an incomplete native speaker. The definition refers to knowledge of the context 'in which that language is used by native speakers' and competence presupposes 'a certain degree' of familiarity with that context. Even in the case where the language is used as a lingua franca, although there will be 'least need' for sociocultural competence, nonetheless lingua franca speakers should 'be aware of the sociocultural implications of the language forms they are using' (1986:63).

Again the implication of there being only one set of sociocultural implications for a language appears to refer to native speakers.

There are two kinds of reason for criticising the use of the native speaker as a model, in which van Ek is just one of many. The first is a pragmatic educational one which has been recognised widely in recent years. It is the problem of creating an impossible target and consequently inevitable failure. The requirement that learners have the same mastery over a language as an (educated) native speaker ignores the conditions under which learners and native speakers learn and acquire a language. I suspect it is linked to a belief that if bilinguals can speak two languages perfectly, then so can learners of a foreign language. This view is uninformed because it does not take into account the literature which shows that few if any bilinguals are 'perfect' in linguistic competence, even less so in sociolinguistic or sociocultural competence.

The second ground for criticism of the native speaker model is that, even were it possible, it would create the wrong kind of competence. It would imply that a learner should be linguistically schizophrenic, abandoning one language in order to blend into another linguistic environment, becoming accepted as a native speaker by other native speakers. This linguistic schizophrenia also suggests separation from one's own culture and the acquisition of a native sociocultural competence, and a new sociocultural identity. The strains involved in this process, even if it were desirable and possible, are related to the psychological stress of 'culture shock' (Furnham & Bochner, 1986) and could be permanently damaging (cf. Paulston (1992) for a personal description of 'being bicultural').

As I shall argue in more detail later, the more desirable outcome is a learner with the ability to see and manage the relationships between themselves and their own cultural beliefs, behaviours and meanings, as expressed in a foreign language, and those of their interlocutors, expressed in the same language— or even a combination of languages— which may be the interlocutors' native language, or not. The value of van Ek's model is that it identifies a number of components or aspects of communicative and interactional ability for further analysis. It does so by taking a starting point in the analysis of where and how a foreign language might be used, rather than in the analysis of language isolated from use. It also takes into account the place where foreign languages are most widely taught schools and other educational institutions— and their functions and goals in their society. However, complex though van Ek's analysis may be, it does not take into account all the social factors necessary for the analysis. The history of language teaching is the history of increasing understanding of the nature of language and the attempts to incorporate new discoveries into methods and objectives. There is no reason to believe that we have reached the end of that development. It is partly a function of changes in language use leading to changes in the nature of language, and therefore subject to yet further societal change. All we can do here is attempt to take analyses such as that by van Ek the further steps required by more recent discoveries.

An obvious direction for this work is to introduce discoveries related to van Ek's linguistic and sociolinguistic competences. More detailed analysis of the grammar of a language, for example, has implications for the specification of linguistic competence. On the other hand, there are other perspectives which are just as important and perhaps less familiar to the FLT profession, those related to sociocultural and social competence for example. It is these that we shall pursue here because they throw light on non-linguistic aspects of communication and on an understanding of communication as human interaction, not just as exchange of information.

## Non-verbal communication

The first area is one which van Ek's analysis does not cover and which is seldom dealt with at more than a superficial level by FL teachers. In his classic discussion of 'The Psychology of Interpersonal Behaviour', Argyle (1983) identifies eight dimensions of non-verbal communication:

* facial expression
* gaze
* gestures and other bodily movements
* bodily posture
* bodily contact
* spatial behaviour
* clothes and appearance
* non-verbal aspects of speech

and four functions in which these modes of non-verbal communication can operate:

* communicating interpersonal attitudes and emotions
* self-presentation
* rituals
* supporting verbal communication

He points out that there is variation in non-verbal communication between cultures and that 'when people from two different cultures meet, there is infinite scope for misunderstanding and confusion' (Argyle, 1983:189). He deals briefly with the ways of overcoming such problems and suggests that language learning is a valuable but time-consuming approach to other cultures, as are modes of social skills learning which prepare people for contact with other cultures.

Poyatos (1992) addresses these issues very much from the perspective of the foreign language teacher, arguing that traditional FLT is too narrow in its concerns. Language teachers should be concerned with 'the triple reality of speech (language, paralanguage and kinesics)' and that these should be seen within a broader context of cultural signs of all kinds. He identifies ten dimensions of communication where the learner may meet problems, the first four of which are familiar to the language teacher, but are insufficient as a basis for intercultural communication:

* phonetics/phonemics
* morphology
* syntax
* vocabulary
* paralanguage (e.g. tongue clicks, meaningful use of loudness and whispering)
* kinesics (e.g. communicative gestures, manners and postures)
* proxemics (e.g. personal or intimate distances between peers, parents, acquaintances)
* chemical/dermal (e.g. tear-shedding, blushing)
* body-adaptors/object-adaptors (e.g. cosmetics, clothes, occupational artefacts)
* built and modified environments (e.g. status objects such as homes and gardens)

Poyatos then proposes an approach to determining a syllabus and a methodology for a course in non-verbal communication, dealing above all with the inter-relationships between language, paralanguage and kinesics. Unlike Argyle, who acknowledges the difficulty of acquiring the modes of non-verbal communication of other cultures, Poyatos seems to assume that they can in fact be taught, together with or separate from verbal communication. Argyle suggests the alternative of skills and sensitivity training in view of the difficulty, but neither Argyle nor Poyatos question Whether, as an ideal, the learner should attempt to acquire the non-verbal communication of a native speaker. Poyatos sees the problems of learning as including the reduction of 'interference' from the learner's own non-verbal system in order to imitate the native-speaker.

Yet precisely because many aspects of non-verbal communication, although learned within a given cultural environment, are unconscious, the language learner may not be able to control them, or wish to give up what feels like a part of their personality, to acquire the non-verbal communication of others. Here again, therefore, it is important that the learner be able to see similarities and difference and to establish a relationship between their own and other systems, rather than imitate a native-speaker.

## Inter-group and cross-cultural relations

A second line of enquiry which may surprise FL teachers by its minimal concern for language, is the research into communication and interaction between groups, pursued by those who might be broadly described as cross-cultu-ral psychologists. In an overview of 'the study of cross-cultural competence', Ruben emphasises how the work he is reviewing arises out of 'practical problems encountered by individuals living and working overseas, and by their institutional sponsors' (Ruben, 1989: 229). The problems are described in psychological terms and the general model he offers is dominated by skills in interpersonal relationships:

(Cross-cultural) competence has various facets:
 (1) Relational-Building and Maintenance Competence: Competence associated with the establishment and maintenance of positive relationships.
 (2) Information-Transfer Competence: Competence associated with

the transmission of information with minimum loss and distortion.

(3) Compliance-Gaining Competence: Competence associated with persuasion and securing an appropriate level of compliance and/or co-operation. (1989:233)

The origins of this model in studies of business people working on projects in other countries are perhaps betrayed in the third competence particularly. What appears to be naive to FL teachers is the following statement:

> Certainly some knowledges are important to competence— at least some facets of competence as previously mentioned. Knowledge of language, for instance, is obviously important to cross-cultural information transfer. Is such knowledge — and perhaps knowledge of cultural and communication rules — not equally important to compliance-gaining and relationship-building? (1989:234)

On the other hand, this kind of model reminds the FL teacher of the importance of seeing linguistic competence in a wider context. The model begins to expand and add detail to van Ek's notion of 'social competence' and 'sociocultural competence'.

The significance of linguistic competence is down-graded even further in the perspective taken by Gudykunst (1994), who argues that 'the processes operating when we communicate interculturally are the same as when we communicate intraculturally' (1994:x). It is not then surprising when he devotes only two pages to 'second-language competence'. His model of the 'competent communicator' focuses on psychological factors, and he makes the preliminary point that the judgement about competence in communication is one which is context-dependent and made by others in the context rather than in some absolute sense. His definition is therefore of 'perceived competence' and the components are as follows (Gudykunst, 1994:159ff.):

Motivation: made up of a number of needs:
- * for a sense of security as a human being
- * for a sense of predictability
- * for a sense of group inclusion
- * to avoid diffuse anxiety
- * for a sense of a common shared world
- * for symbolic/material gratification
- * to sustain our self-conceptions

Knowledge: this includes cultural and linguistic knowledge but the implication is that foreign language competence is not essential: 'If we are familiar with or fluent in other people's language, for example, we can usually understand them better when they speak our language than if we know nothing about their language' (Gudykunst, 1994:169). Other kinds of knowledge are given more emphasis:
- * knowledge of how to gather information;
- * knowledge of personal similarities, as well as understanding differences;
- * knowledge of alternative interpretation (this is not related to linguistic semantics but to interpretation of behaviour).

Skills: those skills in particular which are directly related to reducing uncertainty and anxiety:
- * ability to be mindful, above all being 'cognitively aware' of the process of communication rather than the intended outcome;
- * ability to tolerate ambiguity, to deal effectively with situations even when there is little objective information present and outcomes are difficult to predict;

* ability to manage anxiety;
* ability to empathise, involving cognitive, affective and communication components;
* ability to adapt, especially adapting behaviour to the expectations of others;
* ability to make accurate predictions and explanations of others' behaviour.

As suggested earlier, such a model is surprisingly lacking in reference to linguistic competence, mentioned only as a possible supportive factor. It could also be criticised for its categorisations of knowledge, skills and psychological factors. For example, 'how to gather information' might be better categorised as a skill, whereas 'ability to tolerate ambiguity' is a psychological trait rather than a skill, and is more related to issues of 'motivation'. The value of this model however lies less in the detail than in the perspective it suggests. Gudykunst is concerned to produce a practical guide to intergroup communication, one which will help in the management of the conflict 'inevitable in any relationship'. His approach reminds FL teachers that, since they have now become committed to FLT which prepares learners for face-to-face interaction with people of other (linguistic) groups, there are new psychological factors which have to be taken into account. FLT cannot confine its interest to the psychology of the learning or acquisition of linguistic and sociolinguistic competence, as it has hitherto.

One reaction to this situation is refusal to 'overload the boat', that is to accept responsibility for other than linguistic and sociolinguistic competence. This attitude is defended by referring to the limited amount of time available in most FLT courses, especially in the general education system. This is obviously an important issue. It can be resolved either by reducing the scope of the linguistic and sociolinguistic competences being pursued, or by extending the time and the nature of the activities in courses. For example, FL teachers are often responsible for 'visits and exchanges' and need to take account of the factors Gudykunst identifies in order to ensure that learners profit from and learn during visits and exchanges. They need to be aware of the Motivation, Knowledge and Skills involved and the learning theories which help them to plan the activities to ensure learning takes place (Whalley, 1997).

## Communication and Interaction

One of the needs which Gudykunst includes in his characterisation of 'motivation' is 'the need for a sense of a common shared world'. The qualities of the 'competent communicator', which he identifies, are the psychological preconditions for satisfying this need, but a common shared world has to be created in interaction with other people. It is not simply there, waiting to be discovered and accessed.

One of the defining characteristics of a social group is the shared world which its members accept, and they in turn are accepted as members because they subscribe to the beliefs, beha-viours and meanings of that shared world. This is however not a static condition. People become members of a group through a process of socialisation over time, and when they are members, they are constantly negotiating their common understanding of details, which over time may become major changes in their beliefs, behaviours or meanings. This much has been demonstrated in the work of symbolic interactionists (cf. O'Keefe & Delia, 1985).

A further dimension is added by the work of Bourdieu (1990) who argues that, within a society, power is differentially held by different social groups. They ensure that access to membership, to a 'field' of activity, is carefully controlled by requiring would-be members to have a specific cultural capital, which can be acquired only in particular educational institutions (Bourdieu, 1989). Christensen (1994) has taken Bourdieu's theory as the basis for considering how FLT should prepare learners for interaction with speakers of other languages. He writes from the particular perspective of Western Europe and its concern with political and social integration, an issue to which we shall return later, but his argument is that Bourdieu's concepts of 'field' and 'capital' should be used to describe what FLT should focus on. FLT should not introduce learners to a 'culture', to a particular combination of beliefs, behaviours and meanings dominant in a specific society, precisely because they are dominant and represent the interests of a powerful minority. Christensen is not explicit about how Bourdieu's concepts can be used in FLT but one can see that the aims might be expressed in terms of providing learners with the means of interacting with any speaker of another language, whatever field or capital they bring to the interaction, and on another occasion (1993) he argued that 'the quest for culture as essence and object has to be abandoned in favour of method, i.e. a process of investigation where every single social encounter potentially involves different values, opinions and world-views'. Thus learners are not limited to interaction only with those who have access to the dominant cultural capital. Instead their own cultural capital, even if not dominant in their own society, is valued in any interaction, as is the cultural capital of their interlocutors. This is particularly important for those learners who do not have access to the dominant culture in their own or another society and who are therefore not attracted by the worlds which FLT offers them. It is also important when the language is a lingua franca, and neither interlocutor is familiar with the cultural capital of the other.

Christensen's view makes very explicit the issue of power and access to power in society, as argued by Bourdieu, and its significance for FLT, and European integration. He argues with others (e. g. Becher, 1996) that European integration cannot take place for the individual— whatever the institutional changes — if they feel cut off from the fields and cultures promoted in schools, including in the FLT classroom. With respect to FLT, therefore, he argues against representation of a society's culture, because this inevitably means the choice of the culture which a dominant group has managed to make the 'national' culture of the society, even though it is accessible only to that group, not to the many other people in the society. Specifically, he argues against the adoption of Geertz's (1975:89) definition of culture as 'an historically transmitted pattern of meanings embodied in symbols, a system of inherited conceptions expressed in a symbolic form by means of which men communicate, perpetuate and develop their knowledge about attitudes towards life' (see Byram, 1989a: 82). Apart from the fact that this 'pattern of meanings' is likely to be only that of the dominant group, this definition is too static, not allowing for the negotiation and change which go on within social groups and societies as a whole.

The implication of this interactionist perspective is that FLT should not attempt to provide representations of other cultures, but should concentrate on equipping learners with the means of accessing and analysing any cultural practices and meanings they encounter, whatever their status in a society. This would be a complete reversal of recent traditions in FLT where the provision of information about a country has been the major and sometimes only approach to equipping learners with sociocultural competence. The information has, moreover, been mainly about the institutions of a society and their history, complemented by an intuitive selection of representations of 'everyday life'. To replace this approach with one which focuses on processes and methods of analysing social processes and their outcomes, is to take seriously the issues of social power in FLT, to provide learners with critical tools and to develop their critical understanding of their own and other societies.

It may however be possible and desirable to combine these two approaches. First of all let us consider why learners need knowledge about the (dominant) culture of a society. Analysis of individuals' social identity defines this as that part of an individual's self-concept which derives from their knowledge of their membership of a social group (or groups) together with the value and emotional significance attached to that membership (Tajfel, 1978:63; Vivian & Brown, 1995). The beliefs, behaviours and meanings which make up the practices of the group are what might be the 'content' or informational dimension of FLT, provided that a means is found to ensure that learners do not perceive these as 'objective' and fixed, but changing and negotiated over time by members of the group. Secondly, since individuals belong to many groups, the analy-sis of the social world to which they belong may in principle prioritise some groups over others. Bourdieu suggests that, in economically advanced societies, economic divisions are powerful and proposes that description of a society should be in those terms, but he also points out that:

> the fact remains that the strength of economic and social differences is never such that one cannot organise agents by means of other principles of division ethnic, religious or national, for instance. (1990:132)

It has been the tradition of FLT to analyse in terms of national divisions and national identity, tacitly accepting the fact that this is also above all the analysis of the culture of a dominant elite. Is this tradition justified?

The learner of a foreign language is likely to use the language in contact with people from another country, either a country where the language is spoken natively or a country whose language they do not speak. In the latter case, the foreign language serves as a lingua franca. In other situations, the learner meets people from their own country (for example Anglophone Canadians learning French) but from a different ethnic group. In these three situations, the contact with someone from another group will reinforce their contrasting identities. As Tajfel says:

> The characteristics of one's group as a whole (...) achieve most of their significance in relation to perceived differences from other groups and the value connotations of these differences (...) the definition of a group (national or racial or any other) makes no sense unless there are other groups around. (1978:66)

So, in the first two cases, the defining characteristics of the encounter will be those of national group identity, whereas in the third encounter, it will be intra-national ethnic differences which dominate.

The argument for developing learners' understanding of the beliefs, behaviours and meanings of the national group is then that it helps learners in international communication and interaction. It is assumed that all interaction will make some reference to national identity and cultural beliefs and practices, even if the people involved are not part of the elite social group which has imposed them on the nation. A similar argument applies to the third case, of inter-ethnic communication. In the case of lingua franca, however, learners cannot acquire knowledge of all the national identities and cultures with which they may come into contact. In this case, the introduction to the national culture of a country where the language is spoken natively can serve as an example, but must be combined with developing in learners the methods to cope with other situations, based on this example. This supports the argument for a focus on methods, as well as content. It might also be support for an exclusive focus on methods, as we saw Christensen arguing earlier, but would this be justified?

The advantages, presented so far, of an emphasis on 'method', of providing learners with the means to analyse and thereby understand and relate to, whatever social world their interlocutors inhabit, are twofold. Method ensures that the representation of a society only in terms of the dominant elite culture is undermined; it is not the focus or perhaps even present at all in the course of study. Second, the emphasis on method prepares learners for encounters with cultural practices which have not been presented to them, and, in the case of lingua franca, cannot be anticipated. A third advantage is that through learning methods of analysis learners can also be encouraged to identify the ways in which particular cultural practices and beliefs maintain the social position and power of particular groups. The analysis can become critical. Furthermore, the analysis can be comparative, turning learners' attention back on their own practices, beliefs and social identities — and the groups to which they do or do not belong- and this analysis too can be critical (Byram, 1997a).

A fourth point will become relevant later when I propose a model of Intercultural Communicative Competence which is based on the concept of the 'intercultural speaker', but let it be raised here too in the discussion of power relationships in communication. There has long been an assumption in FLT that 'the native speaker is always right' (Kramsch, 1998). Native speaker intuitions are called upon to resolve doubts about grammatical issues, idiomatic usage and even pronunciation, although the latter is a problematic area. Language learners aspire to the mastery of grammar and idiom of the educated native speaker using the standard language, and their accuracy is usually evaluated against that norm. Insofar as a minority of learners can attain the norm with respect to the grammar and linguistic competence, this approach seems acceptable. Even though it condemns the majority of learners to 'failure', it can be argued that convergence to the norm is needed to ensure efficient communication among foreign spea-kers of a language, just as a standard language is required for native speakers. There is no doubt, however, that in both cases those who master the norm— which in practice is the same standardised language— have a potential advantage: over foreign speakers, and non-standard native speakers. When they take advantage of that potential, they exercise power over their interlocutors.

A similar situation may arise with respect to culture. The native speaker, especially if they are a member of the dominant group in a society, has the possibility of exercising power over the foreign speaker. The native speaker is 'always right', if both native and foreign speaker have an expectation in common that the learner shall acquire the culture (s) of a country where the language is spoken natively. The advantage of an FLT approach emphasising analysis of the interaction is that it allows learners to see their role not as imitators of native speakers but as social actors engaging with other social actors in a particular kind of communication and interaction which is different from that between native speakers. In this international interaction, both interlocutors have a significant but different role, and the foreign speaker who knows something both of the foreign culture and of their own, is in a position of power at least equal to that of the native speaker. I shall return to this point in Chapter 2, in a closer definition of the 'intercultural speaker'.

The advantages of representing a national culture and cultural identity the need to prepare learners for international interactions— can therefore be combined with the advantages of a focus on critical and comparative method. The national culture will be seen as only one of the sets of cultural practices and beliefs to which an interlocutor subscribes— or is at least aware of as a framework for their actions and identity—and yet it provides learners with a basis for interaction. The learner has also acquired methods for transfer to other situations and the means of coping with new cultural practices and identities.

Finally, we must remember that FLT has a particular contribution to make to the preparation of learners for encounter with otherness, a contribution which complements that of other subject areas in the general education curriculum, notably human geography (McPartland et al., 1996). FLT is centrally concerned with communication in a foreign language. The significance of this is not only the practical question of linguistic competence for communication, central though that is, but also the relationship between the language and cultural practices and beliefs of a group. Since language is a prime means of embodying the complexity of those practices and beliefs, through both reference and connotations (Byram, 1998a), and the interplay of language and identity (Le Page & Tabouret-Keller, 1985), the acquisition of a foreign language is the acquisition of the cultural practices and beliefs it embodies for particular social groups, even though the learner may put it to other uses too. It is also the relativisation of what seems to the learner to be the natural language of their own identities, and the realisation that these are cultural, and socially constructed. Teaching for linguistic competence cannot be separated from teaching for intercultural competence.

## Teaching Intercultural Communication in Context

In discussing whether there should be 'content' as well as 'method' in the cultural dimension of FLT, I gave three simple examples of intercultural communication:

* between people of different languages and countries where one is a native speaker of the language used;
* between people of different languages and countries where the language used is a lingua franca;
* and between people of the same country but different languages, one of whom is a native speaker of the language used.

This is a reminder that FLT always takes place in a particular context and that the nature of the Intercultural Communicative Competence required is partly dependent on context. Furthermore, if someone acquires ICC as a consequence of being taught in a formal sense, then they are part of a social institution which has its aims and purposes decided in part by external societal factors. We saw from the discussion of van Ek's model of communicative competence that he placed it firmly within a general educational framework, where the justification for FLT is partly in terms of its contribution to the personal development of the learner.

It is evident from this that before attempting a descriptive model of ICC, we need to consider to what extent contexts of communication and educational institutions might have an influence on the model. I shall discuss the case of FLT as part of general education, from primary through to lifelong, adult education. Some institutions may not claim to have general educational aims, such as those which train people for short placements in another country, but even these would not reject any educational development which takes place incidentally.

Let us consider some cases, starting with one where the function of the foreign language includes the concept of lingua franca. The Arab Gulf

States have a general agreed approach to education, including FLT, to which each state subscribes. It may then formulate its own aims and purposes within the framework. The 'United Formula for Goals of Subjects in General Education Stages in the Arab Gulf States' includes the following foreign language objectives:

At the end of the secondary stage students should:
* acquire a favourable attitude to the English language;
* acquire a good understanding of English speaking people on the condition that the above will not lead to the creation of a hostile or indifferent attitude to the students' Arab/Islamic culture.

Taking the specifications in more detail, in Qatar we find that they include aims which are orientated to communication with native speakers of English, for reasons of technological progress and as a means of understanding one's own as well as the culture of others:

To acquire a basic communicative competence in order to be able to use English appropriately in real life situations, to appreciate the value of learning English as a means of communication with English speaking people, and to gain access to their knowledge in various fields and to the technology which has international currency.

To expand one's own cultural awareness by learning about the cultural heritage of English speaking peoples and by so doing to arrive at a livelier appreciation of both cultures.

They also include lingua franca aims, both instrumental— to pursue studies— and liberal to develop harmonious relationships:

To provide the potential for pursuing academic studies or practical training in

English speaking countries or in countries where English is, for some subjects, the medium of instruction.

To increase by means of a common language the possibility of understanding, friendship and co-operation with all people who speak that language.

There is also an unusual and interesting particular aim for English as a lingua franca which may be a tacit purpose in many education systems but is here made explicit:

To exploit one's command of English in order to spread in the world a better understanding and appreciation of one's own religion, culture, and values and to influence world public opinion favourably towards one's people and their causes.
(Abu Jalalah, 1993:22-23)

One might infer from the final statement that there is a need to change unfavourable opinions in the world. Events in the Gulf States in the early 1990s clearly created some unfavourable perceptions and, though these statements are all from an earlier date, they might be considered all the more pertinent. The kind of ICC required to fulfil these aims would involve learners acquiring an understanding of those unfavourable perceptions, and how to respond to them. The underlying theme is that FLT should provide opportunities for interaction with people from other countries but should not threaten or undermine the Arab and Islamic identity of learners themselves. A certain fear of 'Western' influences lies behind this, which may be justified by the increase in English-language television and other visual media (Al-Hail, 1995) and by a fear of 'linguistic imperialism' (Phillipson, 1992) although as Pennycook (1994) has shown, this view is easily over-simplified. Furthermore, as argued earlier with support from Tajfel, the encounter with otherness itself creates a clearer sense of one's own identity, an identity which some Arab governments wish to reinforce.

In a second case, Canada, the role of FLT with respect to the teaching of 'core French' is seen by some teachers as creating a better understanding of and potential for interaction with francophone Canadians (C. Leblanc et al., 1990). Their recommendation is that learners' awareness of cultures and cultural identities should begin with their own but be gra-dually extended outwards, to the regional, provincial, national and international. However the main source of cultural understanding is 'la presence desfrancophones (in Canada), Ieur histoire (eh ce qu'elle permet d'expliquer le present), les parlers francophones, le quotidien des francophones et la dimension internationale de la francophonie' (R. Leblanc, 1990:10). Although there is no explicit statement about attitudes towards francophone Canadians, it is evident in recommendations for pedagogy that there is an intention to create more harmonious relationships.

> A un niveau avance une prise de conscience des prejuges dominants peut etre benefique. Il s'agira avant tout de mettre en valur le caractere exagere des stereotypes, non de forcer des attitudes positives fi l'egard des francophones. Il ne faut pas sous-estimer les jeunes en evitant ou en sur-simplifiant un sujet difficile. (C. Leblanc et al., 1990:39)

As in the case of the Arab Gulf States, the political context, this time within the state, is clearly influencing the aims and methods of FLT. The increased support for Quebec separatism in the mid-1990s made the concerns of these authors, representatives of the 'Association canadienne des professeurs de langues secondes', all the more relevant.

A third example is the European situation. The increasing integration and co-operation between European states is a consequence of political union in the West and the opening of political frontiers in the East and Centre. Two political organisations reflect and influence these changes, and have introduced a 'European' perspective into education and FLT. The Council of Europe has related these changes directly to FLT through a programme of research and development with the title 'Language Learning for European Citizenship'. In this context, 'European Citizenship' was susceptible of an interpretation referring to closer political unification and also, more loosely, as 'citizenship in Europe', without necessarily implying closer political unity. The intention was to emphasise 'the strengthening of the individual's independence of thought and action combined with social responsibility as a citizen in a participatory pluralist democratic society'. This would combine 'autonomy with the idea of an emerging European identity and political convergence' (Trim, 1996) As well as encouraging development in specific areas of FLT— such as FLT in the primary school or in upper secondary— the programme focuses upon ways to facilitate mobility between states; the Council of Europe includes both East and West. One purpose was to produce a 'Common European Framework for Language Teaching and Learning' which will enable all involved— teachers, learners, examiners, curriculum designers— to define their work and relate it to a commonly recognised description of aims and objectives and levels of assessment for different aspects of communicative competence. If successful this will influence national definitions of aims, objectives and assessment, and the underlying interpretation of 'communicative competence'.

The European Union has a more limited membership and comprises Western European countries only, although Eastern European countries hope to join and its influence is therefore wider than its current membership. The European Community, as it then was, also introduced a programme for education to encourage a 'European Dimension' in schools, universities and other institutions. Here, too, the concept of mobility across frontiers is fundamental and is formulated in terms of economic and social advantages:

> (the measures introduced should help to) make young people aware of the advantages which the Community represents, but also of the challenges it involves, in opening up an enlarged economic and social area to them. (Bulletin of the European Communities, 5 (1988):10).

There is also an explicit reference to 'European identity', which is not defined precisely but associated with knowledge about European civilisation:

> (the measures introduced should help to) strengthen in young people a sense of European identity and make clear to them the value of European civilisation and of the foundations on which the European peoples intend to base their development today, that is in particular the safeguarding of the principles of democracy, social justice and respect for human rights. [Bulletin of the European Communities, 5 (1988):10]

The scope of the European Dimension is to include 'all appropriate disciplines, for example, literature, languages, history, geography, social sciences, economics and the arts' [Bulletin of the European Communities, 5 (1988):11].

The effect on FLT varies from one member state to another. In Britain, the curriculum for England and Wales reflects European Union membership in that schools must offer an official EU language as a foreign language and they may offer, in addition, a non-EU language if demand

and resources permit; they may not offer a non-EU language as the only foreign language. This is a tangible policy consequence. Other consequences are less easily traced directly to the European Dimension, since the dominant foreign languages have always been French, German and Spanish. Nonetheless, in a report written in preparation for the introduction of the national curriculum, there are several references to the significance of membership of the European Community/Union, including specific discussion of the document cited above:

> European awareness is thus one aspect of international awareness and fits well with one of the main aims of modern language learning, namely, the development in learners of sensitivity to the culture (in its widest sense) of the communities whose languages are being studied. (DES, 1990:49)

The report goes on to emphasise that it places 'a high value on cultural awareness', and suggests a number of approaches and methods to put this into operation, including collaboration with teachers of other subjects. It concludes by saying:

> In these and other ways learners can come to identify with the experience and perspectives of people in the countries and communities where the language is spoken. This should both contribute to meeting the requirements and objectives of the European Community. Resolution on the European Dimension and place these within the broader international context. (DES, 1990:49)

It is therefore clear that European policy has a direct effect on national policy and, as a consequence of the specific recommendations for practice, works through to the school classroom. The kind of cultural awareness which FLT is expected to develop in learners is defined in terms deriving from the socio-political context. In a more recent development, the European Commission (1996) has suggested in a White Paper, that all European citizens should speak three languages. This could imply two compulsory foreign languages in British school curricula rather than one at present. It remains to be seen whether this political demand will be followed too.

A fourth case is the United States, where language learning is not obligatory during compulsory schooling, and where many learners have an obligatory course during the first phase of their higher education. This is not to say that schools do not have a significant role in FLT, and there are a wide range of languages taught, and a variety of approaches to the teaching and learning process. There are immersion courses for Anglophone pupils of primary school age in European and East Asian languages. There are dual language programmes in which anglophone pupils are taught together with children who already have some competence in the language in question because of their home background. There are 'less commonly taught' languages such as Arabic, Chinese, Hebrew, Japanese, Portuguese and Russian, as well as the dominant European languages, French German and Spanish. The aims vary in part as a function of the language for the individual and society. Many children study a language because it has 'heritage' significance for them and their parents. The role of Spanish in the United States, where estimates suggest that there will be more speakers of Spanish than of English by the first decades of the next century, means that the aims and purposes are quite different from those for French and German. In a document setting 'National Standards' for language learning in schools, the variety of aims and purposes is acknowledged and an enriched definition of goals for language learning is proposed:

> Regardless of the reason for study, foreign languages have something to offer to everyone. It is with this philosophy in mind that the standards task force identi-

fied five goal areas that encompass all these reasons: Communication, Cultures, Connections, Comparisons, and Communities— five C's of foreign language education. Communication, or communicating in languages other than English, is at the heart of second language study, whether the communication takes place face-to-face, in writing, or across centuries through the reading of literature. Through the study of other languages? Students gain a knowledge and understanding of the cultures that use that language; in fact, students cannot truly master the language until they have also mastered the cultural contexts in which the language occurs. Learning languages provides connections to additional bodies of knowledge that are unavailable to monolingual English speakers. Through comparisons and contrasts with the language being studied, students develop greater insight into their own language and culture and realise that multiple ways of viewing the world exist. Together, these elements enable the student of languages to participate in multilingual communities at home and around the world in a variety of contexts and in culturally appropriate ways. (Standards for Foreign Language Learning, 1996:23)

It is significant however that the authors feel they have to anticipate the argument that many Americans will not need a foreign language after school either because of the strength of English as a world language or because they are unlikely to travel outside the United States. They argue from the significance of cultural learning and the acquisition of intercultural competence:

> Even if students never speak the language after leaving school, for a lifetime they will retain the crosscultural skills and knowledge, the insight, and the access to a world beyond traditional borders. (Standards for Foreign Language Learning, 1996:24)

In these circumstances, it is particularly important that learning focused on a language which may never be used outside school— such as German or Russian— should give a high priority to the acquisition of skills, attitudes and knowledge which are transferable to situations both within and beyond national frontiers where cultural awareness and sensitivity is required. The acquisition of another language, or even part of one, may be less important and less feasible in the time available than the application of such transferable competences, including the knowledge of how to manage communication in intercultural interactions (Brecht & Walton, 1995).

## Assessment in Context of Intercultural Communicative Competence

We have seen that the formulation of objectives for FLT is influenced by contextual factors. Clearly formulated objectives are essential to proper assessment, and assessment itself is therefore indirectly affected by contextual factors. If, for example, the Gulf States objective of being able to influence world opinion with respect to one's own culture is taken seriously, then assessment should include some kind of measure of learners' ability to do this.

Social factors affect assessment more directly too. FLT as part of general education usually takes place in an institution which has the responsibility of guaranteeing the abilities of their graduates. There are therefore very careful processes involved in certification. In some societies more than others, certification is crucial to the individual's future; it has the function of a laissez-passer through the narrow gates of access to further education, promotion and success. Where large numbers of people wish to use their certificates outside the country of issue, the question of mutual recognition becomes crucial. This is increasingly the case in Europe, and the aim of the Council of Europe's, 'Common European Framework for Language Learning and Teaching', mentioned above, is to facilitate mutual recognition.

Because certification and its guarantees are crucial to learners and their employers or educators, they have to be open to scrutiny and susceptible of reasoned justification, all the more so where mutual recognition is sought. One approach to this is to concentrate only on those aspects of ICC which can be clearly designated and measured. Yet this does not take account of our increasing recognition of the complexity of communication and interaction across cultural and linguistic borders. There is a risk of over-simplifying and misrepresenting a learner's ability in order to ensure objectivity in measurement. The social pressure for clarity in certification cannot however be ignored and has to be taken into account in the assessment of those aspects of ICC which have only recently been recognised and not yet fully described and defined for assessment purposes.

Problems of certification within educational institutions are compounded if learners' competence acquired in other circumstances is also to be recognised and certificated. There are practical difficulties which arise from not being able to use techniques of continuous assessment within the teaching process. It can also be argued that competence acquired outside institutional settings and without the guidance of a teacher, will not necessarily have involved general educational processes and experiences. Should there be certification, and therefore assessment, of a level of general education, of a capacity for insight, of an acquisition of certain humane values and morals, of a potential to act in accordance with these?

We have seen in this chapter that the definition of ICC is a complex matter. There are different theoretical emphases which can determine our understanding of what is involved and how widely the concept should be defined. Should we emphasise knowledge of cultures and cultural practices or rather the capacity and skills of conscious analysis of intercultural interaction? Should we include non-verbal communication? Should we pay attention to psychological traits or focus only on capacity to act? We have also seen that definitions are in practice influenced by social and political factors, by the fact that FLT often takes place within institutions of general education subject to the requirements of society. When we consider assessment, similar social factors have also to be taken into account: assessment is not simply a technical matter for it is often associated with certification and increasingly with recognition across political frontiers.

Our task in the next chapter is thus not an easy one: to offer a definition and description of ICC which is general enough to be of significance but nonetheless takes into account the issues raised in this chapter.

## Notes

1. I do not intend to include here a comprehensive review of the literature. This has been done on a number of occasions: Byram, 1989; Knapp & Knapp-Pot-thoff, 1990; Dirven & Putz, 1993; Jaeger, 1995.
2. Habermas's work was much less influential in language teaching dominated by English as a Foreign Language, perhaps because of the level of abstraction and the language barrier. It is however particularly well used as a basis for discussing sociocultural competence by Melde (1987) discussed in detail in Byram, Morgan et al. (1994).
3. This work was part of the internal development papers for the Council of Europe's proposed Common European Framework.
4. I shall use this rather awkward phrase instead of reviewing the literature on defining culture, or attempting to produce my own water-tight

definition. The phrase is a description of those aspects of culture, however defined, which are important for my purposes and which will become evident throughout the text. I shall discuss the issues in more detail in Chapter 2.

5. Poyatos (1993) gives a wide-ranging and thorough account of this 'triple structure of communication' and other paralinguistic phenomena, including examples from different cultures, but does not develop further his proposals for a syllabus.

[From: Byram, M. 1997, *Teaching and Assessing Intercultural Communicative Competence*. Clevedon: Multilingual Matters. Chapter 1, pp. 7-30]

## 导读：跨文化交际能力的界定与描述

本文主要界定和描述跨文化交际能力（Intercultural Communicative Competence）。作者主要从外语教学的角度出发，通过从其他学科吸取一些有益的见解来建立一个对教学和评估有帮助的跨文化交际能力模型。同时，作者还考虑到如何把该模型与特定的背景联系起来。

### 交际能力（communicative competence）

"交际能力"这一概念是 Hymes (1972) 针对 Chomsky 的"语言能力"（linguistic competence）而提出的。Hymes 认为语言学家如果想了解母语习得的过程，不仅需要注意语法上的能力，还应当注意恰当使用语言的能力是如何形成的。"交际能力"的提出，使外语教学理论很快将社会语言学的因素包括进来，然而却缺乏一个定义明确的社会文化方面的阐释。

Hymes 提出这个概念的时候并没有考虑到外语教学方面。这个空当被后来的 Canale & Swain (1980) 及 Van Ek (1988) 填补了。他们把对"交际能力"的解释用于外语教学当中。作者主要就 Van

Ek 的模型作为出发点进行讨论。

Van Ek 提出了他的"全方位外语学习目标框架"。他强调说外语教学不仅要关心交际能力的培训，还应当注意学习者自身和社会性的发展。框架内容包括了"社会能力"、"自治的培养"、"社会责任心的培养"，这些内容与前面所提到的交际能力是一致的，但是都不是放在最中心和最明确的位置上的。在 Canale & Swain 对交际能力的解释中没有提到这些观点。尽管如此，作者认为跨文化传播能力（ICC）被传授的背景和社会对外语教师的要求这些因素不能被忽略，因此，作者还是采用 Van Ek 的理论来进行讨论。

当然，作者也承认这样定义交际能力或是跨文化交际能力使概念变得更加复杂。就拿对这种能力的评价而言，评价自制力或者社会责任心不仅技术上复杂而且还牵涉到伦理问题。对于 Van Ek 而言，他关心的不是这些，他只是关心目标和内容，对于方法没有太多注意。最终，也许只有对跨文化交际能力中的部分要素进行评价。Van Ek 的交际能力模型由六个方面组成，分别是：语言能力（linguistic competence）、社会语言能力（sociolinguistic competence）、语域能力（discourse competence）、策略能力（strategic competence）、社会文化能力（socio-cultural competence）、社会能力（social competence）。在这个模型当中，语言能力（linguistic competence）和社会文化能力（socio-cultural competence）是解释得不够充分和明确的。因此，在作者的这篇文章中，主要的方向就是瞄准这两个方面。作者同时又从另外一个角度谈到了一些同样重要的方面。只是这些方面对于外语教学来说属于相对生疏的一些因素。首先我们从非言语交际（non-verbal communication）入手，Argyle（1983）列出了非言语交际的八个方面：表情、目光、手势和身体动作、身体姿势、身体接触、空间行为、衣服和容貌、话语的非言语部分。这八个方面可以起到以下四个作用：传达个人态度和感情；自我展示；礼仪；帮助言语交际。在非言语领域的交流中，当一种文化的人接触到另外一种文化的人，很容易产生误解，因为每种文化的非言语交际都是不同的。

尽管在一个特定文化环境里学到非言语交际，但是，很多非言语交际的很多方面都是无意识的。语言学习者也许无法控制它们，或者想放弃他们自身文化所包含的东西，去接受其他文化的非言语交际行为。

## 族群内和文化间关系

外语教师不太熟悉的另外一条研究途径是：一些跨文化心理学家在对不同族群的交际和互动研究中很少考虑语言因素。Ruben（1989）在对跨文化能力进行研究时说，进行这项研究完全是在出于国外生活和工作的个人所碰到的一系列困难。这些困难都是用心理学的方式来进行解释的。他所给出的模型也主要是由人际关系技巧所组成。Ruben 对跨文化能力归纳了三个层面：建立和保持关系的能力；传递信息的能力；获取协调的能力。这个模型对于外语教师来说，是要把语言能力放在一个更广阔的背景之下。

Gudykunst（1994）认为同一文化的人的交流与跨文化间交流是一样的。这也使得语言能力的重要性进一步下降。Gudykunst 的"有能力的交流者"的模型主要集中于心理学因素。因此，这种能力是一种"被感知的能力"，具体包括以下几个因素：动机、知识和能力。动机由一系列的需要所组成，包括安全感、预测性、集体归属感、避免焦虑、与他人享有同感、象征或物质报偿、保持自我意识。知识主要包括收集信息、寻找相似和不同、寻求其他解释。技能主要是：思维敏捷、容忍歧义、控制焦虑、调动所有感官、适应能力、对别人的想法和行为作出正确的判断。

正如上面所说的那样，这个模型缺乏语言能力的重视，只是把其当做是一个支持的因素。尽管这个模型也存在一些弱点，但是对于外语教师而言，在帮助学习者做好面对其他语言文化的人时，需要把心理因素考虑在内。

## 交流和互动

在 Gudykunst（1994）所归纳出的动机这一因素当中包括一种

与他人有同感的需要，在他认为，成为有能力的交流者的心理先决条件就是在与他人交流的过程中建立一种同感。在社会群体当中，其中一个决定性的特征就是具有共同的信念、思想等。然而，这也并不是一个静止的状态。在一个群体中，成员们曾经共同拥有的信念将随着时间而改变。Bourdieu（1990）的著作中进一步阐释了这个问题，他认为不同社会群体的人拥有不同的权力。Christensen（1994）把 Bourdieu 的观点引入到外语教学当中，认为外语教学不应只教会学生少数拥有权利资本人的信仰、行为，而是教学生与另外一种语言的人交流的方法，不论他是什么领域的，拥有多少权力和资本，这样学生不会把交际圈仅仅局限在少数人身上。这对于外语教学来说也就意味着外语教师应该教会学生了解和分析他们所遇到的文化的方式，而不是向他们展示那些文化。这对于目前的外语教学来说是个彻底的改变，因为目前传授文化是最主要甚至是惟一的培养学习者跨文化能力的方法。这种做法的可取之处是强调方法论，给学生提供一种方法去分析，这样可以帮助他们更好理解他们的对话者处在一个什么样的社会里，同时通过分析，也就鼓励学生进行比较和采用一种批判的眼光来对待文化。

## 在情景中教授跨文化交际

在外语教学中，是否应该把内容和方法结合起来一直是一个讨论的话题。作者首先列出了三种情形，借以提出外语教学总是出现在一个特定的环境当中，跨文化交际能力的形成部分依赖于情景。

如果要给出一个跨文化交际能力的描述性模型，首先必须考察情景在多大程度上影响模型。作者认为外语教学是通识教育的一部分，从初级教育到终生成人教育。作者以阿拉伯国家的教育大纲为例，列举出了外语教学相关的一些教学目标。卡塔尔的教学大纲明确指出要通过培养学生与英语国家人士进行交谈的能力，来促进科技的进步并作为了解自我文化和他国文化的手段。同时还包括通用语目的，一方面是为了能够出国深造，另一方面是为了与英语国家人士建立和谐的关系。

在加拿大，法语教学的目的是为了让学生更好了解和更好地与当地说法语的加拿大人进行交流和沟通。尽管没有明确表示对说法语加拿大人的态度，但是，从外语教学中我们可以看出人们还是希望与他们建立一种和谐的关系。

在欧洲，随着国家一体化和合作的不断加强，这使得教育和外语教学也逐步欧洲化。因此，外语教学也进入了小学，目的主要是要促进欧洲人员的流动，也是为了建立欧洲共同外语教学框架，结果是不断强化"欧洲公民"概念。这种欧洲化意识也是国际化意识的一个方面，也符合目前现代外语学习的主要目标。

在美国的义务教育当中，外语教学不是作为必修的，只是在高等教育的第一年有语言必修课。这并不代表学校不担当外语教学的任务，而是在美国有众多语言教育，并且教学的方式也非常多。对于个人和社会来说，学习外语的目的是不同的，很多儿童学习语言是为了保留他们民族的语言。不论是出于什么原因，对于每个人来说，外语都能为他们提供所需。因此，美国外语教育的目标是：交流、文化、联系、比较、社团。

## 跨文化交际能力的评价

从上面我们已经看到了外语教学的目标受到学习背景的影响。显然，目标对于恰当评价学生是十分重要的。因此，背景对评价产生间接的影响。例如，海湾国家制定了希望本国的文化受到重视，并且能够影响世界其他国家的看法的目标，那么评价也应该把对这方面的考察列入其中。

社会因素对于评价的影响更为直接。在一些国家，学历对于个人的前途十分重要。当大量的人员希望自己的学历在重视学历的其他国家能够使用的时候，学历的相互承认也就变得十分重要。这在欧洲已经成了一个越来越重要的话题。对于学历的评价，一种方法就是对于跨文化交流能力各个方面的考察，因为操作性比较强。当然，如果考虑到目前交流的复杂性，评价就显得很有挑战性了。

## 结束语

我们在这篇文章当中看到跨文化交际能力（ICC）是一个非常复杂的问题。理论上，对于跨文化交际能力包含哪些内容，学者们各有侧重。我们也看到定义受到了社会和政治因素的影响，因为外语教学要受到社会要求的制约。当考虑到评价的时候，社会因素也被考虑在内，评价不仅仅是个技术性问题，同时还和跨国界的学历的承认紧紧联系在一起。

**Questions for reflection:**

1. What's the main characteristics of Van Ek's framework for comprehensive foreign language learning objectives?
2. Why do some people criticize the use of the native speaker as a model?
3. Why does the author think that learning focused on a language may never be used outside school?
4. On assessing the intercultural communicative competence, what factors should be considered?
5. What's the implication of interactionist perspective for FLT?

# For a Flexible Model of Intercultural Understanding

Lothar Bredella

Because understanding is a complex and contested term, I will attempt to clarify it in the first part of my contribution. Some critics argue that we should refrain from intercultural understanding altogether because it is a form of violence; for when we claim to understand others, we are in reality imposing our categories and interests on them. Other critics stress that intercultural understanding should be limited because it threatens one's own cultural identity. I will outline here what I consider to be the central aspects of intercultural understanding. In the second part of my contribution I will present several positions which explore the tension between assimilation to a foreign culture and the preservation of one's original cultural and ethnic identity. The result of these considerations will make it clear that we need a flexible model of intercultural understanding in which it is legitimate to preserve one's cultural identity and to change it.

## I. The Nature of Intercultural Understanding

### 1. Is Intercultural Understanding Possible and Desirable?

At the end of his essay "The Limits of Understanding" Theo Harden makes the following comment:

> He/she has to be able to draw the line exactly where "understanding" becomes a threat to his/her identity. Instead of creating the illusion that it is possible to "understand" a foreign culture it is therefore probably wiser to prepare the learner for the difficult position of the respected outsider, who, no matter how much he/she might try, will never fully "understand" and will never be fully "understood." (Harden 2000:120f.)

These words lead right to the core of the contemporary discussion about intercultural understanding. Let me first state that I agree with Harden when he says that we will never be "fully" understood. Yet this is not restricted to intercultural understanding. All understanding is limited. I have, however, difficulties to accept Harden's idea that the belief in understanding is an illusion and that therefore we should prepare the learner for the position of the respected outsider. I do not see how the belief that understanding is an illusion leads to the concept of the language learner as a respected outsider. This raises the question what Harden means by understanding. Does he believe that understanding others implies that we become identical with them? Do we as Germans, for example, have to become Americans in order to understand them and is understanding an illusion because we cannot bring about such a change? However, this would be a problematic concept of understanding. The ethnologist who understands members of a foreign culture does not need to become one of them. We can understand fascists without becoming identical with them or approving of what they think and do. In one of my classes students said that we should not read Toni Morrison's *Beloved* because we are not slaves. It is true that there is an unbridgeable gulf between reading about slaves and being a slave, but this does not mean that we cannot understand them. *Beloved* would lose its *raison d'etre* without the belief in understanding what we have not experienced.

In the first sentence of the quotation, Harden assumes that understanding is possible but that we should stop understanding others when it threatens our identity. This view implies that understanding does not enrich our identity but endangers it and that our needs decide how far we understand others. Such a view seems to justify egocentrism and ethnocentrism. We cease to understand others whenever we feel that it could threaten our stereotypes and prejudices. A different concept of understanding would stress that we have an obligation to understand others and to correct our negative images of them.

Harden believes that those who want to understand a foreign culture will not be fully accepted by the members of that culture. I agree with this view and would even go a step further. Those who understand a foreign culture might even be rejected by it. Yet this experience does not justify the conclusion that understanding is an illusion. It only demonstrates that there is a distinction between understanding a foreign culture and being accepted by it. Let us imagine a Nigerian student in Germany who is well informed about the German culture but is mistreated by Germans because he is a foreigner. It would be cynical to infer from the hostility towards foreigners that it is impossible to understand the German culture.

*In East of Eden* John Steinbeck describes Lee, a Chinese-American, who was born in the United States in the middle of the 19th century and attended the University of California. He speaks English fluently. He has assimilated, but the dominant culture regards Chinese-Americans as inassimilable and forces him to speak pidgin English because a Chinese-American who speaks English fluently would be considered to be untrustworthy and regarded as an impostor. The debate about multiculturalism stresses how people have suffered under enforced assimilation but ignores the suffering which results from the refusal of allowing assimilation (cf. Bredella, 1999).

I have already mentioned that understanding has been criticized as an act of violence, because we dominate others by imposing our categories on them. This view is brilliantly expressed in Edward Said's famous book *Orientalism*: "In short, Orientalism [is] a Western style for dominating, restructuring, and having authority over the Orient" (1978:3). In a similar way, James Clifford argues that ethnologists who want to understand foreign cultures must realize that they are constructing nothing but "powerful 'lies' of exclusion and rhetoric" (1986a:7). Clifford also reveals the dilemma of such a view: If it is true that we can only construct "powerful lies" about others, we should stop writing about them. Clifford, however, is not willing to do that. Hence he tells us: "If we are condemned to tell stories we cannot control, may we not at least tell stories we believe to be true" (1986b:121). Yet, this piece of advice encourages us to practice self-deception.

It is a central paradox of our time that in a period of world-wide migration, we are often told that understanding is neither possible nor desirable. Therefore we need a closer look at what understanding means. Its critics believe that we can protect ourselves and others by denying the possibility of understanding. We should no longer be interested in others but only in ourselves. The gulf between cultures is regarded as unbridgeable. The belief that we cannot understand others has become widely accepted. Jerome Rothenberg describes the contemporary situation in the following words: "It has become fashionable to deny the possibility of crossing the boundaries that separate people of different races and cultures: to insist instead that black is the concern of the black, red of red, and white of white" (Rothenberg in Standiford 1982:171). Yet the belief in the impossibility of understanding has also found its severe critics. Henry Louis Gates is one of them. For him it is not possible to respect others without understanding them: "There is no tolerance without respect— and no respect without knowledge" (Gates 1992: XV). For Gates the belief that Whites cannot understand Blacks is "as offensive as saying that I can't teach Milton because I'm not blind. Or that my friend Stanley Fish can't teach Milton because he's not a seventeenth-century Protestant" (Gates in Rowell 1991:452). And he stresses the consequence of the belief in the impossibility of understanding: "The whole enterprise of scholarship is predicated on the recognition that culture is communicable; that this is its nature; otherwise how can you teach?" (ibid. 453). Even Said, who in *Orientalism* stresses the impossibility of understanding other cultures, in another publication points out the ethnocentric consequences of a belief that only Blacks can understand Blacks, only Jews can understand Jews and only Germans can understand Germans (cf. Said 1986:55). According to Clifford Geertz ethnologists have not confirmed our ethnocentric beliefs and interests but, on the contrary, have corrected them:

> We have been the first to insist on a number of things: that the world does not divide into the pious and superstitious; that there are sculptures in jungles and paintings in deserts; that political order is possible without centralized power and principled justice without codified rules; that the norms of reason were not fixed in Greece, the evolution of morality not consummated in England. (Geertz, 1984:275)

In the opinion of Geertz the belief that we cannot understand what others think and feel leads to self-complacency (cf. Geertz, 1986:112).

## 2. Can We Understand What We Have Not Experienced?

In the debate about reading, critics of understanding have pointed out that we do not understand what the text says but project into the text what we want to find in it. Hence reading is in reality writing. This subjective paradigm of reading is well described by Norman Holland:

> In reading, I bring to a text schemata from previous literary experiences, from my historical or critical knowledge, my sense of human nature, my values, my preferences in language, my politics, my metabolism. — I bring all these things to bear on the text, and the text feeds back to me what I bring to it either positively or not at all. It rewards my hypotheses or, so to speak, ignores them. That is all the text does, for it is I who am in control. It is I who ask questions of the text and I who hear and interpret its answers. (Holland, 1985:7)

Holland makes clear by his long list of things which the reader brings to the text that the text has no chance to make itself heard. It is the reader who is in control. Yet one wonders how readers acquired their historical and critical knowledge, their sense of human nature, etc., if they are incapable of perceiving new things. If Holland's concept of reading were true, literary texts could not confuse and contradict us but only confirm our prior knowledge and interests. Obviously the process of understanding is more complex than the subjective paradigm assumes. When Agnes Heller in her book *A Theory of Feelings* discusses the question of whether we can understand what we have not experienced, she comes to the conclusion:

> We need never have been in Othello's shoes in order to experience his jealousy; in fact, we need never have been jealous at all. We need not have been madly in love, to be moved to tears by the death of Tristan and Isolde, we need never have felt desire for vengeance in order to feel through Electra's rancor. Of course, this does not mean that we are jealous along with Othello, in love along with Tristan, or desire vengeance along with Electra, but rather that we are to empathize with these feelings, because we understand the situations that have elicited them and the feelings themselves. (Heller, 1979:122f.)

These words underscore that we do not have to be Othello in order to be able to understand him. On the contrary, if we were identical with him we could not understand how he is manipulated by Jago. In order to understand him, we must put ourselves in his position and imagine what he thinks and feels, given his character, beliefs and values, and we must respond to what he does, feels and thinks. Since there is a distance between him and us, we can feel compassion for him.

Whereas the subjective paradigm assumes that we cannot help but impose our categories and interests on the text, a closer analysis of the reading process reveals that readers of literary texts put themselves in the position of others and tend to evaluate what they understand in an "objective" way because their personal interests are not threatened. Hence Nussbaum introduces the concept of the "judicious spectator" for understanding and evaluating literary texts:

> The judicious spectator is, first of all, a spectator. That is, he is not personally

involved in the events he witnesses, although he cares about the participants as a concerned friend. He will not, therefore, have such emotions and thoughts as relate to his own personal safety and happiness; in that sense he is without bias and surveys the scene before him with a certain sort of detachment. (Nussbaum 1995:73)

In contrast to the subjective paradigm, the concept of the judicious spectator highlights that the aesthetic distance gives the readers the opportunity to be more "objective":

The device of the judicious spectator is aimed above all at filtering out that portion of anger, fear, and so on, that focuses on the self. If my friend suffers an injustice, I become angry on his behalf; but according to Smith, that anger lacks the special vindictive intensity of much anger at wrongs done to oneself. Again, if my friend is grieving for the loss of a loved one, I will share his grief, but not, it appears, its blinding and disabling excess. (Nussbaum, 1995:74)

The analysis of the process of understanding literary texts supports the belief that we can understand what we have not experienced. Understanding means that we become aware of what is different. We can only speak of intercultural understanding if we can distinguish between the foreign culture and our own. If it were true that we create the foreign culture by writing about it, then intercultural understanding would indeed be impossible. Therefore the belief that there is another culture out there which we can understand is the presupposition for understanding a foreign culture. This is also valid for understanding the past. Michael Standford expresses this idea in the following words:

First, this book is based on the assumption that there was a real past for historians to study—a past that existed quite independently of our knowledge of it. Like a distant galaxy, it remains beyond our reach but not beyond the possibility of our knowing it better. To suppose that what is present, either spatially or temporally, is more real than what is remote is more parochialism. (Standford, 1987:26)

We must, of course, recognize that our understanding of the past and the foreign culture is *our* construction. But this insight does not justify the conclusion that understanding is an illusion. The belief that we cannot know anything about the foreign culture or the past because such knowledge is *our* construction is a form of psychological reductionism. The object disappears in the process of understanding. Such a psychological reductionism cannot explain that we acquire a shared knowledge.

For intercultural understanding it is essential that we take the others' perspective. Such a goal includes what Michael Byram calls a process of *decentralization*. We relativize our perspective and learn to see the world through the eyes of others: "They [the native and the foreign language speaker] need the ability to decentre and take up the other's perspective on their own culture, anticipating and where possible resolving dysfunctions in communication and behavior" (Byram, 1997:42). Learning a foreign language and understanding a foreign culture means to cross borders and appreciate differences. Its purpose is to overcome ethnocentrism.

It is essential for intercultural understanding to see the world through the others' eyes, but we must also ask the question of whether the others' perspective is correct. This implies that we must distinguish between what the others *think* their culture is like and what it really *is*. It seems that the latter question is misleading because it cannot be answered. Yet let us suppose that we study the *Civil Rights Movement* in the United States and understand how the segregationists see their world. Should we take their views at face value? Obviously not. Therefore intercultural understanding must be more than taking the others' perspective. "Understanding someone," writes Charles Taylor, "cannot simply mean adopting his point of view, for otherwise a good account would never be the basis for a more clairvoyant practice" (Taylor, 1985:118).

These considerations indicate that intercultural understanding includes the ability to evaluate what we understand. Relativists will argue that such an evaluation is impossible because there are no transcultural values and each culture can only be evaluated in its own frame of reference. It is true, we must be very careful in evaluating other cultures from our perspectives. Yet a relativist view would, for example, imply that a fascist culture cannot be criticized because it can only be evaluated by fascist values. Richard Rorty says about this relativism: "We have become so open-minded that our brains have fallen out" (Rorty 1991:208). Relativists want to avoid ethnocentrism at all cost. Therefore they refrain from evaluating other cultures from the outside. Yet Zygmunt Bauman points out that relativism itself can be a form of ethnocentrism:

> If I consider corporal punishment degrading and bodily mutilations inhuman, letting the others practice them in the name of their right to choose (or because I cannot believe anymore in the universality of moral rules) amounts to the reassertion of my own superiority: "they may wallow in barbarities I would never put up with ... that serves them right, those savages." (Bauman, 1992:XXIII).

We must be aware of the danger of ethnocentrism in evaluating other cultures. Wittgenstein reminds us of the consequences when we apply our values uncritically: "Think what happens when missionaries convert natives" (Wittgenstein quoted in Putnam, 1998:171). Yet there are situations when we must defend certain language games and criticize others. Wittgenstein himself would criticize "a language game that involved ordeal by fire" (Putnam, 1998:172).

In the first part of my contribution I have attempted to clarify the concept of understanding and have stressed the distinction between understanding the foreign culture and becoming a member of it. Yet such a distinction must be relativized because we are influenced by what we understand. And there are foreign language learners who want to change their identity by learning a foreign language. Claire Kramsch describes their desire in the following words:

> The foreign language might be for many a way out. Through necessity and peer pressure if they are immigrants in a new country, through romantic transference if they are yearning for new adventures in their home environment, the desire to shed one's old identity and to identify with others, to become "one of them", to act, talk, think like them, is often a strong incentive for foreign language learning. (Kramsch, 1997:3)

The central question for a pedagogy of intercultural understanding is how do we evaluate the desire for changing one's cultural identity? How do we evaluate assimilation and preservation of one's cultural identity? In the second part of my contribution I will analyze different positions as they have been presented in novels, autobiographies and interviews.

## II. The Tension between Assimilation and Preservation of One's Cultural Identity

### 1. Farhana Sheikh: *The Red Box*

In this novel, Raisa Ahmed writes her thesis about the identities of young

Pakistani women in England. We as readers learn how she interviews Nasreen Ehsan and Tahira Rashid who are both fifteen years old. Nasreen is proud of her Pakistani and Moslem identity and wants to preserve it in England. She is convinced that the Pakistani culture is superior to the English one:

> And if you follow the rules, then you're going to get on well. Whereas with English people, because they see other boys, the boys see them, then they're going to feel more inclined to leave their husbands. Whereas in our religion, in our way of life, it's more strict. I mean, the women cover their whole body so that the men can't even look, can't even think, oh she's beautiful. They have self-respect, they won't let other men see them .... (Sheikh, 1991:29)

For Nasreen it is "natural" for women to stay at home and raise their children: "Only women have children; women are supposed to have children and most women in the world— not just eastern women— do look after them and do the house things. So it must be natural" (Ibid. 130). According to this concept of multiculturalism, many cultures should live side by side in one society. In contrast to Nasreen, Tahira wants to be integrated. She is not interested in preserving her Pakistani culture, but wants to live like other young English women: "This is really my country, so I should really do what English people do" (Ibid. 28). She suffers from the pressure her mother, her brothers and her relatives apply to make her behave like a Pakistani girl. For her it is not "natural" to bring up children: "I ain't wild about having kids. I don't want to cook and clean for them and I don't want to go out to work. Not just 'cos it'll mean double the work, but 'cos the work I'll end up doing won't be worth it" (Ibid. 131).

The novel accepts both attitudes as legitimate, but it also indicates that it would be illusory to assume that the two girls can freely decide whether to preserve their identity or assimilate to the dominant culture. Tahira, who wants to be integrated, must experience that the English do not acknowledge her as one of them. And Nasreen's emphasis on her Pakistani and Moslem identity is to some extent the effect of the rejection she experiences as a Pakistani in England.

Stuart Hall points out that he regarded himself as a British subject when he came to England from the Caribbean in the 1950s but had to experience that he was not welcome. This rejection led to identity politics, which stresses that one should be proud of one's cultural and ethnic identity, "the constitution of some defensive collective identity against the practices of a racist society" (Hall, 1991:52). Such a reaction is understandable but it is also restrictive because many of the immigrants in Britain belong to many cultures and want to see the British part of their identity recognized. Hall admires the film *My Beautiful Laundrette* because it shows that it is futile to reduce people to one identity:

> If you have seen *My Beautiful Laundrette* you will know that it is the most transgressive text there is. Anybody who is Black, who tries to identify it, runs across the fact that the central characters of this narrative are two gay men. What is more, anyone who wants to separate the identities into their two clearly separate points will discover that one of these Black gay men is white and one of these Black gay men is brown. (Hall, 1991:60)

Assimilation becomes a painful experience if one feels that one should be ashamed of one's cultural identity. In an interview Frank Paci describes in detail how he suffered because his Italian identity was regarded as inferior in Canada:

> What I remember most distinctly, however, was this tremendous pressure to transform myself by repudiating my Italian background. It didn't occur to me that the two cultures and languages could co-exist within me. One of the effects of this pressure of assimilation— which, of course, is experienced by all immigrants in varying degrees— is that it made me very much ashamed of my parents and their ways. In my teen years the shame became contempt. I was very much influenced by school and the media to view my parents and their ways as foreign to my true sensibility. I was only disowning part of myself, of course. So, I wasn't so much struggling with others for acceptance as struggling within myself. (Paci, 1990:229)

In such a context the emphasis on the value of one's collective identity could help to overcome shame and self-hatred and offer security and protection. The most significant symbol of such a re-evaluation of one's degraded collective identity is the slogan "Black is beautiful." Therefore Kwame Anthony Appiah is for Black Power as long as it helps correct the degrading images of Blacks and builds up a positive self-image: "If I had to choose between the world of *Uncle Tom's Cabin* and Black Power, I would of course choose in each case the latter." But he also adds: "I would like not to have to choose. I would like other options" (Appiah, 1994:163). In another context he points out that "identity politics" puts too much emphasis on race: "There is a danger in making racial identities too central to our conceptions of ourselves" (Appiah, 1996:32). The strong emphasis on cultural, ethnic and racial identities forgets that we possess complex and multifarious identities:

> They lead people to forget that they have occupations or professions, are fans of clubs and groups. And they then lead them, in obliterating the identities they share with people outside their race or ethnicity, away from the possibility of identification with others. (Appiah, 1996:103)

The emphasis on our cultural and ethnic identities ignores what we share with others and exclusively directs our attention to the differences between them and us. Therefore a pedagogy of intercultural understanding should take this problematic nature of identity politics into account:

> Collective identities have a tendency, if I may coin a phrase, to "go imperial," dominating not only people of other identities, but the other identities, whose shape is exactly what makes each of us what we individually and distinctively are. (Ibid.)

In a similar way Steven C. Rockefeller is critical of the identity politics: "To elevate ethnic identity, which is secondary, to a position equal in significance to, or above, a person's universal identity is to weaken the foundations of liberalism and to open the door to intolerance" (Rockefeller, 1994:88). Like Rockefeller, Michael Ignatieff sees the dangers of a multiculturalism which regards one's own collective identity as the final frame of reference: "Being only oneself is what ethnic nationalism will not allow. When people become by terror and exaltation, to think of themselves as patriots first, individuals second, they have embarked on a path of ethical abdication" (Ignatieff, 1993:248).

These considerations indicate that a pedagogy of intercultural understanding must acknowledge the desire to maintain one's cultural and ethnic identity but must also take into account the reasons why it has been criticized:
— The preservation of one's collective identity demands that individuals disregard their personal needs and interests. The collective identity goes "imperial."
— Identity politics is based on a hermeneutics of contrasts. The differences between them and us are stressed and the similarities are

ignored.

—Other cultures are seen as threats to one's own cultural identity.

## 2. Eric Liu: *The Accidental Asian*

*The Accidental Asian* is the autobiography of Eric Liu, a successful Chinese-American who, among other things, wrote speeches for President Bill Clinton. Liu is critical of the belief that he should preserve his Chinese identity because such a belief assumes that every man or woman of Chinese origin has something Chinese in them, no matter where they are born. Liu finds this essentialist concept of culture expressed in the following proverb: "You can take a Chinese out of China, but you can't take China out of a Chinese" (Liu, 1998:10). For Liu one is not a Chinese because one's ancestors are Chinese but because one decides to preserve one's Chinese identity in a foreign culture: "And whether it [Chinese culture] is transmitted to Overseas Chinese depends, ultimately, on consent rather than descent. Chineseness isn't a mystical, more authentic way of being, it's a decision to act Chinese" (Ibid. 10). Liu, who regards himself as an American, is aware of the fact that multiculturalists accuse him of having betrayed his Chineseness:

> The assimilist is a traitor to his kind, to his class, to his own family. He cannot gain the world without losing his soul. To be sure, something *is* lost in any migration, whether from place to place or from class to class. But something is gained as well. And the result is always more complicated than the monochrome language of "whiteness" and "authenticity" would suggest. (Ibid. 36)

We have seen in *East of Eden* that in the United States of the 19th century Chinese-Americans were regarded as inassimilable. At the end of the twentieth century, assimilation is possible for Asian-Americans, but multiculturalists tell them to reject it. Liu highlights this paradoxical situ-ation when he says: "Walls that once existed to keep a minority *out* [are] now maintained to keep them *in*" (Ibid. 77).

For Liu a culture which allows assimilation will be changed by accepting the people who had been excluded. Therefore assimilation brings about change whereas multiculturalism preserves the status quo: the powerlessness of the minorities: "The vocabulary of 'assimilation' has remained fixed all this time: fixed in whiteness, which is still our metonym for power; and fixed in shame, which is what the colored are expected to feel for embracing the power" (Ibid. 35). Yet if he accepts the power which assimilation makes possible, he can change the meaning of whiteness.

Bharati Mukherjee criticizes multiculturalism for similar reasons. The idea that immigrants should preserve their languages and cultures is well-meant but excludes them from power and social mobility: "The intention was good. But if, in a multicultural system, unequal value is put on the various cultures, then I'm afraid that marginalization tends to work against the non-white immigrant" (Mukherjee, 1990:6).

Multiculturalism starts from the assumption that the preservation of one's language and culture is an ethical act. Yet Mukherjee questions it:

> Letting go of the old culture, allowing the roots to wither is natural; change is natural. But the unnatural thing is to hang on, to retain the old world. What is the point of hanging on to a culture that's thousands of miles away, and that probably not you, not your children, not your grandchildren, will ever see? Why not adjust and accommodate to the world around you? (Ibid. 8)

Neil Bissoondath is also critical of multiculturalism because it can easily lead to "a kind of gentle cultural, ethnic, Canadian apartheid":

> I would be more comfortable knowing that I was a Canadian, and not an ethnic, not a Trinidian Canadian or a West Indian Canadian; I don't know what those things mean anyway. To be called a Trinidian Canadian to me conjures a picture of someone who, in March or April, whenever they have the carnival in Toronto, dresses up in a costume to jump and dance in the streets, while drinking illegally. That has nothing to do with me. " (Bissoondath, 1990:315)

Himani Bannerji points out that immigrants cannot go on living in the new culture as they lived in the old one. They and their children would go crazy if they were to preserve their original identity:

> Now, if you ask, can we reproduce Indian culture here [in Canada], I don't think it is possible. I don't think you can transplant. I don't think the issue is culture; the issue is politics. Neither Tinni not Guatam [her children] can be raised in Toronto as though we were in Delhi or Calcutta, and if we wanted to do that we would go crazy and the children would go crazy. We both know many such cases. They [our children] don't have to shut themselves off from everything around here, saying it isn't us. It *is* us; we are here. We are different from what we were. (Bannerji 1990:147)

She accuses multiculturalism of "the fossilization and a reification of cultural forms that we brought twenty years ago" and adds: "We must not carry on as though India is not changing. Things are going on, and people are not sitting here worrying about the need to preserve culture because the culture is living" (Ibid. 148). Josef Skvorecky points out that assimilation is inevitable and that it is ironic "that most of the folk dances and songs that the ethnic dance groups do at officially sponsored events [in Canada] are no longer done in the hills of Bohemia or Poland or wherever" (Skvorecky, 1990:30).

Liu is afraid of the possibility that the minorities who claim that their identity is not shaped by the *nation* but by their *descent* will be rejected in critical situations by "those who belong to the nation" (Liu, 1998: 123). An essentialist concept of culture which implies that you cannot take the China out of a Chinese will justify racist statements like the following which was published in the *Los Angeles Times* at the outbreak of the war between the United States and Japan: "A viper is nonetheless a viper wherever the egg is hatched— so a Japanese-American, born of Japanese parents, grows up to be a Japanese not an American" (Ibid. 119).

Liu criticizes multiculturalism for imposing on him a Chinese-American identity. Mukherjee criticizes it for preventing immigrants from social mobility and developing new identities. Bissoondath and Bannerji stress that change is inevitable and that the preservation of one's cultural identity leads to fossilization of cultural forms and to the reduction of culture to folklore.

## 3. Eva Hoffman: *Lost in Translation*

In her autobiography Eva Hoffman, who came from Poland to Canada when she was 13 years old, describes the difficult process of learning English and of adapting to the North American culture. She describes her process of assimilation and feels that she has to justify this process in an age of multiculturalism. In one of her reflections she begins with a statement from Adorno, who asked refugees not to assimilate in order to preserve their integrity:

> A bracingly uncompromising idea of integrity: but I doubt that Adorno could have maintained it over a lifetime without the hope of returning home— without

having a friendly audience back there for his dialectical satires. The soul can shrivel from an excess of critical distance, and if I don't want to remain in arid internal exile for the rest of my life, I have to find a way to lose my alienation without losing my self. (Hoffman, 1989:209)

Like Liu and Mukherjee she knows that without learning English she would be excluded from social mobility: "I have to make myself a steel breastplate of achievement and good grades, so that I'll be able to get out- and get in, so that I can gain entry into the social system from where I stand, on a precarious ledge" (Ibid. 157). She is aware of the fact that she will be accused of giving in to the dominant culture but she stresses that there is not only a social reason but also a psychological one for learning English. The inability to express oneself leads to violence: "And if one is perpetually without words, if one exists in the entropy of inarticulateness, that condition itself is bound to be an enraging frustration" (Ibid. 124). If one cannot understand the signs of the new culture, one will "fall out of the net of meaning into the weightlessness of chaos" (Ibid. 151). Hoffman stresses the necessity of learning the second language: "We want to be able to give voice accurately and fully to ourselves and our sense of the world" (Ibid. 124).

Assimilation is a complex process in a multicultural society. In the novel *Almost a Woman* by Esmeralda Santiago, Negi, the protagonist, who came from Puerto Rico to the United States as a child, becomes a dancer in "the new Japanese-inspired production for Children's Theater" in New York and plays the role of a member of Indian royalty. Her Puerto Rican friend Jaime is worried about the loss of their cultural and ethnic identity: "There's something wrong with this. We should be out there fighting for the rights of our people. We need to champion *our* art and theater. Let the Hindus worry about their own" (Santiago, 1998:286). Yet Negi does not accept this line of argument. Her interest in the Indian dance does not mean that she is against Puerto Rican culture and for Indian culture: "My devotion to Indian dance, I argued, wasn't part of a conspiracy to promote their civilization over Puerto Rico's" (Ibid.). Like Appiah and Rockefeller, Negi stresses the need for the development of her own personal identity which will profit from the influences of many different cultures. Yet for Jaime, the multiculturalist, her devotion to Indian dance is part of a conspiracy and a betrayal of her Puerto Rican culture: "If we lose Puerto Ricans to other cultures, we lose Puerto Rican culture" (Ibid.). Negi, however, contradicts him: "Why should I be less Puerto Rican if I danced Bharata Natyam? Were ballet dancers on the island less Puerto Rican because their art originated in France? What about pianists who performed Beethoven? Or people who read Nietzsche?" (Ibid. 286f.). It is probably one of the most irritating consequences of multiculturalism that it tends to regard the understanding of the foreign culture as a threat to one's own cultural identity and therefore regards intercultural understanding with suspicion. Whenever we learn something from the foreign culture we seem to betray our own. Although Negi does not approve of Jaime's arguments, he succeeds in making her feel guilty: "Jaime's judgment of me made me question my loyalty to my people" (Ibid. 287).

Like Negi, Tomson Highway stresses that he cannot help being influenced by the many cultures which surround him, so that assimilation is inevitable: "I can't help but be influenced by the fact that I've seen *Superman* or Joan Collins or *Archie* comic books, or for that matter, that I've heard the works of Beethoven. They are all irreparably, irretrievably, a part of my imagination now" (Highway, 1990:354). In an illuminating essay "Minority Cultures and the Cosmpolitan Alternative" Jeremy Waldron points out that for our well-being and self-realization we need cultural stimulation, but it need not come from our own culture, it can come from various cultures: "Meaningful options may come to us, as items or fragments from a variety of cultural sources" (Waldron, 1992: 783). Hoffman, Negi and Waldron stress that we should not refrain from being interested in foreign cultures. They are not a threat to but an enrichment of our personal identities.

## 4. Yasmine Gooneratne: *A Change of Skies*

In this novel the central theme is how immigrants from Sri Lanka should relate to the Australian culture: Should they preserve their Asian identity or should they assimilate to the Australian culture? Mr. Kyako from Sri Lanka, who is the leader of the Asian community in Sydney, fights for the preservation of Asian identities in Australia. Therefore, he asks Bharat Mangala-Davansinha, who has come as a guest professor of linguistics to Southern Cross University in Sydney, to write a guide for Asian migrants in Australia. Such a guide should help them succeed economically in Australia without assimilating to the Australian culture. Yet while Bharat is writing the guide his thoughts take a different direction. First of all, he changes the title. He writes a guide not for migrants but for immigrants which is a decisive change. For Kyako there can only be migrants because they will never give up their Asian cultures, but immigrants, according to Bharat, are faced with the question:

> There is a question I still ask myself after many years in an alien country: when is it exactly that the immigrant throws overboard every other idea, every other possible destination, and decides that here, and in no other place, he will make his home? (Gooneratne, 1991:151)

For Bharat, such a decision includes a moment of liberation from the norms and values of one's original culture: "Until we choose where we shall settle, and decide (in our own time) to make ourselves known, displaced people such as ourselves enjoy a liberty that others may well envy" (Ibid. 281). Especially for Bharat's wife, Navaranjini, life in Australia gives her the opportunity to change from "a tradition-minded helpmeet to her intellectual hubby" (Ibid. 293) to a successful writer of an intercultural cookbook. At first, she does not even dare to mention her intention of writing a book to her husband because "he'd pour scorn on the very idea that I could do anything with a book beyond listing it in a bibliography" (Ibid. 200).

*A Change of Skies* severely criticizes the ethnocentrism of those who want to preserve their original identity in the new culture and refuse to recognize the culture which has accepted them. For Mrs. Kyako the Australians are "brutes": "My husband warned me from the start: 'Be careful, Padmini,' he said. 'Always be on your guard! These people are not like us. They only know violence'" (Ibid. 81). And later she adds: "As my husband is always saying to me, 'Padmini, Padmini, what can you expect of barbarians and exconvicts?'" (Ibid. 82). In a highly ironic scene, a religious ceremony is to take place in Bharat's and Navaranjini's house. Mr. Kyako arrives before the other guests to make sure that everything is allright. He assures Bharat that he is very satisfied with what he sees, but is upset by some Keyt paintings. Since they show naked women, Bharat believes that Mr. Kyako is against them for moral and religious reasons. But he must learn that Mr. Kyako objects to these paintings for cultural reasons. He is against them because they were not produced by a Sinhalese artist but by one of "Dutch extraction" and because they show Indian influences:

> Mr. Keyt may be a good artist (even though I may not personally care for his work), but he does not represent those traditions [...] Mr. Keyt does not re-

present our good Sinhala traditions because he cannot, Bharat. How can he? He is, I am told, of Dutch extraction. A Burgher. And, I am informed, "Mr. Koyako added with serious displeasure, "that his painting reveals Indian influences." (Ibid. 91)

The preservation of one's cultural purity seems to be the logic consequence of a multiculturalism which regards assimilation as betrayal and stresses the differences between them and us. For Gertrud Nunner-Winkler this emphasis on "the right to difference" and purity is very problematic because it is an expression of the fear of mixing. She points out that after the Holocaust it is no longer possible to argue for racial purity, but the demand for the right to difference and cultural purity can fulfill the same function: "Underlying the manifest demand for a 'right to difference' is the same old racist structure: namely, a deep-seated phobia of interbreeding" (Nunner-Winkler, 1998: 280). Several times, *A Change of Skies* refers to the atrocities of the civil war between the Sinhalese and the Tamils in Sri Lanka and indicates that these atrocities are committed because people believe that they must defend their language and culture.

## Conclusion

In the first part of my paper I attempted to clarify the concept of intercultural understanding: I stressed the differences between understanding others, of becoming identical with them and being accepted by those whom we understand. It is essential for intercultural understanding that we take on the others' perspective and consider it critically. Such a goal makes it necessary to enter into a dialogue with others in which our own views are at stake.

The debate about assimilation or preservation of one's original cultural and ethnic identity can help us develop a flexible model for intercultural understanding. Intercultural understanding is based on the recognition of the differences between cultures but we must not essentialize them and must not ignore that we might have more in common with members of a foreign culture than with members of our own. We must acknowledge the individual identities of others and must not reduce them to their collective identity. We must further consider that the goal of intercultural understanding is not necessarily the preservation of one's cultural and ethnic identity. We must also recognize— and this is a justification for intercultural understanding— that our identities are not threatened but enriched by what we understand.

## References

Appiah, Kwame Anthony (1994). Identity, Authenticity, Survival: Multicultural Societies Social Reproduction. In: Charles Taylor (ed.), *Multiculturalism*. Princeton: Princeton University Press, pp. 149-163.

Appiah, Kwame Anthony (1996). Race, Culture, Identity: Misunderstood Connections. In: Kwame Anthony Appiah & Amy Gutman, *Color Conscious: The Political Morality of Race*. Princeton, NJ: Princeton University Press, pp. 30-105.

Bannerji, Himani (1990). The Other Family. Interview by Arun Mukherjee. In: Hutcheon & Richmond, pp. 141-152.

Baumann, Zygmunt (1992). *Intimations of Postmodernity*. London: Routledge.

Bissoondath, Neil (1990). Dancing. Interview by Aruna Srivastava. In: Hutcheon & Richmond, pp. 297-320.

Bredella, Lothar (1999). Nightmares of Misrecognition in Multicultural Texts. In: Carin Freywald & Michael Porsche (eds.), *The American Dream. Festschrift for Peter Freese*. Essen: Die Blaue Eule, pp. 79-96.

Byram, Michael (1997). *Teaching and Assessing Intercultural Communicative Competence*. Clevedon: Multilingual Matters.

Clifford, James (1986a). Introduction: Partial Truths. In: James Clifford & George E. Marcus (eds.), *Writing Culture. The Poetics and Politics of Ethnography*. Berkeley et al.: University of California Press, pp. 1-26.

Clifford, James (1986b). An Ethnographic Allegory. In: James Clifford & George E. Marcus (eds.), *Writing Culture. The Poetics and Politics of Ethnography*. Berkeley et al.: University of California Press, pp. 98-121.

Gates, Henry Louis, Jr. (1992). *Loose Canons. Notes on the Cultural Wars*. New York & Oxford: Oxford University Press.

Geertz, Clifford (1984). Distinguished Lecture: Anti-Anti-Relativism, *American Anthropologist*, LXXXVI, pp. 264-278.

Geertz, Clifford (1986). The Uses of Diversity, *Michigan Quarterly Review*, Winter, pp. 105-123.

Gooneratne, Yasmine (1991). *A Change of Skies*. Sydney: Picador.

Hall, Stuart (1991). Old and New Identities, Old and New Ethnicities, In: Anthony D. King (ed.), *Culture, Globalization and the World-System*. New York: MaCmillan, pp. 41-68.

Harden, Theo (2000). The Limits of Understanding, In: Theo Harden & Arnd Witte (eds.), *The Notion of Intercultural Understanding in the Context of German as a Foreign Language*. Oxford et al.: Lang.

Heller, Agnes (1979). *A Theory of Feelings*. Assen: Van Gorcum.

Highway, Tomson (1990). The First and Founding Nations Respond. Interview by Ann Wilson. In: Hutcheon & Richmond, pp. 350-355.

Hoffman, Eva (1989). *Lost in Translation. A Life in a New Language*.

New York et al.: Penguin.

Holland, Norman (1985). Reading Readers Reading. In: Charles R. Cooper (ed.), *Researching Responses to Literature and the Teaching of Literature. Points of Departure*. Norwood, NJ: Ablex, pp. 3-21.

Hutcheon, Linda & Richmond, Marion (eds.) (1990). *Other Solitudes: Canadian Multicultural Fictions*. Toronto: Oxford University Press.

Ignatieff, Michael (1993). *Blood and Belonging. Journeys into the New Nationalism*. London: BBC Books.

Kramsch, Claire (1997). Culture and Self in Language Learning. The British Council, Bulgaria: Conference Papers. http://britcoun.org/bulgaria/eltconf/papers/cell/index.htm, 1-7.

Liu, Eric (1998). *The Accidental Asian*. New York: Vintage.

Mukherjee, Bharati (1990). Imagining Ourselves', Interview with Bill Moyers. In: Andie Tucher (ed.) & Bill D. Moyers, *A world of Ideas II*. New York: Doubleday, pp. 3-10.

Nunner-Winkler, Gertrud (1998). Normal Elements of Ethnocentrism. In: Dieter Haselbach (ed.), *Multiculturalism in a World of Leaking Boundaries*. Muster: LIT, pp. 279-308.

Nussbaum, Martha C. (1995). *Poetic Justice. The Literary Imagination and Public Life*. Boston: Beacon Press.

Paci, Frank (1990). The Stone Garden. Interview by Joseph Pivato. In: Hutcheon & Richmond, pp. 219-234.

Putnam, Hilary (1998). *Renewing Philosophy*. Cambridge, Mass.: Harvard University Press.

Rockefeller, Stephen C. (1994). Comment. In: Charles Taylor et al., *Multiculturalism. Examining the Politics of Recognition*. (ed. and introd. by Amy Gutman) Princeton: Princeton University Press, pp. 87-98.

Rorty, Richard (1991). *Objectivity, Realism, and Truth*. Cambridge UP.

Rowell, Charles H. (1991) An Interview with Henry Louis Gates, Jr.

*Callaloo* 14.2, pp. 444-463.

Said, Edward W. (1978) *Orientalism*. New York: Vintage Books.

Said, Edward W. (1986) Intellectuals in the Post-Colonial World. *Salmagundi*, 70 (71), pp. 44-64.

Santiago, Esmeralda (1998). *Almost a Woman*. New York: Vintage Books.

Sheikh, Farhana (1991). *The Red Box*. London: Women's Press.

Skvorecky, Josef (1990). From *The Engineer of Human Souls*. Interview by Sam Solecki. In: Hutcheon & Richmond, pp. 141-152.

Standford, Michael (1986). *The Nature of Historical Knowledge*. Oxford & New York: Basil Blackwell.

Standiford, Lester (1982). Worlds Made of Dawn. Characteristic Image and Incident in Native American Imaginative Literature. In: Houston A. Baker Jr. (ed.), *Three American Literatures: Essays on Chicano, Native American, and Asian-American Literatures for Teachers of American Literature*. New York: Modern Language Association of America, pp. 168-196.

Taylor, Charles (1985). *Philosophy and the Human Sciences. Philosophical Papers Ⅱ*. Cambridge: Cambridge University Press.

Waldron, Jeremy (1992). Minority Cultures and the Cosmopolitan Alternative. *University of Michigan Journal of Law Reform*, 24 (3), pp. 751-793.

[From: Byram, M. (2001) *Developing Intercultural Competence in Practice*, Clevedon: Multilingual Matters]

## 导读：跨文化理解的一种灵活模式

本文主要介绍跨文化理解最本质的方面，并且对于外国文化同化和保留自身文化和种族特征之间的紧张现象进行了探讨。最终的结论是需要建立一个更加灵活的跨文化理解的模式，使得保留或改变自己的文化特征成为可能。

## 跨文化理解的本质

Theo Harden（2000）在"理解的局限"一文中提出跨文化理解可能对自己的文化身份构成威胁，并且当他人文化威胁到自身文化时，就应该停止去理解那种文化。在跨文化交际中，永远不会存在"完全理解"和"完全被理解"。作者也认为理解不可能是充分和完全的，但是，作者并不赞同 Harden 所提出的理解他人文化就是把自己的文化和他人文化等同起来，也不赞成理解他人文化不仅不能丰富我们自身文化，反而威胁自身的文化。作者认为理解他人文化到什么程度是受我们的需要所决定的。

Harden 认为一个想要了解他国文化的人是不会被该文化所在国家的人充分接受的。作者也同意这个观点，但是这并不能导致 Harden 所说的"理解是个幻想"这个结论。在我们的社会里，我们常常听到人们说理解既不可能，也没有必要。很多人认为当我们拒绝理解的时候可以保护自己和别人。然而，这种观点也受到了猛烈的抨击，Henry Louis Gates（1992）认为如果没有理解就不可能做到尊重他人："没有理解就没有尊重，没有尊重就没有宽容。"

那我们是否能够理解我们所没有经历过的事情呢？在关于阅读的争论中，反对理解的学者认为我们并不理解文中的内容，而只是进入到文中寻找我们想要寻找的东西。阅读便成了一种主观性很强的写作。这种观点是把读者假设成不断把自己的想法和兴趣强加在文章之上。另外一种观点认为读者和作品之间的美感距离使得读者有机会更加"客观"，并且认为读者可以理解所没有经历过的事。理解的过程就是意识到不同的过程。如果我们能够区分他国文化和本国文化，我们就可以说做到了跨文化理解。在跨文化理解中，最重要的是站在他人的角度来看待问题，即通过他人的眼睛来看待问题。学习一种语言、了解一种文化也就意味着跨越国界，尊重差异，目的是克服"民族中心论"。

## 文化同化与保留自身文化的冲突

在《红盒子》(*The Red Box*) 这篇小说中,作者描述了两位在英国的巴基斯坦裔女性,其中一位女性 Nasreen Ehsan 对自己国家的文化非常自豪,希望在英国继续保持这种文化传统。而另外一位女性 Tahira Rashid 则是想融入到英国文化当中。她对保持自己的文化不感兴趣。她希望能像英国女性那样生活。这部小说认为这两种态度都是合理的,但是对于实际上这两位女士是否能够自由选择到底是保持自己的文化身份还是同化到主流文化里只是一个幻想而已。

同化对于那些觉得自己文化低人一等的人来说是一种痛苦的经历。在这种情况下,把重点转移到一个人整体的身份上能够克服自卑,并且提供安全感和保护。其中最突出的一个例子就是"黑色是美丽的"。但是,从另外一方面来说,过分注重自身的文化和种族身份会忽略我们与其他文化的共同点,把注意力过分引向与他人的区别上。因此,在外语教学中,应当把这种"身份政治"的负面因素考虑在内。

在 Eric Liu (1998) 的自传 *The Accidental Asian* 中,他自己作为一个为总统 Bill Clinton 写演讲稿的成功华裔美国人来说,他不主张要保持自身的文化,因为这样一来,他认为就是每个中国血统的中国人,无论他在什么地方出生,在他身上都存在中国式的东西。对于刘而言,一个人称为中国人并不是因为他祖先是中国人,而是因为他决定在异国文化中保留自身的文化。自称为美国人的刘也意识到多元文化对他对中国文化的背叛的指责。刘认为,文化的同化带来了文化的变迁,同时文化多元主义又保持了现状。刘对于多元主义强加在他身上的华裔身份持反对态度。

在 13 岁从波兰移民到加拿大的 Eva Hoffman 的自传中,她讲述了学习英语的过程和逐步适应北美文化的经历。与刘相似的是,她知道如果不学会英语,就将被社会淘汰,就不可能在社会立足。

Hoffman（1989）认为学习英语不仅有社会因素，同时还有心理因素：无法表达自己只会导致暴力。

在 Yasmine Gooneratne（1991）的小说 A Change of Skies 主要讲述的是斯里兰卡的移民如何适应到澳大利亚的文化当中。这篇小说严厉抨击了那些极力保持自身文化的民族中心论者，因为他们拒绝接纳他人的文化。保持自身文化的纯洁性似乎是多元文化主义产生的逻辑后果，但是多元文化主义视同化是一种背叛，同时承认并强调文化之间的差异。很多学者认为这种看重文化的纯洁性存在很多问题，是害怕文化融合的一种表现。

## 结束语

在文章中，作者首先明确了跨文化理解的概念，作者强调理解和等同他人之间的区别。对于跨文化理解来说，站在他人角度非常重要。关于同化和保持自身文化身份的讨论建立了一个非常灵活的跨文化理解的模型。跨文化理解是建立在对不同文化之间不同的承认之上，同时，我们还应该看到文化间的共同之处。跨文化理解的目标不一定是要保留自身的文化身份，跨文化理解不是我们身份的威胁而是不断丰富我们身份的有利工具。

**Questions for reflection：**

1. What does intercultural understanding really mean?
2. Why does the author think "standing in other's shoes" is important for intercultural understanding?
3. Why do people who understand a foreign culture might even be rejected by it?
4. What's the tension between assimilation and preservation of one's culture like?
5. What's the essence of the proposed flexible model for intercultural understanding?

# Tandem Learning as an Intercultural Activity

Jane Woodin

The purpose of this chapter is to show how learners can benefit from reciprocal arrangements to develop their intercultural competence in the context of tandem learning in a university. They work face-to-face or through email. In this article the diaries kept by those meeting in person are analysed to describe the development of their intercultural competence. The chapter thus suggests ways in which tandem learning can be developed to put emphasis on intercultural competence.

## Introduction

The Modern Languages Teaching Centre at the University of Sheffield was set up in 1993 to provide service language teaching to non-specialist undergraduates (i. e. those taking degrees in Science, Engineering or Social Sciences)①. We take a broadly communicative approach to language learning, with an emphasis on practical language skills. In the year 1999-2000, approximately 700 undergraduates took language courses with our Centre.

The University of Sheffield operates a modular system, which means, for example, that a first year engineering undergraduate who takes modules to the value of 120 credits may be required to take modules to the value of 100 credits from courses offered within his or her department. The re-

---

① Some of the information and data presented in this article was also used as the basis of a paper presented at the conference, The New Communicators: Graduates with Languages (University of Nottingham, July 2000)

maining 20 credits can be taken from any course which is offered to them from other departments across the university; many of them choose to take a language with the Modern Languages Teaching Centre (MLTC).

Tandem learning—collaborative learning between native speakers and learners of each other's language— is particularly relevant to higher education contexts, as it is practically very easy to organise. Large numbers of students come from many countries in Europe under the 'Erasmus' scheme. In particular, Erasmus students from French, German, Italian and Spanish-speaking countries are highly sought after, these being the most commonly-studied languages in UK universities.

The concept of tandem learning① is complex but its overarching principles are as follows:

**Autonomy**: You are responsible for your own learning;
**Reciprocity**: You are responsible for ensuring mutual benefit.
(http://www.slf.ruhr-uni-bochum.de/learning/idxeng11.html)

Students are therefore active participants in their own learning and clearly have the opportunity of setting their own agenda.

Students studying with the Modern Languages Teaching Centre can take part in tandem learning either face-to-face or through email, and either as an informal activity or as an assessed part of their degree course. The

---

① A comprehensive bibliography can be found on the website of the International Email Tandem Network, address: http://www.slf.ruhr-uni-bochum.de/email/infen.html

project described here is concerned with the experience of students undertaking tandem learning face-to-face, as a formal 10-credit module. This is available to students with language proficiency equivalent to Advanced-Level or higher i. e. a level usually reached after 6-8 years of language learning in secondary school.

The tandem module① has proved hugely successful in particular because students have a high degree of control over what they choose to learn and how they go about it, and they have far more opportunity to practise their speaking than in a language class. By way of illustration, some of the comments made by students about the module include the following:

*The ability to manage your own learning and learn from a native*
*Manage own learning and at my own pace and in my own way and choose what I wanted to talk about*
*You can talk about things which aren't in books*
*You choose what you learn— no restrictions.*
*Autonomy and access to native speakers*
*Improve my language learning skills in a relaxed atmosphere.*
(Comments from student evaluation of English-Spanish tandem course in response to the question *What do you like best about the tandem module?* Spring semester, 1999)

The students from other European Union countries, studying under the ERASMUS scheme, consistently report that they find it hard to make English friends when they come to study in the UK; this is particularly difficult for those who only come to study for one twelve-week semester.

---

① The framework for the face-to-face tandem module was developed by Lesley Walker with input from the Centre's core teaching team.

Tandem learning, therefore, is a real opportunity to get to know English students, practise English and (as is often the case) socialise more closely with them.

## Outline of the Tandem Module

The face-to-face tandem module runs over one twelve-week semester. Its format is broadly as follows:

*Week* 1: Get to know your partner, prioritise your main learning aims for the semester, plan your personal learning goals, methods and materials to help you achieve your aims, together with advice from your tutor. Agree time and place for tandem session, discuss effective ways of working with your partner.

*Weeks* 2-5: Attend (optional) session with tutor for advice on filling in diary. Continue with tandem sessions with partner. Complete tandem diary page after each tandem session (10 pages to be completed over the semester). Use ready-made tandem learning sheets if desired.

*Week* 6: Together with your tandem partner, attend a counselling session with your tutor, to review your learning and your goals, making changes where necessary.

*Weeks* 7-10: Continue with tandem sessions and diary completion.

*Weeks* 11-12: Undertake speaking test (mini tandem session), hand in diary together with a report of the semester, self-and peer assessment grades. Speaking test and diary are graded by tutors (each worth 35% of the final grade), self-assessment is on your development of autonomy (worth 10%), your progress in language learning (10%). Peer-assessment is on your partner's development in the language (also worth 10%) The tandem diary[①] offers students a basic structure for them to follow.

---

[①] The tandem diary was also developed by Lesley Walker at the University of Sheffield; copies of the diary can be obtained from the Modern Languages Teaching Centre at the university.

Initially they are required to prioritise the main areas of learning for themselves (they are asked to rank the following in order of priority for them: *Range of vocabulary*, *Sentence structures*, *Accuracy*, *Pronunciation/Intonation*, *Listening*, *Cultural knowledge*, *Techniques for language learning and Independent study skills*). They can also choose their own areas to focus on; one of the most popular areas chosen by students themselves is *Fluency*. Once the general learning areas have been prioritised, students are then required to translate their "wish list" into realistic, manageable goals. This is done with the aid of the tutor. For example, a student who has chosen *Range of vocabulary* as one of their priorities will identify specific areas where they would like to develop their vocabulary (such as informal language spoken by students, or vocabulary related to engineering). They will then devise activities together with the tutor which will enable them to achieve their goals by the end of the semester. Such activities, in the case of engineering vocabulary, might include finding a written text on an aspect of engineering from the Worldwide-web, reading it before the tandem session and then summarising it to their tandem partner. The tutor also helps students to devise activities which are commensurate with their level of language proficiency, enabling them to progress without setting goals which are too easy or difficult for them to achieve.

The process of turning priorities into manageable learning goals is one which is difficult for many students, particularly those who are not used to evaluating and monitoring their own learning. Once the process of setting goals and the means by which they will be achieved is completed, students arrange with their tandem partners the tandem sessions themselves; these take place at times and places mutually agreed between partners. Each week, students fill in a page in their learner diary, recording their progress. The diary pages contain the following headings to help guide them:

*Vocabulary and new expressions;*
*Cultural information;*
*Sentence structures/Accuracy;*
*Did I fully achieve today's goal or not?*
*Next Step;*
*Observation of self and partner (How can I learn from the way I learn and from the way my partner learns?)*

Students are informed that these headings serve as a guide; they can write their diary on separate pages if they prefer, or they can leave out certain sections some weeks if they are not relevant to them. It is the students' diary entries which have revealed evidence of the intercultural nature of tandem learning.

## Evidence from the Tandem Diaries of the Development of Intercultural Communicative Competence (ICC)

One of the aims of the tandem module is "To enable students to develop proficiency in... intercultural awareness" (MLTC Student Guide, 1999-2000).

In fact, the tandem learning module does not directly assess students' intercultural communicative competence, although it is implicit in some areas of assessed work. For example, if a student has chosen the development of cultural knowledge as one of their goals, then they will be assessed on whether they have achieved this or not. However, regardless of whether students have chosen the development of cultural knowledge as their goal, there is evidence that they are in fact developing their intercultural communicative competence through tandem learning. The fact that most of them do not tend to choose cultural knowledge as one of their main priorities means that one can assume that the evidence which they provide of developing their ICC is not driven by a desire to succeed in the module, but is a genuine product of the tandem relationship.

The evidence of aspects of ICC comes from a number of tandem diaries, seventeen of which were examined in detail; these were all from students undertaking the tandem module during the Autumn semester 1999. Nine were from native English students and eight from native Spanish students.

By its very nature, tandem learning is an intercultural activity; in order to achieve their learning goals, learners must exchange ideas, opinions and negotiate ways of working with their partners. In undertaking all of this, they are communicating directly with speakers of another language/culture. One area which provides evidence for the development of ICC is that of the choice of topics discussed by students. The choice of topics discussed was extremely varied, ranging from an exchange of personal information, to debates on homosexual parenting. A rough categorisation has been attempted below, using the work of Robinson (1985:7). She found that when teachers were asked the question "What does culture mean to you?" the following categories were most commonly reported:

- Products (literature, folklore, art, music, artefacts)
- Ideas (beliefs, values, institutions)
- Behaviours (customs, habits, dress, foods)

A rough analysis of the topics mentioned by tandem learners in the "Cultural Information" section of their diaries revealed that certain topics were more popular than others. The number of times each topic was mentioned is noted below:

| **Products:** | **Ideas** | **Behaviours** |
|---|---|---|
| Literature – 3 | Beliefs – 10 | Customs— 14 |
| Folklore – 7 | Values – 18 | Habits— 15 |
| Art – 4 | Institutions – 29 | Dress— 5 |
| Music – 0 | | Foods— 9 |
| Artefacts – 0 | | Leisure— 10 |

The lack of emphasis upon products is interesting. Some of this may be due to the fact that all of the students had visited Spain, some for holidays, others for a period of study. Other possible reasons for this could be that many of the students were also following courses in Spanish/English literature and cinema, or had access to this kind of information in other places. The relationship with their tandem partner, however, allowed them to exchange views on the way Spanish/English people think, similarities and differences between institutions (by far the most popular being the education system, but covering also the job market, government and politics).

Topics which were brought up by students which do not appear to fit into the above categories include:

Getting to know your partner (9). For obvious reasons, this was the most common topic for the first tandem session.
Geography of each other's country (7) (for example, regions, climate, principal cities)
History (3)
Transport (2)
Language/gestures: (15)

Feelings: (2)

Practicalities and conventions: (3) (For example, travelling in another country, structuring essays)

It is interesting to note that quite a number of students wrote aspects of language under the section "Cultural Information". Typical instances include the use of idioms, and phrases related to card playing or drinking, as well as the use of gestures.

Possibly at the time of Robinson's study, teachers saw language as an area separate from culture, whereas nowadays, the cultural weight of language is far more accepted (see for example, Kramsch, 1993).

The students' contributions under the heading Cultural information were also analysed in the light of Byram's factors of intercultural communication (1997):

|  | Skills<br>Interpret and relate<br>(*savoir comprendre*) |  |
|---|---|---|
| **Knowledge**<br>Of self and other;<br>of interaction;<br>individual and societal<br>(*savoirs*) | **Education**<br>Political education<br>Critical cultural awareness<br>(*savoirs' engager*) | **Attitudes**<br>Relativising self<br>Valuing others (*savoir être*) |
|  | Skills<br>Discover and/or interact<br>(*savoir apprendre/faire*) |  |

(Byram, 1997:34)

The criteria for each of these five *savoirs* were used to evaluate the kind of experience that tandem learning was giving the students. Below are some examples from the students' entries which illustrate how they are developing some of the aspects of ICC.

**Attitudes** (*Savoir être*):
Simply by taking part in tandem learning, the student is fulfilling an aspect of Byram's criteria, covered in *Attitudes*. (*Willingness to seek out or take up opportunities to engage with otherness in a relationship of equality, distinct from seeking out the exotic or to profit from others.* (Byram, 1997:57))

The relationship of equality is defined by the nature of the tandem course and the tandem principles themselves. Byram also states that the *Attitudes* category involves the speaker being interested in a range of social groups within a society and not only that represented in the dominant culture (Ibid. 58). With such topics discussed as those mentioned above, students are clearly demonstrating interest in a wide range of social groups.

Similarly, the native Spanish tandem students are displaying a readiness for experiencing different stages of interaction and adaptation with another culture (criteria (d) of Byram's *Attitudes*). For example, Jaime① commented that he and his partner discussed personal feelings about being in the UK: "We talked about the changes for me in Sheffield.... all those little things which you don't realise you miss until they are not there..." (Jaime Week 9).

---

① All names of participants have been changed to ones in keeping with their sex and nationality.

**Knowledge** (*savoirs*):
This is the category for which there was the largest amount of evidence in the tandem diaries. This is possibly not surprising; students with largely linguistic goals often choose different aspects of society to discuss with their partner in order to improve their language. They are, of course, improving their cultural knowledge at the same time.

Some examples of evidence which satisfies the *Knowledge* category are presented here.

One pair of students discussed legends: "We also discovered that the English think that St. George saved England from the dragon, and the Spanish think he saved Spain" (Gail, Week 8). The same student also commented that she and her partner discussed Spain and Britain entering the European Union, but did not give details as to exactly what was discussed (Gail, Week 2). This is evidence of the development of an understanding of historical and contemporary relationships between one's own and one's interlocutor's country (criterion (a) in the *Knowledge* category, Ibid: 59).

One tandem pair decided to study gestures; they used a ready-prepared tandem sheet as a basis for their discussion (Nadia, Week 2). They came to the conclusion that the majority of gestures are similar between Spanish and English cultures, but that kissing is used very differently. This activity clearly contributes to students' knowledge of the types of misunderstanding between interlocutors of different cultural origins. (criterion (c) in the *Knowledge* category, Ibid: 59).

Through the comparison of heroes (stimulated by a tandem sheet on legends), one tandem pair discussed how some of Spain's heroic legends are quite recent, for example from the civil war or the war with France:

> David and I discussed how this wasn't true for England and came to the conclusion that most war heroes come from either civil wars or from wars which are fought on their own land. English war heroes are from a time when we had civil wars, so our heroes/legends are principally from hundreds of years ago. (Gail, Week 8)

This is evidence of their having considered the national memory of each others' country, [see criterion d) and e)] of the *Knowledge* category, Ibid: 59.

Another student discussed with her partner the regional stereotypes in Spain (Alice, Week 7). Another commented on how it is interesting to know the different regional accents "although trying to identify them would be difficult" (David, Week 6). Still another pair discussed the different countries which make up the United Kingdom (Rocío, Week 2).

Education systems are compared by a number of tandem pairs, some in direct relation to the courses which they are currently studying (Annie, Weeks 7 and 8, Charlotte, Week 9). The topic of religion is also considered by a number of tandem pairs, particularly in terms of its importance at Christmas (Marisa, Week 2) or comparatively with the UK (Caroline, Week 6). (This is evidence for criterion h) *Of Knowledge: The processes and institutions of socialisation in one's own and one's interlocutor's country* (Ibid: 60).

Byram's criterion (f) in the *Knowledge* category covers social distinctions and their principal markers, in one's own country and in one's interlocutors (Ibid: 60). Evidence of this is apparent in the tandem pairs who discussed the roles of women (Caroline, Week 3), homosexuality (Cathy, Week 6), under age sex (Alice, Week 11) or the British attitudes towards certain professions, such as waiters and teachers (David, Week 3). These kinds of topics appear to be relatively popular with the tandem partnerships.

As revealed in the rough analysis of topics earlier, a large number of institutions and perceptions of them are discussed (fulfilling criterion (j): *Institutions and perceptions of them, which impinge on daily life within one's own and one's interlocutor's country and which conduct and influence relationships between them* (Ibid: 60)). Some examples include the following:

- "David told me about the *prensa rosa*, which are gossip type magazines and papers like "Hola" (Gail, Week 9).
- One student reported how the police in Spain are cracking down more on drink driving than before, information which she gleaned from her partner. (Polly, Week 4). Another student specifically chose to discuss banking customs, as he felt he needed to understand them better, in England (David, Week 4).
- The same student chose to understand more about the relationship between the House of Commons and the House of Lords in England, at a time when this topic was in the news. (David, Week 9).
- Another pair chose to compare the Spanish and the British royal families (Annie, Week 10).

Public behaviour in terms of meals is discussed (María, Weeks 1 and 5) as are forms of public meeting (Charlotte, Week 7; Gail, Week 7; Alice, Week 1). Less is reported with regard to taboos, which Byram includes under criterion (k) (*The processes of social interaction in one's interlocutor's country* (Ibid: 60)). Taboos are possibly a risky topic to discuss with one's tandem partner.

**Skills of interpreting and relating** (*Savoir comprendre*):
The aspect of this category most evident in the tandem diaries is the ability to identify ethnocentric perspectives in a document or event and explain their origins (Ibid: 61). One student reported that the television in England is of higher quality than in Spain, but notes that the news in England is "self-centred"; that there is little information about Europe. (María, Week 3). She did not, however, report having attempted to explain the origins of this difference.

**Skills of discovery and interaction** (*savoir apprendre/faire*):
Many students discussed documents, whether written or recorded, with their tandem partner; some also identified the significant references within and across cultures. [See criterion (a) *Elicit from an interlocutor the concepts and values of documents or events and develop an explanatory system susceptible of application to other phenomena*, and (b) *Identify significant references within and across cultures and elicit their significance and connotations* (*Ibid*: 61-62)].

One student compared student life in Spain and England with her partner and then came to the conclusion that the reasons for the differences largely come from the fact that Spanish students tend to study near where they live (Cathy, Week 5).

In a discussion about homosexual families, the same student reported in her diary:

One of my arguments for adoption by homosexual couples was that two mothers or two fathers are better than the "one parent family" which is so common in Britain nowadays. Carolina disagreed with me on this point—she thinks that the concept of the single parent family is not as widely accepted in Spain as it is here—and that there are few. (Cathy, Week 6)

Another commented, on discussion with her partner on the topic of tobacco and drink:

Interesting to debate these—it gave me an insight into Spanish young person's opinions on these topics. Despite our cultural difference we saw eye-to-eye on almost all of the topics. ... We decided that European young people are much more alike than a few generations ago. For example, the fact that Spain is a Catholic country no longer seems to affect the opinions of the young people." (Gail, Week 6)

**Critical Cultural Awareness/Political Education** (*savoir s'engager*): This involves: *An ability to evaluate, critically, and on the basis of explicit criteria, perspectives, practices and products in one's own and other cultures and countries* (Ibid: 63).

As mentioned previously, although all the *savoirs* overlap, this is the one category which underlies all the other ones, focusing on comparison and evaluation. Evidence exists of students' evaluating information which they have gleaned. One example is that given previously of Cathy who concluded that the differences in studying habits between Spain and England stemmed largely from the fact that Spanish students tend to study near where they live. Another student reported that she and her partner discussed the availability of alcohol, bleach etc. and related this to the attitudes towards safety in each country (Annie, Week 3).

While there does exist significant evidence from the tandem diaries of some aspects of critical cultural awareness, there is little evidence of students' having evaluated on the basis of *explicit* criteria.

## Developments

To summarise, it certainly appears that the face-to-face tandem relationship does offer opportunities for developing Intercultural Communicative Competence. The evidence from the tandem diaries does not fit neatly into all the categories, however. Neither does it necessarily fulfil each of the criteria in their entirety. For example, concepts and values were elicited from documents, but students did not apply explanations to other phenomena [see *Skills of discovery and interaction* (a)].

It appears that students are interested in their partners' culture coupled with a desire to know more, but students do not seem to take the further step of a deeper analysis, such as questioning attitudes or drawing conclusions from information. It may be that in order to achieve these, students will require further support of their tutor.

This begs the following questions:

1) To what degree can a student who partially fulfils criteria be considered interculturally competent? Byram argues that the ideal to be reached will depend upon the context, and that different contexts will require different descriptions of intercultural competence (Ibid: 79-81). The evidence, as described above from student diaries, could therefore inform the future development of a tandem learning syllabus designed for developing intercultural communicative competence.

2) How much does the layout of the diary dictate what students actually report is happening? As mentioned previously, the sub-heading "Cultural information" may well give them the impression that they should largely report facts and knowledge. What is interesting from their entries is the emphasis on the *Ideas* and *Behaviours* topics as opposed to the *Products* (See earlier). Scrutiny of diaries along with video evidence of tandem session could well provide some answers to this question.

3) Clearly with tutor input it would be possible to enable students to fulfil criteria more fully. For example, with prompting from the tutor, students could take steps to reflect on how their own country is perceived by others (See *Knowledge*). But to what degree will this tutor interference inhibit students' development of autonomy? Since, together with language learning, this is the main aim of the tandem module, it would appear that an insistence of undertaking certain intercultural tasks would remove some of the emphasis on autonomous learning. It might be fitting, therefore, to consider tandem modules with different aims, or a broader intercultural syllabus which incorporates tandem learning as one of its components.

In order to enable learners to take the necessary steps with regard to analysis and evaluation, one may well wish to consider some of the following possible modifications:

- At the start of their tandem learning venture, students can be sensitised to the possibilities of development of their intercultural communicative competence. This could be done by the inclusion on the list of priorities aspects such as
- identification of differences and similarities between my country and that of my partner;

- identification of the main stereotypes which exist of each of our countries as seen from the other;
- understanding of possible reasons for the existence of these.

Similar questions to cover other aspects of ICC could well be devised, to make it easier for students to analyse and evaluate.
- Tandem learners could be encouraged to analyse more through the simple inclusion of further questions in the diary sheets; for example the inclusion of a heading of "Cultural aspects" —your analysis and/or conclusions might draw out a slightly deeper reflection on the topics discussed.
- Some tandem sessions could be extended to involve two or more tandem pairs in group discussion. This could provide students with situations which take them further than their tandem relationship normally allow. For example, a group of English students and a group of Spanish students could be given different points of view to argue on a topic, and be encouraged to identify at the end of the debate any differences in interaction patterns between the English and the Spanish students.

If cultural aspects of tandem learning are more directly assessed, students may well be more inclined to focus more closely on intercultural aspects. This would of course have the effect of lessening the degree of student autonomy over the tandem process.
- Ironically, however, what has been particularly interesting about this study has been the fact that students have not seen the cultural aspects as being assessed (except in the case of one or two who chose cultural aspects as a personal learning goal) and so what they have reported is clearly what they have gleaned regardless of outside requirements. This has offered the unique opportunity to understand

further the points at which intervention from the tutor may be necessary in order to enable them to develop their ICC further.

What is certainly clear from the evidence presented above, is that the acquisition of intercultural competence is a process. Learning is not necessarily a linear process, but students may well wish to revisit these issues at a later date, possibly outside the tandem relationship (see Byram, 1997:75). The definition of culture itself as a process is supported by many (see for example, Robinson, 1985, or Street, 1991). Tandem learners, whether consciously or unconsciously, are engaging in this process actively. To cite a Spanish student:

> From my point of view... the most important goal for me and which I am really proud of having achieved, is having integrated fully into my group of friends... because this means that I am like one of them, and so I can talk about anything, any topic or problem which I like, freely, and it's this way that I have learnt the street language, the language which is used by young people; that is, the language which you can't learn in any book, no matter how good it is. (Marisa, Tandem Report, end of semester 1999).

## References

Walker, L. (1996) *Introducing the Face-to-Face Tandem Learning Module: Integrating Autonomy into the University Curriculum* (unpublished dissertation).

Byram, M. (1997) *Teaching and Assessing Intercultural Communicative Competence*, Clevedon: Multilingual Matters.

Kramsch, C. (1993) *Context and Culture in Language Teaching*, Oxford: Oxford University Press.

Robinson, G. N. (1985) *Crosscultural Understanding*, Oxford: Pergamon.

Street, B. (1997) Culture is a Verb, in Graddol, D. L., Thompson, L., & Byram, M. (eds.) *Language and Culture*, Clevedon: Multilingual Matters.

[From: Byram, M. (2001) *Developing Intercultural Competence in Practice*, Clevedon: Multilingual Matters]

## 导读:跨文化活动中的协作学习模式

本文主要介绍在大学里通过协作式学习模式培养学生跨文化能力。学生通过面对面或者通过发送电子邮件的方式进行相互式学习。在本文当中,作者对学生们每次会面所记下的日记进行分析以查看他们跨文化能力是否得到了提高。同时,本文还对协作式学习如何把重点放在对学生跨文化能力的培养上提出了建议。

### 背景简介

本文中提到的谢弗尔德大学的现代语言教学中心于1993年成立,是专门为工程、社会科学等专业的毕业生提供语言教学服务的机构。协作式学习,也即是讲当地语言的人与讲其他语言的人的一种协作性学习。协作式学习是一个比较复杂的概念,但是主要包含两个方面的原则:自主性和互益性。这种学习模式被证明非常成功。学生可以自主选择他们想要学习的东西,并且对如何学习也可以进行操纵,这样一来,他们拥有了比在语言课堂上更多的机会来练习口语。

来自于欧盟国家,并正在"ERASMUS"计划下学习的学生说他们常常发现在英国学习很难交上英国朋友,尤其是对于那些只在英国进行为期十二周学习的学生而言。协作式学习因此提供了一个很好的机会来了解英国学生,与他们进行交流、练习英语。

## 协作式学习

面对面的协作模式持续十二周,其基本步骤主要是:

第一周:了解伙伴,列出这学期的主要学习目标,寻找一些相关的学习资料,并从导师那里征求建议。确定见面的时间和与伙伴合作的有效方式。

第二至第五周:参加导师组织的见面会,通过做记录来寻求建议。同时,继续与伙伴之间的合作学习。每次见面完后完成一份记录。

第六周:与伙伴一起,与导师见面,总结最近的学习情况,看看哪里需要调整。

第七至十周:继续协作式学习和日记记录。

第十一至十二周:进行口语测试,学生需交上所有的记录、一份学期总结报告、自我评价和同伴评价。口语测试和所作的记录由导师打分。

同伴评价主要是基于对方语言能力,协作学习日记提供给学生一个基本的标准。首先他们主要确定学习的主要方面,例如词汇量、句子结构、准确性、语音语调、听力、文化知识、语言学习策略和独立学习技巧。学生也可以选择自己的学习侧重点,其中被学生认为是最重要的往往是"流利"。

把首要目标转为可操作的学习目标是一项很难的工作,尤其是对于那些不习惯评定和监控自身学习的学生而言。制定目标和如何实现目标计划一旦完成,学生开始自主安排他们与伙伴见面的方式。作为记录谈话内容的日记主要包含以下一些内容来指导学生:词汇和新短语;文化信息;句子结构/准确性;"我是否达到了今天的目标?";对自己和对方的观察。

协作学习日记对于跨文化交际能力的提高。

协作式模式其中的一个主要目的是"在跨文化意识中培养学

生语言的流利性"。事实上，协作式学习模式并不是直接评价学生的跨文化交际能力。对于跨文化交际能力的培养的证据来自于学生们所作的记录。其中的十七份日记被作者仔细研究过。从本质上来说，协作式学习本身就是一种跨文化交流活动，为了达到一定的学习目的，学习者需要交流思想、意见并商讨如何与伙伴合作。其中一个有趣的现象是学生们谈到的话题，内容涉及广泛，从个人信息甚至到同性恋等话题。当谈到文化的时候，话题可以粗略分为三个方面：产品、思想和行为。

在学生的日记中可以发现，他们很少提到关于产品方面的话题。他们与伙伴之间结成的这种协作的关系使得他们能够就西班牙人和英国人的思维方式交换意见，就教育制度的异同展开讨论。很有趣的是，很多学生把语言方面的一些话题归到了"文化信息"方面，例如习语的使用、与打牌和喝酒有关的短语、手势等。从这点可以看出，语言和文化之间的关系已经为多数人所接受。

通过这种协作式的学习，学生们也学会了如何对待自身文化和他人文化。学生在学习过程中，表现出对其他的文化族群的兴趣，并且积极参与到其中。不论是说当地语言的学生或是外国学生，都从这种协作式学习当中体验到了不同阶段的互动和交流，并且积极适应到另外一种文化里。

在协作式学习中，学生们通过与伙伴讨论社会中的不同的方面来提高他们的语言能力，当然，他们的文化知识也在这个时候得到了不断的提高。通过对比不同国家间对同一事件的态度和反应，或者对某一制度进行比较，学生们从中获取了很多有益的文化方面的知识，并且学生进行联想和解释的能力得到了锻炼和提高，他们通过互相交流的方式，不断去发现新的资料和信息，从中找出重要的相关信息作为参考。

## 7 结束语

从学生们所做的记录可以看出，尽管所显示的材料并非完全符合要求，但是这种面对面的协作式学习方式确实为跨文化交际能力的培养提供了很好的条件。学生在学习的过程中表现出对对方文化的兴趣,并且有强烈的愿望要知道和了解得更多,但是在深入分析和思考方面做得不够。为了能够使学生在学习中更多地加入自己的分析和思考,需要对学习式学习模式作些改进,并且需要导师作进一步的更细致的指导。

**Questions for reflection:**

1. What is tandem learning? What's the main principle of tandem learning?
2. Why is tandem learning an intercultural activity?
3. Are there any weaknesses that exist in the tandem learning?
4. What modifications have been made to improve the tandem learning?
5. What evidence has proved that the acquisition of intercultural competence is a process?